Justice Denied

Justice Denied

THE BLACK MAN IN WHITE AMERICA

Edited by

WILLIAM M. CHACE

Stanford University

and

PETER COLLIER

University of California, Berkeley

Harcourt, Brace & World, Inc.

New York/Chicago/San Francisco/Atlanta

ISBN: 0-15-547760-9
Library of Congress Catalog Card Number: 77-114608
Printed in the United States of America

Preface

The history of the Negro in America is the history of America written in vivid and bloody terms. . . . It is the history of men who tried to adjust themselves to a world whose laws, customs, and instruments of force were leveled against them. The Negro is America's metaphor.

—Richard Wright

Racial conflict may be discussed more widely today than ever before, but it can hardly be considered a creation of the sixties. Although each new generation sees it in a slightly different perspective, the "Negro Problem," as black novelist Richard Wright recognized so clearly, has been an enduring feature of life in America. From the first painful encounter between the man ripped from African soil and the man determined to make him a slave, racism has been a part of our institutions and laws, our culture and ourselves.

The encounter between black and white has increased in complexity with each decade. Often it has erupted in sudden, terrifying violence; but it has also produced a more subtle kind of violence: that seen in the bitterness and frustration of the generations of black people who, instead of taking up weapons, have sought to "adjust themselves," as Wright says, to a land and a people who wanted no part of them. Ever since they were brought to the New World in chains, black people have wanted only to become citizens with all the liberties others enjoy as a birthright. But America has been hostile to this aspiration, and in its hostility, it has made the black man a symbol of its own limitations.

No single book could hope to describe fully the clash between black man and white America, and this one does not pretend to. Rather, this anthology attempts to clarify certain aspects of the confrontation by describing the price black people have been forced to pay for attempted "adjustment" to the heavy burden of prejudice, and by considering some of the strategies they have used to fight racism. It begins with a discussion of the damage done to West African societies during the worst years of the slave trade and concludes with the program of the Black Panther Party. In other words, it moves from the nightmare of slavery to the militant demands for self-determination of the black liberation movement.

But the book is neither an historical survey nor a thorough-going sociological investigation. It is a series of essays which reveal the black man's reaction to the powerful and intransigent forces arrayed against him; the results of the ordeal of being black in the United States; and some of the moments of greatest agony and success.

There are voices from the past. In the first section, for example, "Jenny Proctor's Story" conveys a sense of slavery as a day-to-day reality for a woman who, for a large part of her life, was considered someone's chattel. One may turn to a selection from *The Narrative of the Life of Frederick Douglass, an American Slave* to gain an intimate and vivid sense of the strength of the slaves' desire for freedom. Or one may consider W. E. B. DuBois' study of how the Black Codes of Reconstruction brought slavery back to the South immediately after the conclusion of "The War to End Slavery."

There are also contemporary voices. St. Clair Drake's long essay gives a lucid picture of what it means—economically, educationally, medically —to be a black man after 350 years in America. Eldridge Cleaver discusses the connection between the war in Vietnam and the war raging in the ghettos of this nation. And Malcolm X's speech, "The Ballot or the Bullet," is offered as an eloquent appraisal of the decision which black people face each day: whether to accept the gradual approach to social equality and content themselves with small gains, or to commit violence against a land in which democracy has, for them, never really functioned.

The question at the heart of Malcolm X's speech is the focus of this anthology. As many historians have noted, the conflict between working for gains within the established conventions of American society and the possibility of taking a radical stance outside those conventions is a conflict deep within the black experience. It was present in the decision of some slaves to acquiesce and in the decision of others to rebel; in the debate between moderate and aggressive black abolitionists; in the friction between those who would set up a separate black state and those who would trust in America as they found it. It operates today in the conflict between nonviolence and militancy, between "cultural nationalism" and a revolutionary political posture, between "black capitalism" and the Black Panthers.

Perhaps the clearest expression of this conflict and of the changes it undergoes with each new era is the controversy between Booker T. Washington and W. E. B. DuBois at the beginning of this century. In his own time Washington was important enough to become an advisor to Presidents. In our time, however, he has become known as an advocate of compromise and accommodation. On the other hand, DuBois, shunned by many in his own day, is now appreciated as a man who resisted compromise and whose stern response to Washington contains a sentence which stands as the most prophetic insight into what lay ahead. "The problem of the twentieth century," DuBois wrote, "is the problem of the color-line,—the relationship of the darker to the lighter races of men in Asia and Africa, in America and the islands of the sea."

Filled with racial antagonism and bitterness, our century has been closer in spirit to DuBois' prophecy than to Washington's counsels of accommodation. The flight of blacks to Northern cities has, more often than not, only intensified patterns of rejection and racism. The small-town lynchings have virtually disappeared, only to be replaced by the police-suppressed insurrection in the slum-infested metropolis. The chronic hunger of black people in the rural South persists alongside the chronic hunger of black people in the urban ghetto. In one of the most incisive judgments made upon the quality of racial existence in this country of immense wealth and yet grinding misery is that of Ralph Ellison, who saw that to be black in America was to be "invisible." To be black—despite promises from politicians, the best advice of liberal well-wishers, and tardy, half-hearted acts of Congress—was either not to be seen at all, or only to be seen as an object of concern or of anxiety, as something eliciting either sympathy or hatred.

Justice Denied does not try to make the black American "visible." That would be more than presumptuous; given the nature of American society, it would be impossible. Instead, it tries to indicate the kind of forces that have produced this invisibility as well as those that have resisted it. And it tries to show why, because of the wide variety of forces bearing down upon the black man, the twentieth century belongs, so to speak, to DuBois and those who shared his pessimism about what it held for black people.

William M. Chace
Peter Collier

Contents

"We must come to see, with one of our distinguished jurists, that 'justice too long delayed is justice denied.'"

MARTIN LUTHER KING, JR.

"If you're not part of the solution, then you're part of the problem."

ELDRIDGE CLEAVER

Justice Denied

The

Nightmare

Slavery and Resistance

BASIL DAVIDSON

The Great Distortion

Africa had its own domestic form of slavery before the coming of the Europeans. It was, however, relatively moderate compared to what would develop later on. Beginning in the 1400s and continuing for about 400 years, the slave trade eventually took an estimated 40 million people from Africa. Millions died on the marches from the African interior to the sea; millions more died aboard the slave ships. Of all those captured, less than one-half ever saw the shores of the New World.

America, and particularly the South, with its agrarian economy, was the ultimate focus for this frenzied commerce in human flesh. Although slaves were sold elsewhere, in no other country did slavery flourish so long or so profitably; nowhere else did it become the foundation for a way of life; and no other country created such damaging and long-lasting rationalizations to substantiate the sub-human status of black people. However, while the effects of slavery were ultimately disastrous to America's internal life, American society was not the only one so affected. Africa itself, where the slave's journey began, was permanently altered. The corruption and greed that characterized the European slave traders left their mark on this ravished continent. Like the ghosts of the millions dead and departed, such vestiges of the slave trade, as Basil Davidson shows in the following selection, haunted African culture for centuries to come.

THE SCALE OF THE OVERSEA SLAVE TRADE SO MUCH SURPASSED ANYthing of its kind before or since as to be quite distinct, in its impact on Africa, both from overland slaving—long practiced by the Arabs and many Negro states—and from the domestic slavery of African Iron Age feudalism. It was much more than the merely peripheral bleeding of vitality that was represented by overland slaving. It was quite different, in its catastrophic effects, from the subjection of weak peoples to

THE GREAT DISTORTION   From *The Lost Cities of Africa* by Basil Davidson, by permission of Atlantic Monthly Press, Little, Brown and Co. Copyright © 1959 by Basil Davidson.

stronger peoples that occurred through African warfare and conquest. Often as deadly as the medieval Black Death, which is said to have carried off a third of Europe's population, the oversea slave trade was much worse in its social consequences. For the Black Death was over in a handful of years; but the oversea slave trade endured for more than four centuries. It degraded thought and action, African as well as European, through generations of engrained contempt for human life.

European demand for African slaves had been first satisfied as early as 1444, when a consignment taken north of the Senegal estuary was put ashore at Lisbon; and it was continuously satisfied, for hundreds of years after that, as the Portuguese and their rivals pushed further down the coast and established themselves there. By the early sixteenth century there were parts of Portugal where the number of Negro slaves was said to be larger than the number of native Portuguese. But the demand for slaves in the Caribbean and Brazil was infinitely greater still; looking at the records, it appears as practically insatiable. It enormously and radically swelled the trade. Millions were taken away or perished in the wars that oversea slaving provoked and lived from.

Round figures are deceptively easy to digest. A few examples may stick more instructively in the throat. Thus a Portuguese historian has lately estimated that about one million three hundred eighty-nine thousand slaves were taken from the coast of Angola *alone* in the years between 1486 and 1641, or about nine thousand a year from this never densely populated land. A report to Philip I calculated the number of slaves taken from Angola to Brazil in the years 1575 to 1591 as fifty-two thousand fifty-three, or nearly two thousand a year. Cadornega put the total number of slaves imported into Brazil—mainly from Angola and Mozambique—between 1580 and 1680 as about one million, or about ten thousand a year for a century; the figures, later on, would become larger still. And Angola and Mozambique were only two of many zones of collection.

Liverpool records of a century later show that in the eleven years of 1783 to 1793, about nine hundred Liverpool voyages were made for slaving and carried over three hundred thousand slaves worth about fifteen million pounds; the net return being reckoned as something more than twelve million pounds, or more than a million pounds a year. Barth, in the middle of the nineteenth century, could still complain not only of the Sudanese overland slave trade from Kano and elsewhere, but also of the oversea slaving of American ships in the Bight of Benin. Easily accepted over the centuries, the slave trade proved exceedingly hard to stop.

What the full effects of it really were is difficult and perhaps impossible to say. They were ruinously destructive of society and civilizing growth. At many points they were probably fatal to both. The wars provoked by slaving—and it was oversea slaving that made the pace in most of tropical and southern Africa—had no "progressive" side in that they stimulated rivalry between peoples, and hence invention and initiative, and thus material progress—as some have liked to argue. They were, on the contrary, completely negative in their effects on Africa—they stained and ruined much of the fabric of African society while permitting nothing better to replace it.

As the slaving wars continued, men grew more callous. African demoralization matched European cupidity. Slave revolts, sudden and ferocious in despair, added to the misery and bloodshed. "As very few of the negroes can so far brook the loss of their liberty," says an account of 1788, "and the hardships they endure, as to bear them with any degree of patience, they are ever upon the watch to take advantage of the least negligence in their oppressors. Insurrections are frequently the consequence, which are seldom suppressed without much bloodshed. Sometimes these are successful, and the whole ship's company is cut off. They are likewise always ready to seize every opportunity for committing some act of desperation to free themselves from their miserable state; and notwithstanding the restraint under which they are laid, they often succeed."

The writer was abolitionist, and sympathetic to the slaves. Yet, as Herskovits has shown, "from the beginning vast numbers of negroes refused to accept the slave status without a struggle." When they failed in revolt before they reached the Americas, they revolted there; and Toussaint l'Ouverture of San Domingo was only one of many slaves who reasserted human freedom in the Caribbean or the mainland of America.

One needs to remember this long story of insurrection when considering the native attitudes of West Africa. That the chiefs and some of the tribes of the coasts were easily corrupted into wholesale slave trading is obvious enough: the step from domestic slavery, which they had always practiced, to the sale of slaves was all too easily made. Their attitude might not be the same as that of the Elizabethan slaver, John Hawkins, whose much respected coat-of-arms embodied "a demi-Moor, proper, in chains." It might be different from the state of mind of those European bishops of the Congo who sat, decade after decade, in an ivory chair on the quayside of Luanda, and extended their merciful hand in wholesale baptism of the slaves who were rowed beneath, going in chains to the ships that would carry them upon the "middle passage" to Brazil. But it was substantially at one with both: society permitted slavery, and therefore permitted slaving.

The coastal chiefs and peoples, or some of them, might willingly accept all that, for they were soon linked by trading interest to this insatiable European demand (just as, at other times and places, others would be linked to an Arab demand). But the notion that the whole of African society entered and endured the slaving centuries with greed, docility, or dumb acceptance—a notion somewhat favored by those who have argued, or still argue, the "inherent inferiority" of Negroes and the "slavish nastiness" of African society—has no foundation in the record. The weak might go to the wall; they did not therefore like it. African society had been relatively peaceful and generous and even gentle; the world these peoples were thrown into was one of death and horror. The best and strongest took the first or second chance to resist or revolt; the rest endured. But endurance did not mean acceptance.

It is easy to imagine the process of demoralization—the hunt for a few slaves changing into the hunt for many; and, with that, the gradual ruin of every sentiment of decency and restraint. It is more difficult to measure the ruin which this wholesale slaving visited upon many of the states and societies it cursed. "Gradually," Ihle has written of the Congo, and the same would be true elsewhere,

> the last social links were broken, and the whole structure utterly destroyed. Certainly there had been slaves in the Congo before the coming of the white man. They had formed an organic part of the social framework, however, and had in it their clearly determined place. But after the growth of the slave trade the possession of slaves was transformed into a savage manhunt. Not only did the stronger man sell the weaker, but even the bonds of family life were broken, and parents sold their children or children their parents as generally worthless objects to the Portuguese, who branded them with a hot iron as if they had been sheep.[1]

Something of the measure of this decadence and ruin may be seen from comparing the condition of African peoples who suffered the slaving centuries with the condition of other African peoples—or what can be learned of them, for most of these lay far into the hinterland—who did not. Or one may look, for better understanding of the matter, at the contrasts between European narratives of the fifteenth and sixteenth centuries, when the trade was in its infancy, and European narratives

---

[1] Branding was practiced, of course, by all the European slaving nations.

of three or four hundred years later. These contrasts are especially instructive in the case of the notable kingdom of Benin, not far from the coast of modern Nigeria.

The British fought their way into Benin in 1897; and what they found there was afterwards described by Commander Bacon, who led that expeditionary column. "Truly," says Bacon,

> has Benin been called the city of blood. Its history is one long record of savagery of the most debased kind. In the earlier part of this century, when it was the center of the slave trade, human suffering must here have reached its most acute form; but it is doubtful if even then the wanton sacrifice of life could have exceeded that of more recent times.

The true history of the city-state and empire of Benin, of course, was anything but "one long record of savagery of the most debased kind"; yet at the time Bacon got there it may reasonably have seemed so.

> Blood was everywhere . . . On the right [of the main compound of the king] was a crucifixion tree with a double crucifixion on it, the two poor wretches stretched out facing west, with their arms bound together in the middle . . . At the base were skulls and bones, literally strewn about, the debris of former sacrifices, and down every main road were two or more human sacrifices. . . .

What cupidity and fear and despotism may do to rulers everywhere has been lately seen in Europe and in Asia, while the Aztecs of Mexico, whose society had nothing to do with oversea slaving, were also cursed with ritual murder. Yet the link between the scene that Bacon described and the fact of four centuries of oversea slaving must surely be a crucial one. Colonialist Europe may have succeeded, here and there, in fastening on African minds a sense of special guilt for the slaving centuries; but the truth is that the guilt was shared all round, and that Africans were not the prime movers in the matter. The peoples of the interior of central and southern Africa, beyond the long arm of the slavers, seldom or never reproduced those holocausts. When they did, these were occasional and despotic variants from a generally pacific rule. Nor did medieval Benin suffer in this way.

Four centuries before Bacon's expedition, at a time when slaving had yet to be on any great scale, the Portuguese had found a different scene. Pushing up the delta rivers—"small shippes of fifty tunnes" could go as far as Guato, "nine leagues with a good road" to Benin itself—they found a city-state that was prosperous and greatly skillful in the working of metals and of wood, "about a league long from gate to gate," without

a wall but "surrounded by a large moat, very wide and deep, which
sufficeth for its defence."

"I was there four times," says Pacheco, writing at the end of the fifteenth century. "Its houses are made of mud walls covered with palm
leaves." This city-state had extended its rule over the neighboring countryside and was altogether "about eighty leagues long and forty wide."
It was "usually at war with its neighbours." These wars provided slaves
for domestic use, much as in medieval Europe; but the dignitaries of
Benin, with the coming of Europeans, soon found their profit in selling
them. "We buy [slaves]," adds Pacheco, "at twelve or fifteen brass bracelets each, or for copper bracelets which they prize more."

In spite of warfare with rivals, peace and order were the rule in that
old Benin. The accounts are bare; but so much, at least, they make
plain. In 1486 Affonso d'Aveiro took a small trading and exploring
mission into Benin on behalf of the king of Portugal. He died there, but
before dying had managed to send out a cargo of pepper, the first of that
commodity to reach Europe from the Guinea coast; "and presently,"
says another Portuguese account, "samples of it were sent to Flanders
and to other parts, and soon it fetched a great price and was held in high
esteem."

At the same time the king of Benin—the *oba* as he was called—sent
an ambassador to Portugal "because he desired to learn more about
these lands, the arrival of people from them in his country being regarded as an unusual novelty." And when this ambassador—"a man of
good speech and natural wisdom"—returned to Benin, he brought with
him presents from the king of Portugal, a number of Catholic missionaries, and "new agents of the [Portuguese] king, who were to remain in
that country and to traffic for the said pepper and for other things,
which pertained to the trades of the king." Slaving, that is, was still of
minor importance.

How these agents and missionaries fared in Benin is the substance of
another Portuguese report, characteristically short on descriptive detail
if long on implication, of 1516. "The favour which the king of Benin
accords us," wrote Duarte Pires, then Portuguese royal agent in the city,
"is due to his love of your highness; and thus he pays us high honour
and sets us at table to dine with his son, and no part of his court is hidden from us but all the doors are open."

The missionaries were being well received, says Pires, but Christian
labors much hindered, apparently, by the king's being engaged in warfare with his neighbors. On returning from one of his wars, however,
the king

gave his son and some of his noblemen—the greatest in the kingdom—
so that they might become Christians; and also he ordered a church to
be built in Benin; and they made them Christians straightway; and also
they are teaching them to read, and your highness will be very pleased
to know that they are very good learners.

A tactful report, perhaps; but not a troubled one. By 1554, when the
Englishman Richard Windham got there, he found the king "could
speake the Portugall tongue." Windham bought from him—against goods
and the promise of goods on his next returning—"fourscore tunne of
pepper." But he bought no slaves.

Similar reports, brief and scattered and seldom more than incidental
to the business of mariners and traders, have survived from European
visits to several other kingdoms and city-states along the coast, from the
estuary of the Senegal River in the west to the estuary of the Congo in
the south. They reveal the existence of many centers of tribal power,
often at rivalry, often bound together by feudal ties, invariably working
in metals, with a wide range of religious systems from simple animism
to intricate forms of divine kingship; and offering so many apparent
tokens of similarity with feudal Europe that the Portuguese had no
difficulty in transferring a simple European explanation to many of their
customs. In the kingdoms of the Congo estuary, indeed, they very soon
persuaded the paramount chiefs and counselors to accept titles of nobil-
ity along with baptism, so that counts and dukes and marquises soon
flourished there; though neither titles nor baptism can ever have conveyed the same arrogance of meaning for those who received them as
they undoubtedly conveyed for those who offered them. The painful
hierarchies of Europe were unknown to most of Africa.

These peoples had always believed in a single divine power ruling
the ultimate destinies of their world: the Christian god, in that respect,
was no different from their own—with the difference that baptism, for
them, could be nothing but an amiable ceremony. They had usually
accepted a hierarchy of power—with the difference that their hierarchy
was subject to laws of the collective, while the hierarchy of feudal
Europe had long become a law unto itself. These differences explain
why the titles disappeared and the missionaries failed: neither could
survive the strong pressures of a society which, though feudal in many
of its appearances, was tribal in its essence.

Tribal—but not therefore primitive. Here, of course, it is dangerous
to generalize. Primitive societies existed in Africa then, just as they still
exist here and there in Africa today; although the word "primitive,"
even with them, can be properly applied only in a narrow sense of

material or technological simplicity. But the tribalism of these Negro and Bantu-speaking peoples who had spread and multiplied across the central and southern continent, and some of whom the Portuguese reached in the fifteenth and sixteenth centuries, had long evolved their own Iron Age patterns of society and forms of organization. They had shaped their own original course and evolution, and the word "primitive" could have no more application to them than it could to their contemporaries in Europe. So much is clear, to look no further, from the early art of Ife and Benin.

DANIEL MANNIX AND MALCOLM COWLEY

The Middle Passage

Slavery drowned Africa's cultural vitality as well as its human resources. But the individual slave had little time to worry about his homeland; to him, survival was the immediate and overwhelming problem.

The long march from the African interior to the coast was the first test. Those who managed to endure it were herded onto slave ships; they thus began their voyage to the New World in chains and terror that would be passed on to their children and their children's children. The following selection shows that this "middle passage" to America was the slave's initiation into a systematic degradation designed to strip away his humanity and make him ready for the seller's block. With its sadistic punishments, sexual abuse, and rampant disease, life on the slave ship was a sudden and terrifying preview of what was to come. It was also, however, the origin of the restlessness and resistance that would characterize the black man's response to his enslavement and make the sleep of slave owners in the ante-bellum South an uneasy one.

AS SOON AS AN ASSORTMENT OF NAKED SLAVES WAS TAKEN ABOARD a Guineaman, the men were shackled two by two, the right wrist and

THE MIDDLE PASSAGE From *Black Cargoes: A History of the Atlantic Slave Trade* by Daniel P. Mannix and Malcolm Cowley. Copyright © 1962 by Daniel P. Mannix. All rights reserved. Reprinted by permission of the Viking Press, Inc.

ankle of one to the left wrist and ankle of another. Then they were sent to the hold or, at the end of the eighteenth century, to the "house" that the sailors had built on deck. The women—usually regarded as fair prey for the sailors—and the children were allowed to wander by day almost anywhere on the vessel, though they spent the night between decks in other rooms than the men. All the slaves were forced to sleep without covering on bare wooden floors, which were often constructed of unplaned boards. In a stormy passage the skin over their elbows might be worn away to the bare bones.

William Bosman says, writing in 1701, "You would really wonder to see how these slaves live on board; for though their number sometimes amounts to six or seven hundred, yet by careful management of our masters of ships"—the Dutch masters, that is—"they are so regulated that it seems incredible: And in this particular our nation exceeds all other Europeans; for as the French, Portuguese and English slaveships are always foul and stinking; on the contrary ours are for the most part clean and neat." Slavers of every nation insisted that their own vessels were the best in the trade. Thus, James Barbot, Jr., who sailed on an English ship to the Congo in 1700, was highly critical of the Portuguese. He admits that they made a great point of baptizing the slaves before taking them aboard, but then, "It is pitiful," he says,

> to see how they crowd those poor wretches, six hundred and fifty or seven hundred in a ship, the men standing in the hold ty'd to stakes, the women between decks and those that are with child in the great cabin and the children in the steeridge which in that hot climate occasions an intolerable stench.

This youngest Barbot adds, however, that the Portuguese provided the slaves with coarse thick mats, which were "softer for the poor wretches to lie upon than the bare decks . . . and it would be prudent to imitate the Portuguese in this point." The English never displayed that sort of prudence, and neither did they imitate the Dutch, who had special ships built for the trade, Barbot says, "very wide, lofty and airy betwixt decks, with gratings and scuttles . . . to let in more air. Some also have small ports . . . and that very much contributes to the preservation of those poor wretches who are so thick crowded together."

There were two schools of thought among the Guinea captains, called the "loose-packers" and the "tight-packers." The former argued that by giving the slaves a little more room, with better food and a certain amount of liberty, they reduced the mortality among them and received a better price for each slave in the West Indies. The tight-packers answered that although the loss of life might be greater on each of their voyages, so too were the net receipts from a larger cargo. If many of the survivors were weak and emaciated, as was often the case, they could be fattened up in a West Indian slave yard before being offered for sale. The argument between the two schools continued as long as the trade itself, but for many years after 1750 the tight-packers were in the ascendant. So great was the profit on each slave landed alive in the West Indies that hardly a captain refrained from loading his vessel to her utmost capacity. The hold of a slaving vessel was usually about five feet high. That seemed like waste space to the Guinea merchants, so they built a shelf or platform in the middle of it, extending six feet from each side of the vessel. When the bottom of the hold was completely covered with flesh, another row of slaves was packed on the platform. If there was as much as six feet of vertical space in the hold, a second platform might be installed above the first, sometimes leaving only twenty inches of headroom for the slaves; they could not sit upright during the whole voyage. The Reverend John Newton writes from personal observation:

> The cargo of a vessel of a hundred tons or a little more is calculated to purchase from 220 to 250 slaves. Their lodging rooms below the deck which are three (for the men, the boys and the women) besides a place for the sick, are sometimes more than five feet high and sometimes less; and this height is divided toward the middle for the slaves to lie in two rows, one above the other, on each side of the ship, close to each other like books upon a shelf. I have known them so close that the shelf would not easily contain one more.
>
> The poor creatures, thus cramped, are likewise in irons for the most part which makes it difficult for them to turn or move or attempt to rise or to lie down without hurting themselves or each other. Every morning, perhaps, more instances than one are found of the living and the dead fastened together.

Dr. Falconbridge stated in his Parliamentary testimony that "he made the most of the room," in stowing the slaves, "and wedged them in. They had not so much room as a man in his coffin either in length or breadth. When he had to enter the slave deck, he took off his shoes to avoid crushing the slaves as he was forced to crawl over them." Taking off shoes on entering the hold seems to have been a widespread custom among surgeons. Falconbridge "had the marks on his feet where [the slaves] bit and pinched him."

In 1788 Captain Parrey of the Royal Navy was sent to measure such of the slave vessels as were then lying at Liverpool and to make a report to the House of Commons. He discovered that the captains of many slavers possessed a chart showing the dimensions of the ship's half deck, lower deck, hold, platforms, gunroom, orlop, and great cabin, in fact of every crevice into which slaves might be wedged. Miniature black figures were drawn on some of the charts to illustrate the most effective method of packing in the cargo.

On the *Brookes,* which Captain Parrey considered to be typical, every man was allowed a space six feet long by sixteen inches wide (and usually about two feet, seven inches high); every woman, a space five feet, ten inches long by sixteen inches wide; every boy, five feet by fourteen inches; every girl, four feet, six inches by twelve inches. The *Brookes* was a vessel of 320 tons. By the law of 1788 it was permitted to carry 454 slaves, and the chart, which later became famous, showed how and where 451 of them could be stowed away. Captain Parrey failed to see how the captain could find room for three more. Nevertheless, Parliament was told by reliable witnesses, including Dr. Thomas Trotter, formerly surgeon of the *Brookes,* that before the new law was passed she had carried 600 slaves on one voyage and 609 on another.

Taking on slaves was a process that might be completed in a month or two at Bonny or Luanda. On the Gold Coast, where slaves were less plentiful, it might last from six months to a year or more. Meanwhile the captain was buying Negroes, sometimes one or two a day, sometimes a hundred or more in a single lot, while haggling over each purchase.

Those months when a slaver lay at anchor off the Guinea Coast, taking on her cargo, were the most dangerous stage of her triangular voyage. Not only was her crew exposed to African fevers and the revenge of angry natives; not only was there the chance of her being taken by pirates or by a hostile man-of-war; but also there was the constant threat of a slave mutiny. Captain Thomas Phillips says, in his account of a voyage made in 1693–1694:

> When our slaves are aboard we shackle the men two and two, while we lie in port, and in sight of their own country, for 'tis then they attempt to make their escape, and mutiny; to prevent which we always keep centinels upon the hatchways, and have a chest full of small arms, ready loaden and prim'd, constantly lying at hand upon the quarter-deck, together with some granada shells; and two of our quarter-deck guns, pointing on the deck thence, and two more out of the steerage, the door of which is always kept shut, and well barr'd; they are fed

twice a day, at 10 in the morning, and 4 in the evening, which is the time they are aptest to mutiny, being all upon deck; therefore all that time, what of our men are not employ'd in distributing their victuals to them, and settling them, stand to their arms; and some with lighted matches at the great guns that yaun upon them, loaden with partridge, till they have done and gone down to their kennels between decks.

The danger of mutiny was greatest when all the slaves on board belonged to a single tribe, especially if it was one of the warlike tribes from the Gold Coast. On the other hand, the Gold Coast slaves despised other Negroes, and this fault of theirs proved useful to the white men. Phillips says,

> We have some 30 or 40 gold coast negroes, which we buy . . . to make guardians and overseers of the Whidaw negroes, and sleep among them to keep them from quarreling; and in order, as well as to give us notice, if they can discover any caballing or plotting among them, which trust they will discharge with great diligence; . . . when we constitute a guardian, we give him a cat of nine tails as a badge of his office, which he is not a little proud of, and will exercise with great authority.

In spite of such precautions, mutinies were frequent on the coast, and some of them were successful. Even a failed mutiny might lead to heavy losses among the slaves and the sailors. James Barbot, Sr., of the *Albion-Frigate,* made the mistake of providing his slaves with knives so they could cut their meat. The slaves tore pieces of iron from the forecastle door, broke off their shackles, and killed the guard at the entrance to the hatchway. Before the mutiny was quelled, twenty-eight slaves either had been shot dead or had thrown themselves overboard. Bosman went through two mutinies. In the second of these the slaves would have mastered the ship had it not been aided by a French and an English vessel. About twenty slaves were killed. William Snelgrave survived more perils on the coast than any other Guinea captain of the early eighteenth century. Among the perils were three mutinies, one at Old Calabar, when there were four hundred slaves on his father's ship and only ten sailors not disabled by fever, and the other two on the Gold Coast. Both the Gold Coast mutinies were led by Coromantees, against hopeless odds. About the first of these he says:

> This Mutiny began at Midnight. . . . Two Men that stood Centry at the Forehatch way . . . permitted four [slaves] to go to that Place, but neglected to lay the Gratings again, as they should have done;

whereupon four more Negroes came on Deck . . . and all eight fell on the two Centries who immediately called out for help. The Negroes endeavoured to get their Cutlaces from them, but the Lineyards (that is the Lines by which the Handles of the Cutlaces were fastened to the Men's Wrists) were so twisted in the Scuffle, that they could not get them off before we came to their Assistance. The Negroes perceiving several white Men coming towards them, with Arms in their Hands, quitted the Centries and jumped over the Ship's Side into the Sea. . . .

After we had secured these People, I called the Linguists, and ordered them to bid the Men-Negroes between Decks be quiet; (for there was a great noise amongst them). On their being silent, I asked, "What had induced them to mutiny?" They answered, "I was a great Rogue to buy them, in order to carry them away from their own Country, and that they were resolved to regain their Liberty if possible." I replied, "That they had forfeited their Freedom before I bought them, either by Crimes or by being taken in War." . . . Then I observed to them, "That if they should gain their Point and escape to the Shore, it would be of no Advantage to them, because their Countrymen would catch them, and sell them to other Ships." This served my purpose, and they seemed to be convinced of their Fault.

Mutinies were frequent during the years from 1750 to 1788, when Liverpool merchants were trying to save money by reducing the size of their crews. A small crew weakened by fever was no match for the slaves, especially if it had to withstand a simultaneous attack from the shore. On January 11, 1769, the *Nancy* out of Liverpool, Captain Williams, was lying at anchor off New Calabar. She had 132 slaves on board, who managed to break their shackles and assail the crew. The slaves were unarmed, but "it was with great difficulty, though [the crew] attacked them sword in hand, to make them submit." Meanwhile the natives on shore heard the fighting and swarmed aboard the *Nancy* from their canoes. They seized the slaves (whom they later resold to other ships, as Captain Snelgrave had prophesied) and looted the cargo. There was a wild scene of plunder, with black men running through the vessel, breaching rum casks, throwing ships' biscuit and salt beef into the canoes, and robbing the sailors of everything they possessed. Afterward they cut the cables and set the *Nancy* adrift. Another slaver lying in the river sent a boat to rescue Captain Williams and the surviving seamen. The vessel, however, was wrecked.

William Richardson, a young sailor who shipped on a Guineaman in 1790, tells of going to the help of a French vessel on which the slaves had risen while it was at anchor in a bay. The English seamen jumped into their boats and pulled hard for the Frenchman, but by the time they reached it there were "a hundred slaves in possession of the deck and others tumbling up from below." The French vessel had its netting rigged—a customary precaution for slavers lying at anchor—and the nets prevented the Englishmen from boarding. Even after they had broken through the nets, the slaves put up a desperate resistance. "I could not but admire," Richardson says, "the courage of a fine young black who, though his partner in irons lay dead at his feet, would not surrender but fought with his billet of wood until a ball finished his existence. The others fought as well as they could but what could they do against fire-arms?"

There are fairly detailed accounts of fifty-five mutinies on slavers from 1699 to 1845, not to mention passing references to more than a hundred others. The list of ships "cut off" by the natives—often in revenge for the kidnaping of freemen—is almost as long. On the record it does not seem that Africans submitted tamely to being carried across the Atlantic like chained beasts. Edward Long, the Jamaica planter and historian, justified the cruel punishments inflicted on slaves by saying,

> The many acts of violence they have committed by murdering whole crews and destroying ships when they had it in their power to do so have made these rigors wholly chargeable on their own bloody and malicious disposition which calls for the same confinement as if they were wolves or wild boars.

For "wolves or wild boars" a modern reader might substitute "men who would rather die than be enslaved."

As long as a vessel lay at anchor, the slaves could dream of seizing it. If they managed to kill the crew, as they did in perhaps one mutiny out of ten, they could cut the anchor cable and let the vessel drift ashore. That opportunity was lost as soon as the vessel put to sea. Ignorant of navigation, which they regarded as white man's magic, the slaves were at the mercy of the captain. They could still die, but not with any hope of regaining their freedom.

The captain, for his part, had finished the most dangerous leg of his triangular voyage. Now he had to face only the ordinary perils of the sea, most of which were covered by his owners' insurance against fire, shipwreck, pirates and rovers, letters of mart and counter-mart, barratry, jettison, and foreign men-of-war. Among the risks not covered by insurance, the greatest was that the cargo might be swept away by disease. The underwriters refused to issue such policies, arguing that they would expose the captain to an unholy temptation. If insured against disease among his slaves, he might take no precautions against it and might try to make his profit out of the insurance.

The more days at sea, the more deaths among his cargo, and so the captain tried to cut short the next leg of his voyage. If he had shipped his slaves at Bonny or Old Calabar or any port to the southward, he might call at one of the Portuguese islands in the Gulf of Guinea for an additional supply of food and fresh water, usually enough, with what he had already, to last for three months. If he had traded on the Windward Coast, he made straight for the West Indies. Usually he had from four to five thousand nautical miles to sail—or even more, if the passage was from Angola to Virginia. The shortest passage—that from the Gambia River to Barbados—might be made in as little as three weeks, with favoring winds. If the course was much longer, and if the ship was be-calmed in the doldrums or driven back by storms, it might take more than three months to cross the Atlantic, and slaves and sailors would be put on short rations long before the end of the Middle Passage.

On a canvas of heroic size, Thomas Stothard, Esq., of the Royal Academy, depicted "The Voyage of the Sable Venus from Angola to the West Indies." His painting is handsomely reproduced in the second volume of Bryan Edwards' *History of the West Indies,* where it appears beside a poem on the same allegorical subject by an unnamed Jamaican author, perhaps Edwards himself. In the painting the ship that carries the Sable Venus is an immense scallop shell, in which she sits upright on a velvet throne. Except for bracelets, anklets, and a collar of pearls, she wears nothing but a narrow embroidered girdle. Her look is soft and sensuous, and in grace she yields nothing—so the poem insists—to Botticelli's white Venus,

> In FLORENCE, where she's seen;
> Both just alike, except the white,
> No difference, no—none at night
> The beauteous dames between.

The joint message of the poem and the painting is simple to the point of coarseness: that slave women are preferable to English girls at night, being passionate and accessible; but the message is embellished with a wealth of classical details, to show the painter's learning. Two legendary dolphins draw the bark of Venus toward the West. Triton leads one of them, while blowing his wreathed horn. Two mischievous loves gambol about the other dolphin. There are cherubs above the woolly head of Venus, fanning her with ostrich plumes. In the calm distance a grampus discharges his column of spray. Cupid, from above, is shooting an arrow

at Neptune, who strides ahead bearing the Union Jack. As the poet
(who calls the dolphins "winged fish") describes the idyllic scene:

> The winged fish, in purple trace
> The chariot drew; with easy grace
>   Their azure rein she guides:
> And now they fly, and now they swim;
> Now o'er the wave they lightly skim,
>   Or dart beneath the tides.

Meanwhile the Sable Venus, if she was a living woman borne from
Angola to the West Indies, was roaming the deck of a ship that stank of
excrement, so that, as with any slaver, "You could smell it five miles
down wind." She had been torn from her husband and her children, she
had been branded on the left buttock, and she had been carried to the
ship bound hand and foot, lying in the bilge at the bottom of a dugout
canoe. Now she was the prey of the ship's officers, in danger of being
flogged to death if she resisted them. Her reward if she yielded was a
handful of beads or a sailor's kerchief to tie around her waist.

Here is how she and her shipmates spent the day.

If the weather was clear, they were brought on deck at eight o'clock
in the morning. The men were attached by their leg irons to the great
chain that ran along the bulwarks on both sides of the ship; the women
and half-grown boys were allowed to wander at will. About nine o'clock
the slaves were served their first meal of the day. If they were from the
Windward Coast, the fare consisted of boiled rice, millet, or cornmeal,
which might be cooked with a few lumps of salt beef abstracted from the
sailors' rations. If they were from the Bight of Biafra, they were fed
stewed yams, but the Congos and the Angolans preferred manioc or
plantains. With the food they were all given half a pint of water, served
out in a pannikin.

After the morning meal came a joyless ceremony called "dancing the
slaves." "Those who were in irons," says Dr. Thomas Trotter, surgeon
of the *Brookes* in 1783, "were ordered to stand up and make what mo-
tions they could, leaving a passage for such as were out of irons to dance
around the deck." Dancing was prescribed as a therapeutic measure, a
specific against suicidal melancholy, and also against scurvy—although
in the latter case it was a useless torture for men with swollen limbs.
While sailors paraded the deck, each with a cat-o'-nine-tails in his right
hand, the men slaves "jumped in their irons" until their ankles were
bleeding flesh. One sailor told Parliament, "I was employed to dance the
men, while another person danced the women." Music was provided by

a slave thumping on a broken drum or an upturned kettle, or by an African banjo, if there was one aboard, or perhaps by a sailor with a bagpipe or a fiddle. Slaving captains sometimes advertised for "A person that can play on the Bagpipes, for a Guinea ship." The slaves were also told to sing. Said Dr. Claxton after his voyage in the *Young Hero,* "They sing, but not for their amusement. The captain ordered them to sing, and they sang songs of sorrow. Their sickness, fear of being beaten, their hunger, and the memory of their country, &c, are the usual subjects."

While some of the sailors were dancing the slaves, others were sent below to scrape and swab out the sleeping rooms. It was a sickening task, and it was not well performed unless the captain imposed an iron discipline. James Barbot, Sr., was proud of the discipline maintained on the *Albion-Frigate.* "We were very nice," he says

> in keeping the places where the slaves lay clean and neat, appointing some of the ship's crew to do that office constantly and thrice a week we perfumed betwixt decks with a quantity of good vinegar in pails, and red-hot iron bullets in them, to expel the bad air, after the place had been well washed and scrubbed with brooms.

Captain Hugh Crow, the last legal English slaver, was famous for his housekeeping. "I always took great pains," he says, "to promote the health and comfort of all on board, by proper diet, regularity, exercise, and cleanliness, for I considered that on keeping the ship clean and orderly, which was always my hobby, the success of our voyage mainly depended." Consistently he lost fewer slaves in the Middle Passage than the other captains, some of whom had the filth in the hold cleaned out only once a week. A few left their slaves to wallow in excrement during the whole Atlantic passage.

At three or four in the afternoon the slaves were fed their second meal, often a repetition of the first. Sometimes, instead of African food, they were given horse beans, the cheapest provender from Europe. The beans were boiled to a pulp, then covered with a mixture of palm oil, flour, water, and red pepper, which the sailors called "slabber sauce." Most of the slaves detested horse beans, especially if they were used to eating yams or manioc. Instead of eating the pulp, they would, unless carefully watched, pick it up by handfuls and throw it in each other's faces. That second meal was the end of their day. As soon as it was finished they were sent below, under the guard of sailors charged with stowing them away on their bare floors and platforms. The tallest men were placed amidships, where the vessel was widest; the shorter ones were tumbled into the stern. Usually there was only room for them to sleep on their sides, "spoon fashion." Captain William Littleton told Parliament that slaves in the ships on which he sailed might lie on their backs if they wished—"though perhaps," he conceded, "it might be difficult all at the same time."

After stowing their cargo, the sailors climbed out of the hatchway, each clutching his cat-o'-nine-tails: then the hatchway gratings were closed and barred. Sometimes in the night, as the sailors lay on deck and tried to sleep, they heard from below "an howling melancholy noise, expressive of extreme anguish." When Dr. Trotter told his interpreter, a slave woman, to inquire about the cause of the noise, "she discovered it to be owing to their having dreamt they were in their own country, and finding themselves when awake, in the hold of a slave ship."

More often the noise heard by the sailors was that of quarreling among the slaves. The usual occasion for quarrels was their problem of reaching the latrines. These were inadequate and hard to find in the darkness of the crowded hold, especially by men who were ironed together in pairs.

> In each of the apartments [says Dr. Falconbridge] are placed three or four large buckets, of a conical form, nearly two feet in diameter at the bottom and only one foot at the top and in depth about twenty-eight inches, to which, when necessary, the negroes have recourse. It often happens that those who are placed at a distance from the buckets, in endeavoring to get to them, tumble over their companions, in consequence of their being shackled. These accidents, although unavoidable, are productive of continual quarrels in which some of them are always bruised. In this situation, unable to proceed and prevented from going to the tubs, they desist from the attempt; and as the necessities of nature are not to be resisted, they ease themselves as they lie.

In squalls or rainy weather, the slaves were never brought on deck. They were served their two meals in the hold, where the air became too thick and poisonous to breathe. Says Dr. Falconbridge,

> For the purpose of admitting fresh air, most of the ships in the slave-trade are provided, between the decks, with five or six air-ports on each side of the ship, of about six inches in length and four in breadth; in addition to which, some few ships, but not one in twenty, have what they denominate wind-sails.

These were funnels made of canvas and so placed as to direct a current of air into the hold. "But whenever the sea is rough and the rain heavy," Falconbridge continues, it becomes necessary to shut these and every other conveyance by which the air is admitted. . . . The negroes' rooms very soon become intolerably hot. The confined air, rendered noxious by the effluvia exhaled from their bodies and by being repeatedly breathed, soon produces fevers and fluxes which generally carry off great numbers of them.

Dr. Trotter says that when tarpaulins were thrown over the gratings, the slaves would cry, "Kickeraboo, kickeraboo, we are dying, we are dying." "I have known," says Henry Ellison, a sailor before the mast, "in the Middle Passage, in rains, slaves confined below for some time. I have frequently seen them faint through heat, the steam coming through the gratings, like a furnace." Falconbridge gives one instance of their sufferings.

> Some wet and blowing weather [he says] having occasioned the portholes to be shut and the grating to be covered, fluxes and fevers among the negroes ensued. While they were in this situation, I frequently went down among them till at length their rooms became so extremely hot as to be only bearable for a very short time. But the excessive heat was not the only thing that rendered their situation intolerable. The deck, that is, the floor of their rooms, was so covered with the blood and mucus which had proceeded from them in consequence of the flux, that it resembled a slaughter-house. . . . Numbers of the slaves having fainted they were carried upon deck where several of them died and the rest with great difficulty were restored. It had nearly proved fatal to me also. The climate was too warm to admit the wearing of any clothing but a shirt and that I had pulled off before I went down; notwithstanding which, by only continuing among them for about a quarter of an hour, I was so overcome with the heat, stench and foul air that I nearly fainted; and it was only with assistance that I could get on deck. The consequence was that I soon after fell sick of the same disorder from which I did not recover for several months.

Not surprisingly, the slaves often went mad. Falconbridge mentions a woman on the *Emilia* who had to be chained to the deck. She had lucid intervals, however, and during one of these she was sold to a planter in Jamaica. Men who went insane might be flogged to death, to make sure that they were not malingering. Some were simply clubbed on the head and thrown overboard.

While the slaves were on deck they had to be watched at all times to keep them from committing suicide. Says Captain Phillips of the *Hannibal,* "We had about 12 negroes did wilfully drown themselves, and others starv'd themselves to death; for," he explained, " 'tis their belief that when they die they return home to their own country and friends again." This belief was reported from various regions, at various periods of the trade, but it seems to have been especially prevalent among the Ibo of eastern Nigeria. In 1788, nearly a hundred years after the *Hannibal*'s voyage, Ecroide Claxton was the surgeon who attended a shipload of Ibo. "Some of the slaves," he testified,

> wished to die on an idea that they should then get back to their own country. The captain in order to obviate this idea, thought of an expedient viz. to cut off the heads of those who died intimating to them that if determined to go, they must return without heads. The slaves were accordingly brought up to witness the operation. One of them by a violent exertion got loose and flying to the place where the nettings had been unloosed in order to empty the tubs, he darted overboard. The ship brought to, a man was placed in the main chains to catch him which he perceiving, made signs which words cannot express expressive of his happiness in escaping. He then went down and was seen no more.

Dr. Isaac Wilson, a surgeon in the Royal Navy, made a Guinea voyage on the *Elizabeth,* Captain John Smith, who was said to be very humane. Nevertheless, Wilson was assigned the duty of whipping the slaves. "Even in the act of chastisement," Wilson says, "I have seen them look up at me with a smile, and, in their own language, say, 'presently we shall be no more.' " One woman on the *Elizabeth* found some rope yarn, which she tied to the armorer's vise; she fastened the other end round her neck and was found dead in the morning. On the *Brookes* when Thomas Trotter was her surgeon, there was a man who, after being accused of witchcraft, had been sold into slavery with his whole family. During his first night on shipboard he tried to cut his throat. Dr. Trotter sewed up the wound, but on the following night the man not only tore out the sutures but tried to cut his throat on the other side. From the ragged edges of the wound and the blood on his fingers, he seemed to have used his nails as the only available instrument. His hands were tied together after the second wound, but he then refused all food, and he died of hunger in eight or ten days.

"Upon the negroes refusing to take food," says Falconbridge,

> I have seen coals of fire, glowing hot, put on a shovel and placed so near their lips as to scorch and burn them. And this has been accompanied with threats of forcing them to swallow the coals if they persisted in refusing to eat. This generally had the required effect;

but if the Negroes still refused, they were flogged day after day. Lest flogging prove ineffective, every Guineaman was provided with a special instrument called the "speculum oris," or mouth opener. It looked like a pair of dividers with notched legs and with a thumbscrew at the blunt end. The legs were closed and the notches were hammered between the slave's teeth. When the thumbscrew was tightened, the legs of the instrument separated, forcing open the slave's mouth; then food was poured into it through a funnel.

Even the speculum oris sometimes failed with a slave determined to die. Dr. Wilson reports another incident of his voyage on the *Elizabeth,* this one concerning a young man who had refused to eat for several days. Mild means were used to divert him from his resolution, "as well as promises," Wilson says,

> that he should have anything he wished for; but still he refused to eat. He was then whipped with the cat but this also was ineffectual. He always kept his teeth so fast that it was impossible to get anything down. We then endeavored to introduce a Speculum Oris between his teeth but the points were too obtuse to enter and next tried a bolus knife but with the same effect. In this state he was for four or five days when he was brought up as dead to be thrown overboard. . . . I finding life still existing, repeated my endeavours though in vain and two days afterwards he was brought up again in the same state as before. . . . In his own tongue he asked for water which was given him. Upon this we began to have hopes of dissuading him from his design but he again shut his teeth as fast as ever and resolved to die and on the ninth day from his first refusal he died.

One deadly scourge of the Guinea cargoes was a phenomenon called "fixed melancholy." Even slaves who were well fed, treated with kindness, and kept under relatively sanitary conditions would often die one after another for no apparent reason; they simply had no wish to live. Fixed melancholy seems to have been especially rife among the Ibo and among the food-gathering tribes of the Gaboon, but no Negro nation was immune to it. Although the disease was noted from the earliest days of the trade, perhaps the best description of it was written by George Howe, an American medical student who shipped on an illegal slaver in 1859:

> Notwithstanding their apparent good health [Howe says] each morning three or four dead would be found, brought upon deck, taken by the arms and heels, and tossed overboard as unceremoniously as an empty bottle. Of what did they die? And [why] always at night? In the barra-

coons it was known that if a Negro was not amused and kept in motion, he would mope, squat down with his chin on his knees and arms
clasped about his legs and in a very short time die. Among civilized
races it is thought almost impossible to hold one's breath until death
follows. It is thought the African can do so. They had no means of
concealing anything and certainly did not kill each other. One of the
duties of the slave-captains was when they found a slave sitting with
knees up and head drooping, to start them up, run them about the
deck, give them a small ration of rum, and divert them until in a normal condition.

It is impossible for a human being to hold his breath until he dies.
Once he loses consciousness, his lungs fill with air and he recovers. The
simplest explanation for the slaves' ability to "will themselves dead" is
that they were in a state of shock as a result of their being carried
through the terrifying surf into the totally unfamiliar surroundings of
the ship. In certain conditions shock can be as fatal as physical injury.
There may, however, be another explanation. The communal life of
many tribes was so highly organized by a system of customs, relationships, taboos, and religious ceremonies that there was practically nothing
a man or a woman could do that was not prescribed by tribal law. To
separate an individual from this complex system of interrelationships and
suddenly place him, naked and friendless, in a completely hostile environment was in some respects a greater shock than any amount of physical brutality.

Dr. Wilson believed that fixed melancholy was responsible for the
loss of two-thirds of the slaves who died on the *Elizabeth*. "No one who
had it was ever cured," he says, "whereas those who had it not and yet
were ill, recovered. The symptoms are a lowness of spirits and despon-
dency. Hence they refuse food. This only increases the symptoms. The
stomach afterwards got weak. Hence the belly ached, fluxes ensued, and
they were carried off." But flux, or dysentery, is an infectious disease
spread chiefly by food prepared in unsanitary conditions. The slaves,
after being forced to wallow in filth, were also forced to eat with their
fingers. In spite of the real losses from fixed melancholy, the high death
rate on Guinea ships was due to somatic more than to psychic afflictions.

Along with their human cargoes, crowded, filthy, undernourished, and
terrified out of the wish to live, the ships also carried an invisible cargo
of microbes, bacilli, spirochetes, viruses, and intestinal worms from one
continent to another; the Middle Passage was a crossroads and market-
place of diseases. From Europe came smallpox, measles (less deadly to
Africans than to American Indians), gonorrhea, and syphilis (which last

Columbus's sailors had carried from America to Europe). The African diseases were yellow fever (to which the natives were more resistant than white men), dengue, blackwater fever, and malaria (which was not specifically African, but which most of the slaves carried in their bloodstreams). If anopheles mosquitoes were present, malaria spread from the slaves through any new territories to which they were carried. Other African diseases were amoebic and various forms of bacillary dysentery (all known as "the bloody flux"), Guinea worms, hookworm (possibly African in origin, but soon endemic in the warmer parts of the New World), yaws, elephantiasis, and leprosy.

The particular affliction of the white sailors after escaping from the fevers of the Guinea Coast was scurvy, a deficiency disease to which they were exposed by their monotonous rations of salt beef and sea biscuits. The daily tot of lime juice (originally lemon juice) that prevented scurvy was almost never served on merchantmen during the days of the legal slave trade, and in fact was not prescribed in the Royal Navy until 1795. Although the slaves were also subject to scurvy, they fared better in this respect than the sailors, partly because they made only one leg of the triangular voyage and partly because their rough diet was sometimes richer in vitamins. But sailors and slaves alike were swept away by smallpox and "the bloody flux," and sometimes they went blind from various forms of ophthalmia, the worst of which seems to have been a gonorrheal infection of the eyes.

Smallpox was feared more than other diseases, since the surgeons had no means of combating it until the end of the eighteenth century. One man with smallpox infected a whole vessel, unless—as sometimes happened—he was tossed overboard when the first scabs appeared. Captain Wilson of the *Briton* lost more than half his cargo of 375 slaves by not listening to his surgeon. It was the last slave brought on board who had the disease, says Henry Ellison, who made the voyage. "The doctor told Mr. Wilson it was the small-pox," Ellison continues.

> He would not believe it, but said he would keep him, as he was a fine man. It soon broke out amongst the slaves. I have seen the platform one continued scab. We hauled up eight or ten slaves dead of a morning. The flesh and skin peeled off their wrists when taken hold of, being entirely mortified.

But dysentery, though not so much feared, could cause as many deaths. Ellison testifies that he made two voyages on the *Nightingale,* Captain Carter. On the first voyage the slaves were so crowded that thirty boys "messed and slept in the long boat all through the Middle Passage, there being no room below"; and still the vessel lost only five or six slaves in all, out of a cargo of 270. On the second voyage, however, the *Nightingale* buried "about 150, chiefly of fevers and flux. We had 250 when we left the coast."

Dr. Claxton sailed from Bonny on the *Young Hero,* Captain Molyneux. "We had 250 slaves," he says,

> of whom 132 died, chiefly of the flux. . . . The steerage and the boys' room were insufficient to receive the sick, so greatly did the disorder prevail. We were therefore obliged to place together those that were and those that were not diseased, and in consequence the disease and mortality spread more and more.

The hold was swimming with blood and mucus. Toward the end of her voyage the *Young Hero* met another vessel with almost the same name —the *Hero,* Captain Wilson—and learned that she had lost 360 slaves, more than half her cargo. Most of them had died of smallpox. When moved from one place to another, they left marks of their skin and blood upon the deck, and the other surgeon told Claxton that it was "the most horrid sight he had ever seen."

The average mortality in the Middle Passage is impossible to state accurately from the surviving records. Some famous voyages were made without the loss of a single slave, as notably by Captains John Newton, William Macintosh, and Hugh Crow. On one group of nine voyages between 1766 and 1780, selected at random, the vessels carried 2362 slaves and there were no epidemics of disease. The total loss of slaves was 154, or about 6½ per cent. On another list of twenty voyages compiled by Thomas Clarkson the abolitionist, the vessels carried 7904 slaves and lost 2053, or 26 per cent. Balancing high and low figures together, the English Privy Council in 1789 arrived at an estimate of 12½ per cent for the average mortality in the Middle Passage. That comes close to the percentage reckoned long afterward from the manifests of French vessels sailing from Nantes. Between 1748 and 1782 the Nantes slaves bought 146,799 slaves and sold 127,133 on the other side of the Atlantic. The difference of 19,666 would indicate a loss of 13 per cent in the voyage.

Of course there were further losses. To the mortality in the Middle Passage, the Privy Council added 4½ per cent for the deaths of slaves in harbors before they were sold, and 33 per cent for deaths during the seasoning process, making a total of 50 per cent. If those figures are correct (U. B. Phillips, the author of *American Negro Slavery,* thinks they are somewhat high), then only one slave was added to the New World labor force for every two purchased on the Guinea Coast.

To keep the figures in perspective, it might be added that the mortality among slaves in the Middle Passage was possibly no greater than that of white indentured servants or even of free Irish, Scottish, and German immigrants in the North Atlantic crossing. On the better commanded Guineamen it was probably much less, and for a simple economic reason. There was no profit in a slaving voyage until the Negroes were landed alive and sold; therefore the better captains took care of their cargoes. If the Negroes died in spite of good care, the captains regarded their deaths as a personal affront. "No gold-finders," lamented Captain Phillips of the *Hannibal,* who lost nearly half of his cargo from the bloody flux,

> can endure so much noisome slavery as they do who carry negroes; for those have some respite and satisfaction, but we endure twice the misery; and yet by their mortality our voyages are ruin'd, and we pine and fret our selves to death, to think that we should undergo so much misery, and take so much pains to so little purpose.

It was different on the North Atlantic crossing, where even the hold and steerage passengers paid their fares before coming aboard, and where it was of little concern to the captain whether they lived or died.

After leaving the Portuguese island of São Thomé—if he had watered there—a slaving captain bore westward along the equator for a thousand miles, and then northwestward toward the Cape Verde Islands. This was the tedious part of the Middle Passage. Along the equator the vessel might be delayed for weeks by calms or storms; sometimes it had to return to the African coast for fresh provisions. Then, "on leaving the Gulf of Guinea," says the author of a *Universal Geography* published in the early nineteenth century,

> . . . that part of the ocean must be traversed, so fatal to navigators, where long calms detain the ships under a sky charged with electric clouds, pouring down by turns torrents of rain and of fire. This *sea of thunder,* being a focus of mortal diseases, is avoided as much as possible, both in approaching the coasts of Africa and those of America.

It was not until reaching the latitude of the Cape Verde Islands that the vessel fell in with the Northeast Trades and was able to make a swift passage to the West Indies.

Ecroide Claxton's ship, the *Young Hero,* was one of those delayed for weeks before reaching the trade winds. "We were so streightened for provisions," he testified, "that if we had been ten more days at sea, we must either have eaten the slaves that died, or have made the living slaves *walk the plank,*" a term, he explained, that was widely used by Guinea captains. There are no authenticated records of cannibalism in the Middle Passage, but there are many accounts of slaves killed for various reasons. English captains believed that French vessels carried poison in their medicine chests, "with which they can destroy their negroes in a calm, contagious sickness, or short provisions." They told the story of a Frenchman from Brest who had a long passage and had to poison his slaves; only twenty of them reached Haiti out of five hundred. Even the cruelest English captains regarded this practice as Latin, depraved, and uncovered by their insurance policies. In an emergency they simply jettisoned part of their cargo.

The most famous case involving jettisoned slaves was that of the *Zong* out of Liverpool, Luke Collingwood master. The *Zong* had left São Thomé on September 6, 1781, with a cargo of four hundred and forty slaves and a white crew of seventeen. There was sickness aboard during a slow passage; more than sixty Negroes died, with seven of the seamen, and many of the remaining slaves were so weakened by dysentery that it was a question whether they could be sold in Jamaica. On November 29, after they had already sighted land in the West Indies, Captain Collingwood called his officers together. He announced that there were only two hundred gallons of fresh water left in the casks, not enough for the remainder of the voyage. If the slaves died of thirst or illness, he explained, the loss would fall on the owners of the vessel; but if they were thrown into the sea it would be a legal jettison, covered by insurance. "It would not be so cruel to throw the poor sick wretches into the sea," he argued, "as to suffer them to linger out a few days under the disorders to which they were afflicted."

The mate, James Kelsal, demurred at first, saying there was "no present want of water to justify such a measure," but the captain outtalked him. To quote from a legal document,

> The said Luke Collingwood picked, or caused to be picked out, from the cargo of the same ship, one hundred and thirty-three slaves, all or most of whom were sick or weak, and not likely to live; and ordered the crew by turns to throw them into the sea; which most inhuman order was cruelly complied with.

A first "parcel," as the sailors called them, of fifty-four slaves went overboard that same day, November 29. A second parcel, this time of forty-two, followed them on December 1, still leaving thirty-six slaves out of those condemned to be jettisoned. (One man seems to have died from natural causes.) Also on December 1 there was a heavy rain and the sailors collected six casks of water, enough to carry the vessel into port. But Collingwood stuck to his plan, and the last parcel of condemned slaves was brought on deck a few days later. Twenty-six of them were handcuffed, then swung into the sea. The last ten refused to let the sailors come near them; instead they vaulted over the bulwarks and were drowned like the others.

On December 22 the *Zong* dropped anchor in Kingston harbor after a passage of three months and sixteen days. Collingwood sold the remainder of his slaves, then sailed his vessel to England, where his owners claimed thirty pounds of insurance money for each of the one hundred and thirty-two jettisoned slaves. The underwriters refused to pay, and the case was taken to court. At a first trial the jury found for the owners, since "they had no doubt . . . that the case of slaves was the same as if horses had been thrown overboard." The underwriters appealed to the Court of Exchequer, and Lord Mansfield presided. After admitting that the law supported the owners of the *Zong,* he went on to say that "a higher law [applies to] this very shocking case." He found for the underwriters. It was the first case in which an English court ruled that a cargo of slaves could not be treated simply as merchandise.

Often a slave ship came to grief in the last few days of the Middle Passage. It might be taken by a French privateer out of Martinique, or it might disappear in a tropical hurricane, or it might be wrecked on a shoal almost in sight of its harbor. There was a famous wreck on Morant Keys off the eastern end of Jamaica; the sailors took refuge on a sandspit with a scanty store of provisions but plenty of rum, then massacred the slaves who tried to follow them. Only thirty-three Negroes survived (and were later exposed for sale in Kingston) out of about four hundred. On a few ships there was an epidemic of suicide at the last moment. Thus, when the *Prince of Orange* anchored at St. Kitts in 1737, more than a hundred Negro men jumped overboard. "Out of the whole," Captain Japhet Bird reported,

> we lost 33 of as good Men Slaves as we had on board, who would not endeavour to save themselves, but resolv'd to die, and sunk directly down. Many more of them were taken up almost drown'd, some of them died since, but not the Owners Loss, they being sold before any Discovery was made of the Injury the Salt Water had done them. . . .

> This Misfortune was owing to one of their Countrymen, who came on
> board and in a joking manner told the Slaves that they were first to
> have their Eyes put out, and then to be eaten, with a great many other
> nonsensical Falsities.

These, however, were exceptional misfortunes, recounted as horror
stories in the newspapers of the time. Usually the last two or three days
of the Middle Passage were a comparatively happy period. All the slaves,
or all but a few, might be released from their irons. When there was a
remaining stock of provisions, the slaves were given bigger meals—to
fatten them for market—and as much water as they could drink. Sometimes on the last day—if the ship was commanded by an easy-going
captain—there was a sort of costume party on deck, with the women
slaves dancing in the sailors' cast-off clothing. Then the captain was
rowed ashore to arrange for the disposition of his cargo.

There were several fashions of selling the slaves. In a few instances
the whole cargo was consigned to a single rich planter, or to a group
of planters. More often a West Indian factor took charge of retail sales,
for a commission of 15 per cent on the gross amount and 5 per cent
more on the net proceeds. When the captain himself had to sell his
slaves, he ferried them ashore, had them drawn up in a ragged line of
march, and paraded them through town with bagpipes playing, before
exposing them to buyers in the public square. J. G. Stedman, a young
officer in the Scots Brigade employed as a mercenary by the Dutch in
their obstinate efforts to suppress the slave revolts in Surinam, witnessed
such a parade. "The whole party was," he says, ". . . a resurrection of
skin and bones . . . risen from the grave or escaped from Surgeon's
Hall." The slaves exposed for sale were "walking skeletons covered over
with a piece of tanned leather."

But the commonest method of selling a cargo was a combination of
the "scramble"—to be described presently—and the vendue or public
auction "by inch of candle." First the captain, probably with the West
Indian factor at his side, went over the cargo and picked out the slaves
who were maimed or diseased. These were carried to a tavern and auc-
tioned off, with a lighted candle beside the auctioneer; bids were received until an inch of candle had burned. The price of these "refuse"
slaves sold at auction was usually less than half of that paid for a healthy
Negro; sometimes it was as little as five or six dollars a head. "I was
informed by a mulatto woman," Falconbridge says, "that she purchased
a sick slave at Grenada, upon speculation, for the small sum of one
dollar, as the poor wretch was apparently dying of the flux." There were

some slaves who could not be sold for even a dollar, and they were often left to die on the wharfs without food or water.

There were horse traders' methods of hiding the presence of disease. Yaws, for example, could be concealed by a mixture of iron rust and gunpowder, a practice which Edward Long, the Jamaica historian, denounces as a "wicked fraud." Falconbridge tells of a Liverpool captain who

> boasted of his having cheated some Jews by the following stratagem: A lot of slaves, afflicted with the flux, being about to be landed for sale, he directed the surgeon to stop the anus of each of them with oakum. . . . The Jews, when they examine them, oblige them to stand up, in order to see if there be any discharge; and when they do not perceive this appearance, they consider it as a symptom of recovery. In the present instance, such an appearance being prevented, the bargain was struck, and they were accordingly sold. But it was not long before a discovery ensued. The excruciating pain which the prevention of a discharge of such an acrimonious nature occasioned, not being to be borne by the poor wretches, the temporary obstruction was removed, and the deluded purchasers were speedily convinced of the imposition.

The healthy slaves remaining after an auction were sold by "scramble," that is, at standard prices for each man, each woman, each boy, and each girl in the cargo. The prices were agreed upon with the purchasers, who then scrambled for their pick of the slaves. During his four voyages Falconbridge was present at a number of scrambles. "In the *Emilia*," he says,

> at Jamaica, the ship was darkened with sails, and covered round. The men slaves were placed on the main deck, and the women on the quarter deck. The purchasers on shore were informed a gun would be fired when they were ready to open the sale. A great number of people came on board with tallies or cards in their hands, with their own names upon them, and rushed through the barricado door with the ferocity of brutes. Some had three or four handkerchiefs tied together, to encircle as many as they thought fit for their purpose.

For the slaves, many of whom thought they were about to be eaten, it was the terrifying climax of a terrifying voyage. Another of Falconbridge's ships, the *Alexander*, sold its cargo by scramble in a slave yard at Grenada. The women, he says, were frightened out of their wits. Several of them climbed over the fence and ran about Saint George's town as if they were mad. In his second voyage, while lying in Kingston harbor, he saw a sale by scramble on board the *Tyral,* Captain Macdonald. Forty or fifty of the slaves jumped overboard—"all of which, however," Falconbridge told the House of Commons, "he believes were taken up again."

STANLEY M. ELKINS

Shock and Detachment

The newly-captured slave underwent not one, but a series of dehumanizing experiences—"shocks," as Stanley M. Elkins calls them. Capture in the homeland, marches to the coast, the middle passage, the auctioneer's block—the total impact was immense and bewildering to those who survived. These shocks neutralized the system of values and pattern of culture from which the slave had taken his identity as an African. Suddenly he found himself in a foreign environment, in psychological limbo. How much, if any, of his African identity survived the experiences he suffered is a subject for conjecture. What is clear is that by the time he reached his new master, the slave was forced to look in large part to the "peculiar institution" itself for standards of behavior and belief, just as he had to depend on it for food, shelter, and other necessities.

As Elkins points out in the following selection, it was the comprehensiveness of the individual's enslavement and the removal of cultural alternatives that made American chattel slavery such a complete and totalitarian system of human bondage. Elsewhere in *Slavery,* the study from which this excerpt is taken, the author suggests that only Nazism and the concentration camps of World War II are truly analogous to slavery in the power to ravage the human psyche.

Slavery, of course, existed in Africa. But there was a sharp distinction between the domestic slavery prevalent among the tribes themselves and the state into which the deported captives would ultimately

SHOCK AND DETACHMENT   Reprinted from *Slavery: A Problem in American Institutional and Intellectual Life* by Stanley M. Elkins. By permission of The University of Chicago Press and Stanley M. Elkins. © 1959 by The University of Chicago. Universal Library Edition, 1963 by arrangement with the University of Chicago Press.

be delivered by the Europeans. There was little in the one that could prepare a man for what he would experience in the other. The typical West African slave was a recognized member of a household and possessed numerous rights. "A slave," according to R. S. Rattray, writing of Ashanti society, "might marry; own property; himself own a slave; swear an 'oath'; be a competent witness; and ultimately might become heir to his master."[1]

A closely knit family structure stood at the base of all political, economic, and legal institutions, whose efficiency in turn depended on the discipline enforced within the family. Throughout West Africa the authority of the elders was accepted without question. Despite wide variation in political organization—ranging from small independent units to large empires—all assumed the rule of law rather than simple despotism. The king was never absolute; he ruled with the advice of a council of elders and in accordance with traditional law and custom. Just as authority was carefully graded from the family to the chief—and, in the larger units, to the king—so the law itself was administered by an intricate system of inferior and superior courts. African political institutions, moreover, were developed in sufficient complexity that they were able to provide stable governments for groups as large as two hundred thousand, some of them lasting for centuries.[2]

One of the most famous of these governments was the Ashanti, located in the heart of the slaving area. Ashanti emerged as a powerful feudal state about 1700, when one of the tribal rulers persuaded his fellow chiefs to recognize him as the *Asantehene,* king of all the Ashantis. A meaningful comparison between such a society and those of medieval Europe would be difficult, but the political federation of the Ashantis, their traditional constitution, their tax and revenue structure, and their military system—a system that enabled them to wage extended campaigns with armies as large as thirty or forty thousand—entitles one to argue that they must have had an institutional life at least as sophisticated as that of Anglo-Saxon England.[3]

---

[1] R. S. Rattray, *Ashanti Law and Constitution* (Oxford: Clarendon Press, 1929), p. 38. See also *ibid.,* pp. 33–46; Herskovits, *Dahomey,* I, 99–100, and II, 97–98. [Melville J. Herskovits, *Dahomey: An Ancient West African Kingdom,* I, II (New York: J. J. Augustin, 1938).]

[2] See, e.g., C. K. Meek, *Law and Authority in a Nigerian Tribe: A Study in Indirect Rule* (London: Oxford University Press, 1937), pp. 88–164, 206–51; Rattray, *Ashanti Law and Constitution,* esp. pp. 75–98; and Herskovits, *Dahomey,* II, 3–48.

[3] In addition to the material in Rattray, see W. E. F. Ward, *A History of the Gold Coast* (London: George Allen & Unwin, 1948), pp. 107–19; and J. D. Fage, *An Introduction to the History of West Africa* (Cambridge: University Press, 1955), pp. 95–98. It was not primarily the rigors of disease and tropical

But returning to the primary problem: no true picture, cursory or extended, of African culture seems to throw any light at all on the origins of what would emerge, in American plantation society, as the stereotyped "Sambo" personality. The typical West African tribesman was a distinctly warlike individual; he had a profound sense of family and family authority; he took hard work for granted; and he was accustomed to live by a highly formalized set of rules which he himself often helped to administer. If he belonged to the upper classes of tribal society —as did many who later fell victim to the slave trade—he might have had considerable experience as a political or military leader. He was the product, in any case, of cultural traditions essentially heroic in nature.

Something very profound, therefore, would have had to intervene in order to obliterate all this and to produce, on the American plantation, a society of helpless dependents.

We may suppose that every African who became a slave underwent an experience whose crude psychic impact must have been staggering and whose consequences superseded anything that had ever previously happened to him. Some effort should therefore be made to picture the series of shocks which must have accompanied the principal events of that enslavement.

The majority of slaves appear to have been taken in native wars,[4]

---

climate that served to keep the Europeans out of the interior for so long, but rather the highly developed governmental and military systems of such West African nations as Ashanti, all of whom had at least one policy in common, an inflexible determination to prevent any non-African middlemen from cutting in on the internal slave trade. Nor was this area a "trackless wilderness"; it was much more thickly populated than was North America at the time of the first colonizing ventures and was crossed by a maze of heavily traveled trading routes. The power of Ashanti, for instance, continued until late in the nineteenth century when the Ashanti armies were finally defeated by the British after a long period, nearly a hundred years, of full-scale warfare. Ward's *History* deals at length with the relations of Ashanti and the British, and with the military campaigns that they waged against each other. See also Dike, *Trade and Politics*, pp. 7–10. [K. Onwuka Dike, *Trade and Politics in the Niger Delta, 1830–1885* (Oxford: Clarendon Press, 1956).]

[4] There were other pretexts, such as crime or debt, but war was probably the most frequent mode of procurement. Snelgrave, *New Account*, p. 158; [William Snelgrave, *A New Account of Some Parts of Guinea, and the Slave Trade* (London: James, John and Paul Knapton, 1734).] "John Barbot's Description," in Donnan, *Documents*, I, 284, 289, 294, 298; [Elizabeth Donnan, *Documents Illustrative of the History of the Slave Trade* (Washington: Carnegie Institution, 1930ff.).] "Observations on the Slave Trade, 1789" [C. B. Wadström] in *ibid.*, II, 599; Matthews, *Voyage to Sierra-Leone*, pp. 145–46, 163. [John Matthews, *A Voyage to the River Sierra-Leone* . . . (London: B. White and Son, 1788).]

which meant that no one—neither persons of high rank nor warriors of prowess—was guaranteed against capture and enslavement.[5] Great numbers were caught in surprise attacks upon their villages, and since the tribes acting as middlemen for the trade had come to depend on regular supplies of captives in order to maintain that function, the distinction between wars and raiding expeditions tended to be very dim.[6] The first shock, in an experience destined to endure many months and to leave its survivors irrevocably changed, was thus the shock of capture. It is an effort to remember that while enslavement occurred in Africa every day, to the individual it occurred just once.[7]

The second shock—the long march to the sea—drew out the nightmare for many weeks. Under the glaring sun, through the steaming jungle, they were driven along like beasts tied together by their necks;

[5] As to "character types," one might be tempted to suppose that as a rule it would be only the weaker and more submissive who allowed themselves to be taken into slavery. Yet it appears that a heavy proportion of the slaves were in fact drawn from among the most warlike. "In a country divided into a thousand petty states, mostly independent and jealous of each other; where every freeman is accustomed to arms, and fond of military achievements; where the youth who has practised the bow and spear from his infancy, longs for nothing so much as an opportunity to display his valour; it is natural to imagine that wars frequently originate from very frivolous provocation." Park, *Travels*, p. 328. [Mungo Park, *Travels and Recent Discoveries, in the Interior Districts of Africa, in the Years, 1796 & 97* (New York: Alexander Brodie, 1801).] "The most potent negroe," wrote William Bosman, "can't pretend to be insured from slavery; for if he ever ventures himself in the wars it may easily become his lot." *New and Accurate Description*, p. 183. [William Bosman, *A New and Accurate Description of the Coast of Guinea* (London: J. Knapton, 1705).] It has often been pointed out that slavery already existed among the tribes themselves and that a considerable proportion of Africans were used to it and had in fact been born into it. It may be doubted, however, if substantial numbers of *these* slaves came to America, for apparently the native chiefs tended to sell only their war captives to the Europeans and to keep their hereditary and customary slaves—together with their most docile captives—for themselves. Park, *Travels*, p. 332. It has even been asserted that in many places the tribal laws themselves forbade the selling of domestic slaves, except for crimes, though apparently it was simple enough to trump up an accusation if one wanted to get rid of a slave. Matthews, *Voyage to Sierra-Leone*, p. 153; Edwards, *History*, II, 312. [Bryan Edwards, *The History, Civil and Commercial, of the British Colonies in the West Indies* (Philadelphia: James Humphreys, 1806).]

[6] "The Wars which the inhabitants of the interior parts of the country, beyond Senegal, Gambia, and Sierra Leona, carry on with each other, are chiefly of a predatory nature, and owe their origin to the yearly number of slaves, which the Mandingoes, or the inland traders suppose will be wanted by the vessels that will arrive on the coast." "Observations" [Wadström], in Donnan, *Documents*, II, 599.

[7] A number of excerpts describing these raids are cited in Thomas Fowell Buxton, *Letter on the Slave Trade to the Lord Viscount Melbourne* (London, 1838), pp. 34–38.

day after day, eight or more hours at a time, they would stagger barefoot over thorny underbrush, dried reeds, and stones. Hardship, thirst, brutalities, and near starvation penetrated the experience of each exhausted man and woman who reached the coast.[8] One traveler tells of seeing hundreds of bleaching skeletons strewn along one of the slave caravan routes.[9] But then the man who must interest us is the man who survived —he who underwent the entire experience, of which this was only the beginning.

The next shock, aside from the fresh physical torments which accompanied it, was the sale to the European slavers. After being crowded into pens near the trading stations and kept there overnight, sometimes for days, the slaves were brought out for examination. Those rejected would be abandoned to starvation; the remaining ones—those who had been bought—were branded, given numbers inscribed on leaden tags, and herded on shipboard.[10]

The episode that followed—almost too protracted and stupefying to be called a mere "shock"—was the dread Middle Passage, brutalizing to any man, black or white, ever to be involved with it. The holds, packed with squirming and suffocating humanity, became stinking infernos of filth and pestilence. Stories of disease, death, and cruelty on the terrible two-month voyage abound in the testimony which did much toward ending the British slave trade forever.[11]

---

[8] Descriptions of the march may be found in Park, *Travels,* pp. 371ff., Buxton, *Letter,* pp. 41–44; Rinchon, *La traite et l'esclavage,* pp. 174–75; [Fr. Dieudonné Rinchon, *La traite et l'esclavage des Congolais par les Europeéns* (Wetteren, Belgium, 1929).] L. Degrandpré, *Voyage à la côte occidentale d'Afrique, fait dans les années 1786 et 1787* (Paris, 1801), II, 48–50.

[9] Buxton, *Letter,* p. 43.

[10] "When these slaves come to fida, they are put in prison all together, and when we treat concerning buying them, they are all brought out together in a large plain; where, by our Chirurgeons, whose province it is, they are thoroughly examined, even to the smallest member, and that naked too both men and women, without the least distinction and modesty. Those which are approved as good are set on one side; and the lame or faulty are set by as *invalides,* which are here called *mackrons.* These are such as are above five and thirty years old, or are maimed in the arms, legs, hands or feet, have lost a tooth, are greyhaired, or have films over their eyes; as well as all those which are affected by any venereal distemper, or with several other diseases." Bosman, *New and Accurate Description,* p. 364. See also Degrandpré, *Voyage,* II, 53–56; Buxton, *Letter,* pp. 47–49; Rinchon, *La traite et l'esclavage,* pp. 188–89; "John Barbot's Description," in Donnan, *Documents,* I, 289, 295; Park, *Travels,* p. 360.

[11] Descriptions of the Middle Passage may be found in *An Abstract of the Evidence Delivered before a Select Committee of the House of Commons in the Years 1790, and 1791; on the Part of the Petitioners for the Abolition of the Slave Trade* (London, 1791); Alexander Falconbridge, *An Account of the Slave Trade on the Coast of Africa* (London: J. Phillips, 1788); Rinchon, *La*

The final shock in the process of enslavement came with the Negro's introduction to the West Indies. Bryan Edwards, describing the arrival of a slave ship, writes of how in times of labor scarcity crowds of people would come scrambling aboard, manhandling the slaves and throwing them into panic. The Jamaica legislature eventually "corrected the enormity" by enacting that the sales be held on shore. Edwards felt a certain mortification at seeing the Negroes exposed naked in public, similar to that felt by the trader Degrandpré at seeing them examined back at the African factories.[12] Yet here they did not seem to care. "They display . . . very few signs of lamentation for their past or of apprehension for their future condition; but . . . commonly express great eagerness to be sold."[13] The "seasoning" process which followed completed the series of steps whereby the African Negro became a slave.

The mortality had been very high. One-third of the numbers first taken, out of a total of perhaps fifteen million, had died on the march and at the trading stations; another third died during the Middle Passage and the seasoning.[14] Since a majority of the African-born slaves who came to the North American plantations did not come directly but were imported through the British West Indies, one may assume that the typical slave underwent an experience something like that just outlined. This was the man—one in three—who had come through it all and lived and was about to enter our "closed system." What would he be like if he survived and adjusted to that?

Actually, a great deal had happened to him already. Much of his past had been annihilated; nearly every prior connection had been severed. Not that he had really "forgotten" all these things—his family and kinship arrangements, his language, the tribal religion, the taboos, the name he had once borne, and so on—but none of it any longer carried much meaning. The old values, the sanctions, the standards, already unreal, could no longer furnish him guides for conduct, for adjusting to the expectations of a complete new life. Where then was he to look for new

---

traite et l'esclavage, pp. 196–209; Edwards, History, II; Brantz Mayer, Captain Canot (New York: D. Appleton, 1854); Averil Mackenzie-Grieve, The Last Years of the English Slave Trade, Liverpool 1750–1807 (London: Putnam, 1941).

[12] Degrandpré, Voyage, II, 55–56.

[13] Edwards, History, II, 340. See also Abstract of Evidence, pp. 46–47, and Falconbridge, Account, pp. 33–36.

[14] Tannenbaum, Slave and Citizen, p. 28. [Frank Tannenbaum, Slave and Citizen (New York: Alfred A. Knopf, 1947).] As for the total exports of slaves from Africa throughout the entire period of the trade, estimates run as high as twenty million. "Even a conservative estimate," notes Mr. Tannenbaum, "would hardly cut this figure in half." Ibid., p. 32.

standards, new cues—who would furnish them now? He could now look to none but his master, the one man to whom the system had committed his entire being: the man upon whose will depended his food, his shelter, his sexual connections, whatever moral instruction he might be offered, whatever "success" was possible within the system, his very security—in short, everything.

E. FRANKLIN FRAZIER

Hagar and Her Children

The slaveholding South adopted the position, bluntly expressed in the periodical literature of the time, that slaves were not men at all, but exotic creatures occupying some ambiguous state between man and beast. At every turn it did what it could to enforce and strengthen this assumption. Marriages between slaves were illegal and commonly ridiculed by the masters as the amusing antics of mimicking children; slave families were capriciously broken up and sold; slave breeding flourished, with the owners picking out and rewarding women who were called "hearty breeders" and men who were "good studs." That all this ignored the most basic desires for human dignity on the part of black people was never considered important because slaves were not thought to have any sense of human dignity.

However, another kind of relationship—as damaging in its immediate and long-range consequences as the fragmentation of black families—came out of slavery: a complex network of covert sexual associations between blacks and whites. Not only did Southern whites debase their black "property" by treating them impersonally as simple cheap laboring beasts, but, as E. Franklin Frazier shows in the following excerpt from his study of black families, those same whites were not above resorting to the slave quarters for their own sexual gratifi-

HAGAR AND HER CHILDREN   Reprinted from *The Negro Family in the U.S.* by E. Franklin Frazier. By permission of The University of Chicago Press and E. Franklin Frazier. Published 1966. Revised and Abridged Edition Copyright 1948, by the Dryden Press, Inc., New York. Original edition © 1939 by The University of Chicago.

cation. This intimacy and the syndrome of guilt and hatred it helped establish left their bold imprint on the history of racism in America.

Nowhere did human impulses and human feelings and senti-ments tend to dissolve the formal relations between master and slave as in their sexual association, from which sprang those anomalous family groups consisting mainly of slave mother and mulatto offspring. But it was often in these very cases of human solidarity created by ties of blood that the ideas and sentiments embodied in the institution of slavery pre-vailed over the promptings of human feeling and sympathy. Where sex-ual association between master and slave was supported by personal attachment and in many cases genuine sentiment, we find the black, and more often mulatto, woman, under the protection of her master's house, playing a double role—a wife without the confirmation of the law and a mistress without the glamour of romance. Where the slave woman was only the means of satisfying a fleeting impulse, we find her rearing her mulatto offspring on the fare of slaves or being sold at a premium on the auction block because of her half-white brood. But whether her children were doomed to servitude or nurtured under the guidance of a solicitous father, they were not unconscious of their relation to the master race.

The admonition contained in the sermon preached at Whitechapel in 1609 for the benefit of adventurers and planters bound for Virginia, that "Abrams posteritie [must] keepe to themselves," was ignored in regard to the Negro as well as to the Indian. But the added injunction that "they may not marry nor give in marriage to the heathen, that are uncir-cumcised" became, except in rare instances, the inexorable policy of the whites in their relation with both of the subordinate races. Intercourse between whites and Negroes began as soon as the latter were introduced into America. In the beginning the sexual association between the two races was not confined to white males and the women of the black race. Colonial records furnish us with numerous instances of bastard children by Negro men and indentured white women. Two instances of this nature are reported by Helen Tunnicliff Catterall. A case brought into the Virginia courts in 1769 by a mulatto in suing for his freedom begins thus:

> A Christian white woman between the year of 1723 and 1765, had a daughter, Betty Bugg, by a negro man. This daughter was by deed in-dented, bound by the churchwardens to serve till thirty-one. Before the expiration of her servitude, she was delivered of the defendant Bugg,

who never was bound by the churchwardens, and was sold by his master to the plaintiff. Being now twenty-six years of age, and having cause of complaint against the plaintiff, as being illy provided with clothes and diet, he brought an action in the court to recover his liberty, founding his claim on three points.

Another case for the following year states that "the plaintiff's grandmother was a mulatto, begotten on a white woman by a negro man, after the year 1705, and bound by the churchwardens, under the law of that date, to serve to the age of thirty-one."

There is also good evidence that intercourse between Negro males and white servant women was sometimes encouraged by white masters who desired to increase the number of their bound servants. Marriages of Negroes and whites, most of whom were indentured servants, seem to have been numerous enough to require the enactment of severe laws for their prevention. But, when the principle of racial integrity and white domination became fixed in the minds of the whites, social censure and severe penalties were reserved, with rare exceptions, for the association of Negro men and white women. Calhoun has given us the following items from the court records of Chester County, Pennsylvania, in 1698: "For that hee . . . contrary to the laws of the government and contrary to his masters consent hath . . . got with child a certain mulato woman called swart Anna. . . . ."

> David Lewis Constable of Haverford returned a negro man of his and a white woman for haveing a baster childe . . . the negro said she intised him and promised him to marry him; she being examined, confest the same . . . the court ordered that she shall receive twenty-one lashes on her beare backe . . . and the court ordered the negroe man never to meddle with any white woman more uppon paine of his life.

As slavery developed into an institution, neither the segregation of the great body of slaves from the masses of the whites nor the mutual antagonism between the "poor whites" and the blacks was an effectual check on the sexual association between the two races. In the cities, especially, where the slaves were released from the control under which they lived on the plantations, and there were many free Negroes, association between the women of the subordinate race and white men assumed in the majority of cases a casual and debasing character. In fact, a traffic in mulatto women especially for prostitution became a part of the regular slave trade in southern cities. The following item appeared in the *Memphis Eagle and Enquirer,* June 26, 1857: "A slave woman is advertised to be sold in St. Louis who is so surpassingly beautiful that

$5,000 has been already offered for her, at private sale, and refused."

Prostitution of slave women became in many cases a private affair and, when in such cases it led to the formation of more or less permanent associations, it merged into that developed and almost socially approved system of concubinage which was found in Charleston, Mobile, and New Orleans. The cities were not, however, the only places where widespread intermixture of the races occurred. Although it is difficult to estimate the extent to which the slaveholders entered into sexual associations with their slaves, there is abundance of evidence of both concubinage and polygamy on the part of the master class. Moreover, although the intercourse between the masters and slave women on the plantations assumed as a rule a more permanent form than similar relations in the cities, the character of these associations varied considerably. Therefore, we shall examine the character of the different types of associations and try to determine the nature of the family groups that grew out of them.

In view of the relations of superordination and subordination between the two races, how far did these associations originate in mere physical compulsion? How far did the women of the subordinate race surrender themselves because they were subject to the authority of the master race? Or was the prestige of the white race sufficient to insure compliance on the part of the black and mulatto women, both slave and free? How far was mutual attraction responsible for acquiescence on the part of the woman?

All these factors were effective in creating the perplexing relationships in which men of the master race and women of the subject race became entangled. That physical compulsion was necessary at times to secure submission on the part of black women, both slave and free, is supported by historical evidence and has been preserved in the traditions of Negro families. A young man in a Negro college writes concerning the birth of his great-great-grandfather on his mother's side:

> Approximately a century and a quarter ago, a group of slaves were picking cotton on a plantation near where Troy, Alabama, is now located. Among them was a Negro woman, who, despite her position as a slave, carried herself like a queen and was tall and stately. The over-seer (who was the plantation's owner's son) sent her to the house on some errand. It was necessary to pass through a wooded pasture to reach the house and the over-seer intercepted her in the woods and forced her to put her head between the rails in an old stake and rider fence, and there in that position my great-great-grandfather was conceived.

In the family history of another college student the story of the circumstances under which the Negro woman had been forced to yield to the sexual assault by her white master had become a sort of family skeleton, well guarded because of the sensitive feelings and pride of the victim. Of her great-grandmother, our informant writes:

> As young as I was when I knew her, I remember distinctly her fierce hatred of white people, especially of white men. She bore marks of brutal beatings she received for attempted escapes, or for talking back to her master or mistress. One mark in particular stands out in my memory, one she bore just above her right eye. As well as she liked to regale me with stories of her scars, this is one she never discussed with me. Whenever I would ask a question concerning it, she would simply shake her head and say, "White men are as low as dogs, child. Stay away from them." It was only after her death, and since I became a woman that I was told by my own mother that she received that scar at the hands of her master's youngest son, a boy of about eighteen years at the time she conceived their child, my grandmother, Ellen. She belonged to a family of tobacco planters I believe, for she often spoke of tobacco, and liked very much to smoke it in an old pipe, which seems to have been almost as old as she. During the time she was carrying Ellen, she was treated more brutally than before, and had to work even harder than ever. But strange to say, after the child was born, and was seen to be white, in appearance at least, the attitude of the whole C——family seemed to soften toward her somewhat, and after this she became a house servant and was taught to sew, and became the family seamstress.

It seems that at times resistance to the white man's passion resulted in sadistical revenge upon the women. The form of punishment administered in the following case bears this implication.

> Thomas James, Jep's second son, had cast his eyes on a handsome young negro girl, to whom he made dishonest overtures. She would not submit to him, and finding he could not overcome her, he swore he would be revenged. One night he called her out of the gin-house, and then bade me and two or three more, strip her naked; which we did. He then made us throw her down on her face, in front of the door, and hold her whilst he flogged her—the brute—with the bull-whip, cutting great gashes of flesh out of her person, at every blow, from five to six inches long. The poor unfortunate girl screamed most awfully all the time, and writhed under our strong arms, rendering it necessary for us to use our united strength to hold her down. He

flogged her for half an hour, until he nearly killed her, and then left her to crawl away to her cabin.[1]

However, in many instances men of the master race did not meet much resistance on the part of the slave women. The mere prestige of the white race was sufficient to secure compliance with their desires. As Miss Kemble observed, the slaves accepted the contempt of their masters to such an extent that "they profess, and really seem to feel it for themselves, and the faintest admixture of white blood in their veins appears at once, by common consent of their own race, to raise them in the scale of humanity." The following incident related by John Thompson, a former slave indicates compliance on the part of a woman who was married to a slave:

> Soon after my arrival in the family, Mr. Thomas let me to one of his sons, named Henry, who was a doctor, to attend his horse. This son was unmarried, lived a bachelor, and kept a cook and waiter. The cook belonged neither to him nor his father, but was hired. She was a good looking mulatto, and was married to a right smart, intelligent man, who belonged to the doctor's uncle. One night, coming home in haste, and wishing to see his wife, he sent me up stairs to request her to come down. Upon going up I found she was in a room with the doctor, the door of which was fast. This I thoughtlessly told her husband, who, upon her coming down a moment after, upbraided her for it. She denied it, and afterwards told the doctor. . . . The doctor was a very intemperate man. As soon as his cook told him her story, he came to his father with the complaint that I had left him without his consent; upon which his father told him to flog me.[2]

Moreover, there were often certain concrete advantages to be gained by surrendering themselves to the men of the master race that overcame any moral scruples these women might have had. In some cases it meant freedom from the drudgery of field labor as well as better food and clothing. Then there was the prospect that her half-white children would enjoy certain privileges and perhaps in time be emancipated.

Mutual attraction also played a part in securing the compliance of the woman. In many cases the intimacies that developed began in the household where the two races lived in close association. The historian

[1] John Brown, *Slave Life in Georgia,* ed., L. A. Chameroozow (London, 1855), pp. 132–33.
[2] John Thompson, *The Life of John Thompson, a Fugitive Slave: Containing His History of Twenty-five Years in Bondage, and His Providential Escape, Written by Himself* (Worcester, 1856), pp. 30–31.

of Alabama, who attempts to place the responsibility for these illicit unions upon the slave woman, refers to the seductiveness of the latter. But it appears that, aside from the prestige of the white race and the material advantages to be gained, these slave women were as responsive to the attractiveness of the white males as the latter were to the charms of the slave women. Hence, slave women were not responsive to the approaches of all white men and often showed some discrimination and preference in the bestowal of their favors. The following incident is from the life of Bishop Loguen's mother, who was the mistress of a white man near Nashville, Tennessee:

> When she was about the age of twenty-four or five, a neighboring planter finding her alone at the distillery, and presuming upon the privileges of his position, made insulting advances, which she promptly repelled. He pursued her with gentle force, and was still repelled. He then resorted to a slaveholder's violence and threats. These stirred all the tiger's blood in her veins. She broke from his embrace, and stood before him in bold defiance. He attempted again to lay hold of her—and careless of caste and slave laws, she grasped the heavy stick used to stir the malt, and dealt him a blow which made him reel and retire. But he retired only to recover and return with the fatal knife, and threats of vengeance and death. Again she aimed the club with unmeasured force at him, and hit the hand which held the weapon, and dashed it to a distance from him. Again he rushed upon her with the fury of a madman, and she then plied a blow upon his temple, which laid him, as was supposed, dead at her feet.[3]

The relations between the white men and the slave women naturally aroused the jealousy and antagonism of the women of the master race. Because of the patriarchal character of the family, it was probably true to some extent, as one traveler related, that "a Southern wife, if she is prodigally furnished with dollars to 'go shopping,' apparently considers it no drawback to her happiness if some brilliant mulatto or quadroon woman ensnares her husband." But, frequently, the wife visited her resentment not only upon the slave woman but upon her husband's mulatto children. In some cases white women arranged marriages for their female slaves as a means of breaking off their husband's attachment. This expedient seemingly failed in the following incident related by a former slave concerning his sister:

> Mistress told sister that she had best get married, and that if she would, she would give her a wedding. Soon after a very respectable

[3] J. W. Loguen, *The Rev. J. W. Loguen, as a Slave and as a Freeman* (Syracuse, N.Y., 1859), pp. 20–21.

young man, belonging to Mr. Bowman, a wealthy planter, and reputed
to be a good master, began to court my sister. This very much pleased
Mistress, who wished to hasten the marriage. She determined that her
maid should be married, not as slaves usually are, but that with the
usual matrimonial ceremonies should be tied the knot to be broken
only by death. The Sabbath was appointed for the marriage, which was
to take place at the Episcopal Church. I must here state that no slave
can be married lawfully, without a fine from his or her owner. Mistress
and all the family, except the old man, went to church, to witness the
marriage ceremony, which was to be performed by their minister, Par-
son Reynolds. The master of Josiah, my sister's destined husband, was
also at the wedding, for he thought a great deal of his man. Mistress
returned delighted from the wedding, for she thought she had accomplished a great piece of work. But the whole affair only enraged her
unfeeling husband, who, to be revenged upon the maid, proposed to
sell her. To this his wife refused consent. Although Mrs. T. had never
told him her suspicions or what my sister had said, yet he suspected
the truth, and determined to be revenged. Accordingly, during another
absence of Mistress, he again cruelly whipped my sister. A continued
repetition of these things finally killed our Mistress, who the doctor
said, died of a broken heart. After the death of this friend, sister ran
away leaving her husband and one child and finally found her way to
the North.[4]

Sometimes white women used more direct means of ridding themselves of their colored rivals. There was always the possibility of selling
them. If they were not able to accomplish this during the lifetime of their
husbands, they were almost certain to get their revenge when the slave
woman's protector died, as witness the following excerpt from the family
history of a mulatto:

> My father's grandmother, Julia Heriot, of four generations ago lived
> in Georgetown, South Carolina. Recollections of her parentage are,
> indeed, vague. Nevertheless, a distinct mixture of blood was portrayed
> in her physical appearance. And, because she knew so little of her
> parents, she was no doubt sold into Georgetown at a very early age
> as house servant to General Charles Washington Heriot. Julia Heriot
> married a slave on the plantation by whom she had two children. Very
> soon after her second child was born an epidemic of fever swept the
> plantation, and her husband became one of the victims. After her hus-
> band's death, she became maid to Mrs. Heriot, wife of General Heriot.
> From the time that Julia Heriot was sold to General Heriot, she had
> been a favorite servant in the household, because of the aptitude which

4 Thompson, *op. cit.*, pp. 33–34.

she displayed in performing her tasks. General and Mrs. Heriot had been so impressed with her possibilities that in a very short time after she had been in her new home, she had been allowed to use the name of Heriot. . . . in the midst of her good fortune, a third child was born to her, which bore no resemblance to her other children. Reports of the "white child" were rumored. General Heriot's wife became enraged and insisted that her husband sell this slave girl, but General Heriot refused.

During the winter of the following year General Heriot contracted pneumonia and died. Before his death, he signed freedom papers for Julia and her three children; but Mrs. Heriot maneuvered her affairs so that Julia Heriot and her three children were again sold into slavery. In the auction of properties Julia Heriot was separated from her first two children. She pleaded that her babies be allowed to remain with her, but found her former mistress utterly opposed to anything that concerned her well-being. Her baby was the only consolation which she possessed. Even the name Heriot had been taken away by constant warnings.

In spite of the moralizing tone of the following excerpt the incidents related are probably authentic:

Among the slaves on Mr. McKiernan's plantation were a number of handsome women. Of these the master was extremely fond, and many of them he beguiled with vile flatteries, and cheated by false promises of future kindness, till they became victims to his unbridled passions. Upon these unfortunate women fell the heavy hatred of their mistress; and year after year, as new instances of her husband's perfidy came to her knowledge her jealousy ran higher, till at length reason seemed banished from her mind, and kindliness became a stranger to her heart. Then she sought a solace in the wine cup; and the demon of intoxication fanned the fires of hatred that burned within her, till they consumed all that was womanly in her nature, and rendered her an object of contempt and ridicule, even among her own dependents.[5]

The resentment of the white woman was likely to be manifested toward the offspring of her husband's relations with the slave woman. A mulatto former slave, after remarking that white women were "always revengeful toward the children of slaves that [had] any of the blood of their husbands in them," tells of his mother's anxiety when he, because of his relation to his master, became the object of the mistress' resentment. Calhoun cites the case of a mistress who, "out of ungrounded

[5] Mrs. Kate E. R. Pickard, *The Kidnapped and the Ransomed: Being the Personal Collections of Peter Still and His Wife "Vina," after Forty Years of Slavery* (New York, 1856), p. 167.

jealousy, had slaves hold a negro girl down while she cut off the forepart of the victim's feet."

Resentment against the mulatto child was especially likely to be aroused if the white father showed it much affection. In South Carolina in 1801 a woman secured alimony from her husband on the grounds that

> he cohabited with his own slave, by whom he had a mulatto child, on whom he lavished his affection; whilst he daily insulted the complainant, and encouraged his slave to do the same. . . . That at dinner one day, he took away the plate from complainant when she was going to help herself to something to eat, and said, when he and the negro had dined she might.[6]

The slave woman's relations with the white males sometimes aroused the antagonism of the entire household. Her relations with the sons in the family were regarded in such cases as an offense against the integrity of the family. In the incident related by Pennington we see her not only as the victim of the sexual desires of the son in the household but also as the object of the affection of her colored father who sought to save her:

> My master once owned a beautiful girl about twenty-four. She had been raised in a family where her mother was a great favourite. She was her mother's darling child. Her master was a lawyer of eminent abilities and great fame, but owing to habits of intemperance, he failed in business, and my master purchased this girl for a nurse. After he had owned her about a year, one of his sons became attached to her, for no honourable purposes; a fact which was not only well-known among all the slaves, but which became a source of unhappiness to his mother and sisters.
>
> The result was that poor Rachel had to be sold to "Georgia." Never shall I forget the heart-rending scene, when one day one of the men was ordered to get "the one-horse cart ready to go into town"; Rachel, with her few articles of clothing, was placed in it, and taken into the very town where her parents lived, and there sold to the traders before their weeping eyes. That same son who had degraded her, and who was the cause of her being sold, acted as salesman, and bill of salesman. While his cruel business was being transacted, my master stood aside, and the girl's father, a pious member and exhorter in the Methodist Church, a venerable grey-headed man, with his hat off, besought that he might be allowed to get some one in the place to purchase his child.

[6] Helen Tunnicliff Catterall (ed), *Judicial Cases concerning American Slavery and the Negro,* Washington, D.C., 1929, II, p. 281.

But no: my master was invincible. His reply was, "She has offended in my family, and I can only restore confidence by sending her out of hearing." After lying in prison a short time, her new owner took her with others to the far South, where her parents heard no more of her.[7]

The white wife often saw in the colored woman not only a rival for her husband's affection but also a possible competitor for a share in his property.

Catterall cites several court cases where this was the chief issue. In Kentucky in 1848 the court held that a white man's will should be rejected because he had disinherited his children. The record of the court stated that

> during the few last years of his life, . . . he [the testator, who died in 1845] seems to have had no will of his own, but to have submitted implicitly to the dictation of a colored woman whom he had emancipated, and whose familiar intercourse with him, had brought him into complete and continued subjection to her influence. . . . The gratification of the wishes of this colored woman, seems to be its leading object. The natural duty of providing for his own children . . . was entirely . . . disregarded.

Probably not many men of the master race became so enamoured of their colored mistresses as to disinherit their wives and children. In fact, where they showed strong attachment for their colored mistresses, attempts were made to prove mental disability. This was the contention set up by the heirs-at-law in a case in South Carolina in 1856:

> Elijah Willis, by his will, dated 1854, bequeathed Amy (his slave mistress), her seven children (some of whom were his own), and their descendants to his executors, directing them "to bring or cause said persons, and their increase, to be brought to . . . Ohio, and to emancipate and set them free." He also bequeathed and devised to his executors all the rest of his property, from the sale of which to purchase lands in one of the free states for said slaves, to stock and furnish the same, and to place said persons in possession thereof. "Elijah Willis, taking with him his negro slave, Amy, and her children, and her mother, in May, 1855, left his home (in South Carolina) . . . for Cincinnati. . . . He arrived in a steamboat, and leaving it at a landing, on the Ohio side . . . he died between the landing and a hack, in which he was about proceeding, with his said negroes, to his lodgings." His heirs-at-law contended that the will was void under the act of 1841, and also "undertook to show insanity, fraud, and undue

[7] J. W. C. Pennington, *The Fugitive Blacksmith; or Events in the History of James W. C. Pennington* (London, 1850), pp. vi–vii.

influence, by proving . . . that the deceased was often under gloomy depression of spirits—avoiding society on account of his connection with Amy, by whom he had several children; that he permitted her to act as the mistress of his house; to use saucy and improper language; that she was drunken, and probably unfaithful to him; and that she exercised great influence over him in reference to his domestic affairs, and in taking slaves from his business, to make wheels for little wagons for his mulatto children, and in inducing him to take off for sale the negro man who was her husband. . . .[8]

When the same contention was made against a will in a Kentucky case in 1831, the court held:

"The fact that the deceased evinced an inclination to marry the slave, Grace, whom he liberated, is not a stronger evidence of insanity than the practice of rearing children by slaves without marriage; a practice but too common, as we all know, from the numbers of our mullatto population. However degrading, such things are, and however repugnant to the institutions of society, and the moral law, they prove more against the taste than the intellect. *De gustibus non disputandum.* White men, who may wish to marry negro women, or who carry on illicit intercourse with them, may, notwithstanding, possess such soundness of mind as to be capable in law, of making a valid will and testament"[9]

The attempt to define as insane the devotion of white men to their colored mistresses and mulatto children was to be expected since such behavior was so opposed to the formal and legal relations of the two races and the principles of color caste. But the human relations between the two races constantly tended to dissolve the formal and legal principles upon which slavery rested. Sexual relations broke down the last barriers to complete intimacy and paved the way for assimilation. There was some basis for the belief expressed by some persons that parental affection would put an end to slavery when amalgamation had gone far enough.

Not all masters, of course, developed a deep and permanent attachment for their mistresses and mulatto children. In some cases men of the master race even sold their own mulatto children. The slave woman was often abandoned and fared no better than other slaves. Neither Booker T. Washington nor his mother received any attention or benefactions from his supposedly white father. Frederick Douglass and his mother apparently derived no advantages from his reputed relation to the master race. After Loguen's mother had borne three children for her

[8] Catterall, *op. cit.,* II, 451.
[9] Catterall, *op. cit.,* I, 318.

master, his passion for her cooled, and he took a white woman for his wife or mistress. But Loguen remembered that, when he was a very small child, "he was the pet of Dave, as his father was also nicknamed, that he slept in his bed sometimes, and was caressed by him." In the adjudication of the South Carolina case cited above, a witness testified that the white father gave his mulatto children "the best victuals . . . from the table" and that "one of the small ones got in his lap." It was the prolonged association between the master and his colored mistress and their mulatto children that gave rise to enduring affections and lasting sentiment.

Although the association between the men of the master race and the slave women was regarded as an assault upon the white family, white children of the masters sometimes manifested an affection for their mulatto half-brothers and half-sisters similar to that of their fathers. The mulatto Clarke tells us that at least one of his mother's white half-sisters respected the tie of blood when the estate was sold:

> When I was about six years of age, the estate of Samuel Campbell, my grandfather, was sold at auction. His sons and daughters were all present, at the sale, except Mrs. Banton. Among the articles and animals put upon the catalogue, and placed in the hands of the auctioneer, were a large number of slaves. When every thing else had been disposed of, the question arose among the heirs, "What shall be done with Letty (my mother) and her children?" John and William Campbell, came to mother, and told her they would divide her family among the heirs, but none of them should go out of the family. One of the daughters—to her everlasting honor be it spoken—remonstrated against any such proceeding. Judith, the wife of Joseph Logan, told her brothers and sisters, "Letty is our own half sister, and you know it; father never intended they should be sold." Her protest was disregarded, and the auctioneer was ordered to proceed. My mother, and her infant son Cyrus, about one year old, were put up together and sold for $500!! Sisters and brothers selling their own sister and her children.[10]

All classes of whites in the South were involved in these associations with the slave women. Some have attempted to place the burden upon the overseers and the landless poor whites, the class from which they were recruited. But there is no evidence that the poor whites were more involved than the men of the master class. In fact, there was always considerable antagonism between the slaves and the overseers and the class to which they belonged. Concubinage was the privilege of those

[10] Catterall, *op. cit.,* II, 469.

classes in the South that were economically well off. In Charleston, South Carolina, and in New Orleans, where the system of concubinage reached its highest development, wealthy bachelors included beautiful mulatto women among their luxuries. Sometimes they developed a serious and permanent affection for these women that culminated in marriage. Clarke, a mulatto, gives the following account regarding his sister:

> Sister was therefore carried down the river to New Orleans, kept three or four weeks, and then put up for sale. The day before the sale, she was taken to the barber's, her hair dressed, and she was furnished with a new silk gown, and gold watch, and every thing done to set off her personal attractions, previous to the time of the bidding. The first bid was $500; then $800. The auctioneer began to extol her virtues. Then $1000 was bid. The auctioneer says, "If you only knew the reason why she is sold, you would give any sum for her. She is a pious, good girl, member of the Baptist church, warranted to be a virtuous girl." The bidding grew brisk. "Twelve!" "thirteen," "fourteen," "fifteen," "sixteen hundred," was at length bid, and she was knocked off to a Frenchman, named Coval. He wanted her to live with him as his housekeeper and mistress. This she utterly refused, unless she were emancipated and made his wife. In about one month, he took her to Mexico, emancipated, and married her. She visited France with her husband, spent a year or more there and in the West Indies. In four or five years after her marriage, her husband died, leaving her a fortune of twenty or thirty thousand dollars.[11]

More often, it seems, the women developed real affection for the men; for, when they were abandoned by the white men who entered legal marriage, these women seldom entered new relationships and in some cases committed suicide.

The colored families of the aristocrats were too well known for the fact to be concealed.

According to William Goodell, a sister of President Madison was reported to have remarked to Rev. George Bourne, a Presbyterian minister in Virginia: "We southern ladies are complimented with the names of wives; but we are only the mistresses of seraglios." While Andrew Johnson was governor of Tennessee, in a speech to the newly emancipated blacks, he chided the aristocracy on their objection to Negro equality by reminding them of their numerous mulatto children in the city of Nashville:

[11] Lewis Clarke, *Narrative of the Sufferings of Lewis and Milton Clarke, Sons of a Soldier of the Revolution* (Boston, 1846), p. 75.

The representatives of this corrupt (and if you will permit me almost to swear a little), this damnable aristocracy, taunt us with our desire to see justice done, and charge us with favoring negro equality. Of all living men they should be the last to mouth that phrase; and, even when uttered in their hearing, it should cause their cheeks to tinge and burn with shame. Negro equality, indeed! Why, pass, any day, along the sidewalks of High Street where these aristocrats more particularly dwell,—these aristocrats, whose sons are now in the bands of guerillas and cutthroats who prowl and rob and murder around our city,—pass by their dwellings, I say, and you will see as many mulatto as Negro children, the former bearing an unmistakable resemblance to the aristocratic owners.[12]

The white masters acknowledged the relationships, gave protection to their colored families, and generally emancipated them. The often-cited case of Thomas Jefferson, who emancipated his colored children, is only a conspicuous example of the numerous aristocratic slaveholders who left mulatto descendants. Only as tradition has cast a halo about the southern aristocracy has an attempt been made to remove this supposed stain from their name.

Numerous mulatto families are traceable to the associations between slaveholders and their slave women. The family background of a mulatto who played a part in Texas politics after the Civil War is similar to that of other mulatto families whose relationship to the master race is well authenticated. From the biography of Cuney, written by his daughter, we learn:

> Norris Wright Cuney was of Negro, Indian and Swiss descent. The Negro and Indian blood came through his mother, Adeline Stuart, for whom free papers were executed by Col. Cuney, and who was born in the State of Virginia. . . . The Caucasian blood of my father came principally from the Swiss family of Cuney's who were among the early settlers of Virginia, coming there with the Archinard family from Switzerland. About the time of the Louisiana purchase, they migrated to the new provinces and became planters in Rapides Parish. . . . When Col. Philip Cuney came to Texas with his family, he settled in Waller County, near Hempstead, on the east side of the Brazos River. Here, in the heart of the cotton and melon belt, he maintained a large plantation and held slaves, among whom was my grandmother, mentioned above, Adeline Stuart, who bore him eight children and whom he eventually set free . . . on May 12, 1846, my father was born at "Sunnyside," the plantation on the Brazos River owned by his father,

---

[12] William Goodell, *American Slave Code in Theory and Practice* (New York, 1853), p. 111.

Col. Philip Cuney. In 1853, when father was seven years of age, the family moved to Houston and the two older boys were sent to Pittsburgh to attend school.[13]

When men of the slaveholding aristocracy renounced the conventional society of their peers, withdrew to the seclusion of their feudal estates, and took as their companions mulatto women, it was natural that deep and permanent sentiment should develop between them and their colored mistresses and children. This was the case with those anomalous family groups in which the woman enjoyed the protection of her master and paramour and occupied a dignified and respected position in relation to her children and other slaves on the plantation. It is not surprising, then, to find in the court cases, contesting the wills of masters who emancipated their mistresses and mulatto children and left them their estates, that the fact of the woman's having "had the influence over him of a white woman and a wife" was cited to show undue influence on her part.

That such associations undermined the moral order upon which slavery rested and made possible the gradual assimilation of the Negro as his blood became more and more diluted by white blood cannot be denied. Within the intimacy of these family groups color caste was dissolved, and the children, who were often scarcely distinguishable from white, took over the ideals, sentiments, and ambitions of their white fathers. Their mothers, who were generally mulattoes and already possessed some of the culture and feeling of the master race, were further assimilated into the white group by their close association with the cultured classes of the South.

We can view this process in John M. Langston's mulatto family that originated on a large plantation in Virginia. Captain Ralph Quarles, according to his mulatto son who was elected to Congress during the Reconstruction,

> believed that slavery ought to be abolished. But he maintained that the mode of its abolition should be by the voluntary individual action of the owner. He held that slaves should be dealt with in such manner, as to their superintendence and management, as to prevent cruelty, always, and to inspire in them, so far as practicable, feelings of confidence in their masters. Hence, he would employ no overseer, but, dividing the slaves into groups, convenient for ordinary direction and employment, make one of their own number the chief director of the force.[14]

[13] Maud Cuney Hare, *Norris Wright Cuney* (New York, 1913), pp. 1–4.
[14] John M. Langston, *From the Virginia Plantation to the National Capital* (Hartford, Conn., 1894), p. 12.

Because of these views and practices in the management of his plantation, Captain Quarles was condemned and finally ostracized. "For twenty years before his death, no white man resided upon his plantation other than Captain Quarles himself." As he spent most of his life among his slaves, naturally, as his son remarks, he found "a woman, a companion for life, among his slaves to whom he gave his affections," and made "the mother of his children."

> The woman, for whom he discovered special attachment and who, finally, became really the mistress of the Great House of the plantation, reciprocating the affection of her owner, winning his respect and confidence, was the one whom he had taken and held, at first, in pledge for money borrowed of him by her former owner; but whom, at last, he made the mother of his four children, one daughter and three sons. Her name was Lucy Langston. Her surname was of Indian origin, and borne by her mother, as she came out of a tribe of Indians of close relationships in blood to the famous Pocahontas. Of Indian extraction, she was possessed of slight proportion of negro blood; and yet, she and her mother, a full-blooded Indian woman, who was brought upon the plantation and remained there up to her death, were loved and honored by their fellow-slaves of every class.

She had been emancipated by Captain Quarles in 1806 after the birth of the first child, a girl. It was after her emancipation that the three sons were born to them in 1809, 1817, and 1829.

The children were the objects of their father's affection and solicitude as well as their mother's love. The oldest boy was educated by his father, who required him to appear

> for his recitations, in his father's special apartments, the year round, at five o'clock in the morning; and be ready after his duties in such respect had been met, at the usual hour, to go with the slave boys of his age to such service upon the plantation as might be required of them.

This boy became so much like his father in physical and mental qualities that Captain Quarles made the significant addition of Quarles to his name. In remarking upon his father's regard for his children, the youngest son wrote:

> Could his tender care of them, in their extreme youth, and his careful attention to their education, as discovered by him as soon as they were old enough for study, be made known, one could understand, even more sensibly, how he loved and cherished them; being only prevented from giving them his own name and settling upon them his entire

estate, by the circumstances of his position, which would not permit either the one or the other. He did for his sons all he could; exercising paternal wisdom, in the partial distribution of his property in their behalf and the appointment of judicious executors, of his will, who understood his purposes and were faithful in efforts necessary to execute them. Thus, he not only provided well for the education of his sons, but, in large measure, made allowance for their settlement in active, profitable business-life.

The mother probably played no small part in the training of their children and in helping to create in them a conception of their superior status. She was described by her son as

a woman of small stature, substantial build, fair looks, easy and natural bearing, even and quiet temper, intelligent and thoughtful, who accepted her lot with becoming resignation, while she always exhibited the deepest affection and earnest solicitude for her children. Indeed, the very last words of this true and loving mother, when she came to die, were uttered in the exclamation, "Oh, that I could see my children once more!"[15]

After a long life together Captain Quarles and his mulatto mistress died in 1834.

The former, as he neared his end, requested and ordered, that Lucy, when she died, should be buried by his side, and, accordingly, upon a small reservation in the plantation, they sleep together their long quiet sleep. While the humblest possible surroundings mark the spot of their burial, no one has ever disturbed or desecrated it.

During his last sickness, Captain Quarles was attended only by Lucy, her children, and his slaves. During the two days his body lay upon its bier, in the Great House, it was guarded, specially and tenderly, by the noble negro slave, who, when his master was taken sick suddenly, and felt that he needed medical assistance, without delay, but a few night before, hurried across the country to the home of the physician, and secured his aid for his stricken owner.

In his will of October 18, 1833, Captain Quarles left a large part of his estate, including lands and bank stock, to his three sons. According to the provisions of the will, if they desired to move into free territory the real estate was to be sold. Soon after the death of their parents the sons departed for Ohio.

This case represents the highest development of family life growing out of the association of the men of the master race with the slave

15 Langston, *op. cit.*, p. 13.

women. At the bottom of the scale was the Negro woman who was raped and became separated from her mulatto child without any violence to her maternal feelings; or the slave woman who submitted dumbly or out of animal feeling to sexual relations that spawned a nameless and unloved half-white breed over the South. Between these two extremes there were varying degrees of human solidarity created in the intimacies of sex relations and the birth of offspring. Sexual attraction gave birth at times to genuine affection; and prolonged association created between white master and colored mistress enduring sentiment. There were instances where white fathers sold their mulatto children; but more often they became ensnared by their affections for their colored offspring. Neither color caste nor the law of slavery could resist altogether the corrosive influence of human feeling and sentiment generated in these lawless family groups. The master in his mansion and his colored mistress in her special house near by represented the final triumph of social ritual in the presence of the deepest feeling of human solidarity.

Jenny Proctor's Story

A mythology arose to justify slavery, created by Southern historians who felt the need to protect their peculiar institution from the criticism of the North. The elements of the myth are familiar even today: that the slaves, thankful for the bounty of the master, loved him and his children and served faithfully; that the master, in turn, provided generously for their needs and pampered them like favorite animals.

While some such warmth of emotion may have existed in certain instances, the broad outlines of this myth bear little relation to the slave's daily lot, as the following reminiscence by an ex-slave suggests. The life of the slave was very harsh. His food was most often refuse from the master's table; he lived with five or six others in one-room cabins and was given a small, usually

JENNY PROCTOR'S STORY   Reprinted from *Lay My Burden Down* edited by B. A. Botkin. By permission of The University of Chicago Press and B. A. Botkin. Copyright 1945 by the University of Chicago. All rights reserved.

inadequate ration of clothing twice a year; he was forbidden any education, deprived of all legal rights, and driven mercilessly to help enthrone King Cotton. To the masters, the slaves were a property to be used and exploited, and occasionally discarded in working a livelihood from the fields. Good treatment, in the cases where it existed, was the realistic businessman's way of insuring that his possessions did not depreciate.

I'S HEAR TELL OF THEM GOOD SLAVE DAYS, BUT I AIN'T NEVER SEEN NO good times then. My mother's name was Lisa, and when I was a very small child I hear that driver going from cabin to cabin as early as 3 o'clock in the morning, and when he comes to our cabin he say, "Lisa, Lisa, git up from there and git that breakfast." My mother, she was cook, and I don't recollect nothing 'bout my father. If I had any brothers and sisters I didn't know it. We had old ragged huts made out of poles and some of the cracks chinked up with mud and moss and some of them wasn't. We didn't have no good beds, just scaffolds nailed up to the wall out of poles and the old ragged bedding throwed on them. That sure was hard sleeping, but even that feel good to our weary bones after them long hard days' work in the field. I 'tended to the children when I was a little gal and tried to clean the house just like Old Miss tells me to. Then soon as I was ten years old, Old Master, he say, "Git this here nigger to that cotton patch."

I recollects once when I was trying to clean the house like Old Miss tell me, I finds a biscuit, and I's so hungry I et it, 'cause we never see such a thing as a biscuit only sometimes on Sunday morning. We just have corn bread and syrup and sometimes fat bacon, but when I et that biscuit and she comes in and say, "Where that biscuit?" I say, "Miss, I et it 'cause I's so hungry." Then she grab that broom and start to beating me over the head with it and calling me low-down nigger, and I guess I just clean lost my head 'cause I knowed better than to fight her if I knowed anything 't all, but I start to fight her, and the driver, he comes in and he grabs me and starts beating me with that cat-o'-nine-tails,[1] and he beats me till I fall to the floor nearly dead. He cut my back all to pieces, then they rubs salt in the cuts for more punishment. Lord, Lord, honey! Them was awful days. When Old Master come to the house, he say, "What you beat that nigger like that for?" And the driver tells him why, and he say, "She can't work now for a week. She pay for

[1] A big leather whip, branching into nine tails.

several biscuits in that time." He sure was mad, and he tell Old Miss she start the whole mess. I still got them scars on my old back right now, just like my grandmother have when she die, and I's a-carrying mine right on to the grave just like she did.

Our master, he wouldn't 'low us to go fishing—he say that too easy on a nigger and wouldn't 'low us to hunt none either—but sometime we slips off at night and catch possums. And when Old Master smells them possums cooking 'way in the night, he wraps up in a white sheet and gits in the chimney corner and scratch on the wall, and when the man in the cabin goes to the door and say, "Who's that?" he say, "It's me, what's ye cooking in there?" and the man say, "I's cooking possum." He say, "Cook him and bring me the hindquarters and you and the wife and the children eat the rest." We never had no chance to git any rabbits 'cept when we was a-clearing and grubbing the new ground. Then we catch some rabbits, and if they looks good to the white folks they takes them and if they no good the niggers git them. We never had no gardens. Sometimes the slaves git vegetables from the white folks' garden and sometimes they didn't.

Money? Uh-uh! We never seen no money. Guess we'd-a bought something to eat with it if we ever seen any. Fact is, we wouldn't-a knowed hardly how to bought anything, 'cause we didn't know nothing 'bout going to town.

They spinned the cloth what our clothes was made of, and we had straight dresses or slips made of lowell. Sometimes they dye 'em with sumac berries or sweet-gum bark, and sometimes they didn't. On Sunday they make all the children change, and what we wears till we gits our clothes washed was gunny sacks with holes cut for our head and arms. We didn't have no shoes 'cepting some homemade moccasins, and we didn't have them till we was big children. The little children they goes naked till they was big enough to work. They was soon big enough though, 'cording to our master. We had red flannel for winter underclothes. Old Miss she say a sick nigger cost more than the flannel.

Weddings? Uh-uh! We just steps over the broom and we's married. Ha! Ha! Ha!

Old Master he had a good house. The logs was all hewed off smooth-like, and the cracks all fixed with nice chinking, plumb 'spectable-looking even to the plank floors. That was something. He didn't have no big plantation, but he keeps 'bout three hundred slaves in them little huts with dirt floors. I thinks he calls it four farms what he had.

Sometimes he would sell some of the slaves off of that big auction block to the highest bidder when he could git enough for one.

When he go to sell a slave, he feed that one good for a few days, then when he goes to put 'em up on the auction block he takes a meat skin and greases all round that nigger's mouth and makes 'em look like they been eating plenty meat and such like and was good and strong and able to work. Sometimes he sell the babes from the breast, and then again he sell the mothers from the babes and the husbands and the wives, and so on. He wouldn't let 'em holler much when the folks he sold away. He say, "I have you whupped if you don't hush." They sure loved their six children though. They wouldn't want nobody buying them.

We might-a done very well if the old driver hadn't been so mean, but the least little thing we do he beat us for it and put big chains round our ankles and make us work with them on till the blood be cut out all around our ankles. Some of the masters have what they call stockades and puts their heads and feet and arms through holes in a big board out in the hot sun, but our old driver he had a bull pen. That's only thing like a jail he had. When a slave do anything he didn't like, he takes 'em in that bull pen and chains 'em down, face up to the sun, and leaves 'em there till they nearly dies.

None of us was 'lowed to see a book or try to learn. They say we git smarter than they was if we learn anything, but we slips around and gits hold of that Webster's old blue-back speller and we hides it till 'way in the night and then we lights a little pine torch,[2] and studies that spelling book. We learn it too. I can read some now and write a little too.

They wasn't no church for the slaves, but we goes to the white folks' arbor on Sunday evening, and a white man he gits up there to preach to the niggers. He say, "Now I takes my text, which is, Nigger obey your master and your mistress, 'cause what you git from them here in this world am all you ever going to git, 'cause you just like the hogs and the other animals—when you dies you ain't no more, after you been throwed in that hole." I guess we believed that for a while 'cause we didn't have no way finding out different. We didn't see no Bibles.

Sometimes a slave would run away and just live wild in the woods, but most times they catch 'em and beats 'em, then chains 'em down in the sun till they nearly die. The only way any slaves on our farm ever goes anywhere was when the boss sends him to carry some news to another plantation or when we slips off way in the night. Sometimes after all the work was done a bunch would have it made up to slip out down to the creek and dance. We sure have fun when we do that, most times on Saturday night.

All the Christmas we had was Old Master would kill a hog and give

[2] Several long splinters of rich pine, of a lasting quality and making a bright light.

us a piece of pork. We thought that was something, and the way Christmas lasted was 'cording to the big sweet-gum backlog what the slaves would cut and put in the fireplace. When that burned out, the Christmas was over. So you know we all keeps a-looking the whole year round for the biggest sweet gum we could find. When we just couldn't find the sweet gum, we git oak, but it wouldn't last long enough, 'bout three days on average, when we didn't have to work. Old Master he sure pile on them pine knots, gitting that Christmas over so we could git back to work.

We had a few little games we play, like Peep Squirrel Peep, You Can't Catch Me, and such like. We didn't know nothing 'bout no New Year's Day or holidays 'cept Christmas.

We had some corn-shuckings sometimes, but the white folks gits the fun and the nigger gits the work. We didn't have no kind of cotton-pickings 'cept just pick our own cotton. I's can hear them darkies now, going to the cotton patch 'way 'fore day a-singing "Peggy, does you love me now?"

One old man he sing:

> Saturday night and Sunday too
> Young gals on my mind.
> Monday morning 'way 'fore day
> Old Master got me gwine.
> Peggy, does you love me now?

Then he whoops a sort of nigger holler, what nobody can do just like them old-time darkies, then on he goes:

> Possum up a 'simmon tree,
> Rabbit on the ground.
> Lord, Lord, possum,
> Shake them 'simmons down.
> Peggy, does you love me now?
> Rabbit up a gum stump,
> Possum up a holler.
> Git him out, little boy
> And I gives you half a dollar.
> Peggy, does you love me now?

We didn't have much looking after when we git sick. We had to take the worst stuff in the world for medicine, just so it was cheap. That old blue mass and bitter apple would keep us out all night. Sometimes he have the doctor when he thinks we going to die, 'cause he say he ain't got anyone to lose, then that calomel what that doctor would give us would pretty nigh kill us. Then they keeps all kinds of lead bullets and asafetida balls round our necks, and some carried a rabbit foot with them all the time to keep off evil of any kind.

Lord, Lord, honey! It seems impossible that any of us ever lived to see that day of freedom, but thank God we did.

FREDERICK DOUGLASS

The Slavebreaker

As late as 1940, in their textbook, *The Growth of the American Republic,* liberal historians Samuel Eliot Morison and Henry Steele Commager said of the slave, "As the Sambo, whose wrongs moved the abolitionists to wrath and tears, there is reason to believe that he suffered less than any other class in the South from its 'peculiar institution.' The majority of slaves were adequately fed, well cared for, and apparently happy . . . although brought to America by force, the incurably optimistic Negro soon became attached to the country and devoted to his 'white folks.' "

Nothing could be further from the truth. The slave hated his condition and resisted attempts to break his spirit. He yearned above all for freedom. One of the best historical examples of this is the life of Frederick Douglass. Born a slave with the name of Frederick Augustus Washington Bailey, Douglass escaped from his master in 1838 and eventually became one of America's leading abolitionists; for decades he was one of the most eloquent and uncompromising black leaders. He condemned slavery and the mentality which had created it, both in the North and abroad.

In the following excerpt from his autobiography, Douglass recounts an experience which today has a special symbolic significance, but which was enacted in a variety of less dramatic ways throughout the history of slavery: the decision not to submit.

THE SLAVEBREAKER Reprinted by permission of the publishers from Frederick Douglass, *Narrative of the Life of Frederick Douglass, An American Slave,* edited by Benjamin Quarles. Cambridge, Massachusetts: The Belknap Press of Harvard University Press. © 1960 by the President and Fellows of Harvard College.

I LEFT MASTER THOMAS'S HOUSE, AND WENT TO LIVE WITH MR. COVEY, on the 1st of January, 1833. I was now, for the first time in my life, a field hand. In my new employment, I found myself even more awkward than a country boy appeared to be in a large city. I had been at my new home but one week before Mr. Covey gave me a very severe whipping, cutting my back causing the blood to run, and raising ridges on my flesh as large as my little finger. The details of this affair are as follows: Mr. Covey sent me, very early in the morning of one of our coldest days in the month of January, to the woods, to get a load of wood. He gave me a team of unbroken oxen. He told me which was the in-hand ox, and which the off-hand one. He then tied the end of a large rope around the horns of the in-hand ox, and gave me the other end of it, and told me, if the oxen started to run, that I must hold on upon the rope. I had never driven oxen before, and of course I was very awkward. I, however, succeeded in getting to the edge of the woods with little difficulty; but I had got a very few rods into the woods, when the oxen took fright, and started full tilt, carrying the cart against trees, and over stumps, in the most frightful manner. I expected every moment that my brains would be dashed out against the trees. After running thus for a considerable distance, they finally upset the cart, dashing it with great force against a tree, and threw themselves into a dense thicket. How I escaped death, I do not know. There I was, entirely alone, in a thick wood, in a place new to me. My cart was upset and shattered, my oxen were entangled among the young trees, and there was none to help me. After a long spell of effort, I succeeded in getting my cart righted, my oxen disentangled, and again yoked to the cart. I now proceeded with my team to the place where I had, the day before, been chopping wood, and loaded my cart pretty heavily, thinking in this way to tame my oxen. I then proceeded on my way home. I had now consumed one half of the day. I got out of the woods safely, and now felt out of danger. I stopped my oxen to open the woods gate; and just as I did so, before I could get hold of my ox-rope, the oxen again started, rushed through the gate, catching it between the wheel and the body of the cart, tearing it to pieces, and coming within a few inches of crushing me against the gate-post. Thus twice, in one short day, I escaped death by the merest chance. On my return, I told Mr. Covey what had happened, and how it happened. He ordered me to return to the woods again immediately. I did so, and he followed on after me. Just as I got into the woods, he came up and told me to stop my cart, and that he would teach me how to trifle away my time, and break gates. He then went to a large gum-tree, and with his axe cut three large switches, and, after trimming them up neatly with his pocket-knife, he ordered me to take off my clothes. I made him no answer, but stood with my clothes on. He repeated his order. I still made him no answer, nor did I move to strip myself. Upon this he rushed at me with the fierceness of a tiger, tore off my clothes, and lashed me till he had worn out his switches, cutting me so savagely as to leave the marks visible for a long time after. This whipping was the first of a number just like it, and for similar offences.

I lived with Mr. Covey one year. During the first six months, of that year, scarce a week passed without his whipping me. I was seldom free from a sore back. My awkwardness was almost always his excuse for whipping me. We were worked fully up to the point of endurance. Long before day we were up, our horses fed, and by the first approach of day we were off to the field with our hoes and ploughing teams. Mr. Covey gave us enough to eat, but scarce time to eat it. We were often less than five minutes taking our meals. We were often in the field from the first approach of day till its last lingering ray had left us; and at saving-fodder time, midnight often caught us in the field binding blades.

Covey would be out with us. The way he used to stand it, was this. He would spend the most of his afternoons in bed. He would then come out fresh in the evening, ready to urge us on with his words, example, and frequently with the whip. Mr. Covey was one of the few slavehold-ers who could and did work with his hands. He was a hard-working man. He knew by himself just what a man or a boy could do. There was no deceiving him. His work went on in his absence almost as well as in his presence; and he had the faculty of making us feel that he was ever present with us. This he did by surprising us. He seldom ap-proached the spot where we were at work openly, if he could do it secretly. He always aimed at taking us by surprise. Such was his cun-ning, that we used to call him, among ourselves, "the snake." When we were at work in the cornfield, he would sometimes crawl on his hands and knees to avoid detection, and all at once he would rise nearly in our midst, and scream out, "Ha, ha! Come, come! Dash on, dash on!" This being his mode of attack, it was never safe to stop a single minute. His comings were like a thief in the night. He appeared to us as being ever at hand. He was under every tree, behind every stump, in every bush, and at every window, on the plantation. He would sometimes mount his horse, as if bound to St. Michael's, a distance of seven miles, and in half an hour afterwards you would see him coiled up in the corner of the wood-fence, watching every motion of the slaves. He would, for this purpose, leave his horse tied up in the woods. Again, he would sometimes walk up to us, and give us orders as though he was upon the point of starting on a long journey, turn his back upon us, and make as though he was going to the house to get ready; and, before he would get half way thither, he would turn short and crawl into a fence-corner, or behind some tree, and there watch us till the going down of the sun.

Mr. Covey's *forte* consisted in his power to deceive. His life was devoted to planning and perpetrating the grossest deceptions. Every thing he possessed in the shape of learning or religion, he made conform to his disposition to deceive. He seemed to think himself equal to deceiving the Almighty. He would make a short prayer in the morning, and a long prayer at night; and, strange as it may seem, few men would at times appear more devotional than he. The exercises of his family devotions were always commenced with singing; and, as he was a very poor singer himself, the duty of raising the hymn generally came upon me. He would read his hymn, and nod at me to commence. I would at times do so; at others, I would not. My non-compliance would almost always produce much confusion. To show himself independent of me, he would start and stagger through with his hymn in the most discordant manner. In this state of mind, he prayed with more than ordinary spirit. Poor man! such was his disposition, and success at deceiving, I do verily believe that he sometimes deceived himself into the solemn belief, that he was a sincere worshipper of the most high God; and this, too, at a time when he may be said to have been guilty of compelling his woman slave to commit the sin of adultery. The facts in the case are these: Mr. Covey was a poor man; he was just commencing in life; he was only able to buy one slave; and, shocking as is the fact, he bought her, as he said, for *a breeder.* This woman was named Caroline. Mr. Covey bought her from Mr. Thomas Lowe, about six miles from St. Michael's. She was a large, able-bodied woman, about twenty years old. She had already given birth to one child, which proved her to be just what he wanted. After buying her, he hired a married man of Mr. Samuel Harrison, to live with him one year; and him he used to fasten up with her every night! The result was, that, at the end of the year, the miserable woman gave birth to twins. At this result Mr. Covey seemed to be highly pleased, both with the man and the wretched woman. Such was his joy, and that of his wife, that nothing they could do for Caroline during her confinement was too good, or too hard, to be done. The children were regarded as being quite an addition to his wealth.

If at any one time in my life more than another, I was made to drink the bitterest dregs of slavery, that time was during the first six months of my stay with Mr. Covey. We were worked in all weathers. It was never too hot or too cold; it could never rain, blow, hail, or snow, too hard for us to work in the field. Work, work, work, was scarcely more the order of the day than of the night. The longest days were too short for him, and the shortest nights too long for him. I was somewhat unmanageable when I first went there, but a few months of this discipline tamed me. Mr. Covey succeeded in breaking me. I was broken in body, soul, and spirit. My natural elasticity was crushed, my intellect languished, the disposition to read departed, the cheerful spark that lingered about my eye died; the dark night of slavery closed in upon me; and behold a man transformed into a brute!

Sunday was my only leisure time. I spent this in a sort of beast-like stupor, between sleep and wake, under some large tree. At times I would rise up, a flash of energetic freedom would dart through my soul, accompanied with a faint beam of hope, that flickered for a moment, and then vanished. I sank down again, mourning over my wretched condition. I was sometimes prompted to take my life, and that of Covey, but was prevented by a combination of hope and fear. My sufferings on this plantation seem now like a dream rather than a stern reality.

Our house stood within a few rods of the Chesapeake Bay, whose broad bosom was ever white with sails from every quarter of the habitable globe. Those beautiful vessels, robed in purest white, so delightful to the eye of freedom, were to me so many shrouded ghosts, to terrify and torment me with thoughts of my wretched condition. I have often, in the deep stillness of a summer's Sabbath, stood all alone upon the lofty banks of that noble bay, and traced, with saddened heart and tearful eye, the countless number of sails moving off to the mighty ocean. The sight of these always affected me powerfully. My thoughts would compel utterance; and there, with no audience but the Almighty, I would pour out my soul's complaint, in my rude way, with an apostrophe to the moving multitude of ships:—

"You are loosed from your moorings, and are free; I am fast in my chains, and am a slave! You move merrily before the gentle gale, and I sadly before the bloody whip! You are freedom's swift-winged angels, that fly round the world; I am confined in bands of iron! O that I were free! O, that I were on one of your gallant decks, and under your protecting wing! Alas! betwixt me and you, the turbid waters roll. Go on, go on. O that I could also go! Could I but swim! If I could fly! O, why was I born a man, of whom to make a brute! The glad ship is gone; she hides in the dim distance. I am left in the hottest hell of unending slav-

ery. O God, save me! God, deliver me! Let me be free! Is there any
God? Why am I a slave? I will run away. I will not stand it. Get caught,
or get clear, I'll try it. I had as well die with ague as the fever. I have
only one life to lose. I had as well be killed running as die standing.
Only think of it; one hundred miles straight north, and I am free! Try it?
Yes! God helping me, I will. It cannot be that I shall live and die a
slave. I will take to the water. This very bay shall yet bear me into freedom. The steamboats steered in a north-east course from North Point.
I will do the same; and when I get to the head of the bay, I will turn
my canoe adrift, and walk straight through Delaware into Pennsylvania.
When I get there, I shall not be required to have a pass; I can travel
without being disturbed. Let but the first opportunity offer, and, come
what will, I am off. Meanwhile, I will try to bear up under the yoke.
I am not the only slave in the world. Why should I fret? I can bear as
much as any of them. Besides, I am but a boy, and all boys are bound
to some one. It may be that my misery in slavery will only increase my
happiness when I get free. There is a better day coming."

Thus I used to think, and thus I used to speak to myself; goaded almost to madness at one moment, and at the next reconciling myself to
my wretched lot.

I have already intimated that my condition was much worse, during
the first six months of my stay at Mr. Covey's, than in the last six. The
circumstances leading to the change in Mr. Covey's course toward me
form an epoch in my humble history. You have seen how a man was
made a slave; you shall see how a slave was made a man. On one of the
hottest days of the month of August, 1833, Bill Smith, William Hughes,
a slave named Eli, and myself, were engaged in fanning wheat. Hughes
was clearing the fanned wheat from before the fan, Eli was turning,
Smith was feeding, and I was carrying wheat to the fan. The work was
simple, requiring strength rather than intellect; yet, to one entirely un-
used to such work, it came very hard. About three o'clock of that day,
I broke down; my strength failed me; I was seized with a violent aching
of the head, attended with extreme dizziness; I trembled in every limb.
Finding what was coming, I nerved myself up, feeling it would never do
to stop work. I stood as long as I could stagger to the hopper with grain.
When I could stand no longer, I fell, and felt as if held down by an
immense weight. The fan of course stopped; every one had his own work
to do; and no one could do the work of the other, and have his own go
on at the same time.

Mr. Covey was at the house, about one hundred yards from the treading-yard where we were fanning. On hearing the fan stop, he left immediately, and came to the spot where we were. He hastily inquired what the matter was. Bill answered that I was sick, and there was no one to bring wheat to the fan. I had by this time crawled away under the side of the post and rail-fence by which the yard was enclosed, hoping to find relief by getting out of the sun. He then asked where I was. He was told by one of the hands. He came to the spot, and, after looking at me awhile, asked me what was the matter. I told him as well as I could, for I scarce had strength to speak. He then gave me a savage kick in the side, and told me to get up. I tried to do so, but fell back in the attempt. He gave me another kick, and again told me to rise. I again tried, and succeeded in gaining my feet; but, stooping to get the tub with which I was feeding the fan, I again staggered and fell. While down in this situation, Mr. Covey took up the hickory slat with which Hughes had been striking off the half-bushel measure, and with it gave me a heavy blow upon the head, making a large wound, and the blood ran freely; and with this again told me to get up. I made no effort to comply, having now made up my mind to let him do his worst. In a short time after receiving this blow, my head grew better. Mr. Covey had now left me to my fate. At this moment I resolved, for the first time, to go to my master, enter a complaint, and ask his protection. In order to [do] this, I must that afternoon walk seven miles; and this, under the circumstances, was truly a severe undertaking. I was exceedingly feeble; made so as much by the kicks and blows which I received, as by the severe fit of sickness to which I had been subjected. I, however, watched my chance, while Covey was looking in an opposite direction, and started for St. Michael's. I succeeded in getting a considerable distance on my way to the woods, when Covey discovered me, and called after me to come back, threatening what he would do if I did not come. I disregarded both his calls and his threats, and made my way to the woods as fast as my feeble state would allow; and thinking I might be overhauled by him if I kept the road, I walked through the woods, keeping far enough from the road to avoid detection, and near enough to prevent losing my way I had not gone far before my little strength again failed me. I could go no farther. I fell down, and lay for a considerable time. The blood was yet oozing from the wound on my head. For a time I thought I should bleed to death; and think now that I should have done so, but that the blood so matted my hair as to stop the wound. After lying there about three quarters of an hour, I nerved myself up again, and started on my way, through bogs and briers, barefooted and bare-headed, tearing my feet sometimes at nearly every step; and after a journey of about seven miles, occupying some five hours to perform it, I arrived at master's store. I then presented an appearance enough to affect any but a heart of iron. From the crown of my head to my feet, I was covered with blood. My hair was all clotted with dust and blood; my shirt was stiff with blood. My legs and feet were torn in sundry places with briers and thorns, and were also covered with blood. I suppose I looked like a man who had escaped a den of wild beasts, and barely escaped them. In this state I appeared before my master, humbly entreating him to interpose his authority for my protection. I told him all the circumstances as well as I could, and it seemed, as I spoke, at times to affect him. He would then walk the floor, and seek to justify Covey by saying he expected I deserved it. He asked me what I wanted. I told him, to let me get a new home; that as sure as I lived with Mr. Covey again, I should live with but to die with him; that Covey would surely kill me; he was in a fair way for it. Master Thomas ridiculed the idea that there was any danger of Mr. Covey's killing me, and said that he knew Mr. Covey; that he was a good man, and that he could not think of taking me from him; that, should he do so, he would lose the whole year's wages; that I belonged to Mr. Covey for one year, and that I must go back to him, come what might; and that I must not trouble him with any more stories, or that he would himself *get hold of me*. After threatening me thus, he gave me a very large dose of salts, telling me that I might remain in St. Michael's that night (it being quite late), but that I must be off back to Mr. Covey's early in the morning; and that if I did not, he would *get hold of me,* which meant that he would whip me. I remained all night, and, according to his orders, I started off to Covey's in the morning (Saturday morning), wearied in body and broken in spirit. I got no supper that night, or breakfast that morning. I reached Covey's about nine o'clock; and just as I was getting over the fence that divided Mrs. Kemp's fields from ours, out ran Covey with his cowskin, to give me another whipping. Before he could reach me, I succeeded in getting to the cornfield; and as the corn was very high, it afforded me the means of hiding. He seemed very angry, and searched for me a long time. My behavior was altogether unaccountable. He finally gave up the chase, thinking, I suppose, that I must come home for something to eat; he would give himself no further trouble in looking for me. I spent that day mostly in the woods, having the alternative before me,—to go home and be whipped to death, or stay in the woods and be starved to death. That night, I fell in with Sandy Jenkins, a slave with whom I was somewhat acquainted. Sandy had a free wife who lived about four miles from Mr. Covey's; and it being Saturday, he was on his way to see her. I told him my circumstances, and he very kindly invited me to go home with him. I went home with him, and talked this whole matter over, and got his advice as to what course it was best for me to pursue. I found Sandy an old adviser. He told me, with great solemnity, I must go back to Covey; but that before I went, I must go with him into another part of the woods, where there was a certain *root,* which, if I would take some of it with me, carrying it *always on my right side,* would render it impossible for Mr. Covey, or any other white man, to whip me. He said he had carried it for years; and since he had done so, he had never received a blow, and never expected to while he carried it. I at first rejected the idea, that the simple carrying of a root in my pocket would have any such effect as he had said, and was not disposed to take it; but Sandy impressed the necessity with much earnestness, telling me it could do no harm, if it did no good. To please him, I at length took the root, and, according to his direction, carried it upon my right side. This was Sunday morning. I immediately started for home; and upon entering the yard gate, out came Mr. Covey on his way to meeting. He spoke to me very kindly, made me drive the pigs from a lot near by, and passed on towards the church. Now, this singular conduct of Mr. Covey really made me begin to think that there was something in the *root* which Sandy had given me; and had it been on any other day than Sunday, I could have attributed the conduct to no other cause than the influence of that root; and as it was, I was half inclined to thing the *root* to be something more than I at first had taken it to be. All went well till Monday morning. On this morning, the virtue of the *root* was fully tested. Long before daylight, I was called to go and rub, curry, and feed, the horses. I obeyed, and was glad to obey. But whilst thus engaged, whilst in the act of throwing down some blades from the lift, Mr. Covey entered the stable with a long rope; and just as I was half out of the loft, he caught hold of my legs, and was about tying me. As soon as I found what he was up to, I gave a sudden spring, and as I did so, he holding to my legs, I was brought sprawling on the stable floor. Mr. Covey seemed now to think he had me, and could do what he pleased; but at this moment— from whence came the spirit I don't know—I resolved to fight; and, suiting my action to the resolution, I seized Covey hard by the throat; and as I did so, I rose. He held on to me, and I to him. My resistance was so entirely unexpected, that Covey seemed taken all aback. He trembled like a leaf. This gave me assurance, and I held him uneasy, causing the blood to run where I touched him with the ends of my fingers. Mr. Covey soon called out to Hughes for help. Hughes came, and, while Covey held me, attempted to tie my right hand. While he was in the act of doing so, I watched my chance, and gave him a heavy kick close under the ribs. This kick fairly sickened Hughes, so that he left me in the hands of Mr. Covey. This kick had the effect of not only weakening Hughes, but Covey also. When he saw Hughes bending over with pain, his courage quailed. He asked me if I meant to persist in my resistance. I told him I did, come what might; that he had used me like a brute for six months, and that I was determined to be used so no longer. With that, he strove to drag me to a stick that was lying just out of the stable door. He meant to knock me down. But just as he was leaning over to get the stick, I seized him with both hands by his collar, and brought him by a sudden snatch to the ground. By this time, Bill came. Covey called upon him for assistance. Bill wanted to know what he could do. Covey said, "Take hold of him, take hold of him!" Bill said his master hired him out to work, and not to help to whip me; so he left Covey and myself to fight our own battle out. We were at it for nearly two hours. Covey at length let me go, puffing and blowing at a great rate, saying that if I had not resisted, he would not have whipped me half so much. The truth was, that he had not whipped me at all. I considered him as getting entirely the worst end of the bargain; for he had drawn no blood from me, but I had from him. The whole six months afterwards, that I spent with Mr. Covey, he never laid the weight of his finger upon me in anger. He would occasionally say, he didn't want to get hold of me again. "No," thought I, "you need not; for you will come off worse than you did before."

This battle with Mr. Covey was the turning-point in my career as a slave. It rekindled the few expiring embers of freedom, and revived within me a sense of my own manhood. It recalled the departed self-confidence, and inspired me again with a determination to be free. The gratification afforded by the triumph was a full compensation for whatever else might follow, even death itself. He only can understand the deep satisfaction which I experienced, who has himself repelled by force the bloody arm of slavery. I felt as I never felt before. It was a glorious resurrection, from the tomb of slavery, to the heaven of freedom. My long-crushed spirit rose, cowardice departed, bold defiance took its place; and I now resolved that, however long I might remain a slave in form, the day had passed forever when I could be a slave in fact. I did not hesitate to let it be known of me, that the white man who expected to succeed in whipping, must also succeed in killing me.

KENNETH STAMPP

A Troublesome Property

Men like Frederick Douglass are rare in any era. But as the following selection from historian Kenneth Stampp's *The Peculiar Institution* shows, resistance by slaves was a condition of everyday life in the ante-bellum South, and not just the action of exceptional men. Resistance took many forms: theft of the master's property, arson, self-mutilation, and others. Most troublesome for the slaveowner and the region in which he lived was the simple act of running away. The slave patrols and the awesome power of the slaveholding states stood against these runaways, but their numbers increased rather than declined, especially with the coming of the Underground Railroad. Sabotage, flight, myriad other ways of indicating dissatisfaction—they were all, Stampp emphasizes, as much a part of slavery as the overseer's whip and the auctioneer's block.

HIS LOOK IS IMPUDENT AND INSOLENT, AND HE HOLDS HIMSELF straight and walks well." So a Louisiana master described James, a runaway slave. There were always bondsmen like James. In 1669, a Virginia statute referred to "the obstinacy of many of them"; in 1802, a South Carolina judge declared that they were "in general a headstrong, stubborn race of people"; and in 1859, a committee of a South Carolina agricultural society complained of the "insolence of disposition to which, as a race, they are remarkably liable." An overseer on a Louisiana plantation wrote nervously about the many "outrageous acts" recently committed by slaves in his locality and insisted that he scarcely had time to eat and sleep: "The truth is no man can begin to attend to Such a business with any Set of negroes, without the Strictest vigilance on his part." It was the minority of slaves whom his discipline could not humble (the "insolent," "surly," and "unruly" ones) that worried this overseer —and slaveholders generally. These were the slaves whose discontent drove them to drastic measures.

Legally the offenses of the rebels ranged from petty misdemeanors to

A TROUBLESOME PROPERTY   From *The Peculiar Institution* by Kenneth Stampp. © Copyright 1956 by Kenneth Stampp. Reprinted by permission of Alfred A. Knopf, Inc. The author's footnotes—of a scholarly nature—have been omitted.

capital crimes, and they were punished accordingly. The master class looked upon any offense as more reprehensible (and therefore subject to more severe penalties) when committed by a slave than when committed by a free white. But how can one determine the proper ethical standards for identifying undesirable or even criminal behavior among slaves? How distinguish a "good" from a "bad" slave? Was the "good" slave the one who was courteous and loyal to his master, and who did his work faithfully and cheerfully? Was the "bad" slave the one who would not submit to his master, and who defiantly fought back? What were the limits, if any, to which a man deprived of his freedom could properly go in resisting bondage? How accountable was a slave to a legal code which gave him more penalties than protection and was itself a bulwark of slavery? This much at least can be said: many slaves rejected the answers which their masters gave to questions such as these. The slaves did not thereby repudiate law and morality: rather, they formulated legal and moral codes of their own.

The white man's laws against theft, for example, were not supported by the slave's code. In demonstrating the "absence of moral principle" among bondsmen, one master observed: "To steal and not to be detected is a merit among them." Let a master turn his back, wrote another, and some "cunning fellow" would appropriate part of his goods. No slave would betray another, for an informer was held "in greater detestation than the most notorious thief."

If slaveholders are to be believed, petty theft was an almost universal "vice"; slaves would take anything that was not under lock and key. Field-hands killed hogs and robbed the corn crib. House servants helped themselves to wines, whiskey, jewelry, trinkets, and whatever else was lying about. Fugitives sometimes gained from their master unwilling help in financing the journey to freedom, the advertisements often indicating that they absconded with money, clothing, and a horse or mule. Thefts were not necessarily confined to the master's goods: any white man might be considered fair game.

Some bondsmen engaged in theft on more than a casual and petty basis. They made a business of it and thus sought to obtain comforts and luxuries which were usually denied them. A South Carolina master learned that his house servants had been regularly looting his wine cellar and that one of them was involved in an elaborate "system of roguery." A planter in North Carolina found that three of his slaves had "for some months been carrying on a robbery" of meat and lard, the leader being "a young carpenter, remarkable for smartness . . . and no less worthy for his lamentable deficiency in common honesty."

If the stolen goods were not consumed directly, they were traded to whites or to free Negroes. This illegal trade caused masters endless trouble, for slaves were always willing to exchange plantation products for tobacco, liquor, or small sums of money. Southern courts were kept busy handling the resulting prosecutions. One slaveholder discovered that his bondsmen had long been engaged in an extensive trade in corn. "Strict vigilance," he concluded, was necessary "to prevent them from theft; particularly when dishonesty is inherent, as is probably the case with some of them." Dishonesty, as the master understood the term, indeed seemed to be a common if not an inherent trait of southern slaves.

The slaves, however, had a somewhat different definition of dishonesty in their own code, to which they were reasonably faithful. For appropriating their master's goods they might be punished and denounced by him, but they were not likely to be disgraced among their associates in the slave quarters, who made a distinction between "stealing" and "taking." Appropriating things from the master meant simply taking part of his property for the benefit of another part or, as Frederick Douglass phrased it, "taking his meat out of one tub, and putting it in another." Thus a female domestic who had been scolded for the theft of some trinkets was reported to have replied: "Law, mam, don't say I's wicked; ole Aunt Ann says it allers right for us poor colored people to 'popiate whatever of de wite folk's blessings de Lord puts in our way." Stealing, on the other hand, meant appropriating something that belonged to another slave, and this was an offense which slaves did not condone.

The prevalence of theft was a clear sign that slaves were discontented, at least with the standard of living imposed upon them. They stole food to increase or enrich their diets or to trade for other coveted commodities. Quite obviously they learned from their masters the pleasures that could be derived from the possession of worldly goods; and when the opportunity presented itself, they "took" what was denied them as slaves.

Next to theft, arson was the most common slave "crime," one which slaveholders dreaded almost constantly. Fire was a favorite means for aggrieved slaves to even the score with their master. Reports emanated periodically from some region or other that there was an "epidemic" of gin-house burnings, or that some bondsman had taken his revenge by burning the slave quarters or other farm buildings. More than one planter thus saw the better part of a year's harvest go up in flames. Southern newspapers and court records are filled with illustrations of this offense, and with evidence of the severe penalties inflicted upon those found guilty of committing it.

Another "crime" was what might be called self-sabotage, a slave deliberately unfitting himself to labor for his master. An Arkansas slave, "at any time to save an hour's work," could "throw his left shoulder out of place." A Kentucky slave made himself unserviceable by downing medicines from his master's dispensary (thus showing a better understanding of the value of these nostrums than his owner). A slave woman was treated as an invalid because of "swellings in her arms"—until it was discovered that she produced this condition by thrusting her arms periodically into a beehive. Yellow Jacob, according to his master's plantation journal, "had a kick from a mule and when nearly well would bruise it and by that means kept from work." Another Negro, after being punished by his owner, retaliated by cutting off his right hand; still another cut off the fingers of one hand to avoid being sold to the Deep South.

A few desperate slaves carried this form of resistance to the extreme of self-destruction. Those freshly imported from Africa and those sold away from friends and relatives were especially prone to suicide. London, a slave on a Georgia rice plantation, ran to the river and drowned himself after being threatened with a whipping. His overseer gave orders to leave the corpse untouched "to let the [other] negroes see [that] when a negro takes his own life they will be treated in this manner." A Texas planter bewailed the loss of a slave woman who hanged herself after two unsuccessful breaks for freedom: "I had been offered $900.00 for her not two months ago, but damn her . . . I would not have had it happened for twice her value. *The fates pursue me.*"

Some runaways seemed determined to make their recapture as costly as possible and even resisted at the risk of their own lives. One advertisement, typical of many, warned than an escaped slave was a "resolute fellow" who would probably not be taken without a "show of competent force." When, after a day-long chase, three South Carolina fugitives were cornered, they "fought desperately," inflicted numerous wounds upon their pursuers with a barrage of rocks, and "refused to surrender until a force of about forty-five or fifty men arrived." In southern court records there are numerous cases of runaway slaves who killed whites or were themselves killed in their frantic efforts to gain freedom.

In one dramatic case, a Louisiana fugitive was detected working as a free Negro on a Mississippi River flatboat. His pursuers, trailing him with a pack of "Negro dogs," finally found him "standing at bay upon the outer edge of a large raft of drift wood, armed with a club and pistol." He threatened to kill anyone who got near him.

> Finding him obstinately determined not to surrender, one of his pursuers shot him. He fell at the third fire, and so determined was he not to be captured, that when an effort was made to rescue him from drowning he made battle with his club, and sunk waving his weapon in angry defiance.

An effort to break up an organized gang of runaways was a dangerous business, because they were often unwilling to surrender without a fight. The fugitives in one well-armed band in Alabama were building a fort at the time they were discovered. Their camp was destroyed after a "smart skirmish" during which three of them were killed. Such encounters did not always end in defeat for the slaves; some runaway bands successfully resisted all attempts at capture and remained at large for years.

Ante-bellum records are replete with acts of violence committed by individual slaves upon masters, overseers, and other whites. A Texan complained, in 1853, that cases of slaves murdering white men were becoming "painfully frequent." "Within the last year or two many murders have taken place, by negroes upon their owners," reported a Louisiana newspaper. And a Florida editor once wrote: "It is our painful duty to record another instance of the destruction of the life of a white man by a slave."

Many masters owned one or more bondsmen whom they feared as potential murderers. A Georgia planter remembered Jack, his plantation carpenter, "the most notoriously bad character and worst Negro of the place." Jack "was the only Negro ever in our possession who I considered capable of Murdering me, or burning my dwelling at night, or capable of committing any act."

Slaves like Jack could be watched closely; but others appeared to be submissive until suddenly they turned on their masters. Even trusted house servants might give violent expression to long pent up feelings. One "first rate" female domestic, while being punished, abruptly attacked her mistress, "threw her down, and beat her unmercifully on the head and face." A "favorite body servant" of a "humane master who rarely or never punished his slaves" one day became insolent. Unwilling to be disciplined, this slave waylaid his owner, "knocked him down with a whiteoak club, and beat his head to a pumice." Here was another reason why it seemed foolish for a master to put his "confidence in a Negro."

At times these acts of violence appeared to be for "no cause"—that is, they resulted from a slave's "bad disposition" rather than from a particular grievance. But more often they resulted from a clash of personalities, or from some specific incident. For example, a slave who had been promised freedom in his master's will, poisoned his master to hasten the day of liberation. A South Carolina bondsman was killed during a fight with an overseer who had whipped his son. In North Carolina a slave intervened while the overseer was whipping his wife, and in the ensuing battle the overseer met his death.

The most common provocation to violence was the attempt of a master or overseer either to work or to punish slaves severely. An Alabama bondsman confessed killing the overseer because "he was a hard down man on him, and said he was going to be harder." Six Louisiana slaves together killed an overseer and explained in their confession that they found it impossible to satisfy him. Three North Carolina slaves killed their master when they decided that "the old man was too hard on them, and they must get rid of him." During one of these crises an overseer called upon his hands to help him punish an "unmanageable" slave: "not one of them paid the least attention to me but kept on at their work." These encounters did not always lead to death, but few plantations escaped without at least one that might easily have ended in tragedy. "Things move on here in the old Style except that now and then a refractory negro has to be taken care of," was the off-hand comment of a planter.

Sometimes a slave who showed sufficient determination to resist punishment managed to get the best of his owner or overseer. A proud bondsman might vow that, regardless of the consequences, he would permit no one to whip him. An overseer thought twice before precipitating a major crisis with a strong-willed slave; he might even overlook minor infractions of discipline.

But an impasse such as this was decidedly unusual; if it had not been, slavery itself would have stood in jeopardy. Ordinarily these clashes between master and slave were fought out to a final settlement, and thus a thread of violence was woven into the pattern of southern bondage. Violence, indeed, was the method of resistance adopted by the boldest and most discontented slaves. Its usual reward, however, was not liberty but death!

HARVEY WISH

American Slave Insurrections Before 1861

The individual acts of flight and violence which Stampp describes culminated in organized slave rebellions. One of the most successful and celebrated of these revolts occurred in 1831 under the leadership of Nat Turner; it eventually claimed about 57 white lives. However, as the following selection shows, it was not the only such outbreak. Historian Herbert Aptheker has estimated that over 250 slave rebellions and conspiracies occurred in the United States during the time of slavery.

In their own time, these insurrections sent waves of hysteria through the South. Today, like Frederick Douglass' resistance against the slavebreaker, they have become especially powerful for black people as reminders of a past that is not without honor.

THE ROMANTIC PORTRAYAL OF ANTE-BELLUM SOCIETY ON THE SOUTH-ern plantation, which depicts the rollicking black against a kindly patriarchal background, has tended to obscure the large element of slave unrest which occasionally shook the whole fabric of the planter's kingdom. Even the abolitionist, eager to capitalize upon such material, could make only vague inferences as to the extent of Negro insurrections in the South. The danger of inducing general panic by spreading news of an insurrection was a particularly potent factor in the maintenance of silence on the topic. Besides, sectional pride, in the face of anti-slavery taunts, prevented the loyal white Southerner from airing the subject of domestic revolt in the press. "Last evening," wrote a lady of Charleston during the Denmark Vesey scare of 1822, "twenty-five hundred of our citizens were under arms to guard our property and lives. But it is a subject not to be mentioned; and unless you hear of it elsewhere, say nothing about it."[1] Consequently, against such a conspiracy of silence

[1] T. W. Higginson, "Gabriel's Defeat," *The Atlantic Monthly*, X (1862), 337–345.

AMERICAN SLAVE INSURRECTIONS BEFORE 1861   By Harvey Wish. Published in the *Journal of Negro History* (July, 1937). Copyright © by The Association for the Study of Negro Life and History, Inc.

the historian encounters unusual difficulties in reconstructing the true picture of slave revolts in the United States.

.   .   .

The desire for freedom on the part of the African, evidenced by his struggle on the slave ships, did not die in the New World. On the plantations of Latin-America, in the British and French Indies, and finally in the American cotton, rice, and sugar fields, the aspirations of the Negro, blocked by the white master, gave birth to plots and uprisings. The lesson of San Domingo particularly was suggestive to both whites and blacks. Repressive black codes and emergency patrols frequently converted the plantation into an armed camp. Governor Robert Y. Hayne of South Carolina declared to the Assembly in 1833, two years after the Nat Turner Insurrection: "A state of military preparation must always be with us, a state of perfect domestic security. A period of profound peace and consequent apathy may expose us to the danger of domestic insurrection."[2]

Professor Thomas R. Dew, militant apologist of slavery, sought, in an address that year before the Virginia Legislature, to minimize the fears of insurrection:

> "This is the evil, after all, let us say what we will, which really operates most powerfully upon the schemers and emancipating philanthropists of those sections where slaves constitute the principal property. . . . We cannot fail to derive the greatest consolation from the fact that although slavery has existed in our country for the last two hundred years, there have been but three attempts at insurrection—one in Virginia, one in South Carolina, and we believe, one in Louisiana—and the loss of lives from this cause has not amounted to one hundred persons in all."[3]

Despite the serious understatement of the number of insurrections, Dew's remarks are actually revelatory of the fears aroused among the planters. A graphic illustration of the cyclic fears of Negro uprisings during the 1830's is afforded by the remarks of several whites of Mississippi in 1859 to Frederick L. Olmsted:

> "Where I used to live (Alabama) I remember when I was a boy—must ha' been about twenty years ago—folks was dreadful frightened

[2] *Message of Governor Robert Y. Hayne to the Senate and House of Representatives of South Carolina* (Columbia, November 26, 1833).
[3] *The Political Register* (Washington, 1833), III (1833), 823.

about the niggers. I remember they built pens in the woods where they could hide and Christmas time they went and got into the pens, fraid the niggers was risin'."[4]

The speaker's wife added her recollection to this comment: "I remember the same time where we was in South Carolina, we had all our things put up in bags so we could tote 'em if we heard they was comin' our way."[5]

Slave outbreaks and plots appeared both North and South during the Colonial period. Sometimes the white indentured servants made common cause with the Negroes against their masters. This was the case in 1663 when a plot of white servants and Negroes was betrayed in Gloucester County, Virginia.[6] The eastern counties of Virginia, where the Negroes were rapidly outnumbering the whites, suffered from repeated scares in 1687, 1709, 1710, 1722, 1723, and 1730.[7] A patrol system was set up in 1726 in parts of the state and later extended. Attempts were made here as elsewhere to check the importation of slaves by high duties.

Two important slave plots, one a serious insurrection, disturbed the peace of New York City in 1712 and 1741. In revenge for ill-treatment by their masters, twenty-three Negroes rose on April 6, 1712, to slaughter the whites and killed nine before they were overwhelmed by a superior force. The retaliation showed an unusual barbarous strain on the part of the whites. Twenty-one Negroes were executed, some were burnt, others hanged, and one broken on the wheel.[8] In 1741 another plot was reported in New York involving both whites and blacks. A white, Hewson (or Hughson), was accused of providing the Negroes with weapons. He and his family were executed; likewise, a Catholic priest was hanged as an accomplice. Thirteen Negro leaders were burnt alive, eighteen hanged, and eighty transported.[9] Popular fears of further insurrections led the New York Assembly to impose a prohibitive tax

[4] Frederick Law Olmsted, *A Journey in the Back Country* (New York, 1860), 203.
[5] *Ibid.*
[6] Ulrich B. Phillips, *American Negro Slavery* (New York, 1918), 472.
[7] William P. Palmer (ed.), *Calendar of Virginia State Papers* (Richmond, 1875), I (1652–1781), 129–130; also James Curtis Ballagh, *A History of Slavery in Virginia* (Baltimore, 1902), 79–80; also Coffin, *Principal Slave Insurrections*, 11. [Joshua Coffin, *An Account of Some of the Principal Slave Insurrections* (New York, 1860).]
[8] Letter of Governor Robert Hunter to the Lords of Trade, in E. B. O'Callaghan (ed.), *Documents Relative to the Colonial History of the State of New York* (Albany, 1855), V (1707–1733), 341–2.
[9] *Gentleman's Magazine*, XI (1741), 441.

on the importation of Negroes. This tax, however, was later rescinded by order of the British Commissioner for Trade and Plantations.[10]

The situation in colonial South Carolina was worse than in her sister states. Long before rice and indigo had given way to King Cotton, the early development of the plantation system had yielded bumper crops of slave uprisings and plots. An insurrection, resulting in the deaths of three whites, is reported for May 6, 1720.[11] Ten years later an elaborate plot was discovered in St. John's Parish by a Negro servant of Major Cordes'. This plan was aimed at Charleston, an attack that was to inaugurate a widespread war upon the planters. Under the pretense of conducting a "dancing bout" in the city and in St. Paul's Parish the Negroes gathered together ready to seize the available arms for the attack. At this point the militia descended upon the blacks and killed the greater number, leaving few to escape.[12]

Owing partly to Spanish intrigues the same decade in South Carolina witnessed many more uprisings. An outbreak is reported for November, 1738.[13] The following year, on September 9, the Stono uprising created panic throughout the southeast. About twenty Angola Negroes assembled at Stono under their captain, Tommy, and marched toward Spanish territory, beating drums and endeavoring to attract other slaves. Several whites were killed and a number of houses burnt or plundered. As the "army" paused in a field to dance and sing they were overtaken by the militia and cut down in a pitched battle.[14] The following year an insurrection broke out in Berkeley County.[15] Charleston was threatened repeatedly by slave plots.[16] These reports are confirmed officially in the petition of the South Carolina Assembly to the King on July 26, 1740. Among the grievances of 1739 the Assembly complained of:

[10] *D.S.T.,* III, 409. [Elizabeth Donnan (ed.), *Documents Illustrative of the Slave Trade to America* (Washington, 1930–5). Abbreviated as D. S. T.] Joshua Coffin also reports plots and actual outbreaks in other slaveholding areas in the Northern Colonies. East Boston is said to have experienced a minor uprising in 1638. In 1723, a series of incendiary fires in Boston led the selectmen to suspect a slave plot and the militia was ordered to police the slaves. Another plot was reported in Burlington, Pennsylvania during 1734. Coffin, *Principal Slave Insurrections,* 10, 11, 12.

[11] Coffin, *Principal Slave Insurrections,* 11.

[12] Edward Clifford Holland, *A Refutation of the Calumnies Circulated Against the Southern and Western States Respecting the Institution and Existence of Slavery* (Charleston, 1822), 68–9, 81.

[13] Ralph Betts Flander, *Plantation Slavery in Georgia* (Chapel Hill, 1933), 24

[14] *Gentleman's Magazine,* X (1740), 127–8.

[15] See the Constable's bill in the *Magazine of American History,* XXV (1891), 85–6.

[16] Edward McGrady, *The History of South Carolina Under the Royal Government* (1719–1776) (New York, 1899), 5.

". . . an insurrection of our slaves in which many of the Inhabitants were murdered in a barbarous and cruel manner; and that no sooner quelled than another projected in Charles Town, and a third lately in the very heart of the Settlements, but happily discovered in time enough to be prevented."[17]

Repercussions of slave uprisings in South Carolina sometimes affected Georgia as well. This was particularly true in 1738.[18] In 1739 a plot was discovered in Prince George County.[19] To many slaves St. Augustine on Spanish soil seemed a welcome refuge from their masters.

Indications of many other insurrections in the American Colonies may be inferred from the nature of early patrol laws: The South Carolina law of 1704 for example contains a reference in its preamble to recent uprisings in that Colony.[20] In the British and French possessions to the south, particularly in the West Indies, affairs were much worse and put the planter of the North in constant fear of importing rebellious slaves and the contagion of revolt.

In considering the insurrections of the national period, it is at once evident that abolitionist propaganda played a relatively minor role despite the charges of southern politicians after 1831. The genealogy of revolt extends much further back than the organized efforts of anti-slavery advocates. It is true, however, that white men played an important role in many Negro uprisings, frequently furnishing arms, and even leadership, as well as inspiration.[21] The motives for such assistance varied from philanthropy to unadulterated self-interest. As might be expected, insurrections tended to occur where King Cotton and his allies were most firmly entrenched and the great plantation system established.

Slave unrest seems to have been far greater in Virginia rather than in the states of the Lower South. Conspiracies like those of Gabriel in 1800 and Nat Turner in 1831 attained national notoriety. The Gabriel plot was developed in the greatest secrecy upon the plantation of a harsh slavemaster, Thomas Prosser, several miles from Richmond. Under the

---

[17] Appendix to Holland, *A Refutation of the Calumnies*, —, 71. Another plot of December 17, 1765, is mentioned in *D.S.T.*, IV, 415.

[18] Flanders, *Plantation Slavery in Georgia*, 24; similarly, South Carolina's slave plots sometimes required the assistance of North Carolina as in the scare of 1766. William L. Saunders (ed.), *Colonial Records of North Carolina* (Raleigh, 1890), VIII (1769–1771), 559.

[19] Jeffrey R. Brackett, *The Negro in Maryland* (Baltimore, 1889), 93.

[20] H. M. Henry, *The Police Control of the Slave in South Carolina* (Vanderbilt University, 1914), 30.

[21] One aspect of this subject is discussed in James Hugo Johnston's article, "The Participation of White Men in Virginia Negro Insurrections," *Journal of Negro History*, XVI (1931), 158–167.

leadership of a young slave, Gabriel, and inspired by the examples of San Domingo and the emancipation of the ancient Israelites from Egypt, some eleven hundred slaves had taken an oath to fight for their liberty. Plans were drawn for the seizure of an arsenal and several other strategic buildings of Richmond which would precede a general slaughter of all hostile whites. After the initial successes, it was expected that fifty thousand Negroes would join the standard of revolt. Beyond this point, the arrangements were hazy.[22] A faithful slave however exposed the plot and Governor James Monroe took rapid measures to secure the co-operation of the local authorities and the federal cavalry. Bloodshed was averted by an unprecedented cloudburst on the day set for the conspiracy and the utter demoralization of the undisciplined "army." Writing to his friend, President Jefferson, the Governor declared: "It (the Gabriel plot) is unquestionably the most serious and formidable conspiracy we have ever known of the kind. While it was possible to keep it secret, which it was till we saw the extent of it, we did so. . . ."[23]

With the opening of the slave trials, hysteria swept the South and many innocent blacks were compelled to pay for this with their lives. Rumors of new plots sprang up everywhere much to the distraction of Monroe. The results of the Gabriel incident were significant. An impetus was given to the organization of the American Colonization Society which took definite form in 1816. The slave patrol laws became very stringent, and the example was copied elsewhere in the South. The incipient feeling of sectional diversity received a new impetus.

Between Gabriel's abortive plot and the Nat Turner uprising, several more incidents occurred which disturbed the sleep of Virginians. In January, 1802, Governor Monroe received word of a plot in Nottaway County. Several Negroes suspected of participation were executed.[24] That same year came disclosures of a projected slave uprising in Goochland County aided by eight or ten white men.[25] Several plots were reported in 1808 and 1809 necessitating almost continuous patrol service.[26] The War of 1812 intensified the apprehensions of servile revolt.

---

[22] Details of the Gabriel Plot are in the *Calendar of Virginia State Papers*, X (1808–1835), 140–173, *et passim;* T. W. Higginson, "Gabriel's Defeat," *The Atlantic Monthly*, X (1862), 337–345; Robert A. Howison, *A History of Virginia* (Richmond, 1848), II, 390–3.

[23] Monroe to Jefferson, September 15, 1800; S. M. Hamilton (ed.), *Writings of James Monroe* (New York, 1893–1903), III, 201. Much of the Gabriel affair can be followed from the letters of Monroe.

[24] Hamilton (ed.) *Writings of James Monroe*, III, 328–9.

[25] James H. Johnston, "The Participation of White Men in Virginia Negro Insurrections," 161.

[26] *Calendar of Virginia State Papers*, X (1808–1835), 31, 62.

Petitions for troops and arms came during the summer of 1814 from Caroline County and Lynchburg.[27] Regiments were called out during the war in anticipation of insurrections along the tidewater area. During the spring of 1816 confessions were wrung from slaves concerning an attack upon Fredericksburg and Richmond. The inspiration for this enterprise was attributed to a white military officer, George Boxley. The latter claimed to be the recipient of divine revelations and the instrument of "omnipotence" although he denied any intention of leading an insurrection. His relatives declared that he was insane, but his neighbors in a complaint to the governor showed serious misgivings on this point:

> "On many occasions he has declared that the distinction between the rich and the poor was too great; that offices were given to wealth than to merit; and seemed to be an advocate for a more leveling system of Government. For many years he has avowed his disapprobation of the slavery of the Negroes and wished they were free."[28]

Boxley was arrested but escaped. About thirty Negroes were sentenced to death or deportation in consequence.

The years preceding the Nat Turner insurrection brought further news of plots discovered. During the middle of July, 1829, the governor received requests for aid from the counties of Mathews, Gloucester, the Isle of Wight and adjacent counties.[29] The ease with which "confessions" were obtained under duress casts doubt upon the reality of such outbreaks, but the reports are indicative of the ever-present fear of attack.

Nat Turner's insurrection of August 21, 1831, at Southhampton, seventy miles from Richmond, raised fears of a general servile war to their highest point. The contemporary accounts of the young slave, Nat, tend to overemphasize his leanings towards mysticism and under-state the background of unrest.[30] As a "leader" or lay preacher, Nat Turner exercised a strong influence over his race. On the fatal August night, he led his followers to the plantations of the whites killing fifty-five before the community could act. The influence of the Southhampton insurrection upon the South was profound. Gradually the statesmen of that section began to reexamine their "peculiar" institution in the rival aspects of

[27] *Ibid.,* 367, 388.
[28] *Calendar of Virginia State Papers,* X, 433–6.
[29] *Ibid.,* 567–9.
[30] Thomas Gray (ed.), *Nat Turner's Confession* (Richmond, 1832); Samuel Warner (ed.), *The Authentic and Impartial Narrative of The Tragical Scene of the Twenty Second of August, 1831,* New York, 1831 (A Collection of accounts by eye witnesses); and William Sidney Drewry, *Slave Insurrections in Virginia, 1830–1865* (Washington, 1900), *passim.*

humanitarianism, the race problem, and the economic requirements for a cheap labor supply. How the friends of emancipation failed is familiar history. The immediate results were also far-reaching. Laws against the free Negro were made more restrictive, the police codes of the slave states were strengthened, and Negro education became more than ever an object of suspicion.[31] Virginia's lucrative business of supplying slaves to the lower South was gradually undermined by the recurrent insurrections. Frederic Bancroft, the historian of the domestic slave trade, has written: "Believing that as a result of actual or feared insurrections Virginia and other States were taking pains to sell to the traders the most dangerous slaves and criminal free Negroes, Alabama, Mississippi, Louisiana, and other States passed laws forbidding all importations for sale."[32]

Rumors of slave plots continued to disturb Virginia up to the era of emancipation. During 1856, the state, in common with other slaveholding states, shared in the general feeling that a widespread conspiracy, set for December 25, was maturing. Requests for aid came to the Governor from the counties of Fauquier, King and Queen, Culpeper, and Rappahannock; and particularly from the towns of Lynchburg, Petersburg, and Gordonsville.[33] As for John Brown's visionary deed at Harper's Ferry in the autumn of 1859, the aftermath can be easily imagined. The spectre of a general insurrection again haunted the minds of the white citizenry and large patrols were kept in constant service to prevent Negro meetings of all types.[34]

Maryland and North Carolina, although more fortunate than their slave-ridden neighbor, did not escape unscathed. The news of Nat Turner and John Brown brought panic to the other states. In Maryland, baseless rumors of conspiracies, rather than actual outbreaks, seemed to be the rule. In 1845 a plot was "disclosed" in Charles County, Maryland, and a number of Negroes were subsequently sold out of the state.[35] Ten years later there was general excitement over alleged uprisings in Dorchester, Talbot and Prince George's Counties. Resolutions were adopted at the time by various citizens asking that slaveholders keep

[31] The immediate results of the Nat Turner affair are summarized in John W. Cromwell's "The Aftermath of Nat Turner's Insurrection," *The Journal of Negro History,* V (1920), 208–234.

[32] Frederick Bancroft, *Slave-Trading in the Old South* (Baltimore, 1931), 18.

[33] *Calendar of Virginia State Papers,* XI (1836–1869), 50. Other rumors of unrest during 1856 came from the towns of Williamsburgh and Alexandria, and from Montgomery County. See Laura A. White, "The South in the 1850's as seen by British Consuls," *The Journal of Southern History,* I (1935), 44.

[34] Brackett, *The Negro in Maryland,* 97–99.

[35] Brackett, *The Negro in Maryland,* 96.

their servants at home.[36] The reaction to John Brown's raid of 1859 was more intense than had ever before been experienced over insurrections in Maryland. The newspapers for days were full of nothing else but the Harper's Ferry incident. Large patrols were called out everywhere and talk was general of a concerted uprising of all the slaves in Maryland and Virginia. A martial atmosphere prevailed.[37]

In 1802 an insurrection was reported in Bertie County, North Carolina, necessitating an elaborate patrol system.[38] A decade later, another outbreak in Rockingham County was narrowly averted,[39] and in 1816 further plots were discovered at Tarboro, New Bern, Camden and Hillsboro.[40] Several minor disturbances occurred in 1821 among the slaves of Bladen, Carteret, Jones, and Onslow Counties.[41] On October 6, 1831, a Georgia newspaper reported an extensive slave conspiracy in North Carolina with ramifications in the eastern counties of Duplin, Sampson, Wayne, New Hanover, Lenoir, Cumberland, and Bladen.[42]

Slave plots in South Carolina during the national period seem to have been abortive for the most part, but several of the projects could easily have been uprisings of the first magnitude. During November, 1797, slave trials in Charleston disclosed a plot to burn the city. Two Negroes were hanged and three deported.[43] The Camden plot of June, 1816, was

[36] *Ibid.*, 97.
[37] *Ibid.*, 97–99.
[38] John Spencer Bassett, *Slavery in the State of North Carolina*, Johns Hopkins University Studies in Historical and Political Science, XVII (Baltimore, 1899), 332. The nature of North Carolina laws during 1777–1788 regarding insurrections indicates the keen fears entertained of slave uprisings. One preamble of 1777 begins ". . . Whereas the evil and pernicious practice of freeing slaves in this State, ought at this alarming and critical time to be guarded against by every friend and well-wisher to his country . . . ." This idea is repeated in the insurrection laws of 1778 and 1788. Walter Clark (ed.), *The State Records of North Carolina* (Goldsboro, N.C., 1905), XXIV (1777–1788), 14, 221, 964. The laws regulating manumission were made increasingly stringent for fear of creating a dangerous class of free Negroes.
[39] *Calendar of Virginia State Papers*, X (1808–1835), 120–2.
[40] A. H. Gordon, "The Struggle of the Negro Slaves for Physical Freedom," *Journal of Negro History*, XIII (1928), 22–35.
[41] Hugh T. Lefler (ed.), *North Carolina History told by Contemporaries* (Chapel Hill, 1934), 265.
[42] Milledgeville (Georgia) *Federal Union*, October 6, 1831, quoted in *ibid.;* The repercussion of the Nat Turner insurrection at Murfreesboro, Hertford County, has been graphically described by an eye witness, "It was court week and most of our men were twelve miles away at Winton. Fear was seen in every face, women pale and terror stricken, children crying for protection, men fearful and full of foreboding, but determined to be ready for the worst." Quoted from the Baltimore *Gazette*, November 16, 1831, by Stephen B. Weeks, "The Slave Insurrection in Virginia," *American Magazine of History*, XXV (1891), 456.
[43] H. M. Henry, *The Police Patrol of the Slave in South Carolina*, 150.

a very serious affair and envisaged a concerted attempt to burn the town and massacre its inhabitants. A favorite slave reported the plot to his master, Colonel Chestnut, who thereupon informed Governor Williams. Six of the slave leaders were executed and patrol measures were strengthened.[44]

The outstanding threat of insurrection in the State was the Denmark Vesey plot of 1822. The leader, Denmark, was a free Negro of Charleston, a native of St. Thomas in the West Indies, who had purchased his freedom in 1800 from the proceeds of a lottery prize and had since worked in the city as a carpenter. He desired to emulate the Negro leaders of St. Domingo and win the freedom of his people. Preaching that conditions had become intolerable for the slave, he urged a war against the slave-holder. A white man was to purchase guns and powder for his proposed army; Charleston was to be captured and burnt, the shipping of the town seized, and all would sail away from the West Indies to freedom. Again a "faithful slave"—or spy—exposed the plot and severe reprisals were instituted. Thirty-five Negroes were executed and thirty-seven sold out of the state.[45]

Because of the number of free Negroes involved, the Legislature passed an act preventing such persons from entering the state. To avoid, as far as possible, the contagion of abolitionist and kindred ideas, the purchase of slaves was forbidden from the West Indies, Mexico, South America, Europe, and the states north of Maryland. Slaves, who had resided in these forbidden areas, were likewise denied entrance into South Carolina.[46] A Charleston editor, Benjamin Elliott, penned a sharp reply to the Northern accusations of cruelty, by pointing out that New York in the insurrection of 1741 had executed thirty-five and deported eighty-five. He demanded that the Federal Government act under its power to suppress insurrection.[47] In July, 1829, another plot was reported in Georgetown County[48] and in 1831, the year of Nat Turner's attack, one in Laurens County.[49]

Georgia, like South Carolina, was able to avert the worst consequences

[44] Holland, *A Refutation of the Calumnies,* —, 75.

[45] J. Hamilton (ed.), *An Account of the Late Intended Insurrection* (Boston, 1822); also Holland, *A Refutation of the Calumnies,* —, 77–82; *Niles Register,* XXIII (1822–3), 9–12.

[46] *An Act of the Legislature of South Carolina Passed at the Session in December to prevent Free Negroes and Persons of Color from Entering This State* (Charleston, 1824).

[47] Appendix to Holland, *A Refutation of the Calumnies,* 81.

[48] *J.C.N.,* 340. [Helen H. Catterall (ed.), *Judicial Cases Concerning American Slavery and the Negro,* I, II (Washington, 1926). Abbreviated as J. C. N.]

[49] Henry, *The Police Control of the Slave in South Carolina,* 153.

of repeated slave plots. One was reported in Greene County in 1810;[50] a plan to destroy Atlanta came to light in May, 1819;[51] during 1831, disquieting rumors came from Milledgeville and Laurens County;[52] four years later, a plot for a general uprising on the Coast was disclosed;[53] in 1851 another plot in Atlanta was reported;[54] and in 1860, similar reports came from Crawford and Brooks Counties.[55]

Florida experienced an uprising in March, 1820, along Talbot Island which was put down by a detachment of federal troops.[56] Another was reported in December, 1856, in Jacksonville.[57] Alabama discovered a plot in January, 1837, believed to have been instigated by a free Negro, M'Donald.[58] Mississippi seems to have been the central area of a widespread slave plot in July, 1835, threatening the entire Cotton Kingdom. Far-reaching plans of revolt had been drawn up by a white, John A. Murrell, who enjoyed a reputation as a Negro kidnapper and land pirate. Ten or fifteen Negroes and a number of whites were hanged for participation in the plot.[59]

Next to Virginia, Louisiana had the greatest difficulty among the southern states in coping with repeated attempts at insurrection. Governor Claiborne of the Mississippi Territory received frequent letters concerning plots in various parts of Louisiana. In 1804, New Orleans seems to have been threatened.[60] Several months later another alarm came from the plantations at Pointe Coupee.[61] In 1805, the attempt of a Frenchman to teach the doctrine of equality to slaves, led to general fears of an uprising.[62]

[50] Flanders, *Plantation Slavery in Georgia*, 274.
[51] *Niles Register*, XVI (1819), 213.
[52] Flanders, *Plantation Slavery in Georgia*, 274.
[53] *Niles Register*, XLIX (1935-6), 172.
[54] Flanders, *Plantation Slavery in Georgia*, 275. Georgia suffered in common with the other southern states during the scare of 1856; White, "The South in the 1850's as Seen by British Consuls," 43.
[55] Flanders, *Plantation Slavery in Georgia*, 275–6, 186. The abolitionists were accused of organizing the slave plots of the thirties and thereafter. One New England abolitionist, Kitchel, who opened a school for Negroes in Tarversville, Twigg County, Georgia, in 1835, was driven out of the community because he was said to have incited the slaves to revolt. *Ibid.*, 275.
[56] *J.C.N.*, III, 327.
[57] James Stirling, *Letters from the Slave States* (London, 1857), 299.
[58] *J.C.N.*, III, 141. Alabama had two rumors of slave plots reported in 1860, White, "The South in the 1850's as Seen by British Consuls," 47.
[59] *Niles Register*, XLIX (1835-6), 119; also Elizur Wright (ed.), *Quarterly Anti-Slavery Magazine* (New York, 1837), II, 104–11.
[60] Dunbar, Rowland (ed.), *Official Letter Book of W.C.C. Claiborne* (Jackson, 1917), II (1801–1816), 337–8.
[61] *Ibid.*, III (1804–1806), 6.
[62] *Ibid.*, 187.

An actual outbreak occurred in January, 1811. Beginning from a plantation in the parish of St. John the Baptist, about thirty-six miles above New Orleans, a concerted slave uprising spread along the Mississippi. The Negroes formed disciplined companies to march upon New Orleans to the beating of drums. Their force, estimated to include from 180 to 500 persons, was defeated in a pitched battle with the troops.[63] According to one historian many of those executed were decapitated and their heads placed on poles along the river as an example to others.[64]

Another uprising took place in the same area in March, 1829, causing great alarm before it was suppressed. Two leaders were hanged.[65] Other plots were reported in 1835, 1837, 1840, 1841 and 1842.[66] An uprising occurred in August, 1856, at New Iberia.[67]

The situation in Tennessee, Kentucky, and Texas may be briefly summarized. In Tennessee, plots were disclosed during 1831, 1856, and 1857.[68] Kentucky, in December, 1856, hanged several ringleaders of an attempted insurrection at Hopkinsville, in which a white man was involved.[69] That same year, two Negroes were punished by being whipped to death in Texas for an alleged conspiracy at Columbus, Colorado County.[70]

Owing to the nature of such a study any claim to an exhaustive treatment would be mere pretense. An analysis of slave patrol history alone would suggest the existence of far more conspiracies and outbreaks than those already mentioned. It is clear however that *ante-bellum* society of the South suffered from a larger degree of domestic insecurity than the conventional view would indicate. No doubt many Negroes made the required adjustments to slavery, but the romantic picture of careless abandon and contentment fails to be convincing. The struggle of the Negro for his liberty, beginning with those dark days on the slaveship,

[63] *Ibid.,* V (1809–1811), 93–142.
[64] François Xavier Martin, *The History of Louisiana* (New Orleans, 1829), II, 300–301. During the fall of the following year another plot was reported. *J.C.N.,* III, 449.
[65] *Niles Register,* XXVI (1829), 53.
[66] *Ibid.,* LIII (1837–8), 129; LX (1841), 368; LXIII (1842–3), 212.
[67] V. Alton Moody, *Slavery on the Louisiana Sugar Plantations* (Univ. of Michigan Press, 1924), 41; also Phillips, *American Negro Slavery,* 486. *J.C.N.,* III, 648.
[68] Caleb P. Patterson, *The Negro in Tennessee,* Univ. of Texas Bulletin No. 225 (Austin, February 1, 1922), 49; *J.C.N.,* II, 565–6; Stirling, *Letters from the Slave States,* 294.
[69] *J.C.N.,* 299.
[70] Frederick Law Olmsted, *A Journey Through Texas* (New York, 1857), 513–4; Stirling, *Letters From the Slave States,* 300.

was far from sporadic in nature, but an ever-recurrent battle waged everywhere with desperate courage against the bonds of his master.

LE ROI JONES

Afro-Christian Music and Religion

A distinctive slave culture began to emerge in the ante-bellum South. As LeRoi Jones points out, it combined the slave's vague memories of an African past with the ethos which the white man constantly imposed. Many of the institutions and folkways that resulted from this synthesis persisted after slavery had officially ended. Like the Afro-Christian church, they underwent change in the crucible of the black man's experience, but continued as a cultural response to his ambiguous position as a "free" man in America.

WHEN THE FIRST SLAVES WERE BROUGHT TO THIS COUNTRY, THERE was no idea at all of converting them. Africans were thought of as beasts, and there was certainly no idea held among the whites that, somehow, these beasts would benefit by exposure to the Christian God. As late as the twentieth century there have been books "proving" the Negro's close relationship to lower animals that have been immensely popular in the South. The idea that perhaps slavery could be condoned as a method for converting heathens to the Christian God did not become popular until the latter part of the eighteenth century, and then only among a few "radical" Northern missionaries. There could be no soul-saving activities, N. N. Puckett points out in his book *Folk Beliefs of the Southern Negro,* where there was no soul.[1]

[1] *Folk Beliefs of the Southern Negro* (Chapel Hill, University of North Carolina Press, 1926).

AFRO-CHRISTIAN MUSIC AND RELIGION   From *Blues People: Negro Music in White America* by LeRoi Jones. Reprinted by permission of William Morrow & Co., Inc., Publishers. Copyright © 1963 by LeRoi Jones.

But still Christianity was adopted by Negroes before the great attempts by missionaries and evangelists in the early part of the nineteenth century to convert them. The reasons for this grasping of the white man's religion by the North American Negro are fairly simple. First, his own religion was prohibited in this country. In some parts of the South, "conjuring" or use of "hoodoo" or "devil talk" was punishable by death or, at the very least, whipping. Also, the African has always had a traditional respect for his conqueror's gods. Not that they are always worshiped, but they are at least recognized as powerful and placed in the hierarchy of the conquered tribe's gods.

The growing "social awareness" of the slave can be mentioned as another reason for the African's swift embrace of the white man's God: social awareness in the sense that the African, or at least his progeny, soon realized that he was living in a white man's world. Not only was it an ancient African belief that the stronger tribe's gods were to be revered, but the African was also forced to realize that all the things he thought important were thought by the white man to be primitive nonsense. The constant contact between black and white in the United States must have produced in the black man a profound anxiety regarding the reasons for his status and the reasons for the white man's dominance. The African's belief in "stronger gods" assuaged or explained slavery for the African slave and was, perhaps, a partial explanation for his rapid adoption of pre-missionary Christianity. But for the American slave, Christianity was attractive simply because it was something the white man did that the black man could do also, and in the time of the missionaries, was encouraged to do. The house Negroes, who spent their lives finding new facets of the white culture that they could imitate, were the first to adopt Christianity. And they and their descendants, even today, practice the most European or American forms of Christianity. The various black Episcopal and Presbyterian churches of the North were invariably started by the black freedmen, who were usually the sons and daughters of "house niggers." The strange "melting pot" of the United States, where after a few decades the new African slaves were ridiculed by their "American" brothers because they were African! And this was for purely "social" reasons. That is, the slaves who had come to America only a few years earlier began to apply what they thought were the white man's standards to their own behavior as well as to that of their newly arrived brothers.

> Sinner, what you gonna do
> When de world's on fi-er?

Sinner, what you gonna do
When de World's on fi-er?
Sinner, what you gonna do
When de world's on fi-er?
O my Lawd.[2]

Because the African came from an intensely religious culture, a society where religion was a daily, minute-to-minute concern, and not something relegated to a specious once-a-week reaffirmation, he had to find other methods of worshiping gods when his white *captors* declared that he could no longer worship in the old ways. (The first slaves thought of the white men as captors; it was later, after they had become Americans, that they began to think of these captors as masters and themselves as slaves, rather than captives.) The immediate reaction, of course, was to try to worship in secret. The more impressive rites had to be discarded unless they could be performed clandestinely; the daily rituals, however, continued. The common day-to-day stance of the African toward his gods could not be erased overnight. In fact, many of the "superstitions" of the Negroes that the whites thought "charming" were holdovers from African religions. Even today in many Southern rural areas, strange mixtures of voodoo, or other primarily African fetish religions, and Christianity exist. Among less educated, or less sophisticated, Negroes the particular significance of dreams, luck and lucky charms, roots and herbs, is directly attributable to African religious beliefs. Also, many aphorisms used by Negroes in strictly social situations spring from African religion.

For example, there was recently a rhythm & blues song that talked of "Spreading goober dust all around your bed/When you wake up you find your own self dead." To most whites (and indeed to most modern sophisticated city Negroes) the song was probably catchy but essentially unintelligible. But now in 1963, one hundred years after the Emancipation of slaves, there exists a song integrated somewhat into the mainstream of American society that refers directly to an African religious belief. (A *goober* is what a peanut is called by many Southern Negroes. The word itself comes from the African word *gooba,* which is a kind of African nut. In Africa the ground-up *gooba* was used to conjure with, and was thought to give one person power over another if the ground *gooba* ("goober dust") was spread around the victim's hut. In the

[2] From Howard W. Odum and Guy B. Johnson, *Negro Workaday Songs* (Chapel Hill, University of North Carolina Press, 1926), p. 195.

South, peanut shells spread in front of someone's door supposedly cause
something terrible to happen to him.)

"Never go to bed on an empty stomach," my grandmother has told
me all my life. Perhaps the origins of this seemingly health-conscious
aphorism have been forgotten even by her. But the Africans believed
that evil spirits could steal your soul while you slept if your body was
empty. "If the sun is shining and it is raining at the same time, the
devil's beating his wife." "Sweeping out the house after dark is disre-
spectful." Both these aphorisms I heard when I was younger, and they
are both essentially African. The latter refers to the African's practice
of praying each night for the gods to protect him while he slept from
evil spirits; it was thought that the benevolent gods would actually descend and sit in one's house. Sweeping at night, one might sweep the
guardian out since he was invisible. The "gods" of the African eventually became "The Holy Ghos'" of the American Negro.

And so to "outlaw" the African slave's religion completely was impossible, although the circumstance of slavery did relegate religious practice
to a much smaller area of his life. But the African could not function as a human being without religion; he daily invoked the "conjure
men," herb doctors and root healers, cult priests and sorcerers—the
mystical forces he thought controlled the world. The sorcerer was consulted each day to find out the disposition of the gods toward a man and
his activities, just as we dial our phones for the weather report.

The first attempts by Negroes to openly embrace the white Christ
were rebuffed, sometimes cruelly, because of the Christian theologists'
belief that Africans were beasts, literally, lower animals. "You would
not give oxen the holy scripture." Also, on a slightly more humane level,
it was thought by white Christians that if the Africans were given
Christianity, there could be no real justification for enslaving them, since
they would no longer be heathens or savages. In spite of this, the slaves
did go off into the woods to hold some semblance of a Christian rite
when they could. By the beginning of the nineteenth century, however,
against the wishes of most of the planters and slave owners, attempts
were made to convert the slaves because of the protests of the Quakers
and other religious groups.

Fannie Kemble, in her journal of 1838 and 1839, reported:

> You have heard, of course, many and contradictory statements as to
> the degree of religious instruction afforded to the Negroes of the South,
> and their opportunities of worship, etc. Until the late abolition move-
> ment, the spiritual interests of the slaves were about as little regarded
> as their physical necessities. The outcry which has been raised with

threefold force within the last few years against the whole system has induced its upholders and defenders to adopt, as measures of personal extenuation, some appearance of religious instruction (such as it is), and some pretense at physical indulgences (such as they are), bestowed apparently voluntarily upon their dependents. At Darien a church is appropriated to the especial use of the slaves, who are almost all of them Baptists here; and a gentleman officiates it (of course, white) who, I understand, is very zealous in the cause of the spiritual well-being. He, like most Southern men, clergy or others, jump the present life in their charities to the slaves, and go on to furnish them with all requisite conveniences for the next.[3]

She added:

Some of the planters are entirely inimical to any such proceedings and neither allow their Negroes to attend worship, or to congregate together for religious purposes. . . . On other plantations, again, the same rigid discipline is not observed; and some planters and overseers go even farther than toleration, and encourage these devotional exercises and professions of religion, having actually discovered that a man may become more faithful and trustworthy, even as a slave, who acknowledges the higher influences of Christianity. . . .[4]

The ambivalent attitude of the slave-holders toward the conversion of the slaves to Christianity is further illustrated by another of Miss Kemble's observations: ". . . this man is known to be a hard master; his Negro houses are sheds not fit to stable beasts in; his slaves are ragged, half-naked, and miserable; yet he is urgent for their religious comforts, and writes to Mr. Butler about 'their souls—their precious souls.' "[5]

The Quakers and other religious groups began to realize that the only justification for slavery was that the slaves could be converted to Christianity, and the great missionary and evangelical movements of the nineteenth century began. Some of the churches, such as the Methodist and Baptist, began to send ministers among the slaves to convert them. Soon the grossest disparagement the "religious" Negro could make of another was that he or she was "a heathen." (When I spilled food on the table or otherwise acted with boyish slovenliness, my grandmother would always think to dress me down by calling me "a heathen.")

The emotionalism and evangelism of the Methodists and Baptists ap-

[3] *Op. cit.,* pp. 92–93. [Frances Anne Kemble, *Journal of a Residence on a Georgia Plantation in 1838–1839* (New York, Alfred A. Knopf, 1961).]
[4] *Ibid.,* p. 106.
[5] *Ibid.*

pealed much more to the slaves than any of the other denominations. Also, the Baptists, especially, allowed the Negroes to participate in the services a great deal and began early to "appoint" black ministers or deacons to conduct the services while the missionaries themselves went on to other plantations. And on the poorer plantation the lower-class white was more apt to be Baptist or Methodist than Episcopal or Presbyterian. Another, possibly more important, reason why the Negroes were drawn to the Baptist Church was the method of conversion. Total immersion in water, which is the way Baptists symbolize their conversion to the "true church" and the teachings of Christ, in imitation of Christ's immersion by Saint John "The Baptist," was perhaps particularly attractive to the early slaves because in most of the religions of West Africa the river spirits were thought to be among the most powerful of the deities, and the priests of the river cults were among the most powerful and influential men in African society.

The Christian slave became more of an American slave, or at least a more "Westernized" slave, than the one who tried to keep his older African traditions. The slave masters also learned early that the Africans who had begun to accept the Christian ethic or even some crude part of its dogma were less likely to run away or start rebellions or uprisings. Christianity, as it was first given to the slaves (as Miss Kemble pointed out), was to be used strictly as a code of conduct which would enable its devotees to participate in an afterlife; it was from its very inception among the black slaves, a slave ethic. It acted as a great pacifier and palliative, although it also produced a great inner strength among the devout and an almost inhuman indifference to pain. Christianity was to prepare the black man for his Maker, and the anthropomorphic "heben" where all his "sins and suffering would be washed away." One of the very reasons Christianity proved so popular was that it was the religion, according to older Biblical tradition, of an oppressed people. The struggles of the Jews and their long-sought "Promised Land" proved a strong analogy for the black slaves.

> Mary, don't you weep an' Marthie don't you moan,
> Mary, don't you weep an' Marthie don't you moan;
> Pharaoh's army got drown-ded,
> Oh Mary don't you weep.
>
> I thinks every day an' I wish I could
> Stan' on de rock whar Mose stood

Oh, Pharaoh's army got drown-ded,
Oh Mary don't you weep.

The Christianity of the slave represented a movement away from Africa. It was the beginning of Africa as "a foreign place." In the early days of slavery, Christianity's sole purpose was to propose a metaphysical resolution for the slave's natural yearnings for freedom, and as such, it literally made life easier for him. The secret African chants and songs were about Africa, and expressed the African slave's desire to return to the land of his birth. The Christian Negro's music became an expression of his desire to "cross Jordan" and "see his Lord." He no longer wished to return to Africa. (And one can see, perhaps, how "perfect" Christianity was in that sense. It took the slave's mind off Africa, or material freedom, and proposed that if the black man wished to escape the filthy paternalism and cruelty of slavery, he wait, at least, until he died, when he could be transported peacefully and majestically to the Promised Land.)

Gonna shout trouble over
When I get home,
Gonna shout trouble over
When I get home.

No mo' prayin', no mo' dyin'
When I get home.
No mo' prayin' an' no mo' dyin'
When I get home.

Meet my father
When I get home.
Meet my father
When I get home.

The religious imagery of the Negro's Christianity is full of references to the suffering and hopes of the oppressed Jews of Biblical times. Many of the Negro spirituals reflect this identification: *Go Down, Moses, I'm Marching to Zion, Walk Into Jerusalem Just Like John,* etc. "Crossing the river Jordan" meant not only death but also the entrance into the very real heaven and a release from an earthly bondage; it came to represent all the slave's yearnings to be freed from the inhuman yoke of slavery. But at the time, at least for the early black Christian, this freedom was one that could only be reached through death. The later secular music protested conditions *here,* in America. No longer was the great majority of slaves concerned with leaving this country (except, perhaps, the old folks who sat around and, I suppose, remembered). *This* was their country, and they became interested in merely living in it a little better and a little longer.

The early black Christian churches or the pre-church "praise houses" became the social focal points of Negro life. The relative autonomy of the developing Negro Christian religious gathering made it one of the only areas in the slave's life where he was relatively free of the white man's domination. (Aside from the more formally religious activities of the fledgling Negro churches, they served as the only centers where the slave community could hold strictly social functions.) The "praise nights," or "prayer meetings," were also the only times when the Negro felt he could express himself as freely and emotionally as possible. It is here that music becomes indispensable to any discussion of Afro-Christian religion.

"The spirit will not descend without song."

This is an old African dictum that very necessarily was incorporated into Afro-Christian worship. The Negro church, whether Christian or "heathen," has always been a "church of emotion." In Africa, ritual dances and songs were integral parts of African religious observances, and the emotional frenzies that were usually concomitant with any African religious practice have been pretty well documented, though, I would suppose, rarely understood. This heritage of emotional religion was one of the strongest contributions that the African culture made to the Afro-American. And, of course, the tedious, repressive yoke of slavery must well have served to give the black slave a huge reservoir of emotional energy which could be used up in his religion.

"Spirit possession," as it is called in the African religions, was also intrinsic to Afro-Christianity. "Gettin' the spirit," "gettin' religion" or "gettin' happy" were indispensable features of the early American Negro church and, even today, of the non-middle-class and rural Negro churches. And always music was an important part of the total emotional configuration of the Negro church, acting in most cases as the catalyst for those worshipers who would suddenly "feel the spirit." "The spirit will not descend without song."

The first Afro-Christian music differed from the earlier work songs and essentially nonreligious shouts first of all in its subject matter and content. Secondly, the religious music became much more melodic and musical than the field hollers because it was sung rather than grunted or "hollered." (Though no aspect of Negro song is completely without the shout, if later, only as an element of style.) Also, this religious music was drawn from many sources, and represented, in its most mature stage, an amalgam of forms, styles, and influences.

Christianity was a Western form, but the actual practice of it by the American Negro was totally strange to the West. The American Negro's religious music developed quite similarly, taking its superficial forms (and instrumentation, in many cases) from European or American models, but there the imitation ended. The lyrics, rhythms, and even the harmonies were essentially of African derivation, subjected, of course, to the transformations that American life had brought into existence. The Negro's religious music was his original creation, and the spirituals themselves were probably the first completely *native American* music the slaves made. When I refer to the Negro's religious music, however, I mean not only the spiritual, which is used, I am aware, as a general catchall for all the nonsecular music made by the American black man, but I am referring as well to the church marches, ring and shuffle shouts, "sankeys," chants, camp or meetin' songs, and hymns or "ballits," that the Afro-Christian church produced.

But even as the masses of Negroes began to enter the Christian Church and get rid of their "heathenisms," Africa and its religious and secular traditions could not be completely shaken off. In fact, as Borneman points out: "The Methodist revival movement began to address itself directly to the slaves, but ended up not by converting the Africans to a Christian ritual, but by converting itself to an African ritual."[6]

The more conscientious Christian ministers among the slaves sought to get rid of "all dem hedun ways," but it was difficult. For instance, the Christian Church saw dancing as an evil worldly excess, but dancing as an integral part of the African's life could not be displaced by the still white notes of the *Wesleyan Hymnal*. The "ring shouts" or "shuffle shouts" of the early Negro churches were attempts by the black Christians to have their cake and eat it: to maintain African tradition, however veiled or unconscious the attempt might be, yet embrace the new religion. Since dancing was irreligious and sinful, the Negro said that only "crossing the feet" constituted actual dancing. So the ring shout developed, where the worshipers link arms and shuffle, at first slowly but then with increasing emotional display, around in a circle, singing hymns or chanting as they move. This shuffle, besides getting around the dogma of the stricter "white folks" Christianity also seems derived from African

6 *Loc. cit.*, p. 21. [Ernest Borneman, "The Roots of Jazz," in Nat Hentoff and Albert J. McCarthy, eds., *Jazz* (New York, Rinehart, 1959).]

religious dances of exactly the same nature. "Rocking Daniel" dances and the "Flower Dance" were among the dances that the black Christians allowed themselves to retain. The so-called "sanctified" Protestant churches still retain some of these "steps" and "moo-mens" today. And indeed, the "sanctified" churches always remained closer to the African traditions than any of the other Afro-Christian sects. They have always included drums and sometimes tambourines in their ceremonies, something none of the other sects ever dared do.

A description of a typical Afro-Christian church service is found in H. E. Krehbiel's book. Krehbiel had excerpted it from the May 30, 1867, issue of *The Nation:*

> . . . the benches are pushed back to the wall when the formal meeting is over, and old and young, men and women, sprucely dressed young men, grotesquely half-clad field hands—the women generally with gay handkerchiefs twisted about their heads and with short skirts—boys with tattered shirts and men's trousers, young girls bare-footed, all stand up in the middle of the floor, and when the "sperichil" is struck up begin first walking and by and by shuffling around, one after the other, in a ring. The foot is hardly taken from the floor, and the progression is mainly due to a jerking, hitching motion which agitates the entire shouter and soon brings out streams of perspiration. Sometimes they dance silently, sometimes as they shuffle they sing the chorus of the spiritual, and sometimes the song itself is also sung by the dancers. But more frequently a band, composed of some of the best singers and of tired shouters, stand at the side of the room to "base" the others, singing the body of the song and clapping their hands together or on the knees. Song and dance are alike extreme energetic, and often, when the shout lasts into the middle of the night, the monotonous thud, thud of feet prevents sleep within half a mile of the praise house.[7]

The music that was produced by Negro Christianity was the result of diverse influences. First of all, there was that music which issued from pure African ritual sources and which was changed to fit the new religion—just as the ring shouts were transformed from pure African religious dances to pseudo-Christian religious observance, or the Dahomey river cult ceremonies were incorporated into the baptism ceremony. Early observers also pointed out that a great many of the first Negro Christian religious songs had been taken almost untouched from the great body of African religious music. This was especially true of

---

[7] *Op. cit.,* p. 33. [H. E. Krehbiel, *Afro-American Folksongs* (New York, G. Schirmer, 1914).]

the melodies of certain black Christian spirituals that could also be heard in some parts of Africa.

Maude Cuney-Hare, in her early book *Negro Musicians and Their Music,* cites the experience of a Bishop Fisher of Calcutta who traveled to Central Africa:

> . . . in Rhodesia he had heard natives sing a melody so closely resembling *Swing Low, Sweet Chariot* that he felt that he had found it in its original form: moreover, the region near the great Victoria Falls have a custom from which the song arose. When one of their chiefs, in the old days, was about to die, he was placed in a great canoe together with trappings that marked his rank, and food for his journey. The canoe was set afloat in midstream headed toward the great Falls and the vast column of mist that rises from them. Meanwhile the tribe on the shore would sing its chant of farewell. The legend is that on one occasion the king was seen to rise in his canoe at the very brink of the Falls and enter a chariot that, descending from the mists, bore him aloft. This incident gave rise to the words "Swing Low, Sweet Chariot," and the song, brought to America by African slaves long ago, became anglicized and modified by their Christian faith.[8]

It would be quite simple for an African melody that was known traditionally to most of the slaves to be used as a Christian song. All that would have to be done was change the words (which is also the only basic difference between a great many of the "devil music" songs and the most devout of the Christian religious songs. Just as many high school students put their own words to the tune *Yankee Doodle Dandy,* for whatever purpose, the converted slave had only to alter his lyrics to make the song "Christian"). Of course, the point here is that the slave had *to be able* to change the words, that is, he had to know enough of the language in which the new religion was spoken so that he could make up lyrics in that language. Christian songs in African tongues are extremely rare, for obvious reasons. (What is the word for *God* in any of the African dialects? The answer would be: Which god?)

Almost all parts of the early Negro Christian church service had to do in some way with music, which was also true of the African religions. And not only were African songs transformed into a kind of completely personal Christian liturgical music but African prayers and chants as well. The black minister of an early Christian church (as well as the Negro ministers of today's less sophisticated black churches) himself contributed the most musical and most emotional parts of the church

---

[8] *Op. cit.,* p. 69. [Maud Cuney-Hare, *Negro Musicians and Their Music* (Washington, D.C., Associated Publishers, 1936).]

service. The long, long, fantastically rhythmical sermons of the early
Negro Baptist and Methodist preachers are well known. These men were
singers, and they sang the word of this new God with such passion and
belief, as well as skill, that the congregation had to be moved. The traditional African call-and-response song shaped the form this kind of
worship took on. The minister would begin slowly and softly, then build
his sermon to an unbelievable frenzy with the staccato punctuation of his
congregation's answers. "Have you got good religion?/Certainly, Lord,"
is the way one spiritual goes, modeled on the call-and-response, preacher-
to-congregation type of song. When the preacher and the congregation
reach their peaks, their music rivals any of the more formal Afro-
American musics in intensity and beauty.

> Oh, my Lawd, God, what happened when Adam took de apple?
> (Amen, Amen). Yas, didn't de Lawd tell dat po' foolish sinner not to
> listen to that spiteful wo-man? (Amen, Amen). Yas, Lawd, Did he tell
> him or no? (Amen, Amen, Yas he told him, brother). And what did
> Adam do, huh? Yas, Lawd, after you told him not to, what did he do?
> (Amen, Amen, brother, preach, preach).

Another kind of song that the Negro church produced in America
was one based on European or American religious (and sometimes secular) songs. In these songs the words often remained the same (with, of
course, the natural variances of Negro speech). For instance, Puckett
seemed puzzled by the use of the word *fellom-city* in Negro spirituals.
The word, most old Negroes say, means some kind of peace, so I would
think the word to be *felicity*. The melodies of many of the white Christian and European religious songs which the Negroes incorporated into
their worship remained the same, but the Negroes changed the rhythms
and harmonies of these songs to suit themselves. The very fact that the
Negroes sang these songs in their peculiar way, with not only the idiosyncratic American idiom of early Negro speech but the inflection,
rhythm, and stress of that speech, also served to shape the borrowed
songs to a strictly Negro idiom. And usually, no matter how closely a
Negro spiritual might resemble superficially one of the white hymns
taken from sources like the *Bay Psalm Book,* the *Wesleyan Hymnal,*
the *Anglican Hymnal,* or the *Moody Hymnal,* when the song was actually sung, there could be no mistake that it had been made over into
an original Negro song. A very popular white Christian hymn like *Climb
Jacob's Ladder* is completely changed when sung in the Negro church
as *Climin' Jacob's Ladda. Jesus, Lover of my Soul,* a song out of the
Sankey Hymnal, is changed by the Shouting Baptists of Trinidad into

an unmistakably African song. And, as Herskovits noted, in a great many parts of the West Indies, all the Protestant pseudo-Christian religious songs are called "sankeys."

Rhythmic syncopation, polyphony, and shifted accents, as well as the altered timbral qualities and diverse vibrato effects of African music were all used by the Negro to transform most of the "white hymns" into Negro spirituals. The pentatonic scale of the white hymn underwent the same "aberrations" by which the early musicologists characterized African music. The same chords and notes in the scale would be flattened or diminished. And the meeting of the two different musics, the white Christian hymn and the Negro spiritual using that hymn as its point of departure, also produced certain elements that were later used in completely secular music. The first instrumental voicings of New Orleans jazz seem to have come from the arrangement of the singing voices in the early Negro churches, as well as the models for the "riffs" and "breaks" of later jazz music. The Negro's religious music contained the same "rags," "blue notes" and "stop times" as were emphasized later and to a much greater extent in jazz.

The purely social function of the early Negro Christian churches is of extreme importance if one is trying to analyze any area of American Negro culture. First of all, as I have said, because the church for a long time was the *only* place the slave had for any kind of vaguely human activity. The black churches, as they grew more and more autonomous and freer of the white man's supervision, began to take on social characteristics that, while imitative of their white counterparts in many instances, developed equally, if not more rigid social mores of their own. Not only did the churches sponsor the various social affairs, such as the barbecues, picnics, concerts, etc., but they became the sole arbiters of what kind of affair would be sponsored.

During the time of slavery, the black churches had almost no competition for the Negro's time. After he had worked in the fields, there was no place to go for any semblance of social intercourse but the praise houses. It was not until well after the Emancipation that the Negro had much secular life at all. It is no wonder then that early books about Negro music talked about "the paucity of Negro secular music." The churches called sinful all the "fiddle sings," "devil songs," and "jig tunes"—even the "corn songs" were outlawed by some church elders. Also, certain musical instruments, such as the violin and banjo, were said to be the devil's own. The Negro church, as it was begun, was the only place where the Negro could release emotions that slavery would naturally tend to curtail. The Negro went to church, literally, to be free, and to prepare himself for his freedom in the Promised Land. But as the church grew more established and began to shape itself more and more in its image of the white man's church, the things it desired to achieve for Negroes began to change. The church began to produce social stations as well. The ministers, deacons, elders, trustees, even the ushers, of the Baptist and Methodist churches formed a definite social hierarchy, and that hierarchy dominated the whole of the Negro society. The "back-slider" (the sinning churchgoer) and the "heathen" became in the new theocracy the lowest rungs of the social ladder. And during slavery, the churches controlled by the house Negroes or the "freedmen" imposed even stricter social categories than did the other Negro churches. The churches after a time, of course, became as concerned with social mat-ters as with religion, although all such concerns were still couched in religious terms. And what came to be known as "progress," or "ad-vance," to the growing numbers of willing congregations came to mean merely the imitation of the white man—in practice, if not in theory.

As some indication of this practice, in W. F. Allen's book, published in 1867, when mentioning the "paucity of secular songs" among the Negroes, Allen goes on to say:

> We have succeeded in obtaining only a very few songs of this char-acter. Our intercourse with the colored people has been chiefly through the work of the Freedmen's Commission, which deals with the serious and earnest side of the negro character. . . . It is very likely that if we had found it possible to get at more of their secular music we should have come to another conclusion as to the proportion of the barbaric element.[9]

But the end of slavery had, in many ways, a disintegrating effect on the kind of slave culture the church had made possible. With the legal end of slavery, there was now proposed for the Negro masses a much fuller life *outside* the church. There came to be more and more back-sliders, and more and more of the devil music was heard.

[9] *Slave Songs of the United States* (New York, 1867).

Abolition to Jim Crow

LEON LITWACK

The Black Abolitionists

Some white abolitionists wanted full equality for the black man; most wanted only to abolish the institution of slavery. In the North, headquarters for abolitionism, the movement was often on the defensive, since most people were against ending slavery altogether. Abolitionists' meetings were frequently broken up; frequently also, white mobs stormed the sections of town inhabited by free blacks. In 1829, for instance, white citizens invaded Cincinnati's "Little Africa," killing blacks and eventually driving off half of the town's black population.

There were also internal problems within the movement. Leon Litwack points out in the following selection that some black abolitionists strongly differed with their white allies on crucial questions of tactics and goals. Much of this tension can be felt in the struggle between Frederick Douglass and William Lloyd Garrison. Although both were important leaders in the antislavery movement, they had very different ideas about the methods black men should use to obtain their freedom. As Litwack shows, the abolitionist movement, like Douglass himself, became more radical as time passed and as the ideas of black spokesmen such as David Walker and Henry H. Garnet became more influential.

THE WIDELY PUBLICIZED ACTIVITIES OF WHITE ANTISLAVERY WORKERS and the commanding figures of William Lloyd Garrison, Wendell Phillips, and Theodore Weld have tended to obscure the important and active role of the Negro abolitionist. The antislavery movement was not solely a white man's movement. Through their own newspapers, conventions, tracts, orations, and legislative petitions, Negroes agitated for an end to southern bondage and northern repression. The white abolitionist encountered strong and often violent public opposition, but the Negro abolitionist risked even greater hostility, for his very presence on the antislavery platform challenged those popular notions which had stereotyped his people as passive, meek, and docile. As a common laborer,

THE BLACK ABOLITIONISTS Reprinted from *North of Slavery, the Negro in the Free States, 1790–1860* by Leon F. Litwack. By permission of The University of Chicago Press and Leon F. Litwack. © 1961 by The University of Chicago.

the Negro might be tolerated, even valued, for his services; as an anti-slavery agitator, he was frequently mobbed.

Negro abolitionism preceded by several years the appearance of Garrison and *The Liberator*. Encouraged by the post-Revolutionary emancipation movement, Negroes worked with sympathetic whites to remove the last traces of slavery in the North and to call for its abolition in the South. As early as 1797, four illegally manumitted North Carolina Negroes, who had fled to the North to escape re-enslavement, petitioned Congress to consider "our relief as a people." Three years later, a group of Philadelphia free Negroes appealed directly to Congress to revise the federal laws concerning the African trade and fugitive slaves and to adopt "such measures as shall in due course emancipate the whole of their brethren from their present situation."[1] In addition to legislative petitions, meetings commemorating the abolition of the African slave trade or the end of slavery in a particular state afforded opportunities for such prominent Negro leaders as Peter Williams, Nathaniel Paul, William Hamilton, and Joseph Sidney to voice their sentiments on public issues.[2] The organization of independent churches, Free African societies, Masonic lodges, and anticolonization meetings further intensified a growing race consciousness and helped to arouse the Negro community in several areas to a more vigorous defense of its civil rights.

Four years before the publication of the first issue of *The Liberator,* two Negro leaders, John Russwurm and Samuel E. Cornish, launched the first Negro newspaper—*Freedom's Journal*—in an effort to disseminate useful ideas and information and to attract public attention to the plight of those still in bondage. In the first issue, the editors announced that Negroes had to plead their own cause: "Too long have others spoken for us. Too long has the publick been deceived by misrepresentations."[3] During its two years of publication, *Freedom's Journal* featured articles on the evils of slavery and intemperance, the importance of education and the progress of Negro schools, literary and historical

---

[1] Herbert Aptheker (ed.), *A Documentary History of the Negro People in the United States* (New York, 1951), pp. 39–41.

[2] For a convenient guide to the published addresses of these early Negro leaders, see Dorothy P. Porter, "Early American Negro Writings: A Bibliographical Study," *Papers of the Bibliographical Society of America*, XXXIX (1945), 192–268. Especially valuable for an early Negro's views on national affairs is Joseph Sidney, *An Oration, Commemorative of the Abolition of the Slave Trade in the United States; Delivered before the Wilberforce Philanthropic Association, in the City of New York, on the second of January, 1809* (New York, 1809). Copy in Schomburg Collection, New York Public Library.

[3] *Freedom's Journal*, March 16, 1827.

selections, moral lessons, information on the various Afro-American benevolent societies, and a discussion of colonization. Cornish subsequently withdrew from the partnership and established a short-lived newspaper, *The Rights of All,* and Russwurm abandoned his editorial duties to join the colonizationists.[4]

Negro antislavery agitation took on a more aggressive tone in 1829 as David Walker, a Boston clothing dealer and local agent for *Freedom's Journal,* contributed a powerful tract to abolitionist literature—*Walker's Appeal, in Four Articles.* Addressing his sentiments to the "coloured citizens" of the world, but particularly to those of the United States, Walker described American Negroes as "the most degraded, wretched, and abject set of beings that ever lived since the world began." Indeed, he asked,

> Can our condition be any worse?—Can it be more mean and abject? If there are any changes, will they not be for the better, though they may appear for the worst at first? Can they get us any lower? Where can they get us? They are afraid to treat us worse, for they know well, the day they do it they are gone.

In Walker's estimation, four major factors accounted for this wretched state of affairs: slavery, ignorance, "the preachers of Jesus Christ," and the African colonization movement. Consequently, Negroes had to strive for economic and educational improvement and resist the encroachments of the colonizationists. ("America is as much our country, as it is yours.") The southern Negro, on the other hand, faced an even greater challenge, for he had to strike directly and perhaps violently for his freedom as a natural right. Once that thrust for liberty had been made, Walker advised, "make sure work—do not trifle, for they will not trifle with you—they want us for their slaves, and think nothing of murdering us in order to subject us to that wretched condition—therefore, if there is an *attempt* made by us, kill or be killed." To prevent the outbreak of racial war, Walker warned the white man, recognize the legal rights of Negroes. There can be no mistaking the alternative.

> Remember, Americans, that we must and shall be free and enlightened as you are, will you wait until we shall, under God, obtain our liberty by the crushing arm of power? Will it not be dreadful for you? I speak Americans for your good. We must and shall be free I say, in spite of

---

[4] For some bitter criticism of Russwurm after his conversion to colonization, see Carter G. Woodson (ed.), *Mind of the Negro,* pp. 160–63. As reflected in letters written during the crisis, 1800–1860 (Washington, D.C., 1926), pp. 160–63.

you. . . . And wo, wo, will be to you if we have to obtain our free-dom by fighting.[5]

Within a year after its publication, the apparent popularity—or notoriety—of Walker's pamphlet warranted a third edition. The often violent reaction to its contents and the mysterious death of the author in 1830 undoubtedly assisted its circulation.[6] Indeed, it had already caused some consternation in the North, and it understandably created outright alarm in portions of the South. Already beset by a growing fear of slave uprisings, the South could not afford to tolerate the potentially explosive appeal of a Boston clothing dealer. The governor of North Carolina denounced it as "an open appeal to their [the slaves'] natural love of liberty . . . and throughout expressing sentiments totally subversive of all subordination in our slaves"; the mayor of Savannah wrote to the mayor of Boston requesting that Walker be arrested and punished, and Richmond's mayor reported that several copies of *Walker's Appeal* had been found in the possession of local free Negroes; the governors of Georgia and North Carolina submitted the pamphlet to their state legis-latures for appropriate action; and the Virginia legislature held secret sessions to consider proper measures to prevent the pamphlet's cir-culation. Finally, four southern states—Georgia, North Carolina, Mis-sissippi, and Louisiana—seized upon the pamphlet to enact severe restrictions to cope with such "seditious" propaganda.[7]

The South was not alone in its critical reaction. Walker's medicine for the ills of American Negroes was too strong for many white abo-litionists. "A more bold, daring, inflammatory publication, perhaps, never issued from the press of any country," antislavery publisher Ben-jamin Lundy declared. "I can do no less than set the broadest seal of condemnation on it."[8] Lundy's disciple, William Lloyd Garrison, had just launched his own career as an aggressive antislavery publicist and was more equivocal in his reaction. The editor of *The Liberator* found it difficult to reconcile his belief in nonresistance with his unconcealed admiration of Walker's courage and forthrightness. While deploring

[5] David Walker, *Walker's Appeal, in Four Articles; together with a Preamble, to the Coloured Citizens of the World, but in particular, and very expressly to those of the United States of America, written in Boston, State of Massachusetts, September 28, 1829* (3d ed.; Boston, 1830).
[6] See Vernon Loggins, *The Negro Author* (New York, 1931), p. 86; Woodson (ed.), *Mind of the Negro*, p. 222.
[7] Clement Eaton, "A Dangerous Pamphlet in the Old South," *Journal of Southern History*, II (1936), 323–34.
[8] *Genius of Universal Emancipation*, April, 1830; *The Liberator*, January 29, 1831.

the circulation of this "most injudicious publication" and "its general spirit," Garrison admitted that it contained "many valuable truths and seasonable warnings."[9]

The appearance of *The Liberator* in 1831 and the formation of the American Anti-Slavery Society two years later thus found northern Negroes already engaged in a variety of abolitionist activities. In addition to publishing a newspaper and several antislavery tracts, Negroes had taken steps to co-ordinate their actions through annual national conventions. On September 15, 1830, delegates gathered in Philadelphia's Bethel Church to launch the first in a series of such conventions. Against a background of increasing repressive legislation in the North, the delegates adopted an address to the free Negro population, pointing out that their present "forlorn and deplorable situation" demanded immediate action. Where Negroes were subjected to constant harassment and denied even the right of residence, the most recent and blatant case being Ohio, such action would have to take the form of emigration to Canada. There, the convention advised, Negroes could establish themselves "in a land where the laws and prejudices of society will have no effect in retarding their advancement to the summit of civil and religious improvement." Meanwhile, those Negroes who chose to remain in the United States would have to utilize every legal means to improve their political and economic position. Before adjourning, the delegates called upon Negroes to establish auxiliary societies and send delegates to the next annual convention.[10]

Convening annually up to 1835 and periodically thereafter, the national Negro conventions regularly condemned the American Colonization Society, deprecated segregation and "oppressive, unjust and unconstitutional" legislation, stressed the importance of organization, education, temperance, and economy, and set aside the Fourth of July as a day of "humiliation, fasting and prayer" when Negroes would ask for divine intervention to break "the shackles of slavery."[11] Meanwhile, the formation of auxiliary state organizations, temperance groups, moral-reform societies, and educational associations created an unprecedented amount of unity and activity among northern Negroes, developed new leadership, and contributed mightily to the strength of the newly formed white antislavery societies.

[9] *The Liberator,* January 29, 1831.
[10] "The First Colored Convention," *Anglo-African Magazine,* I (October, 1859), 305–10; Aptheker (ed.), *Documentary History,* pp. 102–7.
[11] Selected proceedings of several of the national Negro conventions may be found in Aptheker (ed.), *Documentary History,* pp. 114–19, 133–37, 141–46, 154–57, 159, 226–33, and 341–57.

While engaged in these independent activities, Negro abolitionists also hailed the appearance of a new militancy among their white supporters; they not only welcomed the publication of *The Liberator* but actually outnumbered white subscribers in the early years. "It is a remarkable fact," William Lloyd Garrison wrote in 1834, "that, of the whole number of subscribers to the *Liberator,* only about one-fourth are white. The paper, then, belongs emphatically to the people of color—it is their organ."[12] In addition to contributing articles and letters to the antislavery press, Negroes also attended and addressed abolitionist conventions and, notwithstanding some opposition, served as members of the executive committee and board of managers of both the American Anti-Slavery Society and its later rival, the American and Foreign Anti-Slavery Society.[13]

Negro abolitionists did not confine their activities to the United States. In the 1840's and 1850's, several of them toured the British Isles to promote antislavery sentiment and raise money for abolitionist enterprises. Englishmen crowded into meeting halls to see and hear leading American Negroes tell of the plight of their people and their own experiences as slaves or freemen. Frederick Douglass, for example, described his years of bondage in the South; William G. Allen told of his narrow escape from an enraged northern mob after proposing to marry a white girl; William and Ellen Craft related their flight to freedom and their subsequent exile to avoid prosecution under the Fugitive Slave Act; and Henry Highland Garnet undoubtedly mentioned the mob that ejected him from a Connecticut boys' academy.[14] While arousing their foreign audiences with these tales of slavery and racial violence, Negroes also found much to amaze them. "Here the colored man feels himself among friends, and not among enemies," one Negro "exile" wrote from England, "among a people who, when they treat him well, do it not in the patronizing (and, of course insulting) spirit, even of hundreds of the American abolitionists, but in a spirit rightly appreciative of the doctrine of human equality."[15] For some of these Negro abolitionists, returning home must have been difficult. After extensive travels in England and Europe, for example, William Wells Brown came back to Philadelphia,

[12] Francis and Wendell P. Garrison, *William Lloyd Garrison, 1805–1879* (4 vols., Boston & New York, 1894), I, 432.
[13] Herbert Aptheker, "The Negro in the Abolitionist Movement," *Essays in the History of the American Negro* (New York, 1945), pp. 154–55; Foner (ed.), *Life and Writings of Frederick Douglass,* I, 33, 426. [(4 vols., New York, 1950–55.)]
[14] Benjamin Quarles, "Ministers Without Portfolio," *Journal of Negro History,* XXXIX (1954), 27–42.
[15] *The Liberator,* July 22, 1853.

only to find himself proscribed from the Chestnut Street omnibus on his
first day home. "The omnibuses of Paris, Edinburgh, Glasgow, and
Liverpool, had stopped to take me up," he recollected, "but what mat-
tered that? My face was not white, my hair was not straight; and,
therefore, I must be excluded from a seat in a third-rate American omnibus."[16]

Both Negro and white abolitionists suffered from internal dissension
over fundamental questions of policy and ideology. While the white anti-
slavery societies split over the issues of political action, nonresistance,
women's rights, disunion, and the nature of the Constitution, Negroes
argued the merits of moral suasion and separate conventions. By 1835,
the American Moral Reform Society, dominated largely by Philadelphia
Negroes, replaced the regular convention movement. Dedicated to "improving the condition of mankind," the new organization urged Negroes
to abandon the use of the terms "colored" and "African," to refrain
from holding separate colored conventions, to integrate as fully as possible into white society, to support the equality of women, and to adopt
the principles of peace, temperance, brotherly love, and nonresistance
"under all circumstances." In adopting such a program, the moral reformers obviously allied themselves with the Garrisonians in the growing
factional struggle within the antislavery movement.

The American Moral Reform Society found little support outside the
Garrisonian strongholds of Philadelphia and Boston. Meanwhile, New
York Negro leaders launched a new weekly newspaper, the *Colored
American,* which expressed dismay over the growing split in abolitionist
ranks and the activities of the moral reformers. Editor Samuel Cornish
noted that the delegates to a recent moral-reform convention had impressed him as "vague, wild, indefinite and confused in their views."
Only drastic reorganization and the adoption of a more vigorous program of action could possibly salvage the society. As for their efforts to
substitute the term "oppressed Americans" for "colored people," Cornish called this sheer nonsense. "Oppressed Americans! *who are they?"*
he asked. "Nonsense brethren!! You are COLORED AMERICANS. The indians are RED AMERICANS, and the white people are WHITE AMERICANS
and *you are good as they, and they are no better than you."*

While scolding the moral reformers, the *Colored American* also engaged in a controversy with the pro-Garrison *National Anti-Slavery
Standard* over the advisability of colored conventions. "We oppose all
exclusive action on the part of the colored people," the *Standard* announced in June, 1840, "except where the clearest necessity demands

16 William Wells Brown, *The American Fugitive in Europe* (Boston, 1855), pp.
312–14.

it." As long as Negroes contented themselves with separate churches, schools, and conventions, public sentiment would remain unaltered. Instead, Negroes should join with their white friends to demand equal rights as men, not as colored persons, and thus confirm the abolitionists' contention that racial distinctions had no place in American society. The moral reformers enthusiastically indorsed the position of the *Standard*. Other Negro leaders, however, immediately condemned it and upheld the need for independent action. The abolitionists had done much for the Negro, Samuel R. Ward wrote to the editor of the *Standard,* but too many of them "best love the colored man at a distance" and refuse to admit or eradicate their own prejudices. In the meantime, Negroes had to meet and act for themselves.

Although the American Moral Reform Society had a short life, the split in white abolitionist ranks continued to undermine Negro unity. By 1840, Garrisonians shared the field of agitation with the American and Foreign Anti-Slavery Society and the Liberty party. New England and Philadelphia Negroes generally supported the American Anti-Slavery Society and condemned the critics of Garrison as unworthy of confidence or support. New York Negroes, on the other hand, not only dissociated themselves from the moral reformers but generally indorsed direct po- litical action and contributed to the leadership and campaigns of the Liberty party. At one point, the *Colored American* attempted to restore some semblance of sanity and unity to abolitionists by urging them to avoid peripheral issues and petty bickering and get back to opposing slavery. "Why . . . make governments or anti-governments—resistance or nonresistance—women's rights or men's rights—Sabbaths or anti- Sabbaths, a bone of contention?" the Negro newspaper asked. "None of these should have any thing to do with our Anti-Slavery efforts. *They are neither parts nor parcels of that great and holy cause,* nor should they be intruded into its measures." Rather than promote abolitionist harmony, however, such sentiments, coupled with the editors' indorse- ment of political action and their refusal to censure Garrison's critics, induced some severe attacks and threats to cut off financial support from the paper. Defending their right to differ with Garrison on any issue and to adopt an independent editorial policy, the editors of the *Colored American* warned Negroes that as long as they permitted white abolition- ists to act and think for them, "so long they will outwardly treat us as men, while in their hearts they still hold us as slaves."[17]

In a desperate effort to retain their hold on the antislavery movement,

[17] *Colored American,* October 7, 14, 1837, May 11, August 17, October 5, 19, November 2, 1839.

Garrison and his associates made every effort to secure Negro support. In Boston and New Bedford, Negro meetings acclaimed Garrison as a "friend and benefactor" and indorsed his antislavery position.[18] Already abandoned by many of his white followers, Garrison expressed gratification over such reactions. The opposition knew, he wrote, "that, so long as I retain the confidence of my colored friends, all of their machinations against me will prove abortive."[19] Had Garrison known that his most important Negro ally, Frederick Douglass, was about to desert him, he would have had much less cause for optimism.

As late as September 4, 1849, Douglass had insisted that he was a loyal Garrisonian abolitionist, and there was little reason to doubt him. According to the tenets of that faith, he had excoriated the Constitution as "a most foul and bloody conspiracy" against the rights of three million slaves, had supported disunion as the most effective means to remove federal protection from the "peculiar institution," had belittled political action as futile and necessarily compromising, and had advocated moral persuasion rather than violence in attacking slavery.[20] Nevertheless, signs of revolt became increasingly apparent. After founding the *North Star* in 1847 against the advice of his Boston friends and moving from New England to Rochester, Douglass carefully re-evaluated his position and listened to the arguments of various New York abolitionists who had already broken with Garrison. Before long, the Negro leader reached the conclusion that disunion would only place the slaves at the complete mercy of the South, that political action constituted "a legitimate and powerful means for abolishing slavery," that southern bondage would probably have to expire in violence, and that the Constitution made no guarantees to slavery but in fact implied its eventual extinction.[21] In May, 1851, Douglass utilized the annual convention of the American Anti-Slavery Society to proclaim his heresy publicly. "There is roguery somewhere," Garrison reputedly declared as he moved to strike the *North Star* from the list of approved abolitionist publications.[22] Douglass had gone over to the enemy.

---

[18] *The Liberator,* June 7, 21, 1839. See also *Eighth Annual Report of the Board of Managers of the Massachusetts Anti-Slavery Society* (Boston, 1840), pp. 36–37; *The Liberator,* October 6, 1837, April 3, 1840; Dwight L. Dumond (ed.), *Letters of James Gillepsie Birney, 1831–1857* (2 vols.; New York, 1938), I, 575–79.

[19] William Lloyd Garrison to Elizabeth Pease, September 1, 1840, Garrison Papers.

[20] Foner (ed.), *Life and Writings of Frederick Douglass,* II, 49–52.

[21] Douglass, *Life and Times,* pp. 322–24; Foner (ed.), *Life and Writings of Frederick Douglass,* II, 52–53, 149–50, 152–53, 155–57.

[22] Foner (ed.), *Life and Writings of Frederick Douglass,* II, 53–54, 155–56.

Although he voiced his new position on the lecture platform and in the *North Star,* Douglass hoped to avert a complete break with Garrison. "I stand in relation to him something like that of a child to a parent," he wrote to Charles Sumner.[23] Nevertheless, Garrisonian anxiety and alarm soon changed to vigorous denunciation and even personal defamation. *The Liberator* now placed Douglass' editorials in the section usually reserved for proslavery sentiments, and it charged that the Negro leader had betrayed his former friends for the sake of financial gain, that he possessed ambitions to become the spokesman of the colored race, and that he had lost much of his moral fervor and influence.[24] When Douglass reduced the size of his newspaper, one Garrisonian gleefully wrote to an English friend that the Negro editor "has the confidence of very few, the respect . . . of none. Do what he may, we shall take no notice of him, and I think his career—on professedly anti-slavery grounds— will soon come to an end." Although Garrison generally allowed his followers to deal editorially with the Negro upstart, he confided to friends that he regarded Douglass as a malignant enemy, "thoroughly base and selfish," "destitute of every principle of honor, ungrateful to the last degree, and malevolent in spirit," and unworthy of "respect, confidence, or countenance." Such was the thoroughness of the Garrison indictment.[25]

Replying to his critics with equal bitterness, Douglass called them "vigilant enemies" and labeled their Negro followers as "practical enemies of the colored people" and contemptible tools. The Garrisonians had first attempted to silence his newspaper, he charged, and now they sought to expel him from the anti-slavery fold as a dangerous heretic. "They talk down there [Boston] just as if the Anti-Slavery Cause belonged to them—and as if all Anti-Slavery ideas originated with them and that no man has a right to 'peep or mutter' on the subject, who does not hold letters patent from them."[26] Douglass also sought to clarify his differences with Garrison, but these appeared to be lost in the bitter editorial war. Before long, Negroes in various parts of the country were meeting to discuss the conflict and to choose sides. Chicago Negroes condemned Garrison's "vile crusade" against "the voice of the

[23] *Ibid.,* II, 210–11.
[24] *The Liberator,* September 16, 23, 30, December 16, 30, 1853.
[25] Samuel May, Jr., to Richard Davis Webb, February 8, 1857, May Papers; William Lloyd Garrison to Samuel J. May, September 5, 1857, September 28, 1860, Garrison Papers.
[26] *Frederick Douglass' Paper,* December 9, 1853; Foner (ed.), *Life and Writings of Frederick Douglass,* II, 270.

colored people"; a Rhode Island convention hailed Douglass as "our acknowledged leader"; and an Ohio gathering decisively defeated a proposal calling on Negroes to abstain from voting in those areas where they enjoyed the franchise. Meanwhile, Garrisonian Negro leaders reiterated the charges of *The Liberator* and claimed to speak for "all the true colored men in the country."[27]

Efforts to reconcile the two antislavery leaders met with no success— only time could heal the deep wounds left by this useless and wasteful struggle. To many Negro and white abolitionists, the entire affair presented a rather sordid and dreary spectacle. "Where is this work of excommunication to end?" Harriet Beecher Stowe wrote Garrison. "Is there but one true anti-slavery church and all others infidels?—Who shall declare which it is."[28] While the dispute helped to reduce the effectiveness of the antislavery movement, it also clearly demonstrated some of the weaknesses in Garrison's ideological and tactical position. Nonresistance, the rejection of political action, disunion, and a proslavery interpretation of the Constitution did not strike many abolitionists in the 1840's and 1850's as being either suitable or realistic weapons with which to abolish southern bondage or northern proscription. Indeed, the final triumph of Garrisonian objectives resulted almost entirely from the employment of strictly non-Garrisonian methods—political agitation and armed force.

Internal dissension hampered but did not stifle the independent activities of Negro abolitionists. Despite the Garrisonian antipathy to "complexional conventions," local and state organizations continued to meet in the 1840's, and several national conventions revived interstate cooperation. On August 15, 1843, Negroes from various states met in Buffalo to consider "their moral and political condition as American citizens." After several heated debates—which partly reflected the growing split in abolitionist ranks—the convention adopted a series of resolutions which denounced the American Colonization Society and the pro-slavery churches, indorsed the Liberty party, stressed the value of temperance, education, the mechanical arts, and agriculture, and attributed the plight of free Negroes—North and South—to the evils of slavery.[29]

Henry Highland Garnet, a New York Negro leader, hoped to secure

[27] Foner (ed.), *Life and Writings of Frederick Douglass*, II, 61–62; *Minutes of the State Convention of the Colored Citizens of Ohio* (Columbus, 1851), pp. 11–12.

[28] Foner (ed.), *Life and Writings of Frederick Douglass*, II, 64.

[29] *National Colored Convention, Buffalo, 1843*, pp. 11, 14–16, 19–22, 25, 27, 31–36.

from the Buffalo delegates a more aggressive stand against slavery. Indicating the cruelties of southern bondage and praising as martyrs those Negroes who had led revolts for freedom, Garnet delivered a powerful plea to the slave population in tones reminiscent of David Walker's *Appeal.* "Brethren arise, arise!" he declared.

> Strike for your lives and liberties. Now is the day and the hour. Let every slave throughout the land do this, and the days of slavery are numbered. You cannot be more oppressed than you have been—you cannot suffer greater cruelties than you have already. *Rather die freemen than live to be slaves.* Remember that you are FOUR MILLIONS! . . . Let your motto be resistance! resistance! RESISTANCE!

Although the Garrisonians had suffered a defeat on the issue of political action, they managed to steer the convention away from such a commitment to physical violence in overthrowing slavery. By a vote of nineteen to eighteen, the delegates refused to indorse Garnet's address. Instead, the convention affirmed its faith in the ultimate righteousness of human government and the abolition of slavery through its instrumentality.[30] Relieved at this outcome, one Garrisonian intimated that Garnet, who had also been one of the first Negroes to indorse the Liberty party, had fallen under the influence of bad advisers. "If it has come to this," Garnet replied, "that I must think as you do, because you are an abolitionist, or be exterminated by your thunder, then I do not hesitate to say that your abolitionism is abject slavery."[31]

Although the Buffalo delegates refused to indorse Garnet's address, its contents and the closeness of the convention vote indicated the emergence of a new militancy among Negro abolitionists. Six years later, Garnet's address and Walker's appeal appeared together in a published pamphlet—reportedly at the expense of an obscure New York farmer, John Brown.[32] An Ohio Negro convention immediately ordered five hundred copies to be "gratuitously" circulated.[33] That same year, a New York Negro editor reminded the governor and legislature of Louisiana that their recent expressions of sympathy for Hungarian rebels might be equally applicable to their own bondsmen. "Strike for your freedom now, at the suggestion of your enslavers," the editor wrote. "Make up

[30] Carter G. Woodson (ed.), *Negro Orators and Their Orations* (Washington, D.C., 1925), pp. 150–57; William M. Brewer, "Henry Highland Garnet," *Journal of Negro History,* XIII (1928), p. 46; *National Colored Convention, Buffalo, 1843,* p. 16.

[31] *The Liberator,* December 3, 1843.

[32] Loggins, *The Negro Author,* p. 192; Woodson (ed.), *Negro Orators and Their Orations,* p. 150.

[33] *Ohio Colored Convention of 1849,* p. 18.

your minds to die, rather than bequeath a state of slavery to your posterity."[34]

By the end of the 1840's, the appeals of Garnet and Walker—once deemed too radical—received growing support in Negro conventions, newspapers, and antislavery tracts. Even Frederick Douglass, who had bitterly opposed Garnet's address, abandoned his previous conviction that moral persuasion and nonresistance alone could abolish slavery. While still a loyal Garrisonian, he created a "marked sensation" in 1849 when he told a Faneuil Hall audience that he would "welcome the intelligence tomorrow, should it come, that the slaves had risen in the South, and that the sable arms which had been engaged in beautifying and adorning the South were engaged in spreading death and devastation there." Three years later, Douglass told the national Free Soil party convention that the slaveholders had forfeited their right to live. The potential horrors of a slave insurrection should no longer be allowed to obstruct the path to freedom. "The slaveholder has been tried and sentenced," he declared in 1857. "He is training his own executioners." The following year, John Brown visited the Douglass home and remained there for several weeks, devoting most of his time to writing financial appeals for a yet unrevealed plan.[35]

[34] Aptheker (ed.), *Documentary History,* pp. 290–91.
[35] *North Star,* June 15, 1849; *Frederick Douglass' Paper,* August 20, 1852; Chambers, *American Slavery and Colour,* p. 174 n.; Foner (ed.), *Life and Writings of Frederick Douglass,* II, 88.

JAMES MCPHERSON

The Colonization Issue

Even with the coming of war and the commitment of Union troops to combat, resistance to the full emancipation of black people was still strong in the North. Northern politicians periodically proposed and explored detours, most of which implied that virtually anything was better than full equality in the political, economic, and social spheres. One alternative, supported by a number of black and white citizens before and during the war, would have had blacks emigrate to Haiti or other apparently hospitable places. As James McPherson here indicates, all such suggestions were founded on the belief that black and white could never live together in peace or equality. Among those who made this judgment in the early 1860s was President Abraham Lincoln.

In MARCH 1862, THE TAMMANY HALL YOUNG MEN'S DEMOCRATIC Club resolved that "we are opposed to emancipating negro slaves, unless on some plan of colonization, in order that they may not come in contact with the white man's labor."[1] Colonization was the magic solution of the Negro question offered by many leading men in the early part of the Civil War. For more than forty years the American Colonization Society and its state auxiliaries, impelled by mixed motives, had sought to solve the race problem by colonizing freed Negroes in Africa. Opposed by abolitionists and by most Negroes, this project was a miserable failure. With the coming of war and the imminent possibility of large-scale emancipation, however, the colonization chimera gained new popularity among conservatives who foresaw the inevitability of emancipation but dreaded its social consequences.

As fugitive slaves began to pour into Union army camps in the summer of 1861, colonization proposals blossomed forth in all parts of the North. Some suggestions envisaged voluntary colonization, others compulsory; still others were vague on the question whether emigration should be voluntary or compulsory. But all colonization plans had one

[1] *Liberator,* May 16, 1862.

THE COLONIZATION ISSUE   From *The Negro's Civil War* by James M. McPherson. © Copyright 1956 by James M. McPherson. Reprinted by permission of Pantheon Books, a division of Random House, Inc.

thing in common: the belief that the Negro and the white man could never live together peacefully as equals. Colonization, therefore, was the only possible solution of the vexing slavery and racial problems.

Embittered by their status as second-class citizens, some Northern Negroes favored emigration from America's hostile environment. In the 1850s a minority of colored men, led by Henry Highland Garnet, Martin R. Delany, and James T. Holly, began to advocate the emigration of Negroes to Haiti or Central America. There they could escape the blighting prejudice of the white man and establish flourishing Negro republics that would disprove the myth of the black man's inability to govern himself.[2] James Redpath, a white, British-born radical, became the organizer of a spectacular but short-lived emigration movement to Haiti. Redpath visited Haiti three times as a reporter for the New York *Tribune* in 1859 and 1860. He came away from the island deeply impressed by its beauty, fertility, and climate. A revolution in 1859 had brought a new president, Fabre Geffrard, to power in Haiti. Eager to develop the country's natural and human resources, Geffrard approached Redpath with a proposition to subsidize the emigration of American Negroes to the island. Geffrard finally won Redpath over to a vision of a powerful, prosperous Haiti which would exhibit the capacity and genius of the Negro race to a skeptical world.[3]

Redpath returned to Boston with a commission as "General Agent of the Haytian Bureau of Emigration." With an initial grant of $20,000 from the Haitian government he opened a central office in Boston in the fall of 1860, and began to recruit agents and establish branch offices in several Northern cities. He published a *Guide to Hayti* (which went through three editions), that described in glowing terms the physical and political characteristics of the island and urged American Negroes to emigrate there for a new and better start in life. Haiti, he told them, was the only country in the Western Hemisphere "where the Black and the man of color are undisputed lords . . . where neither laws, nor prejudice, nor historical memories press cruelly on persons of African descent; where the people whom America degrades and drives from her are rulers, judges, and generals, . . . authors, artists, and legislators." Redpath informed prospective emigrants that the Haitian government would pay fifteen dollars apiece toward their passage expenses, and sell them land at low prices and long-term credits when they arrived. They would be exempt from military service, and eligible for citizenship after one

[2] Leon F. Litwack, *North of Slavery* (Chicago, 1961), pp. 257–62.
[3] James Redpath, *A Guide to Hayti* (Boston, 1st ed., 1860, 2nd and 3rd eds., 1861), pp. 9–11.

year. Complete religious freedom for all immigrants was guaranteed.[4]

Redpath recruited several prominent Negroes as agents and organizers for his Bureau: James T. Holly, Henry Highland Garnet, William Wells Brown, H. Ford Douglass, and J. B. Smith, to name only a few. He established in May 1861 an emigrationist newspaper, the *Pine and Palm,* which was published in both Boston and New York. The New York editor was George Lawrence, a Negro. Redpath's Negro allies gave scores of speeches and published dozens of articles on behalf of the emigration movement. The following selections are representative.

The *Anglo-African* of April 13, 1861, published a letter from an anonymous supporter of emigration:

> Listen! We want our rights. No one is going to *give* them to us, so perforce we must take them. In order to do this, we must have a strong nationality somewhere—respected, feared. . . . We can make of Hayti the nucleus of a power that shall be to the black, what England has been to the white races, the hope of progress and the guarantee of permanent civilization. Look at her position; she is the centre of a circle in whose plane lies Cuba, Central America, and the Southern Slave States. From that centre, let but the fire of Freedom radiate until it shall enkindle, in the whole of that vast area, the sacred flame of Liberty upon the altar of every black man's heart, and you effect at once the abolition of slavery and the regeneration of our race.

George Lawrence wrote:

> Believing that "God hath made of one blood all nations of men for to dwell on the face of the earth," we hold the idea of the absolute inferiority of the negro to be a most damnable heresy, and that it is the bounden duty of those portions of the race who have partially enjoyed the benefits of civilization, to refute the heresy, and convince mankind of their error. . . .
>
> To do it we must escape from the miasmatic influences of prejudice, and the mephitic exhalations of mistaken philanthropy, and establish ourselves where our self-confidence will not be shaken either by the detraction of enemies, or the humiliating misgivings of friends. . . . [It is a] necessity, that we should demonstrate to the world by the upbuilding of black nationalities, our thorough capacity independently to compete with other peoples and our absolute equality to them. . . . Let us, then, not shirk the question, but meet it manfully, hopefully; let us say wherever there is a black man there is a brother, and that out of black men there *shall* arise a nation able to protect itself and defend the weaker portions of the race.[5]

[4] *Ibid.,* p. 9 and *passim.*
[5] *Pine and Palm,* June 22, 1861.

A Washington Negro declared:

> In this city, the question is still discussed by the people of color—
> Shall we go to Hayti, and enjoy the blessings of citizenship in that
> free and independent Republic, or shall we remain in the United States,
> in ignorance and degradation? . . . Let us emigrate to Hayti, where
> we shall be free from the white man's contumely, and where we can
> secure for ourselves and our children after us, a home, a farm, and all
> the rights which citizenship confers. . . . If God ever opened a way
> for the poor despised African to escape from the bondage which he
> endures in this country, it is now—in the offer made to us by the
> Haytian Government. And if we, as a body, possess any desire to prove
> our manhood, let us go energetically to work, and demonstrate to the
> world that we can not only govern ourselves, but that we can only at-
> tain to true greatness when we cease to lean upon the white man for
> support.[6]

Another Negro advocate of emigration was J. Willis Menard. A college graduate, Menard later in the war became the first colored man to
hold a white-collar job in the national government, and during Reconstruction he played an active role in the politics of Louisiana and Florida. But in 1861 he was deeply discouraged by the lowly status of black
men in America. He wrote that

> two hundred and forty-two years of continued administration of in-
> justice to our race on the North American Continent, ought to have
> taught them ere this time that America was not their home, as a race
> or as men and women, but their home only as "moveable chattels"
> and "saleable commodities.". . . Shall we always say, "O America,
> with thy many faults, we love thee still?" No! let us commit to the care
> of God the graves of our fathers, and of those who died by the cruel
> tortures of a slow fire, and go at once to our "promised land!" [Haiti]
> where we will yet be in hearing of the wails and groans of our enslaved
> brothers and sisters, and where we can at any time be summoned to
> help deal the last blow to slavery.
>
> We need have no hope in the present conflict, for the atmosphere of
> North America is interwoven and vocal with the blasting breath of
> negro prejudice. It is the first lesson taught by white parents to their
> children, that the negro is a low, debased animal, not fit for their as-
> sociation nor their equal. . . .
>
> > "Ho! children of the dusky brow!
> > Why will ye wear the chain?

[6] *Ibid.*

A fairer home is waiting you,
In isles beyond the main!"[7]

The opponents of emigration were as eloquent as its proponents. John Rock said in 1860 that

> there are many reasons and much philosophy in abandoning a country and people who have so diligently sought to crush us. But, then, it must be remembered that there is no other country that is particularly inviting to us, and on this account the masses of the colored people, who *think* for themselves, have believed that the same effort made in working our way up in this country, and in civilizing the whites, would accomplish our object as certain and as easy as we could by emigrating to a foreign country, and overcoming the disadvantages of language, climate, low wages, and other obstacles which would tend to embarrass us in a strange country. This being our country, we have made up our minds to remain in it, and to try to make it worth living in.[8]

Frederick Douglass believed that

> the place for the free colored people is the land where their brothers and sisters are held in slavery, and where circumstances might some day enable them to contribute an important part to their liberation . . . because we have seen that the habit of looking away from America for a home, induces neglect to improve such advantages as are afforded by our condition here.

Nevertheless, Douglass declared at the end of 1860 that

> while we have never favored any plan of emigration, and have never been willing to concede that this is a doomed country, and that we are a doomed race in it, we can raise no objection to the present movement toward Hayti. . . . If we go any where, let us go to Hayti. Let us go where we are still within hearing distance of the wails of our brothers and sisters in bonds. Let us not go to Africa, where those who hate and enslave us want us to go; but let us go to Hayti, where our oppressors do not want us to go, and where our influence and example can still be of service to those whose tears will find their way to us by the waters of the Gulf washing all our shores.[9]

But in June 1861, Douglass came out strongly against the Haitian emigration movement:

> Now, this simple overture of benevolence has hardened into a grand scheme of public policy, and claims the acceptance of the whole

[7] *Ibid.,* September 10, 1861.
[8] *Liberator,* February 3, 1860.
[9] *Douglass' Monthly,* III (January, 1861), 386–87.

colored people and their friends. It has become ethnological, philosophical, political and commercial. It has its doctrines of races, of
climates, of nationalities and destinies, and offers itself as the grand
solution of the destiny of the colored people in America. In this aspect
the Haytian Emigration movement challenges criticism, and leaves
room to question its wisdom. . . . It has propagated the favorite
doctrine of all those who despise and hate the colored man, that the
prejudice of the whites is invincible, and that the cause of human freedom and equality is hopeless for the black man in this country. . . .
This attitude of the Haytian Emigration movement compels me to say,
I am not an Emigrationist. . . .

We are Americans, speaking the same language, adopting the same
customs, holding the same general opinions, . . . and shall rise or fall
with Americans; upon the whole our history here has been one of
progress and improvement, and in all the likelihoods of the case, will
become more so; the lines of social and political distinction, marking
unjust and unnatural discriminations against us, are gradually being
effaced; and that upon the fall of slavery, as fall it must, these discriminations will disappear still more rapidly. I hold that all schemes of
wholesale emigration tend to awaken and keep alive and confirm the
popular prejudices of the whites against us. They serve to kindle hopes
of getting us out of the country. . . . I hold that there is no such
thing as a natural and unconquerable repugnance between the varieties
of men. All these artificial and arbitrary barriers give way before
interest and enlightenment. . . . The hope of the world is in Human
Brotherhood; in the union of mankind, not in exclusive nationalities.[10]

The emigration scheme gave rise to an intense and sometimes bitter
debate among American Negroes in 1861. This debate can be traced in
the following documents.

At the end of 1860 James McCune Smith wrote an open letter to
Henry Highland Garnet, the foremost Negro clergyman in New York
City, criticizing Garnet for his acceptance of a position in Redpath's
Emigration Bureau. Dr. Smith's portly figure concealed a passionate and
combative dedication to equal rights. After earning an M.D. degree at
the University of Glasgow in 1837, Smith had returned to practice medicine in New York City, where he became a leader in the city's Negro
community. In his public letter to Garnet he wrote:

More than a quarter of a century ago, you and others, among whom
I was the humblest, pledged yourselves to devote life and energies
to the elevation and affranchisement of the free colored people on this,
the soil which gave them birth, and through their affranchisement, the
emancipation of the slaves of the South. This may be called old-

[10] *Ibid.,* IV (July, 1861), 484.

fashioned doctrine; but it is none the less sound, and our pledges are none the less binding on that account. We are bound by these pledges until one of two things occurs. Either the elevation and affranchisement of our brethren free and enslaved must be accomplished; or the attempt must be proven useless because impossible of accomplishment. . . .

So far from being released, we are more solemnly bound by those pledges to-day than at any time since we made them: for we are hourly approaching that affranchisement for which we are bound to struggle. . . . Is it right, my dear Sir, or is it not rather a wanton shame, when the work goes so nobly on, while the goal is within our reach, is it not a shame that you should lend the weight of your name and the luster of your talents to divert us to other and distant fields of labor? . . . Is it right in you, my dear Sir, is it in accordance with the pledges of your youth to . . . [advise] us to leave the *white man's country*—which is our country before God? . . . Your duty to our people is to tell them to aim higher. In advising them to go to Hayti you direct them to sink lower. . . . We affirm by our lives and conduct that, if degraded, it is not by our innate inferiority, but by the active oppression of those who outnumber us. . . . Our people want to stay, and will stay, at home: we are in for the fight, and will fight it out here. Shake yourself free from these migrating phantasms, and join us with your might and main.[11]

Garnet was not convinced by Smith's argument. Born a slave in Maryland, Garnet was the son of an African chief who had been kidnapped and sold into American slavery. His father's entire family escaped to the North in 1822, where Henry was later educated at Oneida Institute in New York. He served as pastor of several churches in New York State and as a missionary at Jamaica before coming to New York as minister of the Shiloh Presbyterian Church. At the beginning of 1861 he replied to Smith's letter:

You anti-emigrationists seem to desire to see the hundreds of colored men and women who have good trades to stay here and be the drudges and menials of white men, who will not employ or work with them. Go to our hotels and private mansions of the rich, and on board of our steamboats, and you will find many skillful carpenters, masons, engineers, wheelwrights, and blacksmiths, millers, as well as female mechanics, who are wasting their talents for a mere pittance. You will see many of them borne down with discouragement, and they will tell you that the reason they do not work at their trades is, because they have been told over and over again when they have applied for work —"We don't employ niggers."[12]

[11] *Anglo-African*, January 5, 12, 1861.
[12] *Ibid.*, January 19, 1861.

A Negro woman from New York who agreed with Garnet wrote that "it is my firm conviction that we as a mass never can rise to any degree of eminence in this country. Our condition may be ameliorated, and individuals may by dint of severe struggling, manage to keep chin above water and that is about all."[13] The "Haytian Emigration Society" of Toledo adopted the following resolutions on January 14, 1861:

> Whereas, It is common for man, wherever placed on the habitable globe, when deprived of his God-given rights, to devise some means to better his condition, . . . Resolved, That we view in Hayti the chief corner-stone of an Ethiopic empire, and that we see in her the elements of a future that are nowhere to be found on or adjacent to the American continent.
>
> Resolved, That we appeal to the blacks and men of color to form this nucleus around the chief cornerstone in our political edifice of the Antilles, and ere long from that radiating point the sable arm of Africa will belt the tropical regions of the globe.[14]

But a Philadelphia Negro declared that "the idea of a great nationality in Hayti is all humbug; let us build up a nationality for ourselves here."[15] Opposition to colonization was very strong among Massachusetts Negroes, who enjoyed more rights than the colored men of any other state. A meeting of Boston Negroes passed the following resolution in November 1861:

> Whereas, Strenuous efforts are now being made by certain intelligent, but misguided colored men and white men to induce free colored persons, resident in the United States and in the Canadas, to emigrate to Hayti under the mistaken policy of bettering their condition; and whereas, in the present crisis of the history of our race we deem such efforts pernicious, calculated to weaken our strength, by lessening our number, and removing our laboring and able-bodied men; Therefore,
>
> Resolved, That we regard such men with suspicion, and deprecate both their counsel and advice; and we earnestly recommend that if they are sincere in their pretended love and admiration for Hayti, they immediately quit our shores and take up their abode in that country.
>
> Resolved, That under no circumstances will we be induced or persuaded to emigrate from this our native country, until the last fetter has been struck from the limbs of the last slave on this continent, believing that in the accomplishment of this great work, which in our judgment is near at hand, we are to have a word to say and a blow to strike.[16]

13 *Ibid.,* January 26, 1861.
14 *Ibid.,* February 16, 1861.
15 *Ibid.,* March 16, 1861.
16 *Ibid.,* November 16, 1861.

Negro Baptists, meeting in New Bedford, resolved that

> this Convention feel it to be their duty to protest against the operations
> and designs of those in charge of Haytian emigration, and that we look
> upon any body of men who seek our wholesale removal, as is con-
> templated by Mr. James Redpath and his coadjutors, as being charac-
> terized by the same spirit which breathed into existence the old
> American Colonization Society.
>
> Resolved, That we condemn the infamous doctrine . . . that the
> white and black races cannot live together upon this continent in a
> state of freedom and equality.
>
> Resolved, That we feel a deep sense of regret that colored men in
> whom we have confided as our leaders should allow themselves to be
> the tools of a widespread evil, which is discouraging and dividing us
> just at the daybreak of our universal emancipation.[17]

William Wells Brown replied to the arguments of Redpath's critics:

> All the objections to emigration appear to centre in the feeling that
> we ought not to quit the land of our birth, and leave the slave in his
> chains. This view of the case comes at the first glance with some force,
> but on a closer examination, it will be found to have but little weight.
> If it could be shown that our presence here was actually needed, and
> that we could exert an influence, no matter what position we occupied
> in the community, then I agree that duty would require us to remain.
>
> But let us look at facts. It must be confessed that we, the colored
> people of this country, are a race of cooks, waiters, barbers, whitewash-
> ers, bootblacks, and chimney sweeps. How much influence has such a
> class upon a community? . . .
>
> I hold that the descendants of Africa, in this country, will never be
> respected until they shall leave the cook shop and barber's chair and
> the white-wash brush. "They who would be free, themselves must
> strike the blow," means something more than appearing in a military
> attitude. To emigrate to Hayti, and to develop the resources of the
> Island, and to build up a powerful and influential government there,
> which shall demonstrate the genius and capabilities of the Negro, is
> as good an Anti-Slavery work as can be done in the Northern States
> of this Union.
>
> Our opponents do not meet the subject fairly and honestly. To at-
> tempt to connect the Haytian emigration movement with the old and
> hateful colonization scheme, is only to create a prejudice in the minds
> of the people. Originated by a colored nation, in the interests of the
> colored race, conducted and sustained exclusively by the friends or
> members of that nation and that race, it is essentially and diametrically

opposed to the colonization project, which was originated by slave-holders, in the interests of slavery, and conducted and sustained exclu-sively by the friends of bondage, and the haters of the Negro.[18]

And George Lawrence, the New York editor of the *Pine and Palm,* stated that

> if this war should result in the abolition of slavery, as we hope it may, while it strikes the shackles from the slave, it will not ameliorate the condition of the free black man, one iota. Let none such, therefore, taking counsel of his desires, hope for a satisfactory recognition of his claims as the result, even under the most favorable of circumstances, of this war. He may be used (for Uncle Sam's chestnuts are roasting in a pretty hot fire), may be accorded a *quasi* recognition; but so soon as the purposes of the Federal Government may have been served through his instrumentality, he will be rewarded with a mockery of thanks, and unceremoniously thrust aside. Judging the future from the past, can any one doubt it? . . . The scanty pittance of social tolera-tion which is here and there grudgingly doled out to us is only excep-tional, illustrating the more strikingly the rule which everywhere excludes us. And the only way in which we can reasonably expect to change this state of affairs is by assuming the separate position of an independent people, exacting social recognition, and able to enforce it. Why, then, refuse to look our condition fully in the face; why continue to hug a criminal delusion which only tends to deeper degradation?[19]

While the debate continued, Redpath went ahead with the work of recruiting emigrants and sending them to Haiti. Between December 1860 and October 1861, more than one thousand Negroes migrated from the United States to the island republic. But difficulties began to develop. Reports soon filtered back from Haiti of mismanagement, de-lays in the assignments of land grants, disease and death among unaccli-mated colonists, and hostility between the natives and the immigrants. A Pennsylvania Negro who had gone to Haiti in October 1861 returned home four months later and reported that

> Hayti is not the place for a colored American, unless he is a capitalist, and it is utter folly for a poor man to go there and expect to make money or even procure as decent a living there as can be easily ob-tained here. The majority of the emigrants [are] . . . not doing well, earning but little money, enjoying miserable health, generally dissatis-fied with the country, its prospects, its climate, soil, and the "old fogy" modes in which business of all kinds are carried on.[20]

[18] *Pine and Palm,* June 2, 1861.
[19] *Ibid.,* November 16, 1861.
[20] *Anglo-African,* March 15, 1862.

There were other reasons why the Haitian fever soon subsided among American Negroes. Despite the riots and discrimination to which colored men were subjected in 1862–63, the war was opening up new opportunities for Negroes, and many of them exchanged their previous pessimism for the hope of a brighter future in America. For example, William Parham, the Cincinnati schoolteacher, had planned in 1862 to emigrate to Haiti or Jamaica. But by 1863 he had changed his mind, because "the present aspect of things in this country . . . —the injustice and outrage to which we are still subject, notwithstanding—gives evidence of the coming of a better and a brighter day."[21]

Reports of mismanagement and failure continued to come back from Haiti, and applications for emigration began to decline. Finally in October 1862, Redpath suspended publication of the Pine and Palm and resigned as agent of the Haytian Bureau of Emigration. His ill-starred colonization project was an almost total failure. About two thousand emigrants went to Haiti in 1861 and 1862. Most of them either died or returned to the United States. An American commissioner who visited Haiti in 1864 could find only two hundred of the original colonists still living there. On May 5, 1863, a group of New York Negroes held a meeting at Zion Church to welcome back from Haiti several families who had emigrated with high hopes, but who had returned disillusioned and poverty-stricken. Emigration sentiment had been strong in New York in 1861, but now the meeting gave the final burial to Redpath's movement by resolving that "we view with contempt, as our fathers nobly did, the old Hag, the 'American Colonization Society,' its pet daughter, the 'African Civilization Society,' also its deformed child, the Haytian Emigration Movement, and their efforts to remove the colored man from the United States."[22]

But the demise of Redpath's Bureau did not mean the end of the colonization issue. In the first two years of the war the Lincoln administration, supported by a large segment of Northern public opinion, favored the gradual and voluntary colonization of Negroes as the best possible solution of the race problem. Aaron Powell, a lecturer for the American Anti-Slavery Society, reported in 1862 that "unfriendly expressions against the colored people were never more common in my

21 Parham to Jacob C. White, Jr., August 7, 1863, Jacob C. White Papers, Howard University Library. See also Parham to White, March 5, September 7, 1862, and March (?), 1863, White Papers.
22 Liberator, June 12, 1863. See also Willis D. Boyd, "James Redpath and American Negro Colonization in Haiti, 1860–1862," The Americas, XII (1955), 169–82.

hearing. Many Republicans unite with Democrats in cursing the 'niggers,' and in declaring that the slaves, if possibly emancipated by the war, must be removed from the country."[23]

In his message to Congress on December 3, 1861, Lincoln recommended that "steps be taken" to colonize the slaves who had come into Union lines plus any free Negroes who might wish to emigrate. He urged Congress to appropriate money for the acquisition of colonial territory for this purpose.[24] During the 1861–62 Congressional session several colonization bills were introduced, and Congress actually appropriated $600,000 to help finance the voluntary emigration of Negroes freed by the District of Columbia Emancipation Act and the Second Confiscation Act.[25]

Whatever their attitude toward the Haitian movement, most Negroes were angrily opposed to the various colonization proposals advanced in the early war years whose general purpose was to rid the country of the troublesome Negro. The *Anglo-African* labeled Lincoln's message to Congress "a speech to stir the hearts of all Confederates." Instead of colonizing colored men, suggested this Negro newspaper, "any surplus change Congress may have can be appropriated 'with our consent' to expatriate and settle elsewhere the surviving slaveholders."[26] John Rock asked:

> Why is it that the white people of this country desire to get rid of us? Does any one pretend to deny that this is our country? or that much of the wealth and prosperity found here is the result of the labor of our hands? or that our blood and bones have not crimsoned and whitened every battle-field from Maine to Louisiana? Why this desire to get rid of us? Can it be possible that because the nation has robbed us for nearly two and a half centuries, and finding that she can do it no longer and preserve her character among nations, now, out of hatred, wishes to banish, because she cannot continue to rob us? . . .
>
> This nation has wronged us, and for this reason many hate us. (Hear, hear.) The Spanish proverb is, *"Desde que te erre nunca bien te quise"*—Since I have wronged you, I have never liked you. This is true not only of Spaniards and Americans, but of every other class of people. When a man wrongs another, he not only hates him, but tries to make others dislike him. . . .
>
> The black man is a good fellow while he is a slave, and toils for nothing, but the moment he claims his own flesh and blood and bones, he is a most obnoxious creature, and there is a proposition to get rid

23 *National Anti-Slavery Standard,* June 28, 1862.
24 Roy P. Basler, ed., *The Collected Works of Abraham Lincoln* (9 vols., New Brunswick, 1955), V, 48.
25 *U.S. Statutes at Large,* XII, 376–78, 582.
26 *Anglo-African,* December 7, 1861.

of him! He is happy while he remains a poor, degraded, ignorant slave, without even the right to his own offspring. While in this condition, the master can ride in the same carriage, sleep in the same bed, and nurse from the same bosom. But give this same slave the right to use his own legs, his hands, his body and his mind, and this happy and desirable creature is instantly transformed into a miserable and loathsome wretch, fit only to be colonized. . . .

It is true, a great many simple-minded people have been induced to go to Liberia and to Hayti, but, be assured, the more intelligent portion of the colored people will remain here; not because we prefer being oppressed here to being freemen in other countries, but we will remain because we believe our future prospects are better here than elsewhere, and because our experience has proved that the greater proportion of those who have left this country during the last thirty years have made their condition worse, and would have gladly returned if they could have done so. You may rest assured that we shall remain here—here, where we have withstood almost everything. Now, when our prospects begin to brighten, we are the more encouraged to stay, pay off the old score, and have a reconstruction of things.[27]

And at a meeting on April 28, 1862, Boston's Negro leaders made their position perfectly clear in four sharply worded resolutions:

Resolved, That when we wish to leave the United States we can find and pay for that territory which shall suit us best.

Resolved, That when we are ready to leave, we shall be able to pay our own expenses of travel.

Resolved, That we don't want to go now.

Resolved, That if anybody else wants us to go, they must compel us.[28]

On August 14, 1862, President Lincoln met with five colored men from the District of Columbia. This "interview" turned out to be a speech by Lincoln, a curious mixture of condescension and kindness. The President told his listeners that the broad racial differences between Negro and Caucasian made it impossible for them to live together as equals. "Whether it is right or wrong I need not discuss, but this physical difference is a great disadvantage to us both, as I think your race suffer very greatly, many of them by living among us, while ours suffer from your presence." Complete separation of the races was the only solution.

[27] Speech by Rock to the annual convention of the Massachusetts Anti-Slavery Society in Boston, January 23, 1862, printed in the *Liberator,* February 14, 1862.

[28] *Ibid.,* May 2, 1862.

> There is an unwillingness on the part of our people, harsh as it may be, for you free colored people to remain with us. . . . I do not propose to discuss this, but to propose it as a fact with which we have to deal. I cannot alter it if I would. . . . It is better for us both, therefore, to be separated.

Lincoln urged the Negroes to recruit twenty-five, fifty, or a hundred colored families for colonization in Central America, where they could find work in the new coal mines being developed there. He promised them government assistance. The delegation withdrew, telling Lincoln that they would have to think the matter over before replying.[29]

Accounts of this interview were widely publicized in the Northern press. The reaction by articulate Negroes was swift and angry. Frederick Douglass spared no adjectives in his denunciation of Lincoln's speech:

> The President of the United States seems to possess an ever increasing passion for making himself appear silly and ridiculous, if nothing worse. . . . In this address Mr. Lincoln assumes the language and arguments of an itinerant Colonization lecturer, showing all his inconsistencies, his pride of race and blood, his contempt for negroes and his canting hypocrisy. . . . Mr. Lincoln takes care in urging his colonization scheme to furnish a weapon to all the ignorant and base, who need only the countenance of men in authority to commit all kinds of violence and outrage upon the colored people. . . . The tone of frankness and benevolence which he assumes in his speech to the colored committee is too thin a mask not to be seen through. The genuine spark of humanity is missing in it, no sincere wish to improve the condition of the oppressed has dictated it. It expresses merely the desire to get rid of them, and reminds one of the politeness with which a man might try to bow out of his house some troublesome creditor or the witness of some old guilt.[30]

A. P. Smith of Saddle River, New Jersey, published the following reply to Lincoln's proposal:

> Let me tell you, sir, President though you are, there is but one race of men on the face of the earth:—One lord, one faith, one baptism, one God and Father of all, who is above all, and through all, and in all. Physical differences no doubt there are; no two persons on earth are exactly alike in this respect; but what of that? In physical conformation, you, Mr. President, may differ somewhat from the negro, and also from the majority of white men; you may even, as you indicate,

[29] Basler, *Collected Works of Lincoln,* V, 370–75.
[30] *Douglass' Monthly,* V (September, 1862), 707–8.

feel this difference on your part to be very disadvantageous to you; but does it follow that therefore you should be removed to a foreign country? . . .

But were all you say on this point true, must I crush out my cherished hopes and aspirations, abandon my home, and become a pander to the mean and selfish spirit that oppresses me? Pray tell us, is our right to a home in this country less than your own, Mr. Lincoln? . . . Are you an American? So are we. Are you a patriot? So are we. Would you spurn all absurd, meddlesome, impudent propositions for your colonization in a foreign country? So do we. . . .

But say, good Mr. President, why we, why anybody should swelter, digging coal, if there be any in Central America? . . . But, say you: "Coal land is the best thing I know of to begin an enterprise." Astounding discovery! Worthy to be recorded in golden letters, like the Lunar Cycle in the temple of Minerva. "Coal land, sir!" Pardon, Mr. President, if my African risibilities get the better of me, if I do show my ivories whenever I read that sentence! Coal land, sir! If you please, sir, give McClellan some, give Halleck some, and by all means, save a little strip for yourself.

Twenty-five negroes digging coal in Central America! Mighty plan! Equal to about twenty-five negroes splitting rails in Sangamon! . . . Good sir, if you have any nearer friends than we are, let them have that coal-digging job.[31]

Isaiah Wears, a prominent Philadelphia Negro, expressed the opinion of most colored men in his city:

To be asked, after so many years of oppression and wrong have been inflicted in a land and by a people who have been so largely enriched by the black man's toil, to pull up stakes in a civilized and Christian nation, and to go to an uncivilized and barbarous nation, simply to gratify an unnatural wicked prejudice emanating from slavery, is unreasonable and anti-Christian in the extreme. . . . If black men are here in the way of white men, they did not come here of their own accord. Their presence is traceable to the white man's lust for power, love of oppression and disregard of the plain teachings of the Lord Jesus Christ. . . . It is not the negro race that is the cause of the war; it is the unwillingness on the part of the American people to do the race simple justice. . . . The effect of this scheme of colonization, we fear, will be to arouse prejudice and to increase enmity against us, without bringing with it the remedy proposed or designed.[32]

[31] National Anti-Slavery Standard, September 6, 1862.
[32] Christian Recorder, August 23, 1862. Philadelphia Negroes addressed a long Appeal to the President urging him to abandon his colonization ideas. See An Appeal from the Colored Men of Philadelphia to the President of the United States (Philadelphia, 1862).

A mass meeting of colored men at Newtown, Long Island, on August 20 issued an eloquent rejection of Lincoln's colonization proposal:

> We rejoice that we are colored Americans, but deny that we are a "different race of people," as God has made of one blood all nations that dwell on the face of the earth, and has hence no respect of men in regard to color. . . .
>
> This is our country by birth. . . . This is our native country; we have as strong attachment naturally to our native hills, valleys, plains, luxuriant forests, flowing streams, mighty rivers, and lofty mountains, as any other people. . . . This is the country of our choice, being our fathers' country. We love this land, and have contributed our share to its prosperity and wealth. . . .
>
> We have the right to have applied to ourselves those rights named in the Declaration of Independence. . . . When our country is struggling for life, and one million freemen are believed to be scarcely sufficient to meet the foe, we are called upon by the President of the United States to leave this land. . . . But at this crisis, we feel disposed to refuse the offers of the President since the call of our suffering country is too loud and imperative to be unheeded. . . .
>
> In conclusion, we would say that, in our belief, the speech of the President has only served the cause of our enemies, who wish to insult and mob us, as we have, since its publication, been repeatedly insulted, and told that we must leave the country. Hence we conclude that the policy of the President toward the colored people of this country *is a mistaken policy*.[33]

From all over the North came similar protests. But in spite of this cool reception of his colonization suggestion, Lincoln went ahead with plans to send a company of volunteer colonists to Central America. Four years earlier Ambrose W. Thompson, a free-lance American capitalist, had secured control by questionable means of a land grant of two million acres in the northern part of present-day Panama. Thompson incorporated the "Chiriqui Improvement Company" to develop the coal mines and other resources on his land. In 1861 he offered to sell to the American government coal for its navy at half the prevailing price if the government would supply him with Negro colonists to work the mines. Lincoln expressed interest in the offer, and in the summer of 1862 the President appointed Senator S. C. Pomeroy "United States Colonization Agent" to recruit colonists and arrange transportation. Pomeroy issued a pamphlet addressed to "The Free Colored People of the United States," praising the wonderful climate and opportunities for them in Chiriqui.[34]

---

[33] *National Anti-Slavery Standard,* September 13, 1862.
[34] Paul J. Scheips, "Lincoln and the Chiriqui Colonization Project," *Journal of Negro History,* XXXVII (1950), 419–30.

Robert Purvis, the wealthy Negro abolitionist of Philadelphia, was not impressed by the pamphlet. He assured Pomeroy in a public letter that few Negroes wished to be colonized:

> Sir, for more than twenty years the question of colonization agitated and divided this country. The "colored" people stamped it with the seal of their reprobation; the whites acquiesced in the justice of their decision, and the vexed and vexing question was put to rest. Now it is revived; the apple of discord is again thrown into the community, and as though you had not already enough to divide and distract you, a new scheme is hit upon, and deliberately sent upon its errand of mischief. . . .
>
> But it is said this is a question of prejudice—of national antipathy and not to be reasoned about. The President has said, "Whether it is right or wrong, I need not now discuss it." Great God! is justice nothing? Is honor nothing? Is even pecuniary interest to be sacrificed to this insane and vulgar hate? . . .

FREDERICK DOUGLASS

Men of Color, to Arms!

Despite much resistance from Northern whites, black spokesmen constantly advanced the idea that blacks should be allowed to serve in the Union Army. Douglass and others fought hard to make this a reality; they saw the war as an opportunity for black men to win glory and, as Douglass put it, perhaps thinking of slavery days, "wipe out the dark reproaches" against their name. In mentioning in the following speech Denmark Vesey, Nat Turner, and the blacks involved in John Brown's raid at Harpers Ferry, Douglass hoped to remind his followers that black people had many times before asserted their courage to war against oppression.

WHEN FIRST THE REBEL CANNON SHATTERED THE WALLS OF SUMTER and drove away its starving garrison, I predicted that the war then and

MEN OF COLOR, TO ARMS! A speech delivered by Frederick Douglass in Rochester, New York, March 2, 1863. From *Life and Times of Frederick Douglass* by Frederick Douglass (Boston: De Wolfe & Co., 1895).

there inaugurated would not be fought out entirely by white men. Every month's experience during these dreary years has confirmed that opinion. A war undertaken and brazenly carried on for the perpetual enslavement of colored men, calls logically and loudly for colored men to help suppress it. Only a moderate share of sagacity was needed to see that the arm of the slave was the best defense against the arm of the slaveholder. Hence, with every reverse to the national arms, with every exulting shout of victory raised by the slaveholding rebels, I have implored the imperiled nation to unchain against her foes her powerful black hand. Slowly and reluctantly that appeal is beginning to be heeded. Stop not now to complain that it was not heeded sooner. That it should not may or may not have been best. This is not the time to discuss that question. Leave it to the future. When the war is over, the country saved, peace established and the black man's rights are secured, as they will be, history with an impartial hand will dispose of that and sundry other questions. Action! action! not criticism, is the plain duty of this hour. Words are now useful only as they stimulate to blows. The office of speech now is only to point out when, where, and how to strike to the best advantage. There is no time to delay. The tide is at its flood that leads on to fortune. From East to West, from North to South, the sky is written all over, 'Now or never.' Liberty won by white men would lose half its luster. 'Who would be free themselves must strike the blow.' 'Better even die free, than to live slaves.' This is the sentiment of every brave colored man amongst us. There are weak and cowardly men in all nations. We have them amongst us. They tell you this is the 'white man's war'; that you 'will be no better off after than before the war'; that the getting of you into the army is to 'sacrifice you on the first opportunity.' Believe them not; cowards themselves, they do not wish to have their cowardice shamed by your brave example. Leave them to their timidity, or to whatever motive may hold them back. I have not thought lightly of the words I am now addressing you. The counsel I give comes of close observation of the great struggle now in progress, and of the deep conviction that this is your hour and mine. In good earnest, then, and after the best deliberation, I now, for the first time during this war, feel at liberty to call and counsel you to arms. By every consideration which binds you to your enslaved fellow-countrymen and to the peace and welfare of your country; by every aspiration which you cherish for the freedom and equality of yourselves and your children; by all the ties of blood and identity which make us one with the brave black men now fighting our battles in Louisiana and in South Carolina, I urge you to fly to arms, and smite with death the power that would bury the Government and your liberty in the same hopeless grave. I wish I could tell you that the State of New York calls you to this high honor. For the moment her constituted authorities are silent on the subject. They will speak by and by, and doubtless on the right side; but we are not compelled to wait for her. We can get at the throat of treason and slavery through the State of Massachusetts. She was first in the War of Independence; first to break the chains of her slaves; first to make the black man equal before the law; first to admit colored children to her common schools, and she was first to answer with her blood the alarm-cry of the nation, when its capital was menaced by rebels. You know her patriotic governor, and you know Charles Sumner. I need not add more.

Massachusetts now welcomes you to arms as soldiers. She has but a small colored population from which to recruit. She has full leave of the general government to send one regiment to the war, and she has undertaken to do it. Go quickly and help fill up the first colored regiment from the North. I am authorized to assure you that you will receive the same wages, the same rations, the same equipments, the same protection, the same treatment, and the same bounty, secured to white soldiers. You will be led by able and skillful officers, men who will take especial pride in your efficiency and success. They will be quick to accord to you all the honor you shall merit by your valor, and to see that your rights and feelings are respected by other soldiers. I have assured myself on these points, and can speak with authority. More than twenty years of unswerving devotion to our common cause may give me some humble claim to be trusted at this momentous crisis. I will not argue. To do so implies hesitation and doubt, and you do not hesitate. You do not doubt. The day dawns; the morning star is bright upon the horizon! The iron gate of our prison stands half open. One gallant rush from the North will fling it wide open, while four millions of our brothers and sisters shall march out into liberty. The chance is now given you to end in a day the bondage of centuries, and to rise in one bound from social degradation to the place of common equality with all other varieties of men. Remember Denmark Vessey [sic] of Charleston; remember Nathaniel Turner of South Hampton; remember Shields Green and Copeland, who followed noble John Brown, and fell as glorious martyrs for the cause of the slave. Remember that in a contest with oppression, the Almighty has no attribute which can take sides with oppressors. The case is before you. This is our golden opportunity. Let us accept it, and forever wipe out the dark reproaches unsparingly hurled against us by our enemies. Let us win for ourselves the gratitude of our country, and the best blessings of our posterity through all time. The nucleus of this first regiment is now in

camp at Readville, a short distance from Boston. I will undertake to forward to Boston all persons adjudged fit to be mustered into the regiment,
who shall apply to me at any time within the next two weeks.

DUDLEY CORNISH

Second-Class Soldiers

Douglass had been "authorized to assure" his listeners in 1863 that all black
soldiers serving in the Union Army would receive "the same wages, the same
rations, the same equipments, the same protection, the same treatment, and
the same bounty, secured to white soldiers." They received none of these
things. Furthermore, they were given the most inglorious work details available,
usually far from the scene of fighting. As the table drawn up in 1864 by the Chicago *Tribune* (and here presented by historian Dudley Cornish) shows, all
blacks, regardless of rank, were paid the same small sum. The official position
black soldiers would have in the United States Army was established in the
Civil War. It remained a second-class one as late as 1948, when President
Truman issued an executive order finally banning segregation in the armed
forces.

THROUGHOUT THE CIVIL WAR, AMERICAN NEGROES SERVING IN THE
Union Army labored under a double disadvantage: the South refused to
recognize them as soldiers and the North refused to grant them financial
status equal to that enjoyed by white troops. Slowly and with marked
reluctance the Union came to recognize this inequity in pay and allow-
ances. It took two years of sustained effort by prominent officers of
Negro troops, with help from governors, newspaper editors, and senators,
to achieve partial victory in the Army Appropriation Bill of 1864. Com-

SECOND-CLASS SOLDIERS   Reprinted from *THE SABLE ARM: Negro Troops in
the Union Army, 1861–1865,* by Dudley Taylor Cornish. By permission of W. W.
Norton & Company, Inc. Copyright © 1956 by Dudley Taylor Cornish. Copyright
© by W. W. Norton & Company, Inc. The author's footnotes have been omitted.

plete success did not crown their efforts until after the war had been won.

Negro soldiers and their spokesmen argued for equality in financial treatment on two basic assumptions. The first of these was that, since they served with white soldiers, ate the same food, wore the same uniform, worked, fought, and died just as the whites did, they were entitled to the same pay. And since the Negro soldier did his soldier's job at substantially greater personal risk than that of his white contemporaries in the Union Army, it seemed only minimum justice to him to be paid what the rest of the Union Army drew. The second basic assumption was that Secretary of War Stanton had promised Negro soldiers standard army pay in his original authorization to General Rufus Saxton, the first definite War Department authorization for the enrollment of Negroes as soldiers.

This second assumption, which had less weight than the first, was based on the third paragraph of Stanton's orders of August 25, 1862, in which he directed Saxton to raise five thousand "volunteers of African descent." These volunteers and their officers, the orders read, were "to be entitled to and receive the same pay and rations as are allowed by law to volunteers in the service." Volunteers in the service at the time were entitled to $13 per month, $3 of which constituted a clothing allowance, and one ration per day. Unfortunately, Secretary Stanton had shaky legal authority for this "promise" to General Saxton. The only law applicable to the Negro regiments that Saxton was empowered to raise was the Militia Act of July 17, 1862, Section 15 of which provided that colored recruits would be paid "ten dollars per month and one ration, three dollars of which monthly pay may be in clothing." It was on the basis of this legislation that Negro troops were paid for the next two years.

The radicals in Congress had managed to fight through a law authorizing the president to employ Negro soldiers at his discretion, but at the same time they had made it clear that such Negroes were to be second-class soldiers when payday came. Secretary Stanton may have been motivated by the most generous of intentions, but his hands and the hands of the paymaster general were tied by Congress. The secretary of war may have pledged the faith of the federal government in the orders of August 25, as Colonel Thomas Wentworth Higginson charged, but to his question, "is not Congress bound, in all decency, either to fulfill [that pledge] or to disband the regiments?" Congress continued to answer with a stubborn "No!"

It was on the other basic assumption (that Negro soldiers performed duty similar to that of white troops and at greater risk and thus were entitled to the pay of white troops) that some success was finally achieved. When Negro troops had been first proposed and recruited, it was pretty widely understood that they would be used as labor battalions, as service and garrison troops, that they would not be used in the full capacity of soldiers but only as auxiliary forces. White soldiers would continue to bear the brunt of battle; more white troops than before could appear on the fighting fronts, released from rear area and garrison duty in the forts by their Negro auxiliaries. These fighting troops, it was fairly thought, should naturally draw higher pay than garrison and service troops.

There were logical reasons for this point of view. Doubt was widespread that Negroes would be reliable in battle or that they could learn the duties of field soldiers in sufficient time to bear a part in the actual fighting before the South was brought to terms. Because of their being accustomed to the heat and fevers of the South, it was argued that the logical role for Negro troops would be in relieving white soldiers from the work of building fortifications and manning artillery in captured Confederate forts. It was further argued that, in order to prevent a degeneration of the war into savage barbarity, Negro soldiers should be kept within the definite limits of fortifications and out of close contact with their former masters.

Underlying most of this thinking was an awareness of the sensitivity of Northern white soldiers to the charge that they had been unable to bring the South to her knees without calling on the Negro for help on the field of battle. Anti-Negro sentiment in and out of the army added to the strength of that reasoning. The prejudices against Negro soldiers clearly evident among the white troops in the Department of the South during the summer of 1862 could not be overlooked or lightly considered. Equal pay to Negro soldiers would in effect place former slaves on the same level with freeborn Northern whites, and this idea could hardly be tolerated by large segments of the Northern population, particularly in the lower economic strata where competition with cheap Negro labor was both feared and hated. As an example, the *National Intelligencer* of October 17, 1862, reported that the packinghouse workers of Chicago had pledged "not to work for any packer, under any consideration, who will, in any manner, bring negro labor into competition with our labor." To these Chicago workingmen, the obvious purpose of employing Negroes in the packing houses was to reduce white wages "to the lowest possible standard."

After Negro soldiers had proved in combat that they were willing and able to carry the soldier's full burden and that they could make efficient and courageous combat troops, this thinking had to be revised. The raising of regiments of free Northern Negroes, such as the 54th and 55th Massachusetts, also argued for a re-evaluation of thinking that had been based exclusively on plans to arm fugitives from Southern slavery. As Colonel Robert Shaw was quick to inform Governor Andrew, the officers and men of the 54th keenly felt the discrimination in pay. Andrew as quickly wrote Shaw to tell the regiment that there had been a mistake and that "the Secretary of War will cause right to be done as soon as the case is presented to him and shall be fully understood." Shaw and the 54th, however, had moved to the assault of Fort Wagner before the governor's letter reached the Department of the South.

Certain legal doors had already been closed on the case before Governor Andrew had the opportunity to present it to the secretary of war. When the Bureau for Colored Troops was established in May, 1863, Stanton, with his usual thoroughness, had asked the solicitor of the War Department, William Whiting of Boston, for an opinion as to what pay those troops should receive. Whiting, a patent lawyer and moderate Republican, after studying the Militia Act of 1862, concluded that the Negro should be paid as a laborer and not as a soldier. The War Department published this decision as part of General Orders, No. 163, June 4, 1863. The final paragraph announced that "Persons of African descent who enlist . . . are entitled to 'ten dollars per month and one ration; three dollars of which monthly pay may be in clothing.' " Stanton suggested to Governor Tod of Ohio late in June that "For any additional pay or bounty colored troops must trust to State contributions and the justice of Congress at the next session."

Governor Andrew, not satisfied with correspondence, went to Washington in September for talks with Lincoln and various cabinet officers, and while he did secure assurances of fair treatment, he found the national capital so upset by the news of the Chickamauga disaster that action on the Negro soldier pay problem was impossible to secure. As a stopgap measure, Andrew then asked for and got action from the Massachusetts legislature: state money was appropriated to make up the difference in pay for the men of the 54th and 55th. But the men of those regiments were adamant and refused to accept this compromise solution to their problem. A spokesman for the 54th condemned the offer "to pay this regiment the difference between what the United States Government offers us and what they are legally bound to pay us" as tantamount to advertising "us to the world as holding out for *money* and not from *principle*,—that we sink our manhood in consideration of a few more dollars." And, acting on principle, the Massachusetts regiments refused to accept *any* pay until it should be made equal by national legislation to that received by the white troops with whom they fought and died. As a result, they served for some eighteen months without pay other than the $50 bounty given each recruit by the state of Massachusetts upon enlistment.

While Negro soldiers suffered humiliation because of the pay situation, at least they had food, clothing, and occasional shelter. Their families did not always fare so well. In the majority of Northern states, local or state aid was granted the dependents of soldiers in the armies, but state aid was not immediately extended to the families of Negro soldiers. Characteristically, Massachusetts seems to have led the way. Mary Livermore, nurse and worker with the Sanitary Commission, recorded several instances of state assistance to Chicago families of soldiers of the 54th. Governor Andrew, when he learned of the desperate need of some of these families, gave Miss Livermore *"carte blanche* for the relief of the families living in Chicago whose husbands and fathers were enlisted in the 54th." Not until July, 1864, however, did the federal government make any provision for the wives and families of Negro soldiers who had been killed in action or had died of wounds or disease while in federal service. Then, finally, widows and orphans of Negro soldiers were declared entitled to pensions—"provided such widows and orphans were free."

Negro soldiers served under a further financial disadvantage: they were not, until the middle of 1864, entitled to receive the federal bounty of $100 granted to white volunteers from the third month of the war. Curiously enough, Negro recruits were forbidden this small fortune even before their reception into the Union Army had been authorized by the War Department. On August 19, 1862, Assistant Adjutant General Thomas Vincent notified Lieutenant Charles S. Bowman, disbursing officer at Fort Leavenworth, Kansas, that "Recruits for negro regiments will under no circumstances be paid bounty and premiums." General Benjamin F. Butler managed to secure War Department authority for a $10 bounty for Negro recruits in Virginia at the end of November, 1863, but this was limited to Butler's command.

Congress and the War Department seem to have been more interested in conciliating the sensitivities of Border state owners of slaves recruited into the Union Army than in meeting the just demands of Negro soldiers already in the service or of the families of Negroes who had already given their lives in that service. Recruiting instructions issued by presidential order in October, 1863, appointed boards to examine claims of loyal slaveowners whose property had become soldiers of the Union.

Where claims were found valid, such owners were entitled to receive compensation "not to exceed the sum of three hundred dollars, upon filing . . . a valid deed of manumission and release, and making satisfactory proof of title, and any slave so enlisted shall be free." These instructions carried into effect to some degree the president's earlier plan of compensated emancipation.

In his annual report for 1863, Secretary of War Stanton urged Congress to correct the inequity of Negro soldiers' pay. "The colored troops," he pointed out, "have been allowed no bounty, and, under the construction given the department [by Solicitor Whiting], they can only, under existing law, receive the pay of ten dollars per month, white soldiers being paid thirteen dollars per month, with clothing and a daily ration." Stanton spoke directly to the point: "There seems to be inequality and injustice in this distinction, and an amendment authorizing the same pay and bounty as white troops receive, is recommended." Nor did he base his recommendation on mean, legalistic grounds. "Soldiers of the Union," he declared, "fighting under its banner, and exposing their lives in battle to uphold the Government, colored troops are entitled to enjoy its justice and beneficence."

Stanton had carried the case to the highest tribunal. The whole problem lay in the lap of Congress, as Stanton had suggested to the governor of Ohio in June. Both Stanton and Lincoln had implied as much to Frederick Douglass during their interviews with him in midsummer of 1863. Lincoln had suggested that, since Negroes "had larger motives for being soldiers than white men . . . they ought to be willing to enter the service upon any condition," and he had explained that their unequal pay "seemed a necessary concession to smooth the way to their employment at all as soldiers." Ultimately, the president had reassured Douglass, "they would receive the same."

No one could say with any assurance how the Congress would act or when. As the tribunes of the people turned to the task of "equalizing the pay of soldiers," they demonstrated a tendency to be parsimonious and niggardly. The first bill they considered would have granted full soldiers' pay to Negroes only from the beginning of 1864! John Andrew and Thomas W. Higginson and other champions of the Negro soldier went into indignant action to try to get something a little more like the justice and beneficence Stanton had recommended.

Colonel Higginson, in his usual incisive language, set forth the case for United States colored troops in a letter to the New York *Tribune* in January, 1864: "The public seems to suppose that all required justice will be done by the passage of a bill equalizing the pay of all soldiers for the future." This was, for his regiment and others of early origin, "but half the question." He reminded the public that his men had then "been nearly sixteen months in the service, and for them," he insisted, "the immediate issue is the question of arrears." Referring to the initial War Department orders to Saxton, he argued that every man in his regiment understood the matter thoroughly, even if the public did not: every man had "volunteered under an explicit *written assurance* from the War Department that he should have the pay of a white soldier." Further, Higginson insisted, "He knows that for five months the regiment received that pay, after which it was cut down from the promised thirteen dollars per month to ten dollars, for some reason to him inscrutable."

The colonel maintained that there was "nothing mean or mercenary" about most of his men and that, if they could be convinced that the government actually needed the money, they "would serve it barefooted and on half-rations, and without a dollar—for a time." Unfortunately, however, his troops saw white soldiers all around them receiving hundreds of dollars in bounties for re-enlisting "from this impoverished Government, which can only pay seven dollars out of thirteen to its black regiments." Here he referred to the paternalistic practice of withholding the $3 uniform or clothing allowance instead of paying it in cash as was the custom with white soldiers. Federal delay, Higginson concluded, "has already inflicted untold suffering, has impaired discipline, has relaxed loyalty, and has begun to implant a feeling of sullen distrust in the very regiments whose early career solved the problem of the nation, created a new army, and made peaceful emancipation possible."

James Montgomery, colonel of the 2nd South Carolina, urged similar arguments on Senator Henry Wilson of Massachusetts, chairman of the Committee on Military Affairs. "I can certify, most conscientiously," Montgomery wrote,

> that the troops under my command have been second to none in efficiency; while their loyalty and fidelity might put to the blush some who boast of white skins. Could Honorable Senators have seen, as I have seen them; toiling in the trenches before "Wagner," mounting guns, digging, carrying shot and shells for weeks and weeks together; and this under a storm of shot and bursting shells, I know they could not, and would not, withhold so simple an act of justice.

The Chicago *Tribune* early took an interest in the campaign for equal pay for colored troops, and on January 28, 1864, it argued editorially that no additional legislation was necessary to achieve that end. "The fact is," the Chicago paper maintained, "the chief disability of the black race, lies in prejudice and not in law." The blame lay with Stanton. "The War Department at the very outset," the *Tribune* urged,

> could have found no legal bar to obstruct any order it chose to make, recognizing no distinction in its troops of whatever color. All that was required was to take down the barriers of false pride, and caste, and the black soldier and white would stand shoulder to shoulder on the common ground of devotion to country.

Unfortunately, the War Department had, through its solicitor, Mr. Whiting, made the fatal distinction in compliance with the Militia Act of 1862. While Stanton might have corrected the inequity by reversing or disregarding the decision of his solicitor, he had chosen rather to let Congress solve the problem. President Lincoln seemed satisfied to go along with the Stanton choice despite the steady pressure of John Andrew in the spring of 1864. Even Attorney General Edward Bates supported Andrew's position and that of the Chicago *Tribune*. Bates's opinion of April 23 discovered a way around the limitations of the Militia Act as interpreted by Whiting, and the attorney general went so far as to inform the president that his "constitutional obligation to take care that the laws be faithfully executed" made it his duty "to direct the Secretary of War to inform the officers of the Pay Department of the Army" to end the inequality in soldiers' pay. Notwithstanding this strong encouragement to action, Lincoln continued to do nothing in the matter.

The Chicago *Tribune* continued to do what it could, and on May 1 it published an editorial clearly showing what the double standard in pay meant. The Negro soldier "deserves equal pay with the best," the *Tribune* insisted, "and has been promised it. What he receives is this:

	WHITE	COLORED
Sergeant Major	$21	$7
Quartermaster Sergeant	21	7
First Sergeant	20	7
Sergeant	17	7
Hospital Steward	30	7
Corporal	13	7
Private	13	7
Chaplain	100	7

The white soldier is permitted to purchase his clothing himself," the editorial explained, "but from the ten dollars of the colored, three are reserved for this purpose." The *Tribune* gave the editorial the title "Read and Blush." There is, however, little indication that many members of Congress read the item and no evidence to show that they blushed.

The bill finally passed in June granted equal pay to Negro soldiers— retroactive to January 1, 1864. Stubbornly refusing to solve the problem of arrears in pay, Congress provided that "all persons of color who were free on the 19th day of April, 1861, and who have been enlisted and mustered into the military service of the United States, shall from the time of their enlistments be entitled to receive the pay, bounty, and clothing allowed to such persons by the laws existing at the time of their enlistment"—providing the attorney general approved!

This was no solution at all. It simply called on Edward Bates to repeat his decision of two months earlier. This the attorney general did on July 14, and on the next day Stanton issued the necessary order to his paymaster general. On August 18, 1864, the adjutant general's office issued Circular 60, directing commanders of Negro regiments to find out which of their men had been free on April 19, 1861, "the fact of freedom to be determined in each case on the statement of the soldier, under oath, taken in connection with the most reliable information that can be obtained from other sources."

This ruling and directive failed to solve the problem of back pay for all the men of a single colored regiment. Even the Massachusetts regiments had in their ranks men who had not been free in any strict legal sense in the first week of the war. Colonel Edward N. Hallowell, commanding the 54th, devised a way out of the dilemma. Since the circular had failed to provide any particular form of oath, he administered this one to his men: "You do solemnly swear that you owed no man unrequited labor on or before the 19th day of April, 1861. So help you God." This was called the "Quaker Oath" and even those men of the 54th who were fugitive slaves took it as freemen "by God's higher law, if not by their country's." The muster rolls of the companies of the 54th and 55th Massachusetts with the magic word "Free" written after the name of every man who had taken the Hallowell oath went up to Washington for approval, and in October of 1864 the men were mustered for pay, the full pay of soldiers in the service of the United States, retroactive to the time of their enlistment.

Of course this was no solution for other Negro regiments, whose back pay was still withheld from them by the inadequacy of the law. Thomas W. Higginson's indignation knew no bounds. His soldiers, few if any of whom had been free on April 19, 1861, were thus by the peculiar character of the legislation deprived of the arrears in pay which he had all along claimed for them and which were justly due them. He again addressed himself to the editor of the New York *Tribune:* "No one can possibly be so weary of reading of the wrongs done by the Government toward the colored soldiers as I am of writing about them. This is my only excuse for intruding on your columns again." His apologetic tone quickly disappeared as he developed his argument. He pointed out that the men of his regiment were "volunteers, every one," and he argued that "they did not get their freedom by enlisting" under the terms of the Emancipation Proclamation; "they had it already. They enlisted to serve the Government, trusting its honor." That trust had been betrayed. "Now the nation," Higginson charged,

> turns upon them and says: Your part of the contract is fulfilled; we have had your services. If you can show that you had previously been free for a certain length of time, we will fulfill the other side of the contract. If not, we repudiate it. Help yourselves if you can.

Colonel Higginson admitted that the law might at least do justice to most of the men of the Massachusetts regiments and "take their wives and children out of the almshouses," but toward his own regiment, "which had been in service and under fire months before a Northern colored soldier was recruited, the policy of repudiation," he maintained, "has at last been officially adopted." What could his men now do in the face of this official repudiation? "There is no alternative for the officers of the South Carolina regiments," he wrote, "but to wait for another session of Congress." Meanwhile, they would have to continue "to act as executioners for those soldiers who, like Sergeant Walker, refuse to fulfill their share of a contract where the Government has openly repudiated the other share." Walker had been shot for having the men of his company stack arms and refuse to continue to serve as soldiers until they had received the pay they understood had been promised them; he was found guilty of inciting to mutiny. Wearily, Higginson concluded that "If a year's discussion . . . has at length secured the arrears of pay for the Northern colored regiments, possibly two years may secure it for the Southern."

Higginson was right. Section 5 of the Enrollment Act of March 3, 1865, finally brought belated justice to the South Carolina and other Negro regiments recruited in the South before January 1, 1864, in the shape of a provision for their full payment from the date of their original enlistment. The war was over by the time the colored soldiers in this category finally drew their arrears in pay.

It is impossible to measure the harm caused by the federal government's shortsighted and parsimonious policy toward the pay of colored troops. It is impossible to measure human suffering, humiliation, distrust, or the cancer of disloyalty bred of the conviction of having been treated unfairly. It does seem obvious, however, that, had the federal government—Lincoln, Stanton, or the Congress—seen fit to correct the inequalities in the pay of Negro troops more promptly, the results might have been apparent in a measurable increase in Negro enlistments. The adjutant general of Illinois in October of 1863 told Major Foster of the Bureau for Colored Troops that, if "no greater inducements can be offered to enlist these men than the sum named," Governor Yates could not be very optimistic about the prospects for raising a colored regiment in Lincoln's own state. "The colored men of this State," the Illinois official wrote Major Foster, "are generally a good class and can command at home readily from $12 to $15 per month." And without running the risk of death or enslavement. Without the obvious inequity of the distinction in pay, Sergeant Robert Walker would not have been shot for mutiny and there would have been far fewer reports of impaired discipline and relaxed loyalty, such as Higginson made.

It should have been clear to the nation by the fall of 1863 that Negro soldiers were ready and willing to share all the dangers of the soldier's life in full measure, and that their contribution to saving the Union was worth at least $36 per man per annum over what was being paid them. There is no good explanation for the reluctance of the Union to admit its error in this regard and to correct it. The amount of money involved was too small by comparison with the amounts being spent every day of the war to explain the injustice of Negro pay on the basis of Congressional or War Department economy. That it was an error in judgment and an injustice is plain. That the error should have been corrected earlier and ungrudgingly is obvious. That the injustice was stubbornly maintained was unworthy of the cause for which all soldiers, Negro and white, struggled.

W. E. B. DU BOIS

The Black Codes

Even as the war ended and the soldiers, both black and white, were returning home, the enforced inequality and black peonage that had characterized slavery began to appear in a new form. The South established the infamous Black Codes as a strategy for returning the shattered traditions of black deprivation and white power to good working order. The result was a new slavery, one based on law instead of custom. W. E. B. DuBois, perhaps the most influential American black intellectual of this century, here details the determined efforts of the Southern states to subjugate again a people who had not yet experienced their new freedom. As he suggests, the Black Codes were the precursors of the system of legalized oppression black people would be forced to endure until the middle of the twentieth century.

THE WHOLE PROOF OF WHAT THE SOUTH PROPOSED TO DO TO THE emancipated Negro, unless restrained by the nation, was shown in the Black Codes passed after Johnson's accession, but representing the logical result of attitudes of mind existing when Lincoln still lived. Some of these were passed and enforced. Some were passed and afterward repealed or modified when the reaction of the North was realized. In other cases, as for instance, in Louisiana, it is not clear just which laws were retained and which were repealed. In Alabama, the Governor induced the legislature not to enact some parts of the proposed code which they overwhelmingly favored.

The original codes favored by the Southern legislatures were an astonishing affront to emancipation and dealt with vagrancy, apprenticeship, labor contracts, migration, civil and legal rights. In all cases, there was plain and indisputable attempt on the part of the Southern states to make Negroes slaves in everything but name. They were given certain civil rights: the right to hold property, to sue and be sued. The family relations for the first time were legally recognized. Negroes were no longer real estate.

THE BLACK CODES From *Black Reconstruction* by W. E. B. DuBois (New York: Harcourt, Brace & Company, 1935). Reprinted by permission of Mrs. W. E. B. DuBois.

Yet, in the face of this, the Black Codes were deliberately designed to take advantage of every misfortune of the Negro. Negroes were liable to a slave trade under the guise of vagrancy and apprenticeship laws; to make the best labor contracts, Negroes must leave the old plantations and seek better terms; but if caught wandering in search of work, and thus unemployed and without a home, this was vagrancy, and the victim could be whipped and sold into slavery. In the turmoil of war, children were separated from parents, or parents unable to support them properly. These children could be sold into slavery, and "the former owner of said minors shall have the preference." Negroes could come into court as witnesses only in cases in which Negroes were involved. And even then, they must make their appeal to a jury and judge who would believe the word of any white man in preference to that of any Negro on pain of losing office and caste.

The Negro's access to the land was hindered and limited; his right to work was curtailed; his right of self-defense was taken away, when his right to bear arms was stopped; and his employment was virtually reduced to contract labor with penal servitude as a punishment for leaving his job. And in all cases, the judges of the Negro's guilt or innocence, rights and obligations were men who believed firmly, for the most part, that he had "no rights which a white man was bound to respect."

Making every allowance for the excitement and turmoil of war, and the mentality of a defeated people, the Black Codes were infamous pieces of legislation.

Let us examine these codes in detail.[1] They covered, naturally, a wide range of subjects. First, there was the question of allowing Negroes to come into the state. In South Carolina the constitution of 1865 permitted the Legislature to regulate immigration, and the consequent law declared "that no person of color shall migrate into and reside in this State, unless, within twenty days after his arrival within the same, he shall enter into a bond, with two freeholders as sureties . . . in a penalty of one thousand dollars, conditioned for his good behavior, and for his support."

Especially in the matter of work was the Negro narrowly restricted. In South Carolina, he must be especially licensed if he was to follow on his own account any employment, except that of farmer or servant. Those licensed must not only prove their fitness, but pay an annual tax ranging from $10–$100. Under no circumstances could they manufacture or sell liquor. Licenses for work were to be granted by a judge and

[1] Quotations from McPherson, *History of United States During Reconstruction*, pp. 29–44.

were revokable on complaint. The penalty was a fine double the amount
of the license, one-half of which went to the informer.

Mississippi provided that

> every freedman, free Negro, and mulatto shall on the second Monday
> of January, one thousand eight hundred and sixty-six, and annually
> thereafter, have a lawful home or employment, and shall have written
> evidence thereof . . . from the Mayor . . . or from a member of the
> board of police . . . which licenses may be revoked for cause at any
> time by the authority granting the same.

Detailed regulation of labor was provided for in nearly all these states.

Louisiana passed an elaborate law in 1865, to "regulate labor contracts for agricultural pursuits." Later, it was denied that this legislation
was actually enacted; but the law was published at the time and the
constitutional convention of 1868 certainly regarded this statute as law,
for they formally repealed it. The law required all agricultural laborers
to make labor contracts for the next year within the first ten days of
January, the contracts to be in writing, to be with heads of families, to
embrace the labor of all the members, and to be "binding on all minors
thereof." Each laborer, after choosing his employer,

> shall not be allowed to leave his place of employment until the fulfill-
> ment of his contract, unless by consent of his employer, or on account
> of harsh treatment, or breach of contract on the part of the employer;
> and if they do so leave, without cause or permission, they shall forfeit
> all wages earned to the time of abandonment. . . .
>
> In case of sickness of the laborer, wages for the time lost shall be
> deducted, and where the sickness is feigned for purposes of idleness,
> . . . and also should refusal to work be continued beyond three days,
> the offender shall be reported to a justice of the peace, and shall be
> forced to labor on roads, levees, and other public works, without pay,
> until the offender consents to return to his labor. . . .
>
> When in health, the laborer shall work ten hours during the day
> in summer, and nine hours during the day in winter, unless otherwise
> stipulated in the labor contract; he shall obey all proper orders of his
> employer or his agent; take proper care of his work mules, horses,
> oxen, stock; also of all agricultural implements; and employers shall
> have the right to make a reasonable deduction from the laborer's wages
> for injuries done to animals or agricultural implements committed to
> his care, or for bad or negligent work. Bad work shall not be allowed.
> Failing to obey reasonable orders, neglect of duty and leaving home
> without permission, will be deemed disobedience. . . . For any dis-
> obedience a fine of one dollar shall be imposed on the offender. For

all lost time from work hours, unless in case of sickness, the laborer shall be fined twenty-five cents per hour. For all absence from home without leave, the laborer will be fined at the rate of two dollars per day. Laborers will not be required to labor on the Sabbath except to take the necessary care of stock and other property on plantations and do the necessary cooking and household duties, unless by special contract. For all thefts of the laborers from the employer of agricultural products, hogs, sheep, poultry or any other property of the employer, or willful destruction of property or injury, the laborer shall pay the employer double the amount of the value of the property stolen, destroyed or injured, one half to be paid to the employer, and the other half to be placed in the general fund provided for in this section. No live stock shall be allowed to laborers without the permission of the employer. Laborers shall not receive visitors during work hours. All difficulties arising between the employers and laborers, under this section, shall be settled, and all fines be imposed, by the former; if not satisfactory to the laborers, an appeal may be had to the nearest justice of the peace and two freeholders, citizens, one of said citizens to be selected by the employer and the other by the laborer; and all fines imposed and collected under this section shall be deducted from the wages due, and shall be placed in a common fund, to be divided among the other laborers employed on the plantation at the time when their full wages fall due, except as provided for above.

Similar detailed regulations of work were in the South Carolina law. Elaborate provision was made for contracting colored "servants" to white "masters." Their masters were given the right to whip "moderately" servants under eighteen. Others were to be whipped on authority of judicial officers. These officers were given authority to return runaway servants to their masters. The servants, on the other hand, were given certain rights. Their wages and period of service must be specified in writing, and they were protected against "unreasonable" tasks, Sunday and night work, unauthorized attacks on their persons, and inadequate food.

Contracting Negroes were to be known as "servants" and contractors as "masters." Wages were to be fixed by the judge, unless stipulated. Negroes of ten years of age or more without a parent living in the district might make a valid contract for a year or less. Failure to make written contracts was a misdemeanor, punishable by a fine of $5 to $50; farm labor to be from sunrise to sunset, with intervals for meals; servants to rise at dawn, to be careful of master's property and answerable for property lost or injured. Lost time was to be deducted from wages. Food and clothes might be deducted. Servants were to be quiet and orderly and to go to bed at reasonable hours. No night work or outdoor work in bad weather was to be asked, except in cases of necessity, visitors not allowed without the master's consent. Servants leaving employment without good reason must forfeit wages. Masters might discharge servants for disobedience, drunkenness, disease, absence, etc. Enticing away the services of a servant was punishable by a fine of $20 to $100. A master could command a servant to aid him in defense of his own person, family or property. House servants at all hours of the day and night, and at all days of the week, "must answer promptly all calls and execute all lawful orders."

The right to sell farm products "without written evidence from employer" was forbidden in South Carolina, and some other states.

> A person of color who is in the employment of a master, engaged in husbandry, shall not have the right to sell any corn, rice, peas, wheat, or other grain, any flour, cotton, fodder, hay, bacon, fresh meat of any kind, poultry of any kind, animals of any kind, or any other product of a farm, without having written evidence from such master, or some person authorized by him, or from the district judge or a magistrate, that he has the right to sell such product.

There were elaborate laws covering the matter of contracts for work. A contract must be in writing and usually, as in South Carolina, white witnesses must attest it and a judge approve it. In Florida, contracts were to be in writing and failure to keep the contracts by disobedience or impudence was to be treated as vagrancy. In Kentucky, contracts were to be in writing and attested by a white person. In Mississippi, contracts were to be in writing attested by a white person, and if the laborer stopped work, his wages were to be forfeited for a year. He could be arrested, and the fee for his arrest must be paid by the employer and taken out of his wages.

There were careful provisions to protect the contracting employer from losing his labor. In Alabama,

> When any laborer or servant, having contracted as provided in the first section of this act, shall afterward be found, before the termination of said contract, in the service or employment of another, that fact shall be *prima facie* evidence that such person is guilty of violation of this act, if he fail to refuse to forthwith discharge the said laborer or servant, after being notified and informed of such former contract and employment.

Mississippi provided

> that every civil officer shall, and every person may, arrest and carry back to his or her legal employer any freedman, free Negro, or mulatto

who shall have quit the service of his or her employer before the expiration of his or her term of service without good cause; and said officer and person shall be entitled to receive for arresting and carrying back every deserting employee aforesaid the sum of five dollars, and ten cents per mile from the place of arrest to the place of delivery, and the same shall be paid by the employer and held as a set-off for so much against the wages of said deserting employee.

It was provided in some states, like South Carolina, that any white man, whether an officer or not, could arrest a Negro.

Upon view of a misdemeanor committed by a person of color, any person present may arrest the offender and take him before a magistrate, to be dealt with as the case may require. In case of a misdemeanor committed by a white person toward a person of color, any person may complain to a magistrate, who shall cause the offender to be arrested, and, according to the nature of the case, to be brought before himself, or be taken for trial in the district court.

On the other hand, in Mississippi, it was dangerous for a Negro to try to bring a white person to court on any charge.

In every case where any white person has been arrested and brought to trial, by virtue of the provisions of the tenth section of the above recited act, in any court in this State, upon sufficient proof being made to the court or jury, upon the trial before said court, that any freedman, free Negro or mulatto has falsely and maliciously caused the arrest and trial of said white person or persons, the court shall render up a judgment against said freedman, free Negro or mulatto for all costs of the case, and impose a fine not to exceed fifty dollars, and imprisonment in the county jail not to exceed twenty days; and for a failure of said freedman, free Negro or mulatto to pay, or cause to be paid, all costs, fines and jail fees, the sheriff of the county is hereby authorized and required, after giving ten days' public notice, to proceed to hire out at public outcry, at the court-house of the county, said freedman, free Negro or mulatto, for the shortest time to raise the amount necessary to discharge said freedman, free Negro or mulatto from all costs, fines, and jail fees aforesaid.

Mississippi declared that:

Any freedman, free Negro, or mulatto, committing riots, routs, affrays, trespasses, malicious mischief and cruel treatment to animals, seditious speeches, insulting gestures, language or acts, or assaults on any person, disturbance of the peace, exercising the functions of a minister of the gospel without a license from some regularly organized church, vending spirituous or intoxicating liquors, or committing any other misdemeanor, the punishment of which is not specifically provided for by law, shall, upon conviction thereof, in the county court, be fined not less than ten dollars, and not more than one hundred dollars, and may be imprisoned, at the discretion of the court, not exceeding thirty days.

As to other civil rights, the marriage of Negroes was for the first time recognized in the Southern states and slave marriages legalized. South Carolina said in general:

> That the statutes and regulations concerning slaves are now inapplicable to persons of color; and although such persons are not entitled to social or political equality with white persons, they shall have the right to acquire, own, and dispose of property, to make contracts, to enjoy the fruits of their labor, to sue and be sued, and to receive protection under the law in their persons and property.

Florida forbade "colored and white persons respectively from intruding upon each other's public assemblies, religious or other, or public vehicle set apart for their exclusive use, under punishment of pillory or stripes, or both."

Very generally Negroes were prohibited or limited in their ownership of firearms. In Florida, for instance, it was

> unlawful for any Negro, mulatto, or person of color to own, use, or keep in possession or under control any bowie-knife, dirk, sword, firearms, or ammunition of any kind, unless by license of the county judge or probate, under a penalty of forfeiting them to the informer, and of standing in the pillory one hour, or be whipped not exceeding thirty-nine stripes, or both, at the discretion of the jury.

Alabama had a similar law making it illegal to sell, give or rent firearms or ammunition of any description "to any freedman, free Negro or mulatto."

Mississippi refused arms to Negroes.

> No freedman, free Negro, or mulatto, not in the military service of the United States Government, and not licensed to do so by the board of police of his or her county, shall keep or carry firearms of any kind, or any ammunition, dirk, or bowie-knife; and on conviction thereof, in the county court, shall be punished by fine, not exceeding ten dollars, and pay the costs of such proceedings, and all such arms or ammunition shall be forfeited to the informer.

A South Carolina Negro could only keep firearms on permission in writing from the District Judge.

> Persons of color constitute no part of the militia of the State, and no one of them shall, without permission in writing from the district judge

or magistrate, be allowed to keep a firearm, sword, or other military weapon, except that one of them, who is the owner of a farm, may keep a shot-gun or rifle, such as is ordinarily used in hunting, but not a pistol, musket, or other firearm or weapon appropriate for purposes of war . . . and in case of conviction, shall be punished by a fine equal to twice the value of the weapon so unlawfully kept, and if that be not immediately paid, by corporal punishment.

The right of buying and selling property was usually granted but sometimes limited as to land. Mississippi declared:

That all freedmen, free Negroes and mulattoes may sue and be sued, implead and be impleaded in all the courts of law and equity of this State, and may acquire personal property and choses in action by descent or purchase, and may dispose of the same in the same manner and to the same extent that white persons may: *Provided,* that the provisions of this section shall not be so construed as to allow any freedman, free Negro or mulatto to rent or lease any lands or tenements, except in incorporated towns or cities, in which places the corporate authorities shall control the same.

The most important and oppressive laws were those with regard to vagrancy and apprenticeship. Sometimes they especially applied to Negroes; in other cases, they were drawn in general terms but evidently designed to fit the Negro's condition and to be enforced particularly with regard to Negroes.

The Virginia Vagrant Act enacted that

any justice of the peace, upon the complaint of any one of certain officers therein named, may issue his warrant for the apprehension of any person alleged to be a vagrant and cause such person to be apprehended and brought before him; and that if upon due examination said justice of the peace shall find that such person is a vagrant within the definition of vagrancy contained in said statute, he shall issue his warrant, directing such person to be employed for a term not exceeding three months, and by any constable of the county wherein the proceedings are had, be hired out for the best wages which can be procured, his wages to be applied to the support of himself and his family. The said statute further provides, that in case any vagrant so hired shall, during his term of service, run away from his employer without sufficient cause, he shall be apprehended on the warrant of a justice of the peace and returned to the custody of his employer, who shall then have, free from any other hire, the services of such vagrant for one month in addition to the original term of hiring, and that the employer shall then have power, if authorized by a justice of the peace,

to work such vagrant with ball and chain. The said statute specified
the persons who shall be considered vagrants and liable to the penalties
imposed by it. Among those declared to be vagrants are all persons
who, not having the wherewith to support their families, live idly and
without employment, and refuse to work for the usual and common
wages given to other laborers in the like work in the place where they
are.

In Florida, January 12, 1866:

It is provided that when any person of color shall enter into a contract
as aforesaid, to serve as a laborer for a year, or any other specified
term, on any farm or plantation in this State, if he shall refuse or
neglect to perform the stipulations of his contract by willful disobedience of orders, wanton impudence or disrespect to his employer, or his
authorized agent, failure or refusal to perform the work assigned to
him, idleness, or abandonment of the premises or the employment
of the party with whom the contract was made, he or she shall be
liable, upon the complaint of his employer or his agent, made under
oath before any justice of the peace of the county, to be arrested and
tried before the criminal court of the county, and upon conviction
shall be subject to all the pains and penalties prescribed for the punishment of vagrancy.

In Georgia, it was ruled that

All persons wandering or strolling about in idleness, who are able to
work, and who have no property to support them; all persons leading
an idle, immoral, or profligate life, who have no property to support
them and are able to work and do not work; all persons able to work
having no visible and known means of a fair, honest, and respectable
livelihood; all persons having a fixed abode, who have no visible property to support them, and who live by stealing or by trading in, barter-
ing for, or buying stolen property; and all professional gamblers living
in idleness, shall be deemed and considered vagrants, and shall be
indicted as such, and it shall be lawful for any person to arrest said
vagrants and have them bound over for trial to the next term of the
county court, and upon conviction, they shall be fined and imprisoned
or sentenced to work on the public works, for not longer than a year,
or shall, in the discretion of the court, be bound over for trial to the
next term of the county court, and upon conviction, they shall be
fined and imprisoned or sentenced to work on the public works, for
not longer than a year, or shall, in the discretion of the court, be bound
out to some person for a time not longer than one year, upon such
valuable consideration as the court may prescribe.

Mississippi provided

That all freedmen, free Negroes, and mulattoes in this state over the age of eighteen years, found on the second Monday in January, 1866, or thereafter, with no lawful employment or business, or found unlawfully assembling themselves together, either in the day or night time, and all white persons so assembling with freedmen, free Negroes or mulattoes, or usually associating with freedmen, free Negroes or mulattoes on terms of equality, or living in adultery or fornication with a freedwoman, free Negro or mulatto, shall be deemed vagrants, and on conviction thereof shall be fined in the sum of not exceeding, in the case of a freedman, free Negro or mulatto, fifty dollars, and a white man two hundred dollars and imprisoned, at the discretion of the court, the free Negro not exceeding ten days, and the white men not exceeding six months.

Sec. 5 provides that

all fines and forfeitures collected under the provisions of this act shall be paid into the county treasury for general county purposes, and in case any freedman, free Negro or mulatto, shall fail for five days after the imposition of any fine or forfeiture upon him or her, for violation of any of the provisions of this act to pay the same, that it shall be, and is hereby made, the duty of the Sheriff of the proper county to hire out said freedman, free Negro or mulatto, to any person who will, for the shortest period of service, pay said fine or forfeiture and all costs; *Provided,* a preference shall be given to the employer, if there be one, in which case the employer shall be entitled to deduct and retain the amount so paid from the wages of such freedman, free Negro or mulatto, then due or to become due; and in case such freedman, free Negro or mulatto cannot be hired out, he or she may be dealt with as a pauper.

South Carolina declared to be vagrants all persons without fixed and known places of abode and lawful employment, all prostitutes and all persons wandering from place to place and selling without a license; all gamblers; idle and disobedient persons; persons without sufficient means of support; persons giving plays or entertainments without license; fortune-tellers, beggars, drunkards and hunters. If a person of color is unable to earn his support, his near relatives must contribute. Pauper funds were composed of fines paid by Negroes and taxes on Negroes. On the other hand, former slaves who were helpless and had been on plantations six months previous to November 10, 1865, could not be evicted before January 1, 1867.

In Alabama, the "former owner" was to have preference in the apprenticing of a child. This was true in Kentucky and Mississippi. Mississippi

> provides that it shall be the duty of all sheriffs, justices of the peace, and other civil officers of the several counties in this state to report to the probate courts of their respective counties semiannually, at the January and July terms of said courts, all freedmen, free Negroes and mulattoes, under the age of eighteen, within their respective counties, beats, or districts, who are orphans, or whose parent or parents have not the means, or who refuse to provide for and support said minors, and thereupon it shall be the duty of said probate court to order the clerk of said court to apprentice said minors to some competent and suitable person, or such terms as the court may direct, having a particular care to the interest of said minors: *Provided,* that the former owner of said minors shall have the preference when, in the opinion of the court, he or she shall be a suitable person for that purpose.

South Carolina established special courts for colored people, to be created in each district to administer the law in respect to persons of color. The petit juries of these courts were to consist of only six men. The local magistrate "shall be specially charged with the supervision of persons of color in his neighborhood, their protection, and the prevention of their misconduct." Public order was to be secured by the organization of forty-five or more militia regiments.

> Capital punishment was provided for colored persons guilty of willful homicide, assault upon a white woman, impersonating her husband for carnal purposes, raising an insurrection, stealing a horse, a mule, or baled cotton, and house-breaking. For crimes not demanding death Negroes might be confined at hard labor, whipped, or transported; "but punishments more degrading than imprisonment shall not be imposed upon a white person for a crime not infamous."[2]

In most states Negroes were allowed to testify in courts but the testimony was usually confined to cases where colored persons were involved, although in some states, by consent of the parties, they could testify in cases where only white people were involved. In Alabama

> all freedmen, free Negroes and mulattoes, shall have the right to sue and be sued, plead and be impleaded in all the different and various courts of this State, to the same extent that white persons now have by law. And they shall be competent to testify only in open court, and only in cases in which freedmen, free Negroes, and mulattoes are

[2] Simkins and Woody, *South Carolina During Reconstruction,* pp. 49, 50.

parties, either plaintiff or defendant, and in civil or criminal cases, for injuries in the persons and property of freedmen, free Negroes and mulattoes, and in all cases, civil or criminal, in which a freedman, free Negro, or mulatto, is a witness against a white person, or a white person against a freedman, free Negro or mulatto, the parties shall be competent witnesses.

North Carolina, March 10, 1866,

gives them all the privileges of white persons before the courts in the mode of prosecuting, defending, continuing, removing, and transferring their suits at law in equity,

and makes them eligible as witnesses, when not otherwise incompetent, in

all controversies at law and in equity where the rights of persons or property of persons of color shall be put in issue, and would be concluded by the judgment or decree of courts; and also in pleas of the State, where the violence, fraud, or injury alleged shall be charged to have been done by or to persons of color. In all other civil and criminal cases such evidence shall be deemed inadmissible, unless by consent of the parties of record.

Mississippi simply reënacted her slave code and made it operative so far as punishments were concerned.

That all the penal and criminal laws now in force in this State, defining offenses, and prescribing the mode of punishment for crimes and misdemeanors committed by slaves, free Negroes or mulattoes, be and the same are hereby reenacted, and declared to be in full force and effect, against freedmen, free Negroes, and mulattoes, except so far as the mode and manner of trial and punishment have been changed or altered by law.

North Carolina, on the other hand, abolished her slave code, making difference of punishment only in the case of Negroes convicted of rape. Georgia placed the fines and costs of a servant upon the master.

Where such cases shall go against the servant, the judgment for costs upon written notice to the master shall operate as a garnishment against him, and he shall retain a sufficient amount for the payment thereof, out of any wages due to said servant, or to become due during the period of service, and may be cited at any time by the collecting officer to make answer thereto.

The celebrated ordinance of Opelousas, Louisiana, shows the local ordinances regulating Negroes.

No Negro or freedman shall be allowed to come within the limits of the town of Opelousas without special permission from his employer, specifying the object of his visit and the time necessary for the accomplishment of the same.

Every Negro freedman who shall be found on the streets of Opelousas after ten o'clock at night without a written pass or permit from his employer, shall be imprisoned and compelled to work five days on the public streets, or pay a fine of five dollars.

No Negro or freedman shall be permitted to rent or keep a house within the limits of the town under any circumstances, and anyone thus offending shall be ejected, and compelled to find an employer or leave the town within twenty-four hours.

No Negro or freedman shall reside within the limits of the town of Opelousas who is not in the regular service of some white person or former owner, who shall be held responsible for the conduct of said freedman.

No Negro or freedman shall be permitted to preach, exhort, or otherwise declaim to congregations of colored people without a special permission from the Mayor or President of the Board of Police, under the penalty of a fine of ten dollars or twenty days' work on the public streets.

No freedman who is not in the military service shall be allowed to carry firearms, or any kind of weapons within the limits of the town of Opelousas without the special permission of his employer, in writing, and approved by the Mayor or President of the Board.

Any freedman not residing in Opelousas, who shall be found within its corporate limits after the hour of 3 o'clock, on Sunday, without a special permission from his employer or the Mayor, shall be arrested and imprisoned and made to work two days on the public streets, or pay two dollars in lieu of said work.[3]

Of Louisiana, Thomas Conway testified February 22, 1866:

Some of the leading officers of the state down there—men who do much to form and control the opinions of the masses—instead of doing as they promised, and quietly submitting to the authority of the government, engaged in issuing slave codes and in promulgating them to their subordinates, ordering them to carry them into execution, and this to the knowledge of state officials of a higher character, the governor and others. And the men who issued them were not punished except as the military authorities punished them. The governor inflicted no punishment on them while I was there, and I don't know that, up to this day, he has ever punished one of them. These codes were simply the old black code of the state, with the word "slave" expunged,

[3] Warmoth, *War, Politics and Reconstruction,* p. 274.

and "Negro" substituted. The most odious features of slavery were preserved in them. They were issued in three or four localities in the state, not a hundred miles from New Orleans, months after the surrender of the Confederate forces, and years after the issuance of the Emancipation Proclamation.

I have had delegations to frequently come and see me—delegations composed of men who, to my face, denied that the proclamation issued by President Lincoln was a valid instrument, declaring that the Supreme Court would pronounce it invalid. Consequently they have claimed that their Negroes were slaves and would again be restored to them. In the city of New Orleans last summer, under the orders of the acting mayor of the city, Hugh Kennedy, the police of that city conducted themselves towards the freedmen, in respect to violence and ill usage, in every way equal to the old days of slavery; arresting them on the streets as vagrants, without any form of law whatever, and simply because they did not have in their pockets certificates of employment from their former owners or other white citizens.

I have gone to the jails and released large numbers of them, men who were industrious and who had regular employment; yet because they had not the certificates of white men in their pockets they were locked up in jail to be sent out to plantations; locked up, too, without my knowledge, and done speedily and secretly before I had information of it. Some members of the Seventy-Fourth United States Colored Infantry, a regiment which was mustered out but one day, were arrested the next because they did not have these certificates of employment. This was done to these men after having served in the United States army three years. They were arrested by the police under the order of the acting mayor, Mr. Hugh Kennedy. . . .[4]

The aim and object of these laws cannot be mistaken. "In many cases the restraints imposed went to the length of a veritable 'involuntary servitude.' "[5]

Professor Burgess says:

Almost every act, word or gesture of the Negro, not consonant with good taste and good manners as well as good morals, was made a crime or misdemeanor, for which he could first be fined by the magistrates and then consigned to a condition of almost slavery for an indefinite time, if he could not pay the bill.[6]

Dunning admits that "The legislation of the reorganized governments, under cover of police regulations and vagrancy laws, had enacted severe

[4] *Report of the Joint Committee on Reconstruction,* 1866, Part IV, pp. 78–79.
[5] *Atlantic Monthly,* LXXXVII, January, 1910, p. 6.
[6] DuBois, *Reconstruction and Its Benefits,* p. 784.

discriminations against the freedmen in all the common civil rights.''[7]
A recent study says of South Carolina:

> The interests of both races would have been better served had there
> never been a "black code." This would be true even if there had been
> no Northern sentiment to take into account. Economically, the laws
> were impracticable, since they tried to place the Negro in a position
> inferior to that which competition or his labor would have given him.[8]
>
> But it is monotonous iteration to review the early legislation of the
> reconstructed government established under the proclamation of the
> President. In most of the states the laws established a condition but
> little better than that of slavery, and in one important respect far
> worse; for in place of the property interest, which would induce the
> owner to preserve and care for his slave, there was substituted the
> guardianship of penal statutes; and the ignorant black man, innocent
> of any intention to commit a wrong, could be bandied about from
> one temporary owner to another who would have no other interest
> than to wring out of him, without regard to his ultimate condition,
> all that was possible during the limited term of his thraldom.[9]

These slave laws have been defended in various ways. They were
passed in the midst of bitterness and fear and with great haste; they were
worded somewhat like similar vagrancy laws in Northern States; they
would have been modified in time; they said more than they really
meant. All of this may be partly true, but it remains perfectly evident
that the black codes looked backward toward slavery.

This legislation profoundly stirred the North. Not the North of industry and the new manufactures, but the ordinary everyday people
of the North, who, uplifted by the tremendous afflatus of war, had seen
a vision of something fine and just, and who, without any personal affection for the Negro or real knowledge of him, nevertheless were convinced that Negroes were human, and that Negro slavery was wrong;
and that whatever freedom might mean, it certainly did not mean reën-
slavement under another name.

Here, then, was the dominant thought of that South with which Reconstruction must deal. Arising with aching head and palsied hands it
deliberately looked backward. There came to the presidential chair, with
vast power, a man who was Southern born; with him came inconceivable
fears that the North proposed to make these Negroes really free; to give
them a sufficient status even for voting, to give them the right to hold

---

[7] Dunning, *Essays on the Civil War and Reconstruction*, p. 92.
[8] Simkins and Woody, *Reconstruction in South Carolina*, p. 51.
[9] Morse, *Thaddeus Stevens*, American Statesman, pp. 253–254.

office; that there was even a possibility that these slaves might out-vote their former masters; that they might accumulate wealth, achieve education, and finally, they might even aspire to marry white women and mingle their blood with the blood of their masters.

It was fantastic. It called for revolt. It called in extremity for the renewal of war. The Negro must be kept in his place by hunger, whipping and murder. As W. P. Calhoun of Greenville, South Carolina, said as late as 1901: "Character, wealth, learning, good behavior, and all that makes up or constitutes good citizenship in the black man is positively of no avail whatever. Merit cannot win in this case."[10]

[10] Brewster, *Sketches of Southern Mystery,* p. 275.

JOHN HOPE FRANKLIN

Counter Reconstruction

Black people and concerned Northern liberals hoped that Reconstruction would right the great wrongs of the South and bring into being the dream of full equality for the emancipated slaves. The South responded with two weapons: the Black Codes and vigilante groups, the most feared of which was the Ku Klux Klan. But, as John Hope Franklin, the distinguished black historian, here observes, the Klan was only one of many groups whose aim was to terrify the black man into submission, break the will of his allies, and return the South to the rule of violence, repression, and human indignity.

THE REACTION OF THE FORMER CONFEDERATES AND THEIR SUPPORTERS to the taking over of the reconstruction program by Congress could hardly have been unanticipated. When abolitionists had called for an end to slavery in the ante-bellum period, Southerners had said that the

North was making war on their institutions and their way of life. Whenever there had been slave revolts or rumors of them, planters, and even most non-slaveholders, were thrown into a frenzy of preparation for the great upheaval that they seemed to think was inevitable. "We must prepare for any eventuality," they were accustomed to saying; and whether the dangers of which they spoke were real or fancied, they had no intention of being caught short. All too frequently, long before the Civil War came, these fears had erupted with a violence that to some observers made the South appear a dark and bloody land.

Even when the former Confederates were rather firmly in control of Southern state and local governments in the early postwar years, violence was an important part of the pattern of life. In 1866 the head of the Freedmen's Bureau in Georgia complained that numerous bands of ruffians were committing "the most fiendish and diabolical outrages" on the freedmen. The former slaves themselves made many representations to Congress and the President that they were in constant danger of physical harm at the hands of the former Confederates. Northern teachers of freedmen frequently saw their efforts literally turn to ashes as local white opponents set fire to the Negro schools; and the reports of the Bureau contain many instances of bodily harm inflicted upon Northern teachers by those in the South who were unalterably opposed to the education of the former slaves. If violence was an integral part of the old order and even of the new order controlled by former Confederates, it was only natural that it would be a prime factor in any move to oppose the still newer order administered by those whom the former Confederates regarded as natural enemies.

The targets of attack now were, of course, the Union League, the Heroes of America in North Carolina, the Lincoln Brotherhood, a Radical group that flourished in Florida, and other similar organizations. The work of the League was especially reprehensible to the former Confederates. In addition to teaching Negroes what their political rights were and instructing them in the mysteries of voting, the League also fired the self-respect of the former slaves by telling them that they were the social equals of whites. To many who had supported the Lost Cause this was worse than the burning of Atlanta and Sherman's path of devastation from that city to the sea. Another target was the several state militias, which, in addition to being charged with the responsibility of keeping the hated Radical governments in power, frequently boasted of having Negro contingents to participate in the discharge of this responsibility. If Radical governments were to be placed in power by "Negro votes" and were to be kept there by "Negro militias," they invited opposition by every means, including violence, at the disposal of the former Confederates.

The young Tennesseans who organized late in 1865 the frolicking secret lodge that was to be known as the order of the Ku Klux Klan, or the Invisible Empire, could hardly have been unaware of what they were doing. Even if they were bored and impatient with life, as has been claimed in their defense, this was nothing new for young bloods in the village of Pulaski, Tennessee. Nor were wanton attacks on helpless Negroes new. If the young men were looking for fun, they did not have to go beyond the nearest Negro settlement, and furthermore they would be performing a service to the white community if they whipped Negroes to keep them in line. Long before Negroes became a political factor and while the governments of the Southern states were still in the hands of the former Confederates, the Klan organization was being perfected and was spreading to many parts of the South. It described itself as an institution of "chivalry, humanity, mercy, and patriotism." Within a matter of months it had selected its name, adopted its ritual, and had begun to terrorize the Negroes of the area. Soon there were other chapters (dens) with officers bearing such ominous titles as dragons, hydras, titans, furies, and night-hawks.

In the spring of 1867 delegates from several states met in convention at Nashville, placed General Nathan B. Forrest at the head of the organization as the Grand Wizard, and sent its members back to their respective homes fired with a determination to nullify the program of congressional reconstruction that was just getting under way. No longer was it sufficient to frighten or terrorize Negroes by ghoulish dress, weird rituals, and night rides. By social and business ostracism of the white Radicals, by intimidation and any effective means of violence conceivable against Negroes, by the purchase of votes of any sellers, and by glorifying the white race and especially white womanhood, the Klan grimly moved to wreck each and every phase of Radical Reconstruction.

While the Klan made rapid strides in Tennessee, North Carolina, and Alabama, other similar groups were springing up elsewhere. In Louisiana it was the Knights of the White Camellia. In Texas it was the Knights of the Rising Sun. In Mississippi it was the White Line, and on and on throughout the former Confederate states. Scores of other counter-reconstruction organizations flourished in various parts of the South. Among them were the Constitutional Union Guards, the Pale Faces, the White Brotherhood, the White League, the Council of Safety, and the '76 Association. As the months and years went by, more such organizations came into existence. Old or new, large or small, they had one aim in common:

the maintenance and, later, the re-establishment of white supremacy in the South. They had one means in common: any and every kind of intimidation and violence against the Negro and his supporters. Even if they were, in some instances, autonomous and even amorphous, these groups were at least held together loosely by the ideals, aims, and methods which they shared with the Invisible Empire.

It would be a historical fallacy to assert that the Ku Klux Klan and its compatriots were organized to combat the Union League and to overthrow Radical Reconstruction. They came on the scene much too early to support such a view and they were, indeed, too much a reflection of the general character of Southern life to require the unique conditions of Radical Reconstruction to spawn them. Radical Reconstruction was, however, a powerful stimulus for such endeavors, and the struggle against it gave the Klan respectability and a dignity that it had not anticipated. The lawlessness of the Jayhawkers and Bushwhackers of 1865 became the holy crusade of the Klansmen of 1868. Within a matter of months it was being claimed that the "instinct of self-protection" prompted the organization of the Klan. "It was necessary," one of them argued,

> in order to protect our families from outrage and to preserve our own lives, to have something that we could regard as a brotherhood—a combination of the best men in the country, to act purely in self-defense, to repel the attack in case we should be attacked by these people.

The real stimulus, then, to the growth and expansion of Klan activities was not the attacks on innocent white families by Negroes and others but the apparent determination on the part of Negroes and their Radical friends to assume and wield political power. For the former Confederates this was indeed an attack as real as any they could imagine. The oath of the Klansmen to aid those fellow members in distress and "pecuniary embarrassment" was liberally construed, while their promise to protect female friends and widows of Confederate veterans drew into the fold many who would not have been attracted for other reasons. They proceeded on the basis of that ancient principle that the best defense was a well-planned offense. At times wearing hoods and robes, at other times without disguise, they rode over the land at night "terrifying, whipping, or murdering whites and Negroes who, for one reason or another, were to them undesirable." Negro offenses ranged from insolence to voting and holding office. White offenses ranged from participating in Radical governments to associating with Negroes on a basis of equality.

.   .   .

Since the Freedmen's Bureau had been an important factor in the establishment of congressional reconstruction and since it had assisted the Union League in the "political education" of the freedmen, it was viewed by the Klan as another special enemy. Encouraged by President Johnson's opposition to the Bureau and by the widespread opposition among former Confederates to the Bureau since its inception, the Klan proceeded to drive the Bureau out of the political picture altogether. The attack on Bureau officials was systematic and effective. Sometimes they were simply warned to leave town, sometimes they were flogged. An agent of the Bureau in Tennessee slept for months with a revolver under his pillow, "a double-barreled shot gun, heavily charged at one hand and a hatchet at the other, with an inclination to sell the little piece of mortality with which I am entrusted as dearly as possible." Even after the Bureau had been officially disbanded, former employees were marked objects of the wrath of the Klansmen.

Perhaps nothing aroused the hatred of Klansmen as much as the so-called Negro militia units. Conservatives called the units a "dangerous offensive design" to spy on those opposing Radical Reconstruction. Those in the state legislatures sought to block appropriations for the militia and, failing in this, to enjoin the expenditure of the funds that had been appropriated. The opposition moved steadily toward outright violence. The names of Negro militia leaders were recorded in "Dead Books," while in some communities coffins "were paraded through the streets marked with the names of prominent Radicals and labeled with such inscriptions as 'Dead, damned and delivered.' " Negro militiamen were attacked individually and stripped of their weapons, including pocket knives. When they learned through spies of the shipment of arms into the state for the use of the militia, the enemies of Radical Reconstruction would intercept the shipment and either appropriate it for their own use or destroy it altogether.

Personal violence against militiamen, white or Negro, was the favorite weapon of the Klansmen. In South Carolina, Joseph Crews, a white organizer of the Negro militia, carried on a running fight with his bitter enemies for several years. Finally, in 1875, he was ambushed and killed by a shotgun blast. Frequent raids on the homes of militiamen resulted in property being taken, mutilated, or burned. In Marion, Arkansas, a Negro militia captain was murdered on the streets "in broad daylight." After discharging both loads of a double-barreled shotgun into his body, the assailant fired five revolver shots into him and then rode away unmolested. In Mississippi the well-known Negro state senator, Charles Caldwell, had commanded a company of Negro troops that had been ordered to maintain the peace in Clinton. For this deed, Caldwell was lured into a cellar, shot many times there, and then carried into the streets where his body was "grotesquely turned completely over by the impact of innumerable shots fired at close range." Murders, lynchings, drownings were the hazards facing Negro and white militiamen who undertook to support congressional reconstruction in the South.

The more "respectable" members of Southern communities, repelled by these excesses, argued that the terrorist organizations had been taken over by the low, irresponsible elements of the population. They were composed of "drunken and lawless vagabonds" declared one disgusted South Carolinian. They were "ignorant and without education to the last degree" asserted the Democratic minority of a congressional investigating committee. The Klan fell into the hands of "cutthroats and riffraff, for private gain and vengeance," one historian has recently claimed.

. . .

Congressional reconstruction would have no chance of success unless it could put down the lawlessness that was rapidly destroying every semblance of political and economic stability in the South. If they were ever to take a stand and fight for their survival, the state governments realized that the time was now at hand. Governor William G. Brownlow of Tennessee, among the most vigorous defenders of Radical Reconstruction, was outraged that the violent counter-reconstruction movement should have had its formal inception in his state. These "rebellious elements," he declared, were composed of ex-rebel soldiers and their sympathizers, who were "plotting and planning mischief in every respect." The legislature of 1868 complied with his request to enact a law "to preserve the public peace." These and similar measures in other states came to be known as the "Ku Klux laws." Any person belonging to secret organizations engaged in night prowling "to the disturbance of the peace" or sheltering members of such organizations was to be punished by a fine of not less than $500 and imprisonment for a term of not less than five years and was to be "rendered infamous." Informers were to receive one-half the fines if citizens and three-fourths if public officers. There were other provisions, including the assessment ranging from $500 to $5,000 for the state school fund on a county permitting a Klansman to reside within its borders and civil damages ranging from $10,000 to $20,000 in favor of the victim of Klan violence.

Other states followed Tennessee's lead, and within two years there was a network of Ku Klux laws extending across the South designed to combat the counter-reconstruction efforts. In the same year Alabama enacted a similar law and added that "the fact of a man's hiding his face and wearing a costume was *prima facie* evidence of guilt." In the following year Arkansas and North Carolina passed Ku Klux laws, with Mississippi and South Carolina following in 1870 and 1871, respectively. Governors sought to speed the process of destroying the Klan by declaring martial law, appointing special constables, and offering rewards for the apprehension of the night riders. On the whole, the laws were ineffective and their enforcement was generally impossible. As the authorities realized this, they became more desperate. Few means were left to bolster governments that were sagging badly under the weight of counter-reconstruction.

One possibility was military power. In Tennessee full control over the state militia was placed in the governor's hand, and Brownlow did not hesitate to use it. Late in 1868 Governor Powell Clayton declared martial law in thirteen Arkansas counties and sent militiamen into the disturbed areas to maintain the peace. In the summer of 1870 Governor William W. Holden of North Carolina ordered a Union veteran, Colonel George Kirk, to raise troops and put down threatened insurrections in several Piedmont counties. Scores of Ku Klux suspects were arrested and several were hanged for alleged outrages. These and similar measures merely stiffened the resistance of the enemies of reconstruction and strengthened the conviction that the Klan was fully justified. Reports of the number and conduct of Negro troops on a scene of trouble were frequently exaggerated, and even when that was not the case their use was universally condemned by the former Confederates. Unable to predict what dire consequences might flow from the wielding of military power by Negroes and their friends, the Conservatives began to assert that life for them was becoming "unendurable."

As the whites lashed back at the Ku Klux laws and resisted their enforcement with all the resources they could muster, the supporters of reconstruction began desperately to turn to the federal government for support. From the beginning of congressional reconstruction the new governments had kept the authorities in Washington informed of developments. The Northern press followed every incident with lively interest and gave full play to the stream of Ku Klux atrocity stories coming out of the South. At least a portion of the North was becoming aroused. The Republican party in the South was rapidly disintegrating, violence was threatening Northern investments there, and the war and the reconstruction amendments to the Constitution were being nullified by the Klan and its confederates. The Klan was a "hell-born cabal," declared John W. Forney of Philadelphia. It was "another secession snake," the editor of the New York *Tribune* shouted with characteristic directness. Sooner or later, for one reason or another, the federal government would have to take official cognizance of counter reconstruction in the South.

Perhaps no one took very seriously the order of the Grand Wizard in the spring of 1869 that the Invisible Empire was to dissolve, bury or burn its regalia, and destroy its ritual and records. Certainly, the anti-Klan laws enacted by the states did little to discourage the Klan or coerce its dissolution. Nor could the irresponsible violence of the so-called lower elements have filled the Klan with sufficient disgust to cause it to want to dissociate itself from the more extreme counter-reconstruction measures. In the midst of growing criticism and public outrage against the Klan, the dissolution order of the Grand Wizard appears to have been more of a tactical move than an honest effort to reduce the violence associated with the name of the Klan. Such an order, the leaders hoped, would mean that the Klan could no longer be held responsible for hundreds of crimes described in issue after issue of Northern newspapers. And if the work of the Klan was to be effective, whether performed by the white-robed "better elements" or by others, there was no need to invite the criticism of and, perhaps, punishment by those who possessed the means of vengeance. The path to survival and success was underground, and most of those committed to the Klan's objectives followed that path.

The order of dissolution did not, however, divert attention from the Klan. Leaders in Congress became convinced that some measure of federal support was necessary if the reconstructed states were to survive. The enactment of appropriate legislation would provide the ground on which the "Republican party must stand in carrying into effect the Reconstruction," declared Senator John Pool of North Carolina. Without it the "whole fabric of Reconstruction, with all the principles connected with it, amounts to nothing at all, and in the end it will topple and fall." Congress, busily engaged in admitting the last of the Confederate states, soon diverted some of its attention to the defense of the new governments and enacted measures to enforce the reconstruction amendments. At the end of May, 1870, a law was passed designed to protect Negroes exercising the franchise. Persons hindering, obstructing, or controlling qualified electors in their effort to vote were to be fined and imprisoned. The Klan or others in disguise who interfered with anyone in the enjoyment of his constitutional rights were to be found guilty of committing a felony. Federal district and circuit courts were to have jurisdiction, and federal marshals and other officers were to enforce the law.

The first federal intervention was, on the whole, ineffective. Operating underground, the Klan was able to continue its work by threat and by violence. When charges were brought against alleged offenders, witnesses were usually afraid to testify. When they did testify, juries declined to convict. Through the summer and fall conditions in the former Confederate states deteriorated steadily. The Klan was openly active in the Alabama election of August, 1870. Its members paraded in full regalia, despite the Alabama law, the new federal statute, *and* the Grand Wizard's dissolution order of the previous spring. In Mississippi the Klan took on new life in 1870 in order to oppose the establishment of schools for Negroes and to resist the new taxes that it regarded as unreasonable. In North Carolina Governor Holden carried on a running fight with the Klan, and when it appeared that he was not strong enough to cope with the organization, he wired President Grant for support. Holden did not receive any reinforcements and consequently was unable to perpetuate his regime. But he had given the President some indication of the difficulties the reconstruction governments were experiencing, and the President would not forget what he had learned.

In a special message to Congress on December 5, 1870, President Grant declared that "the free exercise of franchise has by violence and intimidation been denied to citizens in several of the states lately in rebellion." On the basis of the information that had come to him regarding conditions in the South, the Senate established a committee of seven to inquire into those conditions. The committee not only examined the voluminous reports turned over to it by the President but called before it a large number of witnesses, from North Carolina—federal and state officials, Klan leaders, and private citizens, white and Negro. The five Republican leaders concluded that the state of North Carolina had insufficient force to cope with the Klan. It was indulging in "a carnival of murders, intimidation, and violence of all kinds." The two Democrats on the committee dissented, declaring that the claim of anarchy in North Carolina was "absurdly untrue."

As a result of the majority report Congress was in a mood to strengthen its legislation of the previous year. On February 28, 1871, it amended the Enforcement Act of May 31, 1870. Supervisors of elections were to be appointed by federal courts, and interference with the discharge of their duties was to be a federal offense, punishable by fine and imprisonment. Federal courts were given jurisdiction over the election supervisors and their work.

Before this law could be tested, a new session of Congress had convened, and the sentiment was strongly favorable to a much more vigorous effort to sustain the new governments in the South. A fresh flood of reports of outrages had come to the attention of the President, and he was ready to take the initiative. Numerous altercations and riots in South Carolina were especially disturbing. They confirmed his growing conviction that life and property were insecure and that the carrying of the mails and the collection of revenue were being endangered. In a special message to Congress he indicated that the power of the states to deal with the problem was inadequate and that he was not certain his own powers were sufficient for such emergencies. Therefore, he recommended legislation to facilitate his enforcement of the law. He then issued a proclamation condemning the lawless elements in South Carolina and ordering them to disperse within twenty days.

Almost immediately Congress responded by drawing up a bill, known as the Third Enforcement Act, which became law on April 20, 1871. Opposition to the bill was bitter, and debate was acrimonious. Not only did Democrats oppose it but several important Republicans spoke out with deep feeling. James A. Garfield in the House called the measure "extreme," while Carl Schurz in the Senate said that the bill gave the President power that he, Schurz, was unwilling to confide in any living man. The majority of members of both houses had been persuaded that the President was justifiably alarmed, and they gave him what he asked for.

The new law, known as the Ku Klux Act, declared that the activity of unlawful combinations constituted a "rebellion against the government of the United States." In areas where such combinations were at work the President could suspend the privilege of the writ of habeas corpus and proclaim martial law. Persons having knowledge of conspiracies could be held responsible for injuries done if they made no effort to prevent the conspirators from carrying out their designs. The President then issued a proclamation calling public attention to the new legislation. He warned that while he would be reluctant to exercise the powers granted him, he would use them "whenever and wherever it shall be necessary to do so." It was not until October 17 that he suspended the writ in nine South Carolina counties that had been especially chaotic and violent during the summer of 1871.

In South Carolina and in other states where the President directed his attention federal troops were used to make arrests and to enforce the law. At the trials in Greenville and Columbia many were found guilty and given fines and prison terms. In Mississippi there were trials under the new law as early as June, 1871, but no convictions. In North Carolina there were hundreds of arrests. Some of the accused confessed their guilt and were released upon providing information that implicated others. By the time the law expired in 1872 there had been hundreds of arrests and some convictions. But the South had not succumbed to federal force. "Short memories," "illness of the defendants," and other reliable alibis frequently destroyed the government's cases. The general attitude of witnesses, the accused, and the public was that the interference by the government was unwarranted and that their previous and current actions were fully justified.

Meanwhile, Congress had injected itself into the reconstruction picture in still another way. At the time the Ku Klux Act was under consideration Congress passed a resolution establishing a joint committee of twenty-one members to "inquire into the condition of the late insurrectionary states." There were five Republicans and two Democrats from the Senate and eight Republicans and six Democrats from the House. Senator John Scott of Pennsylvania was designated chairman. Among the more prominent members from the Senate were Zachariah Chandler of Michigan, Francis P. Blair of Missouri, and New York-born Benjamin F. Rice of Arkansas. From the House, the better-known members were Benjamin F. Butler of Massachusetts, Samuel S. Cox of Ohio and William E. Lansing of New York. Six committee members were from former Confederate states, while Missouri, Delaware, and Kentucky each had one member. On April 20, 1871, the day on which President Grant signed the Ku Klux Act, the joint committee was organized for work. Like its predecessors this committee strengthened vastly the investigative role of Congress. A subcommittee of eight was to hold hearings in Washington, and three subcommittees were to hold hearings in various parts of the South. By the middle of February, 1872, the committee had completed its work and was ready to make its report.

Persons from every segment of the population appeared before the committee. Governors, senators and representatives, state legislators, mayors, and sheriffs; United States Army officers, ex-Confederate generals and other veterans; planters, lawyers, doctors, editors, merchants and artisans; teachers and clergymen; and Negroes "by the score." Wade Hampton and Governor James L. Orr of South Carolina appeared. Former governor Joseph Brown of Georgia, Governor Robert Lindsay of Alabama, and Nathaniel B. Forrest, widely recognized as the Grand Wizard of the Invisible Empire, all gave testimony.

Suspected members of the Klan and former Confederates in general gave little helpful information. Witnesses usually denied membership in the Klan or any knowledge of its activities. Even when they admitted membership in some organization, they could not remember who asked them to join or who were members. General James H. Clanton of

Alabama said that he did not think there had ever been an organization known as the Ku Klux Klan in his state. The testimony of General Forrest and others similarly situated was no more helpful. Indeed, when pressed by members of the committee, some of them became voluble, loosing a flood of invectives and profanities against Negroes and the committee.

Negro witnesses were "more co-operative." Some of them "made good witnesses and told graphic and convincing stories which had the ring of truth," a historian of the Klan has declared. One of them told how he was whipped because he had not lifted his hat when he met a white man on the road. Another related how a Negro was killed by a mob after an altercation with a white man. A Negro woman told how the Klan dragged her husband from their home and lynched him, presumably because he was politically active. Many told of threats and intimidation directed at those Negroes who wielded some political influence or who merely voted. Thus, the Negroes and their friends emphasized the lawless, political character of the Klan, while the former Confederates feigned ignorance of it or claimed that it confined its role to that of peacemaking and law enforcement.

The division within the committee was not unlike the division among the witnesses. The Democratic members criticized the committee for confining its work to six states—North and South Carolina, Georgia, Mississippi, Alabama, and Florida. They argued that the committee's work and its report had been politically inspired, that any violence in the South had been provoked by the corruption of the Republican party and the irresponsible rule of the new governments. The Republicans, who wrote the majority report, recommended continuing protective measures by enforcement of federal laws. This should be maintained until there was "no further doubt of the actual suppression and disarming of . . . [the] widespread and dangerous conspiracy" that it had discovered. The committee urged the North to be patient while the strong feeling engendered by the war gradually subsided. Meanwhile, the South's "reluctant obedience" to federal authority was hoped for, but "less than obedience" the government would not accept.

The report of the joint committee, covering thirteen large volumes, was one of the most extensive that a congressional committee had ever made. Almost as much was gained from what the report did not say as from what it did say. The bellicosity of some of the former Confederate witnesses and the artful evasiveness of some of the others clearly indicated that many Southerners had no intention of accommodating themselves to federal control or congressional reconstruction. The earlier decision of the Klan to go underground paid off handsomely, for the members could now say they knew of no organization whose purpose was to resist the law. Even without the committee's saying so, it was clear that counter reconstruction had been so successful that the new governments in the South could not stand without the most vigorous and direct support of the federal government. And if any of the Republican members had looked to the South for strong party support in the election of 1872, they must have been depressed by what they saw. The reconstruction governments were showing signs of collapse, and the party in power was collapsing even more rapidly.

Counter reconstruction was everywhere an overwhelming success. In the face of violence the Fourteenth and Fifteenth Amendments provided no protection for the Negro citizen and his friends. The federal enforcement laws of 1870 and 1871 proved wholly inadequate, especially when enforcement was left to the meager forces that remained in the South at the time of their enactment. Negroes could hardly be expected to continue to vote when it cost them not only their jobs but their lives. In one state after another, the Negro electorate declined steadily as the full force of the Klan came forward to supervise the elections that federal troops failed to supervise. Towns, counties, and states went Democratic. Overthrow of existing governments became systematic and inevitable. As early as April, 1868, the Democratic convention of South Carolina had said to the Negroes of the state, "It is impossible that your present power can endure, whether you use it for good or ill." Within two years this promise was well on its way to fulfilment in South Carolina and elsewhere.

While the success of counter reconstruction through violence was itself a kind of vindication of violence, it is now clear that reconstruction could have been overthrown even without the use of violence. Except for the exasperation of Grant in 1870 and the Enforcement Acts of 1870 and 1871, the federal government was, more and more, leaving the South to its own devices. Even more important was the enormous prestige that the former Confederates enjoyed. In time they were able to assume leadership in their communities without firing a shot or hanging a single Negro. What they lacked in political strength they made up in economic power. By discharging or threatening to discharge Negro employees who persisted in participating in politics, they could reduce the Negro electorate to a minimum. By refusing to pay taxes to support the expanded and inflated functions of the new governments, they could destroy Radical Reconstruction in a season. But the former Confederates relied on no one method. By political pressure, economic sanctions, *and* violence they brought Radical Reconstruction crashing down almost before it began.

The Black Peril

Southern racism was not always so covert and surreptitious as the kind practiced by the Klan. At times it came forward in unembarrassed bluntness. In the following speech, given on the floor of the Senate on January 21, 1907, Senator Ben Tillman of South Carolina presented an extraordinarily vivid picture of the type of thinking which stood in determined opposition to the aspirations of black people. The speech reveals the extent to which anti-black prejudice is often involved with sexual fear. It also reveals that such prejudice, because of its inherent hysteria, is beyond the reach of rational persuasion. Senator Tillman chose in this speech to direct his remarks against Senator John C. Spooner of Wisconsin; but he was actually speaking against someone else: the black people of America.

TACITUS TELLS US THAT THE "GERMANIC PEOPLE WERE EVER JEALOUS of the virtue of their women." Germans, Saxons, Englishmen, they are practically one, springing from the same great root. That trinity of words, the noblest and holiest in our language, womanhood, wifehood, motherhood, have Saxon origin. I believe with Wordsworth—it is my religion—"A mother is a mother still, the noblest thing alive."

And a man who speaks with lightness or flippancy or discusses cold-bloodedly a matter so vital as the purity and chastity of womanhood is a disgrace to his own mother and unworthy of the love of a good wife.

THE BLACK PERIL   Abridged from a speech delivered by Senator Ben Tillman. From the *Congressional Record*, 59th Congress, 2nd session, 1907, Volume XLI, pp. 1440–1444.

Look at our environment in the South, surrounded, and in a very large number of counties and in two States outnumbered, by the negroes —engulfed, as it were, in a black flood of semi-barbarians. Our farmers, living in segregated farmhouses, more or less thinly scattered through the country, have negroes on every hand. For forty years these have been taught the damnable heresy of equality with the white man, made the puppet of scheming politicians, the instrument for the furtherance of political ambitions. Some of them have just enough education to be able to read, but not always to understand what they read. Their minds are those of children, while they have the passions and strength of men. Taught that they are oppressed, and with breasts pulsating with hatred of the whites, the younger generation of negro men are roaming over the land, passing back and forth without hindrance, and with no possibility of adequate police protection to the communities in which they are residing.

Now let me suppose a case. Let us take any Senator on this floor—I will not particularize—take him from some great and well-ordered State in the North, where there are possibly twenty thousand negroes, as there are in Wisconsin, with over two million whites. Let us carry this Senator to the backwoods in South Carolina, put him on a farm miles from a town or railroad, and environed with negroes. We will suppose he has a fair young daughter just budding into womanhood; and recollect this, the white women of the South are in a state of siege; the greatest care is exercised that they shall at all times where it is possible not be left alone or unprotected, but that can not always and in every instance be the case. That Senator's daughter undertakes to visit a neighbor or is left home alone for a brief while. Some lurking demon who has watched for the opportunity seizes her; she is choked or beaten into insensibility and ravished, her body prostituted, her purity destroyed, her chastity taken from her, and a memory branded on her brain as with a red-hot iron to haunt her night and day as long as she lives. Moore has drawn us the picture in most graphic language:

> One fatal remembrance, one sorrow that throws
> Its bleak shade alike o'er our joys and our woes,
> To which life nothing darker or brighter can bring.
> For which joy hath no balm and affliction no sting.

In other words, a death in life. This young girl thus blighted and brutalized drags herself to her father and tells him what has happened. Is there a man here with red blood in his veins who doubts what impulses the father would feel? Is it any wonder that the whole countryside rises as one man and with set, stern faces seek the brute who has wrought this infamy? Brute, did I say? Why, Mr. President, this crime is a slander on the brutes. No beast of the field forces his female. He waits invitation. It has been left for something in the shape of a man to do this terrible thing. And shall such a creature, because he has the semblance of a man, appeal to the law? Shall men coldbloodedly stand up and demand for him the right to have a fair trial and be punished in the regular course of justice? So far as I am concerned he has put himself outside the pale of the law, human and divine. He has sinned against the Holy Ghost. He has invaded the holy of holies. He has struck civilization a blow, the most deadly and cruel that the imagination can conceive. It is idle to reason about it; it is idle to preach about it. Our brains reel under the staggering blow and hot blood surges to the heart. Civilization peels off us, any and all of us who are men, and we revert to the original savage type whose impulses under any and all such circumstances has always been to "kill! kill! kill!"

I do not know what the Senator from Wisconsin would do under these circumstances; neither do I care. I have three daughters, but, so help me God, I had rather find either one of them killed by a tiger or a bear and gather up her bones and bury them, conscious that she had died in the purity of her maidenhood, than have her crawl to me and tell me the horrid story that she had been robbed of the jewel of her womanhood by a black fiend. The wild beast would only obey the instinct of nature, and we would hunt him down and kill him just as soon as possible. What shall we do with a man who has outbruted the brute and committed an act which is more cruel than death? Try him? Drag the victim into court, for she alone can furnish legal evidence, and make her testify to the fearful ordeal through which she has passed, undergoing a second crucifixion?

. . .

Never in the history of the world has a high-spirited and chivalrous people been called on to face a more difficult and dangerous situation. That a crisis is approaching every thoughtful man must confess. That there is a promise of a safe or happy solution is doubted by all. The Senator from Wisconsin dismisses the question with a wave of the hand and with an admonition to me and others who think like me to keep quiet and be good, urging that he had originally advocated the force bill, but confessed that he was wrong, and that it is better it did not pass. He contends the southern people, black and white, must live together and that the rest of the nation have for the time being left the matter alone; that there has been no discussion among the Republicans in this Chamber such as marked his earlier service in the Senate upon the subject. He says he knows of no better way to precipitate a race conflict than to be always talking about one. And he holds me up as the greatest sinner in that regard. You can not pick up a paper any day but that you will find an appeal from some negro in the North, some convention, some resolution of some kind somewhere denouncing the wrongs done the negroes in the South and demanding justice for them. Those papers circulate in the South. They go everywhere. Our schools, supported by the taxes paid by the white people, are educating these negroes to read such appeals.

.   .   .

I realize that there are millions of good negroes, if they are let alone and not taught heresies and criminal thoughts and feelings and actions. I should like to see this good, easy, good for nothing people given a chance to live. Give them justice; give them equal rights before the law; enable them to get property and keep it, and be protected in its enjoyment; give them life, liberty, and the pursuit of happiness, provided their happiness does not destroy mine.

The Senator from Wisconsin read the other day, with great pathos and effect, the eloquent speech of Henry Grady. There is not a line or a sentence in that noble deliverance to which I do not subscribe. The negroes whom Grady described were the negroes of the old slave days —the negroes with whom he played in childhood, the negroes with whom I played in childhood, the negroes who knew they were inferior and who never presumed to assert equality. For these negroes there is throughout the South a universal feeling of respect and love. I have not got it here, but I have at my home in the city a photograph of one of these. I might term him "Old Black Joe," for he is a full-blooded negro, about 60 years old. He has been living with me thirty-five years. He now has the keys to my home in South Carolina. He has full charge and control over my stock, my plantation. He is in every way a shining example of what the negro can be and how he can get along with the white man peacefully and pleasantly and honorably, enjoying all of his liberties and rights. But he has never meddled with voting. He occupies the same attitude as the white man and the negro do in this District. They do not meddle with voting. I do not hesitate to say, however, that a more loyal friend no man ever had. Every child that I have would share his last crust with that negro to-morrow.

Grady spoke of the loyalty of the slaves during the war, and the Senator from Wisconsin amplified the picture in eloquent phrase. I myself, as a schoolboy of 13, saw the Confederate soldiers as they took their departure for the front to battle for home and liberty. I saw the parting between the husband and his family, kissing one after another of his children, saving the last kiss for the wife and mother, and then turning to the group of faithful slaves and shaking them by the hand, give the parting injunction, "Take care of your mistress and the children." How did the slaves redeem the promise? They all said "Yes, master." How they lived up to the promise history tells. There were in the South at that time 4,000,000 negroes, 800,000 males of adult age. The women and children of the white men who were in the Confederate army were left there, entirely helpless for support and protection, with these negroes. With 800,000 negro men, there is not of record a solitary instance of one white woman having been wronged until near the close of the war, when some of the negro soldiers who had been poisoned by contact with northern ideas come along and perpetrated some outrages.

The negro slave was true to the faith. When Sherman's army marched through South Carolina, leaving behind it a 40-mile breadth of burned houses, the chimneys marking where the habitations of the Confederate soldiers had been, every house that had a plank on it gone, the women and children turned out in the rain and sleet of February to find shelter in the negro cabins, everything to eat burned or having been seized and carried off by the army, I knew some of these slaves to go behind in the track of the army and rake up the corn off the ground where the horses had been fed, wash it and dry it and carry it to the starving wives and children of the white men of the South.

Talk to me about hating these people! I do not do it. We took them as barbarians, fresh from Africa, the first generation we will say, or some of them twice removed, some of them once removed, some of them thrice removed, some of them a fourth removed from barbarism, but the bulk of them only twice. We taught them that there was a God. We gave them what little knowledge of civilization they have to-day. We taught them to tell the truth. We taught them not to steal. We gave them those characteristics which differentiate the barbarian and savage from the civilized man.

·   ·   ·

In 1865 the South, prostrate and bleeding and helpless, a very Niobe of nations, had the dead carcass of slavery chained to it by the fourteenth and fifteenth amendments. For eight years two States labored under it. One after another the others had thrown off for a little while the incubus —not getting loose, but simply getting relief, being able to stand up, to move, to breathe, and to make some progress. But there the carcass hangs, riveted to our civilization. The putrefaction is going on. A return to barbarism is evident in every day of our contact with these people in the South. Relieved from police control, they are no longer compelled, as the Indians have been by the troops, to stay on their reservations. These negroes move where they please. They have a little smattering of education. Some of them have white blood in their veins and taught that they are as good as the white man, they ask, Why not as good as a white woman? And when caste feeling and race pride and every instinct that influences and controls the white women makes them spurn the thought, rape follows. Murder and rape become a monomania. The negro becomes a fiend in human form.

We can not police those people to-day under the fourteenth amendment without taking from the whites their own liberties. In my desperation to seek some remedy to prevent rape and not have the necessity of avenging rape, I have gone so far as to plead with the people of the South to inaugurate a passport system, by which we should keep in control and under supervision all of the wandering classes, white and black.

Race hatred grows day by day. There is no man who is honest, going through the South and conversing with the white people and blacks, but will return and tell you this is true.

Some of the negroes have a good excuse. I will not dispute it. If I were negro I would do probably as they do, but being a white man, I do just as I am doing, and I expect to do so, so help me God, as long as I have breath in my body.

Then I say to you of the North, who are the rulers of the land, who can change this or do something to relieve conditions, what are you going to do about it? Are you going to sit quiet? If nothing else will cause you to think, I notify you, what you already know, that there are a billion dollars or more of northern capital invested in the South in railroads, in mines, in forests, in farm lands, and self-interest, if nothing else, ought to make you set about hunting some remedy for this terrible situation.

C. VANN WOODWARD

Capitulation to Racism

A more complete portrayal of the racist forces which the black American faced is given here by the noted historian, C. Vann Woodward. He shows that the very segregationist measures which some Southerners had once thought mere fantasies became realities at the turn of the century. He shows also that the North, having already compromised the aims of Radical Reconstruction, played its part in allowing racism to assume full power. While the Supreme Court was ruling in favor of certain segregationist policies, the nation as a whole decided that it could not afford to defend the rights of the black man in America at the same time that it was waging racist wars in other lands. Facing pressure from the South and the implications of its foreign imperialism, the United States yielded to Jim Crow.

Up TO THE YEAR 1898 SOUTH CAROLINA HAD RESISTED THE JIM CROW car movement which had swept the western states of the South completely by that time. In that year, however, after several attempts, the proponents of the Jim Crow law were on the eve of victory. The Charleston *News and Courier,* the oldest newspaper in the South and a consistent spokesman of conservatism, fired a final broadside against extremists in behalf of the conservative creed of race policy.

'As we have got on fairly well for a third of a century, including a long period of reconstruction, without such a measure,' wrote the editor, 'we can probably get on as well hereafter without it, and certainly so extreme a measure should not be adopted and enforced without added and urgent cause.' He then called attention to what he considered the absurd consequences to which such a law might lead once the principle of the thing were conceded.

> If there must be Jim Crow cars on the railroads, there should be Jim Crow cars on the street railways. Also on all passenger boats. . . . If there are to be Jim Crow cars, moreover, there should be Jim Crow waiting saloons at all stations, and Jim Crow eating houses. . . .

CAPITULATION TO RACISM   From *The Strange Career of Jim Crow;* Second Revised Edition, by C. Vann Woodward. Copyright © 1966 by Oxford University Press, Inc. Reprinted by permission.

There should be Jim Crow sections of the jury box, and a separate Jim Crow dock and witness stand in every court—and a Jim Crow Bible for colored witnesses to kiss. It would be advisable also to have a Jim Crow section in county auditors' and treasurers' offices for the accommodation of colored taxpayers. The two races are dreadfully mixed in these offices for weeks every year, especially about Christmas. . . . There should be a Jim Crow department for making returns and paying for the privileges and blessings of citizenship. Perhaps, the best plan would be, after all, to take the short cut to the general end . . . by establishing two or three Jim Crow counties at once, and turning them over to our colored citizens for their special and exclusive accommodation.

In resorting to the tactics of *reductio ad absurdum* the editor doubtless believed that he had dealt the Jim Crow principle a telling blow with his heavy irony. But there is now apparent to us an irony in his argument of which the author was unconscious. For what he intended as a *reductio ad absurdum* and obviously regarded as an absurdity became in a very short time a reality, and not only that but a reality that was regarded as the only sensible solution to a vexing problem, a solution having the sanction of tradition and long usage. Apart from the Jim Crow counties and Jim Crow witness stand, all the improbable applications of the principle suggested by the editor in derision had been put into practice—down to and including the Jim Crow Bible.

The South's adoption of extreme racism was due not so much to a conversion as it was to a relaxation of the opposition. All the elements of fear, jealousy, proscription, hatred, and fanaticism had long been present, as they are present in various degrees of intensity in any society. What enabled them to rise to dominance was not so much cleverness or ingenuity as it was a general weakening and discrediting of the numerous forces that had hitherto kept them in check. The restraining forces included not only Northern liberal opinion of the press, the courts, and the government, but also internal checks imposed by the prestige and influence of the Southern conservatives, as well as by the idealism and zeal of the Southern radicals. What happened toward the end of the century was an almost simultaneous—and sometimes not unrelated—decline in the effectiveness of restraint that had been exercised by all three forces: Northern liberalism, Southern conservatism, and Southern radicalism.

The acquiescence of Northern liberalism in the Compromise of 1877 defined the beginning, but not the ultimate extent, of the liberal retreat on the race issue. The Compromise merely left the freedman to the custody of the conservative Redeemers upon their pledge that they would protect him in his constitutional rights. But as these pledges were forgotten or violated and the South veered toward proscription and extremism, Northern opinion shifted to the right, keeping pace with the South, conceding point after point, so that at no time were the sections very far apart on race policy. The failure of the liberals to resist this trend was due in part to political factors. Since reactionary politicians and their cause were identified with the bloody-shirt issue and the demagogic exploitation of sectional animosities, the liberals naturally felt themselves strongly drawn toward the cause of sectional reconciliation. And since the Negro was the symbol of sectional strife, the liberals joined in deprecating further agitation of his cause and in defending the Southern view of race in its less extreme forms. It was quite common in the 'eighties and 'nineties to find in the *Nation, Harper's Weekly,* the *North American Review,* or the *Atlantic Monthly* Northern liberals and former abolitionists mouthing the shibboleths of white supremacy regarding the Negro's innate inferiority, shiftlessness, and hopeless unfitness for full participation in the white man's civilization. Such expressions doubtless did much to add to the reconciliation of North and South, but they did so at the expense of the Negro. Just as the Negro gained his emancipation and new rights through a falling out between white men, he now stood to lose his rights through the reconciliation of white men.

The cumulative weakening of resistance to racism was expressed also in a succession of decisions by the United States Supreme Court between 1873 and 1898 that require no review here. In the *Slaughter House Cases* of 1873 and in *United States* v. *Reese* and *United States* v. *Cruikshank* in 1876, the court drastically curtailed the privileges and immunities recognized as being under federal protection. It continued the trend in its decision on the *Civil Rights Cases* of 1883 by virtually nullifying the restrictive parts of the Civil Rights Act. By a species of what Justice Harlan in his dissent described as 'subtle and ingenious verbal criticism,' the court held that the Fourteenth Amendment gave Congress power to restrain states but not individuals from acts of racial discrimination and segregation. The court, like the liberals, was engaged in a bit of reconciliation—reconciliation between federal and state jurisdiction, as well as between North and South, reconciliation also achieved at the Negro's expense. Having ruled in a previous case (*Hall* v. *de Cuir,* 1877) that a state could not *prohibit* segregation on a common carrier, the Court in 1890 (*Louisville, New Orleans, and Texas Railroad* v.

Mississippi) ruled that a state could constitutionally *require* segregation on carriers. In *Plessy* v. *Ferguson,* decided in 1896, the Court subscribed to the doctrine that 'legislation is powerless to eradicate racial instincts' and laid down the 'separate but equal' rule for the justification of segregation. Two years later, in 1898, in *Williams* v. *Mississippi* the Court completed the opening of the legal road to proscription, segregation, and disfranchisement by approving the Mississippi plan for depriving Negroes of the franchise.

For a short time after the Supreme Court decision of 1883 that held the restrictive parts of the Civil Rights Act unconstitutional, Northern legislatures showed a disposition to protect the rights of Negroes by state action. In the mid-'eighties thirteen states adopted civil rights laws of this sort. In Indiana, however, a study by Emma Lou Thornbrough finds that 'In practice the law proved to be ineffectual in accomplishing its state purpose, and racial patterns [of segregation] remained unchanged by its passage.' The same historian goes further to say that 'Throughout the North there was not only acquiescence among the white population in the 'Southern Way' of solving the race problem but a tendency to imitate it in practice.'

Then, in the year 1898, the United States plunged into imperialistic adventures overseas under the leadership of the Republican party. These adventures in the Pacific and the Caribbean suddenly brought under the jurisdiction of the United States some eight million people of the colored races, 'a varied assortment of inferior races,' as the *Nation* described them, 'which, of course, could not be allowed to vote.' As America shouldered the White Man's Burden, she took up at the same time many Southern attitudes on the subject of race. 'If the stronger and cleverer race,' said the editor of the *Atlantic Monthly,* 'is free to impose its will upon "new-caught, sullen peoples" on the other side of the globe, why not in South Carolina and Mississippi?' The doctrines of Anglo-Saxon superiority by which Professor John W. Burgess of Columbia University, Captain Alfred T. Mahan of the United States Navy, and Senator Albert Beveridge of Indiana justified and rationalized American imperialism in the Philippines, Hawaii, and Cuba differed in no essentials from the race theories by which Senator Benjamin R. Tillman of South Carolina and Senator James K. Vardaman of Mississippi justified white supremacy in the South. The Boston Evening *Transcript* of 14 January 1899, admitted that Southern race policy was 'now the policy of the Administration of the very party which carried the country into and through a civil war to free the slave.' And *The New York Times* of 10 May 1900 reported editorially that 'Northern men . . . no longer denounce the suppression of the Negro vote [in the South] as it used to be denounced in the reconstruction days. The necessity of it under the supreme law of self-preservation is candidly recognized.'

In the South leaders of the white-supremacy movement thoroughly grasped and expounded the implication of the new imperialism for their domestic policies. 'No Republican leader,' declared Senator Tillman,

> not even Governor Roosevelt, will now dare to wave the bloody shirt and preach a crusade against the South's treatment of the negro. The North has a bloody shirt of its own. Many thousands of them have been made into shrouds for murdered Filipinos, done to death because they were fighting for liberty.

And the junior Senator from South Carolina, John J. McLaurin, thanked Senator George F. Hoar of Massachusetts 'for his complete announcement of the divine right of the Caucasian to govern the inferior races,' a position which 'most amply vindicated the South.' Hilary A. Herbert, an advocate of complete disfranchisement of the Negro in Alabama, rejoiced in May 1900 that 'we have now the sympathy of thoughtful men in the North to an extent that never before existed.'

At the very time that imperialism was sweeping the country, the doctrine of racism reached a crest of acceptability and popularity among respectable scholarly and intellectual circles. At home and abroad biologists, sociologists, anthropologists, and historians, as well as journalists and novelists, gave support to the doctrine that races were discrete entities and that the "Anglo-Saxon" or "Caucasian" was the superior of them all. It was not that Southern politicians needed any support from learned circles to sustain their own doctrines, but they found that such intellectual endorsement of their racist theories facilitated acceptance of their views and policies.

At the dawn of the new century the wave of Southern racism came in as a swell upon a mounting tide of national sentiment and was very much a part of that sentiment. Had the tide been running the other way, the Southern wave would have broken feebly instead of becoming a wave of the future.

·   ·   ·

Having served as the national scapegoat in the reconciliation and reunion of North and South, the Negro was now pressed into service as a sectional scapegoat in the reconciliation of estranged white classes and the reunion of the Solid South. The bitter violence and blood-letting recrimination of the campaigns between white conservatives and white radicals in the 'nineties had opened wounds that could not be healed by ordinary political nostrums and free-silver slogans. The only formula powerful enough to accomplish that was the magical formula of white supremacy, applied without stint and without any of the old conservative reservations of paternalism, without deference to any lingering resistance of Northern liberalism, or any fear of further check from a defunct Southern Populism.

The first step in applying the formula was the total disfranchisement of the Negro. In part this was presented as a guarantee that in the future neither of the white factions would violate the white man's peace by rallying the Negro's support against the other. In part disfranchisement was also presented as a progressive reform, the sure means of purging Southern elections of the corruption that disgraced them. The disgrace and public shame of this corruption were more widely and keenly appreciated than the circuitous and paradoxical nature of the proposed reform. To one Virginian, however, it did seem that disfranchising the Negroes 'to prevent the Democratic election officials from stealing their votes' would be 'to punish the man who has been injured'—a topsy-turvy justice at best. In no mood for paradoxes, Southerners generally accepted Negro disfranchisement as a reform, without taking second thought.

The standard devices for accomplishing disfranchisement on a racial basis and evading the restrictions of the Constitution were invented by Mississippi, a pioneer of the movement and the only state that resorted to it before the Populist revolt took the form of political rebellion. Other states elaborated the original scheme and added devices of their own contriving, though there was a great deal of borrowing and inter-change of ideas throughout the South. First of all the plan set up certain barriers such as property or literacy qualifications for voting, and then cut certain loopholes in the barrier through which only white men could squeeze. The loopholes to appease (though not invariably accommo-date) the underprivileged whites were the 'understanding clause,' the 'grandfather clause,' or the 'good character clause.' Some variation of the scheme was incorporated into the constitutions of South Carolina in 1895, Louisiana in 1898, North Carolina in 1900, Alabama in 1901, Virginia in 1902, Georgia in 1908, and Oklahoma in 1910. The restric-tions imposed by these devices were enormously effective in decimating the Negro vote, but in addition all these states as well as the remaining members of the old Confederacy—Florida, Tennessee, Arkansas, and Texas—adopted the poll tax. With its cumulative features and procedures artfully devised to discourage payment, the poll tax was esteemed at first by some of its proponents as the most reliable means of curtailing the franchise—not only among the Negroes but among objectionable whites as well.

But if the Negroes did learn to read, or acquire sufficient property, and remember to pay the poll tax and to keep the receipt on file, they could even then be tripped by the final hurdle devised for them—the white primary. Another of the fateful paradoxes that seemed to dog the history of the progressive movement in the South, the primary system was undoubtedly an improvement over the old convention system and did much to democratize nominations and party control. But along with the progressively inspired primary system were adopted the oppositely inspired party rules, local regulations, and in some cases state laws excluding the minority race from participation and converting the primary into a white man's club. This perverse 'reform' usually followed hard upon, though sometimes preceded, the disfranchisement 'reform.' The state-wide Democratic primary was adopted in South Carolina in 1896, Arkansas in 1897, Georgia in 1898, Florida and Tennessee in 1901, Alabama and Mississippi in 1902, Kentucky and Texas in 1903, Louisiana in 1906, Oklahoma in 1907, Virginia in 1913, and North Carolina in 1915.

The effectiveness of disfranchisement is suggested by a comparison of the number of registered Negro voters in Louisiana in 1896, when there were 130,334 and in 1904, when there were 1,342. Between the two dates the literacy, property, and poll-tax qualifications were adopted. In 1896 Negro registrants were in a majority in twenty-six parishes—by 1900 in none.

In spite of the ultimate success of disfranchisement, the movement met with stout resistance and succeeded in some states by narrow margins or the use of fraud. In order to overcome the opposition and divert the suspicions of the poor and illiterate whites that they as well as the Negro were in danger of losing the franchise—a suspicion that often proved justified—the leaders of the movement resorted to an intensive propaganda of white supremacy, Negrophobia, and race chauvinism. Such a campaign preceded and accompanied disfranchisement in each state. In some of them it had been thirty years or more since the reign of the carpetbagger, but the legend of Reconstruction was revived, refurbished, and relived by the propagandists as if it were an immediate background of the current crisis. A new generation of Southerners was as forcibly impressed with the sectional trauma as if they had lived through it themselves. Symbols and paraphernalia of the Redemption drama were patched up and donned by twentieth-century wearers. Boys who had been born since General U. S. Grant was laid in his tomb paraded in the red shirts of their fathers, and popular Southern novelists glamorized the history of the Ku Klux Klan, the Knights of the White Camelia, and the heroes of the struggle for Home Rule.

.   .   .

Within this context of growing pessimism, mounting tension, and unleashed phobias the structure of segregation and discrimination was extended by the adoption of a great number of the Jim Crow type of laws. Up to 1900 the only law of this type adopted by the majority of Southern states was that applying to passengers aboard trains. And South Carolina did not adopt that until 1898,[1] North Carolina in 1899, and Virginia, the last, in 1900. Only three states had required or authorized the Jim Crow waiting room in railway stations before 1899, but in the next decade nearly all of the other Southern states fell in line. The adoption of laws applying to new subjects tended to take place in waves of popularity. Street cars had been common in Southern cities since the eighties, but only Georgia had a segregation law applying to them before the end of the century. Then in quick succession North Carolina and Virginia adopted such a law in 1901, Louisiana in 1902, Arkansas, South Carolina, and Tennessee in 1903, Mississippi and Maryland in 1904, Florida in 1905, and Oklahoma in 1907. These laws referred to separation within cars, but a Montgomery city ordinance of 1906 was the first to require a completely separate Jim Crow street car. During these years the older seaboard states of the South also extended the segregation laws to steamboats.

The mushroom growth of discriminatory and segregation laws during the first two decades of this century piled up a huge bulk of legislation. Much of the code was contributed by city ordinances or by local regulations and rules enforced without the formality of laws. Only a sampling is possible here. For up and down the avenues and byways of Southern life appeared with increasing profusion the little signs: 'Whites Only' or 'Colored.' Sometimes the law prescribed their dimensions in inches, and in one case the kind and color of paint. Many appeared without requirement by law—over entrances and exits, at theaters and boarding houses, toilets and water fountains, waiting rooms and ticket windows.

A large body of law grew up concerned with the segregation of em-

---

[1] For first-class coaches only, and not until 1900 was the law amended to apply to second class as well.

ployees and their working conditions. The South Carolina code of 1915, with subsequent elaborations, prohibited textile factories from permitting laborers of different races from working together in the same room, or using the same entrances, pay windows, exits, doorways, stairways, 'or windows [sic]' at the same time, or the same 'lavatories, toilets, drinking water buckets, pails, cups, dippers or glasses' at any time. Exceptions were made of firemen, floor scrubbers, and repair men, who were permitted association with the white proletarian elite on an emergency basis. In most instances segregation in employment was established without the aid of statute. And in many crafts and trades the written or unwritten policies of Jim Crow unionism made segregation superfluous by excluding Negroes from employment.

State institutions for the care of the dependent or incapacitated were naturally the subject of more legislation than private institutions of the same sort, but ordinarily the latter followed pretty closely the segregation practices of the public institutions. Both types had usually made it a practice all along. The fact that only Mississippi and South Carolina specifically provided by law for general segregation in hospitals does not indicate that non-segregation was the rule in the hospitals of other states. The two states named also required Negro nurses for Negro patients, and Alabama prohibited white female nurses from attending Negro male patients. Thirteen Southern and border states required the separation of patients by races in mental hospitals, and ten states specified segregation of inmates in penal institutions. Some of the latter went into detail regarding the chaining, transportation, feeding, and working of the prisoners on a segregated basis. Segregation of the races in homes for the aged, the indigent, the orphans, the blind, the deaf, and the dumb was the subject of numerous state laws.

Much ingenuity and effort went into the separation of the races in their amusements, diversions, recreations and sports. The Separate Park Law of Georgia, adopted in 1905, appears to have been the first venture of a state legislature into this field, though city ordinances and local custom were quite active in pushing the Negro out of the public parks. Circuses and tent shows, including side shows, fell under a law adopted by Louisiana in 1914, which required separate entrances, exits, ticket windows, and ticket sellers that would be kept at least twenty-five feet apart. The city of Birmingham applied the principle to 'any room, hall, theatre, picture house, auditorium, yard, court, ball park, or other indoor or outdoor place' and specified that the races be 'distinctly separated . . . by well defined physical barriers.' North Carolina and Virginia interdicted all fraternal orders or societies that permitted members of both races to address each other as brother.

Residential segregation in cities, still rare in the older seaboard towns, developed along five different patterns in the second decade of the century. The type originating in Baltimore in 1910 designated all-white and all-Negro blocks in areas occupied by both races. This experiment was imitated in Atlanta and Greenville. Virginia sought to legalize segregation by a state law that authorized city councils to divide territories into segregated districts and to prohibit either race from living in the other's district, a method adopted by Roanoke and Portsmouth, Virginia. The third method, invented by Richmond, designated blocks throughout the city black or white according to the majority of the residents and forbade any person to live in any block 'where the majority of residents on such streets are occupied by those with whom said person is forbidden to intermarry.' This one was later copied by Ashland, Virginia, and Winston-Salem, North Carolina. A still more complicated law originated in Norfolk, which applied to both mixed and unmixed blocks and fixed the color status by ownership as well as occupancy. And finally New Orleans developed a law requiring a person of either race to secure consent of the majority of persons living in an area before establishing a residence therein. After these devices were frustrated by a Supreme Court decision in 1917, attempts continued to be made to circumvent the decision. Probably the most effective of these was the restrictive covenant, a private contract limiting the sale of property in an area to purchasers of the favored race.

The most prevalent and widespread segregation of living areas was accomplished without need for legal sanction. The black ghettos of the 'Darktown' slums in every Southern city were the consequence mainly of the Negro's economic status, his relegation to the lowest rung of the ladder. Smaller towns sometimes excluded Negro residents completely simply by letting it be known in forceful ways that their presence would not be tolerated. In 1914 there were six such towns in Texas, five in Oklahoma, and two in Alabama. On the other hand there were by that time some thirty towns in the South, besides a number of unincorporated settlements, inhabited exclusively by Negroes. In August 1913, Clarence Poe, editor of the *Progressive Farmer*, secured the unanimous endorsement of a convention of the North Carolina Farmer's Union for a movement to segregate the races in rural districts.

The extremes to which caste penalties and separation were carried in parts of the South could hardly find a counterpart short of the latitudes of India and South Africa. In 1909 Mobile passed a curfew law applying exclusively to Negroes and requiring them to be off the streets by 10 p.m. The Oklahoma legislature in 1915 authorized its Corporation Commission to require telephone companies 'to maintain separate booths for white and colored patrons.' North Carolina and Florida required that textbooks used by the public-school children of one race be kept separate from those used by the other, and the Florida law specified separation even while the books were in storage. South Carolina for a time segregated a third caste by establishing separate schools for mulatto as well as for white and Negro children. A New Orleans ordinance segregated white and Negro prostitutes in separate districts. Ray Stannard Baker found Jim Crow Bibles for Negro witnesses in Atlanta courts and Jim Crow elevators for Negro passengers in Atlanta buildings.

IDA B. WELLS

Lynching Bee

Lynching served as the ultimate manifestation of a deeply harbored hatred of black people. As writers James Weldon Johnson, Jean Toomer, Richard Wright, and James Baldwin have all suggested, lynching in the South was a kind of cathartic, communal, and semi-religious ritual. As such, it encouraged the dangerous feeling that some men are indeed beyond the range of humanity, and allowed the self-righteous to feel that they could accomplish true justice in one swift and horrific act.

In the following selection, the noted black journalist, Ida B. Wells, recreates the circumstances surrounding one particularly brutal "lynching bee." What she describes, however, was by no means an isolated act. In the 1880s and 1890s, there were well over a hundred lynchings a year. Like other forms of racism, mob murder became a social institution.

NEVER IN THE HISTORY OF CIVILIZATION HAS ANY CHRISTIAN PEOPLE stooped to such shocking brutality and indescribable barbarism as that which characterized the people of Paris, Texas, and adjacent communities on the 1st of February, 1893. The cause of this awful outbreak of

LYNCHING BEE by Ida B. Wells. From *A Red Record: Lynchings in the United States 1892–1893–1894* by Ida B. Wells (Chicago, 1895).

human passion was the murder of a four year old child, daughter of a man named Vance. This man, Vance, had been a police officer in Paris for years, and was known to be a man of bad temper, overbearing manner and given to harshly treating the prisoners under his care. He had arrested Smith and, it is said, cruelly mistreated him. Whether or not the murder of his child was an act of fiendish revenge, it has not been shown, but many persons who know of the incident have suggested that the secret of the attack on the child lay in a desire for revenge against its father.

In the same town there lived a Negro, named Henry Smith, a well known character, a kind of roustabout, who was generally considered a harmless, weak-minded fellow, not capable of doing any important work, but sufficiently able to do chores and odd jobs around the houses of the white people who cared to employ him. A few days before the final tragedy, this man, Smith, was accused of murdering Myrtle Vance. The crime of murder was of itself bad enough, and to prove that against Smith would have been amply sufficient in Texas to have committed him to the gallows, but the finding of the child so exasperated the father and his friends, that they at once shamefully exaggerated the facts and declared that the babe had been ruthlessly assaulted and then killed. The truth was bad enough, but the white people of the community made it a point to exaggerate every detail of the awful affair, and to inflame the public mind so that nothing less than immediate and violent death would satisfy the populace. As a matter of fact, the child was not brutally assaulted as the world has been told in excuse for the awful barbarism of that day. Persons who saw the child after its death, have stated, under the most solemn pledge to truth, that there was no evidence of such an assault as was published at that time, only a slight abrasion and discoloration was noticeable and that mostly about the neck. In spite of this fact, so eminent a man as Bishop Haygood deliberately and, it must also appear, maliciously falsified the fact by stating that the child was torn limb from limb, or to quote in his own words, "First outraged with demoniacal cruelty and then taken by her heels and torn asunder in the mad wantonness of gorilla ferocity."[1]

Nothing is farther from the truth than that statement. It is a cold blooded, deliberate, brutal falsehood which this Christian (?) Bishop uses to bolster up the infamous plea that the people of Paris were driven

---

[1] Bishop Atticus Green Haygood of the Methodist Episcopal Church, South, president of Emory College and director of the John F. Slater Fund's educational program for Negroes in the South, wrote on lynching in "The Black Shadow in the South," *The Forum*, XVI (October, 1893), 167–175.

to insanity by learning that the little child had been viciously assaulted, choked to death, and then torn to pieces by a demon in human form. It was a brutal murder, but no more brutal than hundreds of murders which occur in this country, and which have been equalled every year in fiendishness and brutality, and for which the death penalty is prescribed by law and inflicted only after the person has been legally adjudged guilty of the crime. Those who knew Smith, believe that Vance had at some time given him cause to seek revenge and that this fearful crime was the outgrowth of his attempt to avenge himself of some real or fancied wrong. That the murderer was known as an imbecile, had no effect whatever upon the people who thirsted for his blood. They determined to make an example of him and proceeded to carry out their purpose with unspeakably greater ferocity than that which characterized the half crazy object of their revenge.

For a day or so after the child was found in the woods, Smith remained in the vicinity as if nothing had happened, and when finally becoming aware that he was suspected, he made an attempt to escape. He was apprehended, however, not far from the scene of his crime and the news flashed across the country that the white Christian people of Paris, Texas and the communities thereabout had deliberately determined to lay aside all forms of law and inaugurate an entirely new form of punishment for the murder. They absolutely refused to make any inquiry as to the sanity or insanity of their prisoner, but set the day and hour when in the presence of assembled thousands they put their helpless victim to the stake, tortured him, and then burned him to death for the delectation and satisfaction of Christian people.

Lest it might be charged that any description of the deeds of that day are exaggerated, a white man's description which was published in the white journals of this country is used. The *New York Sun* of February 2d, 1893, contains an account, from which we make the following excerpt:

PARIS, TEX., Feb. 1, 1893.—Henry Smith, the negro ravisher of 4-year-old Myrtle Vance, has expiated in part his awful crime by death at the stake. Ever since the perpetration of his awful crime this city and the entire surrounding country has been in a wild frenzy of excitement. When the news came last night that he had been captured at Hope, Ark., that he had been identified by B. B. Sturgeon, James T. Hicks, and many other of the Paris searching party, the city was wild with joy over the apprehension of the brute. Hundreds of people poured into the city from the adjoining country and the word passed from lip to lip that the punishment of the fiend should fit the crime—that death by fire was the

penalty Smith should pay for the most atrocious murder and terrible outrage in Texas history. Curious and sympathizing alike, they came on
train and wagons, on horse, and on foot to see if the frail mind of a man
could think of a way to sufficiently punish the perpetrator of so terrible a
crime. Whisky shops were closed, unruly mobs were dispersed, schools
were dismissed by a proclamation from the mayor, and everything was
done in a business-like manner.

About 2 o'clock Friday a mass meeting was called at the courthouse
and captains appointed to search for the child. She was found mangled
beyond recognition, covered with leaves and brush as above mentioned.
As soon as it was learned upon the recovery of the body that the crime
was so atrocious the whole town turned out in the chase. The railroads
put up bulletins offering free transportation to all who would join in the
search. Posses went in every direction, and not a stone was left unturned.
Smith was tracked to Detroit on foot, where he jumped on a freight train
and left for his old home in Hempstead County, Arkansas. To this
county he was tracked and yesterday captured at Clow, a flag station on
the Arkansas & Louisiana railway about twenty miles north of Hope.
Upon being questioned the fiend denied everything, but upon being
stripped for examination his undergarments were seen to be spattered
with blood and a part of his shirt was torn off. He was kept under heavy
guard at Hope last night, and later on confessed the crime.

This morning he was brought through Texarkana, where 5,000 people awaited the train. . . . At that place speeches were made by prominent Paris citizens, who asked that the prisoner be not molested by
Texarkana people, but that the guard be allowed to deliver him up to the
outraged and indignant citizens of Paris. Along the road the train
gathered strength from the various towns, the people crowded upon the
platforms and tops of coaches anxious to see the lynching and the negro
who was soon to be delivered to an infuriated mob.

Arriving here at 12 o'clock the train was met by a surging mass of
humanity 10,000 strong. The negro was placed upon a carnival float
in mockery of a king upon his throne, and, followed by an immense
crowd, was escorted through the city so that all might see the most inhuman monster known in current history. The line of march was up
Main street to the square, around the square down Clarksville street to
Church street, thence to the open prairies about 300 yards from the
Texas & Pacific depot. Here Smith was placed upon a scaffold, six feet
square and ten feet high, securely bound, within the view of all be-
holders. Here the victim was tortured for fifty minutes by red-hot iron
brands thrust against his quivering body. Commencing at the feet the

brands were placed against him inch by inch until they were thrust against the face. Then, being apparently dead, kerosene was poured upon him, cottonseed hulls placed beneath him and set on fire. In less time than it take to relate it, the tortured man was wafted beyond the grave to another fire, hotter and more terrible than the one just experienced.

Curiosity seekers have carried away already all that was left of the memorable event, even to pieces of charcoal. The cause of the crime was that Henry Vance when a deputy policeman, in the course of his duty was called to arrest Henry Smith for being drunk and disorderly. The Negro was unruly, and Vance was forced to use his club. The Negro swore vengeance, and several times assaulted Vance. In his greed for revenge, last Thursday, he grabbed up the little girl and committed the crime. The father is prostrated with grief and the mother now lies at death's door, but she has lived to see the slayer of her innocent babe suffer the most horrible death that could be conceived.

Words to describe the awful torture inflicted upon Smith cannot be found. The Negro, for a long time after starting on the journey to Paris, did not realize his plight. At last when he was told that he must die by slow torture he begged for protection. His agony was awful. He pleaded and writhed in bodily and mental pain. Scarcely had the train reached Paris than this torture commenced. His clothes were torn off piecemeal and scattered in the crowd, people catching the shreds and putting them away as mementos. The child's father, her brother, and two uncles then gathered about the Negro as he lay fastened to the torture platform and thrust hot irons into his quivering flesh. It was horrible—the man dying by slow torture in the midst of smoke from his own burning flesh.

BOOKER T. WASHINGTON

Atlanta Exposition Address

In the face of Jim Crow and lynching, black people, especially in the South, were powerless. Enunciating this sense of helplessness, Booker T. Washington gained immense support, from both blacks and whites. In his time, he became the most important black leader in the country, primarily because whites found his message of gradualism, compromise, and conciliation attractive. Washington believed that entrenched white hostility would disappear with time and with evidence of real black achievement within the framework of the *status quo*. He asked black people to be patient and work diligently. The following speech, delivered at the opening of The Cotton States and International Exposition at Atlanta in 1895, shows how determined Washington was to separate economic progress from political freedom. He responded to the mood of the United States at the beginning of the twentieth century, and, according to his critics, helped perpetuate it.

ONE THIRD OF THE POPULATION OF THE SOUTH IS OF THE NEGRO RACE. No enterprise seeking the material, civil, or moral welfare of this section can disregard this element of our population and reach the highest success. I but convey to you, Mr. President and Directors, the sentiment of the masses of my race when I say that in no way have the value and manhood of the American Negro been more fittingly and generously recognized than by the managers of this magnificent Exposition at every stage of its progress. It is a recognition that will do more to cement the friendship of the two races than any occurrence since the dawn of our freedom.

Not only this, but the opportunity here afforded will awaken among us a new era of industrial progress. Ignorant and inexperienced, it is not strange that in the first years of our new life we began at the top instead of at the bottom; that a seat in Congress or the state legislature was more sought than real estate or industrial skill; that the political conven-

ATLANTA EXPOSITION ADDRESS From *Up from Slavery: An Autobiography* by Booker T. Washington (New York: Doubleday, Page and Co., 1901).

tion or stump-speaking had more attraction than starting a dairy farm or truck garden.

A ship lost at sea for many days suddenly sighted a friendly vessel. From the mast of the unfortunate vessel was seen a signal: "Water, water; we die of thirst!" The answer from the friendly vessel at once came back: "Cast down your bucket where you are." A second time the signal, "Water, water; send us water!" ran up from the distressed vessel, and was answered: "Cast down your bucket where you are." And a third and fourth signal for water was answered, "Cast down your bucket where you are." The captain of the distressed vessel, at last heeding the injunction, cast down his bucket, and it came up full of fresh, sparkling water from the mouth of the Amazon River. To those of my race who depend upon bettering their condition in a foreign land, or who under-estimate the importance of cultivating friendly relations with the South-ern white man who is their next-door neighbor, I would say: "Cast down your bucket where you are"—cast it down in making friends, in every manly way, of the people of all races by whom we are surrounded.

Cast it down in agriculture, mechanics, in commerce, in domestic service, and in the professions. And in this connection it is well to bear in mind that whatever other sins the South may be called to bear, when it comes to business, pure and simple, it is in the South that the Negro is given a man's chance in the commercial world, and in nothing is this Exposition more eloquent than in emphasizing this chance. Our greatest danger is that in the great leap from slavery to freedom we may overlook the fact that the masses of us are to live by the productions of our hands, and fail to keep in mind that we shall prosper in proportion as we learn to dignify and glorify common labor, and put brains and skill into the common occupations of life; shall prosper in proportion as we learn to draw the line between the superficial and the substantial, the ornamental gewgaws of life and the useful. No race can prosper till it learns that there is as much dignity in tilling a field as in writing a poem. It is at the bottom of life we must begin, and not at the top. Nor should we permit our grievances to overshadow our opportunities.

To those of the white race who look to the incoming of those of foreign birth and strange tongue and habits for the prosperity of the South, were I permitted I would repeat what I say to my own race, "Cast down your bucket where you are." Cast it down among the eight million Negroes whose habits you know, whose fidelity and love you have tested in days when to have proved treacherous meant the ruin of your firesides. Cast down your bucket among these people who have, without strikes and labor wars, tilled your fields, cleared your forests, builded your railroads and cities, brought forth treasures from the bowels of the earth, and helped make possible this magnificent representation of the progress of the South. Casting down your bucket among my people, helping and encouraging them as you are doing on these grounds, and to education of head, hand, and heart, you will find that they will buy your surplus land, make blossom the waste places in your fields, and run your factories. While doing this, you can be sure in the future, as in the past, that you and your families will be surrounded by the most patient, faithful, law-abiding, and unresentful people that the world has seen. As we have proved our loyalty to you in the past, in nursing your children, watching by the sick-bed of your mothers and fathers, and often following them with tear-dimmed eyes to their graves, so in the future, in our humble way, we shall stand by you with a devotion that no foreigner can approach, ready to lay down our lives, if need be, in defence of yours, interlacing our industrial, commercial, civil, and religious life with yours in a way that shall make the interests of both races one. In all things that are purely social we can be as separate as the fingers, yet one as the hand in all things essential to mutual progress.

There is no defense or security for any of us except in the highest intelligence and development of all. If anywhere there are efforts tending to curtail the fullest growth of the Negro, let these efforts be turned into stimulating, encouraging, and making him the most useful and intelligent citizen. Effort or means so invested will pay a thousand per cent interest. These efforts will be twice blessed—"blessing him that gives and him that takes."

There is no escape through law of man or God from the inevitable:

> The laws of changeless justice bind
> Oppressor with oppressed;
> And close as sin and suffering joined
> We march to fate abreast.

Nearly sixteen millions of hands will aid you in pulling the load upward, or they will pull against you the load downward. We shall constitute one-third and more of the ignorance and crime of the South, or one-third its intelligence and progress; we shall contribute one-third to the business and industrial prosperity of the South, or we shall prove a veritable body of death, stagnating, depressing, retarding every effort to advance the body politic.

Gentlemen of the Exposition, as we present to you our humble effort at an exhibition of our progress, you must not expect overmuch. Starting thirty years ago with ownership here and there in a few quilts and pumpkins and chickens (gathered from miscellaneous sources), remember the path that has led from these to the inventions and production of agricultural implements, buggies, steam engines, newspapers, books, statuary carving, paintings, the management of drug-stores and banks, has not been trodden without contact with thorns and thistles. While we take pride in what we exhibit as a result of our independent efforts, we do not for a moment forget that our part in this exhibition would fall far short of your expectations but for the constant help that has come to our educational life, not only from the Southern states, but especially from Northern philanthropists, who have made their gifts a constant stream of blessing and encouragement.

The wisest among my race understand that the agitation of questions of social equality is the extremest folly, and that progress in the enjoyment of all the privileges that will come to us must be the result of severe and constant struggle rather than of artificial forcing. No race that has anything to contribute to the markets of the world is long in any degree ostracized. It is important and right that all privileges of the law be ours, but it is vastly more important that we be prepared for the exercise of these privileges. The opportunity to earn a dollar in a factory just now is worth infinitely more than the opportunity to spend a dollar in an opera-house.

In conclusion, may I repeat that nothing in thirty years has given us more hope and encouragement, and drawn us so near to you of the white race, as this opportunity offered by the Exposition; and here bending, as it were, over the altar that represents the results of the struggles of your race and mine, both starting practically empty-handed three decades ago, I pledge that, in your effort to work out the great and intricate problem which God has laid at the doors of the South, you shall have at all times the patient, sympathetic help of my race; only let this be constantly in mind, that, while from representations in these buildings of the product of field, of forest, of mine, of factory, letters, and art, much good will come, yet far above and beyond material benefits will be that higher good, that, let us pray God, will come, in a blotting out of sectional differences and racial animosities and suspicions, in a determination to administer absolute justice, in a willing obedience among all classes to the mandates of law. This, this, coupled with our material prosperity, will bring into our beloved South a new heaven and a new earth.

To World War II

W. E. B. DU BOIS

Of Mr. Booker T. Washington and Others

Perhaps the most famous and revealing ideological struggle between two black men in this country was that fought out by Booker T. Washington and W. E. B. DuBois. Washington's "Atlanta Exposition Address" has already been presented; DuBois' response follows. DuBois asserts that Washington's ethic of compromise failed to meet the very goals it established for itself; he also says that Washington ignored other goals essential to the true dignity of the black man. Washington argued for submission and vocational training; DuBois argued for political strength and intellectual training. The racial struggle of the twentieth century has involved much internecine warfare between black intellectuals on precisely the question that is at the center of the DuBois–Washington controversy: the relative merits of strategic compromise and the assertion of power.

Easily the most striking thing in the history of the American Negro since 1876 is the ascendancy of Mr. Booker T. Washington. It began at the time when war memories and ideals were rapidly passing; a day of astonishing commercial development was dawning; a sense of doubt and hesitation overtook the freedmen's sons,—then it was that his leading began. Mr. Washington came, with a single definite programme, at the psychological moment when the nation was a little ashamed of having bestowed so much sentiment on Negroes, and was concentrating its energies on Dollars. His programme of industrial education, conciliation of the South, and submission and silence as to civil and political rights, was not wholly original; the Free Negroes from 1830 up to wartime had striven to build industrial schools, and the American Missionary Association had from the first taught various trades; and Price and others had sought a way of honorable alliance with the best of the South-

OF MR. BOOKER T. WASHINGTON AND OTHERS From *The Souls of Black Folk* (Chicago, 1903) by W. E. B. DuBois. Reprinted by permission of Mrs. W. E. B. DuBois.

erners. But Mr. Washington first indissolubly linked these things; he put enthusiasm, unlimited energy, and perfect faith into this programme, and changed it from a by-path into a veritable Way of Life. And the tale of the methods by which he did this is a fascinating study of human life.

It startled the nation to hear a Negro advocating such a programme after many decades of bitter complaint; it startled and won the applause of the South, it interested and won the admiration of the North; and after a confused murmur of protest, it silenced if it did not convert the Negroes themselves.

To gain the sympathy and coöperation of the various elements comprising the white South was Mr. Washington's first task; and this, at the time Tuskegee was founded, seemed, for a black man, well-nigh impossible. And yet ten years later it was done in the word spoken at Atlanta: "In all things purely social we can be as separate as the five fingers, and yet one as the hand in all things essential to mutual progress." This "Atlanta Compromise" is by all odds the most notable thing in Mr. Washington's career. The South interpreted it in different ways: the radicals received it as a complete surrender of the demand for civil and political equality; the conservatives, as a generously conceived working basis for mutual understanding. So both approved it, and to-day its author is certainly the most distinguished Southerner since Jefferson Davis, and the one with the largest personal following.

Next to this achievement comes Mr. Washington's work in gaining place and consideration in the North. Others less shrewd and tactful had formerly essayed to sit on these two stools and had fallen between them; but as Mr. Washington knew the heart of the South from birth and training, so by singular insight he intuitively grasped the spirit of the age which was dominating the North. And so thoroughly did he learn the speech and thought of triumphant commercialism, and the ideals of material prosperity, that the picture of a lone black boy poring over a French grammar amid the weeds and dirt of a neglected home soon seemed to him the acme of absurdities. One wonders what Socrates and St. Francis of Assisi would say to this.

And yet this very singleness of vision and thorough oneness with his age is a mark of the successful man. It is as though Nature must needs make men narrow in order to give them force. So Mr. Washington's cult has gained unquestioning followers, his work has wonderfully prospered, his friends are legion, and his enemies are confounded. To-day he stands as the one recognized spokesman of his ten million fellows, and one of the most notable figures in a nation of seventy millions. One hesitates, therefore, to criticize a life which, beginning with so little, has done so much. And yet the time is come when one may speak in all sincerity and utter courtesy of the mistakes and shortcomings of Mr. Washington's career, as well as of his triumphs, without being thought captious or envious, and without forgetting that it is easier to do ill than well in the world.

The criticism that has hitherto met Mr. Washington has not always been of this broad character. In the South especially has he had to walk warily to avoid the harshest judgments,—and naturally so, for he is dealing with the one subject of deepest sensitiveness to that section. Twice— once when at the Chicago celebration of the Spanish-American War he alluded to the color-prejudice that is "eating away the vitals of the South," and once when he dined with President Roosevelt—has the resulting Southern criticism been violent enough to threaten seriously his popularity. In the North the feeling has several times forced itself into words, that Mr. Washington's counsels of submission overlooked certain elements of true manhood, and that his educational programme was unnecessarily narrow. Usually, however, such criticism has not found open expression, although, too, the spiritual sons of the Abolitionists have not been prepared to acknowledge that the schools founded before Tuskegee, by men of broad ideals and self-sacrificing spirit, were wholly failures or worthy of ridicule. While, then, criticism has not failed to follow Mr. Washington, yet the prevailing public opinion of the land has been but too willing to deliver the solution of a wearisome problem into his hands, and say, "If that is all you and your race ask, take it."

Among his own people, however, Mr. Washington has encountered the strongest and most lasting opposition, amounting at times to bitterness, and even to-day continuing strong and insistent even though largely silenced in outward expression by the public opinion of the nation. Some of this opposition is, of course, mere envy; the disappointment of displaced demagogues and the spite of narrow minds. But aside from this, there is among educated and thoughtful colored men in all parts of the land a feeling of deep regret, sorrow, and apprehension at the wide currency and ascendancy which some of Mr. Washington's theories have gained. These same men admire his sincerity of purpose, and are willing to forgive much to honest endeavor which is doing something worth the doing. They coöperate with Mr. Washington as far as they conscientiously can; and, indeed, it is no ordinary tribute to this man's tact and power that, steering as he must between so many diverse interests and opinions, he so largely retains the respect of all.

But the hushing of the criticism of honest opponents is a dangerous thing. It leads some of the best of the critics to unfortunate silence and paralysis of effort, and others to burst into speech so passionately and intemperately as to lose listeners. Honest and earnest criticism from those whose interests are most nearly touched,—criticism of writers by readers, of government by those governed, of leaders by those led,—this is the soul of democracy and the safeguard of modern society. If the best of the American Negroes receive by outer pressure a leader whom they had not recognized before, manifestly there is here a certain palpable gain. Yet there is also irreparable loss,—a loss of that peculiarly valuable education which a group receives when by search and criticism it finds and commissions its own leaders. The way in which this is done is at once the most elementary and the nicest problem of social growth. History is but the record of such group-leadership; and yet how infinitely changeful is its type and character! And of all types and kinds, what can be more instructive than the leadership of a group within a group?—that curious double movement where real progress may be negative and actual advance be relative retrogression. All this is the social student's inspiration and despair.

Now in the past the American Negro has had instructive experience in the choosing of group leaders, founding thus a peculiar dynasty which in the light of present conditions is worth while studying. When sticks and stones and beasts form the sole environment of a people, their attitude is largely one of determined opposition to and conquest of natural forces. But when to earth and brute is added an environment of men and ideas, then the attitude of the imprisoned group may take three main forms,—a feeling of revolt and revenge; an attempt to adjust all thought and action to the will of the greater group; or, finally, a determined effort at self-realization and self-development despite environing opinion. The influence of all of these attitudes at various times can be traced in the history of the American Negro, and in the evolution of his successive leaders.

Before 1750, while the fire of African freedom still burned in the veins of the slaves, there was in all leadership or attempted leadership but the one motive of revolt and revenge,—typified in the terrible Maroons, the Danish blacks, and Cato of Stono, and veiling all the Americas in fear of insurrection. The liberalizing tendencies of the latter half of the eighteenth century brought, along with kindlier relations between black and white, thoughts of ultimate adjustment and assimilation. Such aspiration was especially voiced in the earnest songs of Phyllis, in the martyrdom of Attucks, the fighting of Salem and Poor, the intellectual accomplishments of Banneker and Derham, and the political demands of the Cuffes.

Stern financial and social stress after the war cooled much of the previous humanitarian ardor. The disappointment and impatience of the Negroes at the persistence of slavery and serfdom voiced itself in two movements. The slaves in the South, aroused undoubtedly by vague rumors of the Haytian revolt, made three fierce attempts at insurrection,— in 1800 under Gabriel in Virginia, in 1822 under Vesey in Carolina, and in 1831 again in Virginia under the terrible Nat Turner. In the Free States, on the other hand, a new and curious attempt at self-development was made. In Philadelphia and New York color-prescription led to a withdrawal of Negro communicants from white churches and the formation of a peculiar socio-religious institution among the Negroes known as the African Church,—an organization still living and controlling in its various branches over a million of men.

Walker's wild appeal against the trend of the times showed how the world was changing after the coming of the cotton-gin. By 1830 slavery seemed hopelessly fastened on the South, and the slaves thoroughly cowed into submission. The free Negroes of the North, inspired by the mulatto immigrants from the West Indies, began to change the basis of their demands; they recognized the slavery of slaves, but insisted that they themselves were freemen, and sought assimilation and amalgamation with the nation on the same terms with other men. Thus, Forten and Purvis of Philadelphia, Shad of Wilmington, Du Bois of New Haven, Barbadoes of Boston, and others, strove singly and together as men, they said, not as slaves, as "people of color," not as "Negroes." The trend of the times, however, refused them recognition save in individual and exceptional cases, considered them as one with all the despised blacks, and they soon found themselves striving to keep even the rights they formerly had of voting and working and moving as freemen. Schemes of migration and colonization arose among them; but these they refused to entertain, and they eventually turned to the Abolition movement as a final refuge.

Here, led by Remond, Nell, Wells-Brown, and Douglass, a new period of self-assertion and self-development dawned. To be sure, ultimate freedom and assimilation was the ideal before the leaders, but the assertion of the manhood rights of the Negro by himself was the main reliance, and John Brown's raid was the extreme of its logic. After the war and emancipation, the great form of Frederick Douglass, the greatest of American Negro leaders, still led the host. Self-assertion, especially in political lines, was the main programme, and behind Douglass came Elliot, Bruce, and Langston, and the Reconstruction politicians, and, less conspicuous but of greater social significance Alexander Crummell and Bishop Daniel Payne.

Then came the Revolution of 1876, the suppression of the Negro votes, the changing and shifting of ideals, and the seeking of new lights in the great night. Douglass, in his old age, still bravely stood for the ideals of his early manhood,—ultimate assimilation *through* self-assertion, and on no other terms. For a time Price arose as a new leader, destined, it seemed, not to give up, but to re-state the old ideals in a form less repugnant to the white South. But he passed away in his prime. Then came the new leader. Nearly all the former ones had become leaders by the silent suffrage of their fellows, had sought to lead their own people alone, and were usually, save Douglass, little known outside their race. But Booker T. Washington arose as essentially the leader not of one race but of two,—a compromiser between the South, the North, and the Negro. Naturally the Negroes resented, at first bitterly, signs of compromise which surrendered their civil and political rights, even though this was to be exchanged for larger chances of economic development. The rich and dominating North, however, was not only weary of the race problem, but was investing largely in Southern enterprises, and welcomed any method of peaceful coöperation. Thus, by national opinion, the Negroes began to recognize Mr. Washington's leadership; and the voice of criticism was hushed.

Mr. Washington represents in Negro thought the old attitude of adjustment and submission; but adjustment at such a peculiar time as to make his programme unique. This is an age of unusual economic development, and Mr. Washington's programme naturally takes an economic cast, becoming a gospel of Work and Money to such an extent as apparently almost completely to overshadow the higher aims of life. Moreover, this is an age when the more advanced races are coming in closer contact with the less developed races, and the race-feeling is therefore intensified; and Mr. Washington's programme practically accepts the alleged inferiority of the Negro races. Again, in our own land, the reaction from the sentiment of war time has given impetus to race-prejudice against Negroes, and Mr. Washington withdraws many of the high demands of Negroes as men and American citizens. In other periods of intensified prejudice all the Negro's tendency to self-assertion has been called forth; at this period a policy of submission is advocated. In the history of nearly all other races and peoples the doctrine preached at such crises has been that mainly self-respect is worth more than lands and houses, and that a people who voluntarily surrender such respect, or cease striving for it, are not worth civilizing.

In answer to this, it has been claimed that the Negro can survive only through submission. Mr. Washington distinctly asks that black people give up, at least for the present, three things,—

First, political power,

Second, insistence on civil rights,

Third, higher education of Negro youth,—

and concentrate all their energies on industrial education, the accumulation of wealth, and the conciliation of the South. This policy has been courageously and insistently advocated for over fifteen years, and has been triumphant for perhaps ten years. As a result of this tender of the palm-branch, what has been the return? In these years there have occurred:

1. The disfranchisement of the Negro.

2. The legal creation of a distinct status of civil inferiority for the Negro.

3. The steady withdrawal of aid from institutions for the higher training of the Negro.

These movements are not, to be sure, direct results of Mr. Washington's teachings; but his propaganda has, without a shadow of doubt, helped their speedier accomplishment. The question then comes: Is it possible, and probable, that nine millions of men can make effective progress in economic lines if they are deprived of political rights, made a servile caste, and allowed only the most meagre chance for developing their exceptional men? If history and reason give any distinct answer to these questions, it is an emphatic *No*. And Mr. Washington thus faces the triple paradox of his career:

1. He is striving nobly to make Negro artisans business men and property-owners; but it is utterly impossible, under modern competitive methods, for workingmen and property-owners to defend their rights and exist without the right of suffrage.

2. He insists on thrift and self-respect, but at the same time counsels a silent submission to civic inferiority such as is bound to sap the manhood of any race in the long run.

3. He advocates common-school and industrial training, and depreciates institutions of higher learning; but neither the Negro common-schools, nor Tuskegee itself, could remain open a day were it not for teachers trained in Negro colleges, or trained by their graduates.

This triple paradox in Mr. Washington's position is the object of criticism by two classes of colored Americans. One class is spiritually descended from Toussaint the Savior, through Gabriel, Vesey, and Turner, and they represent the attitude of revolt and revenge; they hate the white South blindly and distrust the white race generally, and so far as they agree on definite action, think that the Negro's only hope lies in emigration beyond the borders of the United States. And yet, by the irony of fate, nothing has more effectually made this programme seem hopeless than the recent course of the United States toward weaker and darker peoples in the West Indies, Hawaii, and the Philippines,—for where in the world may we go and be safe from lying and brute force?

The other class of Negroes who cannot agree with Mr. Washington has hitherto said little aloud. They deprecate the sight of scattered counsels, of internal disagreement: and especially they dislike making their just criticism of a useful and earnest man an excuse for a general discharge of venom from small-minded opponents. Nevertheless, the questions involved are so fundamental and serious that it is difficult to see how men like the Grimkes, Kelly Miller, J. W. E. Bowen, and other representatives of this group, can much longer be silent. Such men feel in conscience bound to ask of this nation three things:

1. The right to vote.
2. Civic equality.
3. The education of youth according to ability.

They acknowledge Mr. Washington's invaluable service in counselling patience and courtesy in such demands; they do not ask that ignorant black men vote when ignorant whites are debarred, or that any reasonable restrictions in the suffrage should not be applied; they know that the low social level of the mass of the race is responsible for much discrimination against it, but they also know, and the nation knows, that relentless color-prejudice is more often a cause than a result of the Negro's degradation; they seek the abatement of this relic of barbarism, and not its systematic encouragement and pampering by all agencies of social power from the Associated Press to the Church of Christ. They advocate, with Mr. Washington, a broad system of Negro common schools supplemented by thorough industrial training: but they are surprised that a man of Mr. Washington's insight cannot see that no such educational system ever has rested or can rest on any other basis than that of the well-equipped college and university, and they insist that there is a demand for a few such institutions throughout the South to train the best of the Negro youth as teachers, professional men, and leaders.

This group of men honor Mr. Washington for his attitude of conciliation toward the white South; they accept the "Atlanta Compromise" in its broadest interpretation; they recognize, with him, many signs of promise, many men of high purpose and fair judgment, in this section; they know that no easy task has been laid upon a region already tottering under heavy burdens. But, nevertheless, they insist that the way to truth and right lies in straightforward honesty, not in indiscriminate flattery; in praising those of the South who do well and criticising uncompromisingly those who do ill; in taking advantage of the opportunities at hand and urging their fellows to do the same, but at the same time in remembering that only a firm adherence to their higher ideals and aspirations will ever keep those ideals within the realm of possibility. They do not expect that the free right to vote, to enjoy civic rights, and to be educated, will come in a moment; they do not expect to see the bias and prejudices of years disappear at the blast of a trumpet; but they are absolutely certain that the way for a people to gain their reasonable rights is not by voluntarily throwing them away and insisting that they do not want them; that the way for a people to gain respect is not by continually belittling and ridiculing themselves; that, on the contrary, Negroes must insist continually, in season and out of season, that voting is necessary to modern manhood, that color discrimination is barbarism, and that black boys need education as well as white boys.

In failing thus to state plainly and unequivocally the legitimate demands of their people, even at the cost of opposing an honored leader, the thinking classes of American Negroes would shirk a heavy responsibility,—a responsibility to themselves, a responsibility to the struggling masses, a responsibility to the darker races of men whose future depends so largely on this American experiment, but especially a responsibility to this nation,—this common Fatherland. It is wrong to encourage a man or a people in evil-doing; it is wrong to aid and abet a national crime simply because it is unpopular not to do so. The growing spirit of kindliness and reconciliation between the North and South after the frightful difference of a generation ago ought to be a source of deep congratulation to all, and especially to those whose mistreatment caused the war; but if that reconciliation is to be marked by the industrial slavery and civic death of those same black men, with permanent legislation into a position of inferiority, then those black men, if they are really men, are called upon by every consideration of patriotism and loyalty to oppose such a course by all civilized methods, even though such opposition involves disagreement with Mr. Booker T. Washington. We have no right to sit silently by while the inevitable seeds are sown for a harvest of disaster to our children, black and white.

First, it is the duty of black men to judge the South discriminatingly. The present generation of Southerners are not responsible for the past, and they should not be blindly hated or blamed for it. Furthermore, to no class is the indiscriminate endorsement of the recent course of the South toward Negroes more nauseating than to the best thought of the South. The South is not "solid"; it is a land in the ferment of social change, wherein forces of all kinds are fighting for supremacy; and to praise the ill the South is to-day perpetuating is just as wrong as to condemn the good. Discriminating and broad-minded criticism is what the South needs,—needs it for the sake of her own white sons and daughters, and for the insurance of robust, healthy mental and moral development.

To-day even the attitude of the Southern whites toward the blacks is not, as so many assume, in all cases the same; the ignorant Southerner hates the Negro, the workingmen fear his competition, the money-makers wish to use him as a laborer, some of the educated see a menace in his upward development, while others—usually the sons of the masters— wish to help him to rise. National opinion has enabled this last class to maintain the Negro common schools, and to protect the Negro partially in property, life, and limb. Through the pressure of the money-makers, the Negro is in danger of being reduced to semi-slavery, especially in the country districts; the workingmen, and those of the educated who fear the Negro, have united to disfranchise him, and some have urged his deportation; while the passions of the ignorant are easily aroused to lynch and abuse any black man. To praise this intricate whirl of thought and prejudice is nonsense; to inveigh indiscriminately against "the South" is unjust; but to use the same breath in praising Governor Aycock, exposing Senator Morgan, arguing with Mr. Thomas Nelson Page, and denouncing Senator Ben Tillman, is not only sane, but the imperative duty of thinking black men.

It would be unjust to Mr. Washington not to acknowledge that in several instances he has opposed movements in the South which were unjust to the Negro; he sent memorials to the Louisiana and Alabama constitutional conventions, he has spoken against lynching, and in other ways has openly or silently set his influence against sinister schemes and unfortunate happenings. Notwithstanding this, it is equally true to assert that on the whole the distinct impression left by Mr. Washington's propaganda is, first, that the South is justified in its present attitude toward the Negro because of the Negro's degradation; secondly, that the prime cause of the Negro's failure to rise more quickly is his wrong education in the past; and, thirdly, that his future rise depends primarily on his own efforts. Each of these propositions is a dangerous half-truth. The supplementary truths must never be lost sight of: first, slavery and race-prejudice are potent if not sufficient causes of the Negro's position; second, industrial and common-school training were necessarily slow in planting because they had to await the black teachers trained by higher institutions,—it being extremely doubtful if any essentially different development was possible, and certainly a Tuskegee was unthinkable before 1880; and, third, while it is a great truth to say that the Negro must strive and strive mightily to help himself, it is equally true that unless his striving be not simply seconded, but rather aroused and encouraged, by the initiative of the richer and wiser environing group, he cannot hope for great success.

In his failure to realize and impress this last point Mr. Washington is especially to be criticised. His doctrine has tended to make the whites, North and South, shift the burden of the Negro problem to the Negro's shoulders and stand aside as critical and rather pessimistic spectators; when in fact the burden belongs to the nation, and the hands of none of us are clean if we bend not our energies to righting these great wrongs.

The South ought to be led, by candid and honest criticism, to assert her better self and do her full duty to the race she has cruelly wronged and is still wronging. The North—her co-partner in guilt—cannot salve her conscience by plastering it with gold. We cannot settle this problem by diplomacy and suaveness, by "policy" alone. If worse come to worst, can the moral fibre of this country survive the slow throttling and murder of nine millions of men?

The black men of America have a duty to perform, a duty stern and delicate,—a forward movement to oppose a part of the work of their greatest leader. So far as Mr. Washington preaches Thrift, Patience, and Industrial Training for the masses, we must hold up his hands and strive with him, rejoicing in his honors and glorying in the strength of this Joshua called of God and of man to head the headless host. But so far as Mr. Washington apologizes for injustice, North or South, does not rightly value the privilege and duty of voting, belittles the emasculating effects of caste distinctions, and opposes the higher training and ambition of our brighter minds,—so far as he, the South, or the Nation, does this,—we must unceasingly and firmly oppose them. By every civilized and peaceful method we must strive for the rights which the world accords to men, clinging unwaveringly to those great words which the sons of the Fathers would fain forget: "We hold these truths to be self-evident: That all men are created equal; that they are endowed by their Creator with certain unalienable rights; that among these are life, liberty, and the pursuit of happiness."

GILBERT OSOFSKY

Negro Migration and Settlement, 1890–1914

At the turn of the century, great numbers of black people began to migrate to the North. The impetus to move from the rural South to the urban North was provided by several factors: the virulence of Southern racism, the failure of crops, the apparently expanding horizons of possibility in the North, the opening of the industrial job market with the coming of World War I, and others. In the following essay, sociologist Gilbert Osofsky observes that those who made the trek North were a new generation of blacks, born at one remove from the crippling world of counter-Reconstruction and the venom of men like Ben Tillman. Feeling that they had few roots in a land which had persecuted their parents, and placing their hopes in the promise of the cities, they transformed the demographic patterns of America.

THE MOST IMPORTANT FACTOR UNDERLYING THE ESTABLISHMENT OF Harlem as a Negro community was the substantial increase of Negro population in New York City in the years 1890–1914. That Harlem became the specific center of Negro settlement was the result of circumstance; that *some* section of the city was destined to become a Negro ghetto was the inevitable consequence of the Negro's migration from the South. This pre-World War I population movement, the advance guard of the Great Migration (as the movement of Negroes during the First World War is generally called), laid the foundations for present-day Negro communities in Chicago and Philadelphia as well. These were the formative years for the development of Negro communities throughout the North.

In spite of the high Negro death rate, the colored population increased by "leaps and bounds" in New York City in the early twentieth century. By 1910 there were 91,709 Negroes in the metropolis, the majority southern-born: "A Census of the Negroes in any city of the North," said a speaker at the first organizational meeting of the NAACP in 1909, "would show that the majority of . . . them . . . were more or less recent arrivals from the South." Mary White Ovington, in her excellent study *Half A Man: The Status of the Negro in New York,* found that most of the Negro neighborhoods were populated by southerners. Only 14,309 of the 60,534 Negroes in Manhattan in 1910 were born in New York State. The majority of the others (61 per cent) came from other states, practically all in the South. Virginia, North Carolina, South Carolina, Georgia and Florida, in perfect geographical order, were the major southern sources of New York's migrant population.

Contemporaries in both the North and So'·th, Negro and white, were aware of this movement. Unable to foresee that the First World War would bring even larger numbers of Negroes northward, they were staggered by the myriad problems this migration created for them: "There are more Southern Negroes in the North and West than original Northern ones, and they are coming all . . . the time," wrote a Negro journalist in 1913. "What to do with the needy and those who fall by the wayside is becoming a problem of the greatest magnitude. . . ." Historians, impressed by the enormity of changes that occurred at the time of the "Great War," have tended to overlook or underestimate the significance of the pre-World War I migration of Negroes to northern cities.

Since the end of the Civil War there was a steady but small movement of Negroes northward. It averaged 41,378 persons for each decade between 1870 and 1890. In the following ten years, however, the migration more than doubled as at least 107,796 southern Negroes moved north and west. The Negro populations of the states of New Jersey, Pennsylvania and Illinois increased some two and a half times between 1890 and 1910 and that of New York almost tripled. In 1910, New York City was the second largest Negro urban center in America (just behind Washington, D.C.); Philadelphia was fifth; and Chicago eighth. By 1920, they were ranked first, second and fourth respectively. A total of some 200,000 Negroes migrated from the South and to the North and West, primarily to cities, between 1890 and 1910. In the decade 1900–1910, for the first time since their establishments as states in the early nineteenth century, Mississippi and Louisiana lost Negro population through emigration. Practically every southern state showed the first significant deficit in its Negro birth-residence index (the index that measures population increase and decrease through migration) for the decade 1890–1900. "Prior to 1890," observes one student of population

movement, "the migration of Negroes was not great and seems to have
been local, from state to state, and only to a slight extent out of the
South. But after 1890, the northward direction of the movement has
been steadfastly maintained and has increased in amount decade after
decade." The number of Negroes migrating to the principal southern
cities declined significantly in the years 1890–1900. The Negro population in these cities increased 38.7 per cent between 1880 and 1890, but
the growth amounted to only 20.6 per cent in the next ten years. Northern cities were draining off the residents of, and prospective migrants to,
the larger southern cities at the turn of the century.

.   .   .

There were as many individual and varied reasons for migration as
there were people who moved. The less respectable as well as the educated came north. Negroes themselves characterized some as a "hoodlum
element," "rovers," "wanderers," "vagrants," "criminals in search of a
sporting life." "Many of the worthless people of the race are making their
way northward," said *The New York Age* in an editorial. Some wayward
husbands—the "wandering men" of Negro folk songs—abandoned their
families and responsibilities and sought the anonymity of a city: "I was
raised in the country, I been there all my life/Lord I had to run off and
leave my children and my wife."

Others came north on excursion trains to get a look at the big city
and never returned. One man "heard so much of this town," he said,
"that he decided to look it over." Another stated that he "didn't want
to remain in one little place all my days. I wanted to get out and see
something of the world." Migratory laborers found work on New Jersey,
Pennsylvania and New York farms every spring and summer. Some
traveled back and forth each year; others simply went to the nearest city
when winter came. "Tired of the South," "Wanted to make a change,"
"Ran away from home," were some of the reasons advanced by Negroes
for coming north. All received nominally higher wages in the North, and
this was certainly a great attraction. One woman who came to New York
City from Virginia, for example, said she was "willing to live anywhere,
if the wages were good."

There were also those who fled social proscription and violence in the
South. C. Vann Woodward has described the "Capitulation to Racism"
that characterized the southern attitude toward the Negro from the late
1880's through the early twentieth century. Vast numbers of Jim Crow
laws were passed in these years as the forces which held virulent south-

ern racism in check suddenly crumbled. The conservative, *noblesse oblige* attitude of former Whig leaders ("it is a mark of breeding to treat Negroes with courtesy") was replaced by a violently racist white supremacy movement; the paternalism of a Wade Hampton was followed by the viciousness of a Ben Tillman (whose racist tirades even embarrassed his southern colleagues). Free rein was given to mass aggressions as all forces joined together in an active program of "keeping the Negro down." The great heresy that proclaimed the Negro capable of attaining equality with the white had to be rooted out at all costs, it was argued. There were more Negroes lynched, burned, tortured and disfranchised in the late eighties, nineties and first decade of the twentieth century than at any other time in our history. The militant Negro Ida B. Wells graphically and sadly described this *Red Record* in 1895. It was not surprising to find that the American Colonization Society, organized in 1817, experienced a long-hoped-for revival in the 1890's, and various other plans to colonize Negroes in Africa were rekindled in these years. "I used to love what I thought was the grand old flag, and sing with ecstasy about the stars and stripes," wrote Negro Bishop Henry McNeal Turner of Georgia, "but to the Negro in this country today the American flag is a dirty contemptible rag. . . . Hell is an improvement upon the United States when the Negro is involved." "No man hates this Nation more than I do," Turner said on another occasion. He looked longingly to Africa as the only possible place of Negro freedom.

Negro leaders and the Negro press continually stressed their belief that migration was primarily a movement away from racism: "The large cities of the North and West have had a marvelous increase of Afro-American population in the last ten years, and the increase is growing . . . because of the conditions in the Southern States which make for unrest"; "the terrors of mob wrath." When T. Thomas Fortune, William Lewis Bulkley, and North Carolina educator and politician Edward A. Johnson came north, each emphasized he could no longer live under Jim Crow and racial violence. George Henry White said he left North Carolina because he "couldn't live there and be a man and be treated like a man." He believed that thousands of others would follow him. Booker T. Washington told the Board of Trustees of Tuskegee, in 1903, that "for every lynching that takes place . . . a score of colored people leave . . . for the city."

In general, however, the migration could best be considered not so much a flight from racial violence, as it was a desire for expanded opportunity. This is best summarized in a phrase commonly used by the migrants themselves—the attempt "to better my condition." People moved away from the South in search of a better and more fulfilling life. A Negro shoemaker came north, for example, because he felt "choked" by the "narrow and petty life" he was forced to lead in a small Virginia town. To him, the great attraction of New York City was the "wider scope allowed the Negro." One woman who "never could work . . . in a menial way" was proud that she could earn a living as an independent seamstress in New York. Moving north, wrote DuBois in 1907, offered "the possibility of escaping caste at least in its most aggravating personal features. . . . A certain sort of soul, a certain kind of spirit, finds the narrow repression and provincialism of the South simply unbearable."

.   .   .

The *possibilities* for such movement resulted from two basic changes in American life. One was the overwhelming industrial expansion of the late nineteenth century. The Industrial Revolution created economic opportunities for rural people, Negro and white, and both migrated to industrial and urban centers in the North. For the Negro, hedged about by union restrictions and racial antagonism, employment was usually found in the fringe jobs that an industrial and commercial society creates —as janitors, elevator operators, general laborers of all kinds, long-shoremen, servants. Negro women almost always worked as domestics. During periods of labor disputes, Negroes were commonly found among the strikebreakers.

There was, however, an added factor that influenced Negro migration and distinguished it from the general rural migration to cities. Why, it might be asked, had Negroes not moved in similar numbers in response to industrialization in the 1870's—the period of great social upheaval and dislocation that followed the destruction of slavery? The answer undoubtedly lies in an understanding of the differences between the slave and post-slave generations. The Negroes who came north now were the first descendants of former slaves. They had listened to tales of slavery, gentle and harsh, but had not experienced and lived its blight—the denial of full manhood. To them, *"War, Hell, and Slavery were but childhood tales. . . ."* Their parents and grandparents, psychologically and economically unprepared to enter what contemporaries called the "competition for life," tended to remain as tenants, sharecroppers or laborers on their former plantations or on places similar to them. They continued in freedom to live the only life they had knowledge of. "There were great upheavals in political and labor conditions at the time of emancipation, but there was little shifting in the populations. For the most part, the freedmen stayed on in the states and counties where they had formerly existed as slaves," writes one historian of Negro life. In 1900, practically all southern Negroes continued to work on the land and some 75 per cent remained sharecroppers, tenants and laborers. On one Georgia plantation in 1901, as on others, lived many Negroes who had been slaves there: "I have men," the white owner testified, "who were slaves on the place. . . . They have always lived there and will probably die there, right on the plantation where they were born." "It was predicted [during the Civil War] that the Negroes would leave the . . . fields and fill the towns in case of emancipation," said a southern planter at the turn of the century. "That prediction has not been realized suddenly as we anticipated it would be, but it seems to be approaching."

Those who migrated to the North in the 1890's were a new generation. Many Negroes no longer felt any strong attachment to the soil. They could at least *conceive* of life in a new and different way. For some, the discontented and restless, there was now both the ability and willingness to move. They left a South in which their futures were sealed: "There is absolutely nothing before them on the farm. . . . Working year in and year out with . . . no prospect . . . but to continue until they die." In many rural communities of the South, it was reported in 1907, a "number of youths have expressed their conviction that since their fathers and mothers have accumulated nothing after years on the land, they did not intend to stay on the plantation to repeat the process." A leading Republican politician and defender of Negro civil rights, James S. Clarkson, took a trip to the South in the 1890's and "saw many a grey head . . . talking to the young people . . . encouraging the young people to become content," he wrote a Negro confidant. The migrants who came north were aptly described by George Edmund Haynes as "groping seekers for something better. . . ."

·   ·   ·

Exaggerated accounts of the destitute conditions of migrants were commonly published in the press and every hint of failure was described as destitution. The high Negro mortality rate in northern cities was presented as absolute proof that the Negro could not live in cold climates: "they will take colds and develop pneumonia and consumption . . . and will die there." The Southern Negro Anti-Exodus Association was founded in Virginia in 1905 to "preach the gospel of contentment to the colored people South of Mason and Dixon's line. . . ." When a labor agent was arrested in Georgia, an editorial in the *Age* said:

> If there is one thing the Southern man preaches all the time it is that
> the young Negro is worthless and is not to be mentioned in the same
> breath with the older. . . . The young Negro is pictured as worthless
> and a general nuisance that has been tolerated too long. . . . But as
> yet no one can be found to deny the cold fact that this agent was ar-
> rested to put a stop to the exodus. . . . In spite of all this talk, there
> is a desire to keep the Negro help in the South.

These reactions were a reflection of a basic dichotomy in southern
thought. On the one hand, it was believed that the Negro was worthless,
inefficient, untrustworthy, less faithful than the slave. The failure to use
improved agricultural machinery and in industrialization in general was
often blamed on his ignorance. On the other hand, the Negro was encouraged to remain in the South (and sometimes forced to do so) as the
only source of labor available—"the backbone of the South when it
comes to labor"; "the best labor we could have in the South." With the
failure of attempts to attract European immigrants the reliance of the
South on Negro farmers and laborers became even more evident. In
reality, Southern society fundamentally distrusted the very people it
seemed most hopelessly dependent upon. It was caught in a vise of re-
stricting the migration of Negroes who, at the same time, were looked
upon with the utmost disdain, even denied fully human qualities. This
paradox in southern thought provided a seedbed for bitter racial antagonism. It added an emotionalism to the racial hatreds of these years that
make them stand out, above all others, as a period of great violence.

Race Riot, Chicago, 1919

For most black people, the North proved to be no more hospitable than the South. Blacks met with stubborn resistance from whites who felt that the newcomers threatened their jobs, housing, and social life. Northern cities also had traditions of mob violence against blacks dating back to the appearance of colonies of free Negroes in the previous century. Thus, the deep tensions and traditional prejudice frequently resulted in racial confrontations on the streets of major cities. Springfield, Illinois, felt one of the first major shocks in 1908. Other cities with large black populations, such as East St. Louis and Washington, D.C., were soon beset. Chicago's riot of 1919 is typical of these early-century disturbances. It was also one of the precursors of what is now a virtually permanent fixture in American history: a racial rebellion which yields many deaths, a thorough coverage by the media, and little substantial change to improve the situation which first ignited the passions.

THIRTY-EIGHT PERSONS KILLED, 537 INJURED, AND ABOUT 1,000 REN-dered homeless and destitute was the casualty list of the race riot which broke out in Chicago on July 27, 1919, and swept uncontrolled through parts of the city for four days. By August 2 it had yielded to the forces of law and order, and on August 8 the state militia withdrew.

A clash between whites and Negroes on the shore of Lake Michigan at Twenty-ninth Street, which involved much stone-throwing and re-sulted in the drowning of a Negro boy, was the beginning of the riot. A policeman's refusal to arrest a white man accused by Negroes of stoning the Negro boy was an important factor in starting mob action. Within two hours the riot was in full sway, had scored its second fatality, and was spreading throughout the south and southwest parts of the city. Before the end came it reached out to a section of the West Side and even invaded the "Loop," the heart of Chicago's downtown business district. Of the thirty-eight killed, fifteen were whites and twenty-three

RACE RIOT, CHICAGO, 1919 From *The Negro in Chicago* by The Chicago Commission on Race Relations (Chicago, 1922).

Negroes; of 537 injured, 178 were whites, 342 were Negroes, and the race of seventeen was not recorded.

In contrast with many other outbreaks of violence over racial friction the Chicago riot was not preceded by excitement over reports of attacks on women or of any other crimes alleged to have been committed by Negroes. It is interesting to note that not one of the thirty-eight deaths was of a woman or girl, and that only ten of the 537 persons injured were women or girls. In further contrast with other outbreaks of racial violence, the Chicago riot was marked by no hangings or burnings.

The rioting was characterized by much activity on the part of gangs of hoodlums, and the clashes developed from sudden and spontaneous assaults into organized raids against life and property.

In handling the emergency and restoring order, the police were effectively reinforced by the state militia. Help was also rendered by deputy sheriffs, and by ex-soldiers who volunteered.

In nine of the thirty-eight cases of death, indictments for murder were voted by the grand jury, and in the ensuing trials there were four convictions. In fifteen other cases the coroner's jury recommended that unknown members of mobs be apprehended, but none of these was ever found.

The Commission's inquiry concerning the facts of the riot included a critical analysis of the 5,584 pages of the testimony taken by the coroner's jury; a study of the records of the office of the state's attorney; studies of the records of the Police Department, hospitals, and other institutions with reference to injuries, and of the records of the Fire Department with reference to incendiary fires; and interviews with many public officials and citizens having special knowledge of various phases of the riot. Much information was also gained by the Commission in a series of four conferences to which it invited the foreman of the riot grand jury, the chief and other commanding officers of the Police Department, the state's attorney and some of his assistants, and officers in command of the state militia during the riot.

Background of the Riot

The Chicago riot was not the only serious outbreak of interracial violence in the year following the war. The same summer witnessed the riot in Washington, about a week earlier; the riot in Omaha, about a month later; and then the week of armed conflict in a rural district of Arkansas due to exploitation of Negro cotton producers.

Nor was the Chicago riot the first violent manifestation of race antagonism in Illinois. In 1908 Springfield had been the scene of an outbreak that brought shame to the community which boasted of having been Lincoln's home. In 1917 East St. Louis was torn by a bitter and destructive riot which raged for nearly a week, and was the subject of a Congressional investigation that disclosed appalling underlying conditions.

This Commission, while making a thorough study of the Chicago riot, has reviewed briefly, for comparative purposes, the essential facts of the Springfield and East St. Louis riots, and of minor clashes in Chicago occurring both before and after the riot of 1919.

Chicago was one of the northern cities most largely affected by the migration of Negroes from the South during the war. The Negro population increased from 44,103 in 1910 to 109,594 in 1920, an increase of 148 per cent. Most of this increase came in the years 1916–19. It was principally caused by the widening of industrial opportunities due to the entrance of northern workers into the army and to the demand for war workers at much higher wages than Negroes had been able to earn in the South. An added factor was the feeling, which spread like a contagion through the South, that the great opportunity had come to escape from what they felt to be a land of discrimination and subserviency to places where they could expect fair treatment and equal rights. Chicago became to the southern Negro the "top of the world."

The effect of this influx of Negroes into Chicago industries is reviewed in another section of this report. It is necessary to point out here only that friction in industry was less than might have been expected. There had been a few strikes which had given the Negro the name of "strike breaker." But the demand for labor was such that there were plenty of jobs to absorb all the white and Negro workers available. This condition continued even after the end of the war and demobilization.

In housing, however, there was a different story. Practically no new building had been done in the city during the war, and it was a physical impossibility for a doubled Negro population to live in the space occupied in 1915. Negroes spread out of what had been known as the "Black Belt" into neighborhoods near-by which had been exclusively white. This movement, as described in another section of this report, developed friction, so much so that in the "invaded" neighborhoods bombs were thrown at the houses of Negroes who had moved in, and of real estate men, white and Negro, who sold or rented property to the newcomers. From July 1, 1917, to July 27, 1919, the day the riot began, twenty-four such bombs had been thrown. The police had been entirely unsuccessful in finding those guilty, and were accused of making little effort to do so.

A third phase of the situation was the increased political strength gained by Mayor Thompson's faction in the Republican party. Negro politicians affiliated with this faction had been able to sway to its support a large proportion of the voters in the ward most largely inhabited by Negroes. Negro aldermen elected from this ward were prominent in the activities of this faction. The part played by the Negro vote in the hard-fought partisan struggle is indicated by the fact that in the Republican primary election on February 25, 1919, Mayor Thompson received in this ward 12,143 votes, while his two opponents, Olson and Merriam, received only 1,492 and 319 respectively. Mayor Thompson was re-elected on April 1, 1919, by a plurality of 21,622 in a total vote in the city of 698,920; his vote in this ward was 15,569, to his nearest opponent's 3,323, and was therefore large enough to control the election. The bitterness of this factional struggle aroused resentment against the race that had so conspicuously allied itself with the Thompson side.

As part of the background of the Chicago riot, the activities of gangs of hoodlums should be cited. There had been friction for years, especially along the western boundary of the area in which the Negroes mainly live, and attacks upon Negroes by gangs of young toughs had been particularly frequent in the spring just preceding the riot. They reached a climax on the night of June 21, 1919, five weeks before the riot, when two Negroes were murdered. Each was alone at the time and was the victim of unprovoked and particularly brutal attack. Molestation of Negroes by hoodlums had been prevalent in the vicinity of parks and playgrounds and at bathing-beaches.

On two occasions shortly before the riot the forewarnings of serious racial trouble had been so pronounced that the chief of police sent several hundred extra policemen into the territory where trouble seemed imminent. But serious violence did not break out until Sunday afternoon, July 27, when the clash on the lake shore at Twenty-ninth Street resulted in the drowning of a Negro boy.

The Beginning of the Riot

Events followed so fast in the train of the drowning that this tragedy may be considered as marking the beginning of the riot.

It was four o'clock Sunday afternoon, July 27, when Eugene Williams, seventeen-year-old Negro boy, was swimming offshore at the foot of Twenty-ninth Street. This beach was not one of those publicly maintained and supervised for bathing, but it was much used. Although it flanks an area thickly inhabited by Negroes, it was used by both races, access being had by crossing the railway tracks which skirt the lake shore. The part near Twenty-seventh Street had by tacit understanding come to be considered as reserved for Negroes, while the whites used the part near Twenty-ninth Street. Walking is not easy along the shore, and each race had kept pretty much to its own part, observing, moreover, an imaginary boundary extending into the water.

Williams, who had entered the water at the part used by Negroes, swam and drifted south into the part used by the whites. Immediately before his appearance there, white men, women, and children had been bathing in the vicinity and were on the beach in considerable numbers. Four Negroes walked through the group and into the water. White men summarily ordered them off. The Negroes left, and the white people resumed their sport. But it was not long before the Negroes were back, coming from the north with others of their race. Then began a series of attacks and retreats, counterattacks, and stone-throwing. Women and children who could not escape hid behind débris and rocks. The stone-throwing continued, first one side gaining the advantage, then the other.

Williams, who had remained in the water during the fracas, found a railroad tie and clung to it, stones meanwhile frequently striking the water near him. A white boy of about the same age swam toward him. As the white boy neared, Williams let go of the tie, took a few strokes, and went down. The coroner's jury rendered a verdict that he had drowned because fear of stone-throwing kept him from shore. His body showed no stone bruises, but rumor had it that he had actually been hit by one of the stones and drowned as a result.

On shore guilt was immediately placed upon a certain white man by several Negro witnesses who demanded that he be arrested by a white policeman who was on the spot. No arrest was made.

The tragedy was sensed by the battling crowd and, awed by it, they gathered on the beach. For an hour both whites and Negroes dived for the boy without results. Awe gave way to excited whispers. "They" said he was stoned to death. The report circulated through the crowd that the police officer had refused to arrest the murderer. The Negroes in the crowd began to mass dangerously. At this crucial point the accused policeman arrested a Negro on a white man's complaint. Negroes mobbed the white officer, and the riot was under way.

One version of the quarrel which resulted in the drowning of Williams was given by the state's attorney, who declared that it arose among white and Negro gamblers over a craps game on the shore, "virtually under the protection of the police officer on the beat." Eyewitnesses to the stone-throwing clash appearing before the coroner's jury saw no gambling, but said it might have been going on, but if so, was not visible from the water's edge. The crowd undoubtedly included, as the grand jury declared, "hoodlums, gamblers, and thugs," but it also included law-abiding citizens, white and Negro.

This charge, that the first riot clash started among gamblers who were under the protection of the police officer, and also the charge that the policeman refused to arrest the stone-thrower were vigorously denied by the police. The policeman's star was taken from him, but after a hearing before the Civil Service Commission it was returned, thus officially vindicating him.

The two facts, the drowning and the refusal to arrest, or widely circulated reports of such refusal, must be considered together as marking the inception of the riot. Testimony of a captain of police shows that first reports from the lake after the drowning indicated that the situation was calming down. White men had shown a not altogether hostile feeling for the Negroes by assisting in diving for the body of the boy. Furthermore a clash started on this isolated spot could not be augmented by outsiders rushing in. There was every possibility that the clash, without the further stimulus of reports of the policeman's conduct, would have quieted down.

Chronological Story of the Riot

After the drowning of Williams, it was two hours before any further fatalities occurred. Reports of the drowning and of the alleged conduct of the policeman spread out into the neighborhood. The Negro crowd from the beach gathered at the foot of Twenty-ninth Street. As it became more and more excited, a group of officers was called by the policeman who had been at the beach. James Crawford, a Negro, fired into the group of officers and was himself shot and killed by a Negro policeman who had been sent to help restore order.

During the remainder of the afternoon of July 27, many distorted rumors circulated swiftly throughout the South Side. The Negro crowd from Twenty-ninth Street got into action, and white men who came in contact with it were beaten. In all, four white men were beaten, five were stabbed, and one was shot. As the rumors spread, new crowds gathered, mobs sprang into activity spontaneously, and gangs began to take part in the lawlessness.

Farther to the west, as darkness came on, white gangsters became active. Negroes in white districts suffered severely at their hands. From 9:00 P.M. until 3:00 A.M. twenty-seven Negroes were beaten, seven were stabbed, and four were shot.

Few clashes occurred on Monday morning. People of both races went to work as usual and even continued to work side by side, as customary, without signs of violence. But as the afternoon wore on, white men and boys living between the Stock Yards and the "Black Belt" sought malicious amusement in directing mob violence against Negro workers returning home.

Street-car routes, especially transfer points, were thronged with white people of all ages. Trolleys were pulled from wires and the cars brought under the control of mob leaders. Negro passengers were dragged to the street, beaten, and kicked. The police were apparently powerless to cope with these numerous assaults. Four Negro men and one white assailant were killed, and thirty Negro men were severely beaten in the street-car clashes.

The "Black Belt" contributed its share of violence to the record of Monday afternoon and night. Rumors of white depredations and killings were current among the Negroes and led to acts of retaliation. An aged Italian peddler, one Lazzeroni, was set upon by young Negro boys and stabbed to death. Eugene Temple, white laundryman, was stabbed to death and robbed by three Negroes.

A Negro mob made a demonstration outside Provident Hospital, an institution conducted by Negroes, because two injured whites who had been shooting right and left from a hurrying automobile on State Street were taken there. Other mobs stabbed six white men, shot five others, severely beat nine more, and killed two in addition to those named above.

Rumor had it that a white occupant of the Angelus apartment house had shot a Negro boy from a fourth-story window. Negroes besieged the building. The white tenants sought police protection, and about 100 policemen, including some mounted men, responded. The mob of about 1,500 Negroes demanded the "culprit," but the police failed to find him after a search of the building. A flying brick hit a policeman. There was a quick massing of the police, and a volley was fired into the Negro mob. Four Negroes were killed and many were injured. It is believed that had the Negroes not lost faith in the white police force it is hardly likely that the Angelus riot would have occurred.

At this point, Monday night, both whites and Negroes showed signs of panic. Each race grouped by itself. Small mobs began systematically in various neighborhoods to terrorize and kill. Gangs in the white districts grew bolder, finally taking the offensive in raids through territory "invaded" by Negro home seekers. Boys between sixteen and twenty-two banded together to enjoy the excitement of the chase.

Automobile raids were added to the rioting Monday night. Cars from which rifle and revolver shots were fired were driven at great speed through sections inhabited by Negroes. Negroes defended themselves by "sniping" and volley-firing from ambush and barricade. So great was the fear of these raiding parties that the Negroes distrusted all motor vehicles and frequently opened fire on them without waiting to learn the intent of the occupants. This type of warfare was kept up spasmodically all Tuesday and was resumed with vigor Tuesday night.

At midnight, Monday, street-car clashes ended by reason of a general strike on the surface and elevated lines. The street-railway tie-up was complete for the remainder of the week. But on Tuesday morning this was a new source of terror for those who tried to walk to their places of employment. Men were killed enroute to their work through hostile territory. Idle men congregated on the streets, and gang-rioting increased. A white gang of soldiers and sailors in uniform, augmented by civilians, raided the "Loop," or downtown section of Chicago, early Tuesday, killing two Negroes and beating and robbing several others. In the course of these activities they wantonly destroyed property of white business men.

Gangs sprang up as far south as Sixty-third Street in Englewood and in the section west of Wentworth Avenue near Forty-seventh Street. Premeditated depredations were the order of the night. Many Negro homes in mixed districts were attacked, and several of them were burned. Furniture was stolen or destroyed. When raiders were driven off they would return again and again until their designs were accomplished.

The contagion of the race war broke over the boundaries of the South Side and spread to the Italians on the West Side. This community became excited over a rumor, and an Italian crowd killed a Negro, Joseph Lovings.

Wednesday saw a material lessening of crime and violence. The "Black Belt" and the district immediately west of it were still storm centers. But the peak of the rioting had apparently passed, although the danger of fresh outbreaks of magnitude was still imminent. Although companies of the militia had been mobilized in nearby armories as early as Monday night, July 28, it was not until Wednesday evening at 10:30 that the mayor yielded to pressure and asked for their help.

Rain on Wednesday night and Thursday drove idle people of both races into their homes. The temperature fell, and with it the white heat of the riot. From this time on the violence was sporadic, scattered, and meager. The riot seemed well under control, if not actually ended.

Friday witnessed only a single reported injury. At 3:35 A.M. Saturday incendiary fires burned forty-nine houses in the immigrant neighborhood west of the Stock Yards. Nine hundred and forty-eight people, mostly Lithuanians, were made homeless, and the property loss was about $250,000. Responsibility for these fires was never fixed. The riot virtually ceased on Saturday. For the next few days injured were reported occasionally, and by August 8 the riot zone had settled down to normal and the militia was withdrawn.

E. U. ESSIEN-UDOM

Garvey and Garveyism

Blacks soon discovered that there was no "promised land," that no region in America provided solutions for the myriad problems they had faced since slavery. DuBois and others formed the Niagara Movement to speak out on political issues. (It became the National Association for the Advancement of Colored People in 1909–10.) But no federal legislation was created during the first quarter of the century to guarantee equal rights or opportunities for black people. Urban violence continued, and even the patriotism of blacks serving in the American army during World War I earned them no respect or their people any justice. Returning black veterans were lynched, some while in uniform, and the Ku Klux Klan reorganized into an even more effective terrorist organization in 1919.

At this impasse, the one man who clearly demonstrated an ability to understand the feelings of the black masses was Marcus Garvey, and his organization, the Universal Negro Improvement Association, proved successful where many other groups had failed. Garvey never won the support of certain key black intellectuals, and his message never seemed very attractive to the black middle class. But many others found his gospel of pride and separation very compelling. Much of his philosophy of pan-African nationalism is still alive, and Garvey still stands as one of the most important black leaders of the century.

In this selection, the Nigerian intellectual E. U. Essien-Udom gives a summary of Garvey's life and times; two representative speeches by Garvey follow.

GARVEY AND GARVEYISM   From *The Philosophy and Opinions of Marcus Garvey* or *Africa for the Africans*. Compiled by Amy Jacques Garvey, 2 vols. 1923, 1925; 2nd Edition, two volumes in one, with an introduction by E. U. Essien-Udom, Frank Cass, London; Humanities Press, New York, 1967.

The PHENOMENON GENERALLY DESCRIBED AS "BLACK NATIONALISM" among Negroes in the New World was given the clearest and loudest expression by Marcus Mosiah Garvey, who has been described by his biographer, Edmund D. Cronon,[1] as a "largely self-educated but supremely confident black man." Marcus Mosiah Garvey was born on August 17, 1887 to Marcus and Sarah Garvey in the little town of Saint Ann's Bay, Saint Ann, Jamaica, West Indies.

Garvey's father is said to have been a descendant of the Maroons—these were Africans who, having fled to the hills to establish free communities after the English had captured Jamaica from the Spaniards in 1655, successfully repulsed several British military assaults, and in 1739 gained local autonomy from the white rulers of Jamaica. He was a master mason and was well read. A stern and reticent man, he appears to have been self-centred, and often given to brooding. However, a contemporary has remarked that he stood shoulder-high above the inhabitants of Saint Ann's Bay. Sarah Garvey has been described as the opposite of her husband in every way. A Jewish woman who knew both Sarah and Marcus reports that "she was one of the most beautiful black women" she had seen: ". . . her skin was black and soft as velvet; her eyes jet black, large, liquid and sad. Her voice was gentle and caressing, her figure well shaped and erect. She was a regular Church-goer at the Wesleyan Methodist Church. Mr. Garvey only attended funerals, which were not often. . . ."[2]

The Garveys had eleven children; all but two, Marcus Mosiah and his sister, Indiana, died in childhood. It is said that Sarah Garvey wanted to name her youngest and only surviving son Moses, hoping that he would "be like Moses, and lead his people." His father who believed in astromancy, insisted on naming him Marcus. Said he, "any boy born under the planet Leo—the Lion—when the Sun is in the ascendancy is bound to be a leader in his line." A compromise was struck, Sarah added Mosiah as a middle name; and truly the young man named Marcus Mosiah Garvey later became the "Black Moses" for millions of his race.

The Garveys were not wealthy. Unlike the big plantation owners who sent their children to secondary schools and colleges in England, they

---

[1] Edmund D. Cronon, *Black Moses: The Story of Marcus Garvey and the Universal Negro Improvement Association* (Madison: The University of Wisconsin Press), 1955.

[2] Quoted in *Garvey and Garveyism,* p. 4. [A. Jacques Garvey, Kingston, Jamaica, 1963.]

might have been able to send their only son to Kingston (the Capital) for higher education. Marcus Mosiah indeed had hoped that he would attend school in Kingston but because of his father's involvement in unnecessary court actions, owing to his "stubbornness," he lost his properties including all his lands except the plot where his house stood. Consequently, Marcus Mosiah received his entire formal education at a local elementary school. At 14, he was forced to leave school and was apprenticed to learn printing with his godfather, Mr. Burrowes. Here, Garvey took advantage of a substantial library owned by Mr. Burrowes who allowed him free access to it. Three years later (1904), he left Saint Ann's Bay to seek work as a printer at Kingston.

In Kingston, Garvey found employment at one of Jamaica's largest printing firms, the P. A. Benjamin Company. There, he made rapid advancements so that at 20, Garvey had become a master-printer and foreman. In 1907, he was involved in a strike called by the Printers' Union, the first labour organization to be established in Jamaica. The printers had demanded wage increases and better working conditions. When their demands were not met, they went on strike. Although the management promised an increase in Garvey's pay, the foreman went on strike with the workers. For this, he was blacklisted by his employer. Because his activities as the strike leader had prejudiced private employers against him, Garvey left the Company to work at the Government Printing Office.

His experiences had led Garvey to believe that only organized action could improve the position of the black worker. In 1910, this young man who was increasingly becoming restless started a periodical, the *Garvey's Watchman,* which proved an unsuccessful venture. He then helped to establish the National Club, a political organisation which published *Our Own,* a fortnightly publication. At this time, Garvey associated with one Dr. Love, who was born in the Bahamas and educated in England. Dr. Love, publisher of the *Advocate,* spent the best years of his life in Jamaica where he invested time and money for the uplift of the black masses. His example and support was of considerable importance for Garvey. By now, Garvey had realized that effective cultural and political activities would require full time commitment as well as money. Eventually, he left his job at the Government Printing Office and decided to go to one of his maternal uncles at Costa Rica, where he hoped to earn enough money to return and continue his work in Jamaica.

At Costa Rica, his uncle helped him to get a job as a time-keeper with the United Fruit Company. There, Garvey was terribly disturbed by the plight of the black workers in the United Fruit Company's plantations. He was now more determined than ever before to work for the improvement of the lot of the masses of his race wherever they may be. He gave up his job at the plantation to go to Port Lemon (the Capital) where he protested to the British Consul about the treatment of Jamaican Negroes working on the plantations. His protest fell on deaf ears. Garvey was both disappointed and convinced that no white man would ever "regard the life of a black man equal to that of a white man." At Lemon, he started another paper called *La Nacionale* but he could not sustain it owing to lack of support from the apathetic Negro peasants. His uncle helped him to go to Bocasdel-Toro, Republic of Panama, where he experienced the same abuse and exploitation of the black worker. He worked there for some months, then went to Colon and started another paper called *La Prensa.* Garvey continued his travels in South America. He visited Ecuador, Nicaragua, Spanish Honduras, Columbia, and Venezuela. His experience was the same everywhere: exploitation and abuse of black workers, especially West Indians. Failing to secure the co-operation of British officials in these countries for the protection of British West Indian workers, Garvey returned to Jamaica in 1911, hoping that he could enlist the Jamaican government's sympathy and action for the protection of West Indian black workers in South America. He also hoped to acquaint the Jamaicans at home with the true working conditions in South America. Apparently, Garvey found the British officials at Kingston as equally indifferent to the plight of the Negroes as those officials he had approached in South America.

In 1912, Garvey went to London to learn what he could about the condition of Negroes in other parts of the British Empire. There, he met Duse Mohammed, publisher of the *African Times and Orient Review* (London) and later the *Comet* (Lagos, Nigeria). Through this association with an ardent pan-African nationalist, and contacts with African and West Indian nationalists, students and seamen, Garvey became deeply agitated by the colonial question, especially as it affected his African "fatherland." In addition, he read extensively on Africa.

In London, Garvey had also developed a keen interest in the racial problems in the United States of America. Influenced by Booker T. Washington's autobiography, *Up From Slavery,* Garvey was traumatically struck by the deteriorated position of the Negro people throughout the world. Almost ecstatically Garvey asked himself: "Where is the black man's Government? Where is his King and kingdom? Where is his President, his country, and his ambassador, his army, his navy, his men of big affairs? I could not find them, and then I declared, I will help to make them." This fantastic reaction and resolution is best understood if it is remembered that by the end of the last century practically the whole of Africa, excepting Egypt, Ethiopia and Liberia, were firmly under foreign domination. Similarly, in the New World the optimism which followed the emancipation of African slaves during the 19th century had waned. In the United States especially this ill-founded optimism was totally shattered with the introduction of the "Black Codes" in the South, and the collapse of the Reconstruction. Attempt was made in all but name to re-enslave the Negro masses, and everywhere in the Southern United States they were denied elementary rights of citizenship, were terrorized by physical violence, and, for all practical purposes, "lynched" economically. In Northern United States, Negroes constituted the most depressed bottom of the urban proletariat.

Garvey left England in the summer of 1914 inspired with the idea of "uniting all the Negro peoples of the world into one great body to establish a country and government absolutely their own." He envisaged the coming of "a new world of black men, not peons, serfs, dogs and slaves, but of a nation of sturdy men making their impress upon civilization and causing a new light to dawn upon the human race." Five days after his arrival in Jamaica, he established the Universal Negro Improvement Association and African Communities League (U.N.I.A.) and invited all the Negro people or "persons of Negro or African parentage" to join him in the crusade for rehabilitation of the race. Garvey became the President and Travelling Commissioner of the new organization. He was to be assisted by Thomas Smikle as Vice-President, Eva Aldred as President of the Ladies' Division, and T. A. McCormack as General Secretary; and Amy Ashwood, who later became Garvey's first wife, as Associate Secretary. Between 1914 and March 1916, Garvey laboured to unite the Negro masses in Jamaica, and to educate the "black bourgeoisie" to appreciate their responsibility towards the proletarians among their race. His efforts were largely unsuccessful, partly because of the hostility of the mulattoes to the U.N.I.A. and partly because of the apathy of the under-privileged Negro masses.

Meanwhile, Garvey had learned about Booker T. Washington and the help the latter was receiving from influential whites in the United States. He was particularly interested in Washington's programme at Tuskegee Institute, Alabama, which emphasized industrial and technical education of the Negroes. Garvey believed that the establishment of trade colleges along the same lines would help in improving the skills of Jamaican Negroes. The U.N.I.A.'s campaign to establish trade colleges received support from the white Mayor of Kingston, the Governor of the Island, and a Roman Catholic Bishop, but the scheme was vigorously opposed by "some of these coloured men of the island who did not want to be classified as Negroes but as whites."

In 1915, Garvey wrote to Booker T. Washington who encouraged him to visit Tuskegee. However, he did not visit the United States until March 23, 1916, when he arrived in Harlem, New York. Washington was dead by this time. Garvey's arrival in the United States was timely. With the death of the Sage of Tuskegee, the leadership contest which for nearly twenty years had raged between Washington and Dr. W. E. B. DuBois, who had repudiated the former's philosophy, was far from resolved. In a sense, Garvey was to fill the vacuum left by Washington and, inevitably, he was even more savagely assailed by DuBois and the Negro intelligentsia generally. Thus he inherited all the prejudices of the assimilationist Negro leadership against Washington but none of the support or prestige which the Sage of Tuskegee had enjoyed among Negroes and influential white leaders.

Washington's philosophy enunciated in his celebrated "Atlanta Compromise" address of 1895 has been summed up thusly: "Do not antagonize the white majority. Do not ask for the right to vote. Do not fight for civil liberties or against segregation. Go to school. Work hard. Save money. Buy property. Some day, the other things may come." These were the ideas openly challenged by DuBois who believed that the Negroes' retreat from demanding full social and political equality would leave them in a state of permanent subordination. To mobilize militant Negro opinion in support of full social and political equality (and certainly against Washington's conservatism), DuBois organized the Niagara Movement in 1905. The movement comprised mainly one faction of the Negro elite, but did not directly involve the masses. Its influence on both black and white opinion was probably very limited. However, in 1909, the National Association for the Advancement of Coloured People (N.A.A.C.P.), comprised of several prominent Negroes (including DuBois) and liberal whites, was founded. The N.A.A.C.P., known for its programme of integrating Negroes in the United States and for being largely responsible for destroying the legal basis of Negro subordination, was arraigned against Garvey. At any rate, intense leadership rivalry developed between spokesmen of the Negro elite and Garvey.

Garvey's arrival in the United States in 1916 was timely in another sense. The existence of large concentrations of an urbanized and disillusioned Negro proletariat in the ghettoes of Northern United States provided material for his militant nationalism. Their disillusionment was keener at the end of the First World War in which many Negroes had laid down their lives in defence of democracy abroad. They had hoped that the principles for which they had fought would be extended to them at home. Nearly 400,000 Negroes had served in the armed forces during the War, and Negro civilians at home had patriotically purchased more than $250,000,000 worth of bonds and stamps in the five major Liberty Loan drives.

In spite of their sacrifice, there was little improvement in the status of Negroes. Perhaps the only real change was in the Negro mood itself. The rights of citizenship had not been extended to the vast majority. Everywhere the tempo of violence against Negroes had been intensified during and after the War. In September 1917, Negro soldiers clashed with civilians in Houston (Texas); thirteen of them were speedily and summarily tried and executed; and forty-one others were sentenced to imprisonment for life, but were later pardoned and reinstated. In the same year, East St. Louis was the scene of a violent race riot in which at least forty Negroes lost their lives. In 1919, there were a total of twenty-six race riots in a number of cities throughout the country. The Ku-Klux-Klan reared its ugly head again in 1915 and spread its diabolical influence in twenty-seven states, including three Mid-West states, New York and parts of New England. The number of Negroes lynched annually had also increased during the War years. This was partially the state of affairs during the first few years of Garvey's arrival in the United States.

Garvey established a branch of the Universal Negro Improvement Association (U.N.I.A.) in Harlem in 1917. In two months, he built up a new organisation of about 1,500 members. Five years later, the membership had increased to "several" million Negroes in the United States, the West Indies, Latin America, and Africa. Although reliable figures on total membership of the U.N.I.A. are not available, one million represents the most conservative estimate; Garvey himself suggested six million.

Garvey was a pan-African nationalist. Undoubtedly, his basic commitment and dedication was the total liberation of Africa from alien rule, and the eventual establishment of a united, virile and powerful African state. He was aware that "all of us may not live to see the higher accomplishment of an African empire—so strong and powerful as to compel respect of mankind, but we in our life time can so work and act as to make the dream a possibility within another generation." Every other activity of Garvey was either secondary or instrumental to this basic goal: the acquisition of political power in Africa by "Africans abroad and at home." He tended to analogize, and not without some justification, the problem of New World Negroes with colonialism. After all, the Negroes in diaspora as well as those in Africa were subjected to com-

parable economic exploitation and social discrimination by white rulers
and capitalists. He believed firmly that until Africa was liberated, there
was no real hope for black people anywhere.

Consistent with his pan-African objectives, Garvey tended to regard
the New World Negroes as a vanguard for Africa's liberation from alien
rule. His strategy may be said to have been "selected colonization" of
parts of Africa by pioneering members of his organisation, technicians,
educators, doctors, and others equipped with the means to help in
African reconstruction. His opponents generally seized on this aspect of
his programme and maliciously charged him with proposing a mass
exodus of New World Negroes "back-to-Africa." Mrs. Amy Jacques
Garvey has appropriately summed up seven important principles of his
strategy:

   (i) Awakening and uniting Negroes the world over;
  (ii) Changing the thinking of the aroused to a realization of man-
       hood's potential abilities;
 (iii) Channelling the newly released emotional energies and resent-
       ment into constructive individual and racial interests;
  (iv) Mass sacrificial work and struggle to reach embryonic nation-
       hood—the interim stage;
   (v) Through legislation and otherwise to stress mass education along
       scientific and industrial lines, also character building which are
       the sinews of any nation in peace or war;
  (vi) The preparation of nationalists for the grave responsibilities of
       leading and directing young nations, whose people have been
       denied the principles and advantages of early preparation;
 (vii) The final efforts to unite and keep together the young nations,
       not only in (sic) their own protection, but as leaders of those
       still suffering under Colonial and Protectorate rule.

Given these objectives, it is needless to remark that the *Philosophy
and Opinions of Marcus Garvey* is, in the nature of doctrine and propaganda, meant to arouse and to induce particular type of action. It is also
a record of the reactions and yearnings of the oppressed masses of
Negroes in the New World. Unswerving commitment and dedication to
the cause of the "fatherland" or the race, discipline, sacrifice, and the
quality of self-reliance were required of all members of the U.N.I.A.

Garvey was keenly interested in building up an economic base as an
indispensable unit of racial emancipation, for, said he: "The reliance of
our race upon the progress and achievements of others for a consideration in sympathy, justice and rights is like a dependence upon a broken
stick, resting upon which will eventually consign you to the ground. . . ."

Through effective economic organisation he hoped to establish world-wide co-operation among the Negro people.

Garvey's economic programme included the establishment of the Black Star Steamship Company (which consisted of four ill-fated ships) and the Negro Factory Corporation. He sent to the Republic of Liberia a commercial and industrial mission of technicians who were to establish a settlement there. However, his effort to find a foothold for the U.N.I.A. in this African Republic was foiled, partly by British, French and American pressures on the Liberian President to repudiate the agreements between his government and the U.N.I.A. The U.N.I.A.'s commercial enterprises were complete failures partly because of sheer incompetence, which is often emphasized, but also because of sabotage from within and without.

The movement had other auxiliaries: the African Orthodox Church whose influence spread beyond the United States, the Universal African Legion, a semi-military organization, the Universal Black Cross Nurses, the Universal African Motor Corps, the Juvenile and the Black Flying Eagles, all equipped with officers and uniforms. In 1924, the Negro Political Union was established "to consolidate the political union of the Negro through which the race would express its political opinion." This was Garvey's first effort to participate directly in the domestic politics of the United States. He supported Calvin Coolidge, the Republican Presidential nominee. By this time, however, Garvey had become entangled with the United States Government over the business activities of the U.N.I.A. A weekly newspaper, the *Negro World,* edited by Garvey, was the main propaganda organ of the movement.

Apart from reaching his followers, through the *Negro World,* or other publications, Garvey brought together delegates from local branches at an annual convention. The first Convention was held in New York on August 1, 1920. It was attended by delegates from 25 countries— including countries in the West Indies, Central and South America, and Africa. An estimated 25,000 Negroes including delegates assembled at the Madison Square Garden on August 2, to hear Garvey deliver the keynote address to the Convention. The ceremony opened with the Universal Ethiopian Anthem spiritedly sung by the delegates.

Addressing the Convention, Garvey told his audience,

> We are the descendants of a suffering people; we are the descendants of a people determined to suffer no longer. We shall organize the 400,000,000 Negroes of the world into a vast organization to plant the banner of freedom on the great continent of Africa. . . . If Europe is

for the Europeans, then Africa shall be for the black people of the
world. We say it, we mean it. . . .

The Convention was a spectacular success. Harlemites were in festive
mood and thousands were thrilled by the parade of the U.N.I.A.'s African Legion, the Black Cross Nurses (200 strong and smartly attired in
white), and children, organized into a special auxiliary, marched along
with them. The Convention adopted the "Declaration of Rights of the
Negro Peoples of the World" and unanimously elected 33 year-old Garvey the Provisional President of Africa and President-General and Administrator of the U.N.I.A. A high Executive Council consisting of 18
members was also elected. Together with Garvey, they constituted the
"Provisional Government" of a United Africa. After the members of the
High Executive Council had been sworn in, Garvey conferred them
peerages and knighthoods such as Duke of the Nile. Others were made
Knights of the Distinguished Service Order of Ethiopia, Ashanti and
Mozambique. They were all provided with robes and capes, patterned
after the British orders of chivalry. The Convention was a singular
achievement the like of which had not been known before by the Negro
people in the United States or elsewhere. Garvey had set in motion a
mass movement with wide implications. In doing so, he threatened the
security and courted the dedicated opposition of the established assimila-
tion-oriented Negro leadership. Similarly, he aroused the suspicion of
officials of the United States and the outright opposition of the colonial
powers.

Opposition of Negro leaders to Garvey and Garveyism was both persistent and uncompromising. They resented Garvey as a person. Some, in
fact, employed the most abusive ephithets for describing his physical
appearance. Robert Bagnall, an official of the N.A.A.C.P., for example,
described him as "of unmixed stock . . . with protruding jaws and
heavy jowls, small bright pig-like eyes and rather bull-dog face." In
turn, however, Garvey regarded people like Bagnall as "bastards" who
"hate the Negro blood of their mothers, and endeavour to build up a
society based on colour of skin, and not on achievement and worth."
Garvey's antagonists regarded him as an alien, a Jamaican. He was an
upstart, and had challenged the leadership of the "sons of the soil."
He ought to go back to Jamaica "to carry on his work in his own home
and among his own people and to accomplish some of his ideals. Let him
do it. We will be the first to applaud any success he may have." (The
Crisis said editorially in 1928.) Because he had little formal education,
he was utterly despised by American Negro intellectuals and the rising

black bourgeoisie generally. He was a threat to the leadership of the Negro Church as well, and the founding of the African Orthodox Church further exacerbated the rivalry. The Negro elite had always shied away from mass movements and was repulsed by the U.N.I.A. Garvey was equally opposed to them, and regarded the mulattoes among his opponents as traitors of the Negro race. Ideologically, there was no meeting ground between Garvey and his Negro opponents—churchmen, politicians, trade unionists, socialists or communists. Instead, Garvey found some affinities between his ideas and those of white segregationists in Southern United States. While his opponents considered that Garvey was leading the Negro masses into a blind alley, he regarded their quest for cultural assimilation as leading Negroes ultimately to "racial suicide." His opponents were jubilant when in early January 1922, Garvey was arrested on a charge of using the mail to defraud.

The Black Star Company was Garvey's most ambitious commercial enterprise and his doom. Lacking business acumen himself or competent and honest associates, he risked his honour and movement on a highly competitive shipping business. Garvey's conception of the Black Star Line was not narrowly commercial. It was also thought of as a means of arousing self-confidence in the potentialities of the Negro people throughout the world. He appealed to followers through the pages of the *Negro World* and by mails to buy shares in the Company. He was able to raise substantial sums with which four worthless ships were purchased for a Company managed by some associates who were more cunning than scrupulous. In February 1922, a month after his arrest, Garvey and his associates were indicted and charged with knowingly using "fraudulent representations" and "deceptive artifices" in the sale of stock through the mails, and for advertising and selling space on a mythical ship. Garvey felt that this was a plot by "enemies of the Negro race" and enemies of his movement within the race, an attempt to besmirch his character and cause disaffection among his followers. With his arrest and indictment, opposition of Negro leaders to Garvey and Garveyism was intensified. Spearheaded by Chandler Owen and A. Philip Randolph, editors of the radical *Messenger Magazine,* Garvey's opponents united in August, 1922, under the auspices of a group called the Friends of Negro Freedom. They adopted the slogan "Garvey Must Go!" and demanded the deportation of the Jamaican. While his trial was pending, on January 15, 1923, eight prominent Negroes petitioned the United States Attorney-General, Mr. Harry M. Daugherty, to use his "full influence completely to disband and extirpate" the U.N.I.A. They pleaded that "the Attorney-General should vigorously and speedily push the government's case against Marcus Garvey for using the mails to defraud." The petitioners described the U.N.I.A. as a "vicious movement" and attacked Garvey as "an unscrupulous demagogue, who . . . sought to spread among Negroes distrust and hatred of all white people." The signatories included: Harry H. Pace, John E. Nail, Julia P. Coleman, all businessmen, Robert S. Abbott, Editor and Publisher of the *Chicago Defender,* Chandler Owen, Co-Editor of the *Messenger,* George V. Harris, Editor of the *New York News,* William Pickens, Field Secretary of the N.A.A.C.P., Robert W. Bagnall, Director of Branches of the N.A.A.C.P.

The trial of Garvey and his three associates, which had been delayed for nearly a year, took place in this atmosphere of opposition by influential Negroes and official suspicion. Before the trial began in May, 1923, Garvey had petitioned for the disqualification of Circuit Judge Julian W. Mack, who had been designated the trial judge. He argued that Judge Mack was a member of the National Association for the Advancement of Colored People and that he could not be impartial. Garvey recalled the fact that most of the signatories of the "Garvey Must Go!" petition to the Attorney-General five months earlier were members of the N.A.A.C.P. He observed also the sustained campaign against him and the U.N.I.A. by the *Crisis,* the official organ of the N.A.A.C.P. Garvey concluded that Judge Mack "would be unconsciously swayed to the side of the Government" and pleaded that another judge who was likely to be impartial be named. Judge Mack denied Garvey's motion. Although he admitted that he had contributed to the N.A.A.C.P., he rejected Garvey's conclusion from this fact. Garvey did not help his case when he dismissed his attorney a day after the trial had begun. He suspected his Negro lawyer, Cornelius W. McDougald, of possible complicity with the prosecution. From thence on, Garvey, a lay man who probably had read some law on his own during his first visit to England, pleaded his own case before a white jury.

The Government's case rested on the assumption that Garvey and his co-defendants had knowingly and with criminal intent used the mails to sell Black Star shares fully aware that the Company was in a terrible financial condition. There is little evidence that this was the case. Specifically, Garvey was found guilty of having caused promotional material to be sent through the mails to Benny Dancy, "who had testified with some confusion to having received such matter before he purchased his fifty-three shares of Black Star stock."[3] The verdict, concludes Cronon

---

[3] Cronon, *op. cit.,* p. 118.

who has studied the record of the trial meticulously, "was somewhat strange in that the other three Black Star co-defendants were acquitted of any complicity in the crime."[4] Nevertheless, he was sentenced to five years imprisonment. Was justice done? Mr. Armin Kohn, a white lawyer who handled Garvey's appeal, asked by newspaper reporters to comment on the case, is quoted to have said: "In my twenty-three years of practice at the New York Bar, I have never handled a case in which the defendant has been treated with such manifest unfairness and with such a palpable attempt at persecution as this one."[5] It is infinitely difficult to resist the conclusion that Garvey's conviction was political. However, in 1927, President Coolidge commuted the sentence and in December of that year, Garvey was deported from the United States as an undesirable alien. He returned to Jamaica where he continued to work for Negro emancipation. He later went to London where he established the headquarters of the U.N.I.A. but died there on June 10, 1940.

[4] *Ibid.*
[5] Quoted in *Garvey and Garveyism,* p. 128. After Garvey had dismissed his first lawyer, he retained Mr. Kohn for private consultation during the trial before Judge Mack.

MARCUS GARVEY

Speech Delivered at Madison Square Garden

[See headnote on page 233.]

*In Honor of the Return to America of the Delegation Sent to
Europe and Africa by the Universal Negro Improvement
Association to Negotiate for the Repatriation of
Negroes to a Homeland of Their Own in Africa*

Fellow Citizens:

The coming together, all over this country, of fully six million people of Negro blood, to work for the creation of a nation of their own
in their motherland, Africa, is no joke.

There is now a world revival of thought and action, which is causing
peoples everywhere to bestir themselves towards their own security,
through which we hear the cry of Ireland for the Irish, Palestine for
the Jew, Egypt for the Egyptian, Asia for the Asiatic, and thus we
Negroes raise the cry of Africa for the Africans, those at home and those
abroad.

Some people are not disposed to give us credit for having feelings,
passions, ambitions and desires like other races; they are satisfied to
relegate us to the back-heap of human aspirations; but this is a mistake.
The Almighty Creator made us men, not unlike others, but in His own
image; hence, as a race, we feel that we, too, are entitled to the rights
that are common to humanity.

The cry and desire for liberty is justifiable, and is made holy everywhere. It is sacred and holy to the Anglo-Saxon, Teuton and Latin; to
the Anglo-American it precedes that of all religions, and now come the

SPEECH DELIVERED AT MADISON SQUARE GARDEN   From *The Philosophy and Opinions of Marcus Garvey* or *Africa for the Africans*. Compiled by Amy Jacques
Garvey, 2 vols. 1923, 1925; 2nd Edition, two volumes in one, with an introduction
by E. U. Essien-Udom, Frank Cass, London; Humanities Press, New York, 1967.
The speech was delivered in New York on Sunday, March 16, 1924.

Irish, the Jew, the Egyptian, the Hindoo, and, last but not least, the Negro, clamoring for their share as well as their right to be free.

All men should be free—free to work out their own salvation. Free to create their own destinies. Free to nationally build up themselves for the upbringing and rearing of a culture and civilization of their own. Jewish culture is different from Irish culture. Anglo-Saxon culture is unlike Teutonic culture. Asiatic culture differs greatly from European culture; and, in the same way, the world should be liberal enough to allow the Negro latitude to develop a culture of his own. Why should the Negro be lost among the other races and nations of the world and to himself? Did nature not make of him a son of the soil? Did the Creator not fashion him out of the dust of the earth?—out of that rich soil to which he bears such a wonderful resemblance?—a resemblance that changes not, even though the ages have flown? No, the Ethiopian cannot change his skin; and so we appeal to the conscience of the white world to yield us a place of national freedom among the creatures of present-day temporal materialism.

We Negroes are not asking the white man to turn Europe and America over to us. We are not asking the Asiatic to turn Asia over for the accommodation of the blacks. But we are asking a just and righteous world to restore Africa to her scattered and abused children.

We believe in justice and human love. If our rights are to be respected, then, we, too, must respect the rights of all mankind; hence, we are ever ready and willing to yield to the white man the things that are his, and we feel that he, too, when his conscience is touched, will yield to us the things that are ours.

We should like to see a peaceful, prosperous and progressive white race in America and Europe; a peaceful, prosperous and progressive yellow race in Asia, and, in like manner, we want, and we demand, a peaceful, prosperous and progressive black race in Africa. Is that asking too much? Surely not. Humanity, without any immediate human hope of racial oneness, has drifted apart, and is now divided into separate and distinct groups, each with its own ideals and aspirations. Thus, we cannot expect any one race to hold a monopoly of creation and be able to keep the rest satisfied.

Distinct Racial Group Idealism

From our distinct racial group idealism we feel that no black man is good enough to govern the white man, and no white man good enough to rule the black man; and so of all races and peoples. No one feels that the other, alien in race, is good enough to govern or rule to the exclusion of native racial rights. We may as well, therefore, face the question of superior and inferior races. In twentieth century civilization there are no inferior and superior races. There are backward peoples, but that does not make them inferior. As far as humanity goes, all men are equal, and especially where peoples are intelligent enough to know what they want. At this time all peoples know what they want—it is liberty. When a people have sense enough to know that they ought to be free, then they naturally become the equal of all, in the higher calling of man to know and direct himself. It is true that economically and scientifically certain races are more progressive than others; but that does not imply superiority. For the Anglo-Saxon to say that he is superior because he introduced submarines to destroy life, or the Teuton because he compounded liquid gas to outdo in the art of killing, and that the Negro is inferior because he is backward in that direction is to leave one's self open to the retort "Thou shalt not kill," as being the divine law that sets the moral standard of the real man. There is no superiority in the one race economically monopolizing and holding all that would tend to the sustenance of life, and thus cause unhappiness and distress to others; for our highest purpose should be to love and care for each other, and share with each other the things that our Heavenly Father has placed at our common disposal; and even in this, the African is unsurpassed, in that he feeds his brother and shares with him the product of the land. The idea of race superiority is questionable; nevertheless, we must admit that, from the white man's standard, he is far superior to the rest of us, but that kind of superiority is too inhuman and dangerous to be permanently helpful. Such a superiority was shared and indulged in by other races before, and even by our own, when we boasted of a wonderful civilization on the banks of the Nile, when others were still groping in darkness; but because of our unrighteousness it failed, as all such will. Civilization can only last when we have reached the point where we will be our brother's keeper. That is to say, when we feel it righteous to live and let live.

No Exclusive Right to the World

Let no black man feel that he has the exclusive right to the world, and other men none, and let no white man feel that way, either. The world is the property of all mankind, and each and every group is entitled to a portion. The black man now wants his, and in terms uncompromising he is asking for it.

The Universal Negro Improvement Association represents the hopes and aspirations of the awakened Negro. Our desire is for a place in the world; not to disturb the tranquillity of other men, but to lay down our burden and rest our weary backs and feet by the banks of the Niger, and sing our songs and chant our hymns to the God of Ethiopia. Yes, we want rest from the toil of centuries, rest of political freedom, rest of economic and industrial liberty, rest to be socially free and unmolested, rest from lynching and burning, rest from discrimination of all kinds.

Out of slavery we have come with our tears and sorrows, and we now lay them at the feet of American white civilization. We cry to the considerate white people for help, because in their midst we can scarce help ourselves. We are strangers in a strange land. We cannot sing, we cannot play on our harps, for our hearts are sad. We are sad because of the tears of our mothers and the cry of our fathers. Have you not heard the plaintive wail? It is your father and my father burning at stake; but, thank God, there is a larger humanity growing among the good and considerate white people of this country, and they are going to help. They will help us to recover our souls.

As children of captivity we look forward to a new day and a new, yet ever old, land of our fathers, the land of refuge, the land of the Prophets, the land of the Saints, and the land of God's crowning glory. We shall gather together our children, our treasures and our loved ones, and, as the children of Israel, by the command of God, faced the promised land, so in time we shall also stretch forth our hands and bless our country.

Good and dear America that has succored us for three hundred years knows our story. We have watered her vegetation with our tears for two hundred and fifty years. We have built her cities and laid the foundation of her imperialism with the mortar of our blood and bones for three centuries, and now we cry to her for help. Help us, America, as we helped you. We helped you in the Revolutionary War. We helped you in the Civil War, and, although Lincoln helped us, the price is not half paid. We helped you in the Spanish-American War. We died nobly and courageously in Mexico, and did we not leave behind us on the stained battlefields of France and Flanders our rich blood to mark the poppies' bloom, and to bring back to you the glory of the flag that never touched the dust? We have no regrets in service to America for three hundred years, but we pray that America will help us for another fifty years until we have solved the troublesome problem that now confronts us. We know and realize that two ambitious and competitive races cannot live permanently side by side, without friction and trouble, and that is why the white race wants a white America and the black race wants and demands a black Africa.

Let white America help us for fifty years honestly, as we have helped her for three hundred years, and before the expiration of many decades there shall be no more race problem. Help us to gradually go home, America. Help us as you have helped the Jews. Help us as you have helped the Irish. Help us as you have helped the Poles, Russians, Germans and Armenians.

The Universal Negro Improvement Association proposes a friendly co-operation with all honest movements seeking intelligently to solve the race problem. We are not seeking social equality; we do not seek intermarriage, nor do we hanker after the impossible. We want the right to have a country of our own, and there foster and re-establish a culture and civilization exclusively ours. Don't say it can't be done. The Pilgrims and colonists did it for America, and the new Negro, with sympathetic help, can do it for Africa.

Back to Africa

The thoughtful and industrious of our race want to go back to Africa, because we realize it will be our only hope of permanent existence. We cannot all go in a day or year, ten or twenty years. It will take time under the rule of modern economics, to entirely or largely depopulate a country of a people, who have been its residents for centuries, but we feel that, with proper help for fifty years, the problem can be solved. We do not want all the Negroes in Africa. Some are no good here, and naturally will be no good there. The no-good Negro will naturally die in fifty years. The Negro who is wrangling about and fighting for social equality will naturally pass away in fifty years, and yield his place to the progressive Negro who wants a society and country of his own.

Negroes are divided into two groups, the industrious and adventurous, and the lazy and dependent. The industrious and adventurous believe that whatsoever others have done it can do. The Universal Negro Improvement Association belongs to this group, and so you find us working, six million strong, to the goal of an independent nationality. Who will not help? Only the mean and despicable "who never to himself hath said, this is my own, my native land." Africa is the legitimate, moral and righteous home of all Negroes, and now, that the time is coming for all to assemble under their own vine and fig tree, we feel it our duty to arouse every Negro to a consciousness of himself.

White and black will learn to respect each other when they cease to be active competitors in the same countries for the same things in politics and society. Let them have countries of their own, wherein to aspire and climb without rancor. The races can be friendly and helpful to each other, but the laws of nature separate us to the extent of each and every one developing by itself.

We want an atmosphere all our own. We would like to govern and rule ourselves and not be encumbered and restrained. We feel now just as the white race would feel if they were governed and ruled by the Chinese. If we live in our own districts, let us rule and govern those districts. If we have a majority in our communities, let us run those communities. We form a majority in Africa and we should naturally govern ourselves there. No man can govern another's house as well as himself. Let us have fair play. Let us have justice. This is the appeal we make to white America.

MARCUS GARVEY

An Appeal to the Conscience of the Black Race to See Itself

[See headnote on page 233.]

It IS SAID TO BE A HARD AND DIFFICULT TASK TO ORGANIZE AND KEEP together large numbers of the Negro race for the common good. Many have tried to congregate us, but have failed, the reason being that our characteristics are such as to keep us more apart than together.

The evil of internal division is wrecking our existence as a people, and if we do not seriously and quickly move in the direction of a readjustment it simply means that our doom becomes imminently conclusive.

For years the Universal Negro Improvement Association has been working for the unification of our race, not on domestic-national lines

AN APPEAL TO THE CONSCIENCE OF THE BLACK RACE TO SEE ITSELF From *The Philosophy and Opinions of Marcus Garvey* or *Africa for the Africans*. Compiled by Amy Jacques Garvey, 2 vols. 1923, 1925; 2nd Edition, two volumes in one, with an introduction by E. U. Essien-Udom, Frank Cass, London; Humanities Press, New York, 1967.

only, but universally. The success which we have met in the course of our effort is rather encouraging, considering the time consumed and the environment surrounding the object of our concern.

It seems that the whole world of sentiment is against the Negro, and the difficulty of our generation is to extricate ourselves from the prejudice that hides itself beneath, as well as above, the action of an international environment.

Prejudice is conditional on many reasons, and it is apparent that the Negro supplies, consciously or unconsciously, all the reasons by which the world seems to ignore and avoid him. No one cares for a leper, for lepers are infectious persons, and all are afraid of the disease, so, because the Negro keeps himself poor, helpless and undemonstrative, it is natural also that no one wants to be of him or with him.

Progress and Humanity

Progress is the attraction that moves humanity, and to whatever people or race this "modern virtue" attaches itself, there will you find the splendor of pride and self-esteem that never fail to win the respect and admiration of all.

It is the progress of the Anglo-Saxons that single them out for the respect of all the world. When their race had no progress or achievement to its credit, then, like all other inferior peoples, they paid the price in slavery, bondage, as well as through prejudice. We cannot forget the time when even the ancient Briton was regarded as being too dull to make a good Roman slave, yet today the influence of that race rules the world.

It is the industrial and commercial progress of America that causes Europe and the rest of the world to think appreciatively of the Anglo-American race. It is not because one hundred and ten million people live in the United States that the world is attracted to the republic with so much reverence and respect—a reverence and respect not shown to India with its three hundred millions, or to China with its four hundred millions. Progress of and among any people will advance them in the respect and appreciation of the rest of their fellows. It is such a progress that the Negro must attach to himself if he is to rise above the prejudice of the world.

The reliance of our race upon the progress and achievements of others for a consideration in sympathy, justice and rights is like a dependence upon a broken stick, resting upon which will eventually consign you to the ground.

Self-Reliance and Respect

The Universal Negro Improvement Association teaches our race self-help and self-reliance, not only in one essential, but in all those things that contribute to human happiness and well-being. The disposition of the many to depend upon the other races for a kindly and sympathetic consideration of their needs, without making the effort to do for themselves, has been the race's standing disgrace by which we have been judged and through which we have created the strongest prejudice against ourselves.

There is no force like success, and that is why the individual makes all efforts to surround himself throughout life with the evidence of it. As of the individual, so should it be of the race and nation. The glittering success of Rockefeller makes him a power in the American nation; the success of Henry Ford suggests him as an object of universal respect, but no one knows and cares about the bum or hobo who is Rockefeller's or Ford's neighbor. So, also, is the world attracted by the glittering success of races and nations, and pays absolutely no attention to the bum or hobo race that lingers by the wayside.

The Negro must be up and doing if he will break down the prejudice of the rest of the world. Prayer alone is not going to improve our condition, nor the policy of watchful waiting. We must strike out for ourselves in the course of material achievement, and by our own effort and energy present to the world those forces by which the progress of man is judged.

A Nation and Country

The Negro needs a nation and a country of his own, where he can best show evidence of his own ability in the art of human progress. Scattered as an unmixed and unrecognized part of alien nations and civilizations is but to demonstrate his imbecility, and point him out as an unworthy derelict, fit neither for the society of Greek, Jew nor Gentile.

It is unfortunate that we should so drift apart, as a race, as not to see that we are but perpetuating our own sorrow and disgrace in failing to appreciate the first great requisite of all peoples—organization.

Organization is a great power in directing the affairs of a race or nation toward a given goal. To properly develop the desires that are uppermost, we must first concentrate through some system or method, and there is none better than organization. Hence, the Universal Negro Improvement Association appeals to each and every Negro to throw in his lot with those of us who, through organization, are working for the universal emancipation of our race and the redemption of our common country, Africa.

No Negro, let him be American, European, West Indian or African, shall be truly respected until the race as a whole has emancipated itself, through self-achievement and progress, from universal prejudice. The Negro will have to build his own government, industry, art, science, literature and culture, before the world will stop to consider him. Until then, we are but wards of a superior race and civilization, and the outcasts of a standard social system.

The race needs workers at this time, not plagiarists, copyists and mere imitators; but men and women who are able to create, to originate and improve, and thus make an independent racial contribution to the world and civilization.

Monkey Apings of "Leaders"

The unfortunate thing about us is that we take the monkey apings of our "so-called leading men" for progress. There is no progress in aping white people and telling us that they represent the best in the race, for in that respect any dressed monkey would represent the best of its species, irrespective of the creative matter of the monkey instinct. The best in a race is not reflected through or by the action of its apes, but by its ability to create of and by itself. It is such a creation that the Universal Negro Improvement Association seeks.

Let us not try to be the best or worst of others, but let us make the effort to be the best of ourselves. Our own racial critics criticise us as dreamers and "fanatics," and call us "benighted" and "ignorant," because they lack racial backbone. They are unable to see themselves creators of their own needs. The slave instinct has not yet departed from them. They still believe that they can only live or exist through the good graces of their "masters." The good slaves have not yet thrown off their shackles; thus, to them, the Universal Negro Improvement Association is an "impossibility."

It is the slave spirit of dependence that causes our "so-called leading men" (apes) to seek the shelter, leadership, protection and patronage of the "master" in their organization and so-called advancement work. It is the spirit of feeling secured as good servants of the master, rather than as independents, why our modern Uncle Toms take pride in laboring under alien leadership and becoming surprised at the audacity of the Universal Negro Improvement Association in proclaiming for racial liberty and independence.

But the world of white and other men, deep down in their hearts, have much more respect for those of us who work for our racial salvation under the banner of the Universal Negro Improvement Association, than they could ever have in all eternity for a group of helpless apes and beggars who make a monopoly of undermining their own race and belittling themselves in the eyes of self-respecting people, by being "good boys" rather than able men.

Surely there can be no good will between apes, seasoned beggars and independent minded Negroes who will at least make an effort to do for themselves. Surely, the "dependents" and "wards" (and may I not say racial imbeciles?) will rave against and plan the destruction of movements like the Universal Negro Improvement Association that expose them to the liberal white minds of the world as not being representative of the best in the Negro, but, to the contrary, the worst. The best of a race does not live on the patronage and philanthropy of others, but makes an effort to do for itself. The best of the great white race doesn't fawn before and beg black, brown or yellow men; they go out, create for self and thus demonstrate the fitness of the race to survive; and so the white race of America and the world will be informed that the best in the Negro race is not the class of beggars who send out to other races piteous appeals annually for donations to maintain their coterie, but the groups within us that are honestly striving to do for themselves with the voluntary help and appreciation of that class of other races that is reasonable, just and liberal enough to give to each and every one a fair chance in the promotion of those ideals that tend to greater human progress and human love.

The work of the Universal Negro Improvement Association is clear and clean-cut. It is that of inspiring an unfortunate race with pride in self and with the determination of going ahead in the creation of those ideals that will lift them to the unprejudiced company of races and nations. There is no desire for hate or malice, but every wish to see all mankind linked into a common fraternity of progress and achievement that will wipe away the odor of prejudice, and elevate the human race to the height of real godly love and satisfaction.

ROI OTTLEY AND WILLIAM WEATHERBY

The Depression

There are two realities in the United States, one for whites and another for blacks. During the Depression, the former was bad, but the latter was worse. Black people, particularly those in the cities, felt the harshness of the Depression in a way that most whites did not. Officials in urban areas whose welfare resources were near depletion felt no urge to think first of the blacks who were needy. By 1935, approximately two-thirds of the black people who were employable required public assistance. Fledgling labor unions, pioneered by such men as A. Philip Randolph, were still too weak to provide much help. Other white-dominated labor unions were frankly racist. The days of the CIO were still in the future.

As Roi Ottley and William Weatherby here report, Harlem, which has been the "capital" of black American life during this century, reacted to the Depression in ways peculiar to itself and to its own rich complexities. But it shared with other American communities the desperation and turbulence felt by men without jobs and security. And Harlem, like other American communities under similar pressures, finally exploded in frustration and anger.

BLACK HARLEM, 1929–1935—HAND-TO-MOUTH LIVING HAD BEEN THE rule in Harlem for many years. Though some had tasted of the fatted calf during lush days, more than two thousand Negro families were destitute at the height of prosperity.[1] Before the full effects of the Depression were felt, the average weekly income of a Negro workingman had been eighteen dollars. Sixty per cent of the married women worked, a figure four times higher than that of the native-born white Americans.[2] In twenty-five years Harlem's population had increased more than six hundred per cent to more than 350,000 (equal to the total population of

[1] The New York Charity Organization Society reported 592 Harlem Negro families under their care from 1927 to 1928, and these comprised only 24.7 per cent of all Negro families receiving charity.
[2] Beverly Smith, New York *Herald Tribune,* February 10, 1930.
THE DEPRESSION From *The Negro in New York: An Informal Social History,* edited by Roi Ottley and William J. Weatherby. New York: The New York Public Library and Oceana Publications, Inc. Copyright © 1967, The New York Public Library. Two short verse extracts by Langston Hughes and Abe Hill, respectively, have been omitted.

Rochester, N.Y.), with an average density of 233 persons per acre compared with 133 for the rest of Manhattan. The community had become
a vast swarming hive in which families were doubled and trebled in
apartments meant for one family.[3] But with the financial collapse in
October 1929, a large mass of Negroes were faced with the reality of
starvation and they turned sadly to the public relief. When the few
chanted optimistically, "Jesus will Lead Me and the Welfare will Feed
Me," the many said it was a knowing delusion, for the Home Relief
Bureau allowed only eight cents a meal for food; meanwhile men,
women, and children combed the streets and searched in garbage cans,
many foraging with dogs and cats.

Tenement Dwellings

The crashing drop of wages drove Negroes back to the already
crowded hovels east of Lenox Avenue. In many blocks one toilet served
a floor of four apartments. Most of the apartments had no private bath-
rooms or even the luxury of a public bath. Wherever a tub was found it
usually had been installed in the kitchen. Without exception these tenements were filthy and vermin-ridden. Along Fifth Avenue, between
135th and 138th Streets, were flats with old-fashioned toilets which rarely
flushed and, when they were, they often overflowed on the floors below.
In the winter the gaping holes in the skylights allowed cold air to sweep
down the staircase, sometimes freezing the flush for weeks. Coal grates
provided the only heat. The dwellers scoured the neighborhood for fuel,
and harassed janitors in the surrounding districts were compelled to
stand guard over coal deliveries until they were safely stored in the
cellars. Landlords in this section hired a janitor for nothing more than
a basement to exist in, for which he had to clean six floors, take care of
sidewalk and backyard, haul garbage, make minor repairs, and where
a house had a hot-water furnace he had to stoke it.[4]

---

[3] State of New York, *Report of the New York State Temporary Commission on
the Condition of the Urban Colored Population to the Legislature of the State
of New York* (Albany, J. B. Lyon 1938) 44–56.
[4] More than 85 per cent of these buildings were old-law tenements.
This information—and much of this chapter—is derived from the report of The
Mayor's Commission on Conditions in Harlem, "The Negro in Harlem: A Report on Social and Economic Conditions Responsible for the Outbreak of March
19, 1935" (La Guardia Papers). Although the report was not published at the
time, the *Amsterdam News* (July 18, 1936) later printed a summary, and some
of the commission's findings were also reported in E. Franklin Frazier, "Negro
Harlem: An Ecological Study," *The American Journal of Sociology* XLIII (July
1937) 72–88.—Ed.

10,000 in Dungeons

Many families had been reduced to living below street level. It was estimated that more than ten thousand Negroes lived in cellars and basements which had been converted into makeshift flats. Packed in damp, rat-ridden dungeons, they existed in squalor approaching that of the Arkansas sharecroppers. Floors were of cracked concrete and the walls were whitewashed rock, water-drenched and rust-streaked. There were only slits for windows. A tin can in a corner covered by a sheet of newspaper was the only toilet. There was no running water in some, and no partitions to separate the adults from the curious eyes of the young. Packing boxes were used as beds, tables, and chairs. In winter rags and newspapers were stuffed into the numerous cracks to keep out the wind.

. . .

Shunted off into these run-down sections, Negroes were forced to pay exorbitant rents while landlords relaxed supervision and flagrantly violated the city building and sanitary codes. Compared with twenty to twenty-five per cent of their income generally paid by white families for rent, Negro tenants paid from forty to fifty per cent.[5] More than half of the Negro families were forced to take in lodgers to augment the family income. Frequently whole families slept in one room. Envied was the family who had a night worker as a lodger. He would occupy a bed in the day that would be rented out at night—same room, same bed, same sheets, and same bedbugs. This was described as the "hot bed." If the family had a bathtub, it, too, after being covered with boards, would be rented out.

The artificial scarcity of dwellings was accentuated by white property owners who in making a Negro district had heightened the housing problem of Negroes and thus were able to maintain high rents. A prominent member of the New York City Realty Board is quoted as saying:

> I believe a logical section for Negro expansion in Manhattan is East Harlem. At present this district has reached such a point of deterioration that its ultimate residential pattern is most puzzling. Many blocks have a substantial section of their buildings boarded up or demolished and a goodly percentage of those remaining are in disrepair and in violation of law . . . An influx of Negroes into East Harlem would not work a hardship on the present population of the area, because its

[5] Mayor's Commission Report. (See preceding note.—Ed.)

present residents could move to any other section of New York without the attendant racial discrimination which the Negro would encounter if he endeavored to locate in other districts.[6]

"Last Hired, First Fired"

Discrimination against employment of Negroes had practically closed
the doors to any and all types of occupations. Generally, the poorer half
of the colored population lived on an income which was only forty-six
per cent of that of the poorer half of the white population.[7]

The people of Harlem regarded the public utilities and trade unions
as the chief agencies of discrimination. Particularly were these barriers
extended to white-collar employment. During the period 1930–1935 the
Consolidated Gas Company employed 213 Negroes as porters among
its ten thousand employees; the New York Edison Company, with the
same number of employees, had only sixty-five Negroes, all of whom
were porters, cleaners, and hall men. The New York Telephone Company had a similar situation. The Interborough Rapid Transit Company
had 580 Negroes employed as messengers, porters, and cleaners, out of
ten thousand employees. The Western Union Telegraph Company had
two clerks and two operators and a few messengers employed in Harlem.
Except for this office, Negroes employed by this corporation occupied
the same menial positions as colored employees had in the other public
utilities. The Fifth Avenue Coach Company's policy of excluding Negroes had assumed the aspect of a caste system.

These companies had already placed themselves on record. In January 1927, the *Messenger* published a reply to an inquiry made by the
magazine concerning the employment of Negroes in the Consolidated
Gas Company. The letter signed by the company's vice-president, H. M.
Bundage, said: "Replying to your favor of November 23rd, have to advise that Negroes employed by us render common labor, maid service
and the like. We do not assign Negroes as stenographers, clerks or in-
spectors."

The New York Telephone Company in response to this same inquiry
wrote: "As to the question of employment by the company of persons
of known Negro descent, we might say that we do employ such persons
having some on our payroll at the present time assisting us in the conduct of our restaurant and lounge facilities."

[6] *Report of the New York State Temporary Commission* 49.
[7] Including relief and employed families of all classes together, one-half of all
native white families of New York City had incomes of less than $1,814 yearly,
but one-half of all Negro families had incomes of less than $837.

The trade unions, particularly the craft unions, were active in keeping the large employment fields barred to Negroes. In 1936 Charles L. Franklin, in his book the *Negro Labor Unionist of New York,* listed twenty-four international unions which excluded Negroes by initiation rituals. Out of the sixteen of these unions, covering a membership of 609,789 workers, who answered Franklin's inquiries concerning racial discriminations, thirteen said their restrictions remained. One answered that its constitution had been changed to include Negroes. Another reported that the word "white" had been removed from the constitution, but that this was meaningless since there were no colored telegraphers. Still another declared it had changed its policy and admitted colored lodges but would not have colored representation at its conventions.

Slave Market

After 1930 wage standards all but disappeared. This was particularly true of domestic work, which absorbed the vast majority of Negro women workers who, with the almost complete unemployment of Negro men, were becoming the sole support of the family. Unable to find positions through regular employment agencies or newspaper advertisements, many of them traveled to the Bronx in search of a day's work.[8] Frequent complaints of exploitation caused two young Negro women, Ella Baker and Marvel Cooke, to visit the area and describe their experiences in a magazine article. Here, they said, was

> a street corner market where Negro women are "rented" at unbelievably low rates for housework. The heaviest traffic is at 167th Street and Jerome Avenue where, on benches surrounding a green square, the victims wait grateful at least for some place to sit. At Simpson Street and Westchester Avenue they pose wearily against buildings and lampposts or scuttle about in an attempt to retrieve discarded boxes upon which to sit. Not only is human labor bartered and sold for the slave wage, but human love is also a marketable commodity. Whether it is labor or love, the women arrive as early as eight A.M. and remain as late as one P.M. or until they are hired. In rain or shine, hot or cold, they wait to work for ten, fifteen, and twenty cents per hour.

[8] "The practice of hiring for housework Negro women who congregate on street corners in the Bronx, known as 'domestic slave markets,' was severely condemned by the Bronx Citizens' Committee for the Improvement of Domestic Employees meeting. . . . It was proposed that centers of special agencies be established in the sections where they congregate in order to shelter them in severe weather and also see that prospective employers pay them fair wages."— New York *Times,* December 1, 1939.

They wash floors, clothes, windows and etc. Some had been maids and domestics in wealthy homes. Some were former marginal workers.[9]

Unemployed, the last refuge of these people was the relief offices, but here, they compained, they were often met with red tape and prejudice. At this time it was estimated that more than fifty thousand Negroes were neither working nor receiving relief.

. . .

Negro sharecroppers of the South who had lost their land drifted into the big cities and thousands found their way to Harlem, swelling the total of destitutes. Before the relief system was instituted, Negroes had tried every device from "Hoover block parties"[10] to "house rent parties" to tide over the bleak times. Negro churches took an active part in the feeding of many of the people, for private welfare agencies were flooded with pleas for aid. There was bitter waiting and more bitter street fighting.

In the first month in 1933 the Home Relief Bureau opened its doors and was immediately deluged with thousands of demands for food, clothing, and employment; some even asked for transportation to the South and the West Indies. Nine months later more than twenty-five thousand Negro families were receiving unemployment relief from the city, almost fifty per cent of all the families in Harlem. By 1936 the figure had become twenty-one per cent of the city's entire relief rolls. But Negroes had only nine per cent of the work relief jobs allotted by the Home Relief Bureau.[11] At the same time, the Welfare Department allowed $4.15 for food for two weeks to a male over sixteen years old, an increase over $3.30 in 1934 and $3.55 in 1935.[12]

Negroes made considerable complaint against the manner and the amount of relief distributed. But discrimination is a wisp which cannot be nailed down, and investigations of it were never very fruitful, though standardized relief under Mayor La Guardia's administration (1934–40) reduced the number of complaints. When Negroes received work relief they were assigned chiefly to menial jobs and were given an inferior status despite their previous training and experience.[13]

[9] Ella Baker and Marvel Cooke, "The Bronx Slave Market" *Crisis Magazine* XLII No. 11 (Nov. 1935) 330.
[10] President Hoover called for neighborhood endeavor to raise relief funds for the unemployed. This resulted in numerous "street" or "block" parties at which money was raised.
[11] Mayor's Commission Report.
[12] The city's relief allowance for a male adult was raised to $6.25 by 1939.
[13] Mayor's Commission Report.

The "Lung Block"

Unemployment, congestion, and substandard dwellings took their toll of Negro health. In 1934 a survey of twenty thousand residents of Negro Harlem, chiefly on the relief rolls, revealed three per cent suffering from pulmonary tuberculosis, comprising five per cent of the city's deaths from this disease. One block, especially, was known as the "lung block," where more than three thousand persons resided. The death rate there was twice that of white Manhattan.

"Tuberculosis," wrote Dr Louis T. Wright, a Negro, Fellow of the American College of Surgeons and surgical director of Harlem Hospital,

> we all know, is a disease that is rampant among the poverty stricken of all races. Colored people, therefore, show high morbidity and mortality rates from this condition alone, due to bad housing, inability to purchase food in adequate amounts, having to do laborious work while ill, little or no funds for medical care and treatment.

But most hospitals treating T.B. refused to admit Negro patients or limited the type of ward service available, except Sea View Hospital in Staten Island.

The story was the same with social diseases. For the five-year average from 1929–33 there were more than three thousand venereal cases among Negroes per hundred thousand, twice that among whites.[14] "It is not due to lack of morals," said Dr Wright, "but more directly to the lack of money, since with adequate funds these diseases could have been easily controlled." The real dread of Harlem was and still is pneumonia, in which the death rate was double that among whites. More dreadful was infant mortality, which took a toll of one in ten, twice that of the city as a whole. Twice as many Negro women died in childbirth as white women. A vital commentary on Harlem's health was the Central Harlem Health Center's report that it had filled approximately twenty thousand cavities in children's teeth in a six-month period.

The Morgue

Only one hospital in the city was and is concerned with the health of Negroes—Harlem Hospital, a public institution which has been a sore aggravating the life of the community for many years. Situated in the heart of the Harlem area, it attempted to care for more than 350,000 Negroes and all Puerto Ricans, Italians, and Jews living in East Harlem.

[14] New York Department of Health, Vital Statistics, December 1938.

Harlem Hospital contained 273 beds and 52 bassinets in 1932. Investigators for the Mayor's Commission discovered that "patients were forced to sleep on the floor, on mattresses and on benches, even in the maternity wards. Patients recently operated upon slept on benches or on chairs." Besides being the only city hospital in the community, Harlem Hospital also received Negro patients routed from other institutions in the city.

In 1932 proportionately twice as many people died at Harlem Hospital as at Bellevue Hospital.[15] It was for this reason that Negroes feared going to Harlem Hospital and referred to it fiercely as the "morgue" or "butcher shop." Many cases were refused admittance because of overcrowding; sometimes there were as many as fifteen patients waiting for attention in the emergency clinics. Only three ambulances were available for calls in Harlem in 1932. Most of the other hospitals refused to admit Negroes, and the few that did allow them to enter practiced segregation. In March 1937, the wife of W. C. Handy, composer of St. Louis Blues, lay critically ill in an ambulance more than an hour before the doors of Knickerbocker Hospital while the hospital officials debated whether or not a Negro should be admitted.

The city lacked also sufficient facilities for the training of Negro physicians and nurses. Negro internes were admitted in only three hospitals and Negro staff members only in hospitals "where there was a predominance of Negro patients." The medical staff of Harlem Hospital, Negro newspapers charged, pursued a policy of preventing Negro doctors and nurses from serving. In 1929 there were fifty-seven white doctors and only seven Negroes on the staff, though there were almost three hundred Negro physicians from whom to draw. The problem was identical for Negro nurses; they were admitted to only two training schools in the city—Lincoln Hospital and Harlem Hospital—and these had no white students. Even certain specialized sources were frequently not opened to them.[16]

Bitter Blossom[17]

Crime was the bitter blossom of poverty. The evil effects of bad housing and the lack of recreational facilities caused an alarming increase of juvenile crime. There were more Negro children in New York City

---

[15] Harlem Hospital reported a 11.2 mortality, Bellevue 5.7, and Coney Island Hospital 5 per cent in 1932.

[16] *Report of the New York State Temporary Commission* 31.

[17] Note on 2nd Draft: *"Call it Crime* (less flowery but better)."—Ed.

than in any other city in the world.[18] In 1919, the first year that the Courts of Domestic Relations kept special records of children, a little more than four per cent of the cases arraigned were Negroes. The ratio of Negro children arraigned in the Children's Court increased from 4.2 per cent in 1919 to 11.7 per cent in 1930. By 1938 almost twenty-five per cent of the cases were Negroes. This occurred while the total white children arraigned decreased 38.3 per cent.

The overwhelming bulk of Negroes are Protestant, and since the provisions of the New York State law insist upon neglected children being fostered only within their own religion, this left most of them without care. Only six out of thirty-four Protestant agencies cared for Negro children, though Roman Catholic care was found to be more adequate. During the five-year period 1931–1935, the Children's Court adjudged more than three thousand Negro children to be neglected and assigned most of them to a state institution to solve the problem of food and shelter. More than a third of the boys arrested were charged with offenses involving property, though most of them were arrested for hitching on trolleys, stealing subway rides, selling newspapers after 7:00 P.M., and shining shoes on the streets.[19]

Negro adults were chiefly arrested for their participation in the "policy racket"; a little less than eight per cent were women. Almost fifty per cent of the women arrested in the city during the period 1930–1935 were Negro and eighty per cent of these were charged with prostitution. The widespread operations of the "policy racket," which extracted so much money from the community for the benefit of racketeers, were due to a large extent to the desperate economic conditions of the people who had hoped to gain through luck what had been denied them through labor. A percentage of Negro arrests was the result of "the unconscious or deliberate discrimination on the part of the police force against Negro people."[20]

. . . While Rome Burns

Unemployment mounted to staggering totals as the country sank deeper in the mire of Depression. The Federal, State and City ad-

---

[18] The U.S. Census of 1930 reports 75,123 Negro children under fifteen years of age in this city, 46,580 in Manhattan. Under twenty there were 60,402 in Manhattan and 96,243 in the five boroughs. Owen R. Lovejoy, *The Negro Children of New York* (New York, The Children's Aid Society 1932) 5.

[19] Mayor's Commission Report.

[20] Mayor's Commission Report.

ministrations failed to act in the unemployment crisis at a time when the New York *Times* was acknowledging that bread lines were feeding thousands of people a day. Regarded as only a temporary situation, the relief financing began with popular contribution, for private charity had been overtaxed. When the Depression still did not pass, the city assumed partial support of the unemployed on a pay-as-you-go basis. A day did not pass without demonstrations in front of Harlem's Home Relief offices because of this unhappy plan.

Meanwhile, the affairs of the city had gone from bad to worse. The Seabury investigation began its hearings and turned up evidence which made it apparent that Mayor Walker was in a highly vulnerable position. Particularly was Harlem stirred when Seabury uncovered a vice ring which framed innocent women, a fact which Negro women knew only too well. There were many Negroes with friends who had been so victimized.

After Mayor Walker's resignation in 1932, the new city administration was faced with a relief problem that clamored for attention. It first threatened to tax the Stock Exchange and then borrowed money for relief. The point had been reached where the richest city in the richest country in the world could barely meet the needs of the emergency. Two vital things then happened: Roosevelt was elected President in 1932, and with his support La Guardia became Mayor in 1934. But an impenetrable wall of discrimination and segregation, of despair and unhappiness, had sprung up around Harlem. The appalling specter of sickness, poverty, and death grimly faced the Negro.

Protest

The long-expected explosion came on March 19, 1935, when ten thousand Negroes swept through Harlem destroying the property of white merchants. At the time, the outburst was labeled incorrectly a "race riot." White New York was almost panic-stricken as a nightmare of Negro revolt appeared to be a reality. In the very citadel of America's New Negro, "crowds went crazy like the remnants of a defeated, abandoned, hungry army." So formidable did the demonstration become that the Harlem Merchants' Association, a group of white shopkeepers, demanded unsuccessfully that Governor Lehman send troops to patrol the district.

An absurdly trivial incident furnished the spark. On the afternoon of March 19, a Puerto Rican lad was caught stealing a ten-cent penknife from the counter of a 5-and-10c store at West 135th Street. In resisting his captors, the boy hit them. Incensed at what appeared to be a retaliatory display of brutality by the store's white male employees, the Negro shoppers attacked them. Others spread the alarm that a Negro boy was being beaten. A general alarm brought police reserves. Rumor then followed that the boy had been beaten to death, and Negroes rushed to the scene intent upon "avenging" the "murder."

The police estimated that by 5:30 P.M. more than three thousand persons had gathered. Several step-ladder speakers addressed the crowds, charging the police with brutality and the white merchants with discrimination in employment. They were pulled down by the police and arrested. Two hours later protest leaflets were hurled through the neighborhood by members of the Young Communist League.

Large detachments of uniformed police, plainclothes men, and mounted police charged the crowds. Radio cars were driven on the sidewalks to disperse the people. Instead of withdrawing, the crowds grew in numbers and in hostility. Stirred to traditional anger against the police, they surged through the streets smashing store windows, hurling bricks, stones, and other missiles at the police. The mob broke into bands of three and four hundred and looted stores owned by whites. An anecdote is told of a Chinese laundryman who rushed out on the street and in self-defence hurriedly posted a sign on his store window which read: "Me colored too." On Lenox Avenue, the scene of most of the disorder, laden rioters emerged from shattered shop windows, while women stood on the fringe of crowds and shouted their choice of articles. A more humorous side of this was the case of a ragged youth who entered a wrecked tailor shop, outfitted himself with a new spring coat, complaining bitterly that he would be unable to return for alterations.

Sporadic outbursts continued until the early hours of the morning. Five hundred uniformed policemen, two hundred plainclothes men and mounted police, and fifty radio cars were active in quelling the outburst. At least two hundred stores owned by white merchants were smashed and their goods carried away. The total damage was estimated at more than two million dollars. Three deaths—all Negroes—were reported. Thirty-odd people were hospitalized for bullet wounds, knife lacerations, and fractured skulls, and more than two hundred persons received minor injuries, cuts and abrasions. Some one hundred persons, the majority of them Negroes, were arrested on charges of inciting to violence, unlawful assemblage, and looting. The boy, in the meantime, had actually been released, after the manager had refused to press charges.

". . . Foam on Top the Boiling Water"

Many reasons were offered for the uprising. The daily papers were particularly alarming in their reports, characterizing it as Harlem's worst riot in twenty-five years. The *Daily News* said that "Young Liberator orators whipped the fast-gathering crowds into a frenzy of hysteria . . . apparently to seize the opportunity to raise the issue against the store which had been picketed (by Negroes) for its refusal to hire colored clerks." The *Evening Journal,* manifestly incensed, traced its cause directly to "Communistic agitators circulating lying pamphlets." The *Post* said editorially that it would have been impossible to inflame Harlem's residents "if there had not been discrimination in employment and on relief, and justifiable complaints of high rents." The New York *Sun* derided the district attorney's (Dodge's) attempt to find Red propaganda behind the disturbance. "Actually," said the *Sun,* "Communists are more likely to have been passengers on the ebullience of a volatile population than authors of its effervescence."

Harlem's Negro leaders said that "seeing Red" was an official privilege and divergence, for the disorder had deep social, economic, and political roots. The Rev William Lloyd Imes, pastor of St James' Protestant Episcopal Church, felt that the white merchants were "reaping a harvest that they had sown," because of their refusal to employ Negroes. Channing Tobias, Negro field secretary of the Y.M.C.A., summed up the situation in this manner:

> It is erroneous and superficial to rush to the easy conclusion of District Attorney Dodge and the Hearst newspapers that the whole thing was a Communist plot. It is true there were Communists in the picture. But what gave them their opportunity? The fact that there were and still are thousands of Negroes standing in enforced idleness on the street corners of Harlem with no prospect of employment while their more favored Negro neighbors are compelled to spend their money with business houses directed by white absentee owners who employ white workers imported from every other part of New York City.

The views of the Negro leaders followed almost a uniform pattern. For example, George W. Harris, publisher of Harlem's *News* said:

> They [the rioters] were inspired because the colored people have been denied a decent economic opportunity. Private business, public utilities and the city government have oppressed a despondent Negro population and the result is a magazine of dynamite which it is only too easy

to set off. The City of New York has consistently denied positions to colored boys and girls. . . . The riots were born of impatience at segregation, dominations of underworld leaders, who have found a fertile field for their activities among the credulous Negroes of the neighborhood.

Roy Wilkins, editor of the *Crisis,* felt that it was a great mistake to dismiss the riot as the demonstration of a few agitators and attributed it to "a demonstration induced by discrimination against the Negroes in economics, employment and justice, and living conditions." In a series of articles for the New York *Post,* Rev Adam C. Powell, Jr, pastor of the Abyssinian Baptist Church, sought to prove that the outburst was essentially a social protest.

People's Court

Mayor La Guardia immediately named an investigating committee composed of prominent citizens, of which seven were Negro and five whites.[21] It was known as the Mayor's Commission on Conditions in Harlem, and its report was prepared by E. Franklin Frazier, a professor of sociology at Howard University. The public, anxious to air its grievances, appeared at the public hearings which were conducted by the commission at the Harlem Heights Court. Officials of large firms and utilities were placed on the stand and interrogated by the public and the commissioners alike. The witnesses who appeared also represented welfare and civil employee groups and labor unions. Anyone who had a complaint was welcomed to take the stand. This privilege often caused heated demonstrations by Negroes.[22]

On Saturday afternoons the Mayor's Commission held its public hearings. Hundreds of Negroes would crowd into the small municipal courtroom at West 151st Street, and before a member of the commission who presided as chairman, the people presented their case. Often emotional and incoherent, some timid and reticent, some noisy and inarticulate, but all with a burning resentment, they registered their complaints against the discriminations, the Jim-Crowism, and all the forms of oppression to which they had been subjected.

[21] Its members included Dr. Charles H. Roberts, Oswald Garrison Villard, Mrs. Eunice Hunton Carter, Hubert T. Delany, Countee Cullen, A. Philip Randolph, Judge Charles E. Toney, William Jay Schieffelin, Morris Ernst, Arthur Garfield Hays, Col. John G. Grimley, Rev. John W. Robinson, and Rev. William McCann.
[22] Interview with Arthur Garfield Hays, Nov. 22, 1939.

The testimony carried, despite its tragic character, an undertone of humor when expressed in the Negro idiom. In the relating of a story of the killing of a Negro youth by a white policeman, several Negroes who had been eyewitnesses to the incident were called to the stand. The first witness was a man who approached the stand reluctantly and in a lowered, muffled voice, as though he feared too open a discussion of the shooting or too blatant a knowledge of it might involve him unpleasantly with the police authorities, recounted what he had seen. His impatient audience punctuated his testimony with encouraging shouts of "Aw, man, talk up, you ain't down South!" This co-operation failed to help and the man completed his mutterings and sat down. A clean cut, aggressive, sharp-tongued youth succeeded him. In clear, resonant tones he measured out his answers. When the chairman asked, "Did you see any one throw any milk bottles at the police?," the boy answered, "Man, you know ain't nobody gonna throw no milk bottles at a cop who's got a forty-four [gun] staring him in the face . . . people ain't crazy!" Suddenly remembering the difficulty that the audience had had in hearing the testimony of his mouselike predecessor, he good-naturedly bellowed out, "Am I talkin' loud enough?," and the courtroom displayed its approval with a howl of laughter.

The city's commission turned over its report to Mayor La Guardia in March 1936, one year later. The 35,000-word document was published by the *Amsterdam News,* July 18, 1936. Whereas columns and columns of material appeared in the daily press during the riot, the same papers published only sedate accounts of the report. The *Amsterdam News'* "scoop" went practically unnoticed, except for the *Daily Worker.*

During the 1937 session of the legislature, a commission was named to submit a report on the condition of the urban colored population in New York State before March 1938.[23] The commission submitted its first report in March 1938 and had its tenure extended in order to submit a second report in February 1939. Lester B. Granger, Industrial Secretary of the National Urban League, who served as executive director of the commission, was assigned the task of preparing the first report. Many private agencies launched investigations on various phases affecting Negro life.

[23] The commission was composed of Harold P. Herman, chairman, William T. Andrews, Rev. Michael Mulvoy, John J. Howard, Leon A. Fischel, Walter J. Mahoney, Robert W. Justice, Henry Root Stern, Francis B. Rivers, Mrs. Elizabeth Ross Haynes, Rev. John H. Johnson, and Henri W. Shields.

Deep Social Roots

Both investigations concluded on one note: a Harlem riot in 1935, at the height of modern times, in the great city of New York, must have had deep roots. The conditions confronting Negroes were found to spring from several distinct and closely related causes. As a population of low income, it suffered from conditions that affected low-income groups of all races, but the causes that kept Negroes in this class did not apply with the same force to whites. These conditions were underscored by discrimination against Negroes in all walks of life. The rumor of the death of a boy which spread throughout the community had "awakened the deep-seated sense of wrongs and denials and even memories of injustices in the South." The Mayor's Commission reported as the riot's cause "the smouldering resentments of the people of Harlem against racial discrimination and poverty in the midst of plenty." Together with the diminished wage scale, the relief standards had further lowered the already degraded position of these people. Poverty, it was claimed, had taken its toll in the Negroes' health, morale, and general living conditions. The riot was, in the New York State Temporary Commission's view, "a spontaneous and an incoherent protest by Harlem's population against a studied neglect of its critical problems."

RICHARD WRIGHT

The Ethics of Living Jim Crow

Men caught without jobs in large cities feel one kind of desperation; men caught in the vice of a petty personal racism feel another. In this memoir, Richard Wright, one of the most gifted American writers of this century, chronicles his experiences in a society which allowed him no exit, which

again and again placed him in situations from which he could not escape
with honor. This is a description of how one young man met the system of
Jim Crow which had been codified in the South. It is also a picture of the
unsavory society which supported this system. As black people in Wright's position have discovered, the institution of racism limits and poisons relationships
of every kind. Wright's experience on the job in Memphis showed him that
one of racism's inevitable victims is rational discourse of almost every sort.
The acuity of his understanding of the black man's condition is demonstrated
most remarkably in his classic novel, *Native Son,* about a young black adrift
in Chicago. Here, however, he talks about the South, the stagnation of which
was to remain a fixed aspect of American life until Martin Luther King, Jr.'s
revolution in Montgomery in 1955.

I

MY FIRST LESSON IN HOW TO LIVE AS A NEGRO CAME WHEN I WAS QUITE
small. We were living in Arkansas. Our house stood behind the railroad
tracks. Its skimpy yard was paved with black cinders. Nothing green
ever grew in that yard. The only touch of green we could see was far
away, beyond the tracks, over where the white folks lived. But cinders
were good enough for me and I never missed the green growing things.
And anyhow cinders were fine weapons. You could always have a nice
hot war with huge black cinders. All you had to do was crouch behind
the brick pillars of a house with your hands full of gritty ammunition.
And the first woolly black head you saw pop out from behind another
row of pillars was your target. You tried your very best to knock it off.
It was great fun.

I never fully realized the appalling disadvantages of a cinder environment till one day the gang to which I belonged found itself engaged in
a war with the white boys who lived beyond the tracks. As usual we laid
down our cinder barrage, thinking that this would wipe the white boys
out. But they replied with a steady bombardment of broken bottles. We
doubled our cinder barrage, but they hid behind trees, hedges, and the
sloping embankments of their lawns. Having no such fortifications, we
retreated to the brick pillars of our homes. During the retreat a broken
milk bottle caught me behind the ear, opening a deep gash which bled
profusely. The sight of blood pouring over my face completely demoralized our ranks. My fellow-combatants left me standing paralyzed in the
center of the yard, and scurried for their homes. A kind neighbor saw
me, and rushed me to a doctor, who took three stitches in my neck.

I sat brooding on my front steps, nursing my wound and waiting for
my mother to come from work. I felt that a grave injustice had been

done me. It was all right to throw cinders. The greatest harm a cinder could do was leave a bruise. But broken bottles were dangerous; they left you cut, bleeding, and helpless.

When night fell, my mother came from the white folks' kitchen. I raced down the street to meet her. I could just feel in my bones that she would understand. I knew she would tell me exactly what to do next time. I grabbed her hand and babbled out the whole story. She examined my wound, then slapped me.

"How come yuh didn't hide?" she asked me. "How come yuh awways fightin'?"

I was outraged, and bawled. Between sobs I told her that I didn't have any trees or hedges to hide behind. There wasn't a thing I could have used as a trench. And you couldn't throw very far when you were hiding behind the brick pillars of a house. She grabbed a barrel stave, dragged me home, stripped me naked, and beat me till I had a fever of one hundred and two. She would smack my rump with the stave, and, while the skin was still smarting impart to me gems of Jim Crow wisdom. I was never to throw cinders any more. I was never to fight any more wars. I was never, never, under any conditions, to fight *white* folks again. And they were absolutely right in clouting me with the broken milk bottle. Didn't I know she was working hard every day in the hot kitchens of the white folks to make money to take care of me? When was I ever going to learn to be a good boy? She couldn't be bothered with my fights. She finished by telling me that I ought to be thankful to God as long as I lived that they didn't kill me.

All that night I was delirious and could not sleep. Each time I closed my eyes I saw monstrous white faces suspended from the ceiling, leering at me.

From that time on, the charm of my cinder yard was gone. The green trees, the trimmed hedges, the cropped lawns grew very meaningful, became a symbol. Even today when I think of white folks, the hard, sharp outlines of white houses surrounded by trees, lawns, and hedges are present somewhere in the background of my mind. Through the years they grew into an overreaching symbol of fear.

It was a long time before I came in close contact with white folks again. We moved from Arkansas to Mississippi. Here we had the good fortune not to live behind the railroad tracks, or close to white neighborhoods. We lived in the very heart of the local Black Belt. There were black churches and black preachers; there were black schools and black teachers; black groceries and black clerks. In fact, everything was so solidly black that for a long time I did not even think of white folks, save in remote and vague terms. But this could not last forever. As one grows older one eats more. One's clothing costs more. When I finished grammar school I had to go to work. My mother could no longer feed and clothe me on her cooking job.

There is but one place where a black boy who knows no trade can get a job, and that's where the houses and faces are white, where the trees, lawns, and hedges are green. My first job was with an optical company in Jackson, Mississippi. The morning I applied I stood straight and neat before the boss, answering all his questions with sharp yessirs and nosirs. I was very careful to pronounce my *sirs* distinctly, in order that he might know that I was polite, that I knew where I was, and that I knew he was a *white* man. I wanted that job badly.

He looked me over as though he were examining a prize poodle. He questioned me closely about my schooling, being particularly insistent about how much mathematics I had had. He seemed very pleased when I told him I had had two years of algebra.

"Boy, how would you like to try to learn something around here?" he asked me.

"I'd like it fine, sir," I said, happy. I had visions of "working my way up." Even Negroes have those visions.

"All right," he said. "Come on."

I followed him to the small factory.

"Pease," he said to a white man of about thirty-five, "this is Richard. He's going to work for us."

Pease looked at me and nodded.

I was then taken to a white boy of about seventeen.

"Morrie, this is Richard, who's going to work for us."

"Whut yuh sayin' there, boy!" Morrie boomed at me.

"Fine!" I answered.

The boss instructed these two to help me, teach me, give me jobs to do, and let me learn what I could in my spare time.

My wages were five dollars a week.

I worked hard, trying to please. For the first month I got along O.K. Both Pease and Morrie seemed to like me. But one thing was missing. And I kept thinking about it. I was not learning anything and nobody was volunteering to help me. Thinking they had forgotten that I was to learn something about the mechanics of grinding lenses, I asked Morrie one day to tell me about the work. He grew red.

"Whut yuh tryin' t' do, nigger, get smart?" he asked.

"Naw; I ain' tryin' t' git smart," I said.

"Well, don't, if yuh know whut's good for yuh!"

I was puzzled. Maybe he just doesn't want to help me, I thought. I went to Pease.

"Say, are yuh crazy, you black bastard?" Pease asked me, his gray eyes growing hard.

I spoke out, reminding him that the boss had said I was to be given a chance to learn something.

"Nigger, you think you're *white*, don't you?"

"Naw, sir!"

"Well, you're acting mighty like it!"

"But, Mr. Pease, the boss said . . ."

Pease shook his fist in my face.

"This is a *white* man's work around here, and you better watch yourself!"

From then on they changed toward me. They said goodmorning no more. When I was just a bit slow in performing some duty, I was called a lazy black son-of-a-bitch.

Once I thought of reporting all this to the boss. But the mere idea of what would happen to me if Pease and Morrie should learn that I had "snitched" stopped me. And after all the boss was a white man, too. What was the use?

The climax came at noon one summer day. Pease called me to his work-bench. To get to him I had to go between two narrow benches and stand with my back against a wall.

"Yes, sir," I said.

"Richard, I want to ask you something," Pease began pleasantly, not looking up from his work.

"Yes, sir," I said again.

Morrie came over, blocking the narrow passage between the benches. He folded his arms, staring at me solemnly.

I looked from one to the other, sensing that something was coming.

"Yes, sir," I said for the third time.

Pease looked up and spoke very slowly.

"Richard, *Mr*. Morrie here tells me you called me *Pease*."

I stiffened. A void seemed to open up in me. I knew this was the show-down.

He meant that I had failed to call him Mr. Pease. I looked at Morrie. He was gripping a steel bar in his hands. I opened my mouth to speak, to protest, to assure Pease that I had never called him simply *Pease,* and that I had never had any intentions of doing so, when Morrie grabbed me by the collar, ramming my head against the wall.

"Now, be careful, nigger!" snarled Morrie, baring his teeth. "*I* heard yuh call 'im *Pease!* 'N' if yuh say yuh didn't, yuh're callin' me a *lie,* see?" He waved the steel bar threateningly.

If I had said: No, sir, Mr. Pease, I never called you *Pease,* I would have been automatically calling Morrie a liar. And if I had said: Yes, sir, Mr. Pease, I called you *Pease,* I would have been pleading guilty to having uttered the worst insult that a Negro can utter to a southern white man. I stood hesitating, trying to frame a neutral reply.

"Richard, I asked you a question!" said Pease. Anger was creeping into his voice.

"I don't remember calling you *Pease,* Mr. Pease," I said cautiously. "And if I did, I sure didn't mean . . ."

"You black son-of-a-bitch! You called me *Pease,* then!" he spat, slapping me till I bent sideways over a bench. Morrie was on top of me, demanding:

"Didn't yuh call 'im *Pease?* If yuh say yuh didn't, I'll rip yo' gut string loose with this bar, yuh black granny dodger! Yuh can't call a white man a lie 'n' git erway with it, you black son-of-a-bitch!"

I wilted. I begged them not to bother me. I knew what they wanted. They wanted me to leave.

"I'll leave," I promised. "I'll leave right *now.*"

They gave me a minute to get out of the factory. I was warned not to show up again, or tell the boss.

I went.

When I told the folks at home what had happened, they called me a fool. They told me that I must never again attempt to exceed my boundaries. When you are working for white folks, they said, you got to "stay in your place" if you want to keep working.

II

My Jim Crow education continued on my next job, which was portering in a clothing store. One morning, while polishing brass out front, the boss and his twenty-year-old son got out of their car and half dragged and half kicked a Negro woman into the store. A policeman standing at the corner looked on, twirling his nightstick. I watched out of the corner of my eye, never slackening the strokes of my chamois upon the brass. After a few minutes, I heard shrill screams coming from the rear of the store. Later the woman stumbled out, bleeding, crying, and holding her stomach. When she reached the end of the block, the policeman grabbed her and accused her of being drunk. Silently, I watched him throw her into a patrol wagon.

When I went to the rear of the store, the boss and his son were washing their hands at the sink. They were chuckling. The floor was bloody and strewn with wisps of hair and clothing. No doubt I must have appeared pretty shocked, for the boss slapped me reassuringly on the back.

"Boy, that's what we do to niggers when they don't want to pay their bills," he said, laughing.

His son looked at me and grinned.

"Here, hava cigarette," he said.

Not knowing what to do, I took it. He lit his and held the match for me. This was a gesture of kindness, indicating that even if they had beaten the poor old woman, they would not beat me if I knew enough to keep my mouth shut.

"Yes sir," I said, and asked no questions.

After they had gone, I sat on the edge of a packing box and stared at the bloody floor till the cigarette went out.

That day at noon, while eating in a hamburger joint, I told my fellow Negro porters what had happened. No one seemed surprised. One fellow, after swallowing a huge bite, turned to me and asked:

"Huh! Is tha' all they did t' her?"

"Yeah. Wasn't tha' enough?" I asked.

"Shucks! Man, she's a lucky bitch!" he said, burying his lips deep into a juicy hamburger. "Hell, it's a wonder they didn't lay her when they got through."

III

I was learning fast, but not quite fast enough. One day, while I was delivering packages in the suburbs, my bicycle tire was punctured. I walked along the hot, dusty road, sweating and leading my bicycle by the handle-bars.

A car slowed at my side.

"What's the matter, boy?" a white man called.

I told him my bicycle was broken and I was walking back to town.

"That's too bad," he said. "Hop on the running board."

He stopped the car. I clutched hard at my bicycle with one hand and clung to the side of the car with the other.

"All set?"

"Yes, sir," I answered. The car started.

It was full of young white men. They were drinking. I watched the flask pass from mouth to mouth.

"Wanna drink, boy?" one asked.

I laughed as the wind whipped my face. Instinctively obeying the freshly planted precepts of my mother, I said:

"Oh, no!"

The words were hardly out of my mouth before I felt something hard and cold smash me between the eyes. It was an empty whisky bottle. I saw stars, and fell backwards from the speeding car into the dust of the road, my feet becoming entangled in the steel spokes of my bicycle. The white men piled out and stood over me.

"Nigger, ain' yuh learned no better sense'n tha' yet?" asked the man who hit me. "Ain' yuh learned t' say *sir* t' a white man yet?"

Dazed, I pulled to my feet. My elbows and legs were bleeding. Fists doubled, the white man advanced, kicking my bicycle out of the way.

"Aw, leave the bastard alone. He's got enough," said one.

They stood looking at me. I rubbed my shins, trying to stop the flow of blood. No doubt they felt a sort of contemptuous pity, for one asked:

"Yuh wanna ride t' town now, nigger? Yuh reckon yuh know enough t' ride now?"

"I wanna walk," I said, simply.

Maybe it sounded funny. They laughed.

"Well, walk, yuh black son-of-a-bitch!"

When they left they comforted me with:

"Nigger, yuh sho better be damn glad it wuz us yuh talked t' tha' way. Yuh're a lucky bastard, 'cause if yuh'd said tha' t' somebody else, yuh might've been a dead nigger now."

IV

Negroes who have lived South know the dread of being caught alone upon the streets in white neighborhoods after the sun has set. In such a simple situation as this the plight of the Negro in America is graphically symbolized. While white strangers may be in these neighborhoods trying to get home, they can pass unmolested. But the color of a Negro's skin makes him easily recognizable, makes him suspect, converts him into a defenseless target.

Late one Saturday night I made some deliveries in a white neighborhood. I was pedaling my bicycle back to the store as fast as I could, when a police car, swerving toward me, jammed me into the curbing.

"Get down and put up your hands!" the policemen ordered.

I did. They climbed out of the car, guns drawn, faces set, and advanced slowly.

"Keep still!" they ordered.

I reached my hands higher. They searched my pockets and packages. They seemed dissatisfied when they could find nothing incriminating. Finally, one of them said:

"Boy, tell your boss not to send you out in white neighborhoods after sundown."

As usual, I said:

"Yes, sir."

V

My next job was as hall-boy in a hotel. Here my Jim Crow education broadened and deepened. When the bell-boys were busy, I was often called to assist them. As many of the rooms in the hotel were occupied by prostitutes, I was constantly called to carry them liquor and cigarettes. These women were nude most of the time. They did not bother about clothing, even for bell-boys. When you went into their rooms, you were supposed to take their nakedness for granted, as though it startled you no more than a blue vase or a red rug. Your presence awoke in them no sense of shame, for you were not regarded as human. If they were alone, you could steal sidelong glimpses at them. But if they were receiving men, not a flicker of your eyelids could show. I remember one incident vividly. A new woman, a huge, snowy-skinned blonde, took a room on my floor. I was sent to wait upon her. She was in bed with a thick-set man; both were nude and uncovered. She said she wanted some liquor and slid out of bed and waddled across the floor to get her money from a dresser drawer. I watched her.

"Nigger, what in hell you looking at?" the white man asked me, raising himself upon his elbows.

"Nothing," I answered, looking miles deep into the blank wall of the room.

"Keep your eyes where they belong, if you want to be healthy!" he said.

"Yes, sir."

VI

One of the bell-boys I knew in this hotel was keeping steady company with one of the Negro maids. Out of a clear sky the police descended upon his home and arrested him, accusing him of bastardy. The poor boy swore he had had no intimate relations with the girl. Nevertheless, they forced him to marry her. When the child arrived, it was found to be much lighter in complexion than either of the two supposedly legal parents. The white men around the hotel made a great joke of it. They spread the rumor that some white cow must have scared the poor girl while she was carrying the baby. If you were in their presence when this explanation was offered, you were supposed to laugh.

VII

One of the bell-boys was caught in bed with a white prostitute. He was castrated and run out of town. Immediately after this all the bell-boys and hall-boys were called together and warned. We were given to understand that the boy who had been castrated was a "mighty, mighty lucky bastard." We were impressed with the fact that next time the management of the hotel would not be responsible for the lives of "trouble-makin' niggers." We were silent.

VIII

One night, just as I was about to go home, I met one of the Negro maids. She lived in my direction, and we fell in to walk part of the way home together. As we passed the white night-watchman, he slapped the maid on her buttock. I turned around, amazed. The watchman looked at me with a long, hard, fixed-under stare. Suddenly he pulled his gun and asked:

"Nigger, don't yuh like it?"

I hesitated.

"I asked yuh don't yuh like it?" he asked again, stepping forward.

"Yes, sir," I mumbled.

"Talk like it, then!"

"Oh, yes, sir!" I said with as much heartiness as I could muster.

Outside, I walked ahead of the girl, ashamed to face her. She caught up with me and said:

"Don't be a fool! Yuh couldn't help it!"

This watchman boasted of having killed two Negroes in self-defense.

Yet, in spite of all this, the life of the hotel ran with an amazing smoothness. It would have been impossible for a stranger to detect anything. The maids, the hall-boys, and the bell-boys were all smiles. They had to be.

IX

I had learned my Jim Crow lessons so thoroughly that I kept the hotel job till I left Jackson for Memphis. It so happened that while in Memphis I applied for a job at a branch of the optical company. I was hired. And for some reason, as long as I worked there, they never brought my past against me.

Here my Jim Crow education assumed quite a different form. It was no longer brutally cruel, but subtly cruel. Here I learned to lie, to steal, to dissemble. I learned to play that dual role which every Negro must play if he wants to eat and live.

For example, it was almost impossible to get a book to read. It was assumed that after a Negro had imbibed what scanty schooling the state furnished he had no further need for books. I was always borrowing books from men on the job. One day I mustered enough courage to ask one of the men to let me get books from the library in his name. Surprisingly, he consented. I cannot help but think that he consented because he was a Roman Catholic and felt a vague sympathy for Negroes, being himself an object of hatred. Armed with a library card, I obtained books in the following manner: I would write a note to the librarian, saying: "Please let this nigger boy have the following books." I would then sign it with the white man's name.

When I went to the library, I would stand at the desk, hat in hand, looking as unbookish as possible. When I received the books desired I would take them home. If the books listed in the note happened to be out, I would sneak into the lobby and forge a new one. I never took any chances guessing with the white librarian about what the fictitious white man would want to read. No doubt if any of the white patrons had suspected that some of the volumes they enjoyed had been in the home of a Negro, they would not have tolerated it for an instant.

The factory force of the optical company in Memphis was much larger than that in Jackson, and more urbanized. At least they liked to talk, and would engage the Negro help in conversation whenever possible. By this means I found that many subjects were taboo from the white man's point of view. Among the topics they did not like to discuss with Negroes were the following: American white women; the Ku Klux Klan; France, and how Negro soldiers fared while there; French women; Jack Johnson; the entire northern part of the United States; the Civil War; Abraham Lincoln; U. S. Grant; General Sherman; Catholics; the Pope; Jews; the Republican Party; slavery; social equality; Communism; Socialism; the 13th and 14th Amendments to the Constitution; or any topic calling for positive knowledge or manly self-assertion on the part of the Negro. The most accepted topics were sex and religion.

There were many times when I had to exercise a great deal of ingenuity to keep out of trouble. It is a southern custom that all men must take off their hats when they enter an elevator. And especially did this apply to us blacks with rigid force. One day I stepped into an elevator with my arms full of packages. I was forced to ride with my hat on. Two white men stared at me coldly. Then one of them very kindly lifted my hat and placed it upon my armful of packages. Now the most accepted response for a Negro to make under such circumstances is to look at the white man out of the corner of his eye and grin. To have said: "Thank you!" would have made the white man *think* that you *thought* you were receiving from him a personal service. For such an act I have seen Negroes take a blow in the mouth. Finding the first alternative distasteful, and the second dangerous, I hit upon an acceptable course of action which fell safely between these two poles. I immediately—no sooner than my hat was lifted—pretended that my packages were about to spill, and appeared deeply distressed with keeping them in my arms. In this fashion I evaded having to acknowledge his service, and, in spite of adverse circumstances, salvaged a slender shred of personal pride.

How do Negroes feel about the way they have to live? How do they discuss it when alone among themselves? I think this question can be answered in a single sentence. A friend of mine who ran an elevator once told me:

"Lawd, man! Ef it wuzn't fer them polices 'n' them ol' lynch mobs, there wouldn't be nothin' but uproar down here!"

HEYWOOD PATTERSON AND EARL CONRAD

The Big Frame

The Scottsboro Case, which began in 1931 and finished two decades later, was America's racial *cause célèbre* in the years preceding World War II. Nine black teenagers, the youngest thirteen years old, became involved in a fight with whites on a moving freight train. At the next stop, the black youths were suddenly pulled off by white vigilantes and arrested for the rape of two white women. They protested that they hadn't even seen any women, but the charges held and they were told that they would be tried, convicted, and executed.

Strange and contradictory though it proved to be as the legal proceedings wore on, such a case was not uncommon in the South. However, the extreme youth of the accused and the patent insubstantiality of the evidence against them aroused the nation's sympathy. Instrumental in this process was the International Labor Defense, the legal arm of the American Communist Party, which was just then making a serious attempt to gain the support and membership of black people.

Heywood Patterson, co-author of the following selection, was the most prominent of the Scottsboro Boys, as they became known. He was tried first; it was demonstrated during his trial that the charges against him and the others were based on a combination of perverse lies and Southern sexual hysteria. Three times he was convicted and three times his conviction was reversed by appellate courts, once by the Supreme Court, on various technical grounds. Then, in 1934, he was convicted a fourth and final time and sentenced to seventy-five years in prison. Southern justice dealt with the other eight in a variety of ways, keeping the last one in jail for six years before finally bringing him to trial.

Patterson escaped to Detroit after serving a few years of his sentence for a non-crime which was called at the time "the biggest frame-up of the century." Andrew Wright, the last of the Scottsboro Boys to be paroled, finally left prison nineteen years after he was first arrested.

THE FREIGHT TRAIN LEAVING OUT OF CHATTANOOGA, GOING AROUND the mountain curves and hills of Tennessee into Alabama, it went so slow anyone could get off and back on.

THE BIG FRAME From *Scottsboro Boy*, by Heywood Patterson and Earl Conrad. Copyright 1950 by Earl Conrad. Reprinted by permission of Doubleday & Company, Inc.

That gave the white boys the idea they could jump off the train and pick up rocks, carry them back on, and chunk them at us Negro boys.

The trouble began when three or four white boys crossed over the oil tanker that four of us colored fellows from Chattanooga were in. One of the white boys, he stepped on my hand and liked to have knocked me off the train. I didn't say anything then, but the same guy, he brushed by me again and liked to have pushed me off the car. I caught hold of the side of the tanker to keep from falling off.

I made a complaint about it and the white boy talked back—mean, serious, white folks Southern talk.

That is how the Scottsboro case began . . . with a white foot on my black hand.

"The next time you want by," I said, "just tell me you want by and I let you by."

"Nigger, I don't ask you when I want by. What you doing on this train anyway?"

"Look, I just tell you the next time you want by you just tell me you want by and I let you by."

"Nigger bastard, this a white man's train. You better get off. All you black bastards better get off!"

I felt we had as much business stealing a ride on this train as those white boys hoboing from one place to another looking for work like us. But it happens in the South most poor whites feel they are better than Negroes and a black man has few rights. It was wrong talk from the white fellow and I felt I should sense it into him and his friends we were human beings with rights too. I didn't want that my companions, Roy and Andy Wright, Eugene Williams and myself, should get off that train for anybody unless it was a fireman or engineer or railroad dick who told us to get off.

"You white sonsofbitches, we got as much right here as you!"

"Why, you goddamn nigger, I think we better just put you off!"

"Okay, you just try. You just try to put us off!"

Three or four white boys, they were facing us four black boys now, and all cussing each other on both sides. But no fighting yet.

The white boys went on up the train further.

We had just come out of a tunnel underneath Lookout Mountain when the argument started. The train, the name of it was the Alabama Great Southern, it was going uphill now, slow. A couple of the white boys, they hopped off, picked up rocks, threw them at us. The stones landed around us and some hit us. Then the white fellows, they hopped back on the train two or three cars below us. We were going toward Stevenson, Alabama, when the rocks came at us. We got very mad.

When the train stopped at Stevenson, I think maybe to get water or fuel, we got out of the car and walked along the tracks. We met up with some other young Negroes from another car. We told them what happened. They agreed to come in with us when the train started again.

Soon as the train started the four of us Chattanooga boys that was in the oil tanker got back in there—and the white boys started throwing more rocks. The other colored guys, they came over the top of the train and met us four guys. We decided we would go and settle with these white boys. We went toward their car to fight it out. There must have been ten or twelve or thirteen of us colored when we came on a gang of six or seven white boys.

I don't argue with people. I show them. And I started to show those white boys. The other colored guys, they pitched in on these rock throwers too. Pretty quick the white boys began to lose in the fist fighting. We outmanned them in hand-to-hand scuffling. Some of them jumped off and some we put off. The train, picking up a little speed, that helped us do the job. A few wanted to put up a fight but they didn't have a chance. We had color anger on our side.

The train was picking up speed and I could see a few Negro boys trying to put off one white guy. I went down by them and told them not to throw this boy off because the train was going too fast. This fellow, his name was Orville Gilley. Me and one of the Wright boys pulled him back up.

After the Gilley boy was back on the train the fight was over. The four of us, Andy and Roy Wright, Eugene Williams and myself, we went back to the tanker and sat the same way we were riding when the train left Chattanooga.

The white fellows got plenty sore at the whupping we gave them. They ran back to Stevenson to complain that they were jumped on and thrown off—and to have us pulled off the train.

The Stevenson depot man, he called up ahead to Paint Rock and told the folks in that little through-road place to turn out in a posse and snatch us off the train.

It was two or three o'clock in the afternoon, Wednesday, March 25, 1931, when we were taken off at Paint Rock. . . .

A mob of white farmers was waiting when the train rolled in. They closed in on the boxcars. Their pistols and shotguns pointed at us. They took everything black off the train. They even threw off some lumps of coal, could be because of its color. Us nine black ones they took off from different cars. Some of these Negroes I had not seen before the fight and a couple I was looking at now for the first time. They were rounding up the whites too, about a half dozen of them. I noticed among them two girls dressed in men's overalls and looking about like the white fellows.

I asked a guy who had hold of me, "What's it all about?"

"Assault and attempt to murder."

I didn't know then there was going to be a different kind of a charge after we got to the Jackson County seat, Scottsboro.

They marched us up a short road. We stopped in front of a little general store and post office. They took our names. They roped us up, all us Negroes together. The rope stretched from one to another of us. The white folks, they looked mighty serious. Everybody had guns. The guy who ran the store spoke up for us:

"Don't let those boys go to jail. Don't anybody harm them."

But that passed quick, because we were being put into trucks. I kind of remember this man's face, him moving around there in the storm of mad white folks, talking for us. There are some good white people down South but you don't find them very fast, them that will get up in arms for a Negro. If they come up for a Negro accused of something, the white people go against him and his business goes bad.

After we were shoved into the truck I saw for the first time all us to become known as "The Scottsboro Boys." There were nine of us. Some had not even been in the fight on the train. A few in the fight got away so the posse never picked them up.

There were the four from Chattanooga, Roy Wright, about fourteen; his brother, Andy Wright, nineteen; Eugene Williams, who was only thirteen; and myself. I was eighteen. I knew the Wright boys very well. I had spent many nights at their home and Mrs. Wright treated me as if I were her own son. The other five boys, they were Olen Montgomery, he was half blind; Willie Roberson, he was so sick with the venereal he could barely move around; a fellow from Atlanta named Clarence Norris, nineteen years old; Charlie Weems, the oldest one among us, he was twenty; and a fourteen-year-old boy from Georgia, Ozie Powell. I was one of the tallest, but Norris was taller than me.

All nine of us were riding the freight for the same reason, to go somewhere and find work. It was 1931. Depression was all over the country. Our families were hard pushed. The only ones here I knew were the other three from Chattanooga. Our fathers couldn't hardly support us, and we wanted to help out, or at least put food in our own bellies by ourselves. We were freight-hiking to Memphis when the fight happened.

Looking over this crowd, I figured that the white boys got sore at the whupping we gave them, and were out to make us see it the bad way.

We got to Scottsboro in a half hour. Right away we were huddled into a cage, all of us together. It was a little two-story jimcrow jail. There were flat bars, checkerboard style, around the windows, and a little hallway outside our cell.

We got panicky and some of the kids cried. The deputies were rough. They kept coming in and out of our cells. They kept asking questions, kept pushing us and shoving, trying to make us talk. Kept cussing, saying we tried to kill off the white boys on the train. Stomped and raved at us and flashed their guns and badges.

We could look out the window and see a mob of folks gathering. They were excited and noisy. We were hot and sweaty, all of us, and pretty scared. I laughed at a couple of the guys who were crying. I didn't feel like crying. I couldn't figure what exactly, but didn't have no weak feeling.

After a while a guy walked into our cell, with him a couple of young women.

"Do you know these girls?"

They were the two gals dressed like men rounded up at Paint Rock along with the rest of us brought off the train. We had seen them being hauled in. They looked like the others, like the white hobo fellows, to me. I paid them no mind. I didn't know them. None of us from Chattanooga, the Wrights, Williams, and myself, ever saw them before Paint Rock. Far as I knew none of the nine of us pulled off different gondolas and tankers ever saw them.

"No," everybody said.

"No," I said.

"No? You damn-liar niggers! You raped these girls!"

Round about dusk hundreds of people gathered about the jailhouse. "Let these niggers out," they yelled. We could hear it coming in the window. "If you don't, we're coming in after them." White folks were running around like mad ants, white ants, sore that somebody had stepped on their hill. We heard them yelling like crazy how they were coming in after us and what ought to be done with us. "Give 'em to us," they kept screaming, till some of the guys, they cried like they were seven or eight years old. Olen Montgomery, he was seventeen and came from Monroe, Georgia, he could make the ugliest face when he cried. I stepped back and laughed at him.

As evening came on the crowd got to be about five hundred, most of them with guns. Mothers had kids in their arms. Autos, bicycles, and wagons were parked around the place. People in and about them.

Two or three deputies, they came into our cell and said, "All right, let's go." They wanted to take us out to the crowd. They handcuffed us each separately. Locked both our hands together. Wanted to rush us outside into the hands of that mob. We fellows hung close, didn't want for them to put those irons on. You could see the look in those deputies' faces, already taking some funny kind of credit for turning us over.

High Sheriff Warren—he was on our side—rushed in at those deputies and said, "Where you taking these boys?"

"Taking them to another place, maybe Gadsden or some other jail."

"You can't take those boys out there! You'll be overpowered and they'll take the boys away from you."

The deputies asked for their handcuffs back and beat it out.

That was when the high sheriff slipped out the back way himself and put in a call to Montgomery for the National Guards.

He came back to our cell a few minutes later and said, "I don't believe that story the girls told."

His wife didn't believe it either. She got busy right then and went to the girls' cell not far from ours. We all kept quiet and listened while Mrs. Warren accused them of putting down a lie on us. "You know you lied," she said, so that we heard it and so did the white boys in their cell room. The girls stuck to their story; but us black boys saw we had some friends.

It had been a fair day, a small wind blowing while we rode on the freight. Now, toward evening, it was cool, and the crowd down there was stomping around to keep warm and wanting to make it real hot. When it was coming dark flashlights went on, and headlights from a few Fords lit up the jail. The noise was mainly from the white folks still calling for a lynching party. Every now and then one of them would yell, for us to hear, "Where's the rope, Bill?" or "Got enough rope, Hank?" They were trying to find something to help them to break into jail, begging all the while to turn us fellows over to them.

Round four o'clock in the morning we heard a heavy shooting coming into the town. It was the National Guards. They were firing to let the crowd know they were coming, they meant business, and we weren't to be burned or hung. The mob got scared and fussed off and away while the state soldiers' trucks came through.

I was young, didn't know what it was all about. I believed the National Guard was some part of the lynching bee. When they came into my cell I figured like the others—that we were as good as long gone now.

First guard to walk in, he was full of fun. He asked some of the boys, "Where you want your body to go to?"

Willie Roberson, he had earlier told one of the deputies he was from Ohio, but now he took this guard serious. He said, "Send my body to my aunt at 992 Michigan Avenue, Atlanta." His aunt owned the place at that address. Others told false names, like people do at first when they're arrested.

Charlie Weems, he had a lot of guts. He understood it was a gag. He said, "Just bury me like you do a cat. Dig a hole and throw me in it." He understood the guard was funning, but the others didn't. I didn't very well understand it myself.

After the National Guards told us they were for us, I believed them. I told them right away where I came from, "Just over the state line, Chattanooga, Tennessee."

I don't tell people stories, I tell the truth.

I told the truth about my name and where I came from. I knew that was all right with my people, they would wade through blood for me.

And which they did.

Early the next morning we had breakfast. Then the National Guards led us out of the jail. We were going to Gadsden, Alabama, where it was supposed to be safer. Soon as we filed out of the jailhouse another mob was there screaming the same stuff at us and talking mean to the National Guards. "We're going to kill you niggers!"

"You ain't going to do a goddamned thing," I yelled back at them. That made them wild.

They sat us down among other colored prisoners at the Gadsden jail. It was the same kind of a little old jimcrow lockup as the one at Scottsboro. White guys, they were in cells a little way down the hall. We talked back and forth with them.

We waited to see what the Jackson County law was going to do with us. The Scottsboro paper had something to say about us. In big headlines, editorials and everything, they said they had us nine fiends in jail for raping two of their girls. The editor had come rummaging around the jail himself.

Then we heard that on March 31 we were indicted at Scottsboro. A trial was set for April 6, only a week away. Down around that way they'll hoe potatoes kind of slow sometimes but comes to trying Negroes on a rape charge they work fast. We had no lawyers. Saw no lawyers. We had no contact with the outside. Our folks, as far as we knew, didn't know the jam we were in. I remember the bunch of us packed in the cell room, some crying, some mad. That was a thinking time, and I thought of my mother, Jannie Patterson, and my father, Claude Patterson. I thought of my sisters and brothers and wondered if they had read about us by now.

What little we heard was going on about us we got from the white inmates. Some were pretty good guys. They saw the papers, read them to us, and the guards talked with them. These fellows, they told us the story had got around all over Alabama and maybe outside the state. They told us, "If you ever see a good chance, you better run. They said they're going to give every one of you the death seat."

I couldn't believe that. I am an unbelieving sort.

Came trial time, the National Guards took us to Scottsboro. We had to go down through the country from Gadsden to the county seat. We went in a truck. There were guards in front, at the side and behind. I never trusted these guards too much. They were white folks, Alabama folks at that, and I felt they could as lief knock us off as anyone else. State and federal and county law didn't make much difference to us down there. It was all law, and it was all against us, the way we figured.

Got to Scottsboro and there was just about the same crowd as when we left—only much bigger. For two blocks either way they were thick as bees, bees with a bad sting and going to sting us pretty quick now.

The sixty or seventy National Guards, they got orders to make a lane through the crowd so we could get through. They had rifles, looked smart in their uniform. They could handle the crowd. When the guards formed a tunnel for us to walk through we heard the mob roaring what I heard a thousand times if I heard once:

"We going to kill you niggers!"

Later I found out why the crowd was so big. A "nigger lynching" might be enough to bring out a big crowd anyway, but this day was what they called "First Monday" or "horse-swapping day." First day of each month the Jackson County farmers came down from the hills into Scottsboro to swap horses and mules and talk. They'd bring in their families and have a time of it. It happened our trial opened on the same day so the mountain people living around here had two good reasons to come to town—and there were thousands out. They were gathered around the courthouse square while we colored boys went into the courthouse.

Near the courthouse was a brass band getting ready to celebrate either our burning or hanging, whichever it was going to be.

We boys sat there in court and watched how Judge E. A. Hawkins had a talk with a man named Stephen Roddy. Roddy said he was a lawyer sent in from Chattanooga to help us fellows. I had a hunch when I heard he was from Chattanooga that my folks and the Wrights had got wind of our jam and hired him. But I saw right away he wasn't much for us. Hawkins said to him, "You defending these boys?" Roddy answered, "Not exactly. I'm here to join up with any lawyers you name to defend them. Sort of help out." The judge asked, "Well, you defending them or aren't you?" Words about like that. So Roddy said, "Well, I'm not defending them, but I wouldn't want to be sent off the case. I'm not being paid or anything. Just been sent here to sort of take part." Then the judge, he said, "Oh, I wouldn't want to see you out of the case. You can stay."

Now that was the kind of defense we Scottsboro boys had when we first went on trial.

Right after that Judge Hawkins put a local guy named Milo Moody, an oldish lawyer, to represent us. But he didn't do anything for us. Not a damned thing. He got up and said a few words now and then: but he was against us.

After Moody was set up to be our lawyer, the trials went on. The courtroom was packed. Jammed in, the people were. Standing up in back and along the sides. Not enough seats there. Weems and Norris were tried together. I was tried separate. The rest were tried together. The trials and convictions went on for about two days. The jury kept going in and out of the jury room and coming back with convictions.

That was one jury that got exercise.

I was tried on April 7, the second day of the trials. Solicitor H. G. Bailey, the prosecutor, he talked excited to the jurymen. They were backwoods farmers. Some didn't even have the education I had. I had only two short little periods of reading lessons. But these men passed a decision on my life. . . .

The girls I and the others were accused of raping I saw for the third time in court. The first I saw them was at Paint Rock when we were all picked up. The second was in Scottsboro jail when they were brought to our cell. And now in court. This time they were not wearing men's overalls, but dresses. Victoria Price, the older girl, she was to me a plain-looking woman. Ruby Bates was more presentable.

Solicitor Bailey, he asked me questions. The way he handled me was the same way he handled all of us. Like this:

"You ravished that girl sitting there."

"I ravished nobody, I saw no girl."

"You held a knife to her head while the others ravished her."

"I had no knife. I saw no knife. I saw no girl."

"You saw this defendant here ravish that girl there."

"I saw nobody ravish nobody. I was in a fight. That's all. Just a fight with white boys."

"You raped that girl. You did rape that girl, didn't you?"

"I saw no girl. I raped nobody."

Bailey, he kept firing that story at me just like that. He kept pounding the rape charge against me, against all of us. We all kept saying no, we saw no girls, we raped nobody, all we knew of was a fight.

The girls got up and kept on lying. There was only one thing the people in the courtroom wanted to hear. Bailey would ask, "Did the niggers rape you?"

"Yes," the girls would answer.

That's all the people in that court wanted to hear, wanted to hear "yes" from the girls' mouths.

When Bailey finished with me he said to the jury:

"Gentlemen of the jury, I don't say give that nigger the chair. I'm not going to tell you to give him the electric chair.

"You know your duty.

"I'm not going to tell you to give the nigger a life sentence. All I can say is, *hide him. Get him out of our sight.*

"Hide them. Get them out of our sight.

"They're not our niggers. Look at their eyes, look at their hair, gentlemen. They look like something just broke out of the zoo.

"Guilty or not guilty, let's get rid of these niggers."

I went on trial about nine o'clock in the morning. Within two hours the jury had come back with a conviction. I was convicted in their minds before I went on trial. I had no lawyers, no witnesses for me. All that spoke for me on that witness stand was my black skin—which didn't do so good. Judge Hawkins asked the jurymen: "Have you reached a verdict?"

"Yes."

"Have the clerk read it."

The clerk read it off: "We, the jurymen, find the defendant guilty as charged and fix his punishment as death."

If I recollect right the verdicts against us all were in in two days. All of us got the death sentence except Roy Wright. He looked so small and pitiful on the stand that one juryman held out for life imprisonment. They declared a mistrial for Roy.

No Negroes were allowed in Scottsboro during the entire time. I didn't see a Negro face except two farmers in jail for selling corn. One of the National Guards, he fired a shot through the courtroom window about noon of the day I was convicted. Later he said that was an accident.

On the night of the first day's trials we could hear a brass band outside. It played, "There'll Be a Hot Time in the Old Town Tonight" and "Dixie."

It was April 9 when eight of us—all but Roy Wright—were stood up before Judge Hawkins for sentencing. He asked us if we had anything to say before he gave sentence. I said:

"Yes, I have something to say. I'm not guilty of this charge."

He said, "The jury has found you guilty and it is up to me to pass sentence. I set the date for your execution July 10, 1931, at Kilby Prison. May the Lord have mercy on your soul."

The people in the court cheered and clapped after the judge gave out with that. I didn't like it, people feeling good because I was going to die, and I got ruffed.

I motioned to Solicitor Bailey with my finger.

He came over. I asked him if he knew when I was going to die.

He mentioned the date, like the judge gave it, and I said, "You're wrong. I'm going to die when you and those girls die for lying about me."

He asked me how I knew and I said that that was how I felt.

I looked around. That courtroom was one big smiling white face.

All my life I always loved my own people. I like my kind best because I understand them best. When I was a young man in Chattanooga, before the train ride that ended at Paint Rock, I knew and loved Negro girls, Negro people. My friends were of black color. I knew them as fellow human beings, as good as all others, and needing as good a chance. It was never in me to rape, not a black and not a white woman. Only a Negro who is a fool or a crazy man, he would chance his life for anything like that. A Negro with sound judgment and common sense is not going to do it. They are going to take his life away from him if he does. Every Negro man in the South knows that. No, most Negroes run away from that sort of thing, fear in their hearts. And nine of us boys, most unbeknownst to each other, a couple sick, all looking for work and a chance to live, and rounded up on a freight train like lost black sheep, we did not do such a thing and could not.

I wouldn't make advances on any woman that didn't want me. Too many women from my boyhood on have shown a desire for me so that I don't have to press myself on anyone not wanting me.

My mother and father, they lived together as husband and wife for thirty-seven years, honest working people. They had many children and they taught us to respect the human being and the human form.

I was also taught to demand respect from others.

Now it is a strange thing that what I have just said I never had a chance to say in an Alabama court. No Alabama judge or jury in the four trials I had ever asked me for my views. Nobody asked about my feelings. Those Alabama people, they didn't believe I had any, nor the right to any.

Back in Gadsden jail we could look outside and see where an old gallows was rigged up. Must have gone back to the slavey days. We didn't like nothing at all about the place; we didn't like our death sentence; and we decided to put on a kick. I said to the man who brought me a prison meal, "I don't want that stuff. Bring me some pork chops."

"Huh, pork chops?"

"Yes, pork chops, You got to get it. We're going to die and we can have anything we want."

All the fellows laid down a yell, "Pork chops!"

We crowded up to the bars. We put our hands out and shook fingers at him. We hollered, "Pork chops. Nothing else."

This guy, he went down someplace and got the pork chops. He brought it to us. Just the food I wanted. I always liked pork meats. After we ate, still we weren't satisfied.

The deputies and guards, they were scared of us now like we would make a jailbreak. Our heads were up against those checkerboard bars and we talked sharp.

The sheriff spoke to me because I was raising the most dust. He said, "Look here, nigger. See that gallows. If you don't quieten down I'll take you around to that gallows and hang you myself."

I had a broom in my hand and maybe he wondered what it was or where I got it. He came up to the bars to take a look at what it was. I jiggled the broom in his face. The fellows laughed.

That was the last that sheriff could take by himself. He beat it down-stairs to call Governor B. M. Miller to send in some National Guards.

They came in serious. The cell door banged open. They beat on us with their fists. They pushed us against the walls. They kicked and tramped about on our legs and feet. They beat up most of the fellows, but Eugene Williams and me backed up in the dark of the cell and es-caped the worst part of it.

The state soldiers handcuffed us in twos. They had a big rope. They fastened the rope in between the handcuffs and bound us all together.

We laid up against the walls and against each other like that till night. We were in a quiet misery, unable to move around. When it was night we tried to sleep like that but we couldn't. Morning came and we were still trussed to each other and tired. Day went on, no food, just laying there moaning atop each other; until it was seven o'clock in the evening.

The National Guards came up again. This time they had more rope. I said to the sheriff, "What you going to do, hang us?"

"I'd like to, goddamn your souls," he said.

They roped us together tighter, then chain-gang marched us outside to a big state patrol truck they called the dog wagon. They tied us to the sides so we couldn't make any break, so we couldn't even move. One of the guards asked, "What you guys raise so much hell for?"

"We just don't like that death sentence," I told him.

The kid I was handcuffed to, he slept rough, and by the time we got to the city jail those handcuffs had swollen my wrists.

They couldn't get the handcuffs off. They had to call in a blacksmith to get them loose.

They split up us Scottsboro boys so we couldn't raise any more sand like we had at Gadsden. They put us in with other prisoners two or three to a cell.

About the middle of the night I was stashed into a cell with two other guys. One was called Box Car. He had burgled a boxcar and had a fifteen-year sentence. The other was a lifer. I was played out and fell on the bunk. One of the guys woke me. "Get up."

I raised up and I looked at him.

"Did you bring my money?"

"What money?"

"Jail feed."

I knew what this was, kangaroo business. I had a pair of shears under the mattress. I had brought it from the Gadsden jail. I just rested my hands on the shears and said, "I got nothing."

This guy, he just kept insisting. Told me to get up. He wanted to see

me. "If you don't pay us kangaroo money you know what it means."
"No, what it means?"
"It means we going to whup you."
They asked for twenty-five cents. If I wouldn't pay, it meant I would
get twenty-five licks.
I raised up a little more and I said, "You can see me. In the morning
you can see me."
"Hey, where you say you from?"
"Scottsboro."
"You one of them Scottsboro boys?"
When I told him yes he just gave right over, got tender. He felt sorry
for me, brought me food and tried to give it to me. I was tired and I
didn't accept it. I laid down to sleep, thinking how the word "Scottsboro" touched them. That was when I first learned that this word would
mean special favors in prison—and special torture.

Next day we were together again, all except Roy Wright, while they
fingerprinted us.
Charlie Weems was chewing gum. The jailer, Dick Barnes, told
Weems to spit the gum out. He refused to do it.
Barnes gave Weems a lick across the side of the head for that. Weems
went down. When he got up he stood his distance from the jailer, a little
quieter. Dick Barnes turned on me:
"You like ham and eggs?"
"I don't like nothing." I knew he was talking about the fuss we made
at the other jail over pork chops.
"Patterson, I heard about you up in Gadsden ordering ham and eggs.
You can get it here any time you want it. You love ham and eggs,
don't you?"
"I don't love nothing." He wanted me to say something so he could
beat on me, but I didn't give him the chance.
He changed tone, got serious. His voice dropped like from the high
end of a piano to the low end, and he said, "We got your waters on to
you here. Any time you fellows get funky we got your waters on here."
Right away he showed us what he meant. Took us all down in the
basement where they gave punishment. He looked at me and said,
"Nigger, keep quiet. If you don't behave . . ." He showed where you
hang up by two fingers with your feet not touching the ground. There
was a time limit they would hold you up that way.
It was supposed to frighten us and maybe it did scare some. I didn't
like it either. But I always protested when I didn't like things. Down

South I always talked like I wanted: before Scottsboro, during it, and since.

A few minutes afterward Barnes told a Negro trusty, "I sure like to be there when they execute these guys. You'll smell flesh burning a mile."

I asked the trusty, "How do you know they're going to kill me?"

"That chair sure going to get you," the trusty said.

I didn't believe nothing like that. Two days later there was the first sign Barnes and the trusty might be wrong—and I might be right. . . .

Two guys from New York, head men from the International Labor Defense, brought us pops and candy and gave them to us boys in the visiting room. They were Jewish. Which was okay with me. I worked for Jews in Chattanooga. Did porter and delivery work and such for them and always got along well. They told us the people were up in arms over our case in New York and if they had our say-so they would like to appeal our case.

These were the first people to call on us, to show any feelings for our lives, and we were glad. We hadn't even heard from our own families; they weren't allowed to see us. But these lawyers got in.

About us nine boys unfairly sentenced, they said their organization was doing all it could to wake up the people in this country and Europe.

Jailer Dick Barnes, he came in and listened when these lawyers asked us whether we got the right medical treatment. They suggested to Barnes a doctor should be sent in. Barnes is the kind of a guy, if you are a Negro, you can read hate in his face and his voice. He said, "We got a doctor here. These boys don't need any treatment."

I wanted a doctor and I didn't want the prison doctor. The prison was very filthy. It was making me sick, making us all sick. It was an old jail. The bed lice would get all over you; they would come up close to you to warm up. I said, "Yes, I want a doctor."

Barnes said, "What do you want a doctor? We got any medicine you can name."

"You have any medicine for these lice?" I asked. "One of them stole my cap last night."

The lawyers and the fellows laughed.

After the visitors went Barnes said, "Nigger, you're too smart. If you want to get along with me you just keep your mouth."

Now we knew why we had been getting mail from white folks. The I.L.D., or the Labor Defense, as we got to call them, had been causing around the country. They had told people at meetings and in newspapers to send us letters and cigarettes to make it easier for us in jail. Mail from white people was confusing to me. All my life I was untrusting of them. Now their kind words and presents was more light than we got through the bars of the windows. The next few days the mail got heavier; and the prison officials were upset what to do. We had the money to get whatever we could buy at the jail commissary, and this outside pressure gave us guts. Me, at least. My guts went up so I could demand a bath which Jailer Dick Barnes promised but didn't let me have. "You'll get it Saturday," he said. Saturday came and he put me off: "I haven't got time to fool with you." I got tight with him. "I got to have a bath!" That jacked up the other Scottsboro fellows and all together we raised hell for a bath. Barnes, he came back and let us out three at a time for showers.

Prisoners told me registered mail wasn't supposed to be opened. I found out mine was being opened and even kept from me. I told the guards I wanted to have some words with somebody about it. A little old man named Ervin, he came around. "I got to okay your mail," he said. "I have to look in the mail of all you Scottsboro niggers."

That got me sore. "Now listen, don't you open no letter of mine. If you do I'll see what I can do about it."

Ervin beat it off, and one of my cellmates said, "You can't talk to him like that. He's a chief warden."

"I don't care if he's President Hoover."

From then on, whenever mail came to me, Ervin, he would bring it himself. I opened it, Ervin saw me take out the money, then he'd read the letter.

It went on like that for many days until Barnes got to hate me. I kept after him; he kept after me. I had my own fight in me to begin with and now I had white folks fronting for me. One day he came up to my door and shook his finger at me and said, "I'll have you sent to Kilby tomorrow."

Sure enough, the next day, April 23, Barnes banged on the cell door and said, "Okay, sonofabitch, you and the other niggers get ready. You going to the death row in Kilby. You can't take nothing with you either. . . . I hope they burn that black dick off of you first before they burn the rest of you."

My cigarettes I gave away. Then I walked out the cell.

Outside the jail I was put in a private car, handcuffed to Willie Roberson. Guards were on each side and in the front seat.

That ride I can remember. It was my last good feeling of the outdoors. It was a fast ride for several hours, with the day getting warmer, the sun hotter. There was no talk, even between Willie and me. My eyes took in everything along the roadsides. It was spring, my favorite time of year. I was a tight guy who would not show people tears, but I felt the water behind my lids.

Willie and myself were the first to reach Kilby.

It was a bitter thing to see the door of Kilby Prison, what the free people of Alabama call "the little green gate." Those walls looked so high and hard to get over. They were concrete. We could see guards in the shacks along the wall tops next to their machine guns. Barbed wire stretched on top of the walls all around.

They took us in through steel gates.

Then, death row opened to us . . . a dozen cells facing each other, six to a side, and a thirteenth cell for toilet work.

Right off a guy in the cell opposite, he said, "So you're from Scottsboro. Been reading about you guys. The papers in New York making a big fuss about it. The governor will insist you go now."

"Go where?"

"To the chair . . . it's right there."

I tried twisting my neck and eyes out the front of the cell to see the death room: but it was just out of my sight.

That guy opposite, they called him Gunboat, he kept talking. "Do you want a Bible to make your soul right?" He was holding up a little red book in his hands for us to see. "You going to die tonight, you know. You Scottsboros better get busy with the Lord."

Willie Roberson, he was leaning up against the door with me listening, and he put a frown on. Willie got scared and excited and started talking about things. "You sure we going to die tonight?" he asked. We were both afraid. We didn't know. Sometimes other prisoners, they heard about things before we did.

Another guy in a cell next to Gunboat's was shaking his head from side to side like we should pay no mind to him. This fellow, name of Ricketts, called Gunboat a liar and said, "You fellows ain't going to die tonight. Gunboat don't know nothing about your case."

Gunboat yelled out, "Them guys going to die tonight! Here, take this here Bible!"

Ricketts waved his hands and said, "Keep away from that thing. That Bible never did us niggers any good!"

I never had really read the Bible. Couldn't read much anyway. But I was upset and leaned toward what Gunboat said. . . .

"You better take to the Bible. You got souls and you better clean 'em."

Ricketts put it different. "You ain't got good lawyers, then you're done for. You ain't got white folks to front for you, then you're done for. *But leave that thing alone!"*

"What you heard about us getting the chair tonight?" Willie Roberson asked Gunboat.

"I know. Don't ask how I know."

"You heard something?"

"The Lord tell me so."

"Get that Bible across to me," I said to Gunboat.

"Don't take it!" Ricketts made a last try.

Gunboat, he tied a piece of wood to the end of a string and threw it over in front of my cell door. The Bible was on the other end and I started dragging it across to me.

Just then a tall, rawbony guard named L. J. Burrs saw Gunboat telegraphing the Bible to me. He stopped before our cell and said to Willie and me, "Pray, you goddamned black bastards. You'll still burn anyway."

"Hand me the book, will you?" I said to the guard.

"O-o-h, you goddamned black sonofabitch. What you mean talking like that to me? Don't you know to call me *Captain,* call me *Boss?"*

"I don't call no one Captain. I don't call no one Boss."

"You nigger, you better get right with me before you get right with your Lord. You call me Captain when you talk to me."

He made to open the cell door, like he might come in to beat on me, then he changed his mind. Instead he kicked the Bible under my door and said, "I fix you, Patterson. You the ringleader of all these Scottsboro bastards. We got your record. You going to reckon with me." He walked down by the toilet.

I could hardly make out the words in the book. The little training in reading I had had I never much followed up. Never read no papers, no books, nothing. I did not know how to pronounce things, could not even say "Alabama" so you could understand me. I had to ask prisoners to tell me, and I would try and repeat it. Negroes called this way of speaking "flat talk."

But the Bible felt solid in my hands. I found myself stumbling through the small printed words.

Pretty soon the other fellows came in. They put Weems and Andy Wright in one cell, Powell and Norris together, and Eugene Williams and Olen Montgomery in another cell.

Right off Gunboat, he started to work on all of them, telling them the juice was going on tonight, and to get right with the Lord.

Charlie Weems wasn't easy to fool and he answered, "Aw, I know better than that. Our date set for July 10. They ain't going to do it before. You're a damned liar."

The religious stuff got going, all up and down the death row, them that was there trying to convert those of us just arrived. You see, a man in the death cell, he clings to anything that gives him a little hope.

That kind of talk mixed with the guessing about whether we would die tonight or in July. It went all up and down the twelve cells. My cell number was 222. I told the others my cell number and they told me theirs. Cell number 231 was right next to the chair room and none of us Tennessee and Georgia boys in the Scottsboro case had that one.

Each cell was just big enough for a single cot. Sometimes, when it was crowded in the death row, like now, they would put up a double-deck bed. Then you couldn't move around. One fellow would have to lay up on the bunk while the other could take about three steps forward and turn and take three steps back—if he was nervous and needed to walk.

White and black were in the death row, but mostly Negroes. Around us were desperate men who tried to question us about the Scottsboro case. They were killers, stoolies, and crazy guys. Some hoped to hear something they could carry to the warden so as to escape punishment for their crimes. They got nothing out of us. There was nothing to get out of us anyway. We just kept quiet about the case, all of us.

Night pushed into death row. I knew there were stars outside. The face of the sky I could see and remember clearly because I had looked at it at night all my life. I laid on the top bunk, in a way still feeling I was on a moving freight. Nothing was standing still. I was busy living from minute to minute. Everything was rumbling. I dreamed bad dreams, with freight trains, guards' faces, and courtrooms mixed up with the look of the sky at night.

LUCILLE B. MILNER

Jim Crow in the Army

For many black Americans, the New Deal had been a mixed bag of many promises and small successes. The CIO had come into being with the optimism that black and white workers could unite in full equality and power. The NAACP, once the hope of many, was soon regarded as an organization that was too tepid, too concerned with seeking small practical gains instead of considering the larger economic situation. With the advent of World War II, however, the question of racial equality took on an entirely new reality.

Once again the nation was tested seriously, and once again it failed. Once again America let it be known that the black man was not to be allowed a position of leadership and responsibility at the very moment that the country encountered one of its most serious challenges. This attitude was embodied in segregated army bases, segregated blood banks, and a segregated fighting force. Many black men served only as menials; many served in units largely regarded as jokes by white GI's. As John Oliver Killens notes in his novel, *And Then We Heard the Thunder,* some black soldiers were made to go marching off to war to the humiliating tune of "Darktown Strutter's Ball."

I am a Negro soldier 22 years old. I won't fight or die in vain. If I fight, suffer or die it will be for the freedom of every black, any black man to live equally with other races. . . . If the life of the Negro in the United States is right as it is lived today, then I would rather be dead.

Any Negro would rather give his life at home fighting for a cause he can understand than against any enemy whose principles are the same as our so-called democracy.

JIM CROW IN THE ARMY   by Lucille B. Milner. Reprinted by permission of *The New Republic,* © 1944, Harrison-Blaine of New Jersey, Inc.

Lucille Milner's Note: The letters quoted in this article are in the files of organizations such as the National Association for the Advancement of Colored People. For obvious reasons the names and addresses of the senders are withheld. It is the policy of these organizations to forward copies of letters making serious charges to the proper authorities for investigation. Thus many of the conditions described in the actual letters quoted, or scores of similar ones, have been authenticated by high military and civil officers, and in some cases have been corrected.

A new Negro will return from the war—a bitter Negro if he is disappointed again. He will have been taught to kill, to suffer, to die for something he believes in, and he will live by these rules to gain his personal rights.

STATEMENTS LIKE THESE ARE FOUND OVER AND OVER IN THE HUNDREDS of soldiers' letters received by organizations defending the rights of the colored people. It is impossible to read a dozen of these letters picked at random without feeling their tragic significance. The war attitude of the Negro reflects today's dilemma of his race, in an intensified and critical form. The Negro soldier is deeply patriotic, vividly conscious of our aims in this war, eager to get into the fighting areas. That seems an ideal attitude for a soldier to have, but the truth is that the morale of the colored men in our armed forces is far from ideal. For they are not allowed to express their patriotism, their democracy and their militancy freely. They have fought bravely in every war, from the Revolution on, but still they are not treated like Americans.

The sense of being excluded from the mainstream of military service is expressed in their letters in phrases like these: "We really have nothing to soldier for.". . . "It is not like being in a soldier camp. It is more like being in prison." A soldier at an air base wrote:

> Segregation in the Army is making enemies of the Negro soldier, demoralizing him. You may wonder why they don't rebel. They do, but individually, and as a result, they are either transferred to Southern parts, placed in the guardhouse or given a dishonorable discharge from the army. . . . We keep constantly in mind that army law is WHITE man's law.

The very set-up in our various services proves that a race that has been three centuries on our soil is still considered Negro, rather than American. The fault is not in our pronouncements but in our practice. The Selective Training and Service Act of 1940 said distinctly that there shall be no discrimination against any person because of race or color.

How is this principle reflected in military practice?

The Navy has refused to commission Negroes in any branch of service—in the Navy proper, the Marine Corps and the Coast Guard.[1] While it has admitted Negroes to its fighting ranks, Jim Crowism is practised in training and in service.

The Air Corps has discriminated against Negroes in the most com-

[1] On February 15, 1944, since this article was written, the Secretary of the Navy announced that 22 Negroes will be commissioned.

plicated and costly way, building a segregated air base for Negroes when there was room in established training centers over the country. The annual output of Negro pilots was 200 when it could easily have been five times that number.

The Army trains and commissions colored and white candidates without discrimination, but Jim Crow rules over every Southern camp.

Colored women are excluded from every auxiliary service but the Wacs, and here there is segregation.

With the Army calling for thousands of nurses, they have held down the quota of colored nurses to about 200.

Briefly this is the set-up. It reflects no policy on the part of our command, for the simple reason that no policy exists. It reflects merely today's confusion and the inherited tradition of our services from the prewar days when Southern officers in the Army and Navy had a good deal to do with molding attitudes. The Negro serviceman feels that the general pattern he must follow is this: to be barred from the sea and the air except on "their" terms; to serve on the land mainly in labor or "service of supply" battalions; to endure Jim Crow in every guise, from subtle slights to brutality and death at the hands of both peace officers and military police; to be kept on American soil and excluded from combat service as long as "they" can contrive retraining, or transfer, or some other run-around; in combat service to be kept if possible behind the lines and always out of the headlines, the newsreels and the glory; to come back as a war casualty and find Jim Crow waiting in most of the hospitals in the South.

The racial attitude of the military is a curious anachronism. Despite the gains made on the civilian front in race relations during the last two decades, actual conditions in our camps, most of which are unfortunately in the South, show a reversion to dark and ignorant prejudice. A corporal writes from the Deep South: ". . . It is no secret that the Negro soldier in the South is as much persecuted as is his civilian brother; the conditions existing in this Godforsaken hole which is Camp . . . are intolerable, and may be considered on a par with the worst conditions throughout the South since 1865."

Certain inequalities may not seem important until you think what they mean to the soldiers: post movie theatres and post exchanges barring Negroes in some camps and segregating them in others; guest accommodations for whites only in Southern camps; the fact that in many parts of the South Negro MP's may not carry arms as the whites do; exclusion from the white USO even when none exists for the colored men; overwhelming and widespread troubles about transportation in buses and trains. Candidates for commissions in a few of the training schools may eat, sleep and study together without regard to color—but what then? The white officer is soon sent overseas, the colored officer is apt to be transferred to another camp for "further training." The practice seems to be to keep the Negroes, as far as possible, from overseas duty, to use them at their lowest rather than their highest skills and to retard promotion.

Segregation is the deepest issue between whites and blacks in the services. It is made more bitter by the fact that North and South as well as white and colored are thrown together in the camps and bases. Northern-born Negroes are appalled at meeting Jim Crow on his home ground for the first time, and as a rule the Northern whites are also shocked. But Southern Negroes crossing the Mason-Dixon Line for the first time are confused by the comparative freedom of conditions in the North and West; it is claimed that they become demoralized. Southern white officers and trainees coming North often turn into rabid missionaries for "keeping the niggers in their place."

The soldiers ponder and write a good deal about this crisscross. A private at an air base in the Pacific Northwest writes: "The next sore spot that may respond to lancing is the attitude of the Southern-born or (climate of opinion) Commanding Officers. They try to impose a Dixie viewpoint on a democratic community."

A white boy from New York who had never thought much about racial problems wrote from a Southern camp:

> I feel bitter towards the South and the Southern boys. I used to think that when one talked about the Civil War being fought all over again it was a gag. Not any more. We just had another discussion about the Negro situation. It seems to be the big thing around here. Some Southern boys do believe that the Negro should be treated as a man. They say: "Give them education, give them all the rights we have, but always remember that a white man is always better than a colored man. Let the white man live in one place and the Negro in another.". . . A boy runs into a brick wall when he talks to a Southern boy about the Negro.

From a colored officer in the Deep South:

> The only desire the Negro officers could possibly have is to get completely out of the South. Many of us have never been below the Mason-Dixon Line, and are now being subjected to chain-gang practices and disgraceful and embarrassing verbal abuse. . . . No nursing or recreational facilities have been organized for us. . . . To go to a nearby

city is to invite trouble, not only from civilian police but more often from the military police, who are upheld in any discourtesy, breach of discipline, arrogance and bodily assault they render the Negro officers.

Another young white officer, born in the North, made it a point to discuss race relations with hundreds of men, white and black, gathered from every part of the country at a Southern camp. He reports some reactions:

A white private from Virginia: "Gosh, I just had to salute a damn nigger lieutenant. Boy, that burns me up."

A professedly progressive school-teacher from North Carolina: "Give the Negroes equality of opportunity by all means—by themselves."

A technical sergeant from Texas: "You people up North want to change things overnight. You are heading for a revolution."

The segregation question will be a burning postwar issue. Meanwhile our High Command has the Supreme Court behind it. It has voided laws creating Negro districts in cities, but upheld those compelling separate railroad accommodations, declaring that segregation is not discrimination when the facilities offered both races are substantially the same. Taking the same ground, the Interstate Commerce Commission recently dismissed a complaint filed by eighteen Negro seamen against the Atlantic Coast Line. The men asked for "a bold declaration that segregation in and of itself today must be regarded as constituting an unlawful discrimination." That puts the Negro attitude on segregation in a nutshell. The Commission responded, "What complainants asked us to decide is in its essence a social question and not a question of inequality of treatment."

This makes it lawful, if somewhat grotesque, for incidents like the following to happen. On a crowded troop train going through Texas the colored soldiers were fed behind a Jim Crow curtain at one end of the dining car. In the main section, along with the white folks, a group of German war prisoners dined—and no doubt fed their illusions of race superiority on that Jim Crow curtain.

The assignment of Negro units in the Army to menial jobs is a widespread practice. Colored inductees go to camp for military training and find themselves assigned to service units—cooking, shoveling coal, waiting on the white officers. Entering service, they may find themselves building the Burma Road, or African bases, or encountering winter temperatures of 50 degrees below zero hacking the Alaska Highway or the Canol pipeline out of the Canadian wastes. Meanwhile white units trained at the same time are in the fighting war, where the Negro longs to be. "The sight of masses of Negro soldiers constantly blocked off into separate groups and assigned to menial jobs," a white officer writes, "generates in the mind of the average soldier a powerful feeling of superiority and of being 'different'."

A highly trained Negro technologist turned up in the psychotic ward of a hospital. His Army service was picking up papers around the officers' quarters in a Southern camp. When he was transferred to radio work his mental troubles vanished. Another inductee, a brilliant biochemist, had a fantastic Army career. At the reception center on the Pacific Coast the officers proposed to use his years of medical training to the Army's advantage. He was sent to Camp A for training and assigned to a post in the biological laboratory. Before he could start work he was shipped further east to Camp B, and enrolled for technical training as an armorer. He passed this course with high honors, and was promptly shipped to Camp C—farther west—classed as corporal and assigned to the Army Air Forces. A week later he found himself at Camp D in the Southwest, assigned to labor detail. That meant losing his corporal's stripes gained in another division. He wrote his wife:

> I find that this post is the "Port of Lost Hope.". . . Merciful God, I have not been so close to loss of faith as I am at this moment. . . . All this build-up for something to respect, only to be treated like a brainless gorilla fit for nothing more than a post-hole digger and a stringer of wire, a yard bird. . . . I swear if this was Guadalcanal or Australia or North Africa I would expect nothing and would give everything, even my life. . . . It is mockery, let no one tell you differently, this sudden opening up of the so-called exclusive branches of the services to Negroes. We are trained, become skilled—and then the oblivion of common labor.

It is no secret that the Air Corps wished no Negro inductees. But it was forced to let the color bar down late in 1940 and created ten "Aviation Squadrons (Separate)" which served no specific military need and were assigned to whatever odd jobs of common labor the various air fields could offer. There was no equivalent white organization and these Negro units would probably never have come into existence but for the necessity of making some provision for the Negroes enlisted in the Air Forces.

The Air Corps began by training Negroes for combat aviation in only one branch—pursuit flying. A segregated base was set up near Tuskegee Institute and advanced training was at Selfridge Field. Pursuit flying is the most difficult type of combat aviation. Perhaps the Air

Corps was paying tribute to the Negro; possibly it was trying to discourage him. In any event, the pursuit flyers not only made good in training, but the Ninety-ninth Squadron, the first and only one sent abroad, has won special praise from Secretary of War Stimson and others for its fine spirit and the specialized dive bombing the men were called upon unexpectedly to perform when the squadron was on loan to the British Eighth Army in Italy.

In 1943, schools for bombardiers and navigators were opened to Negroes and the first squadron, known as Squadron 10, was graduated on February 26, 1944, at Hondo, Texas, and will now receive training as bombardiers.

In some respects the Navy, with its ancient and Southern-gentleman traditions, tallies with the policy of the modern Air Command. Between 1922 and 1942 Negroes were "the chambermaids of the Navy," acting as stewards, chefs and messboys. Several months after Pearl Harbor the Navy broke down and admitted colored men as apprentice seamen with the chance of becoming petty officers. It has let down the bars to women —but no dark-skinned women. There are no colored Waves, Spars or Marine Corps Auxiliaries. And since no Negro could be commissioned up to a few weeks ago, there are no Negro chaplains in the Navy.

The Navy trains its seamen in a Jim Crow station near the Great Lakes Naval Training Station. In creating this new all-Negro camp it was thought fitting to name it for a seagoing Negro, and history provided the name of Robert Smalls, a hero of the Civil War. Smalls was a slave who served as pilot of the Confederate gunboat Planter. Early in the war he and his Negro engineer smuggled their families aboard while the white captain was ashore at Charleston. Smalls took the gunboat through the Confederate blockade and delivered it to the Union officers at Port Royal. He was commissioned in the Navy and served for the duration.

At Camp Robert Smalls the colored men took their boot training with no hope of being commissioned like Smalls. Their chief comfort is their white commander, Lt.-Comdr. Daniel C. Armstrong, whose father founded Hampton Institute and brought him up to understand race problems.

It is reliably reported that a large proportion of the Seabees, a remarkable new arm of the service, is colored. Much of the work is stevedoring and the building of naval bases and many of the Negroes who enlisted after Pearl Harbor are highly skilled artisans, college and technical-school graduates. Racial discrimination is thinly camouflaged by ratings

—the Negroes, whatever their qualifications, are kept in lower grades and the men are segregated by grades, not by color. Recently fifteen Negro Seabees who had worked more than a year constructing a naval base in the Caribbean were dishonorably discharged as "unfit." Their real offense was telling their battalion commander, in what he assured them was an off-the-record consultation, that they objected to the Jim Crow conditions at the construction base.

The fact that no Negroes have been commissioned in the Marine Corps and the Coast Guard has not discouraged many youngsters who see a chance for adventurous and tough service in these branches. If they want higher pay and complete surcease from Jim Crow, they join the Merchant Marine. Since the Navy is out of the picture, any Negro who has served fourteen months on a floating unit may enter an Officers' Candidate School in the Merchant Marine. At present three merchant ships with mixed crews are commanded by Negroes—the Booker T. Washington, the Frederick Douglass and the George Washington Carver.

It is hard to decide which is more cruel—this new pattern of murdering the ambition, the skills, the high potential contributions of the gifted Negro, or the old pattern of physical brutality which the Negro-baiters and Klan agents use against the colored man in uniform. Soldiers of both races have been killed in camp riots which have grown out of unequal conditions and mounting tensions. But the Negro soldier is much safer in camp than in some Southern towns or on common carriers. He "finds himself not only outside the protection of the law but even the object of lawless aggression by the officers of the law," in the opinion of Judge William H. Hastie, former Civilian Aide to the Secretary of War, who felt it necessary to resign his high post in protest against the Air Corps policy toward Negroes.

For instance, last Memorial Day at Centerville, Mississippi, the local sheriff intervened in a minor fracas between a white MP and a Negro soldier whose offense was having lost a sleeve button. The two were fighting things out, with the other MP's and the Negro's companions holding back. When the MP began to get the worst of things, he yelled at the sheriff, "Shoot the nigger." The sheriff fired point-blank at the Negro's chest, then asked the MP, "Any more niggers you want killed?"

Another ugly story based on the sworn testimony of eyewitnesses concerns the murder of a colored private in Hampton, Arkansas, last spring. He was trying to protect his sister from assault by a white man who was drunk. A deputy sheriff intervened, and though it was the white man who attacked him, it was the black man who was shot. The deputy sheriff was never apprehended.

Buses and trains mean even more to the Negro soldier than to the white in parts of the country where there is no local Negro population, and he must travel far, or else hope for a visit from his family, in order to mingle with his own kind. The soldiers' letters describe endless troubles with buses and trains. Even when they are being transferred as troops, they are often refused service in the railway restaurants and go hungry for twenty-four hours. The wife and two babies of a Negro chaplain traveled three days to join him without being able to buy anything but cold milk and sandwiches. One gentle little Negro woman, whose soldier-husband was refused coffee at a bus terminal, delivered a sermon to the snappish counter-girl. "Our boys can fight for you," she said. "They are spilling their blood for you on the battlefield, yet you can't serve them a cup of coffee." But the management still refused the coffee. "May the Lord forgive them, for they know not what they do," she said in a quiet tone as they turned and left.

From 1770, when the colored boy Crispus Attucks fell in the Boston Massacre, down through the Battle of San Juan Hill and the Meuse-Argonne offensive, the colored Americans have been collecting their traditions of war and their flags and decorations and trophies. As far as we will let them, they are fighting as Americans today, and yet they are fighting with a difference. This, from a soldier's letter, expresses what is in their hearts: "Those of us who are in the armed services are offering our lives and fortunes, not for the America we know today, but for the America we hope will be created after the war."

The

Awakening

The South and Civil Rights

Edward Aaron

On May 18, 1954, the long struggle waged by the NAACP and other organizations to end the official policy of public school segregation in America came to
a conclusion. In its famous Brown vs. Board of Education decision, the Supreme
Court ruled that such a policy was unconstitutional. But the distance between
the end of an unconstitutional policy and the beginning of a constitutionally
valid one was extraordinarily great. Several Southern states did everything they
could to retard even the "deliberate speed" toward desegregation advised by
the Court. Using random violence and threats, and in the case of one school
system, outright locking of school doors to all children, those defiants of the
Court fought, as they still do, to prevent equal opportunity for education. Mobs
were formed, for example, in Clinton, Tennessee; at Little Rock, Arkansas; and
at the University of Alabama, to stop desegregation. But the most terrifying
violence came from men who were not simply angered at a particular advance
made by black people; ignoring any "issues," they responded with fury to the
realization that times were changing and that the black man could no longer
be locked in a *status quo* rooted in slavery and Jim Crow. Thus Emmet Till was
murdered in 1955 near Money, Mississippi. And thus, as journalist William Bradford Huie here recounts, Edward Aaron was castrated.

In the decade following the second world war the national
Ku Klux Klan all but died. It took new life from the Supreme Court's
Black Monday decision. With no central headquarters but with several
regional leaders, chapters began organizing themselves throughout the
old cotton South.

In 1957 a chapter of about twenty-five members was organized in
the East Lake section of Birmingham. Its most respectable member was
its treasurer, Jesse Mabry, forty-five, who for twenty years had been an

EDWARD AARON From *Three Lives for Mississippi* by William Bradford Huie.
New York: New American Library, Inc., 1965. Reprinted by permission of the
author.

employee and foreman at Perfection Mattress Company. Mabry owned his home in East Lake. He had never been arrested for any offense. His name first reached the newspapers—and police records—when the Negro singer, the late Nat King Cole, was attacked. Cole was singing at the Birmingham Municipal Auditorium when several Klansmen jumped onto the stage, seized him, and attempted to maul him. Police saved him from serious injury. Mabry, for his part in this assault, paid a fine for disorderly conduct.

Mabry's Klan chapter met each Wednesday evening. Its meeting place or "lair" was a crude, empty, cinderblock building, some twenty-five by thirty feet, located on a lonely dirt road about eight miles from Mabry's home. The building was lighted with kerosene lamps and fitted with blackout curtains. White sheets running on wires formed partitions.

On Labor Day, Monday evening, September 2, 1957, the six officers of the chapter met at Mabry's home. They were Joe Pritchett, Bart Floyd, Grover McCullough, William Miller, John Griffin, and Mabry. A Klan chapter's officers often have titles like the Army: the presiding officer or cyclops is a major; under him are captains and lieutenants, their number depending on the size of the chapter.

The business at Mabry's home was this: the chapter had no "captain of the lair." It had a major, Pritchett, and it had five lieutenants, the others. But it hadn't filled the office of captain, and the officers were holding a special meeting to decide which of the lieutenants deserved to be promoted to captain of the lair. Bart Floyd wanted to be captain. He told the others he thought he could qualify. He said he was ready to prove himself worthy of being captain of the lair.

What did Floyd mean by "proving himself"? He meant he was willing to "get nigger blood on his hands." He was ready to show his fellow officers that not only could he put on his robe and hood and "scare a nigger," but that he was also capable of "cutting [castrating] a nigger."

It then became the responsibility of the officers to "put Floyd to the test." They got in two cars. In Floyd's car were Floyd, Mabry, and Miller. In Griffin's car were Griffin, Pritchett, and McCullough. They drove off about 8:30 P.M.

Look at those six men. They thought of themselves as "average Americans." They thought they were a little superior because they were Klan officers. They were also members of the "country club Klan"—Citizens Council. All were members of Protestant churches; all said they believed in God. All had high-school educations and could read and write. Two were high school graduates. Three had served in the Army. The youngest, Miller, was twenty-eight; the oldest, Mabry, was forty-five. Miller

and Griffin worked together in a grocery store; the others held compa-
rable jobs. None had ever been charged with a felony. They had no whiskey with them; they were not drunk or even drinking.

The first stop was at a drugstore where Floyd bought a package of
razor blades and a bottle of turpentine.

One of them thought of a particular Negro and they drove to his
home, but this intended victim was lucky; he wasn't there. They then
went to a Negro roadside spot, the Cabin Club. Pritchett and Floyd went
in, looked around, but found no likely victim. They drove farther and
spotted a Negro couple walking along a country road.

The man was Edward Aaron, thirty-four, a quiet, slender, peaceable
citizen, five foot nine, 148 pounds. He had been born in Barbour County,
Alabama; during the war he had served honorably with the Army's
Quartermaster Corps in England and in the Philippines. He was barely
literate. Since the war he had lived with his mother on the outskirts of
Birmingham, working as a painter's helper and doing other odd jobs,
earning about $600 a year. He had never married—he "couldn't afford
to"; he had never been in jail—"never bothered a living soul." He was
about the least combative Negro male the Klansmen could have found.
His companion was Cora Parker, a respectable woman Aaron and his
family had known for eight years.

Floyd said: "We'll grab him and chase her off."

The cars stopped, and before the Negroes could suspect danger the
Klansmen leaped on Aaron and threw him into the back of Floyd's car.
Aaron said: "Whatya want with me? I ain't done nothin'!" Floyd answered by slugging him with a pistol, then sitting on him while Mabry
drove Floyd's car about six miles to the lair.

At the lair the Klansmen unlocked the door and lighted the lamps.
Then they brought in "the nigger." None of them knew him or had ever
seen him. They didn't ask his name. They addressed him only as *nigger*
or *you black sonofabitch*. Not once did they allow him to stand erect.
They made him crawl out of the car, then crawl to the entrance of the
lair and inside. They made him sit on his knees and watch them put on
their robes and hoods. Pritchett, as Cyclops, put on a red hood adorned
with gold. The hood looked like a pillow case: it had slits for the eyes
but no slits for ears or mouth. Pritchett's robe and the robes and hoods
of the others were white.

Aaron, kneeling in the dirt and lamplight, knew he was helpless. He
didn't even have a pocket knife. There were no houses nearby: he could
scream his head off and no one would hear.

In full regalia Pritchett stood splendidly overlooking the "nigger."

"Look up at me, nigger!" Pritchett ordered. Aaron raised his eyes and Pritchett dramatically raised his hood and looked down at Aaron. "Do you know me, nigger?" Pritchett asked.

"Naw, suh," Aaron replied. "I ain't never seen yuh."

Pritchett kicked him hard in the eye.

Pritchett then lowered his hood and said: "Now look around you, nigger! Look careful. You ever seen any of these gentlemen?"

Aaron looked around and said: "Naw, suh." He ducked as he said it, but Pritchett didn't kick him again.

For half an hour the group baited their helpless victim. With curses, kicks, and four-letter filth they "interrogated the nigger." They knew three "hate" names—Earl Warren; Martin Luther King, who a year earlier had led the Montgomery bus boycott; and a local Negro preacher who was then leading an effort to integrate the railroad station. They used these names in the "interrogation."

"Look at me, nigger! You think you're as good as I am! You think any nigger is as good as a white man!"

"Look here, nigger! You ever heard of a nigger-loving Communist named Earl Warren? You ain't? Well, you ought to learn who he is, because he loves yuh!"

"Look at me, nigger! You got any kids? You think nigger kids should go to school with my white kids? You think you got a right to vote? Or eat where I eat? Or use the same toilet I use?"

Pritchett finally halting the baiting with a "judgment." "All right, nigger, look up at me! Here's my judgment. We're gonna take your life or your nuts. You got your choice. It don't make a damn bit o' difference to us. Which will it be?"

Aaron sank farther into the dirt and began to cry. "Neither one," he said.

Pritchett said he'd choose for him. They'd take his nuts. They were gonna use him to send a little message to Earl Warren and Martin Luther King and all other nigger-lovers.

Pritchett turned to Floyd and snapped: "Do your duty!"

Floyd leaped at Aaron and slugged him with the pistol. He didn't knock him unconscious, but he partially dazed him. The others grabbed Aaron, made him pull off his pants and shorts, and spreadeagled him in the dirt. Floyd jumped between his legs and with a razor blade severed the entire scrotum. Pritchett imperiously held forth a paper cup and Floyd dropped the testicles into it. Then Floyd doused his squirming, bleeding victim with the turpentine.

Pritchett passed the cup of "evidence" to each of the lieutenants, and each nodded agreement that Bart Floyd was now worthy to become captain of the lair. One lieutenant proved himself unworthy: Miller sickened and vomited.

They dressed Aaron, tossed him into a car trunk, drove about eight miles and threw him out on the side of a road. As their cars pulled away he crawled into some bushes. When the cars turned around and started back toward him, Aaron thought they were returning to kill him. He crawled farther and dropped into a small creek about three feet deep. The cars stopped. While helping remove Aaron from the trunk, Pritchett had set the cup of evidence on the pavement and driven off without it. Aaron submerged himself in the creek until Pritchett retrieved his cup and the cars drove off again.

Aaron then managed to crawl to the road and stagger to his feet. Several cars passed him, and one of the motorists telephoned police that a "bloody Negro" was staggering along the road. Police arrived and later testified that Aaron looked like he had been "dipped in blood from the belt down." At the Veterans Administration Hospital in Birmingham a surgeon closed the wound and Aaron was given whole blood. For four days his condition remained critical with his temperature reaching 105. He then began to recover, and after three weeks he was able to leave the hospital.

MARTIN LUTHER KING, JR.

The Montgomery Bus Boycott

In 1947, the Congress of Racial Equality and the Fellowship of Reconciliation led a "Journey of Reconciliation" into certain Southern states to test the degree of compliance given to a Supreme Court decision invalidating segregation on

MONTGOMERY BUS BOYCOTT   Abridged from pp. 43–49, 53–54 in *Stride Toward Freedom* by Martin Luther King, Jr. Copyright © 1958 by Martin Luther King, Jr. By permission of Harper & Row, Publishers, Incorporated.

interstate buses. The result was violence and jailings. But the struggle had
begun, just as it had in the North in 1941 when A. Philip Randolph threatened
to lead a massive march on Washington unless President Roosevelt banned
discriminatory hiring in the nation's defense plants. With such precedents as
these and with growing numbers of adherents to the Gandhian principles of
nonviolent resistance, a new chapter in the struggle for civil rights began.

The most dramatic and successful example of such principles was the Montgomery Bus Boycott of 1955. Led by the Reverend Martin Luther King, Jr.,
E. D. Nixon, and the Reverend Ralph Abernathy, the boycott emptied Montgomery's buses for more than a year. Employing nonviolent methods, the Montgomery Improvement Association, which grew out of the boycott, gathered the
black people of the city together and allowed them to act in an effective way
as a mass movement. The rest of the South soon heard the news. By December,
1956, when lawyers for the NAACP obtained an order desegregating the Montgomery buses, similar struggles were being waged elsewhere.

In the following selection, Dr. King discusses the events which inspired the boycott in Montgomery, and indicates why he felt techniques of nonviolence were
necessary.

ON DECEMBER 1, 1955, AN ATTRACTIVE NEGRO SEAMSTRESS, MRS. ROSA
Parks, boarded the Cleveland Avenue Bus in downtown Montgomery.
She was returning home after her regular day's work in the Montgomery
Fair—a leading department store. Tired from long hours on her feet,
Mrs. Parks sat down in the first seat behind the section reserved for
whites. Not long after she took her seat, the bus operator ordered her,
along with three other Negro passengers, to move back in order to
accommodate boarding white passengers. By this time every seat in the
bus was taken. This meant that if Mrs. Parks followed the driver's command she would have to stand while a white male passenger, who had
just boarded the bus, would sit. The other three Negro passengers immediately complied with the driver's request. But Mrs. Parks quietly
refused. The result was her arrest.

There was to be much speculation about why Mrs. Parks did not obey
the driver. Many people in the white community argued that she had
been "planted" by the NAACP in order to lay the groundwork for a test
case, and at first glance that explanation seemed plausible, since she
was a former secretary of the local branch of the NAACP. So persistent
and persuasive was this argument that it convinced many reporters from
all over the country. Later on, when I was having press conferences three
times a week—in order to accommodate the reporters and journalists

who came to Montgomery from all over the world—the invariable first question was: "Did the NAACP start the bus boycott?"

But the accusation was totally unwarranted, as the testimony of both Mrs. Parks and the officials of the NAACP revealed. Actually, no one can understand the action of Mrs. Parks unless he realizes that eventually the cup of endurance runs over, and the human personality cries out, "I can take it no longer." Mrs. Parks's refusal to move back was her intrepid affirmation that she had had enough. It was an individual expression of a timeless longing for human dignity and freedom. She was not "planted" there by the NAACP, or any other organization; she was planted there by her personal sense of dignity and self-respect. She was anchored to that seat by the accumulated indignities of days gone by and the boundless aspirations of generations yet unborn. She was a victim of both the forces of history and the forces of destiny. She had been tracked down by the *Zeitgeist*—the spirit of the time.

Fortunately, Mrs. Parks was ideal for the role assigned to her by history. She was a charming person with a radiant personality, soft spoken and calm in all situations. Her character was impeccable and her dedication deep-rooted. All of these traits together made her one of the most respected people in the Negro community.

Only E. D. Nixon—the signer of Mrs. Parks's bond—and one or two other persons were aware of the arrest when it occurred early Thursday evening. Later in the evening the word got around to a few influential women of the community, mostly members of the Women's Political Council. After a series of telephone calls back and forth they agreed that the Negroes should boycott the buses. They immediately suggested the idea to Nixon, and he readily concurred. In his usual courageous manner he agreed to spearhead the idea.

Early Friday morning, December 2, Nixon called me. He was so caught up in what he was about to say that he forgot to greet me with the usual "hello" but plunged immediately into the story of what had happened to Mrs. Parks the night before. I listened, deeply shocked, as he described the humiliating incident. "We have taken this type of thing too long already," Nixon concluded, his voice trembling. "I feel that the time has come to boycott the buses. Only through a boycott can we make it clear to the white folks that we will not accept this type of treatment any longer."

I agreed at once that some protest was necessary, and that the boycott method would be an effective one.

Just before calling me Nixon had discussed the idea with Rev. Ralph

Abernathy, the young minister of Montgomery's First Baptist Church who was to become one of the central figures in the protest, and one of my closest associates. Abernathy also felt a bus boycott was our best course of action. So for thirty or forty minutes the three of us telephoned back and forth concerning plans and strategy. Nixon suggested that we call a meeting of all the ministers and civic leaders the same evening in order to get their thinking on the proposal, and I offered my church as the meeting place. The three of us got busy immediately. With the sanction of Rev. H. H. Hubbard—president of the Baptist Ministerial Alliance—Abernathy and I began calling all of the Baptist ministers. Since most of the Methodist ministers were attending a denominational meeting in one of the local churches that afternoon, it was possible for Abernathy to get the announcement to all of them simultaneously. Nixon reached Mrs. A. W. West—the widow of a prominent dentist—and enlisted her assistance in getting word to the civic leaders.

By early afternoon the arrest of Mrs. Parks was becoming public knowledge. Word of it spread around the community like uncontrolled fire. Telephones began to ring in almost rhythmic succession. By two o'clock an enthusiastic group had mimeographed leaflets concerning the arrest and the proposed boycott, and by evening these had been widely circulated.

As the hour for the evening meeting arrived, I approached the doors of the church with some apprehension, wondering how many of the leaders would respond to our call. Fortunately, it was one of those pleasant winter nights of unseasonable warmth, and to our relief, almost everybody who had been invited was on hand. More than forty people, from every segment of Negro life, were crowded into the large church meeting room. I saw physicians, schoolteachers, lawyers, businessmen, postal workers, union leaders, and clergymen. Virtually every organization of the Negro community was represented.

The largest number there was from the Christian ministry. Having left so many civic meetings in the past sadly disappointed by the dearth of ministers participating, I was filled with joy when I entered the church and found so many of them there; for then I knew that something unusual was about to happen.

Had E. D. Nixon been present, he would probably have been automatically selected to preside, but he had had to leave town earlier in the afternoon for his regular run on the railroad. In his absence, we concluded that Rev. L. Roy Bennett—as president of the Interdenominational Ministerial Alliance—was the logical person to take the chair. He agreed and was seated, his tall, erect figure dominating the room.

The meeting opened around seven-thirty with H. H. Hubbard leading a brief devotional period. Then Bennett moved into action, explaining the purpose of the gathering. With excited gestures he reported on Mrs. Parks's resistance and her arrest. He presented the proposal that the Negro citizens of Montgomery should boycott the buses on Monday in protest. "Now is the time to move," he concluded. "This is no time to talk; it is time to act."

So seriously did Bennett take his "no time to talk" admonition that for quite a while he refused to allow anyone to make a suggestion or even raise a question, insisting that we should move on and appoint committees to implement the proposal. This approach aroused the opposition of most of those present, and created a temporary uproar. For almost forty-five minutes the confusion persisted. Voices rose high, and many people threatened to leave if they could not raise questions and offer suggestions. It looked for a time as though the movement had come to an end before it began. But finally, in the face of this blistering protest, Bennett agreed to open the meeting to discussion.

Immediately questions began to spring up from the floor. Several people wanted further clarification of Mrs. Parks's actions and arrest. Then came the more practical questions. How long would the protest last? How would the idea be further disseminated throughout the community? How would the people be transported to and from their jobs?

As we listened to the lively discussion, we were heartened to notice that, despite the lack of coherence in the meeting, not once did anyone question the validity or desirability of the boycott itself. It seemed to be the unanimous sense of the group that the boycott should take place.

The ministers endorsed the plan with enthusiasm, and promised to go to their congregations on Sunday morning and drive home their approval of the projected one-day protest. Their co-öperation was significant, since virtually all of the influential Negro ministers of the city were present. It was decided that we should hold a city-wide mass meeting on Monday night, December 5, to determine how long we would abstain from riding the buses. Rev. A. W. Wilson—minister of the Holt Street Baptist Church—offered his church, which was ideal as a meeting place because of its size and central location. The group agreed that additional leaflets should be distributed on Saturday, and the chairman appointed a committee, including myself, to prepare the statement.

Our committee went to work while the meeting was still in progress.

The final message was shorter than the one that had appeared on the first leaflets, but the substance was the same. It read as follows:

Don't ride the bus to work, to town, to school, or any place Monday, December 5.

Another Negro woman has been arrested and put in jail because she refused to give up her bus seat.

Don't ride the buses to work, to town, to school, or anywhere on Monday. If you work, take a cab, or share a ride, or walk.

Come to a mass meeting, Monday at 7:00 P.M., at the Holt Street Baptist Church for further instruction.

After finishing the statement the committee began to mimeograph it on the church machine; but since it was late, I volunteered to have the job completed early Saturday morning.

The final question before the meeting concerned transportation. It was agreed that we should try to get the Negro taxi companies of the city—eighteen in number, with approximately 210 taxis—to transport the people for the same price that they were currently paying on the bus. A committee was appointed to make this contact, with Rev. W. J. Powell, minister of the Old Ship A.M.E. Zion Church, as chairman.

With these responsibilities before us the meeting closed. We left with our hearts caught up in a great idea. The hours were moving fast. The clock on the wall read almost midnight, but the clock in our souls revealed that it was daybreak.

I was so excited that I slept very little that night, and early the next morning I was on my way to the church to get the leaflets out. By nine o'clock the church secretary had finished mimeographing the 7000 leaflets and by eleven o'clock an army of women and young people had taken them off to distribute by hand.

Those on the committee that was to contact the taxi companies got to work early Saturday afternoon. They worked assiduously, and by evening they had reached practically all of the companies, and triumphantly reported that every one of them so far had agreed to coöperate with the proposed boycott by transporting the passengers to and from work for the regular ten-cent bus fare.

Meanwhile our efforts to get the word across to the Negro community were abetted in an unexpected way. A maid who could not read very well came into possession of one of the unsigned appeals that had been distributed Friday afternoon. Apparently not knowing what the leaflet said, she gave it to her employer. As soon as the white employer received the notice she turned it over to the local newspaper, and the *Montgomery Advertiser* made the contents of the leaflet a front-page story on Saturday morning. It appears that the *Advertiser* printed the story in order to let the white community know what the Negroes were up to; but the whole thing turned out to the Negroes' advantage, since it served to bring the information to hundreds who had not previously heard of the plan. By Sunday afternoon word had spread to practically every Negro citizen of Montgomery. Only a few people who lived in remote areas had not heard of it.

. . .

MY WIFE AND I AWOKE EARLIER THAN USUAL ON MONDAY MORNING. We were up and fully dressed by five-thirty. The day for the protest had arrived, and we were determined to see the first act of this unfolding drama. I was still saying that if we could get 60 per cent coöperation the venture would be a success.

Fortunately, a bus stop was just five feet from our house. This meant that we could observe the opening stages from our front window. The first bus was to pass around six o'clock. And so we waited through an interminable half hour. I was in the kitchen drinking my coffee when I heard Coretta cry, "Martin, Martin, come quickly!" I put down my cup and ran toward the living room. As I approached the front window Coretta pointed joyfully to a slowly moving bus: "Darling, it's empty!" I could hardly believe what I saw. I knew that the South Jackson line, which ran past our house, carried more Negro passengers than any other line in Montgomery, and that this first bus was usually filled with domestic workers going to their jobs. Would all of the other buses follow the pattern that had been set by the first? Eagerly we waited for the next bus. In fifteen minutes it rolled down the street, and, like the first, it was empty. A third bus appeared, and it too was empty of all but two white passengers.

I jumped in my car and for almost an hour I cruised down every major street and examined every passing bus. During this hour, at the peak of the morning traffic, I saw no more than eight Negro passengers riding the buses. By this time I was jubilant. Instead of the 60 per cent coöperation we had hoped for, it was becoming apparent that we had reached almost 100 per cent. A miracle had taken place. The once dormant and quiescent Negro community was now fully awake.

She Walked Alone

In the days of passive resistance in the South, heroes and heroines were legion. Moved by intense moral concern and by a realistic sense that *the* time had come for injustice to be overthrown at last, they behaved with extraordinary courage. One such heroine, Elizabeth Eckford, fifteen years old, was among those who had decided that the doors of Central High School in Little Rock, Arkansas, would no longer remain closed to black people. In September, 1957, she and eight others received a court order allowing them entrance to the school. Prepared by NAACP attorneys Wiley Branton and Thurgood Marshall, the order was at first blocked by Governor Orval Faubus, who closed off Central High School to all black people on the grounds that white mobs would make blood "run in the streets" should desegregation proceed. On September 4, the nine youngsters were turned away from the school by National Guardsmen, armed with bayonets and stationed at the school by Faubus. Elizabeth Eckford was separated from her comrades. Her story follows, as told by Benjamin Fine and Daisy Bates, one of the leaders in the struggle and author of *The Long Shadow of Little Rock.*

D R. BENJAMIN FINE WAS THEN EDUCATION EDITOR OF THE NEW YORK *Times.* He had years before won for his newspaper a Pulitzer prize. He was among the first reporters on the scene to cover the Little Rock story.

A few days after the National Guard blocked the Negro children's entrance to the school, Ben showed up at my house. He paced the floor nervously, rubbing his hands together as he talked.

"Daisy, they spat in my face. They called me a 'dirty Jew.' I've been a marked man ever since the day Elizabeth tried to enter Central. I never told you what happened that day. I tried not to think about it. Maybe I was ashamed to admit to you or to myself that white men and women could be so beastly cruel.

"I was standing in front of the school that day. Suddenly there was a shout—'They're here! The niggers are coming!' I saw a sweet little girl

SHE WALKED ALONE   From *The Long Shadow of Little Rock* by Daisy Bates. New York: David McKay Co., Inc., 1962. Reprinted by permission of the publisher.

who looked about fifteen, walking alone. She tried several times to pass through the guards. The last time she tried, they put their bayonets in front of her. When they did this, she became panicky. For a moment she just stood there trembling. Then she seemed to calm down and started walking toward the bus stop with the mob baying at her heels like a pack of hounds. The women were shouting, 'Get her! Lynch her!' The men were yelling, 'Go home, you bastard of a black bitch!' She finally made it to the bus stop and sat down on the bench. I sat down beside her and said, 'I'm a reporter from *The New York Times,* may I have your name?' She just sat there, her head down. Tears were streaming down her cheeks from under her sun glasses. Daisy, I don't know what made me put my arm around her, lifting her chin, saying, 'Don't let them see you cry.' Maybe she reminded me of my fifteen-year-old daughter, Jill.

"There must have been five hundred around us by this time. I vaguely remember someone hollering, 'Get a rope and drag her over to this tree.' Suddenly I saw a white-haired, kind-faced woman fighting her way through the mob. She looked at Elizabeth, and then screamed at the mob, 'Leave this child alone! Why are you tormenting her? Six months from now, you will hang your heads in shame.' The mob shouted, 'Another nigger-lover. Get out of here!' The woman, who I found out later was Mrs. Grace Lorch, the wife of Dr. Lee Lorch, professor at Philander Smith College, turned to me and said, 'We have to do something. Let's try to get a cab.'

"We took Elizabeth across the street to the drugstore. I remained on the sidewalk with Elizabeth while Mrs. Lorch tried to enter the drugstore to call a cab. But the hoodlums slammed the door in her face and wouldn't let her in. She pleaded with them to call a cab for the child. They closed in on her saying, 'Get out of here, you bitch!' Just then the city bus came. Mrs. Lorch and Elizabeth got on. Elizabeth must have been in a state of shock. She never uttered a word. When the bus pulled away, the mob closed in around me. 'We saw you put your arm around that little bitch. Now it's your turn.' A drab, middle-aged woman said viciously, 'Grab him and kick him in the balls!' A girl I had seen hustling in one of the local bars screamed, 'A dirty New York Jew! Get him!' A man asked me, 'Are you a Jew?' I said, 'Yes.' He then said to the mob, 'Let him be! We'll take care of him later.'

"The irony of it all, Daisy, is that during all this time the national guardsmen made no effort to protect Elizabeth or to help me. Instead, they threatened to have me arrested—for inciting to riot."

Elizabeth, whose dignity and control in the face of jeering mobsters had been filmed by television cameras and recorded in pictures flashed to newspapers over the world, had overnight become a national heroine. During the next few days newspaper reporters besieged her home, wanting to talk to her. The first day that her parents agreed she might come out of seclusion, she came to my house where the reporters awaited her. Elizabeth was very quiet, speaking only when spoken to. I took her to my bedroom to talk before I let the reporters see her. I asked how she felt now. Suddenly all her pent-up emotion flared.

"Why am I here?" she said, turning blazing eyes on me. "Why are you so interested in my welfare now? You didn't care enough to notify me of the change of plans—"

I walked over and reached out to her. Before she turned her back on me, I saw tears gathering in her eyes. My heart was breaking for this young girl who stood there trying to stifle her sobs. How could I explain that frantic early morning when at three o'clock my mind had gone on strike?

In the ensuing weeks Elizabeth took part in all the activities of the nine—press conferences, attendance at court, studying with professors at nearby Philander Smith College. She was present, that is, but never really a part of things. The hurt had been too deep.

On the two nights she stayed at my home I was awakened by the screams in her sleep, as she relived in her dreams the terrifying mob scenes at Central. The only times Elizabeth showed real excitement were when Thurgood Marshall met the children and explained the meaning of what had happened in court. As he talked, she would listen raptly, a faint smile on her face. It was obvious he was her hero.

Little by little Elizabeth came out of her shell. Up to now she had never talked about what happened to her at Central. Once when we were alone in the downstairs recreation room of my house, I asked her simply, "Elizabeth, do you think you can talk about it now?"

She remained quiet for a long time. Then she began to speak.

"You remember the day before we were to go in, we met Superintendent Blossom at the school board office. He told us what the mob might say and do but he never told us we wouldn't have any protection. He told our parents not to come because he wouldn't be able to protect the children if they did.

"That night I was so excited I couldn't sleep. The next morning I was about the first one up. While I was pressing my black and white dress— I had made it to wear on the first day of school—my little brother turned on the TV set. They started telling about a large crowd gathered at the school. The man on TV said he wondered if we were going to show up that morning. Mother called from the kitchen, where she was fixing breakfast, 'Turn that TV off!' She was so upset and worried. I wanted to comfort her, so I said, 'Mother, don't worry.'

"Dad was walking back and forth, from room to room, with a sad expression. He was chewing on his pipe and he had a cigar in his hand, but he didn't light either one. It would have been funny, only he was so nervous.

"Before I left home Mother called us into the living-room. She said we should have a word of prayer. Then I caught the bus and got off a block from the school. I saw a large crowd of people standing across the street from the soldiers guarding Central. As I walked on, the crowd suddenly got very quiet. Superintendent Blossom had told us to enter by the front door. I looked at all the people and thought, 'Maybe I will be safer if I walk down the block to the front entrance behind the guards.'

"At the corner I tried to pass through the long line of guards around the school so as to enter the grounds behind them. One of the guards pointed across the street. So I pointed in the same direction and asked whether he meant for me to cross the street and walk down. He nodded 'yes.' So, I walked across the street conscious of the crowd that stood there, but they moved away from me.

"For a moment all I could hear was the shuffling of their feet. Then someone shouted, 'Here she comes, get ready!' I moved away from the crowd on the sidewalk and into the street. If the mob came at me I could then cross back over so the guards could protect me.

"The crowd moved in closer and then began to follow me, calling me names. I still wasn't afraid. Just a little bit nervous. Then my knees started to shake all of a sudden and I wondered whether I could make it to the center entrance a block away. It was the longest block I ever walked in my whole life.

"Even so, I still wasn't too scared because all the time I kept thinking that the guards would protect me.

"When I got right in front of the school, I went up to a guard again. But this time he just looked straight ahead and didn't move to let me pass him. I didn't know what to do. Then I looked and saw that the path leading to the front entrance was a little further ahead. So I walked until I was right in front of the path to the front door.

"I stood looking at the school—it looked so big! Just then the guards let some white students go through.

"The crowd was quiet. I guess they were waiting to see what was going to happen. When I was able to steady my knees, I walked up to the guard who had let the white students in. He too didn't move. When I tried to squeeze past him, he raised his bayonet and then the other guards closed in and they raised their bayonets.

"They glared at me with a mean look and I was very frightened and didn't know what to do. I turned around and the crowd came toward me.

"They moved closer and closer. Somebody started yelling, 'Lynch her! Lynch her!'

"I tried to see a friendly face somewhere in the mob—someone who maybe would help. I looked into the face of an old woman and it seemed a kind face, but when I looked at her again, she spat on me.

"They came closer, shouting, 'No nigger bitch is going to get in our school. Get out of here!'

"I turned back to the guards but their faces told me I wouldn't get help from them. Then I looked down the block and saw a bench at the bus stop. I thought, 'If I can only get there I will be safe.' I don't know why the bench seemed a safe place to me, but I started walking toward it. I tried to close my mind to what they were shouting, and kept saying to myself, 'If I can only make it to the bench I will be safe.'

"When I finally got there, I don't think I could have gone another step. I sat down and the mob crowded up and began shouting all over again. Someone hollered, 'Drag her over to this tree! Let's take care of the nigger.' Just then a white man sat down beside me, put his arm around me and patted my shoulder. He raised my chin and said, 'Don't let them see you cry.'

"Then, a white lady—she was very nice—she came over to me on the bench. She spoke to me but I don't remember now what she said. She put me on the bus and sat next to me. She asked me my name and tried to talk to me but I don't think I answered. I can't remember much about the bus ride, but the next thing I remember I was standing in front of the School for the Blind, where Mother works.

"I thought, 'Maybe she isn't here. But she has to be here!' So I ran upstairs, and I think some teachers tried to talk to me, but I kept running until I reached Mother's classroom.

"Mother was standing at the window with her head bowed, but she must have sensed I was there because she turned around. She looked as if she had been crying, and I wanted to tell her I was all right. But I couldn't speak. She put her arms around me and I cried."

The Sit-ins

In February, 1960, four black students at North Carolina Agricultural and Technical State College in Greensboro put into action a technique which had been used sporadically, with only mixed success, during the forties and fifties. They held a sit-in at a segregated lunch counter. The results were such that within weeks thousands of young people all over the South began to adopt the tactic. In the next three years, the high point of the "Civil Rights Revolt," tens of thousands of people were arrested for sit-ins and related protests. City after city became involved; Montgomery, Baton Rouge, Atlanta, and Orangeburg, South Carolina, were the scenes of particularly dramatic encounters between stoic young black people and frenzied whites. The attention of the nation was riveted upon this moral spectacle.

What the sit-ins actually achieved was modest in one sense, but great in another. As many people soon learned, the goal of "lunch-counter desegregation" was expensive to win; nor was the segregated South deeply upset by such victories. But the sit-in period coordinated a phalanx of organizations dedicated to destroying racism. In April, 1960, the Student Non-Violent Coordinating Committee was born. In January, 1961, James Farmer, national director of the Congress of Racial Equality, helped launch The Freedom Ride into Alabama and Mississippi. The NAACP accelerated its program of legal defiance of segregation, and even The Urban League, traditionally quite conservative, was soon vigorously defending direct action.

MY STOMACH ALWAYS HURT A LITTLE ON THE WAY TO A SIT-IN. . . . I guess it's the unexpected." Candie Anderson, a white girl attending Fisk University as an exchange student from Pomona College in California, had joined her Negro classmates to demonstrate against segregation in Nashville, Tennessee. It was the explosion of sit-ins throughout the South in early 1960 that led to the formation of the Student Nonviolent Coordinating Committee.

On February 1, 1960, four freshmen at A & T College in Greensboro, North Carolina, took seats at a lunch counter downtown, not knowing

THE SIT-INS   From *SNCC: The New Abolitionists* by Howard Zinn. Reprinted by permission of the Beacon Press. Copyright © 1964, 1965 by Howard Zinn.

they were starting a movement that would soon take on the proportions of a revolution. "For about a week," David Richmond recalled later, "we four fellows sat around the A & T campus, talking about the integration movement. And we decided we ought to go down to Woolworth's and see what would happen." They spent an hour sitting at the Woolworth's counter, with no service. Then the counter was closed for the day, and they went home.

In a matter of days, the idea leaped to other cities in North Carolina. During the next two weeks, sit-ins spread to fifteen cities in five Southern states. Within the following year, over 50,000 people—most were Negroes, some were white—had participated in one kind of demonstration or another in a hundred cities, and over 3600 demonstrators spent time in jail. But there were results to show: by the end of 1961, several hundred lunch counters had been desegregated in scores of cities—in Texas, Oklahoma, the border states of the South, and even as far at Atlanta, Georgia. A wall of resistance, however, apparently impenetrable, faced the student in the rest of Georgia, South Carolina, Alabama, Mississippi, Louisiana—the hard-core Deep South.

It is hard to overestimate the electrical effect of that first sit-in in Greensboro, as the news reached the nation on television screens, over radios, in newspapers. In his Harlem apartment in New York City, Bob Moses, a former Harvard graduate student and mathematics teacher, saw a picture of the Greensboro sit-inners. "The students in that picture had a certain look on their faces," he later told writer Ben Bagdikian, "sort of sullen, angry, determined. Before, the Negro in the South had always looked on the defensive, cringing. This time they were taking the initiative. They were kids my age, and I knew this had something to do with my own life. . . ."

In Atlanta, Morehouse College student Julian Bond, who wrote poetry and thought about being a journalist, reacted quickly to the Greensboro sit-in. He and another student, discussing it in the Yates & Milton drug store across the street from the campus, decided to summon Morehouse men to a meeting. Out of that grew the Atlanta student movement, which six weeks later erupted in one of the largest and best organized sit-in demonstrations of all.

Also in Atlanta, seventeen-year-old Ruby Doris Smith, a sophomore at Spelman College, heard about the Greensboro sit-in and ran home that evening to see it on television:

> I began to think right away about it happening in Atlanta, but I wasn't ready to act on my own. When the student committee was formed in

the Atlanta University Center, I told my older sister, who was on the Student Council at Morris Brown College, to put me on the list. And when two hundred students were selected for the first demonstration, I was among them. I went through the food line in the restaurant at the State Capitol with six other students, but when we got to the cashier, she wouldn't take our money. She ran upstairs to get the Governor. The Lieutenant-Governor came down and told us to leave. We didn't, and went to the county jail.

Charles ("Chuck") McDew, a husky former athlete from Massilon, Ohio, was studying at South Carolina State College in Orangeburg. McDew had never adjusted to South Carolina; he had been arrested three times in his first three months there, and was struck by a policeman for trying to enter the main YMCA. When, during Religious Emphasis Week at the College, some visiting white Protestant ministers had responded negatively to his question about attending their churches, and a rabbi invited him to the temple, he converted to Judaism. With the news of Greensboro being discussed all around him, McDew read in the Talmud: "If I am not for myself, then who is for me? If I am for myself alone, then what am I? If not now, when?" He became a leader of the local sit-in movement.

To these young people, the Supreme Court decision of 1954 was a childhood memory. The Montgomery bus boycott of 1955, the first mass action by Southern Negroes, though also dimly remembered, was an inspiration. The trouble at Little Rock in 1957 was more vivid, with the unforgettable photos of the young Negro girl walking past screaming crowds towards Central High School. The Greensboro sit-ins struck a special chord of repressed emotion, and excitement raced across the Negro college campuses of the South.

Bob Moses, Julian Bond, Ruby Doris Smith, Chuck McDew: all were to become stalwarts in the Student Nonviolent Coordinating Committee. And for so many others in SNCC, the Greensboro sit-in—more than the Supreme Court decision, more than the Little Rock crisis, more than the Montgomery bus boycott, more than the recent declarations of independence by a host of African nations, and yet, perhaps, owing its galvanic force to the accumulation of all these events—was a turning point in their lives. James Forman, studying French in graduate school in the North, began turning his thoughts southward. Exactly what was going on in the minds of so many other students, soon to leave school for "The Movement," remains unknown.

Out of the Nashville, Tennessee, sit-ins, a battalion of future SNCC people took shape. Tall, quiet, Marion Barry, a graduate student in chemistry at Fisk University, who would later become the first chairman of SNCC, took a leading part in the Nashville sit-ins from the beginning. His father, a Mississippi farmer, migrated to Memphis, Tennessee, and Barry went to school there. As an undergraduate at LeMoyne College in Memphis, he publicly protested an anti-Negro remark made by a prominent white trustee of the college, created an uproar in the city, and barely avoided being expelled.

> I came to Fisk . . . inquired about forming a college chapter of the NAACP. . . . But we didn't do much. . . . We had not at any time thought of direct action. . . . In the meantime in Greensboro, N.C., the student movement began February 1, 1960. So we in Nashville decided we wanted to do something about it. . . . I remember the first time I was arrested, about February 27. . . . I took a chance on losing a scholarship or not receiving my Master's degree. But to me, if I had received my scholarship and Master's degree, and still was not a free man, I was not a man at all.

John Lewis, short, fiery, from a small town in Alabama, was also in Nashville as a seminary student when the sit-ins began. He immediately became involved and went to jail four times.

> My mother wrote me a letter and said "Get out of the movement," but I couldn't. . . . I wrote her and said, "I have acted according to my convictions and according to my Christian conscience. . . . My soul will not be satisfied until freedom, justice, and fair play become a reality for all people."

Lewis later followed Marion Barry and Chuck McDew to become Chairman of SNCC.

"Do show yourself friendly on the counter at all times. Do sit straight and always face the counter. Don't strike back, or curse back if attacked. Don't laugh out. Don't hold conversations. Don't block entrances." These were the instructions to sit-in demonstrators in Nashville. They demanded a careful balance of quiet non-resistance and a determined militancy, and perhaps no one better expressed this than Diane Nash, a tiny, slender, campus beauty queen at Fisk, one of the pillars of the Nashville student movement and later a founder of SNCC. When students were being cross-examined at the trials that followed the Nashville demonstrations, one of the standard questions was: "Do you know Diane Nash?" Friendship with her was apparently full of perils.

Twelve days after the Greensboro incident, forty students sat in at Woolworth's in Nashville. There was at first some discussion about whether the white exchange students should go along, but finally the prevailing opinion was in favor. Candie Anderson recalls:

> That first sit-in was easy. . . . It was a Thursday afternoon and it was snowing. There were not many people downtown. Store personnel ran around nervously. . . . My friends were determined to be courteous and well-behaved. . . . Most of them read or studied while they sat at the counters, for three or four hours. I heard them remind each other not to leave cigarette ashes on the counter, to take off their hats, etc. . . . When the sit-in was over we all met in church. There must have been five hundred kids there, and we all sang together. . . .

By the fourth sit-in, tension was mounting rapidly. There was violence that day. Lighted cigarettes were pushed against the backs of girls sitting at the counter. A white sit-inner, on a stool beside a Negro girl, became a special object of attention by the crowd nearby. Someone kept calling him a "nigger-lover." When he didn't respond he was pulled off the stool, thrown to the floor, and kicked. At McClellan's variety store, a white man kept blowing cigar smoke into the face of a Negro sitting at the counter, a Fisk University student named Paul LePrad, who made no move. This infuriated the man. He pulled the student from his stool and hit him. LePrad got back on the stool. He was pulled off again and hit. The police came and arrested LePrad and the seventeen students sitting in with him.

The group at Woolworth's, where Candie Anderson was, heard about this incident. They decided to go to McClellan's to protest.

> There was a rope around the stools, showing that the counter was closed. We climbed over the rope. A policeman stood there and said quite clearly, "Do not sit down," and we sat down. . . . I became suddenly aware of the crowd of people standing behind us. . . . Young kids threw french fried potatoes at us, and gum, and cigarette butts. I looked down the counter at Barbara Crosby in a straight pink skirt and nice white blouse, and at Stephen in a dark suit, with a calculus book. . . . The policemen simply lined up behind us and peeled us two by two off the stools. . . . The crowd in the store . . . shouted out approval. They said about Barbara and me. . . . Oh, white . . . WHITE, WHITE, WHITE! Three paddy wagons were blinking at us from the street. Once more we had to walk through those crowds. Someone spit right in front of me. . . . The TV cameras took lots of pictures and we drove off to the Nashville city jail.

With seventy-six students in jail, a group of NAACP people in Nashville met the next day and pledged support. Fisk University President

Stephen Wright said: "Students have been exposed all their lives to the teachings of the great American scriptures of democracy, freedom, and equality, and no literate person should be surprised that they reflect these teachings in their conduct."

But at white Vanderbilt University in Nashville, where a thirty-one-year-old Negro named James Lawson was enrolled in the Divinity School, it was different. Lawson, a conscientious objector and a pacifist, believed in nonviolent resistance. When the first mass arrests took place, newspapermen quoted him as saying he would advise students to violate the law. The *Nashville Banner* immediately called this "incitation to anarchy" and added: "There is no place in Nashville for flannel-mouthed agitators, white or colored—under whatever sponsorship, imported for preachment of mass disorder; self-supported vagrants, or paid agents of strife-breeding organizations." The Vanderbilt trustees, one of whom was the publisher of the *Nashville Banner,* another of whom was president of one of the large department stores where sit-ins had taken place, voted the next day to give Lawson the choice of withdrawing from the movement or dismissal from the University.

Charging the press with distorting his statements, Lawson refused to leave the movement, and in early March he was expelled, three months before his scheduled graduation. Most of the sixteen faculty members of the divinity school, all white, protested. By May, eleven of them, as well as Dean J. Robert Nelson, had resigned over the refusal of the school to re-admit Lawson, leaving four persons on the divinity school faculty. The *Richmond News Leader* commented: "Good riddance . . . Vanderbilt University will be better off. . . ."

The Nashville sit-ins continued, with arrests, trials, and students deciding to stay in jail in protest rather than pay fines or put up bond. Chief defense lawyer for the students was sixty-two-year-old Z. Alexander Looby, a distinguished Negro attorney, born in Trinidad, the lone Negro member of the Nashville City Council.

On April 19, at five o'clock in the morning, while Looby and his wife were asleep in the backroom of their home, one block away from Fisk University's campus, a bomb exploded on his porch. In her dormitory room, Candie Anderson was awakened by the noise. "Only one time in my life have I heard a sound worse than the one when Mr. Looby's house was bombed," she wrote later. "That was when a girl fainted and I heard her head hit the floor. That's the kind of feeling it left when we heard the explosion. . . . It would have seemed unreal, I think, if the sirens had not kept insistently coming. . . ."

One hundred and forty-seven windows were blown out in Meharry

Medical School across the street, and the front part of the Looby's house was demolished, but the attorney and his wife were not hurt. Perhaps, as James Bevel (who married Diane Nash) said, "The Devil has got to come out of these people." For after the bombing, and after a protest march of 2000 Negroes on City Hall, negotiations for desegregation got under way in earnest. In early May, four theaters and six lunch counters downtown declared an end to the color line. In the meantime, the sit-ins had spread to Chattanooga, Knoxville, Memphis, and Oak Ridge. By late spring, seven Tennessee cities had desegregated some of their lunch counters.

·   ·   ·

The sit-ins were spreading southward now. They were also becoming larger and better organized. In Atlanta, where they were preceded by many meetings and by a sensational full-page ad of eloquent protest in the *Atlanta Constitution* addressed to a startled white community, the sit-ins were planned like a military operation. On March 15, at exactly 11:00 A.M., two hundred students moved into ten downtown restaurants which had been carefully selected because they were connected with city or county or federal government, and were therefore subject to the Fourteenth Amendment's requirement that *public* places may not discriminate. Seventy-six students were arrested, and the city of Atlanta was never the same again.

There was some violence in those first months of the sit-ins. In Jacksonville, Florida, the city was in turmoil for three days: a white sit-in student was attacked in jail and his jaw was broken; a sixteen-year-old Negro boy was pistol-whipped by the Ku Klux Klan; a Negro man unconnected with the demonstrations who went through a police roadblock was shot to death by a white service station attendant. In Atlanta, acid was thrown at sit-in leader Lonnie King. In Frankfort, Kentucky, the gymnasium of a Negro college was set afire. In Columbia, South Carolina, a Negro sit-in student was stabbed. In Houston, Texas, a twenty-seven-year-old Negro was kidnaped and flogged with a chain, and the symbol KKK was carved on his chest.

Mississippi responded with a special savagery. When students marched down the street in Jackson, police used clubs, tear gas, and police dogs. Women, children, and a photographer were beaten by police and bystanders, and some demonstrators were bitten by dogs. In Biloxi, Mississippi, Negroes trying to use a public beach were attacked with clubs and chains by crowds of whites, and ten were wounded by gunfire.

Yet, considering the number of people involved in demonstrations and the intense psychological tremors accompanying this sudden attack by long-quiescent Negroes on the old way of life, violence was minimal. The restraint of the demonstrators themselves was one factor; they gave the least possible excuse for club-happy and trigger-happy policemen, and the most the police could justify, in most cases, was carting them off to jail. The ratio of social change, both immediate and long-term, to the resulting violence, was extremely high.

The sit-ins marked a turning point for the Negro American, subordinate for three hundred years. He was rebelling now, not with the blind, terrible, understandable hatred of the slave revolts, but with skill in organization, sophistication in tactics, and an unassailable moral position. With these went a ferocious refusal to retreat. What had been an orderly, inch-by-inch advance via legal processes now became a revolution in which unarmed regiments marched from one objective to another with bewildering speed.

The idea so long cherished by Southern whites—and by many Northerners too—that the Southern Negro (whether through ignorance or intimidation or a shrewd recognition of reality) was content with the way things were, that only a handful of agitators opposed the system of segregation, was swept aside by the mass marches, demonstrations, meetings. Montgomery had been the first sign of this, and now it was made clear beyond argument that Negroes all across the South had only been waiting for an opportunity to end their long silence.

.   .   .

The sit-ins took the established Negro organizations by surprise. The NAACP had a large membership in the Southern states, had handled thousands of legal cases there, and was a long-established center for Negroes wanting to share their dissatisfactions. But it had not carried on any widespread campaigns of direct protest in the South. The Congress of Racial Equality, or CORE, was a Northern-based organization, with just a few staff members below the Mason-Dixon line. The Southern Christian Leadership Conference, which grew out of the Montgomery boycott and was led by Martin Luther King, Jr., had an office in Atlanta, and was planning various actions in the South, but had engaged in no large-scale movement since Montgomery. Spontaneity and self-sufficiency were the hallmarks of the sit-ins; without adult advice or consent, the students planned and carried them through.

What happened then was that the student movement galvanized the older organizations into a new dynamism, won the support of some of the established Negro leaders who quickly sensed that a new wind was blowing, and left far behind those leaders who could not break either old habits of thinking, or old ties with the white elite.

From the beginning, the students found strong backing in the generation just ahead of them—young Negro professionals in their thirties or early forties, who helped mobilize community support behind the young people. One thinks of Carl Holman, Dr. Clinton Warner, and Whitney Young in Atlanta; also of Dr. Anderson, Slater King and C. B. King in Albany; and of Martin Luther King himself.

On the other hand, the self-interest of some elements in the Negro community had long become enmeshed with that of the whites who held political and economic power, and even the explosive force of the sit-ins could not break that tie. Presidents of state-supported Negro colleges, with an eye on trustees, regents, and state legislatures, lashed out at their student rebels. Faculty members, fearful for their jobs, remained silent. At Southern University in Baton Rouge, whose 5000 students made it the largest Negro institution in the nation, eighteen sit-in leaders were suspended. At Albany State College in Albany, Georgia, the president eventually got rid of forty student demonstrators. At Alabama State and Florida A & M, punishment was swift. Even at some private, church-supported institutions, like Benedict and Allen Colleges in South Carolina, college administrators threatened expulsion for students who joined the sit-in movement and fired the few faculty members who spoke their minds.

Between the unequivocal supporters and the conservative die-hards in the adult Negro community was a third group, whose response to the new militancy of the college generation was complex and curious. These were Negroes ranking high in the social structure of the community, who were beset by a number of conflicting pressures: that of the white side of town, where they had some useful relationships; that of the Negro community at large, which embraced the sit-ins, and on which they were dependent socially and politically; that of their own long resentment against segregation; of a conservatism fundamental to their lofty position; of an uncomfortable feeling of being left in the shadows by the immature upstarts of the student movement. In this confusion of interests, the reaction of such people was often to support the movement publicly, and try privately to keep it within respectable limits.

.   .   .

Throughout the winter of 1960–1961, sit-ins continued, linked only vaguely by SNCC, but creating a warmth of commitment, a solidarity of purpose which spurred awareness of SNCC by students all over the South. They also sustained a vision—or perhaps, knowing SNCC, a set of various visions, which kept Marion Barry, Jane Stembridge, Julian Bond, Diane Nash, Charles Sherrod, Charles Jones, and others, going.

When ten students were arrested in Rock Hill, South Carolina, in February, 1961, the SNCC steering committee, meeting in Atlanta, made its boldest organizational decision up to that date. Four people, it was agreed, would go to Rock Hill to sit in, would be arrested, and would refuse bail, as the first ten students had done, in order to dramatize the injustice to the nation. The Rock Hill action was the start of the jail-no bail policy.

Sit-in veterans Charles Sherrod (Petersburg, Virginia), Charles Jones (Charlotte, North Carolina) and Diane Nash were to go. The fourth person was a relative novice in the movement, Spelman College student Ruby Doris Smith, who talked her older sister out of the trip so she could go instead. "I went home that night to explain to my mother. She couldn't understand why I had to go away—why I had to go to Rock Hill."

Ruby Doris and the others spent thirty days in prison, the first time anyone had served full sentences in the sit-in movement. "I read a lot there: *The Ugly American, The Life of Mahatma Gandhi, Exodus, The Wall Between.* . . . Every day at noon we sang 'We Shall Overcome'. . . ." The fellows had been put on a road gang: Tom Gaither of CORE, Charles Sherrod and Charles Jones of SNCC, and nine others. The captain of the guards took their textbooks away, saying: "This is a prison—not a damned school." He turned out to be wrong.

"Jail-no bail" spread. In Atlanta, in February, 1961, eighty students from the Negro colleges went to jail and refused to come out. I knew some, but not all, of the participants from Spelman, where I taught history and political science. That fall, when a very bright student named Lana Taylor, fair-skinned, rather delicate looking, joined my course on Chinese Civilization, I learned she had been in jail. In early 1964 I came across a reminiscence of Jane Stembridge:

> . . . the most honest moment—the one in which I saw the guts-type truth—stripped of anything but total fear and total courage . . . was one day during 1961 in Atlanta. . . . Hundreds went out that day and filled every lunch counter. . . . There was much humor—like A. D. King coordinating the whole damn thing with a walkie-talkie. . . . The moment: Lana Taylor from Spelman was sitting next to me. The man-

ager walked up behind her, said something obscene, and grabbed her by the shoulders. "Get the hell out of here, nigger." Lana was not going. I do not know whether she should have collapsed in nonviolent manner. She probably did not know. She put her hands under the counter and held. He was rough and strong. She just held and I looked down at that moment at her hands . . . brown, stained . . . every muscle holding. . . . All of a sudden he let go and left. I thought he knew he could not move that girl—ever. . . ."

MARTIN LUTHER KING, JR.

Letter from Birmingham Jail

The Birmingham demonstrations of 1963, perhaps the high-water mark of non-violent protest in the South, coincided with the hundredth anniversary of the Emancipation Proclamation. Directing the contending forces were two men of different backgrounds and natures: Martin Luther King, Jr., head of the Southern Christian Leadership Council and the primary spiritual leader of the non-violent civil rights revolution; and Eugene ("Bull") Connor, head of the Birmingham Police Department, believer in force, and a national symbol of the die-hard attitudes of Southern segregationists. The black forces were made up mainly of high school and college youths. They were beaten, set upon by police dogs, and hit by high-pressure water hoses. Their courage and discipline were remarkable. They filled the city jails to overflowing; other buildings had to be pressed into service to hold them.

LETTER FROM BIRMINGHAM JAIL From *Why We Can't Wait* by Martin Luther King, Jr. Copyright © 1963 by Martin Luther King, Jr. By permission of Harper & Row, Publishers, Inc.
AUTHOR'S NOTE: This response to a published statement by eight fellow clergymen from Alabama (Bishop C. C. J. Carpenter, Bishop Joseph A. Durick, Rabbi Hilton L. Grafman, Bishop Paul Hardin, Bishop Holan B. Harmon, the Reverend George M. Murray, the Reverend Edward V. Ramage and the Reverend Earl Stallings) was composed under somewhat constricting circumstances. Begun on the margins of the newspaper in which the statement appeared while I was in jail, the letter was continued on scraps of writing paper supplied by a friendly Negro trusty, and concluded on a pad my attorneys were eventually permitted to leave me. Although the text remains in substance unaltered, I have indulged in the author's prerogative of polishing it for publication.

The Birmingham demonstrations went far toward) arousing the nation's interest in the situation faced by black people in the South; but almost at the same moment that the protest was achieving its goals, four little black children were killed when a bomb was tossed out of a passing car into a Sunday School class at the 16th Street Baptist Church.

King himself was jailed during the Birmingham demonstrations. While in his cell, he wrote the following letter in response to eight leading white Birmingham churchmen who had urged the city's blacks to withdraw their support from the protest. Combining the principles of Gandhi with his own religious background, King's letter is regarded as the most eloquent expression of the aims of the nonviolent protest movement of the mid-sixties.

April 16, 1963

My Dear Fellow Clergymen:

While confined here in the Birmingham city jail, I came across your recent statement calling my present activities "unwise and untimely." Seldom do I pause to answer criticism of my work and ideas. If I sought to answer all the criticisms that cross my desk, my secretaries would have little time for anything other than such correspondence in the course of the day, and I would have no time for constructive work. But since I feel that you are men of genuine good will and that your criticisms are sincerely set forth, I want to try to answer your statement in what I hope will be patient and reasonable terms.

I think I should indicate why I am here in Birmingham, since you have been influenced by the view which argues against "outsiders coming in." I have the honor of serving as president of the Southern Christian Leadership Conference, an organization operating in every southern state, with headquarters in Atlanta, Georgia. We have some eighty-five affiliated organizations across the South, and one of them is the Alabama Christian Movement for Human Rights. Frequently we share staff, educational and financial resources with our affiliates. Several months ago the affiliate here in Birmingham asked us to be on call to engage in a nonviolent direct-action program if such were deemed necessary. We readily consented, and when the hour came we lived up to our promise. So I, along with several members of my staff, am here because I was invited here. I am here because I have organizational ties here.

But more basically, I am in Birmingham because injustice is here. Just as the prophets of the eighth century B.C. left their villages and carried their "thus saith the Lord" far beyond the boundaries of their home towns, and just as the Apostle Paul left his village of Tarsus and carried the gospel of Jesus Christ to the far corners of the Greco-

Roman world, so am I compelled to carry the gospel of freedom beyond my own home town. Like Paul, I must constantly respond to the Macedonian call for aid.

Moreover, I am cognizant of the interrelatedness of all communities and states. I cannot sit idly by in Atlanta and not be concerned about what happens in Birmingham. Injustice anywhere is a threat to justice everywhere. We are caught in an inescapable network of mutuality, tied in a single garment of destiny. Whatever affects one directly, affects all indirectly. Never again can we afford to live with the narrow, provincial "outside agitator" idea. Anyone who lives inside the United States can never be considered an outsider anywhere within its bounds.

You deplore the demonstrations taking place in Birmingham. But your statement, I am sorry to say, fails to express a similar concern for the conditions that brought about the demonstrations. I am sure that none of you would want to rest content with the superficial kind of social analysis that deals merely with effects and does not grapple with underlying causes. It is unfortunate that demonstrations are taking place in Birmingham, but it is even more unfortunate that the city's white power structure left the Negro community with no alternative.

In any nonviolent campaign there are four basic steps: collection of the facts to determine whether injustices exist; negotiation; self-purification; and direct action. We have gone through all these steps in Birmingham. There can be no gainsaying the fact that racial injustice engulfs this community. Birmingham is probably the most thoroughly segregated city in the United States. Its ugly record of brutality is widely known. Negroes have experienced grossly unjust treatment in the courts. There have been more unsolved bombings of Negro homes and churches in Birmingham than in any other city in the nation. These are the hard, brutal facts of the case. On the basis of these conditions, Negro leaders sought to negotiate with the city fathers. But the latter consistently refused to engage in good-faith negotiation.

Then, last September, came the opportunity to talk with leaders of Birmingham's economic community. In the course of the negotiations, certain promises were made by the merchants—for example, to remove the stores' humiliating racial signs. On the basis of these promises, the Reverend Fred Shuttlesworth and the leaders of the Alabama Christian Movement for Human Rights agreed to a moratorium on all demonstrations. As the weeks and months went by, we realized that we were the victims of a broken promise. A few signs, briefly removed, returned; the others remained.

As in so many past experiences, our hopes had been blasted, and the shadow of deep disappointment settled upon us. We had no alternative except to prepare for direct action, whereby we would present our very bodies as a means of laying our case before the conscience of the local and the national community. Mindful of the difficulties involved, we decided to undertake a process of self-purification. We began a series of workshops on nonviolence, and we repeatedly asked ourselves: "Are you able to accept blows without retaliating?" "Are you able to endure the ordeal of jail?" We decided to schedule our direct-action program for the Easter season, realizing that except for Christmas, this is the main shopping period of the year. Knowing that a strong economic-withdrawal program would be the by-product of direct action, we felt that this would be the best time to bring pressure to bear on the merchants for the needed change.

Then it occurred to us that Birmingham's mayoralty election was coming up in March, and we speedily decided to postpone action until after election day. When we discovered that the Commissioner of Public Safety, Eugene "Bull" Connor, had piled up enough votes to be in the run-off, we decided again to postpone action until the day after the run-off so that the demonstrations could not be used to cloud the issues. Like many others, we waited to see Mr. Connor defeated, and to this end we endured postponement after postponement. Having aided in this community need, we felt that our direct-action program could be delayed no longer.

You may well ask: "Why direct action? Why sit-ins, marches and so forth? Isn't negotiation a better path?" You are quite right in calling for negotiation. Indeed, this is the very purpose of direct action. Nonviolent direct action seeks to create such a crisis and foster such a tension that a community which has constantly refused to negotiate is forced to confront the issue. It seeks so to dramatize the issue that it can no longer be ignored. My citing the creation of tension as part of the work of the nonviolent-resister may sound rather shocking. But I must confess that I am not afraid of the word "tension." I have earnestly opposed violent tension, but there is a type of constructive, nonviolent tension which is necessary for growth. Just as Socrates felt that it was necessary to create a tension in the mind so that individuals could rise from the bondage of myths and half-truths to the unfettered realm of creative analysis and objective appraisal, so must we see the need for nonviolent gadflies to create the kind of tension in society that will help men rise from the dark depths of prejudice and racism to the majestic heights of understanding and brotherhood.

The purpose of our direct-action program is to create a situation so crisis-packed that it will inevitably open the door to negotiation. I therefore concur with you in your call for negotiation. Too long has our beloved Southland been bogged down in a tragic effort to live in monologue rather than dialogue.

One of the basic points in your statement is that the action that I and my associates have taken in Birmingham is untimely. Some have asked: "Why didn't you give the new city administration time to act?" The only answer that I can give to this query is that the new Birmingham administration must be prodded about as much as the outgoing one, before it will act. We are sadly mistaken if we feel that the election of Albert Boutwell as mayor will bring the millennium to Birmingham. While Mr. Boutwell is a much more gentle person than Mr. Connor, they are both segregationists, dedicated to maintenance of the status quo. I have hope that Mr. Boutwell will be reasonable enough to see the futility of massive resistance to desegregation. But he will not see this without pressure from devotees of civil rights. My friends, I must say to you that we have not made a single gain in civil rights without determined legal and nonviolent pressure. Lamentably, it is an historical fact that privileged groups seldom give up their privileges voluntarily. Individuals may see the moral light and voluntarily give up their unjust posture; but, as Reinhold Niebuhr has reminded us, groups tend to be more immoral than individuals.

We know through painful experience that freedom is never voluntarily given by the oppressor; it must be demanded by the oppressed. Frankly, I have yet to engage in a direct-action campaign that was "well timed" in the view of those who have not suffered unduly from the disease of segregation. For years now I have heard the word "Wait!" It rings in the ear of every Negro with piercing familiarity. This "Wait" has almost always meant "Never." We must come to see, with one of our distinguished jurists, that "justice too long delayed is justice denied."

We have waited for more than 340 years for our constitutional and God-given rights. The nations of Asia and Africa are moving with jet-like speed toward gaining political independence, but we still creep at horse-and-buggy pace toward gaining a cup of coffee at a lunch counter. Perhaps it is easy for those who have never felt the stinging darts of segregation to say, "Wait." But when you have seen vicious mobs lynch your mothers and fathers at will and drown your sisters and brothers at whim; when you have seen hate-filled policemen curse, kick and even kill your black brothers and sisters; when you see the vast majority of your twenty million Negro brothers smothering in an airtight cage of poverty in the midst of an affluent society; when you suddenly find your tongue twisted and your speech stammering as you seek to explain to your six-year-old daughter why she can't go to the public amusement park that has just been advertised on television, and see tears welling up in her eyes when she is told that Funtown is closed to colored children, and see ominous clouds of inferiority beginning to form in her little mental sky, and see her beginning to distort her personality by developing an unconscious bitterness toward white people; when you have to concoct an answer for a five-year-old son who is asking: "Daddy, why do white people treat colored people so mean?"; when you take a cross-country drive and find it necessary to sleep night after night in the uncomfortable corners of your automobile because no motel will accept you; when you are humiliated day in and day out by nagging signs reading "white" and "colored"; when your first name becomes "nigger," your middle name becomes "boy" (however old you are) and your last name becomes "John," and your wife and mother are never given the respected title "Mrs."; when you are harried by day and haunted by night by the fact that you are a Negro, living constantly at tiptoe stance, never quite knowing what to expect next, and are plagued with inner fears and outer resentments; when you are forever fighting a degenerating sense of "nobodiness"—then you will understand why we find it difficult to wait. There comes a time when the cup of endurance runs over, and men are no longer willing to be plunged into the abyss of despair. I hope, sirs, you can understand our legitimate and unavoidable impatience.

You express a great deal of anxiety over our willingness to break laws. This is certainly a legitimate concern. Since we so diligently urge people to obey the Supreme Court's decision of 1954 outlawing segregation in the public schools, at first glance it may seem rather paradoxical for us consciously to break laws. One may well ask: "How can you advocate breaking some laws and obeying others?" The answer lies in the fact that there are two types of laws: just and unjust. I would be the first to advocate obeying just laws. One has not only a legal but a moral responsibility to obey just laws. Conversely, one has a moral responsibility to disobey unjust laws. I would agree with St. Augustine that "an unjust law is no law at all."

Now, what is the difference between the two? How does one determine whether a law is just or unjust? A just law is a man-made code that squares with the moral law or the law of God. An unjust law is a code that is out of harmony with the moral law. To put it in the terms of St. Thomas Aquinas: An unjust law is a human law that is not rooted in eternal law and natural law. Any law that uplifts human personality is just. Any law that degrades human personality is unjust. All segregation statutes are unjust because segregation distorts the soul and damages the personality. It gives the segregator a false sense of superiority and the segregated a false sense of inferiority. Segregation, to use the terminology of the Jewish philosopher Martin Buber, substitutes an "I—it" relationship for an "I—thou" relationship and ends up relegating persons to the status of things. Hence segregation is not only politically, economically and sociologically unsound, it is morally wrong and sinful. Paul Tillich has said that sin is separation. Is not segregation an existential expression of man's tragic separation, his awful estrangement, his terrible sinfulness? Thus it is that I can urge men to obey the 1954 decision of the Supreme Court, for it is morally right; and I can urge them to disobey segregation ordinances, for they are morally wrong.

Let us consider a more concrete example of just and unjust laws. An unjust law is a code that a numerical or power majority group compels a minority group to obey but does not make binding on itself. This is *difference* made legal. By the same token, a just law is a code that a majority compels a minority to follow and that it is willing to follow itself. This is *sameness* made legal.

Let me give another explanation. A law is unjust if it is inflicted on a minority that, as a result of being denied the right to vote, had no part in enacting or devising the law. Who can say that the legislature of Alabama which set up that state's segregation laws was democratically elected? Throughout Alabama all sorts of devious methods are used to prevent Negroes from becoming registered voters, and there are some counties in which, even though Negroes constitute a majority of the population, not a single Negro is registered. Can any law enacted under such circumstances be considered democratically structured?

Sometimes a law is just on its face and unjust in its application. For instance, I have been arrested on a charge of parading without a permit. Now, there is nothing wrong in having an ordinance which requires a permit for a parade. But such an ordinance becomes unjust when it is used to maintain segregation and to deny citizens the First-Amendment privilege of peaceful assembly and protest.

I hope you are able to see the distinction I am trying to point out. In no sense do I advocate evading or defying the law, as would the rabid segregationist. That would lead to anarchy. One who breaks an unjust law must do so openly, lovingly, and with a willingness to accept the penalty. I submit that an individual who breaks a law that conscience tells him is unjust, and who willingly accepts the penalty of imprisonment in order to arouse the conscience of the community over its injustice, is in reality expressing the highest respect for law.

Of course, there is nothing new about this kind of civil disobedience. It was evidenced sublimely in the refusal of Shadrach, Meshach and Abednego to obey the laws of Nebuchadnezzar, on the ground that a higher moral law was at stake. It was practiced superbly by the early Christians, who were willing to face hungry lions and the excruciating pain of chopping blocks rather than submit to certain unjust laws of the Roman Empire. To a degree, academic freedom is a reality today because Socrates practiced civil disobedience. In our own nation, the Boston Tea Party represented a massive act of civil disobedience.

We should never forget that everything Adolf Hitler did in Germany was "legal" and everything the Hungarian freedom fighters did in Hungary was "illegal." It was "illegal" to aid and comfort a Jew in Hitler's Germany. Even so, I am sure that, had I lived in Germany at the time, I would have aided and comforted my Jewish brothers. If today I lived in a Communist country where certain principles dear to the Christian faith are suppressed, I would openly advocate disobeying that country's antireligious laws.

I must make two honest confessions to you, my Christian and Jewish brothers. First, I must confess that over the past few years I have been gravely disappointed with the white moderate. I have almost reached the regrettable conclusion that the Negro's great stumbling block in his stride toward freedom is not the White Citizen's Counciler or the Ku Klux Klanner, but the white moderate, who is more devoted to "order" than to justice; who prefers a negative peace which is the absence of tension to a positive peace which is the presence of justice; who constantly says: "I agree with you in the goal you seek, but I cannot agree with your methods of direct action"; who paternalistically believes he can set the timetable for another man's freedom; who lives by a mythical concept of time and who constantly advises the Negro to wait for a "more convenient season." Shallow understanding from people of good will is more frustrating than absolute misunderstanding from people of ill will. Lukewarm acceptance is much more bewildering than outright rejection.

I had hoped that the white moderate would understand that law and order exist for the purpose of establishing justice and that when they fail in this purpose they become the dangerously structured dams that block the flow of social progress. I had hoped that the white moderate would understand that the present tension in the South is a necessary phase of the transition from an obnoxious negative peace, in which the Negro passively accepted his unjust plight, to a substantive and positive peace, in which all men will respect the dignity and worth of human personality. Actually, we who engage in nonviolent direct action are not the creators of tension. We merely bring to the surface the hidden tension that is already alive. We bring it out in the open, where it can be seen and dealt with. Like a boil that can never be cured so long as it is covered up but must be opened with all its ugliness to the natural medicines of air and light, injustice must be exposed, with all the tension its exposure creates, to the light of human conscience and the air of national opinion before it can be cured.

In your statement you assert that our actions, even though peaceful, must be condemned because they precipitate violence. But is this a logical assertion? Isn't this like condemning a robbed man because his possession of money precipitated the evil act of robbery? Isn't this like condemning Socrates because his unswerving commitment to truth and his philosophical inquiries precipitated the act by the misguided populace in which they made him drink hemlock? Isn't this like condemning Jesus because his unique God-consciousness and never-ceasing devotion to God's will precipitated the evil act of crucifixion? We must come to see that, as the federal courts have consistently affirmed, it is wrong to urge an individual to cease his efforts to gain his basic constitutional rights because the quest may precipitate violence. Society must protect the robbed and punish the robber.

I had also hoped that the white moderate would reject the myth concerning time in relation to the struggle for freedom. I have just received a letter from a white brother in Texas. He writes: "All Christians know that the colored people will receive equal rights eventually, but it is possible that you are in too great a religious hurry. It has taken Christianity almost two thousand years to accomplish what it has. The teachings of Christ take time to come to earth." Such an attitude stems from a tragic misconception of time, from the strangely irrational notion that there is something in the very flow of time that will inevitably cure all ills. Actually, time itself is neutral; it can be used either destructively or constructively. More and more I feel that the people of ill will have used time much more effectively than have the people of good will. We will have to repent in this generation not merely for the hateful words and actions of the bad people but for the appalling silence of the good people. Human progress never rolls in on wheels of inevitability; it comes through the tireless efforts of men willing to be co-workers with God, and without this hard work, time itself becomes an ally of the forces of social stagnation. We must use time creatively, in the knowledge that the time is always ripe to do right. Now is the time to make real the promise of democracy and transform our pending national elegy into a creative psalm of brotherhood. Now is the time to lift our national policy from the quicksand of racial injustice to the solid rock of human dignity.

You speak of our activity in Birmingham as extreme. At first I was rather disappointed that fellow clergymen would see my nonviolent efforts as those of an extremist. I began thinking about the fact that I stand in the middle of two opposing forces in the Negro community. One is a force of complacency, made up in part of Negroes who, as a result of long years of oppression, are so drained of self-respect and a sense of "somebodiness" that they have adjusted to segregation; and in part of a few middleclass Negroes who, because of a degree of academic and economic security and because in some ways they profit by segregation, have become insensitive to the problems of the masses. The other force is one of bitterness and hatred, and it comes perilously close to advocating violence. It is expressed in the various black nationalist groups that are springing up across the nation, the largest and best-known being Elijah Muhammad's Muslim movement. Nourished by the Negro's frustration over the continued existence of racial discrimination, this movement is made up of people who have lost faith in America, who have absolutely repudiated Christianity, and who have concluded that the white man is an incorrigible "devil."

I have tried to stand between these two forces, saying that we need emulate neither the "do-nothingism" of the complacent nor the hatred and despair of the black nationalist. For there is the more excellent way of love and nonviolent protest. I am grateful to God that, through the influence of the Negro church, the way of nonviolence became an integral part of our struggle.

If this philosophy had not emerged, by now many streets of the South would, I am convinced, be flowing with blood. And I am further convinced that if our white brothers dismiss as "rabble-rousers" and "outside agitators" those of us who employ nonviolent direct action, and if they refuse to support our nonviolent efforts, millions of Negroes will, out of frustration and despair, seek solace and security in black-nationalist ideologies—a development that would inevitably lead to a frightening racial nightmare.

Oppressed people cannot remain oppressed forever. The yearning for freedom eventually manifests itself, and that is what has happened to the American Negro. Something within has reminded him of his birthright of freedom, and something without has reminded him that it can be gained. Consciously or unconsciously, he has been caught up by the *Zeitgeist,* and with his black brothers of Africa and his brown and yellow brothers of Asia, South America and the Caribbean, the United States Negro is moving with a sense of great urgency toward the promised land of racial justice. If one recognizes this vital urge that has engulfed the Negro community, one should readily understand why public demonstrations are taking place. The Negro has many pent-up resentments and latent frustrations, and he must release them. So let him march; let him make prayer pilgrimages to the city hall; let him go on freedom rides—and try to understand why he must do so. If his repressed emotions are not released in nonviolent ways, they will seek expression through violence; this is not a threat but a fact of history. So I have not said to my people: "Get rid of your discontent." Rather, I have tried to say that this normal and healthy discontent can be channeled into the creative outlet of nonviolent direct action. And now this approach is being termed extremist.

But though I was initially disappointed at being categorized as an extremist, as I continued to think about the matter I gradually gained a measure of satisfaction from the label. Was not Jesus an extremist for love: "Love your enemies, bless them that curse you, do good to them that hate you, and pray for them which despitefully use you, and persecute you." Was not Amos an extremist for justice: "Let justice roll down like waters and righteousness like an ever-flowing stream." Was not Paul an extremist for the Christian gospel: "I bear in my body the marks of the Lord Jesus." Was not Martin Luther an extremist: "Here I stand; I cannot do otherwise, so help me God." And John Bunyan: "I will stay in jail to the end of my days before I make a butchery of my conscience." And Abraham Lincoln: "This nation cannot survive half slave and half free." And Thomas Jefferson: "We hold these truths to be self-evident, that all men are created equal . . ." So the question is not whether we will be extremists, but what kind of extremists we will be. Will we be extremists for hate or for love? Will we be extremists for the preservation of injustice or for the extension of justice? In that dramatic scene on Calvary's hill three men were crucified. We must never forget that all three were crucified for the same crime—the crime of extremism. Two were extremists for immorality, and thus fell below their environment. The other, Jesus Christ, was an extremist for love, truth and goodness, and thereby rose above his environment. Perhaps the South, the nation and the world are in dire need of creative extremists.

I had hoped that the white moderate would see this need. Perhaps I was too optimistic; perhaps I expected too much. I suppose I should have realized that few members of the oppressor race can understand the deep groans and passionate yearnings of the oppressed race, and still fewer have the vision to see that injustice must be rooted out by strong, persistent and determined action. I am thankful, however, that some of our white brothers in the South have grasped the meaning of this social revolution and committed themselves to it. They are still all too few in quantity, but they are big in quality. Some—such as Ralph McGill, Lillian Smith, Harry Golden, James McBride Dabbs, Ann Braden and Sarah Patton Boyle—have written about our struggle in eloquent and prophetic terms. Others have marched with us down nameless streets of the South. They have languished in filthy, roach-infested jails, suffering the abuse and brutality of policemen who view them as "dirty nigger-lovers." Unlike so many of their moderate brothers and sisters, they have recognized the urgency of the moment and sensed the need for powerful "action" antidotes to combat the disease of segregation.

Let me take note of my other major disappointment. I have been so greatly disappointed with the white church and its leadership. Of course, there are some notable exceptions. I am not unmindful of the fact that each of you has taken some significant stands on this issue. I commend you, Reverend Stallings, for your Christian stand on this past Sunday, in welcoming Negroes to your worship service on a nonsegregated basis. I commend the Catholic leaders of this state for integrating Spring Hill College several years ago.

But despite these notable exceptions, I must honestly reiterate that I have been disappointed with the church. I do not say this as one of those negative critics who can always find something wrong with the church. I say this as a minister of the gospel, who loves the church; who was nurtured in its bosom; who has been sustained by its spiritual blessings and who will remain true to it as long as the cord of life shall lengthen.

When I was suddenly catapulted into the leadership of the bus protest in Montgomery, Alabama, a few years ago, I felt we would be supported by the white church. I felt that the white ministers, priests and rabbis of the South would be among our strongest allies. Instead, some have been outright opponents, refusing to understand the freedom movement and misrepresenting its leaders; all too many others have been more cautious than courageous and have remained silent behind the anesthetizing security of stained-glass windows.

In spite of my shattered dreams, I came to Birmingham with the hope that the white religious leadership of this community would see the justice of our cause and, with deep moral concern, would serve as the channel through which our just grievances could reach the power structure.

I had hoped that each of you would understand. But again I have been disappointed.

I have heard numerous southern religious leaders admonish their worshipers to comply with a desegregation decision because it is the law, but I have longed to hear white ministers declare: "Follow this decree because integration is morally right and because the Negro is your brother." In the midst of blatant injustices inflicted upon the Negro, I have watched white churchmen stand on the sideline and mouth pious irrelevancies and sanctimonious trivialities. In the midst of a mighty struggle to rid our nation of racial and economic injustice, I have heard many ministers say: "Those are social issues, with which the gospel has no real concern." And I have watched many churches commit themselves to a completely other-worldly religion which makes a strange, un-Biblical distinction between body and soul, between the sacred and the secular.

I have traveled the length and breadth of Alabama, Mississippi and all the other southern states. On sweltering summer days and crisp autumn mornings I have looked at the South's beautiful churches with their lofty spires pointing heavenward. I have beheld the impressive outlines of her massive religious-education buildings. Over and over I have found myself asking: "What kind of people worship here? Who is their God? Where were their voices when the lips of Governor Barnett dripped with words of interposition and nullification? Where were they when Governor Wallace gave a clarion call for defiance and hatred? Where were their voices of support when bruised and weary Negro men and women decided to rise from the dark dungeons of complacency to the bright hills of creative protest?"

Yes, these questions are still in my mind. In deep disappointment I have wept over the laxity of the church. But be assured that my tears have been tears of love. There can be no deep disappointment where there is not deep love. Yes, I love the church. How could I do otherwise? I am in the rather unique position of being the son, the grandson and the great-grandson of preachers. Yes, I see the church as the body of Christ. But, oh! How we have blemished and scarred that body through social neglect and through fear of being nonconformists.

There was a time when the church was very powerful—in the time when the early Christians rejoiced at being deemed worthy to suffer for what they believed. In those days the church was not merely a thermometer that recorded the ideas and principles of popular opinion; it was a thermostat that transformed the mores of society. Whenever the early Christians entered a town, the people in power became disturbed and immediately sought to convict the Christians for being "disturbers of the peace" and "outside agitators." But the Christians pressed on, in the conviction that they were "a colony of heaven," called to obey God rather than man. Small in number, they were big in commitment. They were too God-intoxicated to be "astronomically intimidated." By their effort and example they brought an end to such ancient evils as infanticide and gladiatorial contests.

Things are different now. So often the contemporary church is a weak, ineffectual voice with an uncertain sound. So often it is an archdefender of the status quo. Far from being disturbed by the presence of the church, the power structure of the average community is consoled by the church's silent—and often even vocal—sanction of things as they are.

But the judgment of God is upon the church as never before. If today's church does not recapture the sacrificial spirit of the early church, it will lose its authenticity, forfeit the loyalty of millions, and be dismissed as an irrelevant social club with no meaning for the twentieth century. Every day I meet young people whose disappointment with the church has turned into outright disgust.

Perhaps I have once again been too optimistic. Is organized religion too inextricably bound to the status quo to save our nation and the world? Perhaps I must turn my faith to the inner spiritual church, the church within the church, as the true *ekklesia* and the hope of the world. But again I am thankful to God that some noble souls from the ranks of organized religion have broken loose from the paralyzing chains of conformity and joined us as active partners in the struggle for freedom. They have left their secure congregations and walked the streets of Albany, Georgia, with us. They have gone down the highways of the South on tortuous rides for freedom. Yes, they have gone to jail with us. Some have been dismissed from their churches, have lost the support of their bishops and fellow ministers. But they have acted in the faith that right defeated is stronger than evil triumphant. Their witness has been the spiritual salt that has preserved the true meaning of the gospel in these troubled times. They have carved a tunnel of hope through the dark mountain of disappointment.

I hope the church as a whole will meet the challenge of this decisive hour. But even if the church does not come to the aid of justice, I have no despair about the future. I have no fear about the outcome of our struggle in Birmingham, even if our motives are at present misunderstood. We will reach the goal of freedom in Birmingham and all over the nation, because the goal of America is freedom. Abused and scorned though we may be, our destiny is tied up with America's destiny. Before the pilgrims landed at Plymouth, we were here. Before the pen of Jefferson etched the majestic words of the Declaration of Independence across the pages of history, we were here. For more than two centuries our forebears labored in this country without wages; they made cotton king; they built the homes of their masters while suffering gross injustice and shameful humiliation—and yet out of a bottomless vitality they continued to thrive and develop. If the inexpressible cruelties of slavery could not stop us, the opposition we now face will surely fail. We will win our freedom because the sacred heritage of our nation and the eternal will of God are embodied in our echoing demands.

Before closing I feel impelled to mention one other point in your statement that has troubled me profoundly. You warmly commended the Birmingham police force for keeping "order" and "preventing violence." I doubt that you would have so warmly commended the police force if you had seen its dogs sinking their teeth into unarmed, nonviolent Negroes. I doubt that you would so quickly commend the policemen if you were to observe their ugly and inhumane treatment of Negroes here in the city jail; if you were to watch them push and curse old Negro women and young Negro girls; if you were to see them slap and kick old Negro men and young boys; if you were to observe them, as they did on two occasions, refuse to give us food because we wanted to sing our grace together. I cannot join you in your praise of the Birmingham police department.

It is true that the police have exercised a degree of discipline in handling the demonstrators. In this sense they have conducted themselves rather "nonviolently" in public. But for what purpose? To preserve the evil system of segregation. Over the past few years I have consistently preached that nonviolence demands that the means we use must be as pure as the ends we seek. I have tried to make clear that it is wrong to use immoral means to attain moral ends. But now I must affirm that it is just as wrong, or perhaps even more so, to use moral means to preserve immoral ends. Perhaps Mr. Connor and his policemen have been rather nonviolent in public, as was Chief Pritchett in Albany, Georgia, but they have used the moral means of nonviolence to maintain the immoral end of racial injustice. As T. S. Eliot has said: "The last temptation is the greatest treason: To do the right deed for the wrong reason."

I wish you had commended the Negro sit-inners and demonstrators of Birmingham for their sublime courage, their willingness to suffer and their amazing discipline in the midst of great provocation. One day the South will recognize its real heroes. They will be the James Merediths, with the noble sense of purpose that enables them to face jeering and hostile mobs, and with the agonizing loneliness that characterizes the life of the pioneer. They will be old, oppressed, battered Negro women, symbolized in a seventy-two-year-old woman in Montgomery, Alabama, who rose up with a sense of dignity and with her people decided not to ride segregated buses, and who responded with ungrammatical profundity to one who inquired about her weariness: "My feets is tired, but my soul is at rest." They will be the young high school and college students, the young ministers of the gospel and a host of their elders, courageously and nonviolently sitting in at lunch counters and willingly going to jail for conscience' sake. One day the South will know that when these disinherited children of God sat down at lunch counters, they were in reality standing up for what is best in the American dream and for the most sacred values in our Judaeo-Christian heritage, thereby bringing our nation back to those great wells of democracy which were dug deep by the founding fathers in their formulation of the Constitution and the Declaration of Independence.

Never before have I written so long a letter. I'm afraid it is much too long to take your precious time. I can assure you that it would have been much shorter if I had been writing from a comfortable desk, but what else can one do when he is alone in a narrow jail cell, other than write long letters, think long thoughts and pray long prayers?

If I have said anything in this letter that overstates the truth and indicates an unreasonable impatience, I beg you to forgive me. If I have said anything that understates the truth and indicates my having a patience that allows me to settle for anything less than brotherhood, I beg God to forgive me.

I hope this letter finds you strong in the faith. I also hope that circumstances will soon make it possible for me to meet each of you, not as an integrationist or a civil rights leader but as a fellow clergyman and a Christian brother. Let us all hope that the dark clouds of racial prejudice will soon pass away and the deep fog of misunderstanding will be lifted from our fear-drenched communities, and in some not too distant tomorrow the radiant stars of love and brotherhood will shine over our great nation with all their scintillating beauty.

Yours for the cause of Peace and Brotherhood,

MARTIN LUTHER KING, JR.

JOHN LEWIS

We March Today

Birmingham, with its bombings, police dogs, and violent white politicians, gave the nation a picture of a city, and thus a country, in desperate trouble. The President was moved, and the federal government at last felt obligated to intro- duce some civil rights legislation in Congress. That legislation, later constituting the Civil Rights Act of 1964, attempted to address itself to the entire contempo- rary struggle of the American black man for equality and dignity. But even as the legislation was being drafted, the nature of the struggle was radically chang- ing. The August 1963 March on Washington revealed the extent to which power- ful economic groups opposed the aspirations of black people; it also revealed the extent to which black organizations themselves were at odds with each other.

President Kennedy at first opposed the March, then agreed to support it. The AFL-CIO's national council, in deference to the racist practices of many of its unions, never did support it. By the time of the March, there was serious tension between the older and more conservative NAACP, the religiously-oriented South- ern Christian Leadership Conference, and the more youthful and radical Student Non-Violent Coordinating Committee. The leader of SNCC, at that time, John Lewis, prepared a speech which distressed many moderates and which, be- cause of its unwillingness to commend the Democratic party, was almost cen- sored from the program of speeches to be delivered in Washington. It shows the new toughness of mind which began to control the civil rights movement, and which came to dominate the black struggle in the latter part of the decade.

WE MARCH TODAY FOR JOBS AND FREEDOM, BUT WE HAVE NOTHING to be proud of. For hundreds and thousands of our brothers are not here. They have no money for their transportation, for they are now receiving starvation wages . . . or no wages, at all.

In good conscience, we cannot support the administration's civil rights bill, for it is too little, and too late. There's not one thing in the bill that will protect our people from police brutality. (We favorably call atten- tion to the Kastenmeier Bill—H.R. 7702.)

WE MARCH TODAY by John Lewis. Reprinted from *Liberation*, Vol. VIII, No. 7, September 1963. Reprinted by permission of the author.

This bill will not protect young children and old women from police dogs and fire hoses, for engaging in peaceful demonstrations. This bill will not protect the citizens of Danville, Virginia, who must live in constant fear in a police state. This bill will not protect the hundreds of people who have been arrested on trumped-up charges. What about the three young men—S.N.C.C. field secretaries—in Americus, Georgia, who face the death penalty for engaging in peaceful protest?

The voting section of this bill will not help thousands of black citizens who want to vote. It will not help the citizens of Mississippi, of Alabama, and Georgia, who are qualified to vote, but lack a 6th Grade education. "One man, one vote," is the African cry. It is ours, too. (It must be ours.)

People have been forced to leave their homes because they dared to exercise their right to register to vote. What is in the bill that will protect the homeless and starving people of this nation? What is there in this bill to insure the equality of a maid who earns $5 a week in the home of a family whose income is $100,000 a year?

For the first time in 100 years this nation is being awakened to the fact that segregation is evil and that it must be destroyed in all forms. *Your presence today proves* that you have been aroused to the point of action.

We are now involved in a serious revolution. This nation is still a place of cheap political leaders who build their careers on immoral compromises and ally themselves with open forms of political, economic and social exploitation. What political leader here can stand up and say "My party is the party of principles"? The party of Kennedy is also the party of Eastland. The party of Javits is also the party of Goldwater. Where is *our* party?

In some parts of the South we work in the fields from sun-up to sundown for $12 a week. In Albany, Georgia, nine of our leaders have been indicted not by Dixiecrats but by the Federal Government for peaceful protest. But what did the Federal Government do when Albany's Deputy Sheriff beat Attorney C. B. King and left him half-dead? What did the Federal Government do when local police officials kicked and assaulted the pregnant wife of Slater King, and she lost her baby?

It seems to me that the Albany indictment is part of a conspiracy on the part of the Federal Government and local politicians in the interest of political expediency.

Moreover, we have learned—and you should know—since we are here for Jobs and Freedom—that within the past ten days a spokesman for the administration appeared in secret session before the committee that's writing the civil rights bill and opposed and almost killed a provision that would have guaranteed in voting suits for the first time fair federal district judges.[1] And, I might add, this Administration's bill, or any other civil rights bill—such as the 1960 civil rights act—will be totally worthless when administered by racist judges, many of whom have been consistently appointed by President Kennedy.

I want to know, which side is the Federal Government on?

The revolution is at hand, and we must free ourselves of the chains of political and economic slavery. The nonviolent revolution is saying,

> We will not wait for the courts to act, for we have been waiting for hundreds of years. We will not wait for the President, the Justice Department, nor Congress, but we will take matters into our own hands and create a source of power, outside of any national structure that could and would assure us a victory.

To those who have said, "Be Patient and Wait," we must say that, "Patience is a dirty and nasty word." We cannot be patient, we do not want to be free gradually, we want our freedom, and we want it now. We cannot depend on any political party, for both the Democrats and the Republicans have betrayed the basic principles of the Declaration of Independence.

We all recognize the fact that if any radical social, political and economic changes are to take place in our society, the people, the masses, must bring them about. In the struggle we must seek more than mere civil rights; we must work for the community of love, peace and true brotherhood. Our minds, souls, and hearts cannot rest until freedom and justice exist for *all the people.*

The revolution is a serious one. Mr. Kennedy is trying to take the revolution out of the street and put it in the courts. Listen, Mr. Kennedy, Listen Mr. Congressman, listen fellow citizens, the black masses are on the march for jobs and freedom, and we must say to the politicians that there won't be a "cooling-off" period.

All of us must get in the revolution. Get in and stay in the streets of every city, every village and every hamlet of this nation, until true Freedom comes, until the revolution is complete. In the Delta of Mississippi, in Southwest Georgia, in Alabama, Harlem, Chicago, Detroit, Philadelphia and all over this nation—the black masses are on the march!

[1] [Suits against Southern registrars for their discrimination against black voters. EDS.]

We won't stop now. All of the forces of Eastland, Barnett, Wallace, and Thurmond won't stop this revolution. The time will come when we will not confine our marching to Washington. We will march through the South, through the Heart of Dixie, the way Sherman did. We shall pursue our own "scorched earth" policy and burn Jim Crow to the ground—nonviolently. We shall crack the South into a thousand pieces and put them back together in the image of democracy. We will make the action of the past few months look petty. And I say to you, WAKE UP AMERICA!

ROBERT F. WILLIAMS

Self-Defense Prevents Bloodshed

Nonviolence and passive resistance were the primary strategies of the civil rights movment in the early sixties. By these means, public accommodations were desegregated, and the mood of the country toward the aspirations of black people was somewhat changed; but the intransigence of those wielding power in the South deepened. Men such as Robert F. Williams, who confronted this power as part of their daily lives, became convinced that only armed retaliation could prevent violence against black people. Williams, the opening of whose book *Negroes with Guns* is here presented, was eventually forced to flee the United States to avoid prosecution by federal and state officials. He has since lived in exile in various countries abroad, including Cuba and China. His philosophy evolved in the middle of the nonviolent civil rights movement, and foreshadowed the turn from moral concerns toward actual physical confrontations with power.

IN JUNE OF 1961 THE NAACP CHAPTER OF MONROE, NORTH CAROLINA, decided to picket the town's swimming pool. This pool, built by

SELF-DEFENSE PREVENTS BLOODSHED   From *Negroes with Guns* by Robert F. Williams (New York: Marzani and Munsell, Inc., 1962). Reprinted by permission of the publisher.

WPA money, was forbidden to Negroes although we formed one third the population of the town. In 1957 we had asked not for integration but for the use of the pool one day a week. This was denied and for four years we were put off with vague suggestions that someday another pool would be built. Two small Negro children had meantime drowned swimming in creeks. Now, in 1961, the City of Monroe announced it had surplus funds, but there was no indication of a pool, no indication of even an intention to have a pool. So we decided to start a picket line. We started the picket line and the picket line closed the pool. When the pool closed the racists decided to handle the matter in traditional Southern style. They turned to violence, unlawful violence.

We had been picketing for two days when we started taking lunch breaks in a picnic area reserved for "White People Only." Across from the picnic area, on the other side of a stream of water, a group of white people started firing rifles and we could hear the bullets strike the trees over our heads. The chief of police was on duty at the pool and I appealed to him to stop the firing into the picnic area. The chief of police said, "Oh, I don't hear anything. I don't hear anything at all." They continued shooting all that day. The following day these people drifted toward the picket line firing their pistols and we kept appealing to the chief of police to stop them from shooting near us. He would always say, "Well, I don't hear anything."

The pool remained closed but we continued the line and crowds of many hundreds would come to watch us and shout insults at the pickets. The possibility of violence was increasing to such a proportion that we had sent a telegram to the U.S. Justice Department asking them to protect our right to picket. The Justice Department referred us to the local FBI. We called the local FBI in Charlotte and they said this was not a matter for the U.S. Justice Department; it was a local matter and that they had checked with our local chief of police, who had assured them that he would give us ample protection. This was the same chief of police who had stood idly by while these people were firing pistols and rifles over our heads. This was the same chief of police who in 1957 had placed two police cars in a Klan motorcade that raided the Negro community.

Attempt to Kill Me

On Friday, June 23, 1961, I went into town to make another telephone call to the Justice Department and while I was there I picked up one of the pickets and started back to the line at the swimming pool, which was on the outskirts of town. I was driving down U.S. Highway

74 going east when a heavy car (I was driving a small English car, a Hillman), a 1955 DeSoto sedan, came up from behind and tried to force my lighter car off the embankment and over a cliff with a 75-foot drop. I outmaneuvered him by speeding up and getting in front of him. Then he rammed my car from the rear and locked the bumper and he started a zig-zag motion across the highway in an attempt to flip my light car over. The bumpers were stuck and I didn't use the brake because I didn't want it to neutralize the front wheels.

We had to pass right by a highway patrol station. The station was in a 35-mile-an-hour zone and by the time we passed it the other car was pushing me at 70 miles an hour. I started blowing my horn incessantly, hoping to attract the attention of the highway patrolmen. There were three patrolmen standing on the opposite side of the embankment in the yard of the station. They looked at the man who was pushing and zig-zagging me across the highway and then threw up their hands, laughed, and turned their backs to the highway.

He kept pushing me for a quarter of an hour until we came to a highway intersection carrying heavy traffic. The man was hoping to run me out into the traffic, but about 75 feet away from the highway I was finally able to rock loose from his bumper, and I made a sharp turn into the ditch.

My car was damaged. The brake drum, the wheels, and the bearings had been damaged, and all of the trunk compartment in the rear had been banged in. After we got it out of the ditch, I took the car back to the swimming pool and I showed it to the chief of police. He stood up and looked at the car and laughed. He said, "I don't see anything. I don't see anything at all." I said, "You were standing here when I left." He said, "Well, I still don't see anything." So I told him I wanted a warrant for the man, whom I had recognized. He was Bynum Griffin, the Pontiac-Chevrolet dealer in Monroe. And he said, "I can't give you a warrant because I can't see anything that he's done." But a newspaper-man standing there started to examine my car and when the chief of police discovered that a newspaper man was interested, then he said, "Well, come to the police station and I'll give you a warrant."

When I went to the police station he said, "Well, you just got a name and a license number and I can't indict a man on that. You can take it up with the Court Solicitor." I went to the Court Solicitor, which is equivalent to the District Attorney, and he said, "Well, all you got here is a name and a number on a piece of paper. I can't indict a man on these grounds." I told him that I recognized the man and I mentioned his name. He said, "Wait a minute," and he made a telephone call. He said, "I called him and he said he didn't do that." I again told him that I had recognized the man and that I had the license number of the car that he had used. Finally the Court Solicitor said, "Well, if you insist, I'll tell you what you do. You go to his house and take a look at him and if you recognize him, you bring him up here and I'll make out a warrant for him." I told him that was what the police were being paid for; that they were supposed to go and pick up criminals. So they refused to give me a warrant for this man at all.

"God Damn, The Niggers Have Got Guns!"

The picket line continued. On Sunday, on our way to the swimming pool, we had to pass through the same intersection (U.S. 74 and U.S. 601). There were about two or three thousand people lined along the highway. Two or three policemen were standing at the intersection directing traffic and there were two policemen who had been following us from my home. An old stock car without windows was parked by a restaurant at the intersection. As soon as we drew near, this car started backing out as fast as possible. The driver hoped to hit us in the side and flip us over. But I turned my wheel sharply and the junk car struck the front of my car and both cars went into a ditch.

Then the crowd started screaming. They said that a nigger had hit a white man. They were referring to me. They were screaming, "Kill the niggers! Kill the niggers! Pour gasoline on the niggers! Burn the niggers!"

We were still sitting in the car. The man who was driving the stock car got out of the car with a baseball bat and started walking toward us and he was saying, "Nigger, what did you hit me for?" I didn't say anything to him. We just sat there looking at him. He came up close to our car, within arm's length with the baseball bat, but I still hadn't said anything and we didn't move in the car. What they didn't know was that we were armed. Under North Carolina state law it is legal to carry firearms in your automobile so long as these firearms are not concealed.

I had two pistols and a rifle in the car. When this fellow started to draw back his baseball bat, I put an Army .45 up in the window of the car and pointed it right into his face and I didn't say a word. He looked at the pistol and he didn't say anything. He started backing away from the car.

Somebody in the crowd fired a pistol and the people again started to scream hysterically, "Kill the niggers! Kill the niggers! Pour gasoline on the niggers!" The mob started to throw stones on top of my car. So I opened the door of the car and I put one foot on the ground and stood up in the door holding an Italian carbine.

All this time three policemen had been standing about fifty feet away from us while we kept waiting in the car for them to come and rescue us. Then when they saw that we were armed and the mob couldn't take us, two of the policemen started running. One ran straight to me and he grabbed me on the shoulder and said, "Surrender your weapon! Surrender your weapon!" I struck him in the face and knocked him back away from the car and put my carbine in his face and I told him we were not going to surrender to a mob. I told him that we didn't intend to be lynched. The other policeman who had run around the side of the car started to draw his revolver out of the holster. He was hoping to shoot me in the back. They didn't know that we had more than one gun. One of the students (who was seventeen years old) put a .45 in the policeman's face and told him that if he pulled out his pistol he would kill him. The policeman started putting his gun back into the holster and backing away from the car, and he fell into the ditch.

There was a very old man, an old white man out in the crowd, and he started screaming and crying like a baby and he kept crying, and he said, "God damn, God damn, what is this God damn country coming to that the niggers have got guns, the niggers are armed and the police can't even arrest them!" He kept crying and somebody led him away through the crowd.

Steve Pressman, who is a member of the Monroe City Council, came along and he told the chief of police to open the highway and get us out of there. The chief of police told the City Councilman, "But they've got guns!" Pressman said, "That's OK. Open the highway up and get them out of here!" They opened the highway and the man from the City Council led us through. All along the highway for almost a third of a mile people were lined on both sides of the road. And they were screaming "Kill the niggers! Kill the niggers! We aren't having any integration here! We're not going to swim with niggers!"

By the time we got to the pool, the other students who had gone on had already started the picket line. There were three or four thousand white people milling around the pool. All the city officials were there including the Mayor of Monroe. They had dark glasses on and they were standing in the crowd. And the crowd kept screaming. Then the chief of police came up to me and he said, "Surrender your gun." And I told him that I was not going to surrender any gun. That those guns were legal and that was a mob, and if he wanted those guns he could come to my house and get them after I got away from there. And then he said,

"Well, if you hurt any of these white people here, God damn it, I'm going to kill you!" I don't know what made him think that I was going to let him live long enough to shoot me. He kept saying, "Surrender the gun!" while the white people kept screaming.

The City Councilman reappeared and said that the tension was bad and that there was a chance that somebody would be hurt. He conceded that I had a right to picket and he said that if I were willing to go home he would see that I was escorted. I asked him who was going to escort us home. He said "the police." I told him that I might as well go with the Ku Klux Klan as go with them. I said I would go with the police department under one condition. He asked what that was. I told him I would take one of the students out of my car and let them put a policeman in there and then I could rest assured that they would protect us. And the police said they couldn't do that. They couldn't do that because they realized that this policeman would get hurt if they joined in with the mob.

The officials kept repeating how the crowd was getting out of hand; somebody would get hurt. I told them that I wasn't going to leave until they cleared the highway. I also told them that if necessary we would make our stand right there. Finally they asked me what did I suggest they do, and I recommended they contact the state police. So they contacted the state police and an old corporal and a young man came; just two state patrolmen. Three or four thousand people were out there, and the city had twenty-one policemen present who claimed they couldn't keep order.

The old man started cursing and told the people to move back, to spread out and to move out of there. And he started swinging a stick. Some of the mob started cursing and he said, "God damn it, I mean it. Move out." They got the message and suddenly the crowd was broken up and dispersed. The officials and state police knew that if they allowed the mob to attack us a lot of people were going to be killed, and some of those people would be white.

Two police cars escorted us out; one in front and one behind. This was the first time this had ever been done. And some of the white people started screaming "Look how they are protecting niggers! Look how they are taking niggers out of here!"

As a result of our stand, and our willingness to fight, the state of North Carolina had enforced law and order. Just two state troopers did the job, and no one got hurt in a situation where normally (in the South) a lot of Negro blood would have flowed. The city closed the pool for the rest of the year and we withdrew our picket line.

SYLVESTER CHRISTIE

The Poverty of Rural Blacks Today

The poverty, neglect and disease which characterized the life of many black families was unaffected by the events of protest reported on the nation's television screens. States like Mississippi and Alabama remained poor, and their poorest citizens, of course, were the blacks. Voter registration projects, such as those begun by SNCC in 1961 in Mississippi, were beneficial because they allowed the destitution of black people to become a part of the record later conveyed to the Democratic National Convention in 1964. But such projects did not change the human situation they documented; and the Democratic party virtually ignored the data presented. Nor has the situation changed with the years. The following survey, published in 1967, gives a vivid picture of what life is for the black sharecropper.

During the summer of 1967, the Southern Rural Research Project invited students from all over the U.S. to participate in a massive job of information-gathering in rural Negro areas of Alabama and Mississippi. The students, utilizing a 23-page questionnaire dealing with farm programs and related problems as well as living conditions, interviewed over 1,800 Negro heads of households (representing families of over 10,000 persons).

Nine hundred eighty-six (986) of the interviews were conducted by 14 students in 5 representative blackbelt counties of Alabama. The following is a composite of the living conditions, food and health situations revealed by the answers to their questions . . . and observations of the interviewers.

The Negro farmers interviewed are the invisible people of the South. One million farm Negroes were "lost" by the local white census takers

THE POVERTY OF RURAL BLACKS TODAY   From *The Negro in Rural Alabama: Living, Food and Health Conditions* by Sylvester Christie. This article is reprinted from Vol. 8, No. 2, Spring 1968 issue of *Freedomways*, published at 799 Broadway, New York City.

for the 1960 census.[1] *Services, both federal and state, are equally "lost" on their way to the Negro farmers.*

Living Conditions

The home of the Negro farmer in Alabama is typically an unpainted 3–4 room wood-frame shack for three to five adults and eight to twelve children.

The home is all bedrooms except for one room for cooking with no living room or common room. Each bed is used for two or three adults or up to five children—2 to 3 beds to a room. Those who do not own "spring" mattresses will use fertilizer sacks stuffed with raw cotton or rags—frequently infected with lice, ticks, fleas and roaches. In some cases, children must sleep on the floors with little or nothing underneath them nor any covers for warmth or protection against the swarms of insects, particularly mosquitoes.

In the kitchen, cooking is done for an average of 9 to 11 people. This part of the house is much like a partitioned porch and is only partially cut off from the outdoors by crude doors and paneless windows or shuttered holes in the wall.

The largest piece of furniture in these kitchens is likely to be the woodburning stove. This stove blackens the interior of the house when used for cooking or, less effectively, for heating. The soot also covers the few clothes which hang on nails or a cord in corners of the other rooms. Where electricity is available, there may also be a refrigerator or deep freeze which is used to store vegetables for winter.

Outdoor pumps are the usual source of water in most areas, but some communities of Negro farmers must share wells or walk one to two miles for creek water. Some of these creeks provide foul, stagnant water in which there may be silt and animal droppings. Carrying the day's drinking, cooking and washing water is a considerable task for the mothers and children when they cannot trap enough rainwater. The water is placed in a pan for washing dishes; in a big black iron pot for boiling clothes outdoors; in a tub for use with the washboard and in the same tub to stand up in while "sponge bathing."

There is no piped-in water in these homes and *never* any indoor toilets. Pots are kept inside during the night and bushes are used near the house or wherever the members of the family happen to be. The

[1] *Equal Opportunity in Farm Programs,* U.S. Civil Rights Commission, 1965, p. 9, n. 20.

few outhouses to be found are wooden enclosures containing two slats of wood with space between—covering a hole in the earth and usually inconveniently located in fields—often, by circumstances, uphill from the water supply.

What windows there are in the house are very unlikely to have any glass and are "sealed" (as are the holes and gaps in the walls, ceiling and floors) by use of rags and cardboard. Newspapers cover the walls to both seal the house against the elements by cutting down the draft through the walls and to better reflect the light in the soot-darkened home.

Nevertheless, cold air and rain come in through the walls and ceiling of all the rooms of these shacks. Often a large hole in the floorboards is allowed to remain to permit an escape for rainwater coming through the unrepairable wood roof—all of which contributes to the rat problem. To survive in these homes in winter without expending large amounts of wood, the families dress themselves day and night as heavily as their wardrobe allows.

Although the landowner is obligated to make repairs on the homes, he rarely makes any improvements and promises repairs only on condition of higher rents. The expense of the repairs and the insecurity of his tenancy prohibit the farmer from making the costly repairs himself. House rent, when not included in the crop rent, is usually $10–$15 per month.

Food—Amount and Kind

Breakfast, especially during the seasons of heaviest work, is the largest meal of the day. It is eaten before daylight at those times when the farmer and his family have to be in the fields, otherwise it is eaten at an indefinite time before noon and typically consists of:

Hominy grits	Eggs (up to twice weekly)
Biscuits or cornbread	Meat (occasional small portions
Coffee or water	of chicken or lean pork)

Children going to school are generally unable to pay the daily fee of 25¢ for the school lunch and when peanut butter and jelly sandwiches (occasionally bologna) are not available, they do without the noon meal. The rest of the family will generally skip the midday meal except when engaged in hard work on the farm.

Evening Meal   This final meal consists of vegetables, peas or beans with cornbread or biscuits and maybe leftovers of a hot midday meal—if cooked that day. Most of the year, however, breakfast and the midday meal are spaced far enough apart to avoid the evening meal and the midday meal is eaten late when the children return from school.

The beans and vegetables eaten are those grown in the gardens around the house and are generally okra, collard greens, sweet potatoes and turnips. These are cooked with large quantities of grease and chunks of fat, called "fatback." The fatback is also eaten by itself as a course and is called "whitemeat."

The "filler" in the meal is huge servings of a bread: home cooked biscuits or cornbread and occasionally storebought "lightbread." At times, especially during the winter when the canned vegetables have been used up, bread soaked in syrup becomes a meal in itself.

The drink served with these meals is sometimes coffee, but usually watered down Kool-Aid with little sugar. As an alternative, ice-water is offered. Less than half of the families interviewed drink milk at any time and only a few of these drink it regularly. About twenty per cent of the families own cows that provide milk.

The "meat" meal is usually chicken. Most farm families raise some chickens, but not enough to be able to consume them regularly nor do the hens lay regularly. As a result, chicken and eggs are eaten only about twice a week and come from the farm's resources only part of the time.

Most of the time, the only meat is some pork product, neckbones or just fat. The low cost of these pork products and the ease with which pigs can be raised are the main reasons why pork is eaten over beef. Families possessing pigs or hogs will slaughter as many of them as possible and ration the meat, fat and bones throughout the winter months. Beef is rarely encountered in the rural Negro diet.

Cooking the meals on the wood stove is a laborious task. The stoves discourage any complicated cooking and severely limit the range of variations and the number of dishes that can be prepared. When the preparation of a meal is completed, the pots are left simmering on the stove and the family move to the kitchen and help themselves to the peas, beans, fatback and the cornbread. Since there is rarely enough silverware for the entire family at once, it is used by only a few. There are never enough dishes—those who eat last use the plates of those who have already finished.

When wood becomes especially scarce, cooking is done only every other day or so and portions of the provisions are warmed over. This eliminates the need to buy or haul or purchase wood (at rates up to $4.00 for a two-day supply). The purchase of wood occurs most often among families that live on or near soybean plantations where all wood land has been stripped away.

Wilcox County, Alabama

Description of the Family Home

The B's, a Wilcox County cotton farming family of 10 persons, live in a one-room wooden shack, 3 miles off the main paved road of Coy, Alabama. The dirt road leading to their home, and shared by eight other Negro farm families, is in a state of almost total neglect. In a matter of minutes after a brief summer shower, the ruts and holes turn into impassable mud puddles—and remain in that condition for several days following. During an exceptional rainy season (such as this summer) the puddles do not have a chance to dry up at all. Ordinarily, a small car cannot drive up the road above 5 miles per hour. Aside from an occasional shack, the narrow road is lined on either side by expansive cotton fields.

There is seldom enough table space (and chairs) for the whole family to sit down and eat together. This requires eating in "shifts" and eliminates the pleasure of communal dining and conversation.

At the end of the meal, none of the family will feel hungry, and nothing is ever "left over" for snacks. Some may even feel bloated.

The B's hut squats on a small clearing off the dirt road. The ground in front of the house is sandy—or more often that not—muddy. The shack itself is an almost square (15' x 9') wooden box, with one door and two shuttered windows. The roof is unshingled, the skeleton wood frame covered by a layer of tar paper for protection against the elements. Unlike most Negro farm huts in Wilcox County, the B's house does not have a porch and thus for socializing and relaxing as well as for escaping the intense heat of the closed-in room, the family sits on a large, old—no longer serviceable—horse cart in the front yard. A sawed-off tree stump serves as door step.

The inside room is dark and cluttered. A lone naked bulb dangles from the ceiling. Two foldaway beds (with three children lying widthwise on each) line the walls. Rag quilts on the floor provide beds for the older children. Dust, dirt, paper, and food scraps are swept into a large hole in the floor, left by a rotting plank. It is the same hole through which the rats crawl into the room at night to gnaw at the fertilizer sacks that serve as bedding and linen for the family. The mattresses themselves, despite the attempt to keep up fresh bedding, smell of stale urine. Fleas, flies, and cockroaches vie for room on the beds. Holes in the roof and the walls are tacked up from inside with flattened cardboard boxes—and colored newspaper sheets pasted over the wooden slats both insulate and decorate the hut. The family does not have an "outhouse" or any other toilet facilities. Water is supplied by a pump in the back yard. The shack is heated in the winter by a single fireplace, and the small wood stove used also for cooking.

Except during the cotton picking season, the B's eat two meals a day —usually grits for breakfast and greens and chicken necks—or sometimes field peas for dinner. The bulk of the family's diet is supplied by the vegetable garden and, especially in the fall, from small wild game occasionally caught in the woods nearby: squirrel, possum, wild turkey, etc. About $5 a week is spent on the other food staples: rice, grits, flour, cornmeal, coffee, sugar, fat back, etc.

Mrs. B. is virtually head of the family and manager of the 40-acre cotton and truck farm (rented) in the absence of her husband. She clears, plants, and harvests the land along with the help of six of her eight children—ranging in age from 2 to 16—and of a tractor that she managed to obtain through loans and outside work. It is still only partially paid for. The work day for Mrs. B., as for most Alabama farmers, begins at sunrise and ends at sunset. The family subsists on a gross annual income of $1,200 from the proceeds of the farm.

There is little money to be had for clothing. Mrs. B. works every day in a worn out, torn YWCA porter's dress that someone gave her. The girls wear old slips, polo shirts and material scraps. The youngest child (age 2) goes naked or else wears just a top. The children all seem undersized and underweight for their ages. When they are not working in the fields, the children spend their time sleeping or sitting out in front of the house doing nothing. The two-year-old cannot yet balance himself for walking because of the size of his swollen belly, and the thinness of his legs. He does not yet talk and is just beginning to cut his first teeth. The oozing, crusted sores on his head attract both fleas and flies, which he rarely bothers to brush away. Mrs. B. complains of headaches, fainting and weak spells. She thinks she may have high blood pressure, but cannot afford to get to the doctor for medicine for herself or for the children.

Health Conditions

From birth to death, the Negro farmer and his family in Alabama are denied the rudiments of health care that is generally considered as essential to survival.

Birth   The Negro baby is delivered in the home by a Negro midwife who, though of considerable experience, is trained to a limited degree. The midwife is of little help in difficult births which in these circumstances can become emergencies endangering the life of mother and child. The midwife's job is also complicated by the fact that the minimal medical attention paid the expectant mother in advance of birth does not warn of unforeseen difficulties such as a breech birth.

The homes in which these births occur provide the most deplorable conditions in which an American child could be born. There is sometimes no electricity and almost never any running water. The water used in the delivery comes from a creek or well or perhaps a yard pump and may be polluted with soil or animal waste, including in some instances, the excrement of the family itself.

Heating is attempted with fireplaces and the wood stoves which must also be relied upon to boil water for the delivery. The stoves require considerable quantities of wood and the soot which pours into the air further complicates all attempts for sterility.

The material used in the handling of the child is not likely to have been washed in water hotter than can be tolerated by the hands. The cleanliness of nothing in the house is guaranteed. The home and its furnishings are infested with swarms of flies, fleas, lice, mosquitoes and ticks.

After birth, the mother may be forced to resume her activities within a few days but always within a few weeks of the delivery with a greater or lesser speed dictated by the economic predicament of the moment or the need for labor in the cotton fields.

During the first critical year of its life, the average baby does not see a doctor although he is taken to the clinic for free shots by the nurse. (The typical family is unaware, and unadvised, of other free or low cost health services at the same clinic.) Much more often than is true for the whites of the same area, the children of the farm Negro are stillborn or are born sickly of a sick mother and die during the first year.[2]

In winter, the wind rushing through the cardboard-filled holes defies the small fireplace and kitchen stove making it impossible to adequately heat the home. It is not unknown for babies to freeze to death at night. Mothers describe the health of the children as being much worse during the winter months because of continual exposure to the cold—sometimes below freezing temperatures—when only one room of the home can be warmed and the family groups there.

When the poorest of the mothers is incapable of nursing her child,

---

[2] According to the 1960 Census figures for Alabama, the infant mortality rate for Negroes was almost double that of whites.

the baby receives no milk at all. These most unfortunate babies are sometimes nursed with water—the cloudy water of the wells and creeks.

Childhood During the important years of his greatest growth, the farm child's diet is largely confined to hominy grits, chicken or pork bones, fat, certain vegetables, beans, breads and little or no milk. Even those with milk cows have neither the equipment nor the knowledge of methods to process surplus milk for the period when the cow "dries up." The surplus is instead fed to the pigs.

Toddlers are wrapped in pieces of cloth or wear old undershirts until their turn for the rags of their older sisters and brothers. The problem of clothing the children against the weather often keeps them out of school during the coldest part of the year—during the summer, the token garments suffice. In warm weather, shoes are usually worn only by those who work in the fields. The bare feet of the children are open from bruises and from sores which continuously appear on their feet (as well as other parts of their bodies). It is through such openings in the feet that stomach worms are acquired.

The children under seven commonly have scabs and sores on their heads, arms and legs that remain open and running with pus and blood. These scabs and sores get little medical attention or cleaning and are fed upon by flies and other insects which do not seem to annoy the drowsy children who let the flies climb around their eyes and mouths with no apparent irritation. These sores and infections often spread throughout the family, which only in the rarest cases can afford (or even are aware of) antibiotic treatment.

The youths suffer from swollen stomachs and skimpy hair, while mothers complain of the children's loose teeth and worms or respiratory problems. In one instance, a family sought medical attention for a child of 10 who had lost his fingernails and whose arms and legs were covered with sores and scabs. The condition was diagnosed as probable vitamin deficiency, but the mother, a widow and tenant cotton farmer, was unable to afford further help or medication.

Throughout their childhoods, the children display relatively little interest in each other and play no "make believe" or other games. The children have no toys or dolls. When not working around the house or in the fields, the youths sit idly in the dirt handling sticks or string or remain inside sitting quietly or sleeping. The children always sleep a great deal in school. In spite of this behavior, the mothers who are unfamiliar with noisy, vivacious children, consider the over-all health of their own children to be "as good as it could be" or "normal." These mothers consider what they have described of their children's ills as usual meaningless events in child growth.

While working in the fields, the mother takes her children with her, and keeps them nearby until they are about four years of age and capable of shelling peas and other household tasks. By the time the child is seven, he works full time in the fields—sacrificing much of his education. (White school officials rarely attempt to enforce truancy laws among Negro students.)

Adulthood A child may reach adulthood without ever having been to a doctor unless perhaps he has suffered a serious injury. The dentist is seen for needed extractions—rarely for treatment. During adulthood, the rural Negro begins cycles of dizziness and "falling out." Visits to doctors invariably reveal a need to discontinue starchy and fatty foods such as pork products, especially fatback and cornbread biscuits, beans, peas and grits—the basic diet. The women especially become bloated from this diet and suffer because of their extreme poverty, and in spite of their great industry, the obesity that proverbially afflicts the rich and slothful.

Year in and year out, the Negro farmer and his wife work 8 to 12 hours a day under summer suns, planting, chopping and picking cotton and vegetables and legumes until muscular and joint injuries curtail their enfeebled efforts at making a subsistence income. Complaints of strokes and partial paralysis are common among farmers of middle age. Victims of severe arthritis or strokes often do not go to the doctor—they would be unable to follow his directions because of the cost of the medications or of the foods they may be required to eat.

The adult woman, even when pregnant, continues her heavy schedule of work beginning in early morning with cooking, cleaning, hauling water and preparing children for school until midmorning when she must prepare meals for the rest of the family. The remainder of the morning and the entire afternoon is spent in the cultivation of her vegetable gardens and cornfields and in very strenuous work in the cotton fields until she prepares the evening meal, puts her family to bed and closes the day. The pregnant mother quits her labors as late as three weeks before giving birth. During pregnancy, the mother visits the clinic two or three times but receives the only treatment given to pregnant Negro women—the measuring of weight and blood pressure by a nurse—never a doctor.

By the age of 40, the Negro farm wife has given birth to six to nine children who have the choice of following the unpromising and difficult paths of their parents or leaving their south for a less desirable experiment in one of the urban ghettos. If the child remains, he can expect to repeat an up-till-now unaltered cycle of poverty.

The Urban Crisis

ST. CLAIR DRAKE

The Facts of Black Life

In the early sixties the Southern civil rights crusade had mobilized the conscience of the nation, and a new generation of abolitionists was born. This new
generation fought on moral grounds for a more meaningful Reconstruction. But
moral fervor, from the black man or the white, was apparently not enough.
Awareness of the discrimination and bigotry faced by black people in the South
soon motivated a reevaluation of the black man's role in America.

It also motivated a reevaluation of moral concern as an instrument of change.
It became apparent to many people interested in change that racism was a far
more profound phenomenon than segregated lunchrooms or the bestiality of
Mississippi sheriffs. It was a national phenomenon.

The focus of concern, therefore, shifted gradually to the large urban centers
of the North, and it began to dawn on white America that blacks comprised a
sector of the national population which was "invisible," as Ralph Ellison, the
black novelist, had said. In the following selection, the noted sociologist St. Clair
Drake shows that the invisibility of black people conceals statistics about jobs,
housing, and health which indicate an ordeal of daily desperation. Such a life
was hardly part of white America's public professions about "equality" for
all men.

Folkways and Classways Within the Black Ghetto

Black Ghettos in America are, on the whole, "run down" in appearance and overcrowded, and their inhabitants bear the physical and
psychological scars of those whose "life chances" are not equal to those
of other Americans. Like the European immigrants before them, they
inherited the worst housing in the city. Within the past decade, the white
"flight to the suburbs" has released relatively new and well-kept property

THE FACTS OF BLACK LIFE By St. Clair Drake. Reprinted by permission from
Daedalus, Journal of the American Academy of Arts and Sciences, Boston, Massachusetts, Volume 94, Number 4.

on the margins of some of the old Black Belts. Here, "gilded ghettos" have grown up, indistinguishable from any other middle-class neighborhoods except by the color of the residents' skin.[1] The power mower in the yard, the steak grill on the rear lawn, a well stocked library and equally well stocked bar in the rumpus room—these mark the homes of well-to-do Negroes living in the more desirable portions of the Black Belt. Many of them would flee to suburbia, too, if housing were available to Negroes there.

But the character of the Black Ghetto is not set by the newer "gilded," not-yet run down portions of it, but by the older sections where unemployment rates are high and the masses of people work with their hands —where the median level of education is just above graduation from grade school and many of the people are likely to be recent migrants from rural areas.[2]

The "ghettoization" of the Negro has resulted in the emergence of a ghetto subculture with a distinctive ethos, most pronounced, perhaps, in Harlem, but recognizable in all Negro neighborhoods. For the average Negro who walks the streets of any American Black Ghetto, the smell of barbecued ribs, fried shrimps, and chicken emanating from numerous restaurants gives olfactory reinforcement to a feeling of "at-homeness." The beat of "gut music" spilling into the street from ubiquitous tavern juke boxes and the sound of tambourines and rich harmony behind the crude folk art on the windows of store-front churches give auditory confirmation to the universal belief that "We Negroes have 'soul.' " The bedlam of an occasional brawl, the shouted obscenities of street corner "foul mouths," and the whine of police sirens break the monotony of waiting for the number that never "falls," the horses that neither win, place, nor show, and the "good job" that never materializes. The insouciant swagger of teen-age drop-outs (the "cats") masks the hurt of their aimless existence and contrasts sharply with the ragged clothing and dejected demeanor of "skid-row" types who have long since stopped trying to keep up appearances and who escape it all by becoming "winoes." The spontaneous vigor of the children who crowd streets and playgrounds (with Cassius Clay, Ernie Banks, the Harlem Globe Trotters, and black stars of stage, screen, and television as their role models) and the cheerful rushing about of adults, free from the occupa-

---

[1] Professor Everett C. Hughes makes some original and highly pertinent remarks about new Negro middle-class communities in his introduction to the 1962 edition of Drake and Cayton's *Black Metropolis.* [New York, 1962.]

[2] Pettigrew, *op. cit.,* pp. 180–181. [Thomas F. Pettigrew, *A Profile of the Negro American* (Princeton, N.J., 1964).]

tional pressures of the "white world" in which they work, create an atmosphere of warmth and superficial intimacy which obscures the unpleasant facts of life in the overcrowded rooms behind the doors, the lack of adequate maintenance standards, and the too prevalent vermin and rats.

This is a world whose urban "folkways" the upwardly mobile Negro middle class deplores as a "drag" on "The Race," which the upper classes wince at as an embarrassment, and which race leaders point to as proof that Negroes have been victimized. But for the masses of the ghetto dwellers this is a warm and familiar milieu, preferable to the sanitary coldness of middle-class neighborhoods and a counterpart of the communities of the foreign-born, each of which has its own distinctive subcultural flavor. The arguments in the barbershop, the gossip in the beauty parlors, the "jiving" of bar girls and waitresses, the click of poolroom balls, the stomping of feet in the dance halls, the shouting in the churches are all *theirs*—and the white men who run the pawnshops, supermarts, drug stores, and grocery stores, the policemen on horseback, the teachers in blackboard jungles—all these are aliens, conceptualized collectively as "The Man," intruders on the Black Man's "turf." When an occasional riot breaks out, "The Man" and his property become targets of aggression upon which pent-up frustrations are vented. When someone during the Harlem riots of 1964 begged the street crowds to go home, the cry came back, "Baby, we *are* home!"

But the inhabitants of the Black Ghetto are not a homogeneous mass. Although, in Marxian terms, nearly all of them are "proletarians," with nothing to sell but their labor, variations in "life style" differentiate them into social classes based more upon differences in education and basic values (crystallized, in part, around occupational differences) than in meaningful differences in income. The American caste-class system has served, over the years, to concentrate the Negro population in the low-income sector of the economy. In 1961, six out of every ten Negro families had an income of less than $4000.00 per year. This situation among whites was just the reverse: six out of every ten white families had *over* $4000.00 a year at their disposal. (In the South, eight out of ten Negro families were below the $4000.00 level.) This is the income gap. Discrimination in employment creates a job ceiling, most Negroes being in blue-collar jobs.

With 60 per cent of America's Negro families earning less than $4000.00 a year, social strata emerge between the upper and lower boundaries of "no earned income" and $4000.00. Some families live a "middle-class style of life," placing heavy emphasis upon decorous public behavior and general respectability, insisting that their children "get an education" and "make something out of themselves." They prize family stability, and an unwed mother is something much more serious than "just a girl who had an accident"; pre-marital and extra-marital sexual relations, if indulged in at all, must be discreet. Social life is organized around churches and a welter of voluntary associations of all types, and, for women, "the cult of clothes" is so important that fashion shows are a popular fund raising activity even in churches. For both men and women, owning a home and going into business are highly desired goals, the former often being a realistic one, the latter a mere fantasy.

Within the same income range, and not always at the lower margin of it, other families live a "lower-class life-style" being part of the "organized" lower class, while at the lowest income levels an "unorganized" lower class exists whose members tend always to become *dis*organized—functioning in an anomic situation where gambling, excessive drinking, the use of narcotics, and sexual promiscuity are prevalent forms of behavior, and violent interpersonal relations reflect an ethos of suspicion and resentment which suffuses this deviant subculture. It is within this milieu that criminal and semi-criminal activities burgeon.

The "organized" lower class is oriented primarily around churches whose preachers, often semi-literate, exhort them to "be in the 'world' but not of it." Conventional middle-class morality and Pauline Puritanism are preached, although a general attitude of "the spirit is willing but the flesh is weak" prevails except among a minority fully committed to the Pentecostal sects. They boast, "We *live* the life"—a way of life that has been portrayed with great insight by James Baldwin in *Go Tell it on the Mountain* and *The Fire Next Time*.

Young people with talent find wide scope for expressing it in choirs, quartets, and sextets which travel from church to church (often bearing colorful names like The Four Heavenly Trumpets or the Six Singing Stars of Zion) and sometimes traveling from city to city. Such groups channel their aggressions in widely advertised "Battles of Song" and develop their talent in church pageants such as "Heaven Bound" or "Queen Esther" and fund-raising events where winners are crowned King and Queen. These activities provide fun as well as a testing ground for talent. Some lucky young church people eventually find their fortune in the secular world as did singers Sam Cooke and Nat King Cole, while others remain in the church world as nationally known gospel singers or famous evangelists.

Adults as well as young people find satisfaction and prestige in serving as ushers and deacons, "mothers," and deaconesses, Sunday-school teachers and choir leaders. National conventions of Negro denominations and national societies of ushers and gospel singers not only develop a continent-wide nexus of associations within the organized lower class, but also throw the more ambitious and capable individuals into meaningful contact with middle-class church members who operate as role models for those talented persons who seek to move upward. That prestige and sometimes money come so easily in these circles may be a factor militating against a pattern of delaying gratifications and seeking mobility into professional and semi-professional pursuits through higher education.

Lower-class families and institutions are constantly on the move, for in recent years the Negro lower class has suffered from projects to redevelop the inner city. By historic accident, the decision to check the expansion of physical deterioration in metropolitan areas came at a time when Negroes were the main inhabitants of substandard housing. (If urban redevelopment had been necessary sixty years ago immigrants, not Negroes, would have suffered.) In protest against large-scale demolition of areas where they live, Negroes have coined a slogan, "Slum clearance is Negro clearance." They resent the price in terms of the inconvenience thrust upon them in order to redevelop American cities,[3] and the evidence shows that, in some cities, there is no net gain in improved housing after relocation.

At the opposite pole from the Negro lower class in both life styles and life chances is the small Negro upper class whose solid core is a group in the professions, along with well-to-do businessmen who have had some higher education, but including, also, a scattering of individuals who have had college training but do not have a job commensurate with their education. These men and their spouses and children form a cohesive upper-class stratum in most Negro communities. Within this group are individuals who maintain some type of contact—though seldom any social relations—with members of the local white power élite; but whether or not they participate in occupational associations with their white peers depends upon the region of the country in which they live. (It is from this group that Negro "Exhibit A's" are recruited when white liberals are carrying on campaigns to "increase interracial understanding.") They must always think of themselves as symbols of

[3] The issue of the extent to which Negroes have been victimized by urban redevelopment is discussed briefly by Robert C. Weaver in *The Urban Complex: Human Values in Urban Life* (New York, 1964). See also Martin Anderson, *The Federal Bulldozer: A Critical Analysis of Urban Renewal: 1949–1962* (Cambridge, Mass., 1964).

racial advancement as well as individuals, and they often provide the basic leadership at local levels for organizations such as the N.A.A.C.P. and the Urban League. They must lend sympathetic support to the more militant civil rights organizations, too, by financial contributions, if not action.[4]

The life styles of the Negro upper class are similar to those of the white upper *middle* class, but it is only in rare instances that Negroes have been incorporated into the clique and associational life of this group or have intermarried into it. (Their participation in activities of the white upper class occurs more often than with those whites who have similar life styles because of Negro upper class participation as members of various civic boards and interracial associations to which wealthy white people contribute.) Living "well" with highly developed skills, having enough money to travel, Negroes at this social level do not experience victimization in the same fashion as do the members of the lower class. Their victimization flows primarily from the fact that the social system keeps them "half in and half out," preventing the free and easy contact with their occupational peers which they need; and it often keeps them from making the kind of significant intellectual and social contributions to the national welfare that they might make if they were white. (They are also forced to experience various types of nervous strain and dissipation of energy over petty annoyances and deprivations which only the sensitive and the cultivated feel. Most barbershops, for instance, are not yet desegregated, and taxi drivers, even in the North, sometimes refuse Negro passengers.)

The Negro upper class has created a social world of its own in which a universe of discourse and uniformity of behavior and outlook are maintained by the interaction on national and local levels of members of Negro Greek-letter fraternities and sororities, college and alumni associations, professional associations, and civic and social clubs. It is probable that if all caste barriers were dropped, a large proportion of the Negro upper class would welcome complete social integration, and that these all-Negro institutions would be left in the hands of the Negro middle class, as the most capable and sophisticated Negroes moved into the orbit of the general society. Their sense of pride and dignity does not even allow them to imagine such a fate, and they pursue their social activities and play their roles as "race leaders" with little feeling of inferiority or deprivation, but always with a tragic sense of the irony of it all.

[4] Drake and Cayton, *op. cit.,* Chap. 23, "Advancing the Race."

The Negro middle class covers a very wide income range, and whatever cohesion it has comes from the network of churches and social clubs to which many of its members devote a great deal of time and money. What sociologists call the Negro middle class is merely a collection of people who have similar life styles and aspirations, whose basic goals are "living well," being "respectable," and not being crude. Middleclass Negroes, by and large, are not concerned about mobility into the Negro upper class or integration with whites. They want their "rights" and "good jobs," as well as enough money to get those goods and services which make life comfortable. They want to expand continuously their level of consumption. But they also desire "decent" schools for their children, and here the degree of victimization experienced by Negroes is most clear and the ambivalence toward policies of change most sharp. Ghetto schools are, on the whole, inferior. In fact, some of the most convincing evidence that residential segregation perpetuates inequality can be found by comparing data on school districts in Northern urban areas where *de facto* school segregation exists. (Table 1 presents such data for Chicago in 1962.)

Awareness of the poor quality of education grew as the protest movement against *de facto* school segregation in the North gathered momentum. But while the fight was going on, doubt about the desirability of forcing the issue was always present within some sections of the broad Negro middle class. Those in opposition asked, "Are we not saying that our teachers can't teach our own children as well as whites can, or that our children can't learn unless they're around whites? Aren't we insulting ourselves?" Those who want to stress Negro history and achievement and to use the schools to build race pride also express doubts about the value of mixed schools. In fact, the desirability of race consciousness and racial solidarity seems to be taken for granted in this stratum, and sometimes there is an expression of contempt for the behavior of whites of their own and lower income levels. In the present period one even occasionally hears a remark such as "Who'd want to be integrated with *those* awful white people?"

Marxist critics would dismiss the whole configuration of Negro folkways and classways as a subculture which reinforces "false consciousness," which prevents Negroes from facing the full extent of their victimization, which keeps them from ever focusing upon what they could be because they are so busy enjoying what they are—or rationalizing their subordination and exclusion. Gunnar Myrdal, in *An American Dilemma,* goes so far as to refer to the Negro community as a "patho-

TABLE 1.   Comparison of White, Integrated and Negro Schools
in Chicago: 1962

| | Type of School | | |
Indices of Comparison	White	Integrated	Negro
Total appropriation per pupil	$342.00	$320.00	$269.00
Annual teachers' salary per pupil	256.00	231.00	220.00
Per cent uncertified teachers	12.00	23.00	49.00
No. of pupils per classroom	30.95	34.95	46.80
Library resource books per pupil	5.00	3.50	2.50
Expenditures per pupil other than teachers' salaries.	86.00	90.00	49.00

Adapted from a table in the U.S. Commission on Civil Rights report, *Public Schools, Negro and White* (Washington, D.C., 1962), pp. 241–248.

logical" growth within American society.[5] Some novelists and poets, on the other hand, romanticize it, and some Black Nationalists glorify it. A sober analysis of the civil rights movement would suggest, however, that the striking fact about all levels of the Negro community is the absence of "false consciousness," and the presence of a keen awareness of the extent of their victimization, as well as knowledge of the forces which maintain it. Not lack of knowledge but a sense of powerlessness is the key to the Negro reaction to the caste-class system.

Few Negroes believe that Black Ghettos will disappear within the next two decades despite much talk about "open occupancy" and "freedom of residence." There is an increasing tendency among Negroes to discuss what the quality of life could be within Negro communities as they grow larger and larger. At one extreme this interest slides over into Black Nationalist reactions such as the statement by a Chicago Negro leader who said, "Let all of the white people flee to the suburbs. We'll show them that the Black Man can run the second largest city in America better than the white man. Let them go. If any of them want to come back and integrate with *us* we'll accept them."

It is probable that the Black Belts of America will increase in size rather than decrease during the next decade, for no city seems likely to commit itself to "open occupancy" (although a committee in New York

[5] See section on "The Negro Community as a Pathological Form of an American Community," Chap. 43 of Gunnar Myrdal, *An American Dilemma* (New York, 1944), p. 927.

has been discussing a ten-year plan for dismantling Harlem).[6] And even if a race-free market were to appear Negroes would remain segregated unless drastic changes took place in the job ceiling and income gap. Controlled integration will probably continue, with a few upper- and upper-middle-class Negroes trickling into the suburbs and into carefully regulated mixed neighborhoods and mixed buildings within the city limits.[7] The basic problem of the next decade will be how to change Black Ghettos into relatively stable and attractive "colored communities." Here the social implications of low incomes become decisive.

Social Implications of the Job Ceiling and the Income Gap

Nowhere is direct victimization of Negroes more apparent than with respect to the job ceiling and the income gap; but indirect victimization which is a consequence of direct victimization is often less obvious. For instance, it has been mentioned that family incomes for Negroes are lower than for whites; but family income figures are inadequate tools for careful sociological analysis unless we know which, and how many, members of a family labor to earn a given income. In 1960, half of the white families were being supported by a husband only, while just a few more than a third of the Negro families could depend solely upon the earnings of one male breadwinner. In six out of ten nonwhite families where both a husband and wife were present, two or more persons worked; yet less than half of the white families had both husband and wife working. But even in those families which commanded an income of over $7,000.00 a year, twice as many nonwhite wives had to help earn it as white.[8] One not unimportant consequence is that a smaller proportion of Negro than white wives at this income level can play roles of unpaid volunteers in civic and social work, a fact which should be remembered by those who criticize Negroes in these income brackets for not doing more to "elevate their own people."

One of the most important effects of the income gap and the job ceiling has been the shaping of social class systems within Negro com-

---

[6] A report appeared on the front page of *The New York Times,* April 5, 1965, stating that a commission was at work trying to elaborate plans for "integrating" Harlem by 1975. Columbia University was said to be co-operating in the research aspects of the project.

[7] A successful experiment in "controlled integration" has been described by Julia Abrahamson in *A Neighborhood Finds Itself* (New York, 1959).

[8] Jacob Schiffman, "Marital and Family Characteristics of Workers, March, 1962," in *Monthly Labor Review,* U.S. Department of Labor, Bureau of Labor Statistics, Special Labor Force Report No. 26, January 1963.

munities which differ markedly in their profiles from those of the surrounding white society. Negro class structure is "pyramidal," with a
large lower class, a somewhat smaller middle class, and a tiny upper
class (made up of people whose income and occupations would make
them only middle class in the white society). White class profiles tend
to be "diamond shaped," with small lower and upper classes and a large
middle class. Unpromising "life chances" are reflected in inferior "life
styles," and Black Ghettos are on the whole "rougher" and exhibit a
higher degree of social disorganization than do white communities.

The job ceiling and the income gap do not create classways—for these
reflect educational levels and cultural values, as well as the economic
situation—but job ceiling and income gap do set the limits for realization of class values. It is a fact of American life (whether one approves
of it or not) that as long as Negroes are predominantly lower-class they
will, as a group, have low esteem. Yet, Negroes are victimized in the
sense that the job ceiling and the income gap make it more difficult for
them than for whites to maintain middle-class standards equivalent to
those obtaining among whites. A given life style demands a minimum
level of income, but it is evident that Negroes are victimized in the sense
that their effort as reflected in the acquisition of an education does not
bring equal rewards in terms of purchasing power, for they have less to
spend than their white counterparts at any given educational level. Non-
white family heads in 1960 had a smaller median income than whites
for every educational level. (See Table 2.)[9]

In a sense, getting an education "pays off" for Negroes as for all
other Americans; but while some individuals "get ahead" of other
Negroes, education has not yet raised their earning power to the level of
whites with equivalent training. In fact, the average income for a non-
white family with a male head who had finished high school was less
than that of a white male head who had finished only the eighth grade.
Since any aspects of the caste-class system which make it more difficult
for Negroes than for whites to achieve middle-class norms of family behavior retard the process of eventual "integration," the income differential and the necessity for more members of the family to work operate
in this negative fashion. Even more serious in determining deviations
from general middleclass family norms is the manner in which both income distribution and the occupational structure function to reinforce
the number of families without fathers and to lower the prestige of
Negro males *vis-à-vis* their mates, prospective mates, and children.
Thus a pattern of male insecurity which originated under slavery persists

[9] *Ibid.*

TABLE 2. White and Nonwhite Median
Family Income by Educational
Level, 1960: U.S.A.

Amount of Education in Yrs. of School Completed	White	Nonwhite
Elementary School		
Less than 8 years	$3,656	$2,294
8 years	4,911	3,338
High School		
1–3 years	5,882	3,449
4 years	6,370	4,559
College		
1–3 years	7,344	5,525
4 or more years	9,315	7,875

into the present. In fact, the struggle of Negro men, viewed as a group, to attain economic parity with Negro women has, up to the present, been a losing fight. Norval Glenn, in an exhaustive study of this problem,[10] has concluded that "Among full-time workers, non-white females were, in 1959, less disadvantaged relative to whites than were non-white males." Women were obtaining employment at a relatively faster rate than men and sustained a more rapid proportionate increase in income between 1939 and 1959. According to Glenn, there was an actual reversal in the income growth pattern of Negro males and females during a twenty-year period, and he notes that if their respective rates remain the same it will take twice as long for Negro males to catch up with white males as for Negro women to catch up with white women (93 years to achieve occupational equality and 219 to achieve equality of income). This is a case of *relative* deprivation, of course, but is significant nevertheless. An impressive body of evidence indicates that rather serious personality distortions result from the female dominance so prevalent in the Negro subculture, since the general norms of the larger society stress the opposite pattern as more desirable.

The interplay between caste evaluations and economic and ecological factors has tended not only to concentrate a low-income Negro population within ghettos, but has also concentrated a significant proportion of them in vast public housing projects—sometimes "high rise." In the

[10] Norval D. Glenn, "Some Changes in the Relative Status of American Nonwhites: 1940–1960," *Phylon*, Vol. 24, No. 2 (Summer 1963).

1930's public housing projects were often exciting experiments in interracial living, but there has been a tendency in many cities for them to become ghettos within ghettos. Within housing projects as well as out, a small hard core of mothers without husbands and a larger group of youth without jobs are developing a pattern which social psychologist Frederick Strodtbeck has called "the poverty-dependency syndrome." Here and there an integrated program of professional family services has proved its usefulness, but, in general, family case-work becomes a mere "holding operation."

Only the future will tell whether a large-scale "Poverty Program" coordinated through federally sponsored agencies will break the interlocking vicious circles which now victimize urban Negro populations. The dominant pattern in the American economic system has never been one of racial segregation. In fact, the racial division of labor has always involved considerable close personal contact, while demanding that Negroes play subordinate occupational roles carrying the lesser rewards in terms of economic power and social prestige. Doctrines of racial inferiority originated as dogmas to defend the use of African slave labor and were later used by white workers to defend their own privileged position against Negro competition. Trade union restrictionism reinforces employer preference in maintaining a job ceiling. Often, even when an employer decided it was profitable to use Negro labor, white workers used intimidation or violence against both white employer and black employee.

Access to new roles in the economic structure has occurred during periods of a great shortage of labor, as in the North during both world wars. Negroes entered at the bottom of the hierarchy, but were "last hired and first fired." Yet the job ceiling *was* raised, and, beginning with the organization of industrial unions in the 1930's and reaching a climax in the civil rights movement of the 1960's, ideological factors have reinforced economic interest in breaking the job ceiling. Now, for the first time in American history the full weight of top leadership in labor, industry, and government has been thrown in the direction of "fair employment practices," and public opinion is tolerating an all-out drive against job discrimination (partly because the economy is still expanding). Yet so drastic are the effects of the past victimization of the Negro that any decisive alteration in the caste-class structure without more drastic measures seems remote. Thomas Pettigrew, after an analysis of recent changes, concludes: At the creeping 1950–1960 rate of change, non-whites in the United States would not attain equal proportional representation among clerical workers until 1992, among skilled workers until 2005, among professionals until 2017, among sales workers until 2114, and among business managers and proprietors until 2730![11]

"In Sickness and in Death"

The consequences of being at the bottom in a caste-class system are revealed clearly in comparative studies of morbidity, mortality, and longevity, the latter being a particularly sensitive index to the physical well-being of groups. Comparing Negroes and whites with respect to longevity, Thomas Pettigrew notes that:

> At the turn of this century, the average non-white American at birth had a life expectancy between 32 and 35 years, 16 years less than that of the average white American. By 1960, this life expectancy had risen from 61 to 66 years. . . . But while the percentage gain in life expectancy for Negroes over these sixty odd years has been twice that of whites, there is still a discrepancy of six to eight years. . . .[12]

In other words, Negroes were "catching up," but, as a Department of Labor study pointed out in 1962, they ". . . had arrived by 1959 at about the longevity average attained by whites in 1940."[13] They were twenty years behind in the race toward equality of longevity.

Differences in longevity reflect differences in morbidity rates. Among the communicable diseases, for instance, the Negro tuberculosis rate is three times greater than that of whites, and the rates for pneumonia and influenza are also higher. The incidence of venereal disease is substantially higher among Negroes, although the Public Health Service figure of a syphilis rate ten times larger than that for whites has been questioned in Dr. Ann Pettigrew's study.[14] Twice as many Negro children per thousand as white children suffer from measles, meningitis, diphtheria, and scarlet fever. Given such differences between Negroes and whites in the incidence of specific diseases, it is not surprising to find that the *death* rate from childhood diseases is six times higher among Negroes

---

[11] Pettigrew, *op. cit.,* p. 188.

[12] *Ibid.,* p. 99; see also Marcus S. Goldstein, "Longevity and Health Status of Whites and Non-Whites in the United States," *Journal of the National Medical Association,* Vol. 46, No. 2 (March 1954), p. 83. Among other factors, the author emphasizes the relationship between nutrition and racial mortality differentials.

[13] Marion Haynes, "A Century of Change: Negroes in the U.S. Economy, 1860–1960," *Monthly Labor Review,* U.S. Department of Labor, Bureau of Labor Statistics, December 1962.

[14] Pettigrew (*op. cit.,* p. 87) comments that some research indicates that ". . . these group differences are inflated through disproportionate under-reporting of whites. . . ."

than whites and that the tuberculosis death rate is four times higher in all age groups.[15]

The analysis of mortality rates provides one tool for studying the effects of the caste-class system which victimizes the Negro population. A United States government report for the year 1963 noted that "The age pattern of mortality . . . as in previous years, is similar for each of the color-sex groups—high rates in infancy, lower rates until the minimum is reached during grade-school age, then rising rates for the older age-groups."[16] Although the *pattern* was the same, there were racial differentials in the actual rates; for instance, "The relative increases in the 1963 death rates over the prior years were slightly greater for non-white persons than for white. . . ." There were other differentials too.

The death rate among mothers at childbirth in 1963 was four times greater for nonwhites than for whites (96.9 deaths per 100,000 live births to 24.0). The death rate of nonwhite babies during the first year after birth was almost double the rate for white babies (46.6 per thousand to 25.3 per thousand for males and 36.7 to 19.0 for females.) Prenatal hazards were, as in previous years, greater for nonwhites than for whites. Up to the age of five the nonwhite death rate was twice that for whites, and for older age-groups varied from two to four times the white rate.

·   ·   ·

As for a group of deaths from children's diseases, the pattern of over-representation for nonwhites also prevails. (See Table 3.)

TABLE 3.   Number of Deaths and Rates for Whites and Nonwhites, for Certain Children's Diseases: U.S.A., 1963

Diseases	Cases	Nonwhite	White
Whooping Cough	115	.3	.0
Scarlet Fever	102	.1	.0
Diphtheria	45	.1	.0
Measles	364	.4	.2

[15] The rates cited are from Pettigrew, *op. cit.*, Chap. 4, "Negro American Health."
[16] *Monthly Vital Statistics Report,* National Center for Health Statistics, U.S. Department of Health, Education and Welfare, Public Health Service, Vol. 13 (November 2, 1964), p. 8.

It was once both fashionable and scientifically respectable to explain these differences in terms of differential racial susceptibility to various diseases, but as Thomas Pettigrew points out:

> The many improvements in his situation since 1900 rendered a dramatic increment in the Negro's health, providing solid evidence that corrosive poverty and inadequate medical care were the reasons for his short life span in the past. . . . this difference [between Negro and white rates] can be traced to the diseases which are treatable, preventable and unnecessary.[17]

This is now the generally accepted view among serious students of the problem, and "corrosive poverty" and "inadequate medical care" are aspects of the victimization to which Negroes have been subjected. Further improvement in the health status of Negroes depends upon the eradication of poverty and all its accompanying side effects as well as upon access to adequate medical care.

Much of the "corrosive poverty" has been associated with life in the cotton fields, the logging camps, the mines, and the small-town slums of a poverty-stricken South. Conditions were bad for most people, and the caste-system made them worse for the Negro. Dr. Ann Pettigrew has presented convincing evidence that the massive shift of Negro population into Northern and Western cities during the past two decades has resulted in some health gains for the Negro, and these gains have been due largely to greater access to medical advice and medical care.[18] But, the differentials are still large, even in the North, especially for tuberculosis, pneumonia, and venereal diseases. "Ghettoization," with its associated overcrowding, has been one important factor in keeping these rates high; but for these, as well as for other ailments, hospital discrimination is a primary factor limiting access to adequate medical care.

Patterns of discrimination and segregation by hospitals are prevalent throughout the country. A report prepared in 1962 for circulation to members of the National Medical Association (an organization of Negro physicians)[19] summarized the hospital situation in a sentence, "Things are bad all over," and the report included the bitter comment that "Hospitals under religious auspices have been the most vicious in discrimina-

---

[17] Pettigrew, *op. cit.,* p. 99.

[18] *Ibid.,* pp. 82–94, "Communicable Diseases," and pp. 97–98, "Economics and Physical Health."

[19] It has been demonstrated with data drawn from six Southern states that Negro mothers occupying private rooms in hospitals had a lower death rate among their infants than white mothers on the wards. See H. Bloch, H. Lippett, B. Redner, and D. Hirsch, "Reduction of Mortality in the Premature Nursery," *Journal of Pediatrics,* Vol. 41, No. 3 (September 1952), pp. 300–304.

tion." Conditions were worst in the South where the caste-system has not yet been shattered. In Birmingham, Alabama, for instance, a city of 750,000 people half of whom are Negro, only 1,100 beds were available for whites, and only 500 for Negroes. In Atlanta, Georgia, the South's most progressive city, 4,000 beds were available for whites, but only 600 for Negroes. (Nonwhites were 22.8 per cent of the population of the metropolitan area.) In Augusta, Georgia, a smaller city, twelve beds were set aside for Negroes in the basement of the white hospital but there were no beds for Negro pediatrics or obstetrics patients. The Hill-Burton Act under which federal funds may be secured for aid in building hospitals has a non-discrimination clause, but, generally, it has been evaded or ignored in the South. In one large Texas city a new $6,000,000 hospital constructed with federal aid refused to admit any Negroes until threatened with a suit. (The National Medical Association report emphasized that it was a Catholic hospital.) In Richmond, Virginia, a new "treatment center" accepted Negroes only as out-patients. By 1962, about 2,000 hospitals had been built in the South with federal assistance, and of these 98 would accept no Negroes, while the others stayed within the letter of the law by providing as little space for them as possible. In the few places where Negro physicians are practicing, they usually find it impossible to have their patients hospitalized under their own care since they cannot become members of hospital staffs. (In Elizabeth City, North Carolina, a Negro physician was recently taken on a staff after thirty-two annual applications.) Most Southern local medical societies bar Negroes from membership. (In South Carolina, however, twenty-five of the sixty-five Negro doctors belong to the state medical association, but must hold separate sessions. They can join local societies only if they will agree in advance to stay away from social functions.)

In the more fluid ethnic-class system in the North, patterns of discrimination and segregation vary from city to city. At one extreme is Pittsburgh, Pennsylvania, of which the National Medical Association report simply says, "No hospital problems." A similar assessment is made of Philadelphia. In Gary, Indiana, after a prolonged fight, 85 per cent of the Negro physicians were placed on the staff of some formerly all-white hospitals. When the National Medical Association says that "There is no hospital problem" in these cities, what it really means is that Negro physicians no longer find it difficult to have their patients hospitalized. But the Negro masses still face other problems; for, insofar as they are disproportionately represented in low-income groups, more of them are "charity" patients and must face the more subtle forms of victimization which the poor face everywhere in American hospitals—less careful attention to their needs, psychological and physical, than private patients receive. There is substantial evidence from studies made in one Northern city that such patients are more frequently handled by medical students and interns than by fully trained doctors, and there is reliable statistical evidence indicating that more infants die on the wards than in the rooms of private patients. As important as it is to insist upon the right of Negro doctors to take their patients into hospitals which formerly barred them, other aspects of the Negro health problem must be dealt with, too.

The city of Chicago, with its 900,000 Negroes rigidly segregated into ghettos, reveals the full dimensions of the problem. As recently as 1960 there were no more than 500 beds available to Negroes in private hospitals—one-half bed per 1000 Negroes as compared with 4.5 beds per 1000 whites. A distinguished Negro physician serving as Chairman of a Committee to End Discrimination in Medical Institutions released a statement to the press in October, 1963, in which he said that only thirty-three out of eighty private hospitals admitted Negroes and that:

> Many of these do so on a segregated and discriminating basis. . . . Some hospitals which do admit Negroes place them in the oldest rooms, in basements, in all-Negro wings and often have a quota system limiting the number of Negro patients they will accept. . . . when a Negro becomes ill, he knows he will be accepted at County hospital and is in no mood to have to fight to gain admittance to a private hospital where he will be discriminated against.[20]

The Negro physicians, however, did take up the issue by insisting upon staff appointments so they could take their own patients into these hospitals and insure adequate care for them.

The fight began seriously in 1955 with the passage of an antidiscrimination bill in the City Council and a plea for compliance by Cardinal Stritch. In 1960, after five years of publicity and pleading, only twenty-one of the two hundred fifteen Negro physicians in Chicago held appointments on any private hospital staff outside of the Black Belt, these being at twenty-one of the sixty-eight hospitals of this type. At this point the Mayor appointed a special committee to work on the problem, and a group of ten Negro doctors filed suit under the Sherman and Clayton anti-trust acts against fifty-six hospitals, the Illinois Hospital Association, the Chicago Medical Society, the Chicago Hospital Council, and the Illinois Corporations operating Blue Cross and Blue Shield medical pre-

---

[20] Dr. Arthur G. Falls' statement was released through the Chicago Urban League on October 20, 1963, having been sent out on October 16th with a "hold." (Copy in files of Chicago Urban League, C.E.D.)

payment plans. They took this action, they said, "to thwart the more subtle and sophisticated techniques" being used to evade the issue.[21]

In response to these pressures (and to the general atmosphere regarding civil rights), forty-two of the sixty-eight hospitals in the city had given one hundred two staff appointments to sixty-four of the city's two hundred twenty-five Negro doctors by 1965. (Only eighty-eight of these, however, "permit the physician to admit his private patients.") The downward trend in the number of Negro physicians choosing to practice in Chicago was arrested. For a city which ranked only fourth from the bottom among fourteen cities on degree of hospital integration, the breakthrough has been a major victory.[22] One measure of the extent of the Negro's victimization is the fact that scores of physicians had to spend their money and invest time which could have been devoted to research or professional development in fighting for access to hospital facilities.

The victory of the Chicago Negro doctors has alleviated the plight of paying patients who now have a wider choice of hospitals, though not necessarily closer to their homes. (Because of the fear of being "swamped" by Negro patients, some hospitals near the Black Belt have interposed stronger barriers against Negro doctors than have those farther away.) As early as 1949, a health survey of Chicago pointed out that

> A serious problem faced by the Blue Cross Plan for hospital care in this area is its inability to fulfil its obligations to the 50,000 Negro subscribers, since they are not accepted by all the member hospitals. . . . Many of the subscribers must be admitted to Cook County Hospital under the guise of emergencies. . . .

Six years later, the Packinghouse Workers Civil and Community Committee complained that "Our union has struggled and won hospital benefits for all our members, but a great number of UPWA-CIO members who are Negroes are being cheated out of those benefits. . . ." With over 100,000 insured Negroes and less than 1,000 beds available to them in private hospitals they are still being cheated, and not they alone.[23]

[21] These actions are discussed in the Presidential Address delivered to the Institute of Medicine of Chicago, January 14, 1960, by Dr. Franklin C. McLean, "Negroes and Medicine in Chicago." (Mimeographed copy in files of Chicago Urban League).

[22] The 1965 assessment is from a statement by Dr. Robert G. Morris, circulated in mimeographed form by the Chicago Urban League. The standard work on the problems facing Negro physicians in Dietrich C. Reitzes, *Negroes and Medicine* (Cambridge, Mass., 1958).

[23] Summarized from documents on file with Chicago Urban League.

Chicago Negroes have been forced by hospital discrimination to use the facilities of four or five hospitals within the Black Belt and the large but overcrowded Cook County Hospital which should be serving only those who cannot pay and emergency cases. By 1960, almost two-thirds of all the Negro babies delivered in a hospital were being born at Cook County. Some white hospitals near the Black Ghetto closed down their maternity wards rather than serve Negroes. A prominent white physician delivering an address in 1960 in favor of widening access to hospital care stressed that this was unfair both to the paying patients who were denied the right to choose and to the indigent who were being deprived of space at the Cook County Hospital by Negroes who could pay. He said: Cook County Hospital is even being used to absorb a large number of Negro patients unwanted by the voluntary hospitals even though they may be able and willing to pay . . . the Chicago public would not tolerate this misuse of a tax-supported hospital. . . . for an equivalent number of non-Negro patients. . . .[24] Placing Negroes on the hospital staffs has not solved the fundamental problem of the shortage of beds available to a rapidly expanding Negro population. To build new hospital facilities in the Black Belt *before* eliminating segregation in *all* hospitals would be considered bad strategy by most Negro leaders and a "sell-out" by the militants. The Chicago paradigm has general relevance and is not applicable only to the local scene.

Hospital discrimination is only one facet of a complex process involving both direct and indirect victimization which leads to a lower level of physical and mental well-being among Negroes and which is reflected in morbidity and mortality rates. Health hazards for most of the Negro population begin even before birth, and they affect both mother and child. These hazards are greatest in the rural South, but they exist in urban situations as well, both Northern and Southern. Premature births occurred 50 per cent more frequently among Negroes than among whites during 1958–1959 and maternal mortality rates among Negroes were four times higher.[25] A higher proportion of Negro mothers failed to receive prenatal care, and a higher proportion died in childbirth. The most authoritative testimony on the disadvantaged position of the Negro expectant mother has been supplied by an eminent obstetrician, Dr. Philip F. Williams, who has called attention to the fact that "one survey of maternal mortality is cited which found errors in judgment and technique as well as neglect on the part of the physician, as much as fifty

[24] Dr. F. C. McLean, cited in 21 *supra*.
[25] Note Pettigrew, *op. cit.*, p. 97, which cites "lack of prenatal care, poor family health education, inadequate diet and inexpert delivery" as factors.

per cent more frequently in the case of Negro than white mothers." He pointed out, too, that Negro women who were pregnant and those who had babies were victims of a set of interlocking conditions which included a lack of concern by husbands and putative fathers, a relatively high exposure to gonorrhea and syphilis, and, in the South ". . . a scarcity of physicians that has resulted in an inferior grade of attendance at birth (the untrained midwife). . . ."[26] In both North and South, hospital facilities are still inadequate and all of these factors combine to create a situation ". . . more or less adversely affecting the chances of survival of the Negro mother at childbirth." They affect the chances of the baby's surviving, too. Studies made soon after World War II revealed that, for Negroes as compared with whites, fewer Negro babies were delivered in hospitals and therefore more of them died at birth or during the first year after (and more died before they could be born, too). Immunization of children was less common among Negroes and childhood diseases more prevalent and more often fatal.[27] Negro children, on the average, received fewer of the benefits of deliberately planned feeding, and fewer parents, in proportion, ate according to the more advanced nutritional standards.

Insofar as the job ceiling, the income gap, and Ghettoization preserve and reinforce lower-class behavior patterns among Negroes to a greater extent than in the general society, the general health status of the Negro will be affected. For instance, a less adequate nutritional level than is found among whites is one factor often cited in accounting for the poorer average health status of Negroes. It is conceivable that Negroes could improve their nutritional status immediately by altering their present patterns of food consumption, but this is likely to occur less as a result of education and propaganda than as a by-product of changes in the caste-class situation. Except in wartime or during depressions, food habits are among the most difficult to change, unless change is related to mobility strivings. Maximizing the opportunity for Negroes to achieve the values and norms of the general American middle class is likely to do more to change the eating habits of the Negro population than all of the written or spoken exhortations of home economists or the most seductive of television commercials. A shift in social class supplies the motivation to

---

[26] Philip F. Williams, "Material Welfare and the Negro," *Journal of American Association,* Vol. 132, No. 11 (November 16, 1946), pp. 611–614.

[27] M. Gover and J. B. Yaukey, "Physical Impairments of Members of Low-Income Farm Families," *Public Health Reports,* Vol. 61, No. 4 (January 25, 1946), and Marion E. Altenderfer and Beatrice Crowther, "Relationship Between Infant Mortality and Socio-economic Factors in Urban Areas," *Public Health Reports,* Vol. 64, No. 11 (March 18, 1949), pp. 331–339.

change, and such a shift is dependent upon an increase in the number and proportion of Negroes entering white-collar occupations.

Maintaining a style of living consonant with any occupational roles demands a minimum level of income. Success in improving the health status of the Negro population may ultimately depend upon an indirect rather than a frontal assault. One student of the problem gives us a clue to the strategy when he observes that ". . . the much lower income level of the American Negro, to the extent that it is a measure of standard of living, explains, in part at least, the differences in health status and longevity between whites and non-whites in the United States."[28] Carefully controlled studies "point up the intimate relationship between physical illness and economic . . ."[29] to use Dr. Ann Pettigrew's expression. Economic factors not only partially explain, or serve as indices of, the causes of divergent morbidity and mortality rates, but they also give us the clues to a strategy for change, namely, working toward a continuously rising standard of living. Whether hope or pessimism is warranted depends upon the possibility of drastically changing the economic status of the Negro over the next decade, of eliminating economic "victimization."

. . .

The Identification Problem

Some of the most damaging forms of indirect victimization manifest themselves at the psychological level. The Black Ghetto and the job ceiling are the key variables in accounting for differences in morbidity and mortality rates, and for the persistence of subcultural behavior patterns which deviate from middle-class norms. At the subjective level they also determine the crucial points of social reference for the individual Negro when answering the questions "Who am I today?" and "What will I be tomorrow?" The Black Ghetto forces him to identify as a Negro first, an American second, and it gives him geographical "roots." The job ceiling is an ever present reminder that there are forces at work

[28] Marcus S. Goldstein, op. cit., p. 93.
[29] Dr. Ann Pettigrew cites a study carried out in Chicago, using 1950 data, in which, when Negroes and whites of the same economic level were compared, mortality rates were about the same although the rates for Negroes as a group when compared with those for whites as a group were higher. Other studies using the same body of data indicate sharp differences in mortality rates as between laborers and skilled workers among Negroes, a situation similar to that found among whites (Pettigrew, op. cit., p. 98).

which make him a second-class American. But the Black Ghetto and the job ceiling are only two components of a caste-class system now undergoing revolutionary transformation—an institutional complex which includes the courts, schools, churches, voluntary associations, media of mass communication, and a network of family units. Like all other persons, the individual Negro receives his orientation to this social nexus first from his family and later from his peer group. Exposure to schools and the mass media continues the process of socialization and personality formation while membership in voluntary associations provides a tie to the class system and constitutes an aid to upward mobility.

The white middle-class is the reference group for those who are mobile; yet the entire system operates to emphasize identity with "The Race," since defensive solidarity must be maintained against the white world. Inner conflicts are inevitable; and conventional, as well as idiosyncratic, adjustments to this situation have been thoroughly studied. Ann Pettigrew suggests that ". . . the perception of relative deprivation, the discrepancy between high aspirations and actual attainments . . . is a critical psychological determinant of mental disorder. And certainly racial discrimination acts to bar the very achievements which the society encourages individuals to attempt."[30] A disparity in psychosis rates reflects this discrepancy, but for most Negroes the reaction to oppression is less severe. Neither insanity nor suicide is a *typical* Negro reaction.

Both Negroes and whites are "victims" of one persisting legacy of the slave trade—the derogation of "negroidness." The idea that a dark skin indicates intellectual inferiority is rapidly passing, but at the esthetic level derogatory appraisal of thick lips, kinky hair, and very dark skin is still prevalent. That many Negroes reject their own body image is evident from advertisements for skin lighteners in the major Negro publications,[31] and Negro children in experimental situations begin to reject brown dolls for white ones before the age of five.[32] The ever present knowledge that one's negroid physiognomy is evaluated as "ugly" lowers self-esteem and, therefore, weakens self-confidence. The rise of the new

[30] *Ibid.*, p. 80.
[31] *Ebony*, a well-edited, widely circulated, popular weekly magazine which concentrates upon the display of what its editor calls "Negro achievement" carries skin-lightener advertisements routinely. *Ebony's* African imitator, *Drum*, also carries such advertisements.
[32] The classical study in this field is Kenneth B. Clark and Mamie P. Clark, "Racial Identification and Preference in Negro Children," which has been made widely accessible through T. M. Newcomb and E. L. Hartley's *Readings in Social Psychology* (New York, 1947), pp. 169–178.

African states has given a psychological "lift" to those American Negroes who still look more African than *metis,* but extreme Negro physical traits are still a source of inner disquiet—especially for women. (There is no equivalent in America of the African cult of *negritude* whose poets ideal-ize the black woman.) These negative esthetic appraisals are part of a larger stereotype-complex which equates Africa with primitiveness and savagery and considers Negro ancestry a "taint." A frontal assault on a world-wide scale is necessary to undo this propaganda of the slave era which still exists as a form of cultural lag which has lost even the excuse of the functional utility it once had in rationalizing an integral part of the Western economic system—Negro slavery.[33]

[33] Analyses of the genesis of the derogatory stereotypes of Africa and Africans may be found in Kenneth Little, *Negroes in Britain* (London, 1948), and Philip Curtin, *The Image of Africa* (Madison, Wisc., 1964). See also "Toward an Evaluation of African Societies," by St. Clair Drake, in *Africa Seen by American Negro Scholars* (New York, 1958).

KENNETH CLARK

The Psychology of the Ghetto

By the mid-sixties, most Americans knew about and perhaps sympathized with the articulated aspirations of blacks in the South. But, as the introduction to the previous selection pointed out, the slums of the big cities were still largely unknown, unseen, and unimagined. They remained so until the appearance of guns and Molotov cocktails riveted the country's attention on them. When the ghettos became visible, what Americans finally saw was shocking: malnourished children eating plaster from the walls to fill their empty stomachs; young men leading lives of suicidal crime; huge, impoverished families packed into roach- and rat-infested dwellings.

But these stark images of everyday life are just one facet of the black ghetto. The psychological malaise suffered by those who live within its rigid yet invis-

THE PSYCHOLOGY OF THE GHETTO From pp. 63–74, "The Psychology of the Ghetto" in *Dark Ghetto* by Kenneth B. Clark. Copyright © 1965 by Kenneth B. Clark. By permission of Harper & Row, Publishers, Incorporated.

ible boundaries is another. In the following selection, Kenneth Clark suggests that the cumulative experience of black people teaches them that they
are ignored and segregated because they are worthless and because white
society, while still controlling their lives, has no room for them. As he notes,
it is the ability of the ghetto to cause self-hatred that is ultimately most
destructive.

Human beings who are forced to live under ghetto conditions
and whose daily experience tells them that almost nowhere in society are
they respected and granted the ordinary dignity and courtesy accorded
to others will, as a matter of course, begin to doubt their own worth.
Since every human being depends upon his cumulative experiences with
others for clues as to how he should view and value himself, children
who are consistently rejected understandably begin to question and
doubt whether they, their family, and their group really deserve no more
respect from the larger society than they receive. These doubts become
the seeds of a pernicious self- and group-hatred, the Negro's complex
and debilitating prejudice against himself.

The preoccupation of many Negroes with hair straighteners, skin
bleachers, and the like illustrate this tragic aspect of American racial
prejudice—Negroes have come to believe in their own inferiority. In
recent years Negro men and women have rebelled against the constant
struggle to become white and have given special emphasis to their "Negroid" features and hair textures in a self-conscious acceptance of
"negritude"—a wholehearted embracing of the African heritage. But
whether a Negro woman uses hair straightener or whether she highlights
her natural hair texture by flaunting *au naturel* styles, whether a Negro
man hides behind a neat Ivy League suit or wears blue jeans defiantly in
the manner of the Student Nonviolent Coordinating Committee (SNCC),
each is still reacting primarily to the pervasive factor of race and still not
free to take himself for granted or to judge himself by the usual standards of personal success and character. It is still the white man's society
that governs the Negro's image of himself.

Fantasy Protections

Many Negroes live sporadically in a world of fantasy, and fantasy
takes different forms at different ages. In childhood the delusion is a
simple one—the child may pretend that he is really white. When Negro
children as young as three years old are shown white- and Negro-
appearing dolls or asked to color pictures of children to look like them-

selves, many of them tend to reject the dark-skinned dolls as "dirty" and "bad" or to color the picture of themselves a light color or a bizarre shade like purple. But the fantasy is not complete, for when asked to identify which doll is like themselves, some Negro children, particularly in the North, will refuse, burst into tears, and run away. By the age of seven most Negro children have accepted the reality that they are, after all, dark skinned. But the stigma remains; they have been forced to recognize themselves as inferior. Few if any Negroes ever fully lose that sense of shame and self-hatred.

To the Negro child the most serious injury seems to be in the concept of self-worth related directly to skin color itself. Because school is a central activity at this age, his sense of inferiority is revealed most acutely in his lack of confidence in himself as a student, lack of motivation to learn, and in problems of behavior—a gradual withdrawal or a growing rebellion. The effects of this early damage are difficult to overcome, for the child who never learns to read cannot become a success at a job or in a society where education and culture are necessary. In addition, there is the possibility that poor teaching, generally characteristic of the ghetto schools, tends to reinforce this sense of inferiority and to give it substance in the experience of inferior achievement. The cycle that leads to menial jobs and to broken homes has then begun; only the most drastic efforts at rehabilitation can break that cycle.

The obsession with whiteness continues past childhood and into adulthood. It stays with the Negro all his life. Haryou recorded a conversation between teen-age boys about their hair styles that reflected this obsession.

> *You know, if he go in there with his hair slick up like white, they might go for him better, you know.*
> They might use him for a broom or a mop.
> *Well, why do you wear "brushes?"*
> Why do I wear "brushes?" It's a blind, a front. Are you saying that I'm ignorant?
> *He's a playboy. He like to do his hair like that. He's ashamed of his own hair, you know. He feels bad that he's black and now he wants to be half and half. He wants to be a half-breed.*
> When your great granmammy was taken advantage of in the fields, what was happening then? Have you ever seen a light-skinned African? Have you ever seen an African your color?
> *No.*
> All right then; two bird dogs don't make nothing but a bird dog.
> *You don't have to go all the way, getting your hair slicked.*
> I don't have to go all the way black either, do I?
> *What are you going to do? You can't go all the way white.*

Teen-age Negroes often cope with the ghetto's frustrations by retreat-
ing into fantasies related chiefly to their role in society. There is, for
example, a fantasy employed by many marginal and antisocial teen-
agers, to pretend to knowledge about illicit activities and to a sexual
urbanity that they do not, really, have. They use as their models the
petty criminals of the ghetto, whose colorful, swaggering style of cool
bravado poses a peculiar fascination. Some pretend falsely to be pimps,
some to have contacts with numbers runners. Their apparent admiration
of these models is not total but reflects a curious combination of respect,
of contempt, and, fundamentally, of despair. Social scientists who rely
on questionnaires and superficial interviews must find a way to unravel
this tangled web of pretense if their conclusions are to be relevant.

Among the young men observed at Haryou, fantasy played a major
role. Many of these marginal, upward-striving teen-agers allowed others
to believe that they were college students. One young man told his
friends that he was a major in psychology. He had enrolled in the classes
of a Negro professor with whom he identified, and he described those
lectures in detail to his friends. The fact is that he was a dropout from
high school. Others dressed like college students and went to college
campuses where they walked among the students, attempting to feel a
part of a life they longed for and could not attain. Some carried attaché
cases wherever they went—often literally empty. One carried ordinary
books camouflaged by college bookcovers and pretended to "study" in
the presence of friends. Most of these young men were academically at
the fifth- or sixth-grade reading level; none was in college. Another
youngster who said he was in college planned to become a nuclear physi-
cist. He spoke most convincingly about his physics and math courses and
discussed the importance of Negroes' going into the field. Within a year,
however, he had been dropped for nonattendance from the evening session of the municipal college at which he was enrolled. He had not taken
even a first course in physics and had not been able to pass the elementary course in mathematics. He explained this failure in a complicated story and reported that he now intended to get a job. Later he
described his new job in the executive training program of a high-status
department store downtown. He was saving for college where he would
continue with nuclear physics. He carried an attaché case to work each
day. But the truth was that he was not in an executive training program
at all; he had a job as a stock clerk. Yet the fantasy was one of performance; there was truth in his dreams, for if he had been caught in
time he might have become a scientist. He did have the intellectual potential. But as a Negro, he had been damaged so early in the educational

process that not even the surge of motivation and his basic intelligence could now make his dreams effective. His motivation was sporadic and largely verbal; his plans were in the realm of delusion. To some, this form of social schizophrenia might seem comic, but a more appropriate response is tears, not laughter.

Sex and Status

In Negro adults the sense of inadequate self-worth shows up in lack of motivation to rise in their jobs or fear of competition with whites; in a sense of impotence in civic affairs demonstrated in lethargy toward voting, or community participation, or responsibility for others; in family instability and the irresponsibility rooted in hopelessness.

But, because, in American life, sex is, like business advancement, a prime criterion of success and hence of personal worth, it is in sexual behavior that the damage to Negro adults shows up in especially poignant and tragic clarity. The inconsistency between the white society's view of the Negro as inferior and its sexual exploitation of Negroes has seemed to its victims a degrading hypocrisy. Negroes observe that ever since slavery white men have regarded Negroes as inferior and have condemned interracial marriage while considering illicit sexual relationships with Negro women appropriate to their own higher status. The white man in America has, historically, arranged to have both white and Negro women available to him; he has claimed sexual priority with both and, in the process, he has sought to emasculate Negro men. Negro males could not hold their women, nor could they defend them. The white male tried to justify this restriction of meaningful competition with the paradoxical claim that Negro males were animal-like and brutish in their appetites and hence to be feared and shunned by white women. The ironic fact has been that, given the inferiority of their racial status, Negro males have had to struggle simply to believe themselves men. It has long been an "inside" bit of bitter humor among Negroes to say that Negro men should bribe their wives to silence.

Certain Negro women of status who have married white men report that their choice was related to their discovery that the Negro men they knew were inferior in status, interests, and sophistication and hence unsuitable as partners. Many problems of race and sex seem to follow this principle of the self-fulfilling prophecy. The Negro woman of status may see the Negro male as undesirable as a sexual partner precisely because of his low status in the eyes of whites. Unlike a white female who may reassure herself that the lower the status of the male, the more satisfying he is as a sexual partner, the upper-class Negro female tends to tie sexual desirability to status and exclude many Negro males as undesirable just because their status is inferior. It is a real question whether this "discovery" is based on fact or whether these women are not accepting the white society's assumption of the low status of Negro men and therefore expecting them to be weak. On the other hand, frustrated, thrill-seeking white males or females who have been told all their lives that Negroes are primitive and uninhibited may seek and find sexual fulfillment among the same Negroes who are cool, distant, or hostile in their relationship to other Negroes. In sexual matters it appears that those who expect weakness or gratification often find what they expect.

As Negro male self-esteem rises in the wake of the civil rights movement, one interesting incidental fact is that any Negro woman who is known to be the mistress of a white public official—and particularly any mistress of a segregationist—has been put under a growing pressure to break that relationship. In the past, Negroes tended to suppress their bitterness about such illicit relationships, accepting the white males' evaluation of himself and of them, and in a sense forgiving the Negro woman for submitting to the temptation of protection and economic gain. In the last decade, however, Negro mistresses of white officials are more openly rejected and are regarded as one of the "enemy."

White men were accustomed to possessing Negro women without marriage, but today the fact that a number of white men are married to Negro women of status, particularly those who are well known in the theatrical world, indicates that Negro women are placing higher value upon their own dignity than many other Negro women were permitted to in the past—and so are the white men who marry them. But, though a Negro woman may gain status by marrying into the white community, Negro men, even in the North, remain vulnerable if they seek to cross racial lines and to break this most fearsome of social taboos. When they have done so they have paid a tremendous price—lynching, murder, or a prison sentence in the South, social condemnation in the North—but, above all, the price of their own self-doubt and anxiety. The full complexity of social disapproval and personal doubt is difficult to resist psychologically even when the law allows and protects such nonconformist behavior.

The emerging, more affirmative sexual pride among Negro males may have as one of its consequences an increasing trend toward more open competition between white and Negro males for both white and Negro females. One of the further consequences would probably be an intensification of hostility of white males toward interracial couples and toward the white female participants, reflecting the desire on the part of the white male to preserve his own competitive advantage. One would expect him then to employ his economic and political power—without suspecting the fundamental basis of his antagonism—to maintain the inferior status of the Negro male for as long as possible. An important level of racial progress will have been reached when Negro and white men and women may marry anyone they choose, without punishment, ostracism, ridicule, or guilt.

The Negro Matriarchy and the Distorted Masculine Image

Sexual hierarchy has played a crucial role in the structure and pathology of the Negro family. Because of the system of slavery in which the Negro male was systematically used as a stud and the Negro female used primarily for purposes of breeding or for the gratification of the white male, the only source of family continuity was through the female, the dependence of the child on his mother. This pattern, together with the continued post-slavery relegation of the Negro male to menial and subservient status, has made the female the dominant person in the Negro family. Psychologically, the Negro male could not support his normal desire for dominance. For the most part he was not allowed to be a consistent wage earner; he could not present himself to his wife and children as a person who had the opportunity or the ability to compete successfully in politics, business, and industry. His doubts concerning his personal adequacy were therefore reinforced. He was compelled to base his self-esteem instead on a kind of behavior that tended to support a stereotyped picture of the Negro male—sexual impulsiveness, irresponsibility, verbal bombast, posturing, and compensatory achievement in entertainment and athletics, particularly in sports like boxing in which athletic prowess could be exploited for the gain of others. The Negro male was, therefore, driven to seek status in ways which seemed either antisocial, escapist, socially irresponsible. The pressure to find relief from his intolerable psychological position seems directly related to the continued high incidence of desertions and broken homes in Negro ghettos.

The Negro woman has, in turn, been required to hold the family together; to set the goals, to stimulate, encourage, and to protect both boys and girls. Her compensatory strength tended to perpetuate the weaker role of the Negro male. Negro boys had the additional problem of finding no strong male father figure upon which to model their own behavior, perhaps one of the reasons for the prevalent idea among marginal Negroes that it is not masculine to sustain a stable father or husband relationship with a woman. Many young men establish temporary liaisons with a number of different women with no responsibility toward any. Among Negro teen-agers the cult of going steady has never had the vogue it seems to have among white teen-agers; security for Negroes is found not in a relationship modeled after a stable family—for they have seen little of this in their own lives—but upon the relationship they observed in their own home: unstable and temporary liaisons. The marginal young Negro male tends to identify his masculinity with the number of girls he can attract. The high incidence of illegitimacy among Negro young people reflects this pervasive fact. In this compensatory distortion of the male image, masculinity is, therefore, equated with alleged sexual prowess.

The middle-class white and Negro male often separates women into two categories, good women with whom he will go steady and marry, and others with whom he has and will continue to have sexual relations alone. The lower-class Negro is, in a way, more sophisticated than either in his refusal to make undemocratic distinctions between "good girls" and "others." The consistently higher illegitimacy rate among Negroes is not a reflection of less virtue or greater promiscuity, but rather of the fact that the middle-class teen-agers are taught the use of contraceptives and learn how to protect themselves from the hazards of premarital and illicit sexual contacts. The middle-class girl is able to resort to abortions, or she gives birth secretly, surrendering the child for adoption. In the case of marginal young people, or the upwardly mobile Negro, what contraceptive ideas he has are unreliable; and rarely does the girl participate in protection, in part because it is taken as a sign of masculinity for the male to supervise such matters. Illegitimacy among these groups, therefore, is a consequence, in large part, of poverty and ignorance.

Among Negro middle-class families the attitude toward sex is vastly different from that among marginal and lower-class Negro groups. The middle-class Negro fears he will be identified with the Negro masses from whom he has escaped or tried to escape, and sex is a focal point of anxiety. The middle-class girl is often so rigidly protected that normal sexual behavior is inhibited, or she learns to be sophisticated about the use of contraceptives. For her, as for white middle-class girls, sex is tied to status and aspirations. She wants to make a good marriage—marriage to a white man might even be available—and the motivation to avoid illegitimate pregnancy is great.

The marginal young people in the ghetto, through their tentative and sporadic relationships, are seeking love, affection, and acceptance perhaps more desperately than young people elsewhere. Person-to-person relationships are, for many, a compensation for society's rejection. They are, in a sense, forced to be quite elemental in their demands, and sex becomes more important for them than even they realize. They act in a cavalier fashion about their affairs, trying to seem casual and cool, but it is clear nonetheless that they are dominated by the complexity of their needs.

The girl, like the boy, has no illusions. Unlike the middle-class girl who believes—or demands—that each relationship should be forever, and who tries to hold on to the boy, the marginal Negro lower-class girl is realistic about the facts of the situation. Nor does she expect to hold the boy. Sex is important to her, but it is not, as in middle-class society, a symbol of status, to be used to rise into a better family or a higher income bracket. The marginal Negro female uses her sex, instead, to gain personal affirmation. She is desired, and that is almost enough. The relationship, whatever its social and psychological limitations, is pure in the same sense as innocence—that is, it is not contaminated by other goals. For her and for the boy, sex is time-contained, with its own intrinsic worth and value, not animal in its expression, but related to the urgent human need for acceptance; it is sophisticated, not primitive.

This innocent sophistication includes the total acceptance of the child if a child comes. In the ghetto, the meaning of the illegitimate child is not ultimate disgrace. There is not the demand for abortion or for surrender of the child that one finds in more privileged communities. In the middle class, the disgrace of illegitimacy is tied to personal and family aspirations. In lower-class families, on the other hand, the girl loses only some of her already limited options by having an illegitimate child; she is not going to make a "better marriage" or improve her economic and social status either way. On the contrary, a child is a symbol of the fact that she is a woman, and she may gain from having something of her own. Nor is the boy who fathers an illegitimate child going to lose, for where is he going? The path to any higher status seems closed to him in any case.

Illegitimacy in the ghetto cannot be understood or dealt with in terms of punitive hostility, as in the suggestion that unwed mothers be denied welfare if illegitimacy is repeated. Such approaches obscure, with empty and at times hypocritical moralizing, the desperate yearning of the young for acceptance and identity, the need to be meaningful to some one else even for a moment without implication of a pledge of undying fealty and foreverness. If, when the girl becomes pregnant, the boy deserts or refuses to marry her, it is often because neither can sustain an intimate relationship; both seem incapable of the tenderness that continues beyond immediate gratification. Both may have a realistic, if unconscious, acceptance of the fact that nothing else is possible; to expect—to ask—for more would be to open oneself to the inevitable rejections, hurts, and frustrations. The persistent experience of rejection spills over into the anticipation and acceptance of rejection in a love relationship. This lack of illusion stems from the fact that there can be no illusion in any other area of life. To expose oneself further to the chances of failure in a sustained and faithful relationship is too large to risk. The intrinsic value of the relationship is the only value because there can be no other.

Among most lower-class Negroes, competition in sex is predominantly heterosexual and free. In the Negro middle class sexual freedom and expression are often identified with lower-class status, and many men and women are therefore governed chiefly by their inhibitions and cannot act freely in matters of sex. The men may be impotent, the women frigid, and both afflicted with guilt. Some compensate for the restraints on sexual adequacy and fulfillment through fantasies and boasting about a false prowess. Other middle-class Negro men retreat into noncommittal peripheral relationships with women, avoiding all alternatives—homosexuality, heterosexuality, or verbal bombasts—as risks requiring more ego strength than their resources permit. Instead, a blank and apathetic sexlessness dominates their lives. They withdraw from all commitment to another person seeking refuge from the dangers of personal vulnerability.

Considering the depth and the complexity of the need, aggressive sexual behavior may, for many of the racially damaged, make the difference between personal stability and instability. Until the lower class Negro is free to compete for and to win the socially acceptable rewards of middle-class society, the ghetto's pattern of venereal disease, illegitimacy, and family instability will remain unbroken. But when that time comes, no one can expect destructive sexual activity to cease abruptly. What is more likely is a shift to another, some would say "higher," level of behavior; then the Negro's sexual "misbehavior" will be indistinguishable in all respects from that of the respectables—with full participation in divorce, abortions, adultery, and the various forms of jaded and fashionable middle- and upper-class sexual explorations. There might even be the possibility of sexual fulfillment and health.

The World of the Harlem Child

James Baldwin and others have told of the dangerous maze that ghetto youths must run in reaching their maturity. The life of the criminal, the convict, the pimp, the addict—all can be permanent stops along the way; all are dead-ends. As the following excerpt from Claude Brown's autobiography shows, the primary question is one of survival. Having been initiated into the ghetto's precarious street life, those who do survive and are one day able to come to terms with the forces that affect them are, Brown suggests, very rare.

"Run!"

Where?

Oh, hell! Let's get out of here!

"Turk! Turk! I'm shot!"

I could hear Turk's voice calling from a far distance, telling me not to go into the fish-and-chips joint. I heard, but I didn't understand. The only thing I knew was that I was going to die.

I ran. There was a bullet in me trying to take my life, all thirteen years of it.

I climbed up on the bar yelling, "Walsh, I'm shot. I'm shot." I could feel the blood running down my leg. Walsh, the fellow who operated the fish-and-chips joint, pushed me off the bar and onto the floor. I couldn't move now, but I was still completely conscious.

Walsh was saying, "Git outta here, kid. I ain't got no time to play."

A woman was screaming, mumbling something about the Lord, and saying, "Somebody done shot that poor child."

Mama ran in. She jumped up and down, screaming like a crazy woman. I began to think about dying. The worst part of dying was thinking about the things and the people that I'd never see again. As I lay there trying to imagine what being dead was like, the policeman who had been trying to control Mama gave up and bent over me. He asked

THE WORLD OF THE HARLEM CHILD Reprinted with permission of The Macmillan Company from MANCHILD IN THE PROMISED LAND. Copyright © by Claude Brown 1965.

who had shot me. Before I could answer, he was asking me if I could hear him. I told him that I didn't know who had shot me and would he please tell Mama to stop jumping up and down. Every time Mama came down on that shabby floor, the bullet lodged in my stomach felt like a hot poker.

Another policeman had come in and was struggling to keep the crowd outside. I could see Turk in the front of the crowd. Before the cops came, he asked me if I was going to tell them that he was with me. I never answered. I looked at him and wondered if he saw who shot me. Then his question began to ring in my head: "Sonny, you gonna tell 'em I was with you?" I was bleeding on a dirty floor in a fish-and-chips joint, and Turk was standing there in the doorway hoping that I would die before I could tell the cops that he was with me. Not once did Turk ask me how I felt.

Hell, yeah, I thought, I'm gonna tell 'em.

It seemed like hours had passed before the ambulance finally arrived. Mama wanted to go to the hospital with me, but the ambulance attendant said she was too excited. On the way to Harlem Hospital, the cop who was riding with us asked Dad what he had to say. His answer was typical: "I told him about hanging out with those bad-ass boys." The cop was a little surprised. This must be a rookie, I thought.

The next day, Mama was at my bedside telling me that she had prayed and the Lord had told her that I was going to live. Mama said that many of my friends wanted to donate some blood for me, but the hospital would not accept it from narcotics users.

This was one of the worst situations I had ever been in. There was a tube in my nose that went all the way to the pit of my stomach. I was being fed intravenously, and there was a drain in my side. Everybody came to visit me, mainly out of curiosity. The girls were all anxious to know where I had gotten shot. They had heard all kinds of tales about where the bullet struck. The bolder ones wouldn't even bother to ask: they just snatched the cover off me and looked for themselves. In a few days, the word got around that I was in one piece.

On my fourth day in the hospital, I was awakened by a male nurse at about 3 A.M. When he said hello in a very ladyish voice, I thought that he had come to the wrong bed by mistake. After identifying himself, he told me that he had helped Dr. Freeman save my life. The next thing he said, which I didn't understand, had something to do with the hours he had put in working that day. He went on mumbling something about how tired he was and ended up asking me to rub his back. I had already told him that I was grateful to him for helping the doctor save my life. While I rubbed his back above the beltline, he kept pushing my hand down and saying, "Lower, like you are really grateful to me." I told him that I was sleepy from the needle a nurse had given me. He asked me to pat his behind. After I had done this, he left.

The next day when the fellows came to visit me, I told them about my early-morning visitor. Dunny said he would like to meet him. Tito joked about being able to get a dose of clap in the hospital. The guy with the tired back never showed up again, so the fellows never got a chance to meet him. Some of them were disappointed.

After I had been in the hospital for about a week, I was visited by another character. I had noticed a woman visiting one of the patients on the far side of the ward. She was around fifty-five years old, short and fat, and she was wearing old-lady shoes. While I wondered who this woman was, she started across the room in my direction. After she had introduced herself, she told me that she was visiting her son. Her son had been stabbed in the chest with an ice pick by his wife. She said that his left lung had been punctured, but he was doing fine now, and that Jesus was so-o-o good.

Her name was Mrs. Ganey, and she lived on 145th Street. She said my getting shot when I did "was the work of the Lord." My gang had been stealing sheets and bedspreads off clotheslines for months before I had gotten shot. I asked this godly woman why she thought it was the work of the Lord or Jesus or whoever. She began in a sermonlike tone, saying, "Son, people was gitting tired-a y'all stealing all dey sheets and spreads." She said that on the night that I had gotten shot, she baited her clothesline with two brand-new bedspreads, turned out all the lights in the apartment, and sat at the kitchen window waiting for us to show.

She waited with a double-barreled shotgun.

The godly woman said that most of our victims thought that we were winos or dope fiends and that most of them had vowed to kill us. At the end of the sermon, the godly woman said, "Thank the Lord I didn't shoot nobody's child." When the godly woman had finally departed, I thought, Thank the Lord for taking her away from my bed.

Later on that night, I was feeling a lot of pain and couldn't get to sleep. A nurse who had heard me moaning and groaning came over and gave me a shot of morphine. Less than twenty minutes later, I was deep into a nightmare.

I was back in the fish-and-chips joint, lying on the floor dying. Only, now I was in more pain than before, and there were dozens of Mamas around me jumping up and screaming. I could feel myself dying in a rising pool of blood. The higher the blood rose the more I died.

I dreamt about the boy who Rock and big Stoop had thrown off that roof on 149th Street. None of us had stayed around to see him hit the ground, but I just knew that he died in a pool of blood too. I wished that he would stop screaming, and I wished that Mama would stop screaming. I wished they would let me die quietly.

As the screams began to die out—Mama's and the boy's—I began to think about the dilapidated old tenement building that I lived in, the one that still had the words "pussy" and "fuck you" on the walls where I had scribbled them years ago. The one where the super, Mr. Lawson, caught my little brother writing some more. Dad said he was going to kill Pimp for writing on that wall, and the way he was beating Pimp with that ironing cord, I thought he would. Mama was crying, I was crying, and Pimp had been crying for a long time. Mama said that he was too young to be beaten like that. She ran out of the house and came back with a cop, who stopped Dad from beating Pimp.

I told Pimp not to cry any more, just to wait until I got big: I was going to kill Dad, and he could help me if he wanted to.

This was the building where Mr. Lawson had killed a man for peeing in the hall. I remembered being afraid to go downstairs the morning after Mr. Lawson had busted that man's head open with a baseball bat. I could still see blood all over the hall. This was the building where somebody was always shooting out the windows in the hall. They were usually shooting at Johnny D., and they usually missed. This was the building that I loved more than anyplace else in the world. The thought that I would never see this building again scared the hell out of me.

I dreamt about waking up in the middle of the night seven years before and thinking that the Germans or the Japs had come and that the loud noises I heard were bombs falling. Running into Mama's room, I squeezed in between her and Dad at the front window. Thinking that we were watching an air raid, I asked Dad where the sirens were and why the streets lights were on. He said, "This ain't no air raid—just a whole lotta niggers gone fool. And git the hell back in that bed!" I went back to bed, but I couldn't go to sleep. The loud screams in the street and the crashing sound of falling plate-glass windows kept me awake for hours. While I listened to the noise, I imagined bombs falling and people running through the streets screaming. I could see mothers running with babies in their arms, grown men running over women and children to save their own lives, and the Japs stabbing babies with bayonets, just like in the movies. I thought, Boy, I sure wish I was out there. I bet the Stinky brothers are out there. Danny and Butch are probably out there having all the fun in the world.

The next day, as I was running out of the house without underwear or socks on, I could hear Mama yelling, "Boy, come back here and put a hat or something on your head!" When I reached the stoop, I was knocked back into the hall by a big man carrying a ham under his coat. While I looked up at him, wondering what was going on, he reached down with one hand and snatched me up, still holding the ham under his coat with his other hand. He stood me up against a wall and ran into the hall with his ham. Before I had a chance to move, other men came running through the hall carrying cases of whiskey, sacks of flour, and cartons of cigarettes. Just as I unglued myself from the wall and started out the door for the second time, I was bowled over again. This time by a cop with a gun in his hand. He never stopped, but after he had gone a couple of yards into the hall, I heard him say, "Look out, kid." On the third try, I got out of the building. But I wasn't sure that this was my street. None of the stores had any windows left, and glass was everywhere. It seemed that all the cops in the world were on 145th Street and Eighth Avenue that day. The cops were telling everybody to move on, and everybody was talking about the riot. I went over to a cop and asked him what a riot was. He told me to go on home. The next cop I asked told me that a riot was what had happened the night before. Putting two and two together I decided that a riot was "a whole lotta niggers gone fool."

I went around the corner to Butch's house. After I convinced him that I was alone, he opened the door. He said that Kid and Danny were in the kitchen. I saw Kid sitting on the floor with his hand stuck way down in a gallon jar of pickled pigs' ears. Danny was cooking some bacon at the stove, and Butch was busy hiding stuff. It looked as though these guys had stolen a whole grocery store. While I joined the feast, they took turns telling me about the riot. Danny and Kid hadn't gone home the night before; they were out following the crowds and looting.

My only regret was that I had missed the excitement. I said, "Why don't we have another riot tonight? Then Butch and me can get in it."

Danny said that there were too many cops around to have a riot now. Butch said that they had eaten up all the bread and that he was going to steal some more. I asked if I could come along with him, and he said that I could if I promised to do nothing but watch. I promised, but we both knew that I was lying.

When we got to the street, Butch said he wanted to go across the street and look at the pawnshop. I tagged along. Like many of the stores where the rioters had been, the pawnshop had been set afire. The firemen had torn down a sidewall getting at the fire. So Butch and I just walked in where the wall used to be. Everything I picked up was broken or burned or both. My feet kept sinking into the wet furs that had been burned and drenched. The whole place smelled of smoke and was as dirty as a Harlem gutter on a rainy day. The cop out front yelled to us to get out of there. He only had to say it once.

After stopping by the seafood joint and stealing some shrimp and oysters, we went to what was left of Mr. Gordon's grocery store. Butch just walked in, picked up a loaf of bread, and walked out. He told me to come on, but I ignored him and went into the grocery store instead. I picked up two loaves of bread and walked out. When I got outside, a cop looked at me, and I ran into a building and through the backyard to Butch's house. Running through the backyard, I lost all the oysters that I had; when I reached Butch's house, I had only two loaves of bread and two shrimp in my pocket.

Danny, who was doing most of the cooking, went into the street to steal something to drink. Danny, Butch, and Kid were ten years old, four years older than I. Butch was busy making sandwiches on the floor, and Kid was trying to slice up a loaf of bologna. I had never eaten shrimp, but nobody seemed to care, because they refused to cook it for me. I told Butch that I was going to cook it myself. He said that there was no more lard in the house and that I would need some grease.

I looked around the house until I came up with some Vaseline hair pomade. I put the shrimp in the frying pan with the hair grease, waited until they had gotten black and were smoking, then took them out and made a sandwich. A few years later, I found out that shrimp were supposed to be shelled before cooking. I ate half of the sandwich and hated shrimp for years afterward.

The soft hand tapping on my face to wake me up was Jackie's. She and Della had been to a New Year's Eve party. Jackie wanted to come by the hospital and kiss me at midnight. This was the only time in my life that I ever admitted being glad to see Jackie. I asked them about the party, hoping that they would stay and talk to me for a while. I was afraid that if I went back to sleep, I would have another bad dream.

The next thing I knew, a nurse was waking me up for breakfast. I didn't recall saying good night to Jackie and Della, so I must have fallen asleep while they were talking to me. I thought about Sugar, how nice she was, and how she was a real friend. I knew she wanted to be my girl friend, and I liked her a lot. But what would everybody say if I had a buck-toothed girl friend. I remembered Knoxie asking me how I kissed her. That question led to the first fight I'd had with Knoxie in years. No, I couldn't let Sugar be my girl. It was hard enough having her as a friend.

The next day, I asked the nurse why she hadn't changed my bed linen, and she said because they were evicting me. I had been in the hospital for eleven days, but I wasn't ready to go home. I left the hospital on January 2 and went to a convalescent home in Valhalla, New York. After I had been there for three weeks, the activity director took me aside and told me that I was going to New York City to see a judge and that I might be coming back. The following morning, I left to see that judge, but I never got back to Valhalla.

I stood there before Judge Pankin looking solemn and lying like a professional. I thought that he looked too nice to be a judge. A half hour after I had walked into the courtroom, Judge Pankin was telling me that he was sending me to the New York State Training School for Boys. The judge said that he thought I was a chronic liar and that he hoped I would be a better boy when I came out. I asked him if he wanted me to thank him. Mama stopped crying just long enough to say, "Hush your mouth, boy."

Mama tried to change the judge's mind by telling him that I had already been to Wiltwyck School for Boys for two and a half years. And before that, I had been ordered out of the state for at least one year. She said that I had been away from my family too much; that was why I was always getting into trouble.

The judge told Mama that he knew what he was doing and that one day she would be grateful to him for doing it.

I had been sent away before, but this was the first time I was ever afraid to go. When Mama came up to the detention room in Children's Court, I tried to act as though I wasn't afraid. After I told her that Warwick and where I was going were one and the same, Mama began to cry, and so did I.

Most of the guys I knew had been to Warwick and were too old to go back. I knew that there were many guys up there I had mistreated. The Stinky brothers were up there. They thought that I was one of the guys who had pulled a train on their sister in the park the summer before. Bumpy from 144th Street was up there. I had shot him in the leg with a zip gun in a rumble only a few months earlier. There were many guys up there I used to bully on the streets and at Wiltwyck, guys I had sold tea leaves to as pot. There were rival gang members up there who just hated my name. All of these guys were waiting for me to show. The word was out that I couldn't fight any more—that I had slowed down since I was shot and that a good punch to the stomach would put my name in the undertaker's book.

When I got to the Youth House, I tried to find out who was up at Warwick that I might know. Nobody knew any of the names I asked about. I knew that if I went up to Warwick in my condition, I'd never live to get out. I had a reputation for being a rugged little guy. This meant that I would have at least a half-dozen fights in the first week of my stay up there.

It seemed the best thing for me to do was to cop out on the nut. For the next two nights, I woke up screaming and banging on the walls. On the third day, I was sent to Bellevue for observation. This meant that I wouldn't be going to Warwick for at least twenty-eight days.

While I was in Bellevue, the fellows would come down and pass notes to me through the doors. Tito and Turk said they would get bagged and sent to Warwick by the time I got there. They were both bagged a week later for smoking pot in front of the police station. They were both sent to Bellevue. Two weeks after they showed, I went home. The judge still wanted to send me to Warwick, but Warwick had a full house, so he sent me home for two weeks.

The day before I went back to court, I ran into Turk, who had just gotten out of Bellevue. Tito had been sent to Warwick, but Turk had gotten a walk because his sheet wasn't too bad. I told him I would probably be sent to Warwick the next day. Turk said he had run into Bucky in Bellevue. He told me that he and Tito had voted Bucky out of the clique. I told him that I wasn't going for it because Bucky was my man from short-pants days. Turk said he liked him too, but what else could he do after Bucky had let a white boy beat him in the nutbox? When I heard this, there was nothing I could do but agree with Turk. Bucky had to go. That kind of news spread fast, and who wanted to be in a clique with a stud who let a paddy boy beat him?

The next day, I went to the Youth House to wait for Friday and the trip to Warwick. As I lay in bed that night trying to think of a way out, I began to feel sorry for myself. I began to blame Danny, Butch, and Kid for my present fate. I told myself that I wouldn't be going to Warwick if they hadn't taught me how to steal, play hookey, make homemades, and stuff like that. But then I thought, aw, hell, it wasn't their fault—as a matter of fact, it was a whole lotta fun.

I remembered sitting on the stoop with Danny, years before, when a girl came up and started yelling at him. She said that her mother didn't want her brother to hang out with Danny any more, because Danny had taught her brother how to play hookey. When the girl had gone down the street, I asked Danny what hookey was. He said it was a game he would teach me as soon as I started going to school.

Danny was a man of his word. He was my next-door neighbor, and he rang the doorbell about 7:30 A.M. on the second day of school. Mama thanked him for volunteering to take me to school. Danny said he would have taught me to play hookey the day before, but he knew that Mama would have to take me to school on the first day. As we headed toward the backyard to hide our books, Danny began to explain the great game of hookey. It sounded like lots of fun to me. Instead of going to school, we would go all over the city stealing, sneak into a movie, or go up on a roof and throw bottles down into the street. Danny suggested that we start the day off by waiting for Mr. Gordon to put out his vegetables; we could steal some sweet potatoes and cook them in the backyard. I was sorry I hadn't started school sooner, because hookey sure was a lot of fun.

Before I began going to school, I was always in the streets with Danny, Kid, and Butch. Sometimes, without saying a word, they would all start to run like hell, and a white man was always chasing them. One morning as I entered the backyard where all the hookey players went to draw up an activity schedule for the day, Butch told me that Danny and Kid had been caught by Mr. Sands the day before. He went on to warn me about Mr. Sands, saying Mr. Sands was that white man who was always chasing somebody and that I should try to remember what he looked like and always be on the lookout for him. He also warned me not to try to outrun Mr. Sands, "because that cat is fast." Butch said, "When you see him, head for a backyard or a roof. He won't follow you there."

During the next three months, I stayed out of school twenty-one days. Dad was beating the hell out of me for playing hookey, and it was no fun being in the street in the winter, so I started going to school regularly. But when spring rolled around, hookey became my favorite game again. Mr. Sands was known to many parents in the neighborhood as the truant officer. He never caught me in the street, but he came by my house many mornings to escort me to class. This was one way of getting me to school, but he never found a way to keep me there. The moment my teacher took her eyes off me, I was back on the street. Every time Dad got a card from Mr. Sands, I got bruises and welts from Dad. The beatings had only a temporary effect on me. Each time, the beatings got worse; and each time, I promised never to play hookey again. One time I kept that promise for three whole weeks.

The older guys had been doing something called "catting" for years. That catting was staying away from home all night was all I knew about the term. Every time I asked one of the fellows to teach me how to cat, I was told I wasn't old enough. As time went on, I learned that guys catted when they were afraid to go home and that they slept everywhere but in comfortable places. The usual places for catting were subway trains, cellars, unlocked cars, under a friend's bed, and in vacant news-stands.

One afternoon when I was eight years old, I came home after a busy day of running from the police, truant officer, and storekeepers. The first thing I did was to look in the mailbox. This had become a habit with me even though I couldn't read. I was looking for a card, a yellow card. That yellow card meant that I would walk into the house and Dad would be waiting for me with his razor strop. He would usually be eating and would pause just long enough to say to me, "Nigger, you got a ass whip-pin' comin'." My sisters, Carole and Margie, would cry almost as much as I would while Dad was beating me, but this never stopped him. After each beating I got, Carole, who was two years older than I, would beg me to stop playing hookey. There were a few times when I thought I would stop just to keep her and Margie, my younger sister, from crying so much. I decided to threaten Carole and Margie instead, but this didn't help. I continued to play hookey, and they continued to cry on the days that the yellow card got home before I did.

Generally, I would break open the mailbox, take out the card, and throw it away. Whenever I did this, I'd have to break open two or three other mailboxes and throw away the contents, just to make it look good.

This particular afternoon, I saw a yellow card, but I couldn't find any-thing to break into the box with. Having some matches in my pockets, I decided to burn the card in the box and not bother to break the box open. After I had used all the matches, the card was not completely burned. I stood there getting more frightened by the moment. In a little while, Dad would be coming home; and when he looked in the mailbox, anywhere would be safer than home for me.

This was going to be my first try at catting out. I went looking for somebody to cat with me. My crime partner, Buddy, whom I had played hookey with that day, was busily engaged in a friendly rock fight when I found him in Colonial Park. When I suggested that we go up on the hill and steal some newspapers, Buddy lost interest in the rock fight.

We stole papers from newsstands and sold them on the subway trains until nearly 1 A.M. That was when the third cop woke us and put us off the train with the usual threat. They would always promise to beat us over the head with a billy and lock us up. Looking back, I think the cops took their own threats more seriously than we did. The third cop put us off the Independent Subway at Fifty-ninth Street and Columbus Circle. I wasn't afraid of the cops, but I didn't go back into the subway —the next cop might have taken me home.

In 1945, there was an Automat where we came out of the subway. About five slices of pie later, Buddy and I left the Automat in search of a place to stay the night. In the center of the Circle, there were some old lifeboats that the Navy had put on display.

Buddy and I slept in the boat for two nights. On the third day, Buddy was caught ringing a cash register in a five-and-dime store. He was sent to Children's Center, and I spent the third night in the boat alone. On the fourth night, I met a duty-conscious cop, who took me home. That ended my first catting adventure.

Dad beat me for three consecutive days for telling what he called "that dumb damn lie about sleeping in a boat on Fifty-ninth Street." On the fourth day, I think he went to check my story out for himself. Anyhow, the beating stopped for a while, and he never mentioned the boat again.

Before long, I was catting regularly, staying away from home for weeks at a time. Sometimes the cops would pick me up and take me to a Children's Center. The Centers were located all over the city. At some time in my childhood, I must have spent at least one night in all of them except the one on Staten Island.

The procedure was that a policeman would take me to the Center in the borough where he had picked me up. The Center would assign someone to see that I got a bath and was put to bed. The following day, my parents would be notified as to where I was and asked to come and claim me. Dad was always in favor of leaving me where I was and saying good riddance. But Mama always made the trip. Although Mama never failed to come for me, she seldom found me there when she arrived. I had no trouble getting out of Children's Centers, so I seldom stayed for more than a couple of days.

When I was finally brought home—sometimes after weeks of catting —Mama would hide my clothes or my shoes. This would mean that I couldn't get out of the house if I should take a notion to do so. Anyway, that's how Mama had it figured. The truth of the matter is that these measures only made getting out of the house more difficult for me. I would have to wait until one of the fellows came around to see me.

After hearing my plight, he would go out and round up some of the gang, and they would steal some clothes and shoes for me. When they had the clothes and shoes, one of them would come to the house and let me know. About ten minutes later, I would put on my sister's dress, climb down the back fire escape, and meet the gang with the clothes.

If something was too small or too large, I would go and steal the right size. This could only be done if the item that didn't fit was not the shoes. If the shoes were too small or large, I would have trouble running in them and probably get caught. So I would wait around in the backyard while someone stole me a pair.

Mama soon realized that hiding my clothes would not keep me in the house. The next thing she tried was threatening to send me away until I was twenty-one. This was only frightening to me at the moment of hearing it. Ever so often, either Dad or Mama would sit down and have a heart-to-heart talk with me. These talks were very moving. I always promised to mend my bad ways. I was always sincere and usually kept the promise for about a week. During these weeks, I went to school every day and kept my stealing at a minimum. By the beginning of the second week, I had reverted back to my wicked ways, and Mama would have to start praying all over again.

The neighborhood prophets began making prophecies about my life-span. They all had me dead, buried, and forgotten before my twenty-first birthday. These predictions were based on false tales of policemen shooting at me, on truthful tales of my falling off a trolley car into the midst of oncoming automobile traffic while hitching a ride, and also on my uncontrollable urge to steal. There was much justification for these prophecies. By the time I was nine years old, I had been hit by a bus, thrown into the Harlem River (intentionally), hit by a car, severely beaten with a chain. And I had set the house afire.

HUEY P. NEWTON

A Message

Since the days of slavery, black families have been fragmented and dislocated. Ghetto life has increased this tendency. It is estimated that 25% of these families, excluding those with illegitimate children, are headed by women whose men are absent either because of divorce, desertion, or separation. Approximately 6% of the nation's professional women are black, while just 1% of its professional men are black. Black women have a higher educational level and employment ratio. In a culture that values masculine primacy, black men are often not the breadwinners in their own families.

Such statistics are often used to prove the laziness of the black man. However, at the core of the problem is a society and a set of attitudes which, since slavery, have tried systematically to emasculate the black man and rob him of his self-esteem. In the following selection, Huey P. Newton, founder and leader of the Black Panther Party, explores the painful ambiguity of the black man's position in contemporary society.

THE LOWER SOCIO-ECONOMIC BLACK MALE IS A MAN OF CONFUSION. He faces a hostile environment and is not sure that it is not his own sins that have attracted the hostilities of society. All his life he has been taught (explicitly and implicitly) that he is an inferior approximation of humanity. As a man, he finds himself void of those things that bring respect and a feeling of worthiness. He looks around for something to blame for his situation, but because he is not sophisticated regarding the socio-economic teachings, he ultimately blames himself.

When he was a child, his parents told him that they were not affluent because "we didn't have the opportunity to become educated," or "we did not take advantage of the educational opportunities that were offered to us." They tell their children that things will be different for them if they are educated and skilled, but that there is absolutely nothing other than this occasional warning (and often not even this) to stimulate edu-

A MESSAGE   By Huey P. Newton. From *Black Fire,* Volume III, Number 12, May 3, 1969, published by the Black Student Union of San Francisco State College.

cation. Black people are great worshippers of education, even the lower socio-economic Black person, but at the same time, they are afraid of exposing themselves to it. They are afraid because they are vulnerable to having their fears verified; perhaps they will find that they can't compete with white students. The Black person tells himself that he could have done much more if he had really wanted to. The fact is, of course, that the assumed educational opportunities were never available to the lower socio-economic Black person due to the unique position assigned him in life.

It is a two-headed monster that haunts this man. First, his attitude is that he lacks innate ability to cope with the socio-economic problems confronting him, and second, he tells himself that he has the ability but he simply has not felt strongly enough to try to acquire the skills needed to manipulate his environment. In a desperate effort to assume self-respect, he rationalizes that he is lethargic; in this way, he denies a possible lack of innate ability. If he openly attempts to discover his abilities, he and others may see him for what he is—or is not, and this is the real fear. He then withdraws into the world of the invisible, but not without a struggle. He may attempt to make himself visible by processing his hair, acquiring a "boss mop," or driving a long car, even though he can't afford it. He may father several illegitimate children by several different women in order to display his masculinity. But in the end, he realizes that he is ineffectual in his efforts.

Society responds to him as a thing, a beast, a nonentity, something to be ignored or stepped on. He is asked to respect laws that do not respect him. He is asked to digest a code of ethics that acts upon him but not for him. He is confused and in a constant state of rage, of shame and doubt. This psychological set permeates all his interpersonal relationships. It determines his view of the social system. His psychological set developments have been prematurely arrested. This doubt begins at a very early age and continues through his life. The parents pass it on to the child and the social system reinforces the fear, the shame, and the doubt.

In the third or fourth grade he may find that he shares the classroom with white students, but when the class is engaged in reading exercises, all the Black students find themselves in a group at a table reserved for slow readers. This may be quite an innocent effort on the part of the school system. The teacher may not realize that the Black students feared (in fact, feel certain) that Black means dumb and white means smart. The children do not realize that the head start the children got at home is what accounts for the situation. It is generally accepted that the child is the father of the man; this holds true for the lower socio-economic Black people.

With whom, with what can he, a man, identify? As a child he had no permanent male figure with whom to identify; as a man, he sees nothing in society with which he can identify as an extension of himself. His life is built on mistrust, shame, doubt, guilt, inferiority, role confusion, isolation and despair. He feels that he is something less than a man, and it is evident in his conversation: "the white man is 'THE MAN', he got everything, and he knows everything, and a nigger ain't nothing."

In a society where a man is valued according to occupation and material possessions, he is unskilled and more often than not, either marginally employed or unemployed. Often his wife (who is able to secure a job as a maid cleaning for white people) is the breadwinner. He is therefore viewed as quite worthless by his wife and children. He is ineffectual both in and out of the home. He cannot provide for or protect his family. He is invisible, a non-entity. Society will not acknowledge him as a man. He is a consumer and not a producer. He is dependent upon the white man ('THE MAN') to feed his family, to give him a job, educate his children, serve as the model that he tries to emulate. He is dependent and he hates 'THE MAN' and he hates himself. Who is he? Is he a very old adolescent or is he the slave he used to be?

What did he do to be so BLACK and blue?

MARY FRANCES GREENE AND ORLETTA RYAN

What It's Like to Go to School

While the civil rights movement was reaching its apex of achievement in the South, the "white backlash" was beginning in the North. Black parents began

WHAT IT'S LIKE TO GO TO SCHOOL   Composite of excerpts from *The Schoolchildren: Growing Up in the Slums* by Mary Frances Greene and Orletta Ryan. © Copyright 1964, 1966 by Mary Frances Greene and Orletta Ryan. Reprinted by permission of Pantheon Books, a division of Random House, Inc.

protesting, as they continue to do, against both the *de facto* segregation of black students and the poor conditions of black schools. Many whites responded by organizing into committees to support the sanctity of "the neighborhood school" and to work against programs to achieve school integration through busing. Much of this dialogue, however, has been lost on schools in the heart of the ghetto. They continue to be understaffed, underfinanced, underequipped and unprepared. In the ghetto, as the following report of black schoolchildren's conversation shows, the paramount fact of the child's life remains what it has always been—after class is dismissed, he returns to a world of violence and chaos.

Religion

RICHARD'S CHURCH SENDS HIM TO A SUMMER CAMP SPONSORED BY middle-class Negro members of a small community in Michigan. Asked what they'd think of the writing on third- to fourth-floor stair wall, he says, "Oh, those people wouldn't even know one of those words on the wall. They are church people!"

Curtis brings in a cross at lunch hour he says he found somewhere.

VERNON.   That's a Catholic cross.

CURTIS.   It is not!

VERNON.   It is so, they a body on it, it's Catholic.

(Others are ducking at Curtis's chest to see the cross, and imitate vomiting at the sight.)

RICHARD.   Well, you got to have a cross in my church too! A big cross is at that door.

JOSIE (calls out).   You get communion in that church, boy?

HAROLD.   We do! We gets crackers and cherry pop!

RUBY.   You been *confirmed* in that church?

RICHARD.   I been everything. I been saved. If I gets bumped in the ass by a cab, that cab driver just got to take one look at this card. (Shows card; card gives prescription, ending ". . . and must respect and speak well to members of our race (colored).") We got a lot of baptism too, but not like on 116th Street. I know they got complete diversion there. You got to wear a white gown to the floor for that.

JOSIE (hanging on to Leanore's chair in excitement). *I'm gonna get me that diversion,* my sisters had it. They look so beau-ti-ful in their gowns! The reverend hold you head so you don'ts drownd.

—In my church in the South, when the singing gets glorious, everyone faints!

—Oh, that's *Pentacostal* Church. Christian reform don't do that kinda thing.

VERNON.   In my church everyone gets communion, but you gots to be eleven.

RUBY.   When you eats the crackers, that's eatin up Baby Jesus.

VERNON.   If you go to church every week, my preacher will send you to camp for two weeks. You gotta bring four T shirts and swimming trunks.

RICHARD.   Well, I am a *Christian*. The Catholics prays to the idol Mary. But it ain't wrong to be a Catholic, if it's okay for you. My preacher says I'm going to have salvation, and he musta *read my mind* cause that's just what I got in minds for myself. I go to Sunday School twice a week, and I learn about Adam and Eve—Adam and Eve was stark naked; and the second worst sin. But I forgets what that is. And that's why I gets to go to Michigan in the summer, with the light-skinned Negro people—they never lock doors in Michigan and no one steals nothing.

RUBY.   That's nothing. I'm Baptist and we goes to Atlantic City, but I never heard of Michigan. We goes with lightskin people and we sing beautiful hymns that makes everyone smile.

Addicts

A drizzling day. Richard arrives half an hour late to school. During the night, addicts had stumbled onto a pile of broken plate glass on his street, then into his building to sleep. His father, the superintendent, had found the hall so full of blood at early dawn he'd gone to the police station about getting the addicts out.

RICHARD.   The lieutenant told him, "Dial my private number. I'll send every man in the place out."

MONTY.   They gets blood on the floor because they misses their bein, too.

RICHARD.   They sleep on garbage buckets in the basement. My father tries to get 'em out with his Derringer; but sometimes they get so high they can't get off the piles.

REGGIE.   But they can't help theirself. It's their life. They don't want to hurt no one, just theirselfs.

MONTY.   You has to be so careful with that needle, and be sure you go in your bein, and carry a baby's nipple over the tube or you hurt someone.

REGGIE.   They feel they in the snow—walking in tennis shoes in the snow. They feel like they in another world. I don't mind if I was an addict—they *warm* in winter.

RICHARD.   The reverend at our church, he tried for years to he'p them, but he say he about ready to quit. They do be so greedy, the reverend had four chickens for Christmas for the poor, and the addicts come and eat them all.

RUBY.   Children must stay away from them, they kisses you in a funny way, they wants to expose you. They splits open some candy and fill it with gray powder. They wants you to get funny with them.

MONTY.   An addict always brings his equipment with him. Cover his needle with a *baby's nipple,* and he need a big black belt for his arm so he can set that needle right in his bein.

RICHARD.   They cut when they sees the cops. The cops swing up they billies; they poke to the addicts' chin.

VIRGIL.   Oh, there was an addic', and I was *so* scared. I had my mother's twenty dollars; I was going down to the store. He came up behind me and put a knife on me and say, "Don't turn aroun', *don't breathe."* Sometimes I'm nutty, and I run away! And I was lucky. You gets it right *there.* (Shows on his back.)

Addiction is higher than anything in any book, Mrs. Weiss says. Relatives of school aides may be hooked; parents may be. "In junior high, children go on the needle. Children with their heads down in cafeteria, falling asleep in class. I know of a fifteen-year-old in Jefferson, sister of one of our kids, whose mother is on the needle and got the girl hooked —so she'd keep quiet."

Every doorway in the morning—men with brown paper bags and bottles. Addicts high, standing, leaning, staring. Not drinking. Fifteen in a block on the way to school. Signs in front of every building: "No Loitering, Order of Police." Three addicts are stripped naked at noon on a side street. The police horse off a square around them. Children watch on the way back from lunch as the cops go up each rectum with rubber gloves. ("They private places, they might hi' it.")

Eight bent over a burning ashcan a block down from school, warming gray hands. All night. Someone tips alcohol on the can; blue flame licks up for a moment.

A young addict puts his head in a cab:

ADDICT.   Gimme a dime, that's a' I wan', a dime. . . . Okay, then gi' a cigarette.

DRIVER.   Buddy, I just don't have it.

ADDICT.   Then fuck off.

MONTY.   They keeps moving, and stay together so the cops don't see. They take lights from the hallways; that's why they always so dark. It is *expensive!* A bag of reefers, that cost a buck! And they shares them in the hall.

JOSIE.   You on'y needs blue pills now. The doctor sell them to you for a quarter.—In my block, Brother and Little John are addic'. Little John he's nineteen, he pretty and very light. Has processed hair.

REGGIE.   A lady addic' in our block. I don't know how she have her life. She's an addic'; and she's a lady. There's *nothin* will stop an addic' that needs a fix. They'll cut a head off and mess around with the body. They *gots to do somethin* . . . they won't stop at nothin. But when they attacks you, you gotta fight back. *You gotta do somethin.* I'm gonna pick up detective work when I grow up. You get a Derringer. I'd have my Derringer here, right under my arm. I'd say, "Excuse me, you need a cigarette?" to the addic', and reach up and grab down my Derringer!

RICHARD.   I go to my grandmother's building, she live on the top floor. I like that roof of hers, there's pigeons flyin, but addicts up there too! It's scary! I take my Pepsi bottle and break the top off. Then I'm safe.

VERNON.   I always carry my broken bottle when I go out to someone's building. But they's no addicts in my building.

REGGIE.   You jivin? 122 is full of addicts.

VERNON.   Well, they *don't touch my grandmother.* No addict in our block'd touch my grandmother. They calls her Maw.

RICHARD.   Hey, Mrs. Weiss, that a real diamond or glass?

MRS. WEISS.   Hmmph . . . it is quite real.

RICHARD.   You shouldn' wear that, some addict take and get it off you.

MRS. WEISS.   He'd have to take my arm off to get that, Richard.

RICHARD.   Well that's just what he's gonna do. He's gonna take off your arm if he needs that fix.

NOAH.   My father was addic', but he went down to Florida, got hisself cured. No addic' can work, no addic' ever been known to work, except maybe when he were a small child.

REGGIE. You has to put on coconut butter to cover up the marks cause you can' go round with those hole in you' arm, everyone'll know you.

MALCOLM. But you can't just *start* addict. First sniffin glue; you 'bout nine. Later you goes on reefers on the roof with older kids. My brother smokes reefers but he won't let me come up, he say he'll cut my ass.

—About ten hangs out on *my* block. My super keep them moving in our hall. We live on the first floor, my mom got a police lock on our door. But it's *scary*. They call in soft through the keyhole when my mom be out.

—*My* mother don't answer that door at night. She says Who's there? but don't open it. And she keeps that can of lye by the door.

—My mother too!

MALCOLM. Lye! But you suppose' to use that for the stuffed pipes.

—No, you got to keep that lye. But people do anything with it. A lady in my block, she threw lye in a man's face. He owed her nine dollars, and she needed that. He said, "You better not throw that, there's kids around here." But she didn't even hear that, she was too crazy for her money. Threw it at him and he starts to scream, "My eyes, my eyes!" And the ambulance come, and a lot of people was there. They took him away, I don't know where. But I know when he comes out of that hospital, he's gonna shot her.

.   .   .

Leanore

She spends a morning cleaning her desk whenever my back's turned. Her head goes all the way into the desk with Kleenex; many trips up to the wastebasket with things she's throwing out, into the cabinet to get paste while I'm out in the hall chasing Curtis. She pastes a picture inside her desk top to give it a home atmosphere. "Please get your head out of there, Leanore. Will you, please?" Comes out banging it so hard, it sends shivers through William, Roger, and Monty. "Pardon meee?" Opens her book angrily.

HAROLD (reading). Is . . . th-th-is—

LEANORE (reads at double speed). Eagle befriends this baby bear. Now Eagle has *two* pets. Is *this* the baby bear? *Mama Bear's baby bear?*

(Tears her math paper into one thousand pieces and throws the confetti over her shoulder.)

"I'm going to the washroom," she calls, and walks out. Returns in half an hour.

"No lunch, Leanore, until you finish the math paper."

"You're not keeping me from any lunch—my mother'd love to hear about that. You want a paper? Here, I'll give you a paper." (Tosses blank paper on desk.)

"Well, your mother hasn't answered any of three notes; I should see your mother. Straighten up this afternoon, or I go home with you."

She laughs: "Lady, you better not visit my mother! My mother doesn't want to be bothered."

All afternoon she has the boys on pins and needles. At two o'clock, drops on all fours like a graceful panther, glides halfway up the aisle, stops, calls up something through the rows in a velvety, strange language, so wild the children are shocked.

JOSIE. Shame! I never thought I'd hear a child talk to a teacher like that! Don't you have no mind in your brain, Leanore? Girl, get up.

VERNON. Listen girl, you think you're at home now? No wonder my mother don't want you in our house.

At three o'clock, as the children were lining up and William passed her desk, she snatched his folder of corrected papers and tore it in half. "All right, get your coat, here we go," I said to her, and dismissed the other children. She slipped outside the door and stood laughing. "You wouldn't dare."

"We'll see."

"I'm not going anywhere with you. Fifty times you've said, 'I'll visit your mother,' but I'm on to you."

She dashed away and down the stairs, laughing. I locked the room and in a few moments was following her out of the building. The air was sharp and cold, but boys played with bottles along the curbs or sat eating penny candy—one eating, two looking on. Leanore had appeared ahead, and trailed and shadowed me, always keeping about half a block ahead. She'd cross from one side of the street, cross back, calling insults, running. She didn't think I'd keep going. We reached her block. Adults talked in groups in the store fronts, and at the candy store on her corner, people of different ages stood in coats looking out.

I asked a woman, "Do you know where 153 is? I can't find the number." "No." People stood in the next building hallway—something going on inside. A little boy said, "I'm her brother; her mother's out." (She has no brother.)

At this point I heard my name suddenly called out—Leanore's voice!

She appeared from somewhere in the dark. "Miss Burke, I'm here. Over here!" And she ducked around the fender of a Buick and into a building entrance.

The kid who'd said he was her brother sprinted in after Leanore, announcing me: "Leanore, your teacher's comin!" Then dashed back out and onto the street to tell others. I walked up three flights with Leanore hightailing it ahead of me.

When I knocked a few times, the door opened a crack. "Are you Leanore Hazle's mother?" A woman in plastic curlers peered out: "Yeah, what'd she do?"

It was freezing in the hall. "I'd like to talk to you about Leanore, about her behavior at school." The crack did not get any wider, and from within Leanore's voice screamed, "It's gonna be a lie!" "I wrote you a note," I continued, and with this the door opened. "Listen, miss, the reason I didn't come, I had to go to court. I been very sick. You wanta come in?"

The apartment was spotlessly clean, though dark. Plastic drapes, flowered linoleum, 27-inch television that Mrs. Hazle went to turn down. Big end tables with kewpie dolls and crowds of furniture. Beyond, a bedroom with doubledecker bunks, Leanore stretching out on one and peeking around the door to see what would happen.

Mrs. Hazle fixed a few doilies, pulled shades even, and went out to turn down something bubbling in the kitchen. She re-entered with a baby that she set about diapering, with an appearance of listening while I said, "I've been meaning to come and talk to you about Leanore. She is a nice-looking child who comes to school beautifully groomed, she has a quick mind, shows leadership qualities. However—" The mother was not really listening. I turned to the trouble side: hooky playing, no classwork, language, tormenting of children, leaves seat or room when she pleases, drops small change all over the room—"*Stealing?*" the mother cut in sharply. "Oh, not exactly, it's more that—" "Well, boy, she better not be *stealing,* I'll tell you that much. That'd be just about the next thing I'd hear about that girl. Can't keep her cooped up here, but can't let her go down on that street any more; the neighbors want me to keep her in," said Mrs. Hazle, delivering the last words with a gaze toward the bedroom that hinted at the long antisocial years of Leanore. Leanore was now calling from the bedroom, "Oh, Mama, don't believe this woman, she's a liar herself! Tried to take my lunch money, said it was Iris's, it was mine! She steals money, that's the kind of woman you're talking to, Mama!"

"Leanore answers me back, swears—" ("Dirty lie! This woman lies!")

"—chews gum constantly, obeys no rules, starts fights all day." The longer the list grew, the less I felt that Mrs. Hazle and I took the same view of the list. It sounded like nothing but a list. Particularly when she now stood up, placed the baby on the floor, and walked to a cabinet just inside the kitchen door. She did call, "Go on, go on, I'm diggin you," back over her shoulder.

"I thought if the three of us could talk this over, we could discover a way to correct some of these things. She often leaves the building. I was about to report her truant two different times this semester—" ("Lie! Lie! Mama, don't listen, the only time I leave the room is when I have to get something, like if I have to borrow something in another room, Mama. This woman's been saying she's gonna come up here for three weeks and never came, so you can't believe her! If I do my homework she says it's wrong, that's why I don't do it!")

"Miss Bowser took her as a favor to me for four days and tells me that last year Leanore's behavior was so antisocial she was about to be expelled—" ("Mrs. Bowser's a big, fat black cow!") "—So that's what I've come to tell you, that this is possible again. I've warned Leanore that I might see you, and she always says you can't be bothered." The mother now came out of the kitchen carrying a strap with a buckle.

"I can't be bothered?" She walked into the bedroom. "You told this woman I can't be bothered?" Sounds of strapping began. "Oh, I'll tell you something! You've just about had what you're gonna get out of my life, baby! I'm not going to no court for no kid again!" (Strapping. Cries of "Mama!")

"There's no point in beating her, Mrs. Hazle. We must try to find out what is making her unhappy," I said, going to the door, but inside the strap arm was now working mechanically over Leanore who clung to the bed. The voice droned along with the arm, "Oh yes! I've got a couple of things going for myself now, no one's gonna ruin it! Oh no, no more trouble outa you, girl!" (Strap, strap!) "I've got me this new baby, life looks okay for a little while right now," (strap, strap) "and nothin's gonna go wrong again. No teacher's ever coming here again, no trouble, no judges; I've had it from you! This woman don't want you swearing, chewing gum in your mouth, fighting, and that's what she don't want." (Strap, strap.) "—Shut your mouth—and when you go to that school do that, shut your mouth." (Strap. Pause.) "—Another thing, baby. No guy wants you if you don't have the diploma; they'll sweet-talk you, but they don't want you." (Strap, strap, strap! Nothing could now be heard in the room but the strap going in a burst of new energy, the cries, and the drone.)

"Mrs. Hazle—please!" But just as I spoke, not in answer to my voice but because of some loss of interest on her own part, the strap fell to her side. Staring at Leanore, she wound up, "And when Sidney comes Sunday, he can take you, lock, stock, and barrel, baby. I've got my own scene going; you ain't ruining it again. You can just go up the Hudson this time where they know how to handle kids like you. Where they take those radiator brushes. Remember? Louise there, and she is a forgotten child. No one gonna go to see her; Martin ain't; Ravelle ain't. I got me this baby. You and me are two different parties from now on. I spent a lotta time on you; now I lost interest in you, baby."

At this point an older sister walked in with, "Listen, Mama, I heard about some more things Leanore's been doing," and the mother got in a few more licks, saying, "Yes, Sidney can take you and your stuff in the bag Sunday. Sidney always tellin' me y'got bad blood, but it ain't my bad blood; it's his. And when Farrel comes Tuesday, he can take you, too," she added to the other daughter without looking around or ceasing to strap Leanore. "That bus goes from Forty-second Street right up the Hudson to that school" (strap) "and there's plenty of room."

Here I said goodbye and walked out. The strap stopped, but sobbing still came through the door. I stood in the corridor for a moment. No other sound. Then water began running in the kitchen.

Leanore was very quiet in class the next day but at noon brushed past my desk to snicker and drop a few words stranger than anything in the visit had been: "I never thought you'd come there."

.   .   .

The Children's World

Richard comes in late one morning with a fine German shepherd puppy. He says, "I'm afraid about having him at home; the rats might get him."

MONTY.   You gotta put him up on the kitchen table. If you leave him alone, put a leash on him. Formica top table; they slips on the legs.

RICHARD.   They jump pretty high, though. I hate leaving him alone. I don't know what to do.

—A rat bit my baby sister on the finger. My father's done everything: he sets traps, he beats them, but they tunnel through those walls.

—You got to kill them with orange poison. Traps dangerous, babies get their hands or feet in them. You puts the orange poison on the bread, they swells up and strangles.

—You gots to put the food away. My mother say our neighbor must like rats. She leave all that food around. Leave a dish of corn and rice on the table, they play in it like nothing wrong.

—You leave food, that's just wasting money. Jump up on the table and eat through a forty-cent loaf of bread, right to the other end. Cost you a great expense, not puttin things away. Don't put your bread in a plastic breadbox; they go right through it. Get yourself a tin breadbox.

JASON.   Rats left feet marks across my birthday cake; it had blue flowers on it. My mother has to throw it out.

—My aunt put a roast in the oven and the next day open that oven, and a rat popped right out at her. She screamed and screamed! She ran out of the room. Man, was that rat big!

—My mother don't leave one single food for rats; but even if she don't leave no food around, she still puts that orange powder around, up high so the baby don't get in it.

—No, you puts lye down, very thick aroun' the borders and thick on the floor, and the rat's stomach gets burnt up from that lye. A rat died from that lye. He this long and this fat! (Holding up hands a foot apart.)

—They eat right through wood and plaster, not tin. They's tunnels all through your walls. You need tin—if you can't get flat tin, stick tin can in there, beat 'em flat, till you get tin.

—My mother always plugging up that hole, but she don't know how to hammer it right. Sometimes at that hole I just waits until they comes out. My big brother, he got combat boots, he steps on 'em; if they little, I can kill them with the broom.

—The only good thing is, they don't like to come out in the daytime. They're more for the night. Love garbage, hate light. My mother leaves the hall light on. Never cut lights out when there's rats.

REGGIE.   I dare you to come in my basement, honey. Those dead and alive rats will keep you moving. I always carry a stick or a broken soda bottle. Hide that stick up my arm. Sometimes, in an emergency, I have to go down get the garbage buckets. I'm too scared to even think about it now.

> Your house is so classy,
> You got rats as big as Lassie.

> I went to your house for a piece of cheese.
> A rat jumped up and said, "Heggies, please."

VERNON.   They comes out from behind the refrigerator when you puts the lights on, when you come in from the show. But don't scare me. I sleep in a top bunk.

(Others laugh: "That won't help anything; they climb right up some nights if they want to.")

JOSIE.   I don't want to hear about rats no more—I'm gettin scared!

—They likes the night. Don't come out in the day too much. If all the rats came out around up here, they'd be pushing people off the sidewalk, but they don't. They stay in till it's night.

VERNON.   Rats when they born they red, but when they gets old they long and *gray,* man. My father when he see a baby rat bein born, he say they keep comin and comin.

—Our landlord should live in my house just one day, just one day! But it's no good to bother him, he live out on Long Island and he don't like people to call him up there much.

—You can sue the landlord if the rats eat the baby; otherwise you can't.

VIRGIL.   No point in calling the super; half the time he's drunk. He's a bum, my father said.

—Our super's drunk most of the time, so he don't be sending up the steam. He singing spirituals on Sunday and sends his little kids down to the basement to fix the furnace and big flames leaps out.

—It's bad when he don't send up that steam. My two little sisters has asthma. My mother have to keep the oven on all day.

REGGIE.   Boy, my father ain't that bad, gets drunk but never more than once a month. If he get drunk he send me down to send up the steam. But always he send up the steam.

—Our super never once makes hot water.

—Yeah, us either.

—Those rats look at you! You better not curse them or look back. Don't never curse a rat right to him cause he'll take your clothes—go right into your closet and eat up everything.

—They give you blood poisoning, and their teeth has more germs than to kill an army.

—I'm afraid to go to sleep, they's rats. I'm afraid of the dark, and my room's way down the hall.

—Not me. My cat comes in my bed and saves me.

—You gets yourself a cat. If your cat kills a rat, put it in a newspaper and throw it out back, for the old mean cats to eat. No home cat is gonna truck with no dead thrown-out rat. Before you throw them out, you picks them up with the pliers because he's got every kind of germs on his teeth. And his tail's got germs too. You look out that back window sometime, it make you sick, there's so many cats eating old dead rats.

—Best way to do, always try to break their backs. If you gots combat boots that weigh more you can step on them. That breaks their backs too.

—If you're lucky they come out from the pipe and go right in the bathtub. My mother and me, once we saw eight of them. You hit them with the broom handle and the other person keeps filling the tub with scalding water, and you drown them. The other person keep on hitting with that broom.

—We're gonna move to Brooklyn to a new project where there's no rats.

—My aunt's movin' to Long Island so no rats can get at her baby. There's gonna be hardly any cars on the street. And everyone have their own garden.

—I'm movin' south where there's no rats, just snakes.

RICHARD.   In Michigan, they got very friendly white rats. They never heard of nothing else.

—Rats and cockroaches go together. In my basement you don't see just rats and cats; you see billions of roaches, too.

JOSIE.   Roaches are all right, they washes themselves in sand. But my mother won't let my brother play with them. You can get rid of roaches. But a fly's no good: a fly sits in a dog's mess and then rub its back and front feets together and sit on your food. A roach would never sit on your food.

NOAH.   That's not true! Don't *never* eat grapes or nothing's been in your desk overnight. We had grapes, every cockroach in the neighborhood come sat over those grapes.—I walk into a lady's house and steps on some roaches. She say, "Don't do that. Let my people go."

CURTIS.   Wouldn't you get mad if a rat touched your daughter's head? Wouldn't you kill every one you saw? We're gonna move to the project in Brooklyn. I don't know how, though. My mother's gotta get herself an operation. I guess my uncle's gonna help.

RICHARD.   In Michigan, if you talk about rats, they think you from the outer limits. They country hicks. When first they seen my skin, they call me nigger baby; never seen something like me before. They call like this: "Nig-ger baby! Nig-ger ba-by!" (He demonstrates, skipping in front of desks.) I was ashamed, but they didn't know.

Later Richard speaks of his dog again. The children advise him: "If he be that little, I keep that dog in bed with me. Then you can feel his heart on your heart."

. . .

Teaching. No Effort. No Attention

Harold is the first finished and has three wrong. Teacher: "When you've corrected these, you may read a library book." Harold: "I finished it, so why do I have to correct it?"

He corrects, with tears in his eyes, jabbing the pencil. Breaks the pencil. Then an argument over what to read: "Get a book from the library table." "I read all of 'em." "You read them or you looked at the pictures? . . . Please go get one. . . . Try the story of the lost sailor." "I read it."

Josie's head is down. I've seen her fall asleep in the sun on a bench outside. Utter exhaustion.

Reggie finishes and wants to talk about his new boots.

Teacher: "No, the third problem's wrong—do you see? You added; you didn't multiply. Reggie, please look at the paper. The third problem. Look at what the paper says: three eights are twenty-four; four sixes are twenty-four; two twelves are—?" Repeat. He clamps his lips shut, digs his boot heel in the floor. The button in his head has turned off. He wants to be left alone. Can't watch the numbers. "Please watch my tens frame." Suddenly he clenches his teeth, grabs the paper, stomps back to his desk.

Mrs. Weiss and I stand at the classroom door. "I don't know where to start or finish. That's what I didn't expect. Two weeks ago, five children could do long and short vowels. Now, none of the five know all the vowels. And math. That's the best thing they do. Now I find out they can't do it—today, I say, 'Three twos are six, *five* twos (they expect "four") are—?' Silence."

Mrs. Weiss: "I've gone through it year after year. You think you're batting a thousand—then it blows up on you. They've forgotten everything. No one of them is ever with the school scene."

"Mrs. Weiss, what are they doing? Look at them. What is Reggie doing right now? What is Malcolm doing? Look how they're sitting. Doing nothing because I've stepped out of the door—is that it?"

Not even any noise in the room. Most children have stopped work and sit with vacant stares. Malcolm is looking out the window, his mouth open slack. He is looking on a blank courtyard. There is nothing out there. Reggie is hunched in his seat, angry tears in his eyes. He wanted to talk about the after-shave lotion he was wearing; I had told him to open his reader. He is ruined for the day.

"I thought Virgil was really ticking. He can read. Last week he knew homonyms. When there's a correlation he sees it, shouts it out. Today, I asked him to correct a Rexographed sheet. 'No, I'm not gonna.' 'Virgil. What is it?' Something is always eating them. No one can correct anything. They take it as a personal insult—they've given me the sheet; what do I want from them now? Won't try, can't bear to fail."

Mrs. Weiss: "It's always the children with problems who can't read. For most of these children, life is a burden that they want to put down. They are really very sad children. And the school doesn't work for them. The curriculum has to be overhauled. They hate school; they really do.

"And what comes next for your babies? Sick Jefferson. Jefferson is the terminal date. Kids give each other fixes and have sex in the washrooms, at Jefferson. You know that in the spring there aren't so many wars and rumbles around here any more; the thing is cool it, go on the needle. I know your kids say, 'I ain't goin to Jefferson, that's a *bad* school'; but actually they will—for a while. Then most of them will drop out."

ROBERT CONOT

Mothers' Day Comes Twice a Month

The white world does make its presence known to the ghetto. Its mass media purvey white values and white standards of personal and economic behavior. But it has contacts with ghetto blacks which are even more direct. Two of white

MOTHERS' DAY COMES TWICE A MONTH   From *Rivers of Blood, Years of Darkness* by Robert Conot. Copyright © 1967 by Bantam Books, Inc.

society's most visible and intimidating representatives are the policeman and the social worker, the one representing its law and order and the other its confusing bureaucracy. In addition, there are the white merchants. As Robert Conot shows in his chronicle of the 1965 Watts uprising, these merchants were one of the first targets when the ghetto exploded. In the following selection Conot discusses some of the techniques by which they prey off those whose primary income is the bi-monthly check given grudgingly by the Bureau of Public Assistance.

WHEN COTTER WILLIAMS RETURNED HOME, THE RENT PARTY HIS mother was holding was still going on.

Sara Williams had run into money troubles. Sara Williams had run into money troubles because last mothers' day, the first of August— mothers' day in the projects comes twice a month: the first and the fifteenth, when the checks from the county arrive, and the prices automatically go up a few cents in many stores—the social worker at BPA had told her that her voucher was being temporarily withheld because a mistake had been made. Sara had protested that it wasn't her fault about the mistake, so why should she be *impoverishized* for it?

The worker had replied, "Well, Mrs. Williams, perhaps you haven't been quite truthful with us."

As usual, there was some truth on both sides. When Tommy, her eldest son, now 19, had been sent away to the California Youth Authority Camp as Paso Robles, Sara had not called the BPA to report it— she figured that was the state's business, and since the CYA had taken Tommy, the BPA should know about it. The social worker, however, hadn't discovered it until two months later. What's more, because of a clerical error, Sara had continued to receive Tommy's allotment for another two months after that. That made four months in all that had, somehow, to be repaid to the state. Additionally, there was now some question about Baby Doe: had she dropped out of school; was she still living at home; just exactly what *was* she doing?

So for Sara there had been no check on the first of August. Like everyone else in the projects, if the check didn't come, she was in trouble, bad trouble. Two or three days and then the money, all the money she had, would be gone.

The first thing she had done was pawn her sewing machine. The sewing machine she had bought in March, when she'd had that little extra money. Every mothers' day the project is overrun with salesmen, most of them white. The salesmen peddle everything from appliances like washing and sewing machines to household necessities like towels and thread. The collectors follow after them as street cleaners follow a parade.

The salesman told her that he had a once-in-a-lifetime offer on a sewing machine—his company had gotten thousands of the machines on consignment from a manufacturer on the proviso that they would sell more of them than anyone else in the world, so she, Mrs. Williams, could be the beneficiary of the fix his company had gotten itself into. The machine cost only $95, with a $25 down payment, and surely she could afford that. What's more, the company had a lesson plan, which would provide her with a lesson a month on sewing techniques for a whole year.

So Sara had gone and ordered the machine, and it had been delivered within the week. It had had a lot of little gadgets and things, and it was almost more than she'd expected. She had been really pleased with it.

On mothers' day, the first of the next month, the collector had appeared, and explained to her that, since she had made a $25 down payment, she now owed only $198.60.

There must be some mistake, she had told him, the total cost was only $95, that's what the salesman had told her.

He replied that he didn't know how the salesman could have possibly told her that; it was true that the basic cost of the machine was only $95, but the company didn't just sell the basic machine. The package price, tax included, was a firm $223.60. That included $60 for the attachments, and $60, at $5 each, for the 12 lessons, which would be sent to her every month.

Sara had become very angry and said that the salesman had been nothing but a liar. The collector had agreed with her. The salesman appeared not to have been quite truthful, and the company would certainly look into it. In the meantime, however, this was the bill: $198.60.

She had asked him if she just couldn't have the machine, and forget about all the attachments, lessons and things, and he had replied, "Certainly not!" The company would not sell her an inferior product. As for the lessons, she would never be able to operate the machine properly without them, and might even injure herself—the company could not bear the thought of that!

So she had said she supposed, much as she liked the machine, she would have to give it back, and could she please have her $25 returned.

That would be impossible, the collector had replied, the $25 had signified her good faith, and she now had had the machine almost a month. However, he was determined himself to help her, and so had managed to work out a formula where she would have to pay only $18.83 a month for 12 months in order to buy the machine. Surely that much she could afford. As a matter of fact, if she thought about it, she could probably make more money sewing for other people, or letting other people sew on the machine, than she would have to pay.

So she had bought the machine, and it had become her "negotiable." Almost everyone has some negotiable, some hard goods that they can pawn when the money runs out—which it does periodically. Usually the negotiable is a sewing machine, or a camera, or a gun, or a radio, or an electric kitchen appliance—seldom a tv set. Tv sets aren't considered negotiables. They are necessities.

When the collector had come on the first of August she'd had to tell him that she couldn't pay him, that he'd have to come back on the fifteenth. All right, the collector had agreed, but if she didn't have the money on the fifteenth, "We'll have to come back and pick up our machine!"

That's when she'd taken it down to the pawnshop and gotten a $20 loan—the interest on it was $5 a month.

The $20 lasted her a week, after which she'd decided to hold the rent party. A half dozen neighbors came over to play poker, and, since she was throwing the party, she got a dime out of every kitty. Sometimes, if there was wind that somebody had come into some money, the parties got to be big things; some of the west side gamblers would drift in, and as much as $1,000 might change hands. Usually, though, the party is a neighborhood affair; and the person who throws it is obligated, afterward, to attend any rent party that one of the guests might decide to hold.

When Cotter brought the news that there had been an uprising down on Imperial against the police, they stopped playing, and wanted to know what it was all about. Cotter told them that the police had stopped and raped a pregnant mother, and that the people had gotten angry and driven them out.

(Distorted as Cotter's account was, it gained wide credence in the area because it had a certain basis in fact. The previous month, Mrs. Beverly Tate, of 855 W. 60th St., mother of two, had been out driving with a friend, Herman Overton, when they had been stopped by two police officers, William D. McLeod and Thomas B. Roberts. McLeod had said that there was a warrant outstanding against Mrs. Tate, and told Overton to go on home. After Overton had left, McLeod remarked to his partner that the girl was cute, and, leaving him, had driven her to an isolated location where, according to her, he had raped her, or, more precisely, forced her into an act of oral-genital intercourse. McLeod claimed that she had consented to the act.

(Investigators for the Internal Affairs Division of the police department chose to believe the girl. McLeod was fired and Roberts suspended for six months, and the case was turned over to the District Attorney's office for prosecution. On Friday, August 13, it was presented to the County Grand Jury.

(When the grand jury met, the city was in turmoil, and the white jurors decided to take the word of the white police officers rather than that of the Negro girl. They refused to indict. Commenting, Dist. Att. Evelle J. Younger said, "The conduct on the part of the officers was reprehensible. It is a disgusting, terrible thing. But . . . it isn't a crime unless she refused to consent."

(A month later, Mrs. Tate died under mysterious circumstances while attending a party. Although there was almost certainly no connection between her death and the previous incident, many of the people in the area have their doubts. They have their doubts because vast numbers of them never read a newspaper, and hence rely on word-of-mouth and television for knowledge of what is going on. Word-of-mouth consists of rumors with various degrees of distortion, and television has, for all practical purposes, been unaware that there are Americans whose skins are not white.

(Furthermore, the incident was hardly the first of its kind. It was practically a replay of one that had occurred on Dec. 18, 1961, when Ruth Ball charged that Officer Donald H. Miner had forced her into an act of copulation, her escort, meanwhile, being taken and held in the squad car. When Miss Ball pressed charges, Miner resigned, and the city paid her $1,200 in damages.)

"Shit, baby," said Willie Ridley, "you ain't gonna keep no police out of here. Mr. Charley, he need the police to protect him when he cheat the people. The prophet, he speak right when he say the black man never gonna get no due from the white man. The black man, he got to disintegrate hisself!" Ridley was not a Muslim, because he couldn't go for all that stuff they put on about the women and the drinking and the smoking, and, especially, the eating—like you aren't supposed to eat any kind of nuts or the large-size navy bean, only the small-size navy bean—but he often talked as if he were. He talked as if he were because the Muslim talk gives the black man dignity and power, it makes him feel like he is somebody!

"You right, brother," said Hester LaPlace, Sara's neighbor and Willie's girlfriend. "Police is the ones keeping them blond, blue-eyed Jew devils in business cheatin' us. That why they got us on welfare, so's they can get rich off of us and take all the money out to Beverly Hills!"

"Like they charge a dollar to cash a little bitty check, and you got to buy $5 worth o' stuff that don't 'mount to nothin' to boot!" another agreed.

They were consumed with bitterness against the merchants, a majority of whom are of Mexican, Oriental, or Jewish descent, reflecting the area's ethnic mixture prior to the implosive arrival of Negroes.

"You gets the rich people that lives out in Hollywood, and they buys their groceries cheaper than we cans," Hester continued, "and then they ships their second day goods down here and we poor people have to pay more than they does!"

To a large extent her complaint was justified. Many of the food stores in the area are small, mama-papa operations that are obsolete and can survive only in a poverty area, and only by squeezing out every possible cent. In 1964 a survey conducted by the Los Angeles Times-Mirror Co. showed that in the city's core—the Negro-Mexican area—of 791 stores only 39 were supermarkets, and of the remainder only 29 could be classified Class A. There are 149 Class B markets and the vast majority, 574, are Class C, the lowest rating. These stores cannot afford membership in one of the nonprofit wholesale buying associations; they lack storage space and refrigeration equipment (which means that they have to buy in small quantities); their volume of sales is low—all factors that contribute to the driving up of prices. Inferior cuts of meat are sold because they are cheaper; though, for the reasons stated above, they may be almost as expensive as better cuts sold in Caucasian areas. Bread and vegetables lie on the shelf and become stale and wilted, but must be sold because the margin of profit does not permit writing them off. Kids are constantly running in and out, knocking things off shelves, breaking them, stealing them—the loss from pilferage alone sometimes runs as high as 10 per cent. Land valuations, hence taxes, are high. The cost of fire and burglary insurance borders on the prohibitive.

As a result, it has become a dog-eat-dog world, with the merchants and the customers having nothing in common except a mutual necessity. The customer steals, and the merchant cheats. He charges up to 2½ per cent of a check's amount for cashing it because it is a service he performs and it is important that he make his nickel out of every such service, and because even welfare checks are sometimes fraudulently endorsed.

(Thousands and thousands of persons in the area, lacking drivers' licenses, have no means of personal identification whatever. Hence a merchant can often not be certain that the person cashing a welfare check is the person to whom the check was made out, and there is a small but constant stealing of checks from mail boxes. Lately, some of the more clever recipients have discovered that they can exchange checks, endorse and cash them, then claim that the checks were never received. If, when the canceled check is returned, the signature does not match that of the recipient, there is no proof that the check ever reached the recipient, and the state bounces it and makes out a new voucher. There is no loss to the state, and the over-all amount of such frauds is negligible. But the small merchant who gets stuck with even one $150 or $200 bum check a month is not a very happy fellow.)

"Shit, man," Willie Ridley said, "the ofays is out to keep us where we is, there ain't rhyme or reason they does us the way they is if they wasn't. Like Hester got her window broke, and I say that okay, baby, I fix it for you, I can get the glass for nothin'. And the big-ass project manager, he comes down, and say, 'No man, you can't do that, don't you touch nothing!' And then he get some white feller down, and charge her $5. Ain't that right, baby?"

"Not only that, but Willie, he say he paint the place up, and the man says, 'Don't nobody paint the place but me.' So then he find out that they give me $20 more on my check, and right away he raise the rent $5!"

"You know that scrawny little tree they had out front?" Sara asked. "When the kids come and run over it, the manager, he said I'd have to pay for a new one, and he charge me $12.50. And Cotter," she indicated her son, "he said I'll go out and get you a tree three times that big, and it won't cost you nothin'. But right there the next day was this Japanese man with this little twig that don't look like nothin', and they charge me $12.50!"

"Look, what they do to me!" Ridley went on. "All my life I be working with metal, and then they get a little thing that runs a piece of paper through, and all of a sudden there it is, working my machine and they slap me on the shoulder and say, 'Willie, you be a good man, but we don't need you no more!' Forty-five years old and working a good 30 of them, and they say, Willie, you too old, Willie, you been deplaced! Hester, she go to the BPA for money to feed the kids, and they say you got a husband, and she say Yes, no, you know we live together five years. And they say, too bad, we got no money for you. So then they calls me in and they say: you willing to work? And I say, sure man, I work all my life. So they give me this test and they say it show I be good at hospital work, they gonna train me for hospital work, so they send me down to County General at $1.25 an hour to carry slop buckets, and I say: What you training me for, to be a shit wiper? And they gets all upset at that. But you knows that ain't no work for a man. BPA or no BPA, I just about ready to cut loose!"

"Like Johnnie Lee say," Hester was referring to Johnnie Lee Tillmon, "the only way the soul folk ever gonna get anywhere in the white man's world is to tell him to go his way and we go our, for the only thing he want with us is the exploitation!"

Hester had recently joined *Mothers Anonymous,* an organization of women on welfare aid founded in 1963 by Johnnie Lee Tillmon, herself the mother of six. A large, buxom woman in her late thirties, born in Arkansas, she had, for 18 years worked in a laundry, her highest salary being $67 per week. Separated from her husband, she had developed arthritis, and, as a result, had started receiving welfare aid. Realizing that when her children were 18 she would no longer receive aid and would be "too old to go to school and too young for old age assistance," she had started going to school during the summer in 1962 to supplement her tenth grade—Arkansas level—education.

Training to be a cashier and manager, Mrs. Tillmon works in a small grocery store. It is a store that is this side of the European Middle Ages —but not by very many years.

Not much bigger than 150 square feet, a good portion of it is filled with a jumble of crates and other paraphernalia. Children's toys—with all-year lay-away plans for Christmas purchase—are interspersed with canned goods on the shelves. A nonrefrigerated meat case contains only some wilted lettuce and stray packages of lunch meat. The store caters mostly to kids, and, when school is out, they mill about it as if it were an amusement park.

Mrs. Tillmon, who is afraid to remarry because she doesn't hear from her husband and doesn't know whether or not he got a divorce, has little use for BPA regulations. The minute she applies for public assistance, a woman has no privacy left, she complains. "You can't see a man over two weeks or he has to take on the responsibility of a stepfather—it drives out a man and prevents you from ever getting married. You are supposed to become children and not be interested in keeping company with a man. The check is supposed to make you a hermit. Well, things have to go on, check or no check!"

Her oldest boy has one pair of school pants, which she makes him change as soon as he arrives home. She sews well and makes her own children's clothes. "We might have to eat beans three times a week, but the kids will never drop out because they have no clothes to wear."

There are few women with the strength of character of Mrs. Tillmon, yet her lack of education and sophistication handicap her, and she is able to receive almost no help for Mothers Anonymous, the kind of grass-roots organization that could, potentially, do more than all the programs imposed from the top down. Among her goals are more emphasis on basic education so that kids don't graduate from high school unable to read, write, or spell; the fostering of on-the-job training and rehabilitation; and the dissemination of birth control information to cut down on illegitimacy.

Yet, until very recently, while children multiplied unchecked—the Negro birth rate in Los Angeles is 33.5 per 1,000 population as against 20.0 for Caucasians—social workers for the county were forbidden by fiat to discuss birth control. The Planned Parenthood Association, which wanted to open a number of clinics in the area, was refused federal funds.

"That's right!" said Willie Ridley. "The white man have lived off the sweat of the black man for 300 years, and he ain't gonna let all that nice, free labor go of his own will. He gonna have to be shown!"

"Baby, we gonna show him!" said Cotter. "We gonna meet again to-morrow night, and we gonna show him!"

NATIONAL ADVISORY COMMISSION ON CIVIL DISORDERS

Plainfield, New Jersey

After Watts, the era of the "long, hot summer" came into being. For most Americans, as isolated in their middle-class suburbs as black people were in their ghettoes, it was a time of fearfully new and apocalyptic scenes: National Guardsmen and tanks occupying the inner core of urban centers all over the country; young black men taking up arms and talking of guerrilla warfare; death and destruction on the scale of a small civil war. As this drama became a

PLAINFIELD, NEW JERSEY From *Report of the National Advisory Commission on Civil Disorders* by the National Advisory Commission on Civil Disorders.

seasonal fact of American life, many people condemned the "violence" of the black people involved, the Governor of California going so far as to call them "mad dogs." However, the following example of the genesis of one of these uprisings, from the report of the U.S. Commission on Civil Disorders, suggests that they are not at all the result of random, unmotivated violence, but of a situation generated by the inaction and intransigence of white officialdom.

In the essay that follows this example, Tom Hayden discusses the type of violence that occurred in the Newark rebellion. He shows that people of the black ghetto were the victims of that violence, rather than its perpetrators, and that most of the violence, like the repression behind the conflicts, came from the police and other representatives of a law and order that is racist in nature.

New Jersey's worst violence outside of Newark was experienced by Plainfield, a pleasant, tree-shaded city of 45,000. A "bedroom community," more than a third of whose residents work outside the city, Plainfield had had relatively few Negroes until 1950. By 1967 the Negro population had risen to an estimated 40 percent of the total. As in Englewood, there was a division between the Negro middle class, which lived in the East side "gilded ghetto," and the unskilled, unemployed and underemployed poor on the West side.

Geared to the needs of a suburban middle class, the part-time and fragmented city government had failed to realize the change in character which the city had undergone, and was unprepared to cope with the problems of a growing disadvantaged population. There was no full-time administrator or city manager. Boards, with independent jurisdiction over such areas as education, welfare and health, were appointed by the part-time mayor, whose own position was largely honorary.

Accustomed to viewing politics as a gentleman's pastime, city officials were startled and upset by the intensity with which demands issued from the ghetto. Usually such demands were met obliquely, rather than head-on.

In the summer of 1966, trouble was narrowly averted over the issue of a swimming pool for Negro youngsters. In the summer of 1967, instead of having built the pool, the city began busing the children to the county pool a half-hour's ride distant. The fare was 25 cents per person, and the children had to provide their own lunch, a considerable strain on a frequent basis for a poor family with several children.

The bus operated only on three days in mid-week. On weekends the county pool was too crowded to accommodate children from the Plainfield ghetto.

Pressure increased upon the school system to adapt itself to the changing social and ethnic backgrounds of its pupils. There were strikes and boycotts. The track system created *de facto* segregation within a supposedly integrated school system. Most of the youngsters from white middle-class districts were in the higher track, most from the Negro poverty areas in the lower. Relations were strained between some white teachers and Negro pupils. Two-thirds of school dropouts were estimated to be Negro.

In February 1967 the NAACP, out of a growing sense of frustration with the municipal government, tacked a list of 19 demands and complaints to the door of the city hall. Most dealt with discrimination in housing, employment and in the public schools. By summer, the city's common council had not responded. Although two of the 11 council members were Negro, both represented the East side ghetto. The poverty area was represented by two white women, one of whom had been appointed by the council after the elected representative, a Negro, had moved away.

Relations between the police and the Negro community, tenuous at best, had been further troubled the week prior to the Newark outbreak. After being handcuffed during a routine arrest in a housing project, a woman had fallen down a flight of stairs. The officer said she had slipped. Negro residents claimed he had pushed her.

When a delegation went to city hall to file a complaint, they were told by the city clerk that he was not empowered to accept it. Believing that they were being given the run-around, the delegation, angry and frustrated, departed.

On Friday evening, July 14, the same police officer was moonlighting as a private guard at a diner frequented by Negro youths. He was, reportedly, number two on the Negro community's "ten most-wanted" list of unpopular police officers.

(The list was colorblind. Although out of 82 officers on the force only five were Negro, two of the 10 on the "most-wanted" list were Negro. The two officers most respected in the Negro community were white.)

Although most of the youths at the diner were of high school age, one, in his mid-twenties, had a reputation as a bully. Sometime before 10 P.M., as a result of an argument, he hit a 16-year-old boy and split open his face. As the boy lay bleeding on the asphalt, his friends rushed to the police officer and demanded that he call an ambulance and arrest the offender. Instead, the officer walked over to the boy, looked at him, and reportedly said: "Why don't you just go home and wash up?" He refused to make an arrest.

The youngsters were incensed. They believed that, had the two participants in the incident been white, the older youth would have been arrested, the younger taken to the hospital immediately.

On the way to the housing project where most of them lived, the youths traversed four blocks of the city's business district. As they walked, they smashed three or four windows. An observer interpreted their behavior as a reaction to the incident at the diner, in effect challenging the police officer: "If you won't do anything about that, then let's see you do something about this!"

On one of the quiet city streets two young Negroes, D. H. and L. C., had been neighbors. D. H. had graduated from high school, attended Fairleigh Dickinson University and, after receiving a degree in psychology, had obtained a job as a reporter on the Plainfield *Courier-News*.

L. C. had dropped out of high school, become a worker in a chemical plant, and, although still in his twenties, had married and fathered seven children. A man with a strong sense of family, he liked sports and played in the local baseball league. Active in civil rights, he had, like the civil rights organizations, over the years, become more militant. For a period of time he had been a Muslim.

The outbreak of vandalism aroused concern among the police. Shortly after midnight, in an attempt to decrease tensions, D. H. and the two Negro councilmen met with the youths in the housing project. The focal point of the youths' bitterness was the attitude of the police—until 1966 police had used the word "nigger" over the police radio and one officer had worn a Confederate belt buckle and had flown a Confederate pennant on his car. Their complaints, however, ranged over local and national issues. There was an overriding cynicism and disbelief that government would, of its own accord, make meaningful changes to improve the lot of the lower class Negro. There was an overriding belief that there were two sets of policies by the people in power, whether law enforcement officers, newspaper editors, or government officials; one for white, and one for black.

There was little confidence that the two councilmen could exercise any influence. One youth said:

> You came down here last year. We were throwing stones at some passing cars and you said to us that this was not the way to do it. You got us to talk with the man. We talked to him. We talked with him, and we talked all year long. We ain't got nothing yet!

However, on the promise that meetings would be arranged with the editor of the newspaper and with the mayor later that same day, the youths agreed to disperse.

At the first of these meetings the youths were, apparently, satisfied by the explanation that the newspaper's coverage was not deliberately discriminatory. The meeting with the mayor, however, proceeded badly. Negroes present felt that the mayor was complacent and apathetic, and that they were simply being given the usual lip service, from which nothing would develop.

The mayor, on the other hand, told Commission investigators that he recognized that, "Citizens are frustrated by the political organization of the city," because he, himself, has no real power and "each of the councilmen says that he is just one of the 11 and therefore can't do anything."

After approximately two hours, a dozen of the youths walked out, indicating an impasse and signalling the breakup of the meeting. Shortly thereafter window smashing began. A Molotov cocktail was set afire in a tree. One fire engine, in which a white and Negro fireman were sitting side by side, had a Molotov cocktail thrown at it. The white fireman was burned.

As window smashing continued, liquor stores and taverns were especially hard hit. Some of the youths believed that there was an excess concentration of bars in the Negro section, and that these were an unhealthy influence in the community.

Because the police department had mobilized its full force, the situation, although serious, never appeared to get out of hand. Officers made many arrests. The chief of the fire department told Commission investigators that it was his conclusion that "individuals making fire bombs did not know what they were doing, or they could have burned the city."

At 3 o'clock Sunday morning a heavy rain began, scattering whatever groups remained on the streets.

In the morning police made no effort to cordon off the area. As white sightseers and churchgoers drove by the housing project there was sporadic rock throwing. During the early afternoon such incidents increased.

At the housing project, a meeting was convened by L. C. to draw up a formal petition of grievances. As the youths gathered it became apparent that some of them had been drinking. A few kept drifting away from the parking lot where the meeting was being held to throw rocks at passing cars. It was decided to move the meeting to a county park several blocks away.

Between 150 and 200 persons, including almost all of the rock throwers, piled into a caravan of cars and headed for the park. At approximately 3:30 P.M. the Chief of the Union County Park Police arrived to find the group being addressed by David Sullivan, Executive Director of the Human Relations Commission. He "informed Mr. Sullivan he was in violation of our park ordinance and to disperse the group."

Sullivan and L. C. attempted to explain that they were in the process of drawing up a list of grievances, but the chief remained adamant. They could not meet in the park without a permit, and they did not have a permit.

After permitting the group 10 to 15 minutes grace, the chief decided to disperse them. "Their mood was very excitable," he reported, and "in my estimation no one could appease them so we moved them out without too much trouble. They left in a caravan of about 40 cars, horns blowing and yelling and headed south on West End Avenue to Plainfield."

Within the hour looting became widespread. Cars were overturned, a white man was snatched off a motorcycle, and the fire department stopped responding to alarms because the police were unable to provide protection. After having been on alert until midday, the Plainfield Police Department was caught unprepared. At 6 P.M. only 18 men were on the streets. Checkpoints were established at crucial intersections in an effort to isolate the area.

Officer John Gleason, together with two reserve officers, had been posted at one of the intersections, three blocks from the housing project. Gleason was a veteran officer, the son of a former lieutenant on the police department. Shortly after 8 P.M. two white youths, chased by a 22-year-old Negro, Bobby Williams, came running from the direction of the ghetto toward Gleason's post.

As he came in sight of the police officers, Williams stopped. Accounts vary of what happened next, or why Officer Gleason took the action he did. What is known is that when D. H., the newspaper reporter caught sight of him a minute or two later, Officer Gleason was two blocks from his post. Striding after Williams directly into the ghetto area, Gleason already had passed one housing project. Small groups were milling about. In D. H.'s words: "There was a kind of shock and amazement," to see the officer walking by himself so deep in the ghetto.

Suddenly there was a confrontation between Williams and Gleason. Some witnesses report Williams had a hammer in his hand. Others say he did not. When D. H., whose attention momentarily had been distracted, next saw Gleason he had drawn his gun and was firing at Williams. As Williams, critically injured, fell to the ground Gleason turned and ran back toward his post.

Negro youths chased him. Gleason stumbled, regained his balance, then had his feet knocked out from under him. A score of youths began to beat him and kick him. Some residents of the apartment house attempted to intervene, but they were brushed aside. D. H. believes that, under the circumstances and in the atmosphere that prevailed at that moment any police officer, black or white, would have been killed.

After they had beaten Gleason to death, the youths took D. H.'s camera from him and smashed it.

Fear swept over the ghetto. Many residents—both lawless and law-abiding—were convinced, on the basis of what had occurred in Newark, that law enforcement officers, bent on vengeance would come into the ghetto shooting.

People began actively to prepare to defend themselves. There was no lack of weapons. Forty-six carbines were stolen from a nearby arms manufacturing plant and passed out in the street by a young Negro, a former newspaper boy. Most of the weapons fell into the hands of youths, who began firing them wildly. A fire station was peppered with shots.

Law enforcement officers continued their cordon about the area, but made no attempt to enter it except, occasionally, to rescue someone. National Guardsmen arrived shortly after midnight. Their armored personnel carriers were used to carry troops to the fire station, which had been besieged for five hours. During this period only one fire had been reported in the city.

Reports of sniper firing, wild shooting, and general chaos continued until the early morning hours.

By daylight Monday, New Jersey state officials had begun to arrive. At a meeting in the early afternoon, it was agreed that to inject police into the ghetto would be to risk bloodshed; that, instead, law enforcement personnel should continue to retain their cordon.

All during the day various meetings took place between government officials and Negro representatives. Police were anxious to recover the carbines that had been stolen from the arms plant. Negroes wanted assurances against retaliation. In the afternoon, L. C., an official of the Human Relations Commission, and others drove through the area urging people to be calm and to refrain from violence.

At 8 P.M., the New Jersey attorney general, human relations director, and commander of the state police, accompanied by the mayor, went to the housing project and spoke to several hundred Negroes. Some members of the crowd were hostile. Others were anxious to establish a dialogue. There were demands that officials give concrete evidence that they were prepared to deal with Negro grievances. Again, the meeting was inconclusive. The officials returned to City Hall.

At 9:15 P.M., L. C. rushed in claiming that—as a result of the failure to resolve any of the outstanding problems, and reports that people who had been arrested by the police were being beaten—violence was about to explode anew. The key demand of the militant faction was that those who had been arrested during the riot should be released. State officials decided to arrange for the release on bail of 12 arrestees charged with minor violations. L. C., in turn, agreed to try to induce return of the stolen carbines by Wednesday noon.

As state officials were scanning the list of arrestees to determine which of them should be released, a message was brought to Colonel Kelly of the state police that general firing had broken out around the perimeter.

The report testified to the tension: an investigation disclosed that one shot of unexplained origin had been heard. In response, security forces had shot out street lights, thus initiating the "general firing."

At 4:00 o'clock Tuesday morning, a dozen prisoners were released from jail. Plainfield police officers considered this a "sellout."

When, by noon on Wednesday, the stolen carbines had not been returned, the governor decided to authorize a mass search. At 2:00 P.M., a convoy of state police and National Guard troops prepared to enter the area. In order to direct the search as to likely locations, a handful of Plainfield police officers were spotted throughout the 28 vehicles of the convoy.

As the convoy prepared to depart, the state community relations director, believing himself to be carrying out the decision of the governor not to permit Plainfield officers to participate in the search, ordered their removal from the vehicles. The basis for his order was that their participation might ignite a clash between them and the Negro citizens.

As the search for carbines in the community progressed, tension increased rapidly. According to witnesses and newspaper reports, some men in the search force left apartments in shambles.

The search was called off an hour and a half after it was begun. No stolen weapons were discovered. For the Plainfield police, the removal of the officers from the convoy had been a humiliating experience. A half hour after the conclusion of the search, in a meeting charged with emotion, the entire department threatened to resign unless the state community relations director left the city. He bowed to the demand.

On Friday, seven days after the first outbreak, the city began returning to normal.

The Terror

[See headnote on page 445.]

WE WILL NEVER KNOW THE FULL STORY OF HOW THESE TROOPS AND the police hurt the black people of Newark. But there is now sufficient evidence to establish the main features of their behavior.

The military forces called in to put down the black rebellion were nearly all white. Virtually none of the 250 Negro Newark policemen took part directly in the violent suppression. Only 1.2 per cent of the New Jersey National Guard is black and, according to columnists Evans and Novak on July 22, the organization is "highly social in nature— much like the local chapter of the Moose or Elks. Few Negroes ever try to join." There are five Negroes among 1200 New Jersey state troopers, and many of the white majority are from conservative South Jersey towns where the troopers act as local police. It was understandable that these men would bring into the ghetto racist attitudes that would soon support outright sadism. A captain who commanded helicopter-borne infantry told a *New York Times* reporter on July 14: "They put us here because we're the toughest and the best . . . If anybody throws things down our necks, then it's shoot to kill, it's either them or us, and it ain't going to be us."

On Saturday the 15th, troopers charged up the stairs of the Hayes Homes, shouting, "Get back, you black niggers!" There was shooting up each flight of stairs as they charged. Later, an officer pumped more than thirty bullets into the body of a fallen teen-ager while shouting, "Die, bastard, die!" A Guardsman asked a witness, "What do you want us to do, kill all you Negroes?" A Newark policeman chipped in, "We are going to do it anyway, so we might as well take care of these three now."

These are not isolated examples, but a selection from innumerable

THE TERROR   From *Rebellion in Newark: Official Violence and Ghetto Response* by Tom Hayden. © Copyright 1967 by Tom Hayden. Reprinted by permission of Random House, Inc.

incidents of the kind that were reported throughout the riots. From them, we can draw three conclusions about the soldiers and the police.

Trigger-Happiness Because of Fear, Confusion and Exhaustion

Many of the troops were assigned to round-the-clock duty. During that duty they were under conditions of extreme tension. They were kept moving about by incidents or reports of looting, burning and shooting. They drove at speeds of more than 50 miles per hour; they ran continually along the streets after people. They were surrounded by unfamiliar and hostile faces. There were no foxholes or other shelters from attack. The troopers and Guardsmen knew little or nothing about the terrain. They often were unable to tell the direction of shooting. The New York *Daily News* of July 20 summarized:

> Reporters in the riot area feared the random shots of the guardsmen far more than the shots from snipers . . . Once a frantic voice shouted [over the radio], "Tell those Guardsmen to stop shooting at the roof. Those men they're firing at are policemen." . . . "They were completely out of their depth," said one reporter. "It was like giving your kid brother a new toy. They were firing at anything and everything."

In a report on police behavior for the *New York Times* July 20, Peter Khiss quoted the police radio on Sunday night to this effect: Newark police, hold your fire! State police, hold your fire! . . . You're shooting at each other! National Guardsmen, you're shooting at buildings and sparks fly so we think there are snipers! Be sure of your targets! Khiss adds: "After these appeals, there seemed to be a decrease in sniper alarms."

General and Deliberate Violence Employed Against The Whole Community

On Friday night 10 Negroes were killed, 100 suffered gunshot wounds, 500 were "treated" at City Hospital, and at least as many were arrested or held. By Sunday night another 10 were dead, at least 50 more had gunshot wounds, and another 500 were in jail. People were stopped indiscriminately in the streets, shoved, cursed, and beaten and shot. On Thursday, Joe Price, a veteran of the Korean war and an employee of ITT for fifteen years, was beaten on the head, arms, stomach and legs by five Newark policemen inside the Fourth Precinct. He had protested police harassment of neighborhood teen-agers earlier in the day. Later, Jerry Berfet, walking peacefully on a sidewalk with two women, was stopped by the police who told him to strip, ripped off his clothes, and forced him to run naked down the street. No charges were entered against either man. A Negro professional worker was arrested while driving on a quiet street after the 10 P.M. curfew, beaten unconscious, and then forced to perform what his lawyer describes as "degrading acts" when he revived in the police station.

Troops fired freely and wildly up streets and into buildings at real or imagined enemies.

On Saturday before darkness fell, three women were killed in their homes by police fire. Rebecca Brown, a twenty-nine-year-old nurse's aide, was cut nearly in half as she tried to rescue her two-year-old child by the window. Hattie Gainer, an elderly twenty-year resident of her neighborhood, was shot at her window in view of her three grandchildren. Eloise Spellman was shot through the neck in her Hayes apartment with three of her eleven children present.

A child in Scudder Homes lost his ear and eye to a bullet. A man was shot while fixing his car as police charged after a crowd. When another man told police he was shot in the side, the officer knocked him down and kicked him in the ribs.

The most obvious act of deliberate aggression was the police destruction of perhaps a hundred Negro-owned stores Saturday and Sunday. One witness followed police down Bergen Street for fifteen blocks watching them shoot into windows marked "soul brother." Another store owner observed a systematic pattern. On his block three white-owned stores were looted Thursday night; no Negro stores were damaged. There were no other disturbances on his block until well after midnight Saturday when he received calls that troopers were shooting into the Negro-owned stores or were breaking windows with the butts of their guns.

Was it because the police hated black people indiscriminately? Was it because the police wanted to teach middle-class Negroes that they must take responsibility for what "criminal" Negroes do? Or because the police wanted to prevent Negro-operated stores from gaining an advantage over the looted white merchants? Whatever the reason, the result was summed up clearly by Gustav Heningburg, a Negro who is a lay official of the Episcopal Church. He told the Newark *News* of July 17 that "the nonrioting Negroes are more afraid of the police than the rioters" because the police were retaliating instead of protecting.

Governor Hughes said on Sunday that all reports of excessive behavior would be handled by the troopers' own investigative unit. If charges were proved true, "and after all the police are only human," the Governor was sure that "justice will be done." As for himself, "I felt a thrill of pride in the way our state police and National Guardsmen have conducted themselves."

Cold-Blooded Murder

An evaluation of the deaths so far reported suggests that the military forces killed people for the purposes of terror and intimidation. Nearly all the dead were killed by police, troopers, and Guardsmen. The "crimes" of the victims were petty, vague, or unproven. None were accused by police of being snipers; only one so far is alleged to have been carrying a gun. Several of the dead were engaged in small-scale looting at most. The majority were observers; ten, in fact, were killed inside or just outside their homes. Many were killed in daylight. Nearly all the dead had families and jobs; only a few had previous criminal records. Seven of the dead were women, two were young boys. Of those known to be dead, 5 were killed between Thursday night and dawn Friday: 1 in a hit-and-run car, 1 allegedly shot by mistake by a sniper, 3 others by Newark police. On Friday and Friday night 9 were slain; 9 between Saturday afternoon and late Sunday; 1 on Monday night. All but one or two of these seemed to be police victims.

The July 28th issue of *Life* magazine carried a photo-essay on the death of William Furr. On Saturday afternoon Furr and a few others were carrying cases of beer out of a store that had been looted the previous night. Furr appears in the *Life* photos in the act of looting. The *Life* reporter even shared a can of stolen beer, and was warned by Furr to "get rid of it and run like hell" if the police appeared. Suddenly the police raced up with their sirens off, jumped out of the car with shotguns. Furr, according to the *Life* article, had "part of a six-pack in his left hand." With the *Life* photographer's camera shutter snapping, William Furr ran halfway down the block before two shots from behind dropped him. He died almost immediately, and a twelve-year-old boy, Joe Bass, was severely wounded while standing at the end of the block. A few minutes before Furr had told the *Life* reporter, "When the police treat us like people instead of treating us like animals, then the riots will stop."

The killing of nineteen-year-old James Rutledge will not soon be forgotten in Newark. On Sunday afternoon, he was inside a looted tavern with several other teen-agers hiding from the fire of troopers and police. According to a witness, the troopers burst into the tavern shooting and yelling, "Come out you dirty fucks." James Rutledge agreed to come out from behind a cigarette machine. He was frisked against the wall. Then:

The two troopers . . . looked at each other. Then one trooper who had a rifle shot Jimmy from about three feet away . . . While Jimmy lay on the floor, the same trooper started to shoot Jimmy some more with the rifle. As he fired . . . he yelled "Die, you dirty bastard, die you dirty nigger, die, die . . ." At this point a Newark policeman walked in and asked what happened. I saw the troopers look at each other and smile . . .

The trooper who shot Jimmy remained . . . took a knife out of his own pocket and put it in Jimmy's hand.

Shortly after three men came in with a stretcher. One said, "they really laid some lead on his ass" . . . He asked the state trooper what happened. The trooper said, "he came at me with a knife" . . .

[We remained where we were] for about fifteen minutes, then I got up and walked to the window and knocked a board down.——and—— came over to the window. One state trooper and two National Guardsmen came to the window and said, "Come out or we are going to start shooting" . . .

A National Guardsman said, "What do you want us to do, kill all you Negroes?" I saw a Newark policeman say: "We are going to do it anyway, we might as well take care of these three now." I saw the Newark policeman go over to——point a pistol at his head and say: "How do you feel?" Then he started laughing . . .

For anyone who wonders whether this is an exaggerated youthful horror story, the photographs of James Rutledge's chest and head are available from his mother. There were forty-five bulletholes in his head and body.

Clearly the evidence points to a military massacre and suppression in Newark rather than to a two-sided war. This was not only the conclusion of the Negroes in the ghetto but of private Newark lawyers, professors of constitutional law and representatives of the state American Civil Liberties Union. They have charged that the police were the instrument of a conspiracy "to engage in a pattern of systematic violence, terror, abuse, intimidation, and humiliation" to keep Negroes second-class citizens. The police, according to the lawyers' statement, "seized on the initial disorders as an opportunity and pretext to perpetrate the most horrendous and widespread killing, violence, torture, and intimidation, not in response to any crime or civilian disorder, but as a violent demonstration of the powerlessness of the plaintiffs and their class . . ."

Thus it seems to many that the military, especially the Newark police, not only triggered the riot by beating a cab-driver but then created a climate of opinion that supported the use of all necessary force to suppress the riot. The force used by police was not in response to snipers, looting, and burning, but in retaliation against the successful uprising of Wednesday and Thursday nights.

The action of the troops was supported by civilian authority, which turned the legal and judicial process into an anti-riot weapon. "New Jersey will show its abhorrence of these criminal activities and society will protect itself by fair, speedy and retributive justice," the Governor declared. Not counting hundreds of Negroes swept up by police, held for hours, and released without being charged, 1400 altogether were arrested and detained in jail. Of 829 adults and 144 juveniles interviewed in jail by lawyers during the riot period, more than 80 per cent were charged with looting. Nearly all the other arrests were for minor offenses such as curfew violation. Almost none were for shooting, bombing or arson.[1] Only 85 "dangerous weapons" were confiscated, according to final police reports, and of these only 51 were guns. About 675 of the arrested people—not quite half of them—were reported to have criminal records. But *Life* magazine called this figure "somewhat loaded" since city officials admitted that in half the 675 cases the "criminal records" consisted of arrests but not convictions. The evidence is that most of the prisoners were adults with jobs and families; holding them for several days created serious problems for each.

High bail prevented prisoners from being able to get out of jail. Minimum bond was set at $1,000 for curfew and loitering charges, $2,500 for looting, $5,000 for possession of a gun, $10,000 to $25,000 for other weapons charges. Chief Magistrate James Del Mauro, replying to criticism of the high bail cost, declared in the July 14 Newark *News:* "If they can't afford it, let them stay in jail." As Henry diSuvero of the state American Civil Liberties Union pointed out, this meant that the

---

[1] An earlier, preliminary, breakdown of arrests revealed the following: 473 arrested for breaking and entering (looting, larceny); 50 for curfew violation; 47 for possession or receiving stolen goods; 40 for concealed weapons or possession of weapons; 12 for assault and battery on police, troopers, or guards; 14 for assault and battery (presumably against civilians); 9 for disorderly conduct; 14 for loitering; 3 for failure to give good account of self; 3 for resisting arrest; 3 for resisting arrest after curfew; 1 for unlawfully eluding police; 3 for auto theft; 3 for malicious damage; 3 for possession of marijuana; 2 for failure to obey a policeman; 1 for shooting wife; 1 for impersonating a member of the armed forces; 1 as a material witness; 1 for possession of a gas bomb; 1 for attempted armed robbery; 1 for discharging weapon; 3 for attempted arson; 1 for arson.

concept of "innocent until proven guilty" and the constitutional provision against "excessive bail" was discarded. Thus people were kept off
the streets and, in diSuvero's view, held as "hostages" in the conflict.

During this mass detention no one with the exception of about 150
juveniles, was fed until Saturday and many not until Sunday, even when
food was brought to the jails by friends and relatives of the prisoners.
As the court pens filled up, prisoners were sent to the Newark Street Jail
(condemned as uninhabitable in the 1930s), federal detention facilities,
a state prison, and the armory where Hughes and the troops were head-
quartered. Some of the prisoners were beaten in their cells.

Prisoners were not permitted to receive visitors or make telephone
calls for legal assistance, nor were they allowed to notify friends and
relatives. The right to preliminary hearings was denied. This right, provided for in New Jersey law, compels the prosecutor to demonstrate to
the judge there is "probable cause" to hold the accused; it permits the
defendant to discover the state's case against himself as well. Thus,
merely the word of the arresting officer became sufficient to hold people
without determination of probable cause.

Municipal Court judges started arraigning prisoners at round-the-clock
sessions. One prisoner passed through court every three minutes, according to the *Star-Ledger* of July 16. Pleas by attorneys for the reduction of
bail were ignored except in rare instances.

Starting Monday two Grand Juries heard felony charges and returned,
by week's end, some 500 indictments. With the handing down of an
indictment, which itself is a finding of probable cause, the prisoners lost
forever their right to preliminary hearing. Thus, by agreeing to rush
presentations, the Grand Jury acted more as a rubber stamp for the
prosecutors' requests than a body to ensure an objective check on evidence. The ACLU charge that Hughes was using the judiciary as a
weapon to restore order is supported by this post-riot statement the
Governor gave to *US News & World Report:* "The full measure of the
criminal law should be exacted in these cases. I have insisted on that
from the beginning. I went to the extent of arranging with the appropriate courts for the immediate impaneling of grand juries and presenta-
tion of cases to them."

But the attitude of the courts was perhaps better indicated on July 21
when Newark's Chief Magistrate Del Mauro rejected the attempt by
cab-driver Smith's attorney, Harris David, to file criminal complaints
against the two police who arrested Smith. According to the *Times,*
Del Mauro's words were:

In these times of stress, with all the havoc and destruction, a policeman killed, a fireman killed, more than twenty people killed and $15 million of damage, *I am not accepting a complaint against the police.*

It was this particular man, if I recall from reading the papers, that originally caused the rioting, when he was arrested and rumors swept through the colored community that he had been killed. He has been paroled . . . he is alive and there is nothing wrong with him.

"Mr. Smith," the *Times* reported the next day, "wore a six-inch-wide bandage wrapped tightly around his rib cage" and declined any comment on the advice of his lawyer.

One of the riot's lessons was that the white community, at the highest official levels, gave support to this entire military operation. The Governor stated the necessity of "drawing the line" for all America in Newark; the Governor commented he was "thrilled" by the performance of the troops; the Governor dismissed police brutality charges as "standard operating procedure." City officials were just as implicated. The *Washington Post* of July 24 reported: "There was massive destruction of property—but no deaths—until Newark Mayor Hugh J. Addonizio instructed the city police to use any means necessary to put down the riot . . ." During the height of bloodshed, when Richard Taliaferro was shot in the back on South 8th Street Friday night (the police claimed Taliaferro exchanged shots with them), the Mayor told a Newark *News* reporter: "That's a good show of force in quick time." From the streets to the court room, Negroes' rights were secondary.

In the aftermath of the riot it became clear that substantial citizens of Newark were aware of the magnitude of the police brutality issue. A Committee of Concern, including the Episcopal Bishop, the dean of Rutgers' Newark branch and the dean of Rutgers' Law School, the vice-presidents of the Prudential Insurance Company and of Newark's largest department store, declared that one of the major causes of the riot was the feeling among Negroes that the police are the "single continuously lawless element operating in the community." The solid citizens agreed that this Negro view had merit; indeed, they said "independent observers" agreed with it. Since their statement implied a prior awareness of the problem, the question could be asked why they had taken no action previously to solve the problem. If *Life* magazine could express worry that the Negro community did not turn in the snipers in its midst, would it not be proper to worry why the white community never turned in the violent element in its midst?

The riot made clear that if something is not done about the police immediately, the fears of white society will be transformed into reality: whites will be facing a black society that will not only harbor, but welcome and employ snipers. The troops did not instill fear so much as a fighting hatred in the community. Many people, of every age and background, cursed the soldiers. Women spit at armored cars. Five-year-old kids clenched bottles in their hands. If the troops made a violent move, the primitive missiles were loosed at them. People openly talked of the riot turning into a showdown and, while a great many were afraid, few were willing to be pushed around by the troops. All told there were more than 3000 people arrested, injured, or killed; thousands more witnessed these incidents. From this kind of violence, which touches people personally, springs a commitment to fight back. By the end of the weekend many people spoke of a willingness to die.

Jimmy Cannon was one such person. He was the uncle riding with ten-year-old Eddie Moss when the Guardsmen shot through the car and the young boy's head was ripped open. Jimmy put the car, blood, bullet-holes and all, into a private garage as proof of what happened. Then he was beaten on the street corner by police who found him there. Jimmy learned how to fight during four years in the Marines. "I don't hold any grudges against you," he told a white person who interviewed him. "I'm just for rights, not for violence. This thing is wrong. I've faced a lot of things, but this is bad, and I just don't care anymore. I am to the point where I just don't care."

Black Power

C. ERIC LINCOLN

The Black Muslims

The Black Muslim movement began in Detroit in 1930 with the appearance of an unknown black man who called himself W. D. Farad Muhammad. Farad (later known as The Prophet) told blacks of the Detroit ghetto that he had come from the Holy City of Mecca to instruct them about Armageddon, the black man's final battle against the race which had so long oppressed him.

The conditions were right for The Prophet's message to be heard. Black people had been migrating to the North in great numbers since the turn of the century. They sought a promised land, but, as previous articles have made so clear, they found instead simply a less schematic version of the hardship and deprivation they had already known in the South. They were the hardest hit of any in the urban setting by the Depression. Farad's following therefore multiplied quickly; as he established the first of the Muslims' Temples of Islam, he refined the religion and complex ideology of black superiority that has primarily characterized the group he called "The Nation of Islam in the West."

In 1934, Farad disappeared as mysteriously as he had come. But his preaching had made 8,000 converts, whom, along with his mantle of leadership, he bequeathed to a young man named Elijah Poole. Elijah Muhammad, as he was later called, went on to spread the Word to almost every major city in the country which had a significant black population.

By 1963, under the leadership of Elijah Muhammad and the prime minister-ship of the charismatic Malcolm X, Muslim membership, although officially secret, was conservatively estimated at 250,000. The following selection is excerpted from C. Eric Lincoln's book, *The Black Muslims in America,* published in 1961 when the group was beginning to reach its greatest power; at that time, it was considered a dangerous threat to the country's racial *status quo.* Since then, however, its influence has declined, primarily because of the schism be-tween Elijah and Malcolm X, but also because many of the Muslims' non-religious tenets have been absorbed by more militant, secular movements.

THE BLACK MUSLIMS From *The Black Muslims in America* by C. Eric Lincoln. Reprinted by permission of the Beacon Press, copyright © 1961 by C. Eric Lincoln.

Lures for the True Believer

TO CLINCH THE CONVERSION OF THOSE TRUE BELIEVERS WHO APPROACH
the Movement in simple curiosity, Muhammad offers the lure of personal rebirth. The true believer who becomes a Muslim casts off at last
his old self and takes on a new identity. He changes his name, his
religion, his homeland, his "natural" language, his moral and cultural
values, his very purpose in living. He is no longer a Negro, so long despised by the white man that he has come almost to despise himself.
Now he is a Black Man—divine, ruler of the universe, different only in
degree from Allah Himself. He is no longer discontent and baffled,
harried by social obloquy and a gnawing sense of personal inadequacy.
Now he is a Muslim, bearing in himself the power of the Black Nation
and its glorious destiny. His new life is not an easy one: it demands
unquestioning faith, unrelenting self-mastery, unremitting hatred. He
may have to sacrifice his family and friends, his trade or profession, if
they do not serve his new-found cause. But he is not alone, and he now
knows *why* his life matters. He has seen the truth, and the truth has set
him free.

When he has seen the light and has decided to join the Movement, the
potential convert is made to pass through a number of barriers before
he is admitted. First he is given a copy of the following letter, which he
himself must copy by hand:

Address
City and State
Date

Mr. W. F. Muhammad
4847 So. Woodlawn Avenue
Chicago 15, Illinois

Dear Savior Allah, Our Deliverer:

*I have been attending the teachings of Islam by one of your Ministers, two
or three times. I believe in It, and I bear witness that there is no God but
Thee, and that Muhammad is Thy Servant and Apostle. I desire to reclaim
my Own. Please give me my Original name. My slave name is as follows:*

Name
Address
City and State

The applicant's letter is sent to Chicago, where it is scrutinized. If it
contains any errors, it is returned and must be recopied correctly. If the

letter is perfect, the applicant receives a questionnaire concerning his marital status and dependents. When this and other forms have been completed and approved, the convert enters his new life as a member of the Black Nation of Islam.

To commemorate his rebirth, the convert drops his last name and is known simply by his first name and the letter X. To facilitate identification among Muslims having the same first name and belonging to the same temple, numbers are prefixed to the X. Thus the first man named John to join the temple is named John X; the second becomes John 2X; and so on. Some temples have gone as high as X to the "17th power"! At a later date, Muhammad may grant the convert a new—that is, an "original"—surname, such as Shabazz.

The symbol X has a double meaning: implying "ex," it signifies that the Muslim is no longer what he was; and as "X," it signifies an unknown quality or quantity. It at once repudiates the white man's name and announces the rebirth of Black Man, endowed with a set of qualities the white man does not know. "In short," Malcolm X explains, " 'X' is for mystery. The mystery confronting the Negro as to who he was before the white man made him a slave and put a European label on him. That mystery is now resolved. But 'X' is also for the mystery confronting the white man as to what the Negro has become." That mystery will be resolved only when the teachings of Elijah Muhammad have been received by enough Negroes to counter "three hundred years of systematic brainwashing by the white man." When the Lost Nation of Islam in the West has learned its true identity, has gained a realistic appreciation of its past accomplishments and has seen the "truth about the white man," then the white man will see the Negro in a new light—"and he will have no reason to rejoice."

Most Muslims also retain their "slave" surnames for use in such pragmatic affairs as signing checks. On these occasions, however, the surname is always preceded by an X to indicate that the Muslim repudiates it. On other occasions, Muslims may use the surname Shabazz. For example, when Malcolm X toured Egypt and several other Moslem countries in Africa and Asia in the summer of 1959, he traveled as Malik Shabazz "so that my brothers in the East would recognize me as one of them." If he had used his "European" name (Malcolm Little), he explained, he would have been rejected as an imposter or ridiculed for retaining that symbol of the white man's ownership.

This change of name is, of course, only the most outward token of rebirth. Perhaps the deepest change promised—and delivered—is the release of energies that had been dammed or buried in the old personality. This release may account in part for the regeneration of criminals, alcoholics and narcotic addicts which is a hallmark of the Movement. At the other extreme, it is often apparent in a change from gentle bewilderment to dogmatic and barely leashed hostility. "When I was in the Pacific," said a Muslim veteran of World War II,

> I prayed to God every day that He would not let me die in the jungle, fighting some Japanese who had never done anything to me. I was a Christian then. Now I pray to Allah to let me live to help my people find out who their real enemies are, right here in America.

Recruitment

In pursuit of his goal to make Muslims out of Negro Christians and the unchurched, Muhammad has an ambitious program of recruitment. His ministers go into jails and penitentiaries, pool halls and bars, barbershops and drugstores to talk about Islam. They invade the college campuses, the settlement houses and the YMCAs. Young Muslim brothers pass out literature in front of the Negro Christian churches on Sunday morning, inviting the Christians to attend lectures at the Muslim temples in the afternoon. They speak from street corners and in parks, and they distribute literature wherever large crowds of Negroes are gathered. Invariably, the proselytizers are young, personable, urbane and well-dressed men of confidence and conviction.

It is a Muslim boast that although the Negro intellectual will be hardest to reach ("he has been brainwashed more thoroughly than any of the rest of us"), he will ultimately have no choice other than to embrace Islam. He can never be more than marginally acceptable to the white man, so "he will have nobody to lead and no one to honor him when the common people have all become Muslims." Muhammad himself has a sort of calculated patience with the Negro upper classes. He regards them as doubly cursed: "they have stayed in the white man's schools too long, learning nothing of themselves," and they are fervid in their "hopes that the white man is going to change and treat them like men instead of boys." Malcolm X is more philosophical:

> The American Black Man has worked hard to accomplish something and to be somebody. The whole system was against him, but some made it to a point where the white man will show some isolated individuals a little respect; not much, but more than he shows the rest of us. That man isn't going to join us until the white man is more respectful of us than of him.[1]

·   ·   ·

[1] From an interview with Malcolm X.

Dramatic productions, songs and other such entertainment are effective recruiting devices. "People who can put on a drama like that—and who wrote it themselves are not just 'everyday' folks," a Boston taxi driver remarked. But Muhammad does not make entertainment ability the chief attraction of his Movement. Indeed, he is careful to emphasize that the Negro has already done too much singing and dancing, when he should have been giving his attention to more serious matters like factories and supermarkets. Apart from the public meetings and publications, a good deal of recruiting is done in jails and prisons, among men and women whose resentment against society increases with each day of imprisonment. Here their smoldering hatred against the white man builds up to the point of explosion. But Muhammad's ministers are trained to prevent any such release; they are adept at channeling aggression and hostility into a kind of leakproof reservoir for future use. No act of violence or retaliation against the white man is permitted. Instead, Muslims who join the sect while in prison invariably improve in behavior and outlook. Every Muslim *must* respect constituted authority—no matter what the authority may be. This is one of the cardinal rules of membership in the sect.

The black prisoner is reminded that he is in an institution administered by whites, guarded by whites, built by whites. Even the chaplains are white, "to continue to force upon you the poisonous doctrine that you are blessed by being persecuted." The judge who tried him, the jury who heard his case, the officers who arrested him—all were white. Can he, then, be justly imprisoned?

> If in fact you *did* steal, from whom did you steal? Only the white man has anything, and if you stole from him, you got but a fraction of what he owes you. Did you kill? If you killed a white man, they murder us at will. They decorate their trees with the bodies of our people. Or they kill us by "law," but they cannot enforce the same "law" to protect us or let us vote.[2]

If prisoners have committed crimes against other black men, they are told they committed these "unnatural acts" out of frustration and the inability to "see who the real devil is." "You may have killed your black brother with your hand, but in your heart you have tried to kill your true tormentor."

When the prisoner is discharged, he is "not wanted by the Christian churches who teach love and forgiveness," but a readymade fellowship awaits him at the Muslim temple. The new brother is welcomed and

[2] From a series of Muslim interviews.

immediately made to feel a part of the group. A job is found for him, usually in one of the Muslim enterprises, and in a short time he is indistinguishable from any other Muslim. The routine of work, coupled with the obligations of the temple, leave him little time for regression or for any contacts with the criminal element.

Occasionally, a man or woman will join the Muslims "to keep out of trouble" or to find help in trying to overcome addiction to dope or alcohol. One woman in Milwaukee said that she joined "because I was tired of hating myself every time I looked in the mirror."

Muhammad's reclamation program promises a kind of moral and social perfectionism, which is available to all who adopt Islam. In his public addresses, he chides the Negro community for its juvenile delinquency, which is "caused by parental immortality" and "rips apart the seams of the Christian society." In Islam, echoes Malcolm X, "we don't have any delinquency, either juvenile or adult, and if Mr. Muhammad is given a chance he will clean up the slums and the ghettos—something all the leaders and the social workers and the policemen put together have not been able to do."

The Muslims visualize the reclamation of thousands of Negroes who, through ignorance, despair and defeat, have found themselves in the gutter or in jail. They have had some impressive successes in rehabilitating certain categories of social outcasts, including narcotic addicts and alcoholics. Muhammad operates on the premise that "knowledge of self" and of the "truth about the white man"—when tied in with a constructive program, such as building the "Black Nation"—is sufficient to reclaim the most incorrigible. "By nature," the Muslims are taught, "you are divine." Their social tragedies are caused by the white devil's "tricknology," but truth and hard work will soon make them free.

Visit to a Temple

The real recruitment is done in the temples, for there the import of Muhammad's message may be heard at best advantage. The temple is typically located in the area of densest concentration in the black ghetto. In this way, the bars, pool halls and chicken shacks—all crowded with potential converts—are readily accessible to the proselytizing Muslim brothers. Conversely, the temple is in a neighborhood familiar and convenient to most of those to whom its basic appeal is directed. On Wednesday nights the clean-shaven, dark-suited Muslims may be seen posted near the liquor stores or canvassing the bars and cafes, "fishing for the dead"—that is, inviting the most lost of the Lost Nation to repair to the nearby temple to learn the truth about themselves and their future.

On Sunday mornings the crusading brothers may station themselves outside the Christian churches—High-Church or apostolic, cathedral, or store-front, it doesn't matter to the self-confident Muslims, for the message they have is ultimately intended for the entire Black Nation. They march silently up and down in front of the churches, passing out handbills inviting the Christians to come to the Muslim temple that afternoon "to hear the truth." The "pickets" are polite and friendly, quietly dressed and soft-spoken. But most impressive of all is their self-assurance, their utter confidence in their "program for the Black Man which does not require you to love those who do not love you."

The temple itself may be a vacant store or a lodge hall, if the Muslims have but newly organized or if the Movement has not yet caught on in that vicinity. Where the size of the congregation warrants, the Muslims have typically bought abandoned Jewish temples or Christian churches as the whites have fled from the changing neighborhood. Occasionally the nascent Muslim organizations meet in Negro churches or even in funeral chapels.

Arriving at the temple, the new visitor may discover that it has a number rather than a name. A large sign across the front of the building or a signboard on the temple lawn may proclaim it to be, say, MUHAMMAD'S TEMPLE OF ISLAM NO. 5. However, because law enforcement and other agencies have shown increasing interest in the Movement in recent times, the wily Muslim leader has now stopped numbering his temples in order to keep the strength of the Movement secret.

The lawn bulletin, as in Christian churches, announces the speaker for the day. Nationally popular speakers other than Muhammad include Malcolm X of New York, Louis X of Boston and Wallace Muhammad, the Messenger's son, who leads the Philadelphia temple. Whenever a program of unusual importance is held at a local temple, it is supported by busloads of Muslims from all nearby cities and from national headquarters in Chicago. At a rally held by the Atlanta Temple in September 1960, Muslim caravans came from as far away as Boston and Los Angeles. This kind of mobility promotes a rather widespread cohesiveness within the brotherhood; most of the ministers eventually become known to all other ministers and to congregations scattered across the country.

The Negro visitor is welcomed at the entrance to the temple by a committee of the dark-suited brethren. The white visitor is politely but firmly turned away, with an explanation that "this is a meeting for the victims of the white man and not for the white man himself." It may be further explained that what will be said in the temple "may sound offensive" to white people and that white visitors who become offended may find themselves in danger; consequently "it will be better for all concerned if only black people attend."

Negroes are readily admitted and are shown into the temple with elaborate courtesy and ceremony. In an anteroom just off the sanctuary, a Muslim sister waits to record the visitors' names and addresses, which are then added to the temple's mailing list. Following this registration, the visitor is asked to submit to "a little ceremony we always go through." The "little ceremony" is, in fact, an elaborate and systematic search for concealed weapons. All pocket knives, nail files and any other instruments capable of inflicting serious injury are taken from the visitor and checked in a plastic bag, along with lip rouge, chewing gum, cigarettes and all other "articles of defilement." The visitor is asked to open his wallet and remove his money. Both the wallet and the money are then examined, but the owner is permitted to retain these.

Two Muslims are assigned to go over each new arrival, and they do it with a thoroughness that would delight the heart of a police sergeant. Pockets must be turned inside out; coat lapels, collars and trouser cuffs are all given attention. The trouser legs must be raised to show that nothing is concealed in the socks. While the visitor's arms are held aloft, a Muslim brother places his outspread hands on either side of the neck and in one continuous sweep carefully trails them down the sides of the body to the ankles. The armpits and the inside of a man's legs are given close attention. Women are given similar treatment in a room set aside for that purpose.

The Muslims are remarkably adept in the business of the "ceremony." The whole thing takes only about a minute and is done with as little inconvenience and embarrassment to the bewildered newcomer as possible. On special occasions, such as when the Messenger or Malcolm X is speaking, a double line of perhaps fifty to sixty Muslim brothers is assigned to this detail, thus enabling several thousand people to be "cleared" and seated within an hour or two preceding the meeting. At the big meetings the paramilitary FOI[3] is in charge, and Muslims as well as non-Muslims are searched.

Once the visitor has been cleared, he is escorted into the sanctuary by one of the Muslims. The entrance to this room is typically guarded on the inside by two members of the FOI, who stand, one on each side of the doorway, facing the front of the room. If there is a double entrance (as in most churches), guards are posted at each. The entrances near

[3] [Fruit of Islam. EDS.]

the chancel at the front of the room are similarly guarded. There may also be two guards flanking the speaker, one on each side; or there may be a guard opposite the front row of seats on each side of the room. The escort will lead the visitor to the front of the room, making certain that all seats on the front row are filled first, and so on with the succeeding rows. Men are seated to the right, women to the left. There is no mixed seating whatsoever.

Before the minister enters to deliver the main lecture for the day, one of the brothers may instruct the audience in a Muslim prayer or in the understanding of certain Arabic phrases. The prayer posture may be taught—palms upward, face to the East—and its meaning explained.

There is a flurry of excitement when the minister enters. He walks rapidly to the lectern and bows slightly, with his palms up and slightly extended. Then he smiles at his congregation and greets them in Arabic: *"As-salaam alaikum!"* ("Peace be unto you!") The greeting is returned in unison: *"Wa-alaikum salaam!"* ("And unto you be peace!") This exchange is usually made three times, after which the minister launches immediately into his address, which is the heart of the service and usually lasts two or three hours. Unlike the traditional Christian sermon, it is not confined to a single topic each week. Instead, the minister attempts every week to present the entire gamut of Muhammad's teachings. He speaks almost without pause and is interrupted only by the changing of the guard—a ceremony in which, at intervals, the guards at the rear of the hall march forward, exchange phrases in Arabic with the guards down front and then exchange stations with them.

Throughout the lecture, the audience is attentive and earnest. It is eager and seems enraptured by its exclusive possession of the truth; yet it is always restrained. There are no "happy" people in the congregation, and the foot-thumping, head-wagging-amen stereotype of the store-front Negro churchgoer is conspicuously absent. There is no singing and no "shouting." Emotional displays are limited to frequent ejaculations of "That's right!" when the minister scores a point upon which there is wide agreement. Often, the minister asks a rhetorical question for emotional effect. He may wonder, for example, "Now what do you think would happen if you tried to do some of the things the Constitution says you have a right to do?" At this there is an uneasy rumble of snickering, interspersed with the cynical response: "Now *that's* a good question, Brother Minister! That's a *good* question!"

While the minister lectures, money receptacles are in continuous circulation, and the challenge to "support your own" is insistently urged by young ushers moving among the audience. The receptacles are not inconspicuous: they are plastic wastebaskets or large brown paper bags. Such collections are a recent innovation. The Muslim brothers formerly took no public offerings and announced proudly: "Islam takes care of its own." Now they explain that, since Muhammad has become well-known and "his aims and integrity are established," the public can be permitted to contribute toward his work, "especially the proposed building of an Islamic Center in Chicago."

The minister nearly always begins his lecture by writing several Arabic phrases on a blackboard, explaining that Arabic is the original language of the Black Man and that he must begin to relearn the language of which the white man has deprived him. The first phrase is the Muslim greeting: *As-salaam alaikum.* The proper response is then written and explained: *Wa-alaikum salaam.* "It is proper," the minister explains, "to begin the study of Islam and the worship of Allah in the presence of peace. Islam is the religion of peace, and Muslims should be at peace with each other and, insofar as is possible, with all others."

Peace having been disposed of, the minister launches into a long discussion of the primacy of the Black Man and his remarkable accomplishments. To this end, he cites pertinent passages from the Islamic Quran, the Old Testament and other literature, as well as the writings of Muhammad himself. The hearers are reminded that their earlier knowledge of themselves and their past has been derived from the spurious teachings of the white man, who has "prostituted truth and defiled history to serve his own ends." Black Men must no longer accept the white man's teachings at face value. They must search out the facts and make intelligent judgments for themselves. The ministers will help them, for "the Messenger knows the truth about the white man" and he has taught his ministers well.

Often the minister reads passages from well-known historical, sociological or anthropological works and finds in them inconspicuous references to the Black Man's true history in the world. Black Men in Asia and Africa were enjoying advanced civilizations when the white man was eating his meat raw in the caves of Europe. Yet the whites, through their control of informational media (including the black preachers), have succeeded in making the so-called Negroes accept themselves as inferior.

Black Men sat on the thrones of Egypt and Ethiopia, fought beside the Romans in conquering the savages of Britain, discovered America long before Columbus and then piloted the ship on which Columbus sailed. Black Men ruled Spain and Southern Europe, reigned as popes in the Eternal City of Rome and built great civilizations on the west coast of Africa. They produced many Moslem scholars of whom the white

Christians profess to be ignorant, though the white civilization has stolen much knowledge from them. But the whites have taught the so-called Negro nothing of all this, and he has a mental block against searching out the information for himself. The so-called Negro doesn't want to know about his own history; he wants to know about the white man's history. He has been taught that his own history will only deposit him in the jungle, whereas the white man's history begins with Socrates dying nobly to illustrate a moral principle.

.   .   .

The audience is urged to give the Christian religion "back to the white man," for it is a religion of slavery and death. Negroes must also "give the white man back the names he has labeled you with," for these are badges of slavery. "If a Chinaman tells you his name is 'Whitfield,' you know there's something wrong somewhere. Well, there's also something wrong about a Black Man named 'Jones'."[4] Wherever the white man's name is attached to the so-called Negro, it is a symbol of possession. "Every time you sign your name you tell the world you're still the white man's chattel. If your body happens to be partly free, you're still his chattel in mind."

At this point, the minister may point to a painting which, in most temples, hangs on the wall behind the lectern. On the right half of the canvas are shown the symbols of Islam—the star and crescent—and the legend "Freedom-Justice-Equality." On the left are depicted the American flag, the Christian cross and a Negro hanging by his neck from a tree. These three, the minister explains, are the symbols of Christianity and what it has offered the Black Man. But now the Black Man has a choice: Islam, or continued abuse in subservience to the white Christians.

The men are reminded that they have been helpless even when their homes have been invaded. Resistance, even to protect their families, has meant death. Further, their economic conditions are so contrived that they must send their womenfolk out to work in the homes and offices of Christian white men. This is no accident: the white man controls the economy, and he knows the Black Man is at his mercy. He deliberately "castrates" the Black Man by paying his wife higher wages, so that the male is no longer head of his family. The wife then comes to despise her husband and to admire the white man, who is economically independent. And the white man not only employs the Black Man's women but proceeds "forthwith to send them home to their black husbands with blue-

4 From an interview with Malcolm X.

eyed babies." "These same robbers," says Muhammad, "disgrace and corrupt them with all kinds of diseases besides spotting up [their] children like the animal family."[5]

> We stand by with folded arms, cowards to the core, and allow the human brute . . . to take our women . . . the most priceless gift of a nation. . . . We cannot produce a pure, chaste nation with a "free-for-all" woman. If we [cannot] protect her from the human beast's advances, we should kill ourselves and our women.[6]

Christianity is dealt with summarily. It is considered a religion of ignominy and disgrace for the Black Man, but of great convenience and practicality for the white man. For the white man neither believes its teachings nor makes any attempt to practice them. The white man wants the so-called Negro to accept Christianity and live according to its teachings; but he then laughs at the so-called Negro for being a fool.

> "Love thy neighbor"; I have yet to meet one white man that loved his neighbor. . . . "Thou shalt not kill"; I have yet to meet such a Christian. . . . Where is a good Christian among this race?[7]

> . . . you fear and love [the white Christians] though you are even disgraced, beaten and killed by them, from your ministers of their slavery religion . . . down to the lowly, ignorant man in the mud. You have made yourselves the most foolish people on earth by loving and following after the ways of Slavemasters, whom Allah has revealed to me to be none other than real devils, and that their so-called Christianity is not His religion, nor the religion of Jesus or any other prophet of Allah (God).[8]

The audience is encouraged to disavow a religion which worships "a dead Jesus and his dead disciples," for such behavior distracts them from the business of trying to live in *this* world. "The white man has 'given you Jesus' while he has robbed you blind." Heaven is right here, and we must try to share in it now, rather than after death. Jesus has not "gone anywhere." "No one after death has ever gone any place but where they were carried. There is no heaven or hell other than on earth for you and me, and Jesus was no exception. His body is still . . . in Palestine and will remain there.[9]

With this transition, the minister next gives his attention to the Messenger's economic program. The hearers are chided for thriftlessness,

---

[5] "Mr. Muhammad Speaks," September 20, 1958.
[6] "Mr. Muhammad Speaks," June 6, 1959.
[7] *Ibid.,* April 18, 1959.
[8] *Ibid.,* May 2, 1959.
[9] *Ibid.*

conspicuous consumption and living beyond their means. Such self-indulgence will not build the Black Nation. The white man still owns the so-called Negro, because the white man owns the factories, the land, the houses and everything else needed for survival. When he decides to kill a Negro, he does not shoot him—except for amusement. "All he needs to do is to deny the Negro a job, and he will soon be just as dead." The Negro, in an attempt to protect himself against economic reprisal, adapts a posture of servility. "The so-called Negro's principles are always in pawn to the Slavemaster. The white man can make him bark and roll over any day in the week!" He is no more than a "free slave," for he dares not assert his manhood, no matter what indignities are heaped upon him or what atrocities are directed his way.

"Mr. Muhammad has an economic program," the minister continues, "which, if followed, will soon free the Black Man and make him equal to the other nations of the world." But the Black Man must be prepared to work: "Many of us, the so-called Negroes, today are so lazy that we are willing to suffer anything rather than go to work. It is true that God has come to sit us in heaven, but not a heaven wherein we won't have to work."[10]

Integration comes under heavy attack. It is anathema to the Movement, and the minister is trained to denounce it with especial vehemence. He may read from Muhammad's *The Supreme Wisdom,* in which the Messenger condemns integration as a kind of social opiate.

> The Slavemaster's children are doing everything in their power to prevent the so-called Negroes from accepting their own God and salvation, by putting on a great show of false love and friendship.
>
> This is being done through "integration," as it is called; that is, so-called Negroes and whites mixing together such as in schools, churches, and even intermarriage. . . . The poor slaves really think they are entering a condition of heaven with their former slaveholders, but it will prove to be their doom.
>
> Today . . . we are living in a time of great separation between the blacks and white. . . . The so-called Negroes must now return to their own; nothing else will solve the problem.[11]

The integration controversy is presented as a private quarrel between Northern and Southern whites:

> The Northern whites don't really care about the Negroes, but they don't like it because the crackers in the South disgrace the country and embarrass the nation. They can't keep out of the Black Man's

[10] Elijah Muhammad, *The Supreme Wisdom* (2nd ed.), p. 19.
[11] *Ibid.*

bed, and they have to keep lynching Negroes to try to keep it covered up. Now today, this makes for bad international relations. But the Southern cracker isn't going to clean himself up and stay on his side of town just to please the Yankees or to put the country in a better light. He can't. He was born a dog, and he'll be a dog. But he'll get up on Sunday morning and look pious in his pew![12]

The minister denounces integration as a stratagem of the white man to insure his survival in a world he has managed badly. The white man's time is up, and he knows it. He has no friends anywhere. He now hopes that by integrating with the rising Black Man, he can avoid paying for the long list of crimes he has perpetrated against humanity. So he has undertaken to "sweetheart" with the only people who are stupid enough to listen, the dupes he has trained to love him.

If the so-called American Negro were not so much in love with his deceivers, he would be preparing to be master now, rather than continuing to be satisfied as a free slave. For the white man's doom is sure.

The minister then speaks again of Islam, the religion of "peace, justice and equality." It is the *only* religion, he asserts, in which the Black Man in America—or anywhere else in the world—can find communion in brotherhood. Islam is hateful to the white man because it "equalizes" him, and "the white man would rather be dead than to be equal." But there are as many professing believers in Islam alone as there are white men in the entire world, and all non-white men everywhere are *by nature* Muslims, whether they profess it or not. The white race is thus hopelessly outnumbered by the Muslim brotherhood, which stretches across the world.

The *Holy Quran* of Islam is the "book which makes a distinction between the God of the righteous and the God of evil." This is the book which the Slavemaster has willfully kept from the blacks in America, for it contains all knowledge: "the Guidance of Light and Truth and of Wisdom and Judgment." "This book the *Holy Quran Sharrieff,* pulls the cover off the covered and shows the nation for the first time that which deceived 90 per cent of the people of the earth without knowledge of the deceiver."[13] At present, the *Holy Quran* must be taught by the leaders, but all Muslims should learn Arabic (which is taught at some temples) so that they may read it for themselves in the original. Meanwhile, only those translations approved by Muhammad should be used.[14]

Near the end of the meeting and at the conclusion of the minister's

[12] From a series of interviews with Muslims.
[13] *The Supreme Wisdom,* p. 51.
[14] A translation by Maulana Muhammed Ali and one by Allama Yusuf Ali are approved for the followers of Elijah Muhammad. [This footnote has been abbreviated here. EDS.]

lecture, the congregation is asked whether it agrees with what has been said. Any who do not agree are asked to state the points of disagreement, so that the minister may try to provide "the clarification necessary to unity." If the minister cannot provide a satisfactory answer, he promises to relay the question to the Messenger himself for resolution. No questions or problems are deemed beyond the capacities of the Messenger, for "it is because of his wisdom and insight that he has been chosen leader of the Black Nation."

When all questions raised from the floor by "those not yet returned to Islam" have been spoken to, the minister invites those who believe what they have heard and who have the courage of their convictions to come forward and declare for Islam. There are rarely more than fifteen or twenty in any one meeting; but in a three-hour lecture before 8,500 persons in Los Angeles' Olympic Auditorium, "Mr. Elijah Muhammad . . . persuaded more than 143 Christians to renounce Christianity and embrace Islam."[15]

Those who elect to join are warmly welcomed by the Muslim brotherhood and are assigned to classes of instruction. Those who are impressed, but are not yet willing to separate themselves from the Christian tradition, are urged to continue attending the public meetings, in the expectation that they will eventually overcome this hesitation. The merely curious and those suspected of being "stooges for the FBI" are not encouraged to return.

[15] *Los Angeles Herald-Dispatch,* February 20, 1960.

MALCOLM X

The Ballot or the Bullet

As *The Autobiography of Malcolm X* shows, the man born Malcolm Little was in every way an extraordinary human being. Although he was not part of the nationally recognized civil rights elite, his influence proved to be the most pervasive and long-lasting of all. He, more than any other, understood the depth of the conflict between the races; and he was finally the spokesman who could understand, share, and give voice to the experience of the black masses, their anger as much as their pain.

While he was the leading voice of the Black Muslims, and later, after he had split with Elijah Muhammad, Malcolm X emphasized that racism was not an anomaly in American democracy, but was deeply imbedded in the system and in the national character. At a time when others were urging black people to stand behind the liberal Democratic coalition, Malcolm was saying that blacks should organize for their *own* power. He did much to internationalize America's racial conflict by relating it to the struggle of the "people of color" all over the world.

By the time of his assassination, Malcolm X—along with the urban insurrections which coincided with his rise to national prominence—had altered the nature of America's dialogue on race and racism. He had charted a course for the new black militancy, which, after his death, made "Black Power" as appropriate a rallying cry for the spirit of the late sixties as "Black and White Together" had been for the earlier part of the decade.

"The Ballot or the Bullet," a speech given in Cleveland in 1964, shows Malcolm's characteristic intellectual and oratorical style. In the essay that follows it, black actor-director Ossie Davis, who delivered Malcolm's funeral eulogy, assesses the meaning his life had for black people.

MR. MODERATOR, BROTHER LOMAX, BROTHERS AND SISTERS, FRIENDS and enemies: I just can't believe everyone in here is a friend and I don't want to leave anybody out. The question tonight, as I understand it, is "The Negro Revolt, and Where Do We Go From Here?" or "What Next?" In my little humble way of understanding it, it points toward either the ballot or the bullet.

Before we try and explain what is meant by the ballot or the bullet, I would like to clarify something concerning myself. I'm still a Muslim, my religion is still Islam. That's my personal belief. Just as Adam Clayton Powell is a Christian minister who heads the Abyssinian Baptist Church in New York, but at the same time takes part in the political struggles to try and bring about rights to the black people in the country; and Dr. Martin Luther King is a Christian minister down in Atlanta, Georgia, who heads another organization fighting for the civil rights of black people in this country; and Rev. Galamison, I guess you've heard of him, is another Christian minister in New York who has been deeply involved in the school boycotts to eliminate segregated education; well, I myself am a minister, not a Christian minister, but a Muslim minister; and I believe in action on all fronts by whatever means necessary.

Although I'm still a Muslim, I'm not here tonight to discuss my religion. I'm not here to try and change your religion. I'm not here to argue or discuss anything that we differ about, because it's time for us to submerge our differences and realize that it is best for us to first see that we have the same problem, a common problem—a problem that will make you catch hell whether you're a Baptist, or a Methodist, or a Muslim, or a nationalist. Whether you're educated or illiterate, whether you live on the boulevard or in the alley, you're going to catch hell just like I am. We're all in the same boat and we all are going to catch the same hell from the same man. He just happens to be a white man. All of us have suffered here, in this country, political oppression at the hands of the white man, economic exploitation at the hands of the white man, and social degradation at the hands of the white man.

Now in speaking like this, it doesn't mean that we're anti-white, but it does mean we're anti-exploitation, we're anti-degradation, we're anti-oppression. And if the white man doesn't want us to be anti-him, let him stop oppressing and exploiting and degrading us. Whether we are Christians or Muslims or nationalists or agnostics or atheists, we must first learn to forget our differences. If we have differences, let us differ in the closet; when we come out in front, let us not have anything to argue about until we get finished arguing with the man. If the late President Kennedy could get together with Khrushchev and exchange some wheat, we certainly have more in common with each other than Kennedy and Khrushchev had with each other.

If we don't do something real soon, I think you'll have to agree that we're going to be forced either to use the ballot or the bullet. It's one or the other in 1964. It isn't that time is running out—time has run out! 1964 threatens to be the most explosive year America has ever witnessed. The most explosive year. Why? It's also a political year. It's the year when all of the white politicians will be back in the so-called Negro community jiving you and me for some votes. The year when all of the white political crooks will be right back in your and my community with their false promises, building up our hopes for a letdown, with their trickery and their treachery, with their false promises which they don't intend to keep. As they nourish these dissatisfactions, it can only lead to one thing, an explosion; and now we have the type of black man on the scene in America today—I'm sorry, Brother Lomax—who just doesn't intend to turn the other cheek any longer.

Don't let anybody tell you anything about the odds are against you. If they draft you, they send you to Korea and make you face 800 million Chinese. If you can be brave over there, you can be brave right here.

These odds aren't as great as those odds. And if you fight here, you will at least know what you're fighting for.

I'm not a politician, not even a student of politics; in fact, I'm not a student of much of anything. I'm not a Democrat, I'm not a Republican, and I don't even consider myself an American. If you and I were Americans, there'd be no problem. Those Hunkies that just got off the boat, they're already Americans; Polacks are already Americans; the Italian refugees are already Americans. Everything that came out of Europe, every blue-eyed thing, is already an American. And as long as you and I have been over here, we aren't Americans yet.

Well, I am one who doesn't believe in deluding myself. I'm not going to sit at your table and watch you eat, with nothing on my plate, and call myself a diner. Sitting at the table doesn't make you a diner, unless you eat some of what's on that plate. Being here in America doesn't make you an American. Being born here in America doesn't make you an American. Why, if birth made you American, you wouldn't need any legislation, you wouldn't need any amendments to the Constitution, you wouldn't be faced with civil-rights filibustering in Washington, D.C., right now. They don't have to pass civil-rights legislation to make a Polack an American.

No, I'm not an American. I'm one of the 22 million black people who are the victims of Americanism. One of the 22 million black people who are the victims of democracy, nothing but disguised hypocrisy. So, I'm not standing here speaking to you as an American, or a patriot, or a flag-saluter, or a flag-waver—no, not I. I'm speaking as a victim of this American system. And I see America through the eyes of the victim. I don't see any American dream; I see an American nightmare.

These 22 million victims are waking up. Their eyes are coming open. They're beginning to see what they used to only look at. They're becoming politically mature. They are realizing that there are new political trends from coast to coast. As they see these new political trends, it's possible for them to see that every time there's an election the races are so close that they have to have a recount. They had to recount in Massachusetts to see who was going to be governor, it was so close. It was the same way in Rhode Island, in Minnesota, and in many other parts of the country. And the same with Kennedy and Nixon when they ran for president. It was so close they had to count all over again. Well, what does this mean? It means that when white people are evenly divided, and black people have a bloc of votes of their own, it is left up to them to determine who's going to sit in the White House and who's going to be in the dog house.

It was the black man's vote that put the present administration in Washington, D.C. Your vote, your dumb vote, your ignorant vote, your wasted vote put in an administration in Washington, D.C., that has seen fit to pass every kind of legislation imaginable, saving you until last, then filibustering on top of that. And your and my leaders have the audacity to run around clapping their hands and talk about how much progress we're making. And what a good president we have. If he wasn't good in Texas, he sure can't be good in Washington, D.C. Because Texas is a lynch state. It is in the same breath as Mississippi, no different; only they lynch you in Texas with a Texas accent and lynch you in Mississippi with a Mississippi accent. And these Negro leaders have the audacity to go and have some coffee in the White House with a Texan, a Southern cracker—that's all he is—and then come out and tell you and me that he's going to be better for us because, since he's from the South, he knows how to deal with the Southerners. What kind of logic is that? Let Eastland be president, he's from the South too. He should be better able to deal with them than Johnson.

In this present administration they have in the House of Representatives 257 Democrats to only 177 Republicans. They control two-thirds of the House vote. Why can't they pass something that will help you and me? In the Senate, there are 67 senators who are of the Democratic Party. Only 33 of them are Republicans. Why, the Democrats have got the government sewed up, and you're the one who sewed it up for them. And what have they given you for it? Four years in office, and just now getting around to some civil-rights legislation. Just now, after everything else is gone, out of the way, they're going to sit down now and play with you all summer long—the same old giant con game that they call filibuster. All those are in cahoots together. Don't you ever think they're not in cahoots together, for the man that is heading the civil-rights filibuster is a man from Georgia named Richard Russell. When Johnson became president, the first man he asked for when he got back to Washington, D.C., was "Dicky"—that's how tight they are. That's his boy, that's his pal, that's his buddy. But they're playing that old con game. One of them makes believe he's for you, and he's got it fixed where the other one is so tight against you, he never has to keep his promise.

So it's time in 1964 to wake up. And when you see them coming up with that kind of conspiracy, let them know your eyes are open. And let them know you got something else that's wide open too. It's got to be the ballot or the bullet. The ballot or the bullet. If you're afraid to use an expression like that, you should get on out of the country, you should get back in the cotton patch, you should get back in the alley.

They get all the Negro vote, and after they get it, the Negro gets nothing in return. All they did when they got to Washington was give a few big Negroes big jobs. Those big Negroes didn't need big jobs, they already had jobs. That's camouflage, that's trickery, that's treachery, window-dressing. I'm not trying to knock out the Democrats for the Republicans, we'll get to them in a minute. But it's true—you put the Democrats first and the Democrats put you last.

Look at it the way it is. What alibis do they use, since they control Congress and the Senate? What alibi do they use when you and I ask, "Well, when are you going to keep your promise?" They blame the Dixiecrats. What is a Dixiecrat? A Democrat. A Dixiecrat is nothing but a Democrat in disguise. The titular head of the Democrats is also the head of the Dixiecrats, because the Dixiecrats are a part of the Democratic Party. The Democrats have never kicked the Dixiecrats out of the party. The Dixiecrats bolted themselves once, but the Democrats didn't put them out. Imagine, these lowdown Southern segregationists put the Northern Democrats down. But the Northern Democrats have never put the Dixiecrats down. No, look at that thing the way it is. They have got a con game going on, a political con game, and you and I are in the middle. It's time for you and me to wake up and start looking at it like it is, and trying to understand it like it is; and then we can deal with it like it is.

The Dixiecrats in Washington, D.C., control the key committees that run the government. The only reason the Dixiecrats control these committees is because they have seniority. The only reason they have seniority is because they come from states where Negroes can't vote. This is not even a government that's based on democracy. It is not a government that is made up of representatives of the people. Half of the people in the South can't even vote. Eastland is not even supposed to be in Washington. Half of the senators and congressmen who occupy these key positions in Washington, D.C., are there illegally, are there unconstitutionally.

I was in Washington, D.C., a week ago Thursday, when they were debating whether or not they should let the bill come onto the floor. And in the back of the room where the Senate meets, there's a huge map of the United States, and on that map it shows the location of Negroes throughout the country. And it shows that the Southern section of the country, the states that are most heavily concentrated with Negroes, are the ones that have senators and congressmen standing up filibustering and doing all other kinds of trickery to keep the Negro from being able to vote. This is pitiful. But it's not pitiful for us any longer; it's actually pitiful for the white man, because soon now, as the Negro awakens a little more and sees the vise that he's in, sees the bag that he's in, sees the real game that he's in, then the Negro's going to develop a new tactic.

These senators and congressmen actually violate the constitutional amendments that guarantee the people of that particular state or county the right to vote. And the Constitution itself has within it the machinery to expel any representative from a state where the voting rights of the people are violated. You don't even need new legislation. Any person in Congress right now, who is there from a state or a district where the voting rights of the people are violated, that particular person should be expelled from Congress. And when you expel him, you've removed one of the obstacles in the path of any real meaningful legislation in this country. In fact, when you expel them, you don't need new legislation, because they will be replaced by black representatives from counties and districts where the black man is in the majority, not in the minority.

If the black man in these Southern states had his full voting rights, the key Dixiecrats in Washington, D.C., which means the key Democrats in Washington, D.C., would lose their seats. The Democratic Party itself would lose its power. It would cease to be powerful as a party. When you see the amount of power that would be lost by the Democratic Party if it were to lose the Dixiecrat wing, or branch, or element, you can see where it's against the interests of the Democrats to give voting rights to Negroes in states where the Democrats have been in complete power and authority ever since the Civil War. You just can't belong to that party without analyzing it.

I say again, I'm not anti-Democrat, I'm not anti-Republican, I'm not anti-anything. I'm just questioning their sincerity, and some of the strategy that they've been using on our people by promising them promises that they don't intend to keep. When you keep the Democrats in power, you're keeping the Dixiecrats in power. I doubt that my good Brother Lomax will deny that. A vote for a Democrat is a vote for a Dixiecrat. That's why, in 1964, it's time now for you and me to become more politically mature and realize what the ballot is for; what we're supposed to get when we cast a ballot; and that if we don't cast a ballot, it's going to end up in a situation where we're going to have to cast a bullet. It's either a ballot or a bullet.

In the North, they do it a different way. They have a system that's known as gerrymandering, whatever that means. It means when Negroes become too heavily concentrated in a certain area, and begin to gain too much political power, the white man comes along and changes the district lines. You may say, "Why do you keep saying white man?" Because it's the white man who does it. I haven't ever seen any Negro changing any lines. They don't let him get near the line. It's the white man who does this. And usually, it's the white man who grins at you the most, and pats you on the back, and is supposed to be your friend. He may be friendly, but he's not your friend.

So, what I'm trying to impress upon you, in essence, is this: You and I in America are faced not with a segregationist conspiracy, we're faced with a government conspiracy. Everyone who's filibustering is a senator—that's the government. Everyone who's finagling in Washington, D.C., is a congressman—that's the government. You don't have anybody putting blocks in your path but people who are a part of the government. The same government that you go abroad to fight for and die for is the government that is in a conspiracy to deprive you of your voting rights, deprive you of your economic opportunities, deprive you of decent housing, deprive you of decent education. You don't need to go to the employer alone, it is the government itself, the government of America, that is responsible for the oppression and exploitation and degradation of black people in this country. And you should drop it in their lap. This government has failed the Negro. This so-called democracy has failed the Negro. And all these white liberals have definitely failed the Negro.

So, where do we go from here? First, we need some friends. We need some new allies. The entire civil-rights struggle needs a new interpretation, a broader interpretation. We need to look at this civil-rights thing from another angle—from the inside as well as from the outside. To those of us whose philosophy is black nationalism, the only way you can get involved in the civil-rights struggle is give it a new interpretation. That old interpretation excluded us. It kept us out. So, we're giving a new interpretation to the civil-rights struggle, an interpretation that will enable us to come into it, take part in it. And these handkerchief-heads who have been dillydallying and pussyfooting and compromising—we don't intend to let them pussyfoot and dillydally and compromise any longer.

How can you thank a man for giving you what's already yours? How then can you thank him for giving you only part of what's already yours? You haven't even made progress, if what's being given to you, you should have had already. That's not progress. And I love my Brother Lomax, the way he pointed out we're right back where we were in 1954. We're not even as far up as we were in 1954. We're behind where we were in 1954. There's more segregation now than there was in 1954. There's more racial animosity, more racial hatred, more racial violence today in 1964, than there was in 1954. Where is the progress?

And now you're facing a situation where the young Negro's coming up. They don't want to hear that "turn-the-other-cheek" stuff, no. In Jacksonville, those were teenagers, they were throwing Molotov cocktails. Negroes have never done that before. But it shows you there's a new deal coming in. There's new thinking coming in. There's new strategy coming in. It'll be Molotov cocktails this month, hand grenades next month, and something else next month. It'll be ballots, or it'll be bullets. It'll be liberty, or it will be death. The only difference about this kind of death—it'll be reciprocal. You know what is meant by "reciprocal"? That's one of Brother Lomax's words, I stole it from him. I don't usually deal with those big words because I don't usually deal with big people. I deal with small people. I find you can get a whole lot of small people and whip hell out of a whole lot of big people. They haven't got anything to lose, and they've got everything to gain. And they'll let you know in a minute: "It takes two to tango; when I go, you go."

The black nationalists, those whose philosophy is black nationalism, in bringing about this new interpretation of the entire meaning of civil rights, look upon it as meaning, as Brother Lomax has pointed out, equality of opportunity. Well, we're justified in seeking civil rights, if it means equality of opportunity, because all we're doing there is trying to collect for our investment. Our mothers and fathers invested sweat and blood. Three hundred and ten years we worked in this country without a dime in return—I mean without a *dime* in return. You let the white man walk around here talking about how rich this country is, but you never stop to think how it got rich so quick. It got rich because you made it rich.

You take the people who are in this audience right now. They're poor, we're all poor as individuals. Our weekly salary individually amounts to hardly anything. But if you take the salary of everyone in here collectively it'll fill up a whole lot of baskets. It's a lot of wealth. If you can collect the wages of just these people right here for a year, you'll be rich —richer than rich. When you look at it like that, think how rich Uncle Sam had to become, not with this handful, but millions of black people. Your and my mother and father, who didn't work an eight-hour shift, but worked from "can't see" in the morning until "can't see" at night, and worked for nothing, making the white man rich, making Uncle Sam rich.

This is our investment. This is our contribution—our blood. Not only did we give of our free labor, we gave of our blood. Every time he had a call to arms, we were the first ones in uniform. We died on every battlefield the white man had. We have made a greater sacrifice than anybody who's standing up in America today. We have made a greater contribution and have collected less. Civil rights, for those of us whose philosophy is black nationalism, means: "Give it to us now. Don't wait for next year. Give it to us yesterday, and that's not fast enough."

I might stop right here to point out one thing. Whenever you're going after something that belongs to you, anyone who's depriving you of the right to have it is a criminal. Understand that. Whenever you are going after something that is yours, you are within your legal rights to lay claim to it. And anyone who puts forth any effort to deprive you of that which is yours, is breaking the law, is a criminal. And this was pointed out by the Supreme Court decision. It outlawed segregation. Which means segregation is against the law. Which means a segregationist is breaking the law. A segregationist is a criminal. You can't label him as anything other than that. And when you demonstrate against segregation, the law is on your side. The Supreme Court is on your side.

Now, who is it that opposes you in carrying out the law? The police department itself. With police dogs and clubs. Whenever you demonstrate against segregation, whether it is segregated education, segregated housing, or anything else, the law is on your side, and anyone who stands in the way is not the law any longer. They are breaking the law, they are not representatives of the law. Any time you demonstrate against segregation and a man has the audacity to put a police dog on you, kill that dog, kill him, I'm telling you, kill that dog. I say it, if they put me in jail tomorrow, kill—that—dog. Then you'll put a stop to it. Now, if these white people in here don't want to see that kind of action, get down and tell the mayor to tell the police department to pull the dogs in. That's all you have to do. If you don't do it, someone else will.

If you don't take this kind of stand, your little children will grow up and look at you and think "shame." If you don't take an uncompromising stand—I don't mean go out and get violent; but at the same time you should never be nonviolent unless you run into some nonviolence. I'm nonviolent with those who are nonviolent with me. But when you drop that violence on me, then you've made me go insane, and I'm not responsible for what I do. And that's the way every Negro should get. Any time you know you're within the law, within your legal rights, within your moral rights, in accord with justice, then die for what you believe in. But don't die alone. Let your dying be reciprocal. This is what is meant by equality. What's good for the goose is good for the gander.

When we begin to get in this area, we need new friends, we need new allies. We need to expand the civil-rights struggle to a higher level—to the level of human rights. Whenever you are in a civil-rights struggle, whether you know it or not, you are confining yourself to the jurisdiction of Uncle Sam. No one from the outside world can speak out in your behalf as long as your struggle is a civil-rights struggle. Civil rights comes within the domestic affairs of this country. All of our African brothers and our Asian brothers and our Latin-American brothers cannot open their mouths and interfere in the domestic affairs of the United States. And as long as it's civil rights, this comes under the jurisdiction of Uncle Sam.

But the United Nations has what's known as the charter of human rights, it has a committee that deals in human rights. You may wonder why all of the atrocities that have been committed in Africa and in Hungary and in Asia and in Latin America are brought before the UN, and the Negro problem is never brought before the UN. This is part of the conspiracy. This old, tricky, blue-eyed liberal who is supposed to be your and my friend, supposed to be in our corner, supposed to be subsidizing our struggle, and supposed to be acting in the capacity of an adviser, never tells you anything about human rights. They keep you wrapped up in civil rights. And you spend so much time barking up the civil-rights tree, you don't even know there's a human-rights tree on the same floor.

When you expand the civil-rights struggle to the level of human rights, you can then take the case of the black man in this country before the nations in the UN. You can take it before the General Assembly. You can take Uncle Sam before a world court. But the only level you can do it on is the level of human rights. Civil rights keeps you under his restrictions, under his jurisdiction. Civil rights keeps you in his pocket. Civil rights means you're asking Uncle Sam to treat you right. Human rights are something you were born with. Human rights are your God-given rights. Human rights are the rights that are recognized by all nations of this earth. And any time any one violates your human rights, you can take them to the world court. Uncle Sam's hands are dripping with blood, dripping with the blood of the black man in this country. He's the earth's number-one hypocrite. He has the audacity—yes, he has—imagine him posing as the leader of the free world. The free world!—and you over here singing "We Shall Overcome." Expand the civil-rights struggle to the level of human rights, take it into the United Nations, where our African brothers can throw their weight on our side, where our Asian brothers can throw their weight on our side, where our Latin-American brothers can throw their weight on our side, and where 800 million Chinamen are sitting there waiting to throw their weight on our side.

Let the world know how bloody his hands are. Let the world know the hypocrisy that's practiced over here. Let it be the ballot or the bullet. Let him know that it must be the ballot or the bullet.

When you take your case to Washington, D.C., you're taking it to the criminal who's responsible; it's like running from the wolf to the fox. They're all in cahoots together. They all work political chicanery and make you look like a chump before the eyes of the world. Here you are walking around in America, getting ready to be drafted and sent abroad, like a tin soldier, and when you get over there, people ask you what you are fighting for, and you have to stick your tongue in your cheek. No, take Uncle Sam to court, take him before the world.

By ballot I only mean freedom. Don't you know—I disagree with Lomax on this issue—that the ballot is more important than the dollar? Can I prove it? Yes. Look in the UN. There are poor nations in the UN; yet those poor nations can get together with their voting power and keep the rich nations from making a move. They have one nation—one vote, everyone has an equal vote. And when those brothers from Asia, and Africa and the darker parts of this earth get together, their voting power is sufficient to hold Sam in check. Or Russia in check. Or some other section of the earth in check. So, the ballot is most important.

Right now, in this country, if you and I, 22 million African-Americans —that's what we are—Africans who are in America. You're nothing but Africans. Nothing but Africans. In fact, you'd get farther calling yourself African instead of Negro. Africans don't catch hell. You're the only one catching hell. They don't have to pass civil-rights bills for Africans. An African can go anywhere he wants right now. All you've got to do is tie your head up. That's right, go anywhere you want. Just stop being a Negro. Change your name to Hoogagagooba. That'll show you how silly the white man is. You're dealing with a silly man. A friend of mine who's very dark put a turban on his head and went into a restaurant in Atlanta before they called themselves desegregated. He went into a white restaurant, he sat down, they served him, and he said, "What would happen if a Negro came in here?" And there he's sitting, black as night, but because he had his head wrapped up the waitress looked back at him and says, "Why, there wouldn't no nigger dare come in here."

So, you're dealing with a man whose bias and prejudice are making him lose his mind, his intelligence, every day. He's frightened. He looks around and sees what's taking place on this earth, and he sees that the pendulum of time is swinging in your direction. The dark people are waking up. They're losing their fear of the white man. No place where he's fighting right now is he winning. Everywhere he's fighting, he's fighting someone your and my complexion. And they're beating him. He can't win any more. He's won his last battle. He failed to win the Korean War. He couldn't win it. He had to sign a truce. That's a loss. Any time Uncle Sam, with all his machinery for warfare, is held to a draw by some rice-eaters, he's lost the battle. He had to sign a truce. America's not supposed to sign a truce. She's supposed to be bad. But she's not bad any more. She's bad as long as she can use her hydrogen bomb, but she can't use hers for fear Russia might use hers. Russia can't use hers, for fear that Sam might use his. So, both of them are weaponless. They can't use the weapon because each's weapon nullifies the other's. So the only place where action can take place is on the ground. And the white man can't win another war fighting on the ground. Those days are over. The black man knows it, the brown man knows it, the red man knows it, and the yellow man knows it. So they engage him in guerrilla warfare. That's not his style. You've got to have heart to be a guerrilla warrior, and he hasn't got any heart. I'm telling you now.

I just want to give you a little briefing on guerrilla warfare because, before you know it, before you know it—It takes heart to be a guerrilla warrior because you're on your own. In conventional warfare you have tanks and a whole lot of other people with you to back you up, planes over your head and all that kind of stuff. But a guerrilla is on his own. All you have is a rifle, some sneakers and a bowl of rice, and that's all you need—and a lot of heart. The Japanese on some of those islands in the Pacific, when the American soldiers landed, one Japanese sometimes could hold the whole army off. He'd just wait until the sun went down, and when the sun went down they were all equal. He would take his little blade and slip from bush to bush, and from American to American. The white soldiers couldn't cope with that. Whenever you see a white soldier that fought in the Pacific, he has the shakes, he has a nervous condition, because they scared him to death.

The same thing happened to the French up in French Indochina. People who just a few years previously were rice farmers got together and ran the heavily-mechanized French army out of Indochina. You don't need it—modern warfare today won't work. This is the day of the guerrilla. They did the same thing in Algeria. Algerians, who were nothing but Bedouins, took a rifle and sneaked off to the hills, and de Gaulle and all of his highfalutin' war machinery couldn't defeat those guerrillas. Nowhere on this earth does the white man win in a guerrilla warfare. It's not his speed. Just as guerrilla warfare is prevailing in Asia and in parts of Africa and in parts of Latin America, you've got to be mighty naive, or you've got to play the black man cheap, if you don't think some day he's going to wake up and find that it's got to be the ballot or the bullet.

I would like to say, in closing, a few things concerning the Muslim Mosque, Inc., which we established recently in New York City. It's true we're Muslims and our religion is Islam, but we don't mix our religion with our politics and our economics and our social and civil activities— not any more. We keep our religion in our mosque. After our religious services are over, then as Muslims we become involved in political action, economic action and social and civic action. We become involved with anybody, anywhere, any time and in any manner that's designed to eliminate the evils, the political, economic and social evils that are afflicting the people of our community.

The political philosophy of black nationalism means that the black man should control the politics and the politicians in his own community; no more. The black man in the black community has to be re-educated into the science of politics so he will know what politics is supposed to bring him in return. Don't be throwing out any ballots. A ballot is like a bullet. You don't throw your ballots until you see a target, and if that target is not within your reach, keep your ballot in your pocket. The political philosophy of black nationalism is being taught in the Christian church. It's being taught in the NAACP. It's being taught in CORE meetings. It's being taught in SNCC [Student Nonviolent Coordinating Committee] meetings. It's being taught in Muslim meetings. It's being taught where nothing but atheists and agnostics come together. It's being taught everywhere. Black people are fed up with the dillydallying, pussyfooting, compromising approach that we've been using toward getting our freedom. We want freedom *now,* but we're not going to get it saying "We Shall Overcome." We've got to fight until we overcome.

The economic philosophy of black nationalism is pure and simple. It only means that we should control the economy of our community. Why should white people be running all the stores in our community? Why should white people be running the banks of our community? Why should the economy of our community be in the hands of the white man? Why? If a black man can't move his store into a white community, you tell me why a white man should move his store into a black community. The philosophy of black nationalism involves a re-education program in the black community in regards to economics. Our people have to be made to see that any time you take your dollar out of your community and spend it in a community where you don't live, the community where you live will get poorer and poorer, and the community where you spend your money will get richer and richer. Then you wonder why where you live is always a ghetto or a slum area. And where you and I are concerned, not only do we lose it when we spend it out of the community, but the white man has got all our stores in the community tied up; so that though we spend it in the community, at sundown the man who runs the store takes it over across town somewhere. He's got us in a vise.

So the economic philosophy of black nationalism means in every church, in every civic organization, in every fraternal order, it's time now for our people to become conscious of the importance of controlling the economy of our community. If we own the stores, if we operate the businesses, if we try and establish some industry in our own community, then we're developing to the position where we are creating employment for our own kind. Once you gain control of the economy of your own community, then you don't have to picket and boycott and beg some cracker downtown for a job in his business.

The social philosophy of black nationalism only means that we have to get together and remove the evils, the vices, alcoholism, drug addiction, and other evils that are destroying the moral fiber of our community. We ourselves have to lift the level of our community, the standard of our community to a higher level, make our own society beautiful so that we will be satisfied in our own social circles and won't be running around here trying to knock our way into a social circle where we're not wanted.

So I say, in spreading a gospel such as black nationalism, it is not designed to make the black man re-evaluate the white man—you know him already—but to make the black man re-evaluate himself. Don't change the white man's mind—you can't change his mind, and that whole thing about appealing to the moral conscience of America—America's conscience is bankrupt. She lost all conscience a long time ago. Uncle Sam has no conscience. They don't know what morals are. They don't try and eliminate an evil because it's evil, or because it's illegal, or because it's immoral; they eliminate it only when it threatens their existence. So you're wasting your time appealing to the moral conscience of a bankrupt man like Uncle Sam. If he had a conscience, he'd straighten this thing out with no more pressure being put upon him. So it is not necessary to change the white man's mind. We have to change our own mind. You can't change his mind about us. We've got to change our own minds about each other. We have to see each other with new eyes. We have to see each other as brothers and sisters. We have to come together with warmth so we can develop unity and harmony that's necessary to get this problem solved ourselves. How can we do this? How can we avoid jealousy? How can we avoid the suspicion and the divisions that exist in the community? I'll tell you how.

I have watched how Billy Graham comes into a city, spreading what he calls the gospel of Christ, which is only white nationalism. That's what he is. Billy Graham is a white nationalist; I'm a black nationalist. But since it's the natural tendency for leaders to be jealous and look upon a powerful figure like Graham with suspicion and envy, how is it possible for him to come into a city and get all the cooperation of the church leaders? Don't think because they're church leaders that they don't have weaknesses that make them envious and jealous—no, everybody's got it. It's not an accident that when they want to choose a cardinal [as Pope] over there in Rome, they get in a closet so you can't hear them cussing and fighting and carrying on.

Billy Graham comes in preaching the gospel of Christ, he evangelizes the gospel, he stirs everybody up, but he never tries to start a church. If he came in trying to start a church, all the churches would be against him. So, he just comes in talking about Christ and tells everybody who gets Christ to go to any church where Christ is; and in this way the church cooperates with him. So we're going to take a page from his book.

Our gospel is black nationalism. We're not trying to threaten the existence of any organization, but we're spreading the gospel of black nationalism. Anywhere there's a church that is also preaching and practicing the gospel of black nationalism, join that church. If the NAACP is preaching and practicing the gospel of black nationalism, join the NAACP. If CORE is spreading and practicing the gospel of black nationalism, join CORE. Join any organization that has a gospel that's for the uplift of the black man. And when you get into it and see them pussyfooting or compromising, pull out of it because that's not black nationalism. We'll find another one.

And in this manner, the organizations will increase in number and in quantity and in quality, and by August, it is then our intention to have a black nationalist convention which will consist of delegates from all over the country who are interested in the political, economic and social philosophy of black nationalism. After these delegates convene, we will hold a seminar, we will hold discussions, we will listen to everyone. We want to hear new ideas and new solutions and new answers. And at that time, if we see fit then to form a black nationalist party, we'll form a black nationalist party. If it's necessary to form a black nationalist army, we'll form a black nationalist army. It'll be the ballot or the bullet. It'll be liberty or it'll be death.

It's time for you and me to stop sitting in this country, letting some cracker senators, Northern crackers and Southern crackers, sit there in Washington, D.C., and come to a conclusion in their mind that you and I are supposed to have civil rights. There's no white man going to tell me anything about *my* rights. Brothers and sisters, always remember, if it doesn't take senators and congressmen and presidential proclamations to give freedom to the white man, it is not necessary for legislation or proclamation or Supreme Court decisions to give freedom to the black man. You let that white man know, if this is a country of freedom, let it be a country of freedom; and if it's not a country of freedom, change it.

We will work with anybody, anywhere, at any time, who is genuinely interested in tackling the problem head-on, nonviolently as long as the enemy is nonviolent, but violent when the enemy gets violent. We'll work with you on the voter-registration drive, we'll work with you on rent strikes, we'll work with you on school boycotts—I don't believe in any kind of integration; I'm not even worried about it because I know you're not going to get it anyway; you're not going to get it because you're afraid to die; you've got to be ready to die if you try and force yourself on the white man, because he'll get just as violent as those crackers in Mississippi, right here in Cleveland. But we will still work with you on the school boycotts because we're against a segregated school system. A segregated school system produces children who, when they graduate, graduate with crippled minds. But this does not mean that a school is segregated because it's all black. A segregated school means a school that is controlled by people who have no real interest in it whatsoever.

Let me explain what I mean. A segregated district or community is a community in which people live, but outsiders control the politics and the economy of that community. They never refer to the white section as a segregated community. It's the all-Negro section that's a segregated community. Why? The white man controls his own school, his own bank, his own economy, his own politics, his own everything, his own community—but he also controls yours. When you're under someone else's control, you're segregated. They'll always give you the lowest or the worst that there is to offer, but it doesn't mean you're segregated just because you have your own. You've got to *control* your own. Just like the white man has control of his, you need to control yours.

You know the best way to get rid of segregation? The white man is more afraid of separation than he is of integration. Segregation means that he puts you away from him, but not far enough for you to be out of his jurisdiction; separation means you're gone. And the white man will integrate faster than he'll let you separate. So we will work with you against the segregated school system because it's criminal, because it is absolutely destructive, in every way imaginable, to the minds of the children who have to be exposed to that type of crippling education.

Last but not least, I must say this concerning the great controversy over rifles and shotguns. The only thing that I've ever said is that in areas where the government has proven itself either unwilling or unable to defend the lives and the property of Negroes, it's time for Negroes to defend themselves. Article number two of the constitutional amendments provides you and me the right to own a rifle or a shotgun. It is constitutionally legal to own a shotgun or a rifle. This doesn't mean you're going to get a rifle and form battalions and go out looking for white folks, although you'd be within your rights—I mean, you'd be justified; but that would be illegal and we don't do anything illegal. If the white man doesn't want the black man buying rifles and shotguns, then let the government do its job. That's all. And don't let the white man come to you and ask you what you think about what Malcolm says—why, you old Uncle Tom. He would never ask you if he thought you were going to say, "Amen!" No, he is making a Tom out of you.

So, this doesn't mean forming rifle clubs and going out looking for people, but it is time, in 1964, if you are a man, to let that man know. If he's not going to do his job in running the government and providing you and me with the protection that our taxes are supposed to be for, since he spends all those billions for his defense budget, he certainly can't begrudge you and me spending $12 or $15 for a single-shot, or double-action. I hope you understand. Don't go out shooting people, but any time, brothers and sisters, and especially the men in this audience—some of you wearing Congressional Medals of Honor, with shoulders this wide, chests this big, muscles that big—any time you and I sit around and read where they bomb a church and murder in cold blood, not some grownups, but four little girls while they were praying to the same god the white man taught them to pray to, and you and I see the government go down and can't find who did it.

Why, this man—he can find Eichmann hiding down in Argentina somewhere. Let two or three American soldiers, who are minding somebody else's business way over in South Vietnam, get killed, and he'll send battleships, sticking his nose in their business. He wanted to send troops down to Cuba and make them have what he calls free elections—this old cracker who doesn't have free elections in his own country. No, if you never see me another time in your life, if I die in the morning, I'll die saying one thing: the ballot or the bullet, the ballot or the bullet.

If a Negro in 1964 has to sit around and wait for some cracker senator to filibuster when it comes to the rights of black people, why, you and I should hang our heads in shame. You talk about a march on Washington in 1963, you haven't seen anything. There's some more going down in '64. And this time they're not going like they went last year. They're not going singing "We Shall Overcome." They're not going with white friends. They're not going with placards already painted for them. They're not going with round-trip tickets. They're going with one-way tickets.

And if they don't want that non-nonviolent army going down there, tell them to bring the filibuster to a halt. The black nationalists aren't going to wait. Lyndon B. Johnson is the head of the Democratic Party. If he's for civil rights, let him go into the Senate next week and declare himself. Let him go in there right now and declare himself. Let him go in there and denounce the Southern branch of his party. Let him go in there right now and take a moral stand—right now, not later. Tell him, don't wait until election time. If he waits too long, brothers and sisters, he will be responsible for letting a condition develop in this country which will create a climate that will bring seeds up out of the ground with vegetation on the end of them looking like something these people never dreamed of. In 1964, it's the ballot or the bullet. Thank you.

OSSIE DAVIS

On Malcolm X

[See headnote on page 479.]

Mr. Davis wrote the following in response to a magazine editor's question: Why did you eulogize Malcolm X?

YOU ARE NOT THE ONLY PERSON CURIOUS TO KNOW WHY I WOULD eulogize a man like Malcolm X. Many who know and respect me have written letters. Of these letters I am proudest of those from a sixth-grade class of young white boys and girls who asked me to explain. I appreciate your giving me this chance to do so.

You may anticipate my defense somewhat by considering the following fact: no Negro has yet asked me that question. (My pastor in Grace Baptist Church where I teach Sunday school preached a sermon about Malcolm in which he called him a "giant in a sick world.") Every one of the many letters I got from my own people lauded Malcolm as a man, and commended me for having spoken at his funeral.

At the same time—and this is important—most of them took special pains to disagree with much or all of what Malcolm said and what he stood for. That is, with one singing exception, they all, every last, black, glory-hugging one of them, knew that Malcolm—whatever else he was or was not—*Malcolm was a man!*

White folks do not need anybody to remind them that they are men. We do! This was his one incontrovertible benefit to his people.

Protocol and common sense require that Negroes stand back and let the white man speak up for us, defend us, and lead us from behind the scene in our fight. This is the essence of Negro politics. But Malcolm said to hell with that! Get up off your knees and fight your own battles. That's the way to win back your self-respect. That's the way to make

ON MALCOLM X by Ossie Davis. From *The Autobiography of Malcolm X* by Malcolm X, with the assistance of Alex Haley (New York: Grove Press, Inc., 1966). Reprinted by permission of Ossie Davis.

the white man respect you. And if he won't let you live like a man, he certainly can't keep you from dying like one!

Malcolm, as you can see, was refreshing excitement; he scared hell out of the rest of us, bred as we are to caution, to hypocrisy in the presence of white folks, to the smile that never fades. Malcolm knew that every white man in America profits directly or indirectly from his position vis-à-vis Negroes, profits from racism even though he does not practice it or believe in it.

He also knew that every Negro who did not challenge on the spot every instance of racism, overt or covert, committed against him and his people, who chose instead to swallow his spit and go on smiling, was an Uncle Tom and a traitor, without balls or guts, or any other commonly accepted aspects of manhood!

Now, we knew all these things as well as Malcolm did, but we also knew what happened to people who stick their necks out and say them. And if all the lies we tell ourselves by way of extenuation were put into print, it would constitute one of the great chapters in the history of man's justifiable cowardice in the face of other men.

But Malcolm kept snatching our lies away. He kept shouting the painful truth we whites and blacks did not want to hear from all the housetops. And he wouldn't stop for love nor money.

You can imagine what a howling, shocking nuisance this man was to both Negroes and whites. Once Malcolm fastened on you, you could not escape. He was one of the most fascinating and charming men I have ever met, and never hesitated to take his attractiveness and beat you to death with it. Yet his irritation, though painful to us, was most salutary. He would make you angry as hell, but he would also make you proud. It was impossible to remain defensive and apologetic about being a Negro in his presence. He wouldn't let you. And you always left his presence with the sneaky suspicion that maybe, after all, you *were* a man!

But in explaining Malcolm, let me take care not to explain him away. He had been a criminal, an addict, a pimp, and a prisoner; a racist, and a hater, he had really believed the white man was a devil. But all this had changed. Two days before his death, in commenting to Gordon Parks about his past life he said: "That was a mad scene. The sickness and madness of those days! I'm glad to be free of them."

And Malcolm was free. No one who knew him before and after his trip to Mecca could doubt that he had completely abandoned racism, separatism, and hatred. But he had not abandoned his shock-effect statements, his bristling agitation for immediate freedom in this country not only for blacks, but for everybody.

And most of all, in the area of race relations, he still delighted in twisting the white man's tail, and in making Uncle Toms, compromisers, and accommodationists—I deliberately include myself—thoroughly ashamed of the urbane and smiling hypocrisy we practice merely to exist in a world whose value we both envy and despise.

But even had Malcolm not changed, he would still have been a relevant figure on the American scene, standing in relation as he does, to the "responsible" civil rights leaders, just about where John Brown stood in relation to the "responsible" abolitionist in the fight against slavery. Almost all disagreed with Brown's mad and fanatical tactics which led him foolishly to attack a Federal arsenal at Harpers Ferry, to lose two sons there, and later to be hanged for treason.

Yet, today the world, and especially the Negro people, proclaim Brown not a traitor, but a hero and a martyr in a noble cause. So in future, I will not be surprised if men come to see that Malcolm X was, within his own limitations, and in his own inimitable style, also a martyr in that cause.

But there is much controversy still about this most controversial American, and I am content to wait for history to make the final decision.

But in personal judgment, there is no appeal from instinct. I knew the man personally, and however much I disagreed with him, I never doubted that Malcolm X, even when he was wrong, was always that rarest thing in the world among us Negroes: a true man.

And if, to protect my relations with the many good white folks who make it possible for me to earn a fairly good living in the entertainment industry, I was too chicken, too cautious, to admit that fact when he was alive, I thought at least that now, when all the white folks are safe from him at last, I could be honest with myself enough to lift my hat for one final salute to that brave, black, ironic gallantry, which was his style and hallmark, that shocking *zing* of fire-and-be-damned-to-you, so absolutely absent in every other Negro man I know, which brought him, too soon, to his death.

Power and Racism

During the civil rights struggle, the young black activists of SNCC and other organizations had gained first-hand knowledge of how entrenched white power operates. They had also heard the message of Malcolm X, seen the urban ghettoes explode in violence, and noted that the North reacted with a "backlash" when the struggle spread from Mississippi and Alabama to Los Angeles and Chicago. Unsatisfied with token changes that came about through federal legislation, doubting the ability of moral suasion to bring about fundamental change, and feeling that the American social system was corrupt, they chose another course: the organization of black people—without the presence of large numbers of white liberals—into social, political and economic units that would allow them to determine the course and content of their own lives. Thus, in 1966, the slogan "Black Power" was born on James Meredith's Mississippi March Against Fear.

"Black Power" was more than a slogan, however, and more than rhetoric. As the following selection shows, Stokely Carmichael and the other SNCC militants envisioned it as the call for a program that would allow black people to make a serious bid for power and to take responsibility for those areas of their lives that others had always controlled.

ONE OF THE TRAGEDIES OF THE STRUGGLE AGAINST RACISM IS THAT UP to now there has been no national organization which could speak to the growing militancy of young black people in the urban ghetto. There has been only a civil rights movement, whose tone of voice was adapted to an audience of liberal whites. It served as a sort of buffer zone between them and angry young blacks. None of its so-called leaders could go into a rioting community and be listened to. In a sense, I blame ourselves —together with the mass media—for what has happened in Watts, Harlem, Chicago, Cleveland, Omaha. Each time the people in those cities saw Martin Luther King get slapped, they became angry; when they saw four little black girls bombed to death, they were angrier; and when nothing happened, they were steaming. We had nothing to offer that

POWER AND RACISM From *The New York Review of Books*, September 22, 1966. Originally titled "What We Want." Reprinted by permission of the Student Nonviolent Coordinating Committee.

they could see, except to go out and be beaten again. We helped to build their frustration.

For too many years, black Americans marched and had their heads broken and got shot. They were saying to the country, "Look, you guys are supposed to be nice guys and we are only going to do what we are supposed to do—why do you beat us up, why don't you give us what we ask, why don't you straighten yourselves out?" After years of this, we are at almost the same point—because we demonstrated from a position of weakness. We cannot be expected any longer to march and have our heads broken in order to say to whites: come on, you're nice guys. For you are not nice guys. We have found you out.

An organization which claims to speak for the needs of a community —as does the Student Nonviolent Coordinating Committee—must speak in the tone of that community, not as somebody else's buffer zone. This is the significance of black power as a slogan. For once, black people are going to use the words they want to use—not just the words whites want to hear. And they will do this no matter how often the press tries to stop the use of the slogan by equating it with racism or separatism.

An organization which claims to be working for the needs of a community—as SNCC does—must work to provide that community with a position of strength from which to make its voice heard. This is the significance of black power beyond the slogan.

Black power can be clearly defined for those who do not attach the fears of white America to their questions about it. We should begin with the basic fact that black Americans have two problems: they are poor and they are black. All other problems arise from this two-sided reality: lack of education, the so-called apathy of black men. Any program to end racism must address itself to that double reality.

Almost from its beginning, SNCC sought to address itself to both conditions with a program aimed at winning political power for impoverished Southern blacks. We had to begin with politics because black Americans are a propertyless people in a country where property is valued above all. We had to work for power, because this country does not function by morality, love, and nonviolence, but by power. Thus we determined to win political power, with the idea of moving on from there into activity that would have economic effects. With power, the masses could *make or participate in making* the decisions which govern their destinies, and thus create basic change in their day-to-day lives.

But if political power seemed to be the key to self-determination, it was also obvious that the key had been thrown down a deep well many years earlier. Disenfranchisement, maintained by racist terror, made it impossible to talk about organizing for political power in 1960. The right to vote had to be won, and SNCC workers devoted their energies to this from 1961 to 1965. They set up voter registration drives in the Deep South. They created pressure for the vote by holding mock elections in Mississippi in 1963 and by helping to establish the Mississippi Freedom Democratic Party (MFDP) in 1964. That struggle was eased, though not won, with the passage of the 1965 Voting Rights Act. SNCC workers could then address themselves to the question: "Who can we vote for, to have our needs met—how do we make our vote meaningful?"

SNCC had already gone to Atlantic City for recognition of the Mississippi Freedom Democratic Party by the Democratic convention and been rejected; it had gone with the MFDP to Washington for recognition by Congress and been rejected. In Arkansas, SNCC helped thirty Negroes to run for School Board elections; all but one were defeated, and there was evidence of fraud and intimidation sufficient to cause their defeat. In Atlanta, Julian Bond ran for the state legislature and was elected—twice—and unseated—twice. In several states, black farmers ran in elections for agricultural committees which make crucial decisions concerning land use, loans, etc. Although they won places on a number of committees, they never gained the majorities needed to control them.

All of the efforts were attempts to win black power. Then, in Alabama, the opportunity came to see how blacks could be organized on an independent party basis. An unusual Alabama law provides that any group of citizens can nominate candidates for county office and, if they win 20 per cent of the vote, may be recognized as a county political party. The same then applies on a state level. SNCC went to organize in several counties such as Lowndes, where black people—who form 80 per cent of the population and have an average annual income of $943—felt they could accomplish nothing within the framework of the Alabama Democratic Party because of its racism and because the qualifying fee for this year's elections was raised from $40 to $500 in order to prevent most Negroes from becoming candidates. On May 3, five new county "freedom organizations" convened and nominated candidates for the offices of sheriff, tax assessor, members of the school boards. These men and women are up for election in November—if they live until then. Their ballot symbol is the black panther: a bold, beautiful animal, representing the strength and dignity of black demands today. A man needs a black panther on his side when he and his family must endure—as hundreds of Alabamians have endured—loss of job, eviction, starvation, and sometimes death, for political activity. He may also need a gun and SNCC reaffirms the right of black men everywhere to defend themselves when threatened or attacked. As for initiating the use of violence, we hope that such programs as ours will make that unnecessary; but it is not for us to tell black communities whether they can or cannot use any particular form of action to resolve their problems. Responsibility for the use of violence by black men, whether in self-defense or initiated by them, lies with the white community.

This is the specific historical experience from which SNCC's call for "black power" emerged on the Mississippi march last July. But the concept of "black power" is not a recent or isolated phenomenon: It has grown out of the ferment of agitation and activity by different people and organizations in many black communities over the years. Our last year of work in Alabama added a new concrete possibility. In Lowndes County, for example, black power will mean that if a Negro is elected sheriff, he can end police brutality. If a black man is elected tax assessor, he can collect and channel funds for the building of better roads and schools serving black people—thus advancing the move from political power into the economic arena. In such areas as Lowndes, where black men have a majority, they will attempt to use it to exercise control. This is what they seek: control. Where Negroes lack a majority, black power means proper representation and sharing of control. It means the creation of power bases from which black people can work to change statewide or nationwide patterns of oppression through pressure from strength—instead of weakness. Politically, black power means what it has always meant to SNCC: the coming-together of black people to elect representatives and *to force those representatives to speak to their needs.* It does not mean merely putting black faces into office. A man or woman who is black and from the slums cannot be automatically expected to speak to the needs of black people. Most of the black politicians we see around the country today are not what SNCC means by black power. The power must be that of a community, and emanate from there.

SNCC today is working in both North and South on programs of voter registration and independent political organizing. In some places, such as Alabama, Los Angeles, New York, Philadelphia, and New Jersey, independent organizing under the black panther symbol is in progress. The creation of a national "black panther party" must come about; it will take time to build, and it is much too early to predict its success. We have no infallible master plan and we make no claim to exclusive knowledge of how to end racism; different groups will work in their own different ways. SNCC cannot spell out the full logistics of self-determination but it can address itself to the problem by helping black communities define their needs, realize their strength, and go into action along a variety of lines which they must choose for themselves. Without knowing all the answers, it can address itself to the basic problem of poverty; to the fact that in Lowndes County, 86 white families own 90 per cent of the land. What are black people in that county going to do for jobs, where are they going to get money? There must be reallocation of land, of money.

Ultimately, the economic foundations of this country must be shaken if black people are to control their lives. The colonies of the United States—and this includes the black ghettoes within its borders, north and south—must be liberated. For a century, this nation has been like an octopus of exploitation, its tentacles stretching from Mississippi and Harlem to South America, the Middle East, southern Africa, and Vietnam; the form of exploitation varies from area to area but the essential result has been the same—a powerful few have been maintained and enriched at the expense of the poor and voiceless colored masses. This pattern must be broken. As its grip loosens here and there around the world, the hopes of black Americans become more realistic. For racism to die, a totally different America must be born.

This is what the white society does not wish to face; this is why that society prefers to talk about integration. But integration speaks not at all to the problem of poverty, only to the problem of blackness. Integration today means the man who "makes it," leaving his black brothers behind in the ghetto as fast as his new sports car will take him. It has no relevance to the Harlem wino or to the cottonpicker making three dollars a day. As a lady I know in Alabama once said, "the food that Ralph Bunche eats doesn't fill my stomach."

Integration, moreover, speaks to the problem of blackness in a despicable way. As a goal, it has been based on complete acceptance of the fact that in order to have a decent house or education, blacks must move into a white neighborhood or send their children to a white school. This reinforces, among both black and white, the idea that "white" is automatically better and "black" is by definition inferior. This is why integration is a subterfuge for the maintenance of white supremacy. It allows the nation to focus on a handful of Southern children who get into white schools, at great price, and to ignore the 94 per cent who are left behind in unimproved all-black schools. Such situations will not change until black people have power—to control their own school boards, in this case. Then Negroes become equal in a way that means something, and integration ceases to be a one-way street. Then integration doesn't mean draining skills and energies from the ghetto into white neighborhoods; then it can mean white people moving from Beverly Hills into Watts, white people joining the Lowndes County Freedom Organization. Then integration becomes relevant.

Last April, before the furor over black power, Christopher Jencks wrote in a *New Republic* article on white Mississippi's manipulation of the anti-poverty program:

> The war on poverty has been predicated on the notion that there is such a thing as *a community* which can be defined geographically and mobilized for a collective effort to help the poor. This theory has no relationship to reality in the Deep South. In every Mississippi county there are *two* communities. Despite all the pious platitudes of the moderates on both sides, these two communities habitually see their interests in terms of conflict rather than cooperation. Only when the Negro community can muster enough political, economic and professional strength to compete on somewhat equal terms, will Negroes believe in the possibility of true cooperation and whites accept its necessity. En route to integration, the Negro community needs to develop greater independence—a chance to run its own affairs and not cave in whenever "the man" barks . . . Or so it seems to me, and to most of the knowledgeable people with whom I talked in Mississippi. To OEO, this judgment may sound like black nationalism . . .

Mr. Jencks, a white reporter, perceived the reason why America's anti-poverty program has been a sick farce in both North and South. In the South, it is clearly racism which prevents the poor from running their own programs; in the North, it more often seems to be politicking and bureaucracy. But the results are not so different: In the North, non-whites make up 42 per cent of all families in metropolitan "poverty areas" and only 6 per cent of families in areas classified as not poor. SNCC has been working with local residents in Arkansas, Alabama, and Mississippi to achieve control by the poor of the program and its funds; it has also been working with groups in the North, and the struggle is no less difficult. Behind it all is a federal government which cares far more about winning the war on the Vietnamese than the war on poverty; which has put the poverty program in the hands of self-serving politicians and bureaucrats rather than the poor themselves; which is unwilling to curb the misuse of white power but quick to condemn black power.

To most whites, black power seems to mean that the Mau Mau are coming to the suburbs at night. The Mau Mau are coming, and whites must stop them. Articles appear about plots to "get Whitey," creating an atmosphere in which "law and order must be maintained." Once again, responsibility is shifted from the oppressor to the oppressed. Other whites chide, "Don't forget—you're only 10 per cent of the population; if you get too smart, we'll wipe you out." If they are liberals, they complain, "what about me?—don't you want my help anymore?" These are people supposedly concerned about black Americans, but today they think first of themselves, of their feelings of rejection. Or they admonish, "you can't get anywhere without coalitions," without considering the problems of coalition with whom?; on what terms? (coalescing from weakness can mean absorption, betrayal); when? Or they accuse us of "polarizing the races" by our calls for black unity, when the true responsibility for polarization lies with whites who will not accept their responsibility as the majority power for making the democratic process work.

White America will not face the problem of color, the reality of it. The well-intended say: "We're all human, everybody is really decent, we must forget color." But color cannot be "forgotten" until its weight is recognized and dealt with. White America will not acknowledge that the ways in which this country sees itself are contradicted by being black— and always have been. Whereas most of the people who settled this country came here for freedom or for economic opportunity, blacks were brought here to be slaves. When the Lowndes County Freedom Organization chose the black panther as its symbol, it was christened by the press "the Black Panther Party"—but the Alabama Democratic Party, whose symbol is a rooster, has never been called the White Cock Party. No one ever talked about "white power" because power in this country *is* white. All this adds up to more than merely identifying a group phenomenon by some catchy name or adjective. The furor over that black panther reveals the problems that white America has with color and sex; the furor over "black power" reveals how deep racism runs and the great fear which is attached to it.

Whites will not see that I, for example, as a person oppressed because of my blackness, have common cause with other blacks who are oppressed because of blackness. This is not to say that there are no white people who see things as I do, but that it is black people I must speak to first. It must be the oppressed to whom SNCC addresses itself primarily, not to friends from the oppressing group.

From birth, black people are told a set of lies about themselves. We are told that we are lazy—yet I drive through the Delta area of Mississippi and watch black people picking cotton in the hot sun for fourteen hours. We are told, "If you work hard, you'll succeed"—but if that were true, black people would own this country. We are oppressed because we are black—not because we are ignorant, not because we are lazy, not because we're stupid (and got good rhythm), but because we're black.

I remember that when I was a boy, I used to go to see Tarzan movies on Saturday. White Tarzan used to beat up the black natives. I would sit there yelling, "Kill the beasts, kill the savages, kill 'em!" I was saying: Kill *me*. It was as if a Jewish boy watched Nazis taking Jews off to concentration camps and cheered them on. Today, I want the chief to beat hell out of Tarzan and send him back to Europe. But it takes time to become free of the lies and their shaming effect on black minds. It takes time to reject the most important lie: that black people inherently can't do the same things white people can do, unless white people help them.

The need for psychological equality is the reason why SNCC today believes that blacks must organize in the black community. Only black people can convey the revolutionary idea that black people are able to do things themselves. Only they can help create in the community an aroused and continuing black consciousness that will provide the basis for political strength. In the past, white allies have furthered white supremacy without the whites involved realizing it—or wanting it, I think. Black people must do things for themselves; they must get poverty money they will control and spend themselves, they must conduct tutorial programs themselves so that black children can identify with black people. This is one reason Africa has such importance: The reality of black men ruling their own nations gives blacks elsewhere a sense of possibility, of power, which they do not now have.

This does not mean we don't welcome help, or friends. But we want the right to decide whether anyone is, in fact, our friend. In the past, black Americans have been almost the only people whom everybody and his momma could jump up and call their friends. We have been tokens, symbols, objects—as I was in high school to many young whites, who liked having "a Negro friend." We want to decide who is our friend, and we will not accept someone who comes to us and says: "If you do X, Y, and Z, then I'll help you." We will not be told whom we should choose as allies. We will not be isolated from any group or nation except by our own choice. We cannot have the oppressors telling the oppressed how to rid themselves of the oppressor.

I have said that most liberal whites react to "black power" with the question, What about me?, rather than saying: Tell me what you want me to do and I'll see if I can do it. There are answers to the right question. One of the most disturbing things about almost all white supporters of the movement has been that they are afraid to go into their own communities—which is where the racism exists—and work to get rid of it. They want to run from Berkeley to tell us what to do in Mississippi; let them look instead at Berkeley. They admonish blacks to be nonviolent; let them preach nonviolence in the white community. They come to teach me Negro history; let them go to the suburbs and open up freedom schools for whites. Let them work to stop America's racist foreign policy; let them press this government to cease supporting the economy of South Africa.

There is a vital job to be done among poor whites. We hope to see, eventually, a coalition between poor blacks and poor whites. That is the only coalition which seems acceptable to us, and we see such a coalition as the major internal instrument of change in American society. SNCC has tried several times to organize poor whites; we are trying again now, with an initial training program in Tennessee. It is purely academic today to talk about bringing poor blacks and whites together, but the job of creating a poor-white power bloc must be attempted. The main responsibility for it falls upon whites. Black and white can work together in the white community where possible; it is not possible, however, to go into a poor Southern town and talk about integration. Poor whites everywhere are becoming more hostile—not less—partly because they see the nation's attention focused on black poverty and nobody coming to them. Too many young middle-class Americans, like some sort of Pepsi generation, have wanted to come alive through the black community; they've wanted to be where the action is—and the action has been in the black community.

Black people do not want to "take over" this country. They don't want to "get Whitey"; they just want to get him off their backs, as the saying goes. It was for example the exploitation by Jewish landlords and merchants which first created black resentment toward Jews—not Judaism. The white man is irrelevant to blacks, except as an oppressive force. Blacks want to be in his place, yes, but not in order to terrorize and lynch and starve him. They want to be in his place because that is where a decent life can be had.

But our vision is not merely of a society in which all black men have enough to buy the good things of life. When we urge that black money go into black pockets, we mean the communal pocket. We want to see money go back into the community and used to benefit it. We want to see the cooperative concept applied in business and banking. We want to see black ghetto residents demand that an exploiting landlord or storekeeper sell them, at minimal cost, a building or a shop that they will own and improve cooperatively; they can back their demand with a rent strike, or a boycott, and a community so unified behind them that no one else will move into the building or buy at the store. The society we seek to build among black people, then, is not a capitalist one. It is a society in which the spirit of community and humanistic love prevail. The word love is suspect; black expectations of what it might produce have been betrayed too often. But those were expectations of a response from the white community, which failed us. The love we seek to encourage is within the black community, the only American community where men call each other "brother" when they meet. We can build a community of love only where we have the ability and power to do so: among blacks.

As for white America, perhaps it can stop crying out against "black supremacy," "black nationalism," "racism in reverse," and begin facing reality. The reality is that this nation, from top to bottom, is racist; that racism is not primarily a problem of "human relations" but of an exploitation maintained—either actively or through silence—by the society as a whole. Camus and Sartre have asked, can a man condemn himself? Can whites, particularly liberal whites, condemn themselves? Can they stop blaming us, and blame their own system? Are they capable of the shame which might become a revolutionary emotion?

We have found that they usually cannot condemn themselves, and so we have done it. But the rebuilding of this society, if at all possible, is basically the responsibility of whites—not blacks. We won't fight to save the present society, in Vietnam or anywhere else. We are just going to work, in the way *we* see fit, and on goals *we* define, not for civil rights but for all our human rights.

CHARLES V. HAMILTON

Riots, Revolts and Relevant Response

Although attacked immediately as "reverse racism" by the same official organs of white society which later found it expedient to support programs like black capitalism, the concept of black power quickly captured the imagination of black people. It was the meeting of a slogan with a time that was perfectly ready for it. Young blacks, especially, found in black power an intellectual basis for their new sense of black dignity and pride; they saw in it also militant attitudes and a program of concrete ways to escape their status as second-class citizens.

For intellectuals like Charles Hamilton, however, black power and the re-evaluations of traditional thinking on racial matters that it provoked provided an analytical technique for putting America's racial strife into new perspectives. In the following selection, Hamilton reviews the urban uprisings of the mid-sixties and contends, as others have, that they were not "riots," but desperate exercises of power—denials of the legitimacy of a society which had treated the ghettos like colonies doomed to remain subordinate to the "mother country."

THE UNITED STATES HAS EXPERIENCED, AS OF 1967, ITS FOURTH consecutive summer season of major explosions in its cities' ghettos: burnings, lootings, killings, injuries and mass arrests. The mass media and public officials have consistently referred to these occurrences as riots—race riots. It is clear that the events have become virtually institutionalized; they have become part of what we might call "societal expectations." Around January and February of each year questions will be asked whether we can expect "another long hot summer," what cities we can expect to explode. Local mayors and others will get busy putting

RIOTS, REVOLTS AND RELEVANT RESPONSE by Charles V. Hamilton. From *The Black Power Revolt* edited by Floyd B. Barbour (Boston: Porter Sargent Publisher, 1968). Reprinted by permission of Porter Sargent Publisher.

together remedial summer-time programs to occupy the potential "rioters": give them menial summer jobs; take them on little trips out of the ghettos to nice, green farms on week-ends; provide them with make-shift little swimming pools to splash around in in front of suffocating tenements. And in some places, when the inevitable happens, we can expect a "commission" of "blue-ribboned" persons to be appointed to "investigate" the causes. At times (as in Watts in '64 and Detroit in '67), we will hear great surprise expressed because those places "were not typical ghettos." They either were not like the tall-tenement-type of Harlem ghetto or had an "enlightened" mayor who had received Negro support (and had rewarded that support with Negro appointees to public office). Perhaps we will hear that a certain city was an unexpected target because the anti-poverty program there was "considered" a success.

Invariably, we can expect officials and private commentators to conclude: 1) these are riots having nothing to do with civil rights; 2) only a very small percentage of black people participate; 3) law and order must be maintained. There will be variations, but not too many.

This article will deal with various aspects of the above mentioned expectations. And it will suggest that:

1) what many official and unofficial decision-makers call "riots" is a serious misnomer in terms of understanding what is happening and for charting solutions;

2) the society is confronted with the overt manifestations of repetitive revolts (not *just* riots) against a presumed legitimacy of the system—a presumption held by the larger society. These are revolts born precisely out of a growing alienation from and rejection of many of the basically irrelevant premises and principles of the society;

3) a viable response demands that the decision-makers stop treating the problems solely as matters of control (anti-riot laws, maintaining law and order) or solely as matters of remedial distribution of goods and services (a few jobs here and there, a few housing units remodeled, etc.). It demands that we begin to accept the fact that this is a *systemic* problem, that is, the socio-political, economic system as it now stands is invalid for treating the causes of the revolts.

In other words, if absolutely tight control is clamped on the ghettos—curfews, armed guards, apartheid—this will only increase the danger, not alleviate it. Likewise, if black people are simply *given* more handouts, this will only perpetuate the present status of ghetto colonialism.

Until black people actually have their full share in decision-making power, this society has not begun to address itself to its most crucial problem. And to provide for that, we are talking about the drastic transformation of the *nature* of the socio-political system itself, its values as well as its institutions. Let me deal with each of the three categories separately.

The Misnomer of Riots

We may define an act of rioting as one constituting the unlawful and chaotic destruction of property, such as burning and looting, which, as has occurred in the racial explosions, frequently involves armed sniping at law enforcement and fire officials. In the riot situation, we see people, collectively in small or large groups and individually, breaking into stores, helping themselves to whatever merchandise they can carry, then perhaps applying a match to the premises. We see snipers from rooftops attempting to impede the work of firemen called to put out the fire, etc. These acts are clearly identified by the laws of the larger society as criminal acts. There are statutes on the books spelling out penalties. Invariably, then, we hear that the ghetto explosions are simply riots performed by "hoodlums," the riff-raff, by not more than two or three per cent of the total Negro community. We are told that the "right thinking" Negro community condemns these unlawful acts as much as the property owner whose store has been destroyed. And when the pronouncement is made (usually on the second day) that "law and order must be restored and chaos will not be tolerated," this means that the rioting will be suppressed by whatever military force is available and necessary.

The entire episode is interpreted as an event caused by "mad dogs" (California Governor Ronald Reagan's term) who are interested in getting something for nothing. This opinion is fortified by the view that while only the slightest incident ignited it (an arrest attempt, normally), the flames of excitement are fanned by agitators—inside and outside—who take advantage of mob frenzy to perpetuate the seemingly uncontrollable, emotional situation. Therefore, if the riot was not, in fact, caused by an organized group, it is perpetuated by organized bands who then effectively stir up the people and prolong it.

Thus, whatever effective remedies to end the situation are taken, those control remedies are sanctioned by the overall public. If it is "necessary" to shoot looters (or even those suspected of looting) in the back, this is acceptable. If a person does not respond readily to a national guardsman's command at bayonet point to "move on," the public sanctions the harshest solution to move him on—rifle butt or whatever other means.

The society's full attention is focussed on the acts of looting, burning and sniping. And the entire confrontation is thereby characterized as a "riot."

The fact is that this is a misnomer because the overt, observable acts are the least important of all. In whatever way the society's opinion-leaders decide to characterize the explosions, the fact that black people run through the streets with color television sets and other items on their shoulders is not at all the essence of the problem. It may well be that focussing on such things is the only way this society can relate to the question. But to label the situation as a "riot" and to proceed to deal with it solely in terms of effective control, solely in terms of criminal law enforcement, clearly blinds the decision-makers to the more fundamental problems involved. The goal of the political leaders becomes merely to end the riotous disturbance, to restore "law and order," to impose obedience to duly constituted authority.

Political Legitimacy and Revolts

We cannot term these events riots precisely because, in the minds of many of the people breaking the windows and burning the property, that authority is not duly constituted. They are, in fact, revolts. By this we mean that they are acts which deny the very legitimacy of the system itself. The entire value structure which supports property rights over human rights, which *sanctions* the intolerable conditions in which the black people have been *forced* to live is questioned. They are revolts because the black people are saying that they no longer intend to abide by an oppressive notion of "law and order." That law and that order mean the perpetuation of an *intolerable* status quo. Imbedded in that status quo is an ingrained racist attitude which relegated the black people to a subordinated, suppressed status in the first place. That relegation was deliberate and conscious and vicious, having absolutely nothing to do with inaccurate views about the basic character of the black man. That status quo meant that black people would continue to be sacrificed to a more valued goal of maximizing profits from the colonized ghetto. That status quo meant that the traditional political procedures for alleviating one's ills were not sufficient.

Black people are told that if they have grievances they should take them to court or to the "bargaining table." Occasionally they are told that they must pursue the traditional political processes of the ballot.

But we know that these accepted principles of legitimacy are no longer applicable to vast masses of black people in the ghetto. These people have become alienated from those principles. For them, the system is no longer legitimate. By this we mean that the institutions of the society (the courts, the traditional political parties, the police, the educational institutions) are no longer seen as willing or able to meet the pressing needs of a majority of black people—*qua* black people—in this society. If an individual black person wishes to escape the oppression, he must renounce his black heritage, act as if he were white, conform to white standards and ideas of himself, and maybe then he will be permitted to climb out of the muck and mire. This is interpreted to him as conformity to the Anglo-Ethic of Work and Achievement; if he works hard, he will achieve, just like all other minority groups in the past. The fact has come home, however, that the Ethic (if ever it was applicable to white America) has no relevancy in the lives and history of masses of blacks. In addition, the explosions in the ghettos are not participated in by the handful of black middle class, but rather by the large lower class who correctly see themselves as perennial victims of public policy. They know that the system, as it is now constituted, has no intention of making room for them. Too much history to the contrary has shown otherwise.

Therefore, the *revolts* are the overt denials of legitimacy. True, they are threatening "law and order"—not to get a color television set, but to say to the larger society that a wholly new norm of "law and order" must be established. These are revolts against white America's conception of legitimacy vis-à-vis race in this country. This is a legitimacy which says that black people should accept their subordinated and suppressed status, that since they are only ten to twelve per cent of the total population, they must always accept the crumbs which the remaining majority (with all the economic, political and psychological power) is willing to drop down to them. This is a legitimacy which says that in a pluralistic society each group ultimately gets its grievances attended to, that changes do not come "overnight," but rather they come by stages. The accepted legitimacy says that we must pursue a politics of limited objectives, that the "democratic" mystique provides for ultimate alleviation of grievances.

The acts we have been witnessing for the last four consecutive summers are properly described as *revolts* against these anachronistic principles of legitimacy. They are *revolts* which say in no uncertain terms that the black people no longer believe in this system. They no longer believe that they will ever be able to improve their condition—even by stages—through the normal processes. This is *their* conception of socio-political reality; and *their* conception is the relevant one precisely because they are the ones doing the suffering.

Neither is this conception inaccurate. There is more than substantial evidence that while white America was lauding itself on the "progress" it had been making in race relations, the objective fact is that the day-to-day lives of the majority of black people were becoming progressively worse. Housing conditions were deteriorating, not improving; schools in the ghettos were getting worse and worse, not better and better; jobs were becoming hard to find, not easier. And yet we had more civil rights laws, more judicial decisions favoring black people, more white people marching side by side with blacks against segregation and discrimination. These were the surface impressions which covered up the fact that all those outward manifestations of systemic adaptation to black demands were sheer myths. The fact that a few black people received high public office or "made it" in the white world was set forth as living and breathing evidence of "progress," but this was blatantly irrelevant to the daily lives of the masses of blacks. And so when the revolts came, white America was shocked. It had actually believed its rhetoric, its concepts of what was legitimate. White arrogance is so imbedded that it could not allow for any notions contrary to its own.

Thus, the simmering summers of the sixties have been revolts, not just riots, and realization of that fact would be advisable for a society that must now give a response.

The revolts speak to the society in still another way. It has been assumed that oppressed, minority people in the country would ultimately not push their demands to the point of violence. After all, the assumption was that, given a majority in possession of the overwhelming predominance of power, the minority surely would capitulate. This assumption has completely overlooked the fact that the power equation is not *entirely* stacked in favor of the majority. The revolts have been saying: "You see, we too have some modicum of power, if it's only the power to destroy, to disrupt." Like all power, this minority weapon is as useful in the fact of its *potential* threat as in its actual use. Therefore, given clear evidence, now, that black people are willing to destroy their oppressors' property, to disrupt their normal business cycle, it may well be that the white decision-makers will be forced to view the relations between the races in different terms; the cards are *not* all stacked in their favor. The revolts have established the credibility of the blacks' willingness to use their power if they are forced to do so. *Now,* when the ground rules for bargaining are discussed, and when the agenda to be discussed is drawn up, it will not be a completely unilateral affair. The fact is—and apparently this was never quite clear to white America before—that black people have the power at their disposal to deny peace and stability to the larger society.

Relevant Response or Repressive Reaction

At all times it has been clear that the ultimate decisions to change lie with the white community. That community can choose to listen to the demands of the black revolts and attempt seriously to deal with them, or it can diligently pursue a policy of extermination. If it chooses the first alternative, it must be clear what that involves.

Such an alternative clearly means that precisely because this society has lost its legitimacy vis-à-vis the black American, the solutions must take into account the imbedded distrust and suspicion blacks have of whites. Not only must programs be devised and funded to rebuild the black community, but black people must have a major share of the decision-making process. Black people need much more than benefits *from* the decision-making process; they must be viable participants *in* that process. It is not enough to develop and implement a crash educational program for the ghettos; blacks must control their local school systems, just as other ethnic and racial groups control theirs. It is not enough to implement employment programs; black people must have an initial voice in the planning of those programs. It becomes crucial to understand that this does not mean white hand-picked Negro leaders. The black participants must be products of the black community from which they come, and they must, first and foremost, be responsive to that community. I am suggesting that this is the only feasible way at this juncture to establish *legitimacy* in the minds of the black people. We need not talk at this point about the particular new forms or structures that will be devised to implement this. The fact is that those new forms will be devised to fit the particular indigenous situation.

Relevant responses on the part of the larger society will recognize that only when black people feel a personal stake in the society will they move to protect that society. Only then will the society *deserve* protecting. Only then will the society be legitimate.

Thus far, most of the suggested remedies (short of military control) have overlooked this crucial factor of legitimate participation in decision-making. The "maximum feasible participation" formula in the Economic Opportunity Act is a farce and has been sacrificed to the priorities of irrelevant local political parties. Even the investigating committees have overlooked the possible contributions to be made by adding ghetto citizens to their deliberations, officially. All these decisions have been widening the legitimacy gap. And as these things happen, we should not be heard to register shock when the revolts occur time and again. We should not delude ourselves into thinking that incremental, half-hearted, non-participatory solutions will suffice.

The alternatives are clear, and the money used to rediscover this should be diverted to stimulating a relevant response. It is senseless and wasteful to continue mouthing the old clichés, advocating the anachronistic principles, issuing the same meaningless statements. This society is not faced with a traditional type of problem that lends itself to traditional approaches. If the revolts say anything, they speak to this with loud and unmistakable clarity.

JULIUS LESTER

Cultural Nationalism

The models for personal beauty in America have been white and white only, as have been all other cultural standards. Black people have had no choice but to measure themselves, to some extent at least, by those white standards. As Julius Lester points out in the following selection, this situation has done great violence to the black man's conception of himself. He could not, for all his attempts, ever be white; yet his own culture had been almost completely destroyed during slavery and had been left in limbo ever since. Whatever native American culture he did create out of the ambiguous circumstances of his life here was quickly appropriated by the dominant society without recognition of its genesis.

Lester notes that under the influence of Malcolm X, however, and with the coming of black power, blacks began both to rediscover and recreate an identity as Afro-Americans with significant accomplishments and a unique cultural

CULTURAL NATIONALISM   Reprinted from *Look Out, Whitey! Black Power's Gon' Get Your Mama* by Julius Lester. Copyright © 1968 by Julius Lester and used by permission of the publisher, The Dial Press, Inc.

tradition born of their oppression in America. In a process that is far from complete, they began to assert the integrity of the black experience and demand
that its true meaning, so long ignored, be written into the nation's history books.

BLACKS HAVE ALWAYS BEEN MADE TO VIEW THEIR PREDICAMENT IN
terms of whites. They have been the "outs" trying to get "in." This
immediately gives those who are "in" a power. It is their decision
whether or not you will get in. They set the qualifications. Black people
have to qualify for a job or enter a school according to standards set by
whites. Life for a black person can be nothing more than a series of
tests with a nation of white schoolteachers grading every step you take,
every breath you breathe. In the South you can fail the test if you wear
a white shirt and tie. In the North you can fail if you don't wear a shirt
and tie. By saying that America has a "Negro Problem," the burden for
solving it has been put on the one who carries the burden of being oppressed. "If Negroes would do this and do the other, we wouldn't have
this problem." It is always the Negro who is wrong.

It has been impossible for blacks not to fall victims to this white assessment of themselves, while at the same time resisting it. Black people
are what the sociologist Robert Park has characterized as "marginal
men." We exist in two cultural worlds and in two different societies at
the same time, without being totally a part of either. What is more
pathetic and sad than a wedding in the ghetto, the bride in her lovely
white gown posing for pictures on the stoop of a slum building and walking past the fallen garbage cans to a car at the curb to which someone
has tied a few cans to announce the glad tidings as she and her groom
drive away together. She has had her wedding just as it was described in
the magazines. She has had her six-tiered cake with a little white bride
and groom at the top. She has stuffed a piece of cake into her new husband's mouth. She has walked down the aisle with a little girl walking
behind, holding her train. She has done it all, all, including the big diamond on her third finger, left hand, and she would've been more comfortable and gotten her marriage off to a better start if she'd danced for
four hours to James Brown and Aretha, drunk liquor, had a good time,
and then gone to the marital bed with her new husband. But she wanted
it done the way she thought it was supposed to be done. She threw her
bouquet and they threw rice on her.

This is the marginality with which blacks have to live. It is particularly
difficult for the intellectual, who has roots in the black experience, yet
lives a life where he must compete with whites. He has to learn new ways

in those integrated schools, and this learning makes him a stranger to his people while he comes no closer to overcoming his alienation from the white world. "Marginal men" are created whenever two different historical and cultural peoples come into contact.

No black person has escaped this marginality. He has been constantly bombarded by the symbols of the dominant culture. He has seen his own culture ridiculed by whites. Western culture has equated the evil of the world with black—black as sin, "the blackest day of my life," "blackball," etc. There are over sixty synonyms in *Roget's Thesaurus* for black, and all of them have connotations of something not good. Is it any wonder, then, that black people have devoted so much time trying to erase their blackness? They have tried to solve the pain of their marginality by denying what they are, or at least, by hiding it, covering it up, because to deny it has been impossible.

Since the earliest days of slavery a program of cultural genocide has been conscious on the part of whites, because the success of their lives depended on it. First, the white man tried to stamp out any vestiges of culture in Africans. Blacks from the same tribes were not allowed to remain together. Thus, Africans from different tribes found that they could communicate in only one language—English. The white man then moved to reinforce this by saying that blacks had never contributed anything to civilization. And any knowledge that spoke to the contrary was suppressed. Next came the creation of class distinctions among the blacks. The house servant received more favors than did the field hand. The mulatto was the most prized of all and was quite often educated by the master, his father. In some instances, whites were so successful in wiping out feelings of separate identity in the slaves that there was a small number of black slaveholders in the South.

This program of cultural genocide was backed up by laws forbidding blacks to do, in essence, anything whites didn't want them to do. This amounted to everything except work. The law's authority came from the barrel of a gun or the noose of a rope. Even after the laws were off the books, custom did not change. A nigger is a nigger is a nigger.

Yet, while whites were denigrating black culture, they were stealing it. While saying that blacks had no culture, ol' boss on the plantation didn't have a ball where John didn't fiddle and Sam pick the banjo. Some slaves were professional musicians who did nothing but make music when the white man wanted music. Whites loved to go to black churches for the music. The heard jazz in New Orleans and tried to imitate it. They couldn't, but they recorded it, got the money, and had their thing called "legitimate." This process has never abated. King Oliver and Paul Whiteman (appropriate name) were contemporaneous band leaders, but who earned the money? Not black King Oliver. The musical contribution of black people is recognized today. Jazz is the only indigenous music America has, but now the ploy is to say, well, it may be true that this is Negro music, but now it belongs to the world. Says who? We didn't give it to anybody. You came and got it, took the money and the credit, and then come back and tell me what a great thing I've done by giving the world this music.

The dances whites have tried to do have come from blacks. The mambo, samba, tango, merengue, are all religious dances from Africa, Brazil, or Haiti. These dances have been divested of meaning by people of an alien culture. The twist, watusi, boogaloo, and monkey have come from the black community and have been appropriated by whites who have no idea that these are, in essence, religious dances, rich with sexual adumbrations.

The white attitude toward black culture is another instance where the rhetoric has been the reverse of the actions, for whites have not failed to adopt the music, dance, speech, and fashions of a culture that they have declared nonexistent. (Men's fashions invariably come from the ghetto and generally there is a two-year lag before they enter white America. In women's fashions, 1967 seemed to be the year that African designs were to be appropriated by white America. The February *Harper's Bazaar* featured clothes modeled on African dresswear. The clothes were beautiful, but those white skins killed the vibrancy of the colors.)

Even though blacks have believed what whites told them, that which was uniquely black within them refused to be stilled. The black preacher tried to preach a logical sermon, going deliberately from point to point, but he just couldn't do it. He had to shout and get happy. He had to throw his arms in the air and move around, jump up and down and roundabout. He had to do what the spirit said, do it like the spirit told him to.

The uniqueness of black culture can be explained in that it is a culture whose emphasis is on the nonverbal, i.e., the nonconceptual. The lives of blacks are rooted in the concrete daily experience. When the black preacher shouts, "God is a living God!" don't argue. Get ready to shake hands with the Lord Almighty. "I talked to God this morning and I said, 'Now, listen here, Lord. You got to do something about these white folks down here. Lord, they giving us a hard time. You got to do something!' " God is like a personal friend, an old buddy, whom you talk to man-to-man. The black church congregation doesn't want to be told about God, it wants to feel Him, see Him, and touch Him. It is the preacher's responsibility to see that they do.

In black culture it is the experience that counts, not what is said. The rhythm-and-blues singer and the gospel quartets know that their audiences want to feel the song. The singers are the physical embodiment of the emotions and experiences of the community. They are separate from the community only in that they have the means to make the community experience through music that no-good man who left, the pain of loneliness, the joy of love, physical and religious.

Perhaps the essence of the nonverbalism of black culture is found in rhythm. In any speech by Martin Luther King, one can hear his unconscious understanding of black rhythm and voice timbre. It is there, in the black preacher, the music, and the day-to-day speech. It is there in the color sense of black people. It is there, not only in the way we dance, but in the way we walk. It is African, not American.

With Western culture's emphasis upon the verb, the result has been the creation of a subject-object relationship between man and his experience. The verb-oriented culture separates man from his experience in such a way that for a man to relate his experience he must set himself on one side, the experience on the other, and the verb in between to connect the two. Thus, for example, for the German mystic Meister Eckhart to state his oneness with God, he had to say "I am God," which to his congregation sounded like the highest egotism. If Meister Eckhart had been African, he would simply have been possessed by the rhythm of his particular god and exemplified the dynamic Oneness.

This difference between verb-oriented and non-verb-oriented cultures is most apparent when one considers art in the two cultures. The artist is essentially a revolutionary whose aim is to change people's lives. He wants people to live better, and one way of doing it is to make them see, hear, and feel what he has seen, felt, and heard. The artist is not concerned with beauty, but with making man's life better. Thus, it is an insult when a work of music is applauded for the pleasant vibrations which have come to the ear. The Western concept of art is, in essence, antiart. If the listeners had opened their beings to the music, it would be impossible for them to applaud. If they applauded, it would not be a polite coming together of the hands in rapid motion, but exulting cries. People would run out into the streets and hug everyone in sight, shout, throw off their clothes, and become new men. Instead, they respond by saying, "How beautiful!" Poor Van Gogh. He sacrificed his life to put on canvas the way he saw the world, and his reward is people who can't see beyond the vibrant colors and the agitated brushstrokes. Once something is called "art," it is put in a category. It is no longer something to be experienced directly; it is to be commented upon, studied, and understood. To understand is not to experience. Yet, Western culture and education are aimed at the rational.

The black man knows the inherent irrationality of life. Thus, black culture is aimed at the experience. The congregation responds to the preaching by patting the foot and shouting. The blues singer's audience yells back at him, "Take you time, now. Tell it." The audience demands that the performer (preacher, singer, or what have you) relate to them at this level. It is his responsibility. White teen-agers go to hear the Beatles and scream through their entire performance. It isn't because of the music. Their screams obliterate it. It is because of an involvement with the singers. Yet, you never hear a black teen-ager gush over the Temptations like whites do over the Beatles. You will hear black teen-agers sing every line of the Temptations' current song and all their past ones. You will see them imitate every movement the performers make on stage. You can sit in restaurants in the black community and if a particularly meaningful record is played on the jukebox, every person in the place will suddenly start singing.

These two very different cultures met under what cannot be considered auspicious circumstances. The dominant culture sought to destroy the new one. It did not totally succeed, but through slavery, intimidation, and murder it did create in the members of the minority culture a desire to deny that culture and assume the characteristics and ways of the dominant one. The black American may feel that black is bad, but even while he is saying it one can hear in the rising and falling of his voice the sound of the African dialects and drums.

Of the minority groups in this country, blacks are the only one having no language of their own. Language serves to insulate a group and protect it from outsiders. Lacking this strong protection, black people are more victims of the American lie of assimilation than the Puerto Rican, Italian, or Jew, who can remove himself from America with one sentence in his native language. America is not a melting pot. It is a nation of national minorities, each living in well-defined areas and retaining enough of the culture of the native land to maintain an identity other than that of an American. The black person also has two native lands: America and Africa. But both have deliberately been denied him.

This denial of America and Africa has created the central psychological problem for the black American. Who am I? Many avoid their blackness as much as possible by trying to become assimilated. They remove all traces of blackness from their lives. Their gestures, speech, habits, cuisine, walk, everything they can consciously control, becomes as "American Dream" as possible. Generally, they are the "responsible ones," the undercover, button-down-collar Uncle Toms who front for the white man at a time of "racial crisis," reassuring white folks that "responsible Negroes deplore the violence and looting and we ask that law and order be allowed to prevail." A small minority avoid the crux of their blackness by going to another extreme. They identify completely with Africa. Some do so to the extent of wearing African clothes, celebrating African holidays, and speaking Swahili. They, however, are only unconsciously admitting that the white man is right when he says American blacks have nothing of their own.

For other blacks the question of identity is only now being solved by the realization of those things that are theirs. Black people do have a language of their own. The words may be English, but the way a black person puts them together and the meaning that he gives them creates a new language. He has another language, too, and that language is rhythm. This has been recognized by black people for some time, and they call it "soul." In Africa they speak of negritude. The two are the same. It is the recognition of those things uniquely ours which separate us from the white man.

This consciousness has come about through the teachings of the Honorable Elijah Muhammad, Malcolm X, and most recently, SNCC. More than any other person, Malcolm X was responsible for the growing consciousness and new militancy of black people. He said aloud those things which blacks had been saying among themselves. He even said those things we had been afraid to say to each other. His clear, uncomplicated words cut through the chains on black minds like a giant blowtorch. His words were not spoken for the benefit of the press. He was not concerned with stirring the moral conscience of America, because he knew—America has no moral conscience. He spoke directly and eloquently to black men, analyzing their situation, their predicament, events as they happened, explaining what it all meant for a black man in America.

Now blacks are beginning to study their past, to learn those things that have been lost, to re-create what the white man destroyed in them, and to destroy that which the white man put in its stead. They have stopped being Negroes and have become black men, in recognition of this new identity, their real identity. In the November, 1967, *Ebony,* Lerone Bennett, Jr., quotes Ossie Davis on the difference between a Negro and a black man.

I am a Negro. I am clean, black and I smile a lot. Whenever I want something—to get a job in motion pictures, for instance, or on television or to get a play produced on Broadway, whenever I need a political favor—I got white folks. White folks have money. I do not. White folks have power. I do not. All of my needs—financial, artistic, social, my need for freedom—I must depend on white folks to supply. That is what is meant by being a Negro.

Malcolm X used to be a Negro, but he stopped. He no longer depended upon white folks to supply his needs—psychologically or sociologically—to give him money or lead his fight for freedom or to protect him from his enemies or to tell him what to do. Malcolm X did not hate white folks, nor did he love them. Most of all, he did not need them to tell him who he was. Above all, he was determined to make it on his own. . . . Malcolm was a man, a black man! A black man means not to accept the system as Negroes do but to fight hell out of the system as Malcolm did. It can be dangerous. Malcolm was killed for it. . . .[1]

Blacks now realize that "Negro" is an American invention which shut them off from those of the same color in Africa. They recognize now that part of themselves is in Africa. Some feel this in a deeply personal way, as did Mrs. Fannie Lou Hamer of Mississippi, who cried when she was in Africa, because she knew she had relatives there and she would never be able to know them. Her past would always be partially closed to her.

All across the country now one can find blacks wearing their hair "Afro" style. For the girls it means they no longer go to the beauty parlor to have their hair straightened with hot combs. They wear it as it was before the hot combs and grease got to it. Howard University's Homecoming Queen of 1966 was a former SNCC worker who wears her hair *au naturel*. For the men it means letting the hair grow long. Not only is this true of young blacks directly involved in "the movement," but of teen-agers in the urban centers.

This new cultural awareness has produced numerous conferences of black intellectuals around the country in the past couple of years. Newspapers and small magazines have sprung up whose sole purpose is the furtherance of black consciousness. Friends are often admonished to "think black." People are often criticized for "sounding too much like whitey." When a man is rude to a black woman, he is criticized for not treating his "sister" properly. You no longer "hang out" on the block with your friends, you "hang out with the brothers."

[1] "What's In a Name," *Ebony,* November, 1967.

Black consciousness is more than this, however. It is fundamental to Black Power. Anne Braden defined black consciousness when she wrote:

> Negroes . . . need to eliminate from their thinking and feeling the patterns that have been put there by a society that is essentially built on the concept of the superiority of the white man. . . . Negroes need to reject the unconscious idea that what is white is better. And because they do live in a society that holds to that idea, they will begin to think and feel differently only when they realize their own history, their own worth as a people, their own ties with dark-skinned people elsewhere in the world.[2]

Black consciousness is an essential part of speaking and defining for ourselves. It is the foundation for Black Power.

[2] Anne Braden, "The SNCC Trends: Challenge to White America," *The Southern Patriot,* May, 1966.

ELDRIDGE CLEAVER

Domestic Law and International Order

In a 1966 position paper on the war in Vietnam, the Student Nonviolent Coordinating Committee (SNCC) stated, "We take note of the fact that 16% of the draftees from this country are Negro, called on to stifle the liberation of Vietnam, to preserve a 'democracy' which does not exist for them at home." Black critics of the war pointed out bitterly that the huge sums spent to fight it could easily rebuild the nation's ghettos and alleviate the hardship and suffering of those who live there. They also asserted that because of the inequities of the draft and the social system underlying it, the number of black youths fighting and dying in Vietnam was disproportionately large, and that the black veterans who returned faced joblessness and discrimination.

The war escalated at a time when the black power movement was gaining strength and when black people were becoming more sensitive to the workings of racism in America and abroad. In an address on Vietnam, the Reverend Martin Luther King, Jr., called the United States government "the greatest purveyor of violence in the world today," Stokely Carmichael and others charged that the war was "racist" in nature, a war against "people of color" waged by white power. In the selection which follows, Eldridge Cleaver argues that racism necessarily resorts to armed force to maintain its power; he asserts that the same "system" which sends United States troops to pacify Vietnam also sends white police to maintain the status quo of the black ghetto.

THE POLICE DEPARTMENT AND THE ARMED FORCES ARE THE TWO ARMS of the power structure, the muscles of control and enforcement. They have deadly weapons with which to inflict pain on the human body. They know how to bring about horrible deaths. They have clubs with which to beat the body and the head. They have bullets and guns with which to tear holes in the flesh, to smash bones, to disable and kill. They use force, to make you do what the deciders have decided you must do.

Every country on earth has these agencies of force. The people everywhere fear this terror and force. To them it is like a snarling wild beast which can put an end to one's dreams. They punish. They have cells and prisons to lock you up in. They pass out sentences. They won't let you go when you want to. You have to stay put until they give the word. If your mother is dying, you can't go to her bedside to say goodbye or to her graveside to see her lowered into the earth, to see her, for the last time, swallowed up by that black hole.

The techniques of the enforcers are many: firing squads, gas chambers, electric chairs, torture chambers, the garrote, the guillotine, the tightening rope around your throat. It has been found that the death penalty is necessary to back up the law, to make it easier to enforce, to deter transgressions against the penal code. That everybody doesn't believe in the same laws is beside the point.

Which laws get enforced depends on who is in power. If the capitalists are in power, they enforce laws designed to protect their system, their way of life. They have a particular abhorrence for crimes against property, but are prepared to be liberal and show a modicum of compassion for crimes against the person—unless, of course, an instance of the latter is combined with an instance of the former. In such cases, nothing can stop them from throwing the whole book at the offender. For instance, armed robbery with violence, to a capitalist, is the very epitome of evil. Ask any banker what he thinks of it.

If Communists are in power, they enforce laws designed to protect their system, their way of life. To them, the horror of horrors is the speculator, that man of magic who has mastered the art of getting something with nothing and who in America would be a member in good standing of his local Chamber of Commerce.

"The people," however, are nowhere consulted, although everywhere everything is done always in their name and ostensibly for their betterment, while their real-life problems go unsolved. "The people" are a rubber stamp for the crafty and sly. And no problem can be solved without taking the police department and the armed forces into account. Both kings and bookies understand this, as do first ladies and common prostitutes.

The police do on the domestic level what the armed forces do on the international level: protect the way of life of those in power. The police patrol the city, cordon off communities, blockade neighborhoods, invade homes, search for that which is hidden. The armed forces patrol the world, invade countries and continents, cordon off nations, blockade islands and whole peoples; they will also overrun villages, neighborhoods, enter homes, huts, caves, searching for that which is hidden. The policeman and the soldier will violate your person, smoke you out with various gases. Each will shoot you, beat your head and body with sticks and clubs, with rifle butts, run you through with bayonets, shoot holes in your flesh, kill you. They each have unlimited firepower. They will use all that is necessary to bring you to your knees. They won't take no for an answer. If you resist their sticks, they draw their guns. If you resist their guns, they call for reinforcements with bigger guns. Eventually they will come in tanks, in jets, in ships. They will not rest until you surrender or are killed. The policeman and the soldier will have the last word.

Both police and the armed forces follow orders. Orders. Orders flow from the top down. Up there, behind closed doors, in antechambers, in conference rooms, gavels bang on the tables, the tinkling of silver decanters can be heard as icewater is poured by well-fed, conservatively dressed men in hornrimmed glasses, fashionably dressed American widows with rejuvenated faces and tinted hair, the air permeated with the square humor of Bob Hope jokes. Here all the talking is done, all the thinking, all the deciding. Gray rabbits of men scurry forth from the conference room to spread the decisions throughout the city, as News. Carrying out orders is a job, a way of meeting the payments on the house, a way of providing for one's kiddies. In the armed forces it is also a duty, patriotism. Not to do so is treason.

Every city has its police department. No city would be complete without one. It would be sheer madness to try operating an American city
without the heat, the fuzz, the man. Americans are too far gone, or else
they haven't arrived yet; the center does not exist, only the extremes.
Take away the cops and Americans would have a coast-to-coast free-
for-all. There are, of course, a few citizens who carry their own private
cops around with them, built into their souls. But there is robbery in
the land, and larceny, murder, rape, burglary, theft, swindles, all brands
of crime, profit, rent, interest—and these blasé descendants of Pilgrims
are at each other's throats. To complicate matters, there are also rich
people and poor people in America. There are Negroes and whites, Indians, Puerto Ricans, Mexicans, Jews, Chinese, Arabs, Japanese—all
with equal rights but unequal possessions. Some are haves and some are
have-nots. All have been taught to worship at the shrine of General
Motors. The whites are on top in America and they want to stay there,
up there. They are also on top in the world, on the international level,
and they want to stay up there, too. Everywhere there are those who
want to smash this precious toy clock of a system, they want ever so
much to change it, to rearrange things, to pull the whites down off their
high horse and make them equal. Everywhere the whites are fighting to
prolong their status, to retard the erosion of their position. In America,
when everything else fails, they call out the police. On the international
level, when everything else fails, they call out the armed forces.

A strange thing happened in Watts, in 1965, August. The blacks, who
in this land of private property have all private and no property, got
excited into an uproar because they noticed a cop before he had a
chance to wash the blood off his hands. Usually the police department
can handle such flare-ups. But this time it was different. Things got out
of hand. The blacks were running amok, burning, shooting, breaking.
The police department was powerless to control them; the chief called
for reinforcements. Out came the National Guard, that ambiguous hy-
brid from the twilight zone where the domestic army merges with the
international; that hypocritical force poised within America and capable
of action on either level, capable of backing up either the police or the
armed forces. Unleashing their formidable firepower, they crushed the
blacks. But things will never be the same again. Too many people saw
that those who turned the other cheek in Watts got their whole head
blown off. At the same time, heads were being blown off in Vietnam.
America was embarrassed, not by the quality of her deeds but by the
surplus of publicity focused upon her negative selling points, and a little
frightened because of what all those dead bodies, on two fronts, implied.

Those corpses spoke eloquently of potential allies and alliances. A community of interest began to emerge, dripping with blood, out of the ashes of Watts. The blacks in Watts and all over America could now see the Viet Cong's point: both were on the receiving end of what the armed forces were dishing out.

So now the blacks, stung by the new knowledge they have unearthed, cry out: *"POLICE BRUTALITY!"* From one end of the country to the other, the new war cry is raised. The youth, those nodes of compulsive energy who are all fuel and muscle, race their motors, itch to do something. The Uncle Toms, no longer willing to get down on their knees to lick boots, do so from a squatting position. The black bourgeoisie call for Citizens' Review Boards, to assert civilian control over the activity of the police. In back rooms, in dark stinking corners of the ghettos, self-conscious black men curse their own cowardice and stare at their rifles and pistols and shotguns laid out on tables before them, trembling as they wish for a manly impulse to course through their bodies and send them screaming mad into the streets shooting from the hip. Black women look at their men as if they are bugs, curious growths of flesh playing an inscrutable waiting game. Violence becomes a homing pigeon floating through the ghettos seeking a black brain in which to roost for a season.

In their rage against the police, against police brutality, the blacks lose sight of the fundamental reality: that the police are only an instrument for the implementation of the policies of those who make the decisions. Police brutality is only one facet of the crystal of terror and oppression. Behind police brutality there is social brutality, economic brutality, and political brutality. From the perspective of the ghetto, this is not easy to discern: the TV newscaster and the radio announcer and the editorialists of the newspapers are wizards of the smoke screen and the snow job.

What is true on the international level is true also at home; except that the ace up the sleeve is easier to detect in the international arena. Who would maintain that American soldiers are in Vietnam on their own motion? They were conscripted into the armed forces and taught the wisdom of obeying orders. They were sent to Vietnam by orders of the generals in the Pentagon, who receive them from the Secretary of Defense, who receives them from the President, who is shrouded in mystery. The soldier in the field in Vietnam, the man who lies in the grass and squeezes the trigger when a little half-starved, trembling Vietnamese peasant crosses his sights, is only following orders, carrying out a policy and a plan. He hardly knows what it is all about. They have him wired-up tight with the slogans of TV and the World Series. All he knows is that he has been assigned to carry out a certain ritual of duties.

He is well trained and does the best he can. He does a good job. He may want to please those above him with the quality of his performance. He may want to make sergeant, or better. This man is from some hicky farm in Shit Creek, Georgia. He only knew whom to kill after passing through boot camp. He could just as well come out ready to kill Swedes. He will kill a Swede dead, if he is ordered to do so.

Same for the policeman in Watts. He is not there on his own. They have all been assigned. They have been told what to do and what not to do. They have also been told what they better not do. So when they continually do something, in every filthy ghetto in this shitty land, it means only that they are following orders.

It's no secret that in America the blacks are in total rebellion against the System. They want to get their nuts out of the sand. They don't like the way America is run, from top to bottom. In America, everything is owned. Everything is held as private property. Someone has a brand on everything. There is nothing left over. Until recently, the blacks themselves were counted as part of somebody's private property, along with the chickens and goats. The blacks have not forgotten this, principally because they are still treated as if they are part of someone's inventory of assets—or perhaps, in this day of rage against the costs of welfare, blacks are listed among the nation's liabilities. On any account, however, blacks are in no position to respect or help maintain the institution of private property. What they want is to figure out a way to get some of that property for themselves, to divert it to their own needs. This is what it is all about, and this is the real brutality involved. This is the source of all brutality.

The police are the armed guardians of the social order. The blacks are the chief domestic victims of the American social order. A conflict of interest exists, therefore, between the blacks and the police. It is not solely a matter of trigger-happy cops, of brutal cops who love to crack black heads. Mostly it's a job to them. It pays good. And there are numerous fringe benefits. The real problem is a trigger-happy social order.

The Utopians speak of a day when there will be no police. There will be nothing for them to do. Every man will do his duty, will respect the rights of his neighbor, will not disturb the peace. The needs of all will be taken care of. Everyone will have sympathy for his fellow man. There will be no such thing as crime. There will be, of course, no prisons. No electric chairs, no gas chambers. The hangman's rope will be the thing of the past. The entire earth will be a land of plenty. There will be no crimes against property, no speculation.

It is easy to see that we are not on the verge of entering Utopia: there are cops everywhere. North and South, the Negroes are the have-nots. They see property all around them, property that is owned by whites. In this regard, the black bourgeoisie has become nothing but a ridiculous nuisance. Having waged a battle for entrance into the American mainstream continually for fifty years, all of the black bourgeoisie's defenses are directed outward, against the whites. They have no defenses against the blacks and no time to erect any. The black masses can handle them any time they choose, with one mighty blow. But the white bourgeoisie presents a bigger problem, those whites who own everything. With many shackled by unemployment, hatred in black hearts for this system of private property increases daily. The sanctity surrounding property is being called into question. The mystique of the deed of ownership is melting away. In other parts of the world, peasants rise up and expropriate the land from the former owners. Blacks in America see that the deed is not eternal, that it is not signed by God, and that new deeds, making blacks the owners, can be drawn up.

The Black Muslims raised the cry, *"WE MUST HAVE SOME LAND!" "SOME LAND OF OUR OWN OR ELSE!"* Blacks in America shrink from the colossus of General Motors. They can't see how to wade through that thicket of common stocks, preferred stocks, bonds and debentures. They only know that General Motors is huge, that it has billions of dollars under its control, that it owns land, that its subsidiaries are legion, that it is a repository of vast powers. The blacks want to crack the nut of General Motors. They are meditating on it. Meanwhile, they must learn that the police take orders from General Motors. And that the Bank of America has something to do with them even though they don't have a righteous penny in the bank. They have no bank accounts, only bills to pay. The only way they know of making withdrawals from the bank is at the point of a gun. The shiny fronts of skyscrapers intimidate them. They do not own them. They feel alienated from the very sidewalks on which they walk. This white man's country, this white man's world. Overflowing with men of color. An economy consecrated to the succor of the whites. Blacks are incidental. The war on poverty, that monstrous insult to the rippling muscles in a black man's arms, is an index of how men actually sit down and plot each other's deaths, actually sit down with slide rules and calculate how to hide bread from the hungry. And the black bourgeoisie greedily sopping up what crumbs are tossed into their dark corner.

There are 20,000,000 of these blacks in America, probably more. Today they repeat, in awe, this magic number to themselves: there are

20,000,000 of us! They shout this to each other in humiliated astonishment. No one need tell them that there is vast power latent in their mass. They know that 20,000,000 of anything is enough to get some recognition and consideration. They know also that they must harness their number and hone it into a sword with a sharp cutting edge. White General Motors also knows that the unity of these 20,000,000 ragamuffins will spell the death of the system of its being. At all costs, then, they will seek to keep these blacks from uniting, from becoming bold and revolutionary. These white property owners know that they must keep the blacks cowardly and intimidated. By a complex communications system of hints and signals, certain orders are given to the chief of police and the sheriff, who pass them on to their men, the footsoldiers in the trenches of the ghetto.

We experience this system of control as madness. So that Leonard Deadwyler, one of these 20,000,000 blacks, is rushing his pregnant wife to the hospital and is shot dead by a policeman. An accident. That the sun rises in the east and sets in the west is also an accident, by design. The blacks are up in arms. From one end of America to the other, blacks are outraged at this accident, this latest evidence of what an accident-prone people they are, of the cruelty and pain of their lives, these blacks at the mercy of trigger-happy Yankees and Rebs in coalition against their skin. They want the policeman's blood as a sign that the Viet Cong is not the only answer. A sign to save them from the deaths they must die, and inflict. The power structure, without so much as blinking an eye, wouldn't mind tossing Bova to the mob, to restore law and order, but it knows in the vaults of its strength that at all cost the blacks must be kept at bay, that it must uphold the police department, its Guardian. Nothing must be allowed to threaten the set-up. Justice is secondary. Security is the byword.

Meanwhile, blacks are looking on and asking tactical questions. They are asked to die for the System in Vietnam. In Watts they are killed by it. Now—*NOW!*—they are asking each other, in dead earnest: Why not die right here in Babylon fighting for a better life, like the Viet Cong? If those little cats can do it, what's wrong with big studs like us?

A mood sets in, spreads across America, across the face of Babylon, jells in black hearts everywhere.

The Black Panther Party Ten-Point Program

As racial conflict has grown in intensity, and as the lines upon which it is drawn have daily become sharper, new black organizations have been born to respond. Tones of moral persuasion have been replaced by the voices of those whose concerns lie with power and well-disciplined militancy. One of the most controversial of these organizations (controversial because it has been utterly candid about the political efficacy of the shot-gun and the rifle) is the Black Panther Party.

Founded in 1966 by Huey Newton, Bobby Seale, and others in Oakland, California, the Party quickly gained a national following, and by 1969 had established chapters in most of the larger cities of the country. Its growth has derived mainly from its impressive ability to articulate the revolutionary sentiments of young black people. It has reinforced their feeling that a war is going on between black America and white, and that the appropriate stance in such a time is armed self-defense. The Party encourages its members to work within the black community, to develop local leadership, and to be militant against the established representatives of white power and influence, namely, the police. Because it sees its struggle in *political* terms, the Black Panther Party has also won a sizeable following among radical whites. Its slogan has taken the fight into the arena of class conflict and nationalistic aspiration: "Power to the people; Black Power to black people."

The response from most white politicians and police officers has been predictable; they have pursued, fought with, jailed, and attacked in speech and in fact the leaders of the party and many of its members. Huey Newton is now in jail; Eldridge Cleaver is forced into exile; the acting chairman, Bobby Seale, awaits trial in both Illinois and Connecticut; several other Party leaders have been killed by the police. Meanwhile, some of the Panthers' neighborhood programs continue, most notably one which provides a free breakfast for ghetto children. Despite determined opposition, the Black Panthers still stand as a strong symbol of the will to freedom to a great many people, both black and white. The program of the Party, which embodies its resolute spirit, is here reprinted.

THE BLACK PANTHER PARTY TEN-POINT PROGRAM   From *The Black Panther*. Reprinted by permission of the Black Panther Party.

1. We want freedom. We want power to determine the destiny of our Black Community.

We believe that black people will not be free until we are able to determine our destiny.

2. We want full employment for our people.

We believe that the federal government is responsible and obligated to give every man employment or a guaranteed income. We believe that if the white American businessmen will not give full employment, then the means of production should be taken from the businessmen and placed in the community so that the people of the community can organize and employ all of its people and give a high standard of living.

3. We want an end to the robbery by the white man of our Black Community.

We believe that this racist government has robbed us and now we are demanding the overdue debt of forty acres and two mules. Forty acres and two mules was promised 100 years ago as restitution for slave labor and mass murder of black people. We will accept the payment in currency which will be distributed to our many communities. The Germans are now aiding the Jews in Israel for the genocide of the Jewish people. The Germans murdered six million Jews. The American racist has taken part in the slaughter of over fifty million black people; therefore, we feel that this is a modest demand that we make.

4. We want decent housing, fit for shelter of human beings.

We believe that if the white landlords will not give decent housing to our black community, then the housing and the land should be made into cooperatives so that our community, with government aid, can build and make decent housing for its people.

5. We want education for our people that exposes the true nature of this decadent American society. We want education that teaches us our true history and our role in the present-day society.

We believe in an educational system that will give to our people a knowledge of self. If a man does not have knowledge of himself and his position in society and the world, then he has little chance to relate to anything else.

6. We want all black men to be exempt from military service.

We believe that Black people should not be forced to fight in the military service to defend a racist government that does not protect us. We will not fight and kill other people of color in the world who, like black people, are being victimized by the white racist government of America. We will protect ourselves from the force and violence of the racist police and the racist military, by whatever means necessary.

7. We want an immediate end to POLICE BRUTALITY and MURDER of black people.

We believe we can end police brutality in our black community by organizing black self-defense groups that are dedicated to defending our black community from racist police oppression and brutality. The Second Amendment to the Constitution of the United States gives a right to bear arms. We therefore believe that all black people should arm themselves for self-defense.

8. We want freedom for all black men held in federal, state, county and city prisons and jails.

We believe that all black people should be released from the many jails and prisons because they have not received a fair and impartial trial.

9. We want all black people when brought to trial to be tried in court by a jury of their peer group or people from their black communities, as defined by the Constitution of the United States.

We believe that the courts should follow the United States Constitution so that black people will receive fair trials. The 14th Amendment of the U.S. Constitution gives a man a right to be tried by his peer group. A peer is a person from a similar economic, social, religious, geographical, environmental, historical and racial background. To do this the court will be forced to select a jury from the black community from which the black defendant came. We have been, and are being tried by all-white juries that have no understanding of the "average reasoning man" of the black community.

10. We want land, bread, housing, education, clothing, justice and peace. And as our major political objective, a United Nations-supervised plebiscite to be held throughout the black colony in which only black colonial subjects will be allowed to participate, for the purpose of determining the will of black people as to their national destiny.

When, in the course of human events, it becomes necessary for one people to dissolve the political bands which have connected them with another, and to assume, among the powers of the earth, the separate and equal station to which the laws of nature and nature's God entitle them, a decent respect to the opinions of mankind requires that they should declare the causes which impel them to the separation.

We hold these truths to be self-evident; that all men are created equal; that they are endowed by their Creator with certain unalienable rights; that among these are life, liberty, and the pursuit of happiness. **That, to secure these rights, governments are instituted among men, deriving their just powers from the consent of the governed; that, whenever any form of government becomes destructive of these ends, it is the right of the people to alter or to abolish it, and to institute a new government, laying its foundation on such principles, and organizing its powers in such form, as to them shall seem most likely to effect their safety and happiness.** Prudence, indeed, will dictate that governments long established should not be changed for light and transient causes; and, accordingly, all experience hath shown, that mankind are more disposed to suffer, while evils are sufferable, than to right themselves by abolishing the forms to which they are accustomed. **But, when a long train of abuses and usurpations, pursuing invariably the same object, evinces a design to reduce them under absolute despotism, it is their right, it is their duty, to throw off such government, and to provide new guards for their future security.**

MICHAEL THELWELL

Black Studies and White Universities

In 1969, one of the major issues in American education was the question of Black Studies Departments and Ethnic Colleges. At universities and colleges throughout the country, black students charged that the education they were receiving was white-oriented, and that it neither recognized nor responded to their special needs as black people. They demanded an acceleration in the recruitment of black students and the inclusion of black history and culture in the curriculum; paralleling the demands the black power movement was making in a larger social context, they called for power and autonomy over their educational life.

Universities were both unable and, in many cases, unwilling to respond to these demands, and confrontations between blacks and whites broke out on campuses across the nation. One of the most dramatic of these conflicts occurred in the staid Ivy League atmosphere of Cornell University, where black students finally armed themselves and occupied a campus building. The following selection by Michael Thelwell, who was teaching black literature at Cornell during the crisis, is a case study of the black students' revolt at this school as well as a consideration of the broader question of violence on campus.

"All sho'nuff dialogue come from the barrel of a gun."—JUNEBUG J. JONES, CORNELL UNIVERSITY ADDRESS APRIL 21ST (DAY AFTER THE OCCUPATION OF WILLARD STRAIGHT HALL).

"If, as we are constantly being told, there is a white power structure at this university, then it had damned well better start acting like one."— VISITING PROFESSOR (WHITE), CORNELL UNIVERSITY, MAY 1ST.

IF SUNDAY WERE NOT A "SLOW" NEWS DAY, AND IF AMERICANS—PARticularly white Americans—did not have an obsessional love-fear-guilt thing about guns, James A. Perkins, the president of Cornell University,

BLACK STUDIES AND WHITE UNIVERSITIES by Michael Thelwell. From *Ramparts,* Vol. 7, Issue 12, May 1969. Reprinted by permission of the publisher.

would be resting more easily tonight. In fact he might have good reason to be downright pleased with himself and his administration. But for those two factors, Perkins would be able to point to the fact that Cornell was successfully weathering a potentially violent confrontation with its black students and their SDS supporters without large-scale destruction of property, massive police violence, or the "shutting-down" of the university's functions by dissident students—none of which Harvard, Columbia or Berkeley was able to avoid.

But Sunday *is* a slow news day and white America's guilt-ridden fascination with guns becomes paranoid hysteria when those guns are in the hands of young blacks. And the idea—greatly exaggerated by the way— that any part of the white society's governing institutions, even something as innocuous as a university, has "capitulated" or "surrendered" to those armed blacks evokes the beginning of the end, the specter of a black take-over, and blows white America's collective mind. So Perkins' regime, which was—until the appearance of the guns and what they refer to as "that damned picture"[1]—one of the most skillful exponents of the anticipatory compromise, has been shaken to the point where friend and critic give it no better than a 50-50 chance of survival. If the Perkins regime falls, it will be because the press said he "capitulated" to armed blacks—and to capitulate is unforgivable, even if the blacks were right and, as far as anyone could tell, quite determined to fight in dead earnest for their position.

The establishment has many strategies and tactics for dealing with dissent, but its ultimate weapon is violence. (There was no violence at Cornell, but nobody seems to remember that.) Short of violence, the establishment has minor ploys like transforming issues of principle into issues of etiquette (it is bad form for students to disrupt violently the Vice President's speech, even though a rotten egg is not a fire bomb and the Vice President *is* the spokesman for a policy of genocide in Viet-Nam). Another name for this is, of course, hypocrisy, and it is this process at work which has made the focal issue at Cornell the question of guns in the hands of the blacks. But the press in its foolish search for sensationalism has stumbled onto a question which may become crucial for the foreseeable future: *What if blacks and radicals generally refuse to concede the exclusive right to violence to the establishment?*

Traditionally, when the establishment calls for dialogue and negotiation it means *limited* dialogue. That is, it will, as my students say, "dia-

---

[1] [A widely-published, dramatic picture of a black student wearing a bandoleer and holding a rifle. EDS.]

logue with" you until it grows weary or impatient, at which point the language of dialogue becomes the language of the nightstick and the Marines. This certainly has been the nature of all black dialogue with white America in the past. University administrations, despite their loud appeals to reasonable and civilized discourse, have reserved their right to "invoke cloture" by way of the machinery of violence that the system places at their disposal. It is only because the dissenters have tacitly conceded them this prerogative that the violence on university campuses has been "limited," if one considers broken heads and backs to be "limited" violence. Under the pressure of the situation the Cornell blacks were forced to take that option away from Perkins, and faced him with the necessity of choosing between equal negotiation or unlimited violence.

Negotiation from a position of equality becomes, in the language of the establishment, "capitulation." This is what got the trustees, the state legislature, the governor, and the conservative faculty up-tight: the recognition that the rules had been changed and that their traditional position of paternalistic power supported by the threat of violence was not operative. For the first time in four months the university had to *listen* to the blacks; all along they had been pretending to listen. Faced with the alternative of doing either a little "capitulation" or a little killing, they chose to negotiate for real—what is an appropriate response in Harlem, Watts, Newark, or Saigon is clearly inappropriate on an Ivy League campus. The black students violated not only the civilized proprieties but also the notion of aesthetic distance, the notion that white American violence should be kept as far as possible from suburbia.

It is ironic that—with the exception of an episode in which the occupied building was invaded by fraternity jocks intent on acting out their red-blooded white American male fantasies—the Cornell incident was totally nonviolent. To what extent was this due to the presence of those guns? It is not by any means *certain* that, had they not been present, Perkins, under pressure from trustees, faculty and alumni, would have unleashed the cops to break black heads. That this did not happen at Cornell may not be due solely to the presence of those guns, but the black students feel that in this case, at least, the basic effect of the guns was to prevent violence. It is a sad commentary on the society and the university that they are probably right.

Given the relatively peaceful and nondestructive nature of the incident and the fact that the black students emphasized their intention to use their guns only in the event of physical danger to the black women in the building, and that they did not threaten, coerce or intimidate anyone at gunpoint, the response of certain hysterics on the faculty (located interestingly enough in the upper echelons of the history and government departments) is significant.

These gentlemen claim to be hopelessly compromised, that the university is in ruins and chaos, and that "academic freedom" has been ravished—presumably by the phallic rifle barrels. Obviously they are speaking in terms of high and lofty principle, as they must be speaking symbolically when they say that the administration has surrendered and there is "no authority" at Cornell, since the school seems to be functioning no less efficiently than it was before. What does my colleague mean —he is a civilized and humane man—when he calls Perkins a "spineless jellyfish" and calls for the "white power structure to start acting like one"? Would they really have preferred a shoot-out? And to maintain what principle?—their own notion of their privileged class position protected by the coercive machinery of the state?

What exactly is the "trust" that they accuse Perkins of violating? That he did not swiftly and forcibly put the blacks in their place? How? None of these men have, as far as I can see, said a mumbling word against police violence at Harvard. Guns in the hands of the ROTC on this campus, on the hips of the campus cops, and in the hands of certain fraternities who had been arming themselves—this was a matter of public knowledge for weeks—do not seem to concern them. It is no wonder that "liberal" and "intellectual" have become dirty words in the minds of the young.

Given the peaceful nature of the confrontation, the agitation of these men is understandable only in the context of the entire controversy. The "trust" whose violation they bemoan is simply the racist principle that they and their class have the prerogative to run black people's lives. Because underneath the labyrinthine swirls of red tape, due process and rhetoric on both sides, that is what the ultimate issue is. The actual, specific issues that triggered the confrontation are quite trivial.

Here is an abbreviated version of how the issues developed. When James A. Perkins, a Philadelphia Quaker of liberal pretensions, gained the presidency in 1963, he took over a university that embodied, as do most American universities, the best and worst of American society. One thing it did not have was a race problem, since there were virtually no blacks (about six per class year or no more than 24 at any one time). Besides, the few Negroes who were present at that time, rather than preparing the university for what was to come, probably misled them. These were middle-class, "integrated" blacks who were upwardly mobile and who wanted to fit in and belong.

A committee was set up to finance and recruit black students at Cornell and in 1965 a group of 39 arrived. Contrary to popular racist myth, the black students at Cornell were not "so badly prepared as to be unable to handle the academic load," which is a reason given by certain journalists for the agitation. Prior to the "troubles," this first group, which will graduate this year, had lost only three students, and only one for academic reasons. The psychological burdens are far greater than the academic ones, as we shall see.

What was expected, of course, was that these favored blacks would adjust, adapt, and integrate themselves into the life of the campus, happily, gratefully—and uncritically. At the end of four years they would emerge with the skills, manners and attitudes necessary to usher them into the middle-class world of affluence and gracious living. The only problems anyone visualized in that age of innocence were social ones, like what to do about fraternities that discriminate. (Cornell, with some 60 Greek-letter organizations, has not been quite able to shake its reputation as a winter playground for the sons and daughters of the eastern establishment.) But at first even the fraternities cooperated, sponsoring a "soul of blackness week" and setting up a committee to help black prospects cope with the intricacies of "rushing."

For a while everything went according to script. The notion that this almost lily-white institution, which had been conceived, structured, and had functioned without any thought to the educational needs of the black community, would have to undergo very basic adjustments if it were to be really responsive to the practical and psychological needs of blacks, was apparently as unthinkable as any serious suggestion that God might be black. The fact that with three exceptions, and those in the professional schools, the faculty was lily-white and that no courses *at all* dealing *specifically* with the black experience were offered, seems to have escaped notice. Truly Cornell's small black community was without history or identity so far as the institution was concerned.

As the black population grew—it now numbers about 250—the sounds from the black community changed. Blacks began to perceive that integration was not liberation. Cultural integrity for the black community became a goal and instead of white tolerance and liberal sympathy, black folks were talking about Black Power, and not only that but by any means necessary.

Nationally the black community had stopped asking and started demanding. *They* would make the decisions affecting their lives, and *they,* for the first time in their history, would define the terms of their relationship to the white society. Junebug Jabbo Jones—may his tribe increase —the peripatetic black sage who is a legend in his own time, told a gathering of black Ivy Leaguers that "Harvard, Princeton and Yale had ruined more good niggers than whiskey and dope together," and he received a standing ovation.

At Cornell, blacks began to examine their historical situation and the motives of their benefactors. What was the intent of the decision that had brought them to Cornell? Who had made it and who supplied the money? Had white folks suddenly got religion or did the riots have anything to do with it? Were black students in fact partners and beneficiaries in the exploitation of other blacks here and in the Third World? More important, would their education lead them to a never-never-land suspended between the two communities?

They started talking about the role of a class-oriented, culturally chauvinistic, white educational system in dividing the black community and siphoning off and co-opting its leadership. More than that, they saw the well-meaning but somewhat self-congratulatory publicity that the university was sending out (in fairness it was mainly to alumni for purposes of funding the project) as reducing them to laboratory specimens and evidence of the school's new morality.

They demanded an Afro-American studies program from the university shortly after the King assassination. It seems that the students had no clear idea of what the form and structure of such a program should be. But how in reality could they be expected to, given the educational system to which they were accustomed? Some faculty members, for reasons of politics, internal and general, expressed skepticism or outright hostility. But the administration, sensing the temper of the students, set up a committee to give shape to the idea.

This committee, under Professor Chandler Morse, set about its work in a methodical and cautious manner, genuinely concerned, I believe, with exploring all possibilities in order to set up a program that would not be vulnerable to sniping from the established departments nor offensive to even the most conservative sensibility, and which would also satisfy the blacks. This proved impossible, particularly since the no longer diffident blacks were definitely not interested in avoiding any of those contingencies.

Not much of a tangible nature had happened by November of 1969, and the blacks, suspecting that they were witnessing still another example of honky "tricknology," got restive.

They were simultaneously experiencing some guilt at either having "escaped" the ghetto or, in some cases, never having experienced it.

This was exacerbated by a steady stream of black speakers and ideologically articulate students who challenged the group's presence on the white campus as opposed to "working" in the community or at a black school.

Thus the Afro-American studies program became very important as a tangible sign that they were not being "co-opted" and seduced by the Man's system. But to be that, the program had to be free of domination, control, and influence, overt or covert, from and by whites.

Within the Afro organization sentiment for an autonomous black college developed; the group occupied the office of the committee chairman and declared the committee dissolved. This did not sit well with a great many faculty members.

In support of a number of political demands the organization began a series of noisy, disruptive and admittedly abrasive—but essentially non-violent—demonstrations. To emphasize the need for black courses and materials they took a number of books from the library shelves and, finding them irrelevant, tossed them in a heap on the floor. To dramatize their demand for separate eating facilities they danced on tables in the cafeteria at lunch hour. They disrupted the clinic in demanding a black psychiatrist. And when the promised building to house the activities around the program did not materialize, they took over a building and evicted the whites, giving them three minutes to leave. They still have that building, and when the university did not furnish it as rapidly as they wished, a task force liberated furniture from other campus buildings. Now faculty and students alike were murmuring that it was time to teach the blacks a lesson.

When a small group ran through the administration building and into Perkins' office brandishing toy guns (they were obviously on some revolutionary fantasy of their own), it was clear to many whites that they had gone too far. By this time black-white tension was quite high.

The demands were not what was at issue—since even critics had to admit that they were justified, and with each demonstration the speed of administrative implementation perceptibly increased. The sentiment among some whites, mostly faculty, was that the blacks had to be disciplined. Consequently, charges were brought against six brothers for the toy gun incident and the liberation of the furniture.

Despite repeated urgings, promises of merely "symbolic" punishment, and later warnings and threats of suspension, the six refused to appear before the disciplinary committee. Now all the time this committee was saying informally that the charges themselves were not too "serious" they were also threatening suspension for nonappearance. So the issue was clearly the validation of the judiciary by the appearance of the six, not the charges (especially since the committee's mandate provided no mechanism for judgment in absentia).

During this period there was a symposium on South Africa. Cornell did own stock in Chase Manhattan and several other companies involved in business in South Africa, and Perkins himself—a perfect liberal—was on the Chase Manhattan board. (He is also chairman of the board of the United Negro College Fund.) Because of these connections, the black students felt that Perkins was hardly qualified morally or politically to introduce the speakers in the final session.

They planned to disrupt the meeting but one brother got carried away and seized Perkins by the scruff of the neck. (The brother was agitated at the prospect of his scholarship money possibly originating in South African slave labor. The contradictions for black people on a white campus are indeed great.) Anyway, that broke the dam and sentiment was now quite high for swift and irrevocable discipline for blacks. Meanwhile, the six brothers were still adamant.

At the point where the six were to be suspended, 150 blacks appeared before the committee and informed them that the miscreants were not present and would not appear because:

1. The actions against only six constituted selective reprisal and were clearly intended as political intimidation.

2. By insisting on their appearance and hinting at light penalties, the committee was acting out a charade, the purpose of which was a symbolic lynching to appease "racist" elements on the campus.

3. The committee, as an agent of the university, had no legitimacy to judge political actions directed against the university.

4. As a lily-white committee, it was not a jury of any black's peers and was thus illegitimate.

5. As long as black people were in the institution it was necessary for them to reserve the right of political action as a group, and since the six were the agents of the entire body, the entire body was culpable. But they were not about to relegate to whites the right to control the political activities of blacks made necessary by "lingering vestiges of white racism."

The committee—a joint student-faculty affair—saw fit to make no judgment and passed the buck to the Faculty Committee on Student Affairs. This committee examined the Afro-American position and found no merit therein. The six were instructed to appear and did not. At this point the issue became one of conflicts of autonomy. The blacks were trapped in a position of having to back up their statement, and their definition of their "right to political action." The faculty committee—beneath BOMFOG[1] rhetoric dripping with words like "sensitivity," "understanding," and "sympathy"—was affirming its right to judge blacks for political actions. It is thus primarily responsible for creating the situation that the administration then had to deal with.

Pointing to the precedent of labor-management arbitration, the blacks said they wanted neither sympathy, understanding nor sensitivity, but an objective judiciary committee made up of people independent of the university to judge political actions of blacks.

At this point, the action thickens—three white students are discovered beaten up on campus, one of them quite seriously. The allegation was made by one that his assailant(s) were black. The Daily Sun, the campus newspaper, printed a hasty and ill-advised editorial implying that their policy of collective responsibility for political acts made all blacks in the Afro-American Society responsible and that they should "ferret out" the assailants and hand them over. It is not clear that the assailants were in fact black or that, if they were, they were in fact students. But the editorial, hysterical in tone and quite vituperative, was a clear call to white vigilantism. No one on the faculty pointed this out, nor were any voices raised about the prejudicial nature of the Sun's assumptions.

The blacks received word that some fraternities and individual white students were purchasing arms in Ithaca. The blacks followed suit. The matter of the six had now dragged on for over two months and, given the added tension of the muggings, the nerves of both blacks and whites were frayed. But the whites outnumbered the blacks 14,000 to 250. Both sides seemed unable to dismount from the principled positions which they were riding to what seemed an inevitable confrontation.

The judiciary committee suddenly discovered that suspension was not inevitable after all and that they *could* judge the six in absentia. Two months earlier, this decision might have averted trouble. But when they handed down the reprimands, which are purely formal anyway, the atmosphere of heightened tension made it a provocation to both black and white.

That night a cross was burned, by person or persons unknown, at the black women's cooperative house. When the campus police came, they were unable to stay because of a series of false fire alarms that were being triggered all over the campus. The blacks found both actions

[1] Brotherhood-of-Man-Fatherhood-of-God.

equally provocative. The cross speaks for itself and the police action seemed indicative of a callous, even racist, disregard for the safety of black women.

This was Thursday night. The coming weekend was parents' weekend and the blacks moved to occupy Willard Straight Hall, which was to be the focus of activities. When the fraternity men forced their way in, and the blacks heard radio reports concerning five carloads of armed whites (which never materialized, however), they sent out and got their guns.

The rest is history—the arrival of the mass media, the picture of armed blacks leaving the building and the agreement with the administration in which the reprimands were rescinded and promises of legal assistance and no criminal action were made to the blacks. It is this agreement that the faculty found so distasteful.

It is impossible to say for certain just which principles the faculty imagined themselves to be preserving. In the beginning, the black students would probably have settled for a lifting of the suspension threat. As the issue developed and frustrations increased, however, the question became in their minds one of their ultimate powerlessness and what they saw as the university's willingness and ability to assert its power over their lives arbitrarily, however veiled and mild the manifestation of that power. This appeared to them to be simply a new style of paternalism which their new-found concept of black independence forced them to resist. It is interesting that having resisted so successfully and with élan, they now evince a new spirit and unity that is much less up-tight and beleaguered.

The Afro association has now become the Black United Front, and the American blacks are entering into negotiations with Puerto Ricans, American Indians, West Indians and African brothers and inviting them to use the facilities of the liberated building which has now become the Third World Center.

The white students, as a consequence of the "dialogue" which followed the incident, are also much less up-tight than before. It is interesting that while the administration, for reasons of public safety as they put it, made disarmament the first priority, the white students to whom I spoke felt that as long as the blacks pledged to use their guns only in self-defense, and as long as the university, as one administrator said, "could not be responsible for conditions in the general society" that might threaten blacks (some claim to be still receiving threatening phone calls), they saw no reason why the blacks should be forced to disarm. The generation gap again? But it is clear why the administration's priorities are different from the students'.

This is a division which is symptomatic of much more; as long as the universities continue to embody within themselves the best and worst aspects of the society, it will continue. At their best the universities, and particularly the private ones, have represented, however marginally, a tradition of decency and a principled resistance to know-nothingism, political orthodoxy and repression in the general society. Witness the McCarthy era and the movement against Viet-Nam that was launched from American campuses. By expressing a perception of the possibility of man, they have been the incubators of a generation of audacious, impatient, morally committed and idealistic young radicals not committed to the excesses of folly, pride, greed, moral flatulence and violent exploitation that mark their society's relationship to the poor and powerless at home and abroad.

But at their worst, the universities are the agents and beneficiaries of exactly these forces. Without the technical systems and personnel they provide, Viet-Nam would be possible but not easy. Too often the privileged and smug faculty mandarins are flattered to supply the intellectual underpinnings for economic and political imperialism, and are able to coexist with racism in the society and to perpetuate it in the curricula. They grow affluent and powerful by supplying tax and moral loopholes for the heavily burdened pocketbooks and consciences of the rich. And despite their frequent and loud appeals for reasoned discourse as the avenue to "orderly change," they are ultimately no less coercive, inflexible, manipulative, undemocratic and elitist than the class which they serve and whose interests they maintain while professing to scorn its values. As long as this duality continues, the conflict can only intensify. And the society is certainly more violent than the most revolution-intoxicated student can even imagine.